**Regulatory Barriers and the Principle of Non-Discrimination in World Trade Law**

SIE *Studies in International Economics* includes works dealing with the theory, empirical analysis, and evaluation of international policies and institutions, in the area of international macroeconomics and finance, international trade theory and policy, as well as international legal and political economy.



Keith E. Maskus, Peter M. Hooper, Edward E. Leamer, and J. David Richardson, Editors
*Quiet Pioneering: Robert M. Stern and His International Economic Legacy*

Bjarne S. Jensen and Kar-yiu Wong, Editors
*Dynamics, Economic Growth, and International Trade*

Jagdish Bhagwati and Mathias Hirsch, Editors
*The Uruguay Round and Beyond: Essays in Honor of Arthur Dunkel*

Kala Marathe Krishna and Ling Hui Tan
*Rags and Riches: Implementing Apparel Quotas under the Multi-Fibre Arrangement*

Alan V. Deardorff and Robert M. Stern
*Measurement of Nontariff Barriers*

Thomas Cottier and Petros C. Mavroidis, Editors
*The World Trade Forum, Volume I: State Trading in the Twenty-First Century*

Rajesh Chadha, Sanjib Pohit, Alan V. Deardorff, and Robert M. Stern
*The Impact of Trade and Domestic Policy Reforms in India: A CGE Modeling Approach*

Alan V. Deardorff and Robert M. Stern, Editors
*Constituent Interests and U.S. Trade Policies*

Gary R. Saxonhouse and T. N. Srinivasan, Editors
*Development, Duality, and the International Economic Regime: Essays in Honor of Gustav Ranis*

Charles P. Kindleberger
*Essays in History: Financial, Economic, Personal*

Keith Acheson and Christopher Maule
*Much Ado about Culture: North American Trade Disputes*

Alan V. Deardorff and Robert M. Stern
*Social Dimensions of U.S. Trade Policies*

Thomas Cottier and Petros C. Mavroidis, Editors
*Regulatory Barriers and the Principle of Non-Discrimination in World Trade Law*

WORLD TRADE FORUM, VOLUME 2

# Regulatory Barriers and the Principle of Non-Discrimination in World Trade Law

*Thomas Cottier and Petros C. Mavroidis, Editors*

*Patrick Blatter, Associate Editor*

*Ann Arbor*

THE UNIVERSITY OF MICHIGAN PRESS

Published in the United States of America by
The University of Michigan Press
Manufactured in the United States of America
♾ Printed on acid-free paper

2002 2001 2000 1999 4 3 2 1



*A CIP catalog record for this book is available from the British Library.*

ISBN: 0-472-11100-0
ISSN: 1520-3476

## The World Trade Forum

The World Trade Forum was founded in 1997 to offer an opportunity for an international in-depth discussion of issues facing the world trading system. The Forum is organized through the cooperation of the Universities of Bern and Neuchâtel (Switzerland) and the financial support of the Silva Casa Foundation of Bern. Forum participants include academics, practitioners, and professionals from government and from international non government organizations. Representing both the legal and economic communities, the participants bring a wide variety of perspectives to the issues of debate.

Each year, one particular topic is chosen as the focus of that year's forum. The participants invited to the conference are requested to prepare a paper on that topic, and then to present the paper for discussion. Question-and-answer sessions follow each presentation, and a short analysis by an appointed discussant following the presentation of each groups of papers allows for a synthesis of the ideas. At the end of all sessions, a roundtable discussion takes place, in which participants may either make comments on the overall problems of the topic or address questions and suggestions to the other participants in light of the entire series of papers presented.

Following the conference, the authors of the papers revise their submissions for publication in the series of books that accompany the World Trade Forum conferences. An introduction and conclusory analysis by the editors further the synthesis of the topic at hand and aid the reader in determining the overall results of the scholarship. A transcript of the roundtable discussion is included as an annex.

We are most grateful to the Silva Casa Foundation in Bern, Switzerland, for its generous financial support that allows the conferences to take place, as well as for its encouragement to pursue the idea of the World Trade Forum and to the Universities of Bern and Neuchâtel.

The World Trade Forum series has been founded in order to help spread the ideas that arise from the careful consideration of the issue presented to interested persons throughout the world. We sincerely hope that this volume achieves this goal.

## CONTENTS

## Abbreviations and Acronyms

| | |
|---|---|
| AB | Appellate Body (WTO) |
| ACTPN | Advisory Committee for Trade Policy and Negotiations (U.S.) |
| AIM | Act on the Internal Market (Swiss) |
| APEC | Asia-Pacific Economic Cooperation |
| BISD | Basic Instruments and Selected Documents (GATT/WTO) |
| BTAs | Border Tax Adjustments |
| CAA | Agreement on Trade in Civil Aircraft (WTO) |
| CDV | Countervailing Duty |
| CEC | Central European Countries |
| CEN | Comité européen de normalisation |
| CENELEC | Comité européen de normalisation électrotechnique |
| CRS | Computer Reservation System |
| Cst | Constitution |
| DCC | Dormant Commerce Clause |
| DCS | Directly Competitive or Substitutable Products |
| DSU | Understanding on Rules and Procedures Governing the Settlement of Disputes (WTO) |
| EAC | European Accreditation of Certification Bodies |
| EAL | European Accreditation of Laboratories |
| EC | European Community |
| ECJ | European Court of Justice |
| ECR | European Court Reports |
| ECT | European Community Treaty |
| EEA | European Economic Area |
| EEC | European Economic Community |
| EFTA | European Free Trade Agreement |
| Ens | European standards |
| ESBs | European Standards Bodies |
| ETSI | European Telecommunications Standards Institute |
| EU | European Union |
| GATS | General Agreement on Trade in Services (WTO) |
| GATT | General Agreement on Tariffs and Trade (WTO) |
| GPA | Agreement on Government Procurement (WTO) |
| ICH | International Conference on Harmonization of Technical Requirements for the Registration of Pharmaceuticals for Human Use |
| ISO | International Standard Organization |

| | |
|---|---|
| ITC | International Trade Commission (U.S.) |
| MCM | Monetary Compensatory Amount |
| MFN | Most-Favored Nation |
| MRA | Mutual Recognition Agreement |
| MSOs | Market Surveillance Operators |
| MSSBs | Member State Standards Bodies |
| NAFTA | North American Free Trade Agreement |
| OECD | Organization for Economic Cooperation and Development |
| PPMs | Production and Process Methods |
| QR(s) | Quantitative Restriction(s) |
| RBP | Restrictive Business Practice |
| SPS | Agreement on Sanitary and Phytosanitary Measures |
| T.E.D. | Turtle-Excluding-Device |
| TABD | Transatlantic Business Dialogue |
| TBT | Technical Barriers to Trade |
| TEP | Transatlantic Economic Partnership |
| TRIMs | Agreement on Trade-Related Investment Measures (WTO) |
| TRIPs | Agreement on Trade-Related Aspects of Intellectual Property Rights (WTO) |
| TRIS | Technical Regulations and Industry Standards |
| UN-ECE | United Nations Economic Commission for Europe |
| VAT | Value Added Tax |
| VCLT | Vienna Convention on the Law of Treaties |
| WHO | World Health Organization |
| WTO | World Trade Organization |

## Authors and Conference Participants

### Authors

CHRISTOPH BAIL, EC Commission, Brussels, Belgium
AMERICO BEVIGLIA ZAMPETTI, EC Commission, Brussels, Belgium
JACQUES BOURGEOIS, Attorney, Akin & Gump, Brussels, Belgium; College d'Europe, Brugge, Belgium
MARCO BRONCKERS, Attorney, Stibbe Simont, Brussels and University of Leyden, Law School, Belgium
THOMAS COTTIER, Professor, University of Bern, Law School, Bern, Switzerland
WILLIAM DAVEY, University of Illinois, Law School, currently on leave at the WTO, Director, Legal Affairs Division, Geneva, Switzerland
PAUL DEMARET, Professor, University of Liège, Law School and Collège de l'Europe, Brugge, Belgium
PIET EECKHOUT, Herbert Smith Professor of European Law, King's College, Law School, London, U.K.
CRAWFORD FALCONER, Head of Division, Trade directorate, OECD, Paris, France
JEAN-MARIE GRETHER, Professor, University of Neuchâtel, Department of Economics, Neuchâtel, Switzerland
OLIVIER GUILLOD, Professor, Director of the Health Law Institute, University of Neuchâtel, Law School, Neuchâtel, Switzerland
ANTONIOS HANIOTIS, Swiss Federal Office for Foreign Economic Affairs, Bern, Switzerland
GARY HORLICK, Attorney, O'Melveny and Myers, Washington DC, USA
ROBERT L. HOWSE, Professor, University of Michigan, Law School, Ann Harbor, USA
ROBERT E. HUDEC, Professor, University of Minnesota, Law School, Minneapolis, USA
PATRICK A. LOW, WTO, Director, Economic and Research Analysis Division, Geneva, Switzerland
NATALIE MCNELIS, Attorney, Stibbe Simont, Brussels, Belgium
AADITYA MATTOO, World Bank, Washington D.C., USA
PETROS C. MAVROIDIS, Professor, University of Neuchâtel, Law School, Neuchâtel, Switzerland
PATRICK MESSERLIN, Professor, Institut d'Etudes Politiques, Paris, France
NICOLAS MICHEL, Professor, University of Fribourg, Fribourg, Switzerland

DAMIEN NEVEN, Professor, University of Lausanne, Department of Economics and CEPR, Lausanne, Switzerland

KALYPSO NICOLAIDIS, Professor, Kennedy School of Government, Harvard University, Cambridge, USA

DAVID PALMETER, Attorney, Powell Goldstein, Washington DC, USA

JOOST PAUWELYN, WTO Legal Affairs, Geneva, Switzerland

ERNST-ULRICH PETERSMANN, Professor, University of Geneva, Law School, Geneva, Switzerland

ANDRÉ SAPIR, Professor, Université Libre de Bruxelles, IEE and CEPR, Brussels, Belgium

ROBERT STERN, Professor, University of Michigan, Department of Economics, Ann Harbor, USA

MICHEL WAELBROECK, Professor, Université Libre de Bruxelles, IEE, Brussels, Belgium

## Other Conference Participants

REMO ARPAGAUS, Research Fellow, University of Bern, Bern, Switzerland

PATRICK BLATTER, Research Fellow, University of Neuchâtel, Neuchâtel, Switzerland

ALEXANDRA CAPLAZI, Research Fellow, University of Bern, Bern, Switzerland

PHILIPPE DE CHAMBRIER, Research Fellow, University of Neuchâtel, Neuchâtel, Switzerland

NATALIE ERARD, Research Fellow, University of Neuchâtel, Neuchâtel, Switzerland

YVAN FAUCHÈRE, Research Fellow, University of Neuchâtel, Neuchâtel, Switzerland

MEINHARD HILF, Professor, University of Hamburg, Hamburg, Germany

JEAN LOUIS JUVET, Professor Emeritus, University of Neuchâtel, Neuchâtel, Switzerland

ALVIN KOPSE, Research Fellow, University of Bern, Bern, Switzerland

INGO MEITINGER, Research Fellow, University of Bern, Bern, Switzerland

KRISTA NADAKAVUKAREN SCHEFER, Research Fellow, University of Bern, Bern, Switzerland

FABIENNE RUBIO, Research Fellow, University of Neuchâtel, Neuchâtel, Switzerland

LORENZO SIGISMONDI, Research Fellow, University of Neuchâtel, Neuchâtel, Switzerland

VINCENT STAUFFER, Research Fellow, Neuchâtel, Switzerland

DANIEL WÜNGER, Research Fellow, University of Bern, Bern, Switzerland

## Preface

On August 28 and 29, 1998, over thirty trade professionals met in Neuchâtel, Switzerland for the second annual World Trade Forum Conference. The topic established for the 1998 Conference was how the world trading system addresses the issue of regulatory barriers to trade liberalization.

The various contributors, coming from divergent backgrounds (economics, political science, and law), engaged in a series of discussions on the constraints imposed on the regulatory state by world trade liberalization and how the issue has been tackled so far at different levels: national, regional, and international. Empirical evidence had a prominent part in the discussions; yet the theoretical models were not neglected.

The papers collected here demonstrate disagreements among the contributors on a series of issues: can (and should) law try to be as detailed as possible in order to minimize judicial discretion? What is the appropriate standard of judicial review at the international plane on issues like environmental or health protection touching upon the most sensitive aspects of the regulatory state? How important is (the absence of) democratic legitimacy of international adjudicating bodies? What is the value that we attach on efficiency?

We all agreed that we left the two-day conference with a feeling of satisfaction, mainly due to the cross-fertilization that occurred between the ideas expressed. Indeed, we left the room knowing that we contributed to an already quite comprehensive questionnaire on the issues that need to be addressed in this context.

This volume constitutes our contribution to an existing dialogue that has been taking place for some time now in various fora. Our aim was to provide added impetus to continue this dialogue. The second World Trade Forum convinced its participants that a multi-disciplinary approach in this context is highly recommendable.

The World Trade Forum could not have taken place without the active involvement and support of the participants. We once again want to thank the participants and especially the Silva Casa Foundation, which very generously has been supporting our conferences and largely contributes to their success. Last but not least, we would like to thank our associate editor Patrick Blatter for all his hard work and the people at the University of Michigan Press for their commitment to our project.

The Editors

# Part I: Introduction

# Regulatory Barriers and the Principle of Non-Discrimination in WTO Law: An Overview

*Thomas Cottier and Petros C. Mavroidis*

In Bob Baldwin's well put words, trade liberalization looks like a swamp: as border protection slowly receded, trade negotiators realized that regulatory barriers are equally, if not more, of a threat to trade liberalization. Hence, already during the Tokyo round negotiations, they attempted a first go against this form of protection. Contrary however, to border protection, regulatory protection is often difficult to detect and sometimes even more difficult to appreciate (quantify). Moreover, it often touches upon politically very sensitive issues, since it is rarely decoupled from a public interest rationale: arguably, for example, lawyers provide a public good. And arguably, the society has a strong interest in regulating who and under what conditions would be entitled to supply the said public good. And arguably again, all regulation proposed (imposed?) by domestic Bar Associations is necessary for the public good to be provided in a satisfactory manner. And as a result, the market of lawyers is not easily penetrable (and in fact, penetrated) by foreign lawyers belonging to foreign Bar Associations who also propose (impose?) regulation aiming at securing that the same public good will be provided in a satisfactory manner in their market.

An integration process, the starting-point of which is regulatory diversity, can choose between various ways to integrate, ranging from full harmonization to regulatory diversity. Practice suggests that regulatory diversity can be coupled with an obligation to, in principle, mutually recognize each other's regulatory choices [the most prominent example being the European Union (EU) experience post-*Cassis de Dijon*].

Economic theory suggests that are gains from harmonization (e.g., absence of race to the bottom, transaction costs), but this is the case for regulatory diversity as well (enhanced information stemming about the effectiveness of different regulatory interventions). Consequently, one cannot *a priori* make a definitive statement in favor of one or the other mode of integration. A series of constraints however, (many of them being of political nature) may to a large extent prejudge the choice: for example, harmonization can be facilitated by factors such as the "proximity" of the economies involved, the voting procedures etc. On the other hand, mutual recognition largely depends on some notion of "trust"; consequently, one can easily see how mutual recognition can work between the fifteen members of the EU, a group of rather (albeit with some notable disparities) homogeneous countries, whereas this is not necessarily the case when it comes to pondering on a potential extension of this experience at the multilateral (World Trade Organization, WTO) level.

The WTO model of integration knows of both "negative" and "positive" integration-type of provisions; the former refer to provisions where WTO members are requested to refrain from adopting a particular action (like the Art. XI GATT prohibition to have recourse to quantitative restrictions), whereas the latter refers to provisions requesting from WTO members to adopt a particular conduct (like most of the TRIPs provisions imposing on WTO Members the obligation to guarantee a particular form of protection for intellectual property rights).

But with respect to both, what the WTO contract essentially requires from its Members is to ensure that they will not discriminate either *de jure* or *de facto* between domestic and foreign goods/services/suppliers of services. The WTO contract is not (and should not be interpreted as) an instrument for deregulation. Consequently, governments are free to regulate whenever they deem it appropriate. And when they do deem it appropriate to intervene through regulatory means, WTO Members are, in fields where no harmonized action is called for (like, for example, in the TRIPs), in principle free to enact any legislation they deem appropriate to achieve their stated goals provided that they respect the obligation not to discriminate.

Hence, the WTO is about regulatory diversity. This point was captured in the recent WTO Appellate Body report on *"United States – Import Prohibition of Certain Shrimp and Shrimp Products"* (WT/DS58/AB/R).

The sanctioned by the WTO regulatory diversity can and does affect trade flows. This is the case irrespective of whether governments are authentic about the goals they want to achieve or not (that is in cases where under the guise of a stated social goal, governments actually aim at favoring domestic producers). Indeed, the problem is to distinguish between the authentic and the non-authentic cases.

This area invites contributions from various fields. Economic theory has to a very considerable extent cleared the picture and provided frameworks within which we can test the real intentions of an intervening government. Jurisprudence on the other hand, is still struggling with various (and often mutually exclusive) tests. WTO case law especially is particularly interesting in this respect: in an era where the WTO sees itself becoming the victim of the GATT-success and governments trust it with more and more competence, it is called to manage a continuously increasing portfolio of domestic regulatory interventions having an incidence on international trade.

The WTO at this point in time does not enjoy a clear mandate in this respect. More importantly, the WTO adjudicating process is called to decide on issues without having previously established a clear standard of review: it is one thing to judge whether antidumping duties have been legally or not so imposed; it is an entirely different game to judge whether a decision to ban a product for health reasons is legitimate or not in the presence of conflicting scientific evidence.

And this is a potentially explosive area. We should also not underestimate the probability to see the WTO adjudicating body burdened with questions on which no clear response can be found at the legislative level.

Questions are therefore raised at two levels: at the substantive level, where we continue to ask what should be the appropriate legislative framework within which the legitimacy of regulatory interventions will be judged and at the procedural level where the basic question is what should be the optimal standard of judicial review when the WTO adjudicating bodies are requested to resolve disputes of the type described above.

## 1. An Overview of the Contributions in this Volume

The participants at the second World Trade Forum addressed questions with respect to adjudication concerning regulatory interventions at both the positive and the normative level. There is an overall anxiety (if not dissatisfaction) with the current state of play: true, some steps have been recently taken towards what seems to be the right direction but true as well, the existing framework leaves a lot to be desired.

Participants were inspired by experience in other fora (like the European Union, the United States, Switzerland or the NAFTA). In some respects the federalist example can provide some useful guidance. Participants were also inspired by the experience concerning delineation of the relevant market in the context of antitrust law (on both sides of the Atlantic). And as usual, the conference evidenced substantial cross-fertilization between arguments from the sphere of law, economics, and political science.

Davey and Pauwelyn provide a comprehensive presentation of the GATT/WTO case law on the principle of non discrimination with respect to regulatory barriers (tarifary and non tarifary). They explain the logic behind the rejection of the so-called "aims and effects" test and insist that the new (which in fact is the old) test to establish likeness is not so stringent as to eliminate the possibility for governments to make regulatory distinctions and provide for differential treatment between two otherwise like products. Their analysis is particularly intriguing since they argue that in case their interpretation is accepted, nothing stops governments from operating regulatory distinctions on grounds other than those mentioned in Art. XX GATT (the list of general exceptions).

Mattoo takes us through the logic of national treatment in the GATS context. He acknowledges that his endeavor suffers from a disadvantage which in turn can be seen as an advantage: lack of a critical mass of case law interpreting the obligation to accord national treatment in the context of services. Thus, his hands being free, Mattoo proposes that unless an obligation to justify regulatory distinctions is imposed on WTO Members, the GATS commitments could be void of a substantial part of their content. He proposes a solution inspired by the EC approach according to which regulatory distinctions must be motivated and so must any decisions by the competent bodies rejecting a request for equivalence.

Hudec provides a thorough examination of GATT/WTO case-law in the field of "like products." He finds a discrepancy in the interpretation of the term when applied to product distinctions made by tariffs and when applied to product distinctions made by internal taxes and regulations. In the author's view, governments generally employ a permissive interpretation of the term "like product" with regard to product distinctions in their own national tariffs and this permissive interpretation has been given support in at least one GATT panel ruling. Hudec also finds though, that no such distinction between tariffs and internal measures has as yet been recognized by the dispute settlement rulings that have so far treated the issue.

In his comments to the two papers, Mavroidis acknowledges the tension between regulatory autonomy and trade liberalization. His assessment is that at the current level of integration, the fears about the intrusion of world institutions to domestic democratic regulatory choices are exaggerated. He accepts though that such fears could in the future become reality if no precautionary measures are taken. To his mind, instead of leaving it up to the judiciary to delineate the scope of intrusion, it would be preferable through legislative means to delineate the scope of intervention by the judiciary. In this perspective, he welcomes the inclusion of the "public order" exception in the GATS and recommends an extension of this exception to the GATT.

Howse examines market integration in North America and devotes his research in the way Courts in the United States have interpreted the Commerce Clause. He notices that, notwithstanding the fact that at the United States level there is an additional democratic safety level (the US Congress), the US Supreme Court had in many respects shown a more cautious attitude in disrupting legitimate regulatory outcomes than have done WTO panels. Howse accepts that parts of the recent Appellate Body rulings on *Shrimps/Turtles* and *Hormones* go in the right direction in that they stand for the proposition that a less interventionist approach (more deference to the regulating authority) is commendable. He suggests that for the WTO adjudicating bodies to enhance their legitimacy, a proper understanding of their position in the overall institutional architecture is the *conditio sine qua non*.

Horlick agrees with Howse that we have yet to strike the optimal balance between efficiency and local responsibility and control of our lives. He suggests that we want both, hence the question of striking the right balance. He does take some distance from Howse's approach though based on the idea that governments do not necessarily act in good faith when operating regulatory distinctions and consequently, there is maybe need for a more "interventionist" approach by the judiciary.

Demaret and Eeckhout offer their perspective on the EC experience with respect to market integration. First Demaret, dealing with fiscal barriers in intra-EC trade raises a voice of caution against the way the ECJ has implemented the principle of non discrimination. To his mind, the Court went too far by accepting in the *Danish Cars* case that conformity with Art. 95 ECT does not *ipso facto* amount to conformity under Art. 30 ECT. According to Demaret, the Court should be cautious in the context of Art. 30 ECT especially in the post-*Bosman* era. Eeckhout's contribution is, as its title indicates, a refinement of the *Keck and Mithouard* jurisprudence. For many, this jurisprudence was an unwarranted setback, since it narrowed down the scope of regulations that come under the scope of Art. 30 ECT. Eeckhout disagrees with this point of view. The author forcefully makes the point that in case of absence of *de jure* or *de facto* discrimination, market access will not be impaired. In turn, market access should not be understood as an abstract notion; rulings on Art. 30 ECT should have a concrete dimension concentrating on the specific position in which traders and consumers are found and examine whether they are faced with unjustified hurdles when trying to profit from intra-EC trade liberalization. He adds a word of caution on the possible extension of *Keck and Mithouard* to services, precisely because such an extension would affect other rights acknowledged to private parties by the ECT (Arts. 52, 59 ECT).

Bourgeois in his comments to the two papers focuses on a potential divergence between the two papers in the sense that Demaret's analysis focuses on a strict reading of the non discrimination principle whereas, in the view of Eeckhout, a rights-based approach could take us further. How much further though? The frontier between absence of discrimination and deregulation are sometimes blurred and, in any event, can be easily trespassed. Bourgeois suggests that at the end of the day the only remaining issue is to reconsider the relationship between the legislative and the judiciary which for the time being is unclear at the EC level.

Guillod's paper was the last one presented during the discussion on regional experiences. He focuses on Switzerland, a true federal state and not one in the making like the EC and uses health regulation by cantons in the context of the Act on the Internal Market to illustrate his argument. He notes that it is still unclear whether the Federal Court in Switzerland (the highest court in the country) would accept an extensive notion of public health which is a potential means in the hands of Swiss cantons privileging protectionistic purposes (although there is no evidence suggesting this point). He does not exclude the possibility in the future though for cantons to have intensified recourse to health related legislation which in turn could lead to market segmentation inside a federal state. The Federal Court will then have the opportunity to provide for all necessary refinements. In this case, the EC experience will be, to a large extent, a source of inspiration.

We invited two comments on Guillod's paper. First Haniotis largely shares some of Guillod's conclusions but at the same time points out that Guillod's conclusions should not be exaggerated. In his mind, one could have the impression by reading Guillod's contribution that Switzerland was not an integrated market before the coming into being of the Act on the Internal Market. This is simply not true in Haniotis' view. He points that the aim of the Act was to simply eliminate certain remaining discriminations in the areas of government procurement and professional services and not to undermine the existing level of integration. Grether points out in his contribution that convergence does not depend only on factor mobility but also on inter-regional differences in terms of technology, preferences, and institutions. He reminds us that notwithstanding the fact that swiss cantons have a fairly similar access to technology, they do not share a common linguistic and cultural background and they still keep their sovereignty on some issues such as education, health, and public policy. Difference among them consequently should not be a surprise. Such differences however, one would expect would lead swiss citizens to move around the various cantons. In Grether's opinion "voting with the feet" does not take place too often in Switzerland because swiss often at the ballot (and thus influence public spending directly).

Messerlin and Palmeter take us through the experience with mutual recognition arrangements within the EC and the United States. Messerlin focuses on the rich experience in the EC and in his part of the paper examines the road to market integration in the EC. From the "old" to the "new" approach, from pure mutual recognition in the era of decision making according to unanimity to the dilemma mutual recognition or harmonization in the era of decision making according to qualified majority, the EC experience reveals, in the author's eyes the progressive and somewhat painful realization by the EC authorities of the endless potential complexity of the topic. Palmeter on his part focuses on the US experience which is quasi non existent. And this in turn raises the question whether the "commerce clause" is more compatible form of integration in a federal context with undisputed central authority.

Nicolaidis in her paper focuses on the international dimension of mutual recognition and more especially on the agreement between the EC and the United States in the context of the Transatlantic Economic Partnership. She reaches three basic conclusions: first, that the initiation of the agreement was over-determined in the case of external EC relations and tried to disaggregate the factors that led to such an initiation. Second, a comparative analysis helps us better understand the EC approach. Third, in the long run mutual recognition is not simply about technical requirements but about the equivalence of ensuing market access broadly defined. In her view, a new chapter of international regulatory cooperation would be open warranting an adapted framework of analysis.

In his comments, Beviglia-Zampetti notes that mutual recognition agreements, and the one between the EC and the United States in particular, do not necessarily entail a loss of national sovereignty. They represent a flexible form of integration whereby participants preserve intact their national regulatory processes. To his mind, such agreements foster comity among nations and help avoid conflicts. The challenge for the agreement between the EC and the United States, in the author's view, would be to extend mutual recognition on a plurilateral basis and firmly ground it on the multilateral trading system so as to allow a growing number of countries to enjoy the benefits it can bring.

Neven first notes that the definition of "like products" is crucial in order to determine whether a measure is protectionistic or not. He then expresses his dissatisfaction with the way "like products" are defined in the international trade context and suggests an alternative way to proceed based on antitrust-type considerations. He proposes a two-steps procedure: in the first step, "like products" will be defined in the way "relevant markets" are defined in antitrust. As a second step, he proposes to quantify the extent of rivalry between firms and in case of intense rivalry to dismiss claims about protectionist measures. The first step presents no practical difficulties since it is routinely operated in the context of antitrust. The author acknowledges that practical difficulties do arise with respect to the second step but argues that several quantitative techniques can offer significant help in this context.

Waelbroeck in his comments expresses a skeptical view on Neven's suggested approach. He first makes the point that the same standard, "cross elasticity of demand," is indeed the standard in both the antitrust and the international trade context. Waelbroeck then makes the point that GATT violations may occur even in cases where domestic producers, because of their fierce competition, cannot profit from a tax differential arguably contravening the multilateral trade rules. The author however acknowledges the merits in Neven's intuition and urges him in his comments to take his approach with respect to the need to take into account the intensity of competition between domestic producers one step further.

Bronckers and McNelis examine the application of a market-based definition of "like products," as currently favored by the WTO adjudicating bodies, in the field of antidumping and environment. With respect to the first application, they welcome such an extension and argue in favor of an even more "firm" attitude, in the sense that market-based consideration should be the essential threshold for defining "like products" in the antidumping context. With respect to its application in the field of environment, they offer three comments: first, that the "like product" definition has been circumvented in the evaluation of environmentally inspired trade restrictions under the GATT. Second, that the environmental "aims and effects" of domestic regulation or taxes are no longer relevant to the definition of "like products." And third, that the current market-based approach to defining "like products" will permit some but not all distinctions in regulatory treatment that may be desirable from an environmental perspective.

Stern in his comments provided for an economics-based argument against protectionist tendencies. Acknowledging the merits of regulatory intervention to respond to market failures, he forcefully made the point that many times government intervention is not at all based on sound economics and thus distortions are created. He used contingent protection as an example to illustrate his remarks.

Petersmann focused on the need to advance a constitutional approach of government intervention at the world level. Arguing in favor of a rights-based approach to international trade, he believes that unless a constitutional function is elaborated, suspicion concerning regulatory intervention and at the same time dissatisfaction with pronouncements of the international judiciary will continue to "reign" in international trade relations. Institutional reinforcement and a change in the tone of the substantive integration process are, in his view, the necessary ingredients for future cooperation.

Participants in the conference agreed that the fruitful discussions that they had during the two days in Neuchâtel will have to be continued in other fora and enriched with the input from other sources.

# Part II: Conceptual Issues

CHAPTER 1

# MFN Unconditionality: A Legal Analysis of the Concept in View of its Evolution in the GATT/WTO Jurisprudence with Particular Reference to the Issue of "Like Product"

*William J. Davey and Joost Pauwelyn**

This paper examines the concept of most-favored-nation (MFN) treatment. First, it considers briefly the definition, the history and the arguments for and against MFN obligations. It then examines the way in which the concept has been used in the General Agreement on Tariffs and Trade (GATT) and the Marrakesh Agreement Establishing the World Trade Organization (WTO). The paper then turns to a detailed examination of the concept of like product and how that concept relates to the application of the MFN rule in GATT. The goal of the paper is to set out the current state of affairs concerning the MFN rule in GATT jurisprudence and to consider whether different approaches to the issue might be appropriately followed in the future. Later papers in this volume will critically analyze specific issues related to the MFN concept in more detail.

## 1. Most Favored Nation Treatment Generally

### MFN: Definition and History

A most-favored-nation clause in a treaty between two States typically requires each State to accord to the other State any advantage of the type covered by the treaty that the State accords to a third State. The first use of the MFN concept can be traced to the eleventh century, where the town of Mantua in Italy obtained in its charter from the Holy Roman Emperor, Henry III, the guarantee that it would benefit from all privileges granted to "whatsoever other town."[1] The term "most-favored-nation" first appears at the end of the 17$^{th}$ century.[2] Thereafter, MFN clauses became more common features of commercial treaties. Initially, as the term suggests, MFN treatment was very much a form of discrimination as only a few nations

---

* The views expressed herein are personal and should not be attributed the World Trade Organization. Thanks to Paul Epstein for comments.

benefited from a given MFN clause. Over time, the generalization of MFN obligations, particularly as a result of GATT, has made the MFN concept into a principle of non-discrimination and equal treatment.[3]

There are two variants of the MFN concept, each of which has been common at different points in time. The first variant—the *unconditional* MFN concept—is as described above. If State A has an MFN obligation in favor of State B, then any advantage of the type covered by the obligation that State A grants to State C must also be afforded by State A to State B. This obligation is unconditional. State B benefits from the advantage whether or not it grants a similar advantage to State A. The second variant—the *conditional* MFN concept—is different. Where States A and B have entered into an agreement with a conditional MFN obligation, if State A grants an advantage of the type covered by the agreement to State C, then State A must offer the same advantage to State B. However, it is obligated to grant the advantage only if State B fulfills the conditions of the agreement, which would typically require State B to offer to State A a benefit similar to that offered by State C to State A. Thus, State B's MFN rights are conditional; it obtains the advantage only if it is willing to "pay" for it by conceding an advantage to State A.

The unconditional form of the MFN obligation was used exclusively until the late 18th century.[4] Then in 1778, the United States entered into a treaty with France in which MFN treatment was made conditional on providing the same compensation as had been provided by the third party that obtained the advantage.[5] The use of conditional MFN clauses became more widespread in the early 19th century, but the unconditional form regained its dominance in the second half of the 19th century. However, the United States only began to pursue unconditional MFN agreements in the 1920's.[6] As we will see below, GATT generally enshrines the unconditional MFN concept, although there are significant general exceptions to the MFN requirement.

## The Pros and Cons of Unconditional MFN Treatment

There are several reasons that may be cited to support the application of the unconditional most-favored-nation principle. For example, GATT economists have noted five significant benefits from application of the most-favored-nation treatment.[7] First, in economic terms, application of the MFN rule means that a country's imports will be supplied by the most efficient international supplier. When tariffs are varied according to the source of goods, it is not clear that that will be the case. Second, for trade policy purposes, application of the MFN rule protects bilateral concessions and generalizes them as the basis for the multilateral trading system. In this sense, the MFN principle serves as a positive force for liberalization in the system and, in particular, protects the interests of the small trading countries: the benefits of free trade are multilateralized to all countries, whether rich or poor, weak or strong. Moreover, small trading countries can benefit from concessions without necessarily making concessions themselves. Third, application of the MFN principle promotes better international relations since it avoids the bitterness and tensions that may result from discriminatory policies. Fourth, its application produces domestic benefits in that it simplifies the administration of tariffs and other forms of protection (no origin rules are needed) and it promotes more transparent policies. Finally, it serves as a constraint on the ability of special interests to obtain discriminatory trade measures.

However, the case for MFN treatment is not undisputed. In the first place, while it may be true that the MFN principle is generally in the interest of most countries most of the time, it is not clear that it is always in their interest. For example, it may be possible for some major trading nations to use their economic power in general or in respect of a specific product to gain more in not adhering to unconditional MFN generally, but rather following a conditional-MFN approach. While overall world welfare may not be maximized, these countries may be able to maximize their own welfare in certain circumstances.

Second, while it may be true that the application of the MFN rule promotes multilateralism in some respects, it is also true that the application of the MFN rule results in the so-called "free-rider" problem. There are two aspects of this problem. On the one hand, countries benefit automatically from the liberalization measures of others, whether or not they undertake such measures on their own. This enables smaller trading nations, in particular, to free-ride on the concessions made by others. Thus, they may make fewer concessions themselves. On the other hand, fear of what they view as excessive free-riding may cause major trading nations to agree to less liberalization than they would if reciprocity were required. Again, the result may be fewer concessions if unconditional MFN treatment is required. It is not clear that this fear of free-riding has significantly slowed down the process of multilateral trade liberalization, but it is clear that it is a factor in negotiations. Unless a so-called "critical mass" is willing to make liberalization commitments, some major trading nations may not make commitments.[8] In this respect, it could be argued that it would be better to make progress towards freer trade with smaller groups of countries willing to do so on a reciprocal basis, rather than to wait for the critical mass to emerge.

Against this one could argue that these days more trade barriers exist between non-like-minded countries so that this approach would not significantly liberalize trade anyway. Indeed, in light of the most recent attempt to liberalize investment amongst the OECD countries, the success of such an approach does not seem to be guaranteed either: The OECD negotiations on a Multilateral Agreement on Investment (MAI) have thus far not succeeded. It could be argued that negotiations on investment in the WTO would likely be more successful because of the cross-sectoral trade-offs that could be agreed upon at the WTO. In any event, the recent success of the WTO negotiations on information technology products, telecommunications, and financial services[9] suggests that the problem of critical mass is not at all insurmountable.

Third, the concept of reciprocity is one that is typically used to convince domestic interests that trade liberalization is in their interest. The unconditional MFN principle is, of course, the antithesis of reciprocity, and the perceived lack of reciprocity may sometimes make it more difficult for governments to commit to trade liberalization. This concern is closely related to the foregoing issue and the problem of critical mass.

Overall, it appears that unconditional MFN treatment is the most desirable policy for the world as a whole. While the problems of free riders and the need for perceived reciprocity are significant, they do not counteract the arguments in favor of unconditional MFN.

## 2. MFN in GATT and the WTO

### GATT Article I:1

The basic MFN provision in GATT is Article I, paragraph 1, which provides:

> With respect to customs duties and charges of any kind imposed on or in connection with importation or exportation or imposed on the international transfer of payments for imports or exports, and with respect to the method of levying such duties and charges, and with respect to all rules and formalities in connection with importation and exportation, and with respect to all matters referred to in paragraphs 2 and 4 of Article III, any advantage, favor, privilege or immunity granted by any Member to any product originating in or destined for any other country shall be accorded immediately and unconditionally to the like product originating in or destined for the territories of all other Members.

This provision is often called the most fundamental provision in GATT. It, along with Article II on tariff schedules, may be amended only if all Members accept the amendment.[10]

A number of interpretive issues are presented by the wording of Article I. These issues include: (i) what is the scope of the coverage of Article I:1?; (ii) what is "any advantage, favor, privilege or immunity"?; (iii) how is "originating" defined?; (iv) how is "accorded . . . unconditionally" to be interpreted?; and (v) what is covered by the concept of "like product"? The discussion of the last issue will be postponed to Part III; the other issues are discussed briefly in this section.

*The Scope of GATT Article I:1*

The scope of Article I:1 is defined in its initial clauses. Basically, it covers duties and charges levied on goods or related payment transfers; the methods of levying such duties and charges; all rules and formalities related to importation and exportation; and internal taxation and internal regulations of the type covered by Article III:4. Importantly, and sometimes forgotten, Article I:1 applies to exportation as well as importation.

With respect to "customs duties," Article I:1 applies to both bound and unbound tariffs.[11] With respect to duties and charges, consular taxes fall within this category,[12] as do merchandise processing fees or customs user fees.[13] Similarly, so-called variable levies would seem to fall within the scope of Article I, although no decision has ever been taken as to whether such levies would be consistent with Article I.[14]

The phrases "methods of levying such duties and charges" and "all rules and formalities" have been interpreted to include the application of antidumping rules[15] and countervailing duty rules.[16] It has also been suggested that the phrases include such matters as customs valuation rules[17] and more generally "improved sets of rules," such as those entered into in respect of some GATT provisions in the Tokyo Round.[18]

With respect to the reference to Article III, paragraphs 2 and 4, the Chairman of the Contracting Parties ruled in 1948 that with respect to rebates of excise taxes, Article I:1 would be applicable to any advantage, etc. granted with respect to internal taxes.[19] In 1955 it was proposed to amend Article I:1 to specify that it applied "with respect to the application of internal taxes to exported goods," but the amendment had not been ratified by all Contracting Parties at the time it was abandoned in 1967.[20]

In a recent case, Article I:1 was also found to apply to a tariff-rate quota resulting from compensation negotiations between two Members within the framework of Article XXVIII of GATT, where the results of the negotiations were incorporated into a Member's Schedule.[21]

As a general proposition, it can be said that the scope of Article I:1 has been interpreted broadly in WTO/GATT practice.

*Advantages, Favors, Privileges, and Immunities*

Article I:1 covers advantages, favors, privileges, and immunities granted by a WTO Member to *any* country,[22] including countries which are not WTO Members. Any such advantage, etc. needs to be extended immediately and unconditionally to all WTO Members. Of course, countries which are not WTO Members cannot claim such extension. In other words, an advantage the EC were to give to Russia (to date not a WTO Member), would need to be given also to Mongolia and the Kyrgyz Republic (both WTO Members), but not to Ukraine or the People's Republic of China (to date not WTO Members).

One may also note that only those advantages, etc. "granted . . . to any *product*" are subject to the MFN obligation in Article I:1.[23] Advantages, etc. not linked to the import, export or internal taxation, sale, distribution or use of products but, for example, exclusively linked to producers or service suppliers (without direct or indirect repercussions on the related products), would not seem to be subject to the MFN requirement.

There have been several panel reports that have dealt with the question of what sort of advantages, etc. are covered by Article I:1. For example, in the *US—Customs User Fee* case, the panel, having found that the so-called customs user fee was within the scope of Article I:1, considered whether an exemption from the imposition of that fee, which was afforded to certain developing countries, was an advantage that had to be extended to all contracting parties. Although the panel made no formal finding because the argument had been made by third parties and not the parties to the dispute, its description of the issues suggests that it would have found a violation of Article I.[24]

In a case involving the US countervailing duty law, a panel found that the automatic backdating of the effect of revoking a countervailing duty order without the need to have requested an injury review was an advantage extended to certain contracting parties that had to be extended unconditionally to other contracting parties pursuant to Article I:1.[25] In another case, the panel found that a duty waiver conditioned on certification by a particular government was an advantage.[26] The panel on *Indonesia – Autos* considered both customs duty benefits and internal tax benefits to be advantages of the type covered by Article I:1.[27]

In the panel report on *EC – Bananas,* a number of aspects of the EC import regime for bananas were considered to be advantages and found to violate Article I:1 because they were not accorded to all WTO members. These included:

1. The use of a comparatively less complex licensing procedure for imports of bananas from certain countries (e.g., less data required to be submitted to obtain a license).[28]
2. The allocation of 30 per cent of the import licenses for bananas from one group of countries to operators who had marketed bananas from another group of countries, which was found to provide an incentive for operators to maintain or increase their purchases and sales of bananas from the latter group of countries and thus to constitute an advantage to those bananas.[29]
3. The issuance of import licenses for imports of bananas from certain countries conditional upon the economic activities performed by the operator requesting the license (i.e., upon being a "primary" or "secondary" importer or a ripener) was found to advantage bananas from other countries not subject to such a condition.[30]
4. The grant of so-called hurricane licenses only to operators which included or represented producers from certain countries.[31]
5. The allowance of imports of bananas, at an in-quota tariff, when these bananas were accompanied by an export certificate issued by certain countries.[32] The importance of *EC – Bananas* for Article I:1 lies in the fact that an advantage, etc. under Article I:1 was found to cover not only actual trade but also competitive opportunities: If the contested measure affects the competitive relationship between products with different origins, the measure will be found to confer an advantage.[33] To that extent, the concept of advantage under Article I:1 has thus been interpreted the same way as the notion of less favorable treatment under Article III:4 (calling for an effective equality of opportunities between imports and domestic products).[34]

Finally, it is worth noting that an argument that *less* favorable treatment accorded to a product with respect to one rule or procedure, contrary to Article I:1, is offset by a *more* favorable treatment under another rule or procedure—and that therefore on the whole no violation of Article I:1 can be found—has been rejected.[35]

*"Originating"*

It is generally agreed that under existing WTO/GATT rules, Members have considerable freedom to set their own rules of origin.[36] However, as a result of the Uruguay Round negotiations, the WTO complex of agreements includes an Agreement on Rules of Origin. That agreement established a work program, now expected to be completed in 1999,[37] which will set standard rules of origin for non-preferential purposes. For the moment, the agreement requires several general principles to be followed in the application of rules of origin, such as that rules of origin shall not be used to pursue trade objectives; shall not in themselves create restrictive, distortive or disruptive effects on international trade; and shall be transparent.[38] Disciplines to be observed once the harmonization program has been implemented include the principle that the country of origin of a good needs to be either the country where the good has been wholly obtained or, when more than one country is concerned in the production of the good, the country where the last substantial transformation has been carried out.[39]

In one panel case dealing with origin issues under Article I, the panel examined a US requirement that tuna could not be labeled as "Dolphin Safe" unless certain conditions were met, including conditions specific to tuna from the Eastern Tropical Pacific (ETP). The panel found that since the US considered tuna to originate in the country where the fishing boat was registered (and not the geographical area where the fish was caught), there was no violation of Article I. It did not accept the argument that since tuna from outside the ETP was treated differently than tuna from inside the ETP, there was discrimination of the type covered by Article I.[40]

*"Accorded . . . Unconditionally"*

Article I:1 establishes an unconditional MFN obligation. An advantage given to State A must be accorded to all WTO Members, whether or not they meet any conditions imposed on State A. Thus, any notion of conditioning an advantage on reciprocity would normally run afoul of Article I. For example, in a 1952 working party report, it was noted that a proposal to include a reciprocity clause in a convention on the importation of commercial samples would be inconsistent with Article I.[41] In contrast, in 1955, a working party report saw no reason to disturb a long-standing practice by which some contracting parties accorded special treatment to equipment for diplomatic and consular offices on the basis of reciprocity.[42]

In the panel report on *Belgian Family Allowances,* tax exemptions for products purchased by public bodies made conditional on the existence of a certain system of family allowances to be in force in the exporting country, were found to be inconsistent with the unconditionality principle in Article I:1.[43] Application of the "unconditionally" requirement was also considered by a panel in a case involving an EC provision that required an additional security deposit in respect of imports from countries that were not in a position to guarantee that certain minimum prices would be respected. In the view of the panel, since a guarantee was required in all cases, it was not a violation of Article I:1 for the form to vary depending on whether it was lodged by an individual importer or government.[44] In a case involving a duty waiver made conditional on certification by a particular government, it was found that Article I:1 was violated because this advantage was in fact not made available to other contracting parties, i.e., a case of *de facto* discrimination was established.[45]

Recently, a WTO panel concluded that the grant by Indonesia of customs and tax advantages to cars produced by one company in Korea violated Article I:1 because those advantages were conditional, *inter alia,* on the existence of a contractual relationship between an Indonesian company and the Korean company.[46] According to the panel, advantages granted by a WTO Member cannot be made conditional on, nor even be affected by, the existence of private contractual obligations, such as the existence of a deal between a domestic company designated by the government and a foreign company. Advantages accorded to products of one country (in that case, to Korean cars and parts and components thereof) need to be granted to imported like products from all other WTO Member "immediately and unconditionally." In reaching its conclusion, the panel noted the 1973 working party report on the accession of Hungary, where the GATT Secretariat had expressed the view that the prerequisite of having a co-operation contract in order to benefit from certain tariff treatment appeared to imply conditional MFN treatment and would therefore not be compatible with GATT rules.[47]

## Other MFN or Similar Provisions

There are numerous MFN-like provisions in GATT and other WTO agreements in addition to Article I.1 of GATT. For example, in GATT, Article XIII imposes a sort of MFN requirement on the administration of quotas, subject to a limited exception in Article XIV. GATT's general exceptions provision, Article XX, limits its application to measures that "are not applied in a manner which would constitute a means of arbitrary or unjustifiable discrimination between countries where the same conditions prevail." In addition, there are MFN-like requirements in Article III:7 on international mixing requirements, Article IV(b) concerning films quotas, Article V on transit of goods, Article IX:1 on marks of origin, Article XVII:1 on state trading and Article XVIII:20 concerning measures to assist economic development.

Many of the WTO agreements on trade in goods have MFN provisions. For example, such provisions are found in the Agreement on the Application of Sanitary and Phytosanitary Measures (Articles 2.3 and 5.5)[48] and the Agreement on Technical Barriers to Trade (Articles 2.1 and 5.1), the Agreement on Preshipment Inspection (Article 2.1), the Agreement on Rules of Origin (Article 3(c)) and the Agreement on Import Licensing (Article 1.3).[49] The Agreement on Safeguards also imposes an MFN requirement in respect of allocation of quotas, subject to an exception applicable in certain cases (Article 5.2).[50]

The General Agreement on Trade in Services (GATS) contains an MFN provision in Article II:1, which provides as follows:

> With respect to any measure covered by this Agreement, each Member shall accord immediately and unconditionally to services and service suppliers of any other Member treatment no less favorable than that it accords to like services and service suppliers of any other country.

GATS permits exceptions to this obligation to be specified at the time of its entry into force. In principle, the exemptions should not exceed a period of 10 years. It is noteworthy that the wording of the GATS' MFN requirement resembles the wording of the national treatment requirement of Article III of GATT more than the wording of Article I:1 of GATT. Nonetheless, the Appellate Body has ruled that in interpreting Article II, one should draw inspiration from the interpretation of Article I:1 of GATT notwithstanding the differences in wording.[51]

The Agreement on Trade-Related Aspects of Intellectual Property Rights (the TRIPS Agreement) also contains a general MFN requirement (Article 4, first sentence), subject to certain exceptions listed in the TRIPS Agreement itself (Article 4, second sentence). Article 4, first sentence, provides as follows: "With regard to the protection of intellectual property, any advantage, favor, privilege or immunity granted by a Member to the nationals of any other country shall be accorded immediately and unconditionally to the nationals of all other Members."

### Exceptions to the MFN Obligation

There are two major exceptions to the MFN obligations found in the WTO agreements: the exceptions for customs unions and free trade areas and for special and differential treatment of developing countries. Article I:2 of GATT also provides an exception for historical preferences, but over time, this exception has become quite limited in importance. Interestingly, the exception represented a loss for the United States in the initial GATT negotiations, as it allowed the continuation of the British system of

Commonwealth preferences, although it did limit their expansion.[52] Also, Article IX of the WTO Agreement grants the authority to the Ministerial Conference to waive certain obligations imposed on a WTO Member by a three-fourths majority decision. Such country specific waivers may deviate from the MFN principle.[53]

*Regional Agreements*

*Customs Unions and Free Trade Areas*

Article XXIV of GATT permits in certain circumstances the creation of free trade areas and customs unions. A customs union is defined as the creation of a single customs territory such that duties and other regulations of commerce are eliminated with respect to substantially all the trade between the constituent territories and substantially the same duties and other restrictive regulations of commerce are applied to non-members of the union. A free-trade area is defined as a group of territories where duties and other regulations of commerce are eliminated with respect to substantially all the trade between the constituent territories.[54] Free trade areas and customs unions by their very nature discriminate against non-members. While Article XXIV:4 recognizes the desirability of such entities, it also notes that their purpose should be to facilitate trade between the constituent territories and not to raise barriers to the trade of other contracting parties with such territories. More specifically, Article XXIV:5 requires that following the creation of the area or union, the duties and commercial regulations applied to non-members must not be higher or more restrictive than those applied before creation.[55]

The interpretation of the requirements of Article XXIV has long been a disputed issue in GATT.[56] While there have been long discussions of the various issues in the course of WTO and GATT consideration of various free-trade areas and customs unions, there have been few firm conclusions drawn.[57] In recent years, there has been a proliferation of these entities,[58] which has led to calls for more effective surveillance.[59]

*Mutual Recognition Agreements*

Although they are not free trade areas or customs union, one might also mention under the rubric of regional agreements, the increasing importance of so-called mutual recognition agreements (MRAs), which are typically concluded on either a bilateral or regional basis. MRAs aim at removing trade barriers between the parties thereto related to the differences between them in standards, testing requirements, technical regulations and related procedures. Since they apply only to trade between the parties, they would seem to conflict with the unconditional MFN principle. On the one hand, such agreements offer an effective means of facilitating trade. On the other hand, they also have an impact on the competitive strength of non-participating countries. This is why two WTO agreements encourage Members to negotiate MRAs but at the same time require that they do so in a transparent and open way.

Article 4 of the Agreement on Sanitary and Phytosanitary Measures (SPS Agreement) requires Members to "accept the [SPS] measures of other Members as equivalent . . . if the exporting Member objectively demonstrates to the importing Member that its measures achieve the importing Member's appropriate level of [SPS] protection." It further states that "Members shall, upon request, enter into consultations with the aim of achieving bilateral and multilateral agreements on recognition of the equivalence of specified [SPS] measures." In other words, Members are encouraged to conclude MRAs in the SPS area but should do so equally with all WTO Members which so request. Article 6 of the Agreement on Technical Barriers to Trade includes similar, though more elaborated, rights and obligations. It sums up the different elements which may need to be agreed upon in an MRA and explicitly confirms that the MFN principle applies to MRAs, stating that "Members are encouraged to permit participation of conformity assessment bodies located in the territories of other Members in their conformity assessment procedures under conditions no less favorable than those accorded to bodies located within their territory or the territory of any other country."[60]

*Developing Countries*

There are numerous provisions in WTO agreements that permit more favorable treatment to be given to developing countries.[61] Of particular importance to Article I:1, is the so-called "Enabling Clause,"[62] which essentially allows developed countries to extend tariff preferences to developing countries.[63] The Enabling Clause was adopted at the end of the Tokyo Round and is now part of the GATT acquis through the incorporation clause in the definition of GATT 1994.

It remains unclear, however, whether the Enabling Clause also allows a developed country to discriminate *between* developing countries by granting tariff preferences to certain developing countries only. In practice, the GSP schemes of major trading nations grant preferences to certain developing countries only, with a built in "graduation" among beneficiaries. The preamble to the GSP Decision of 25 June 1975 refers, however, to the unanimous agreement reached at the Second UNCTAD "in favor of the early establishment of a mutually acceptable system of *generalized*, non-reciprocal and *non-discriminatory* preferences beneficial to the developing countries" (emphasis added). An examination of the relevant UNCTAD documents shows that developed countries wanted to grant their preferences following the principle of self-election, whereas developing countries expressed the view that no developing country member should be excluded from a GSP.[64]

## 3. MFN and the Concept of Like Product

The concept of "like product" is a fundamental issue in the application of the MFN obligation in GATT Article I:1: The advantage afforded to one product (originating in or destined for any country) must be afforded to another product (originating in or destined for all other WTO Members) only if the other product is a *like* product.[65]

In this section, the problem related to the like product concept is set in context. Thereafter, GATT definitions of like products are discussed and the application of the like product concept in Article I cases is analyzed. In Part IV, the possibility of a different approach to resolving problems heretofore treated as "like product" problems is considered. In this regard, considerable attention will be devoted to Article III: first, because most of the case law and controversy on the concept of like product developed under Article III; second, because Article I and III, both addressing discrimination, are interrelated, with one and the same measure often challenged under (and found inconsistent with) both provisions.

### Outline of the Problem

Article I:1 deals with differences in treatment between products which result from regulatory distinctions made by governments. If such distinctions are made exclusively on the basis of the origin of the product – rather than on the basis of factors affecting the properties, nature, qualities or end use of the product itself – no doubt Article I:1 would be violated. Such a violation could be referred to as *de jure* discrimination contrary to Article I:1. A simple "but for" test can reveal this kind of violation: "but for" the country of origin, would the products be treated alike? If so, there is a *de jure* discrimination. Origin-based discrimination between products is one extreme. The other extreme consists of regulatory distinctions made between products which are manifestly different. If a WTO Member taxes sales of alcoholic beverages from State A ten times higher than sales of bread from State B, no one will argue that this violates the MFN principle because a product from State A is taxed ten times higher than a product from State B: alcoholic beverages and bread are obviously not "like products."

In many dispute settlement cases neither of these two extremes (*de jure* discrimination or discrimination between manifestly different products) will be submitted for examination. Rather, complaints often concern regulatory distinctions which are not explicitly linked to the origin of a product, but discriminate between different products within the same broader category (e.g., a distinction between cars selling for more than $30,000 and those selling for less;[66] or between vodka and shochu, both being alcoholic beverages[67]). This is where the question of likeness arises in its full complexity: Which differences between products are sufficient to make them not "like," such that governments may treat them differently? Should the "likeness" of products be defined referring only to the physical characteristics of the products as such, taking into account the tariff classification maintained by the country at issue, or should other factors, such as the aim or actual effect of the distinction made between the products also be considered or even be decisive? In cases where there is no *de jure* discrimination, should some kind of a *de facto* discrimination test be imposed, not necessarily in determining likeness of products but under one of the other requirements necessary to establish a violation of the MFN principle? Would such a test avoid the risk that regulatory distinctions not at all related to the origin of the products will be found to be inconsistent with WTO provisions, a result that may not have been intended by the drafters of GATT and that may not be acceptable for some WTO Members?[68] These issues are discussed in the remainder of the paper.

## GATT Definition of Like Product

### *A Different Meaning Provision by Provision and Case by Case*

The concept of "like product" is incorporated in not less than nine Articles of the GATT.[69] It has long been accepted in GATT thinking that the concept may have a different meaning in the different provisions in which it is used.[70] This view has been explicitly adopted by the Appellate Body, which has stated that

> [t]he concept of "likeness" is a relative one that evokes the image of an accordion. The accordion of "likeness" stretches and squeezes in different places as different provisions of the WTO Agreement are applied. The width of the accordion in any one of those places must be determined by the particular provision in which the term "like" is encountered as well as by the context and circumstances that prevail in any given case to which that provisions may apply.[71]

Thus, the concept of like product not only varies depending on the GATT provision in which it is mentioned; it can also be interpreted differently under one and the same provision depending on the particular context and circumstances of the case.[72]

Exactly how "like product" should be interpreted differently in different contexts is not always clear. For example, it has been suggested that the definition of like product as used in Article III:2, first sentence, dealing with discriminatory internal taxation may be narrow, in reflection of the fact that Article III:2, second sentence, also deals with discriminatory internal taxation in respect of the broader class of directly competitive or substitutable products.[73] Since Article III:4, which deals with discriminatory internal regulations in respect of like products, does not have a provision dealing with directly competitive or substitutable products, one can argue that the concept of like product should be interpreted more expansively under Article III:4. On the other hand, it can also be argued that the different language in Articles III:2 and III:4 reflects a decision to impose more stringent obligations in respect of discriminatory internal taxation, which is similar to tariff treatment, than in respect of discriminatory internal regulations, where the effect on the competitive opportunities of imports is less direct.[74] Such a view would lead one to advocate the same narrow interpretation of like product in both Article III:2 and III:4.

In the case of Article I, one can argue that the interpretation of the concept of like product may need to vary depending on the issue presented. For example, the answer to the question of whether a product is like another for purposes of tariffs may not be same as whether a product is like for purposes of the clause of Article I:1 which incorporates Article III:2 and III:4. This issue is explored in more detail below.

*The Classic Test: Physical Characteristics*

The classic GATT statement of the factors to consider in deciding whether two products are like products is found in the working party report on border tax adjustments. That report states in respect of "like or similar products":

> [t]he interpretation of the term should be examined on a case-by-case basis. This would allow a fair assessment in each case of the different elements that constitute a "similar" product. Some criteria were suggested for determining, on a case-by-case basis, whether a product is "similar": the product's end-uses in a given market; consumers' tastes and habits, which change from country to country; the product's properties, nature, and quality.[75]

As will be seen below, the factors listed in this report are those commonly examined by WTO and GATT panels in determining likeness for purposes of Article I:1.

## Application of the MFN Requirement and the Concept of Like Product

### *Overview*

In considering the concept of like product as it is applied under Article I:1 of GATT, it is apparent that it cannot be given the same breadth of meaning with respect to all matters covered by Article I:1. In particular, it would seem useful to consider its meaning in the context of (i) tariff discrimination between products falling under different bindings or tariff lines, (ii) tariff discrimination within one binding or tariff line and (iii) other forms of discrimination.

### *Tariff Discrimination between Products Falling under Different Bindings or Tariff Lines*

This category of cases are those that involve a claim that a product subject to a higher tariff is like a product subject to a lower tariff. The essential issue is to what extent Members can make fine distinctions in their tariff classifications and bindings. Both at the London session of the Preparatory Committee and at the Havana Conference, it was suggested that the method of tariff classification could be used to determine whether products are "like."[76]

There have been three important GATT cases that dealt with this issue, i.e., where a GATT contracting party had either lowered a tariff for certain products only and not for allegedly other like products or reclassified products resulting in different tariffs for allegedly like products.

The first was the *Sardines* case from the early 1950's.[77] As a result of the Torquay negotiations, Germany's duties on sardines remained unbound at 30 per cent; that on sprats was bound at 25 per cent and that on herrings at 20 or 25 per cent. Afterwards, however, Germany lowered its duties on sardines to 14 per cent, without according the same reduction to sprats and herrings. Norway initiated dispute settlement proceedings because the higher tariffs were applied on the fish of greater interest to it. The panel implicitly rejected the claim that the three types of fish were like products for purposes of Article I. It found in Norway's favor, however, on the grounds that Norway had been led by Germany to expect that the three types would continue to receive the same tariff treatment. Thus, Norway was able to establish non-violation nullification or impairment of benefits under Article XXIII:1(b) of GATT.

The second case involved coffee.[78] Spain had been applying a single tariff line for unroasted coffee subject to one tariff rate. It had not bound this rate in GATT. Subsequently, Spain split this one tariff line into five tariff lines, dutiable at two different rates. The effect of the change was apparently to lead to comparatively higher duties on stronger coffee beans. Brazil, which considered itself to have been adversely affected by this reclassification, brought a case against Spain. The panel ruled that unroasted coffee is unroasted coffee, i.e., that it was not possible to distinguish between types of unroasted coffees for tariff purposes. Factors such as differences in taste and aroma resulting from the geographical origin of the coffee, cultivation methods and processing of the beans as well as genetic factors, were not considered to be sufficient to make the products not like.

The third case involved so-called dimension lumber, i.e., lumber finished to certain standard sizes.[79] The Japanese tariff schedule imposed different tariff rates on different kinds of lumber, based on distinctions among various species. These different tariffs had been autonomously introduced by Japan without negotiation. Most of the tariff lines at issue had not been bound by Japan. Canada was of the view that dimension lumber from the species common to Canada was like dimension lumber from other countries, in particular, the United States, and that Canadian lumber was treated less favorably since it was subject to higher duties. The panel noted that likeness for purposes of assessing tariff treatment had to be based on an individual country's tariff schedule and that the concept of "dimension lumber" was extraneous to the Japanese tariff schedule. It was therefore not an appropriate basis for establishing likeness under Article I:1. In the panel's view, Members have considerable discretion in classifying products in their tariff schedules and binding different tariff rates for different products. Accordingly, the panel rejected the Canadian claim.

These cases are not consistent. In particular, the respective approaches of the *Coffee* case and the *Lumber* case are quite different. All in all, it seems that the *Lumber* case is better reasoned. Members should be able to decide exactly which products they wish to make subject to specific tariff bindings. While the WTO agreements, including GATT 1994, broadly aim at trade liberalization, it is recognized that Members should be able to negotiate tariff bindings in light of their particular national interests. The practice of allowing Members to establish fine distinctions in tariff schedules seems supported by GATT practice generally. For example, while there have been several cases where certain alcoholic beverages have been found to be like other alcoholic beverages for purposes of Article III:2, these cases have not led to claims that the tariff treatment afforded to such products must be identical. There have also been examples in the past where the GATT contracting parties seemed to accept that for purposes of applying Article I:1 to tariff rates, distinctions based on weight and value are permissible, even if they might not be in the Article III context. This line of reasoning would thus favor an interpretation of "like product" under Article I:1 that is even narrower than the interpretation of "like product" under Article III.

This approach seems to be confirmed—with respect to tariff classifications specifically mentioned in a Member's schedule—in the recent Appellate Body Report on *EC – LAN Equipment,* where the following was stated:

> Tariff negotiations are a process of reciprocal demands and concessions, of "give and take." It is only normal that importing Members define their offers (and their ensuing obligations) in terms which suit their needs. On the other hand, exporting Members have to ensure that their corresponding rights are described in such a manner in the Schedules of importing Members that their export interests, as agreed in the negotiations, are guaranteed. . . . [T]he fact that Members' Schedules are an integral part of the GATT 1994 indicates that, while each Schedule represents the tariff commitments made by *one* Member, they represent a common agreement among *all* Members.[80]

If the tariff schedule of one Member and the classifications made therein are thus to be fully considered as treaty language agreed upon by all WTO Members vis-à-vis that Member, how then can any tariff discrimination between products explicitly mentioned in such tariff schedule be found to be inconsistent with Article I:1? Following the Appellate Body's point of view in *EC – LAN Equipment,* it would seem that this cannot be the case.

In the subsequent *EC – Poultry* case, however, the Appellate Body ruled that concessions contained in a Member's schedule must be consistent with Article I on the ground that a Member's schedule can only yield rights under GATT, not unilaterally diminish GATT obligations.[81] Even though this means that a concession in a schedule granted only to certain Members will be inconsistent with Article I:1, it would seem that the tariff classifications contained in a schedule (discriminating not between Members but between products) do not diminish obligations under Article I. They rather condition the tariff concessions granted in the schedule specifying to which products each binding applies and thereby clarifying issues of likeness, thus making the classification—which after all was accepted by all WTO Members—legitimate for Article I purposes.[82] However, this conclusion could apply to tariff distinctions between products explicitly mentioned in a Member's schedule, but not necessarily so in cases were a Member unilaterally changes its tariff classification.

Problems of tariff reclassification of products not specifically mentioned in a negotiated schedule, such as those that arose in *Coffee* and *Lumber*, might better be handled as non-violation claims, as was the case in *Sardines*. In those cases, however, the lack of tariff bindings would have complicated bringing a non-violation case. Some argue that no legitimate expectations can arise—and a non-violation claim under GATT can thus not succeed—in cases where no tariff concession has been made.[83] Still, the *EC – LAN Equipment* case would arguably have been better brought as a non-violation case. There, the Appellate Body reversed the panel's finding that the EC's reclassification of certain computer equipment (not specifically mentioned in the EC schedule) under a higher tariff line was contrary to Article II. The Appellate Body rejected the panel's reliance, under Article II, on the legitimate expectations held by the US that LAN equipment would be treated as automatic-data-processing (ADP) machines and not as telecommunication apparatus, subject to higher duties. The Appellate Body did so on the ground that legitimate expectations can only be considered under a non-violation claim.[84] Perhaps if the case had been brought as a non-violation claim, the US might have prevailed.

In conclusion, for purposes of interpreting tariff schedules, WTO/GATT case law accords considerable discretion to Members in subdividing products into different tariff categories for purposes of Article II without fear of violating Article I:1, subject of course to the constraint of the non-violation provision of Article XXIII:1(b).

### *Tariff Discrimination between Products Falling within One Binding or Tariff Line*

In contrast to the situation just described where the discrimination has occurred between products that were in separate tariff bindings or tariff lines, a different situation occurs where there is tariff discrimination in respect of a product that is classified within one tariff binding or tariff line.

A recent example of this arose in *Indonesia—Autos* where Indonesia charged a lower rate of duty on automobiles and parts and components thereof if certain conditions were met (e.g., manufactured by Indonesian nationals under Indonesia's National Car program in the case of autos, or if certain local content requirements were met by the importer in the case of parts and components).[85] However, no such distinction amongst automobiles or amongst parts and components thereof was made in Indonesia's tariff schedule.

In this context, the question arises whether the term "like product" should be interpreted more narrowly than the breadth of a tariff binding. Of course, if the tariff binding in question is a broad ceiling binding, a narrower definition is necessary. However, even if the tariff binding in question is coextensive with a relatively detailed classification, the products thereunder may differ in some respects.[86]

In *Indonesia – Autos* the like product issue would seem to be relatively easy since the criteria used by Indonesia to distinguish between products were explicitly origin-based (a case of *de jure* discrimination). This raises the question of whether it is sufficient that an origin-based distinction is made for there to be a violation of the MFN principle or whether specific examples of like products must be shown. If the latter, it may be difficult to establish discrimination in respect of consumer products that inevitably differ in some respects. As argued above, a simple "but for" test to establish *de jure* discrimination would seem to suffice: If a WTO Member were to levy a tariff of 100 per cent on all products from State A and of 10 per cent on all products from State B, everyone would agree that the MFN principle is breached. There would seem to be no need to determine whether products from State A and State B are like, even though this could be disputed for many products. Trying to determine likeness of actually traded goods would only direct the attention away from an obvious and manifest discrimination (the core issue under Article I) to the disputable issue of likeness, which may be viewed as a peripheral issue. This is consistent with the oft-cited statement that the non-discrimination rules of GATT are designed to protect expectations of competitive relationships, and not actual trade flows: Even if the product subject to the measure is—at the time of examination—not being imported, one should still be able to compare *hypothetical* imports with the actually produced domestic products on the simple ground that the trade restrictive measure at issue may well be the very reason why no imports are currently made.

The Panel on *Indonesia – Autos,* addressing Article I:1 (and in so doing referring back to its examination under Article III:2, first sentence), seems to have followed this approach. However, it still decided first that certain imported automobiles (and parts and components) are like National Cars (and parts and components) imported from Korea, referring to their end use, basic properties, nature, and quality. Only thereafter, the panel noted that the distinction made by Indonesia between automobiles and parts and components was not based on the products *per se,* but rather on such factors as the nationality of the producer or the origin of the parts and components contained in the automobile. To find a violation under Article III:2, first sentence, it then made a hypothetical comparison:

> An imported motor vehicle alike in all aspects relevant to a likeness determination would be taxed at higher rate simply because of its origin or lack of sufficient local content. Such vehicles certainly can exist (and, as demonstrated above, do in fact exist). In our view, such an origin-based distinction in respect of internal taxes suffices in itself to violate Article III:2, without the need to demonstrate the existence of actually traded like products.[87]

With respect to Article I:1, the panel noted that "a legislation itself may violate [Article I] if it could lead in principle to less favorable treatment of the same product."[88] Indeed, the mere fact that products would be treated the same by Indonesia "but for" their origin, would seem to suffice to find a violation: in so doing Indonesia discriminates products in all aspects alike but for their origin.

A hypothetical comparison was also recently used by a panel in an Article III:2 case. In *Canada – Periodicals,*[89] one of the measures at issue was an origin-neutral 80 per cent excise tax applied to the value of all advertising carried by split-run editions of periodicals[90] (irrespective of whether they were of Canadian or foreign origin). Non-split-run periodicals were not subject to the tax. Contrary to the measure examined in *Indonesia – Autos,* the distinction thus made between products was not explicitly origin-based. No *de jure* discrimination contrary to Article III:2, first sentence, could thus be established. However, the panel considered that imported split-run periodicals (taxed at 80 per cent) are "like" domestic non-split-run periodicals (not taxed) and that, therefore, Article III:2, first sentence, was violated. In so doing, the panel made a hypothetical comparison between two editions of the same Canadian-owned magazine printed in the US: The first one being an imported split-run periodical, namely a Canadian edition of the magazine for which also a US edition was being published; the second one being a domestic non-split-run periodical, namely the one and only Canadian edition of the same magazine (the publishers having decided to no longer publish a US edition). Since these two periodicals are only different editions of the same magazine, the panel considered that they are like in all respects. Since one is taxed at 80 per cent and the other not, the panel concluded that Article III:2, first sentence, was violated.[91] The Appellate Body reversed the finding of likeness, mainly on the ground that the panel had used an "incorrect" hypothetical example, namely two editions of the same magazine, both imported products, which could not have been in the Canadian market at the same time.[92] However, instead of looking itself for a correct hypothetical example – the Appellate Body had agreed that hypothetical imports of split-run periodicals have to be considered[93]—it continued its examination of the measure under Article III:2, second sentence, and found a violation.[94] Since the Appellate Body accepted the possibility of using hypothetical examples, one could, for example, make the same comparison as the panel but add to the hypothesis that for the second edition (the domestic non-split-run periodical), the publisher not only decided to give up the US edition but also moved his business from the US to Canada. Then one would no longer compare two imported products, as noted by the Appellate Body. One could also make the following hypothetical comparison: imagine a publisher having to decide where to establish his business and whether or not to publish split-run editions of the first edition of his magazine. If he establishes himself in the US and publishes a split-run edition for the US market, the split-run periodical imported in Canada will be taxed at 80 per cent. If, on the other hand, he establishes his business in Canada and does not publish a split-run for the US market, his very same magazine would not be taxed.[95]

*Other Forms of Discrimination*

The other forms of discrimination covered by Article I:1 address the method, rules, and formalities related to customs administration and matters covered by Article III:2 and III:4.

The *US – Footwear from Brazil* case dealt with advantages related to "rules and formalities."[96] The automatic backdating of the effect of revocation of a pre-existing countervailing duty order granted only to duty-free products and not to dutiable products was considered to be an advantage under Article I:1. The panel then examined whether the products thus distinguished were like. Looking at the products to which this regime had actually been applied (comparing, e.g., automotive glass to non-rubber footwear), the panel found that these products were not like. However, the panel continued its examination and found that in principle duty-free and dutiable products are "like" and found a violation of Article I:1. The criterium used to distinguish between products was not linked to the product itself but to the duty treatment it received, a criterium dependent upon US government policy choices. Thus, identical products could be treated differently depending on whether or not they entered the US market under the US GSP program. The differences linked to such criteria should, indeed, not make products unlike.

Three GATT cases addressed the consistency of measures subject to paragraphs 2 and 4 of Article III with the MFN principle of Article I. First, the Working Party report on *Australian Subsidy on Ammonium Sulfate* addressed the withdrawal of subsidies by Australia for sodium nitrate, which of export interest to the complainant Chile, whereas subsidies were maintained for ammonium sulfate, where there was no such export interest. It was found that the two fertilizers were not like products on the ground that for Australian tariff purposes (as well as in other countries' tariff classification) they were listed as separate items and enjoyed a different treatment. Nevertheless, a case of non-violation was found.[97]

Second, in the panel report on *Belgian Family Allowances,* a different tax was imposed depending on whether or not the exporting country had a certain system of family allowances in place. The tax regime was found to be contrary to Article I:1.[98] Indeed, the criterium used by Belgium to distinguish between products did not relate to the products themselves. The products subject to the distinction could therefore be like, although the panel did not discuss the likeness issue in any detail. Since products were treated differently because of their origin, this would seem to be a case of *de jure* discrimination.

Third, in the panel report on *EEC – Measures on Animal Feed Proteins,* the consistency under Article I:1 of a requirement of different security deposits for different protein products was examined. The panel considered the requirement, which applied to both domestic and imported products, to be a matter covered by Article III and therefore subject to Article I:1 as well. In concluding that the various products at issue were not like, the panel referred to the existence of different tariff duty rates and tariff bindings for the different protein products, their varying protein contents and the different vegetable, animal, and synthetic origins of the products.[99] This conclusion was reached with respect to likeness under both Articles I and III.

More generally, there is an issue of whether the definition of "like product" for purposes of claims raised under Article I:1 on the basis of its incorporation of Article III:2 and III:4 should be the same as that used under Article III:2 and III:4. To avoid a different product coverage under two provisions dealing with the same measure, it would arguably be appropriate when dealing with Article III:4 measures (internal regulations) to maintain the same definition of likeness under both Article I:1 and Article III:4. It should be noted, however, that with respect to internal tax measures (Article III:2 measures), the MFN principle in Article I:1 only covers like products, whereas the national treatment principle in Article III:2 is stricter, prohibiting not only differences in taxation between like products but also between directly competitive or substitutable products. For purposes of consistency, one could argue that in these cases the like product concept should have the same (narrow) meaning under both Article I:1 and Article III:2.[100] On the other hand, to compensate for the narrower coverage of Article I:1, one could argue that like products under that provision, with respect to internal tax measures, should be interpreted more widely. Indeed, the main argument for a narrow interpretation of like products under Article III:2 is that it also covers directly competitive or substitutable products, an argument not valid under Article I:1.

*Likeness under GATS Article II*

The panel on *EC –Bananas,* considered—for the first time—to what extent services and service suppliers of different origin are like. It found that wholesale services are like, irrespective of the origin of the bananas supplied, on the ground that each of the different service activities taken individually was virtually the same and could only be distinguished by referring to the origin of the bananas. Similarly, the panel found that to the extent entities provide these like services, they are like service suppliers.[101] On the latter issue of likeness of service suppliers, it is arguable that a rather broad view was thus taken. Irrespective of whether a supplier is a natural person or a multinational company, a branch or a subsidiary, a reputable company or a company on the verge of collapse, as long as both supply like services, they will be considered to be like service suppliers.[102] The case did not involve differential treatment on the basis of the type of suppliers so it is not clear that the same result would be reached if such differential treatment was clearly presented as an issue.

*Summary*

So far under Article I:1, in interpreting the like product concept, panels have focused on the physical characteristics and similar features of the products involved and not on the aim or effect of the regulation at issue. In particular, panels have recognized tariff differentiation as a legitimate policy tool, subject to the possibility of a non-violation complaint. One can ask, however, whether the problems noted above suggest that a different definition of likeness would be appropriate, one that would perhaps accord governments more discretion in enacting product-based regulations. This issue is treated in the next section.

## 4. Further Thoughts on Like Products and Regulatory Distinctions

### The Aims and Effect Test

In recent years, there has been controversy over whether the above-described focus on physical similarities to determine likeness is appropriate. This has been particularly true in the case of Article III, which requires national treatment in respect of internal taxes and regulations be given to like imported products. Since Article III is directed against protectionist measures, as explained in Article III:1, which provides the context for the rest of Article III, it has been argued that consideration should be given to whether a measure is designed to afford protection in deciding whether products are like. In other words, if a measure does not have the aim and effect of protecting domestic production, then there should be no finding that imported products subject to differential treatment are like the relevant domestic products.

A variant of this so-called aims-and-effect test was first applied in *US—Malt Beverages,* where it was used to conclude that with respect to a law permitting the sale of low-alcoholic, i.e., not regular strength, beer to minors, low-alcoholic beer and regular strength beer were not like products.[103] Accordingly, the claim that all imported beer was entitled to the same treatment as low-alcoholic beer, i.e., that it should be salable to minors, was rejected. Thereafter, the aims-and-effect test was applied in a case involving US environmental regulations related to the fuel efficiency of automobiles. However, that report was never adopted.[104]

In *Japan - Alcohol,*[105] a WTO panel rejected the aims-and-effect test in its interpretation of Article III:2, first sentence (dealing with internal taxation of like products), principally because it was not grounded in treaty language[106] and because its application would have the effect of rendering Article XX superfluous.[107] The panel reached the latter conclusion because instead of the respondent having to invoke Article XX to justify a measure (an invocation that has seldom succeeded in GATT practice), the aims-and-effect test effectively requires the complaining party to show that the challenged measure is *not* the sort that would fall within the scope of the justification permitted by Article XX. The panel's analysis was upheld by the Appellate Body.[108]

However, for tax measures distinguishing between directly competing or substitutable products, the Appellate Body was of the view that Article III:2, second sentence, can only be violated if the measure is separately proven to be "applied . . . so as to afford protection to domestic production," a phrase referred to in Article III:1.[109] Under Article III:2, second sentence, the question of whether there is a trade-distorting *effect*[110] thus becomes crucial. This divergent conclusion with respect to the first and second sentence of Article III:2 was reached because, according to the Appellate Body, only the second sentence (and not the first sentence) explicitly refers to Article III:1, i.e., to the general requirement not to apply internal measures "so as to afford protection to domestic production."[111]

The same reasoning was followed by the Appellate Body in its report on *EC – Bananas* with respect to Article III:4, which refers only to like products, not to directly competing or substitutable products.[112] There it was found that for Article III:4 to be violated a separate consideration of whether the measure affords protection to domestic production is *not* required. This conclusion was again reached—as was the case for Article III:2, first sentence – on the ground that Article III:4 does *not* specifically refer to Article III:1. It may be added that the Appellate Body also rejected the aims-and-effect test under Articles II (MFN) and XVII (national treatment) of GATS.[113]

The rejection of the aims-and-effect test in *Japan – Alcohol* would seem to be a positive development. In determining whether two categories of *products* are like, it is difficult to see why reference should be made to the aims or effect of the contested *measure* which imposes the differential treatment. Nor would it seem to be appropriate to make reference, in such determination, to any other criterium which is not related to objective characteristics of the product itself.[114] If one were to take into account such (more or less subjective) criteria, panels would be able to decide for themselves – in the process of making a decision on likeness – which criteria for distinguishing between products are acceptable under WTO provisions. And this without taking into account the legitimate criteria referred to in Article XX. Since no two products are alike in all respects, stating that two classes of products are like, always presupposes some normative judgment that these products ought to be treated alike. In that sense, a decision on likeness can never be completely objective and the concept of equal treatment is tautological. To avoid such result-oriented decisions on likeness, one should limit relevant differences between products to those which are most objective, namely those linked to the physical characteristics of the product itself.

## Is There a Need for a Discriminatory Effects Test in Article III:2 and III:4?

The debate over the aims-and-effect test or the requirement of proof of protective application—though focused so far on Article III—is important also for Article I and the application of the MFN principle because it highlights the difficult issue of to what extent the WTO agreements should be interpreted so as to limit the discretion of governments. The aims-and-effect test attempted to limit the intrusion of WTO rules into government discretion by asking whether the government action was protectionist. It did so rather artificially in the process of determining the likeness of products. The issue remains, however, whether the non-discrimination obligations of GATT and related instruments should be interpreted flexibly in order to avoid too strict an interpretation of WTO rules which may lead to decisions that some

Member governments will be unwilling to accept because they view them as inappropriate intrusions into domestic regulatory matters. In the end, to fill in the "empty idea of equality,"[115] one needs to refer to substantive rights. In the WTO context, this arguably means that one needs to refer to the right Members have, namely the right that their products not be discriminated *on the basis of their origin.* This raises the question of whether there should be a discriminatory effects test applied in examination of claims under Articles I and III. The following paragraphs explore this possibility, first with respect to Article III and then with respect to Article I. In each case, consideration is given whether such a test could be imposed consistently with the wording of the relevant provision and with the object and purpose of the WTO Agreement.

At the outset, it should be noted that the need for a discriminatory effects test under Article III:2 to address the foregoing concerns is limited. WTO jurisprudence holds that the concept of "like products" should be interpreted narrowly for purposes of Article III:2, first sentence. As a consequence, claims of tax discrimination will more likely be brought under Article III:2, second sentence, which already incorporates a notion of discriminatory effect through its reference to the "so as to afford protection" language of Article III:1. Nonetheless, the possibility of requiring proof of discriminatory effect is explored under Article III:2, first sentence, as well as under Articles I and III:4.

Could a requirement of discriminatory effect be introduced into Article III:2, first sentence, for those cases where no *de jure* discrimination exists?[116] In this regard, it should be noted that Article III:2, first sentence, explicitly provides that the higher-taxed product is to be an *import* and the lower-taxed product a like *domestic* product. If such an approach were introduced, a violation could be found, for example, if the higher-taxed product were predominantly imported and the lower-taxed product predominantly domestically produced.[117] Discriminatory effect might also be proven in other ways, depending on the circumstances of the case (e.g., proof of a protectionist design or structure of the measure, of protective application or effect, etc.). Such a showing could be viewed as an element of the requirement that taxes on imports need be "in excess of" those on like domestic products. Absent a discriminatory effect, it could be argued that taxes on imports were effectively not "in excess of" those on like domestic products.

The same test could be applied to Article III:2, second sentence, be it under the currently imposed "so as to afford protection to domestic production" requirement or, following the approach outlined under Article III:2, first sentence, as part of the requirement that directly competitive or substitutable imported and domestic products be "similarly taxed." Under such an approach, it would be necessary for a complaining party to show that the higher taxed category was predominantly composed of imports. In the event such test would be inappropriate in a given case,[118] the link between imports and higher taxes could be established by proving that the tax differential in its design, structure or effect affords protection to domestic products.[119] Both interpretations would answer the same decisive question: is there discriminatory impact related to origin?

Application of a requirement of discriminatory effect to claims brought under Article III:4 could lead to more significant changes in outcomes, as there is now no similar requirement applied (in contrast to the situation under Article III:2, second sentence). In the case of Article III:4, proof of discriminatory effect could be required in order to demonstrate that imports are treated "less favorably" than like domestic products. Imposing such a requirement would mean that governments would have considerably more flexibility in applying regulatory distinctions to like products since such distinctions would not be held invalid under Article III:4 absent a showing of discriminatory effect. This would allow such distinctions as were made in the *Malt Beverages* case in respect of low-alcoholic beer.

The argument that some proof of discriminatory effect is required under Article III:2 and III:4 could be supported by the wording of these provisions (as explained above), but also by the fact that these provisions need to be interpreted in light of the general purpose of Article III, which is stated in Article III:1 to avoid measures taken so as to afford protection to domestic production, and of the WTO Agreement as a whole. In this connection, it should be recalled that the preamble to the WTO Agreement, third paragraph, sets out "the elimination of discriminatory treatment in international commerce" as one of the means to reach the objectives of the WTO Agreement.

Finally, a requirement of discriminatory effect under Article I:1 could also be required. The word "advantage, etc." in Article I:1 would allow some consideration of origin-based discriminatory effect, in particular since the advantage needs to be granted to products from one country and not to products from another WTO Member. This could call for a link to be established between the disadvantaged product and the complaining WTO Member. For example, proof that this product is, relatively speaking, imported far more frequently from that WTO Member than from the other country which thus *de facto* receives an advantage. It should be recognized, however, that the requirement of discriminatory impact finds less support in the actual wording of Article I than it does in the wording of Article III since Article I does not include a general principle (similar to the one set out in Article III:1) disapproving with measures applied "so as to afford protection." On the other hand, the object and purpose of Article I would seem to be equally clear: only measures giving an advantage (i.e., affording protection) to one country and not to another WTO Member should be prohibited. Moreover, the object and purpose of the WTO Agreement, as mentioned above, applies to Article I as well as Article III.

In light of the foregoing, it could be argued that a discriminatory effect test of some sort could be read into Articles I and III. Doing so would help address concerns raised that Articles I and III as traditionally interpreted may limit the discretion of governments to make appropriate, nondiscriminatory distinctions between products. Would such an approach be desirable? Traditionally, GATT jurisprudence has not concerned itself with actual trade flows, but rather with competitive opportunities. If that approach is to be continued, then the question of discriminatory effects would have to contain an element of potential effect. Could such an element be included without re-creating concerns about government discretion? How would potential effects be measured? Moreover, would such a requirement significantly shift the balance in Article I and III cases against the complaining party? If so, would that be inappropriate? Could such a shift be avoided by allowing the issue of the lack of discriminatory effects to be raised as a defense by the respondent? What treaty basis would there be for creating such a defense? Among others, these questions would have to be considered before making any changes in the present approach.

## NOTES

1. The example is cited in Robert E. Hudec, *Tiger, Tiger in the House: A Critical Evaluation of the Case against Discriminatory Trade Measures,* in THE NEW GATT ROUND OF MULTILATERAL TRADE NEGOTIATIONS: LEGAL AND ECONOMIC PROBLEMS 165, 177 n.11 (Ernst-Ulrich Petersmann & Meinhard Hilf eds. 1988).

2. John H. Jackson, THE WORLD TRADING SYSTEM: LAW AND POLICY OF INTERNATIONAL ECONOMIC RELATIONS 158 (2d ed. 1997).

3. See Hudec, op. cit., at 177. In recognition of this development, there have been proposals in the US Congress to refer to MFN treatment as "normal" trade relations. See INSIDE U.S. TRADE, 13 Sept. 1996.

4. See generally US Executive Branch GATT Studies, *The Most-Favoured-Nation Provision,* quoted in John H. Jackson, William J. Davey & Alan O. Sykes, LEGAL PROBLEMS OF INTERNATIONAL ECONOMIC RELATIONS, 440–442 (3rd ed. 1995).

5. Id. at 441.

6. Id. at 442; John T. Bill Co. v. United States, 104 F.2d 67 (CCPA 1939)(quoting materials explaining US policy shift), in John H. Jackson & William J. Davey, LEGAL PROBLEMS OF INTERNATIONAL ECONOMIC RELATIONS, 435–438 (2nd ed. 1986).

7. GATT Focus, Sept.-Oct. 1984, 3.

8. The first WTO financial services negotiations are an example. The United States declined to accept the results of the negotiations because of its view that the offers of others were insufficient for it to make an MFN-based offer (see, for example, US statement at the 21 June 1995 Meeting of the Committee on Trade in Financial Services, S/FIN/M/5/Rev.1). Later in the second financial services negotiations, the United States did accept the results of the negotiations, although it conditioned its offer, notably in the insurance sector where it reserved the right to discriminate against any WTO Member which compels US nationals to divest from its market (see the US List of Article II (MFN) exemptions, GATS/EL/90/Suppl.3, 2).

9. All of these "agreements" have been made multilateral on an MFN basis, although only part of the WTO membership made commitments. Other Members can still join, however, and make commitments themselves.

10. WTO Agreement, Article X.

11. Panel Report on *Spain – Tariff Treatment of Unroasted Coffee,* adopted on 11 June 1981, BISD 28S/102, para. 4.3.

12. BISD II/12, 7–8.

13. Panel Report on *United States—Customs User Fee,* adopted on 2 February 1988, BISD 35S/245.

14. GATT, ANALYTICAL INDEX: GUIDE TO GATT LAW AND PRACTICE (Updated 6th Edition 1995), hereafter "Analytical Index," 29.

15. Note by the Director-General, dated 29 November 1968, L/3149.

16. Panel Report on *United States—Denial of Most-Favoured-Nation Treatment as to Non-Rubber Footwear from Brazil,* adopted on 19 June 1992, BISD 39S/128, para. 6.8 (hereafter *"US – Footwear from Brazil"*).

17. See Analytical Index, 30.

18. Note by the Director-General, op. cit. in footnote 13.

19. BISD II/12. See also the Panel Report on *Belgian Family Allowances,* adopted on 7 November 1952, BISD 1S/59, where it was found that levying a charge on foreign goods purchased by public bodies when these goods originate in a country whose system of family allowances does not meet specific requirements, is an internal charge, within the meaning of Article III:2, that is inconsistent with Article I:1.

20. Analytical Index, 31.

21. Appellate Body Report on *EC – Measures Affecting the Importation of Certain Poultry Products* (hereafter *"EC – Poultry"*), adopted on 23 July 1998, WT/DS69/AB/R, paras. 96 – 102.

22. In this respect it should be recalled that for WTO purposes the term "country" includes any separate customs territory Member of the WTO (see *Explanatory Notes* to the WTO Agreement). An example is Hong Kong, China, a separate customs territory within the People's Republic of China.

23. See, for example, the Panel Report on *EC – Regime for the Importation, Sale and Distribution of Bananas* (hereafter *"EC – Bananas"*), adopted on 25 September 1997,

WT/DS27/R, para. 7.252: "We note that it is the purpose of the MFN clause to protect foreign *products* from being treated less favorably than like products of any other foreign origin" (emphasis in original).

24. Panel Report on *United States—Customs Users Fee,* adopted on 2 February 1988, BISD 35S/245, 289–290.

25. Panel Report on *US - Footwear from Brazil,* op. cit. The Appellate Body in *EC - Bananas,* op. cit., para. 206, refers to para. 6.9 of this Panel Report as providing a "broad definition" to the term "advantage" in Article I:1.

26. Panel Report on *European Economic Community—Imports of Beef from Canada,* adopted on 10 March 1981, BISD 28S/92.

27. Panel Report on *Indonesia—Certain Measures Affecting the Automobile Industry* (hereafter *"Indonesia – Autos,"*) adopted on 23 July 1998, WT/DS54/R, para. 14.139.

28. Panel Report on *EC –Bananas,* op. cit., paras. 7.188 – 7.193.

29. Ibid., para. 7.194.

30. Ibid., paras. 7.220 – 7.223 and confirmed on appeal, Appellate Body Report, op. cit., para. 206.

31. Ibid., paras. 7.251 – 7.256.

32. Ibid., paras. 7.235 – 7.241 and confirmed on appeal, Appellate Body Report, op. cit., para. 207.

33. Ibid., para. 7.239.

34. Panel Report on *EC – Bananas,* op. cit., paras. 7.179 – 7.182.

35. Panel Report on *US - Footwear from Brazil,* op. cit., para. 6.10. See also Panel Report on *United States – Section 337 of the Tariff Act of 1930,* adopted on 7 November 1989, BISD 36S/345, 387, para. 5.14.

36. See, for example, sub-committee of the Preparatory Committee, Geneva session, EPCT/174, 3.

37. Report of the Committee on Rules of Origin to the Council for Trade in Goods on the Harmonization Work Program, dated 7 July 1998, G/RO/25.

38. Agreement on Rules of Origin, Article 2.

39. Ibid., Article 3.

40. Panel Report on *US – Restrictions on Imports of Tuna,* unadopted, DS21/R, dated 3 September 1991, BISD 39S/155, paras. 5.43 – 5.44.

41. Working Party Report on *International Convention to Facilitate the Importation of Commercial Samples and Advertising Material,* adopted on 7 November 1952, BISD 1S/94, 98 (majority view).

42. Working Party Report on *Schedules and Customs Administration,* adopted on 26 February 1955, BISD 3S/205, 206.

43. Panel Report on *Belgian Family Allowances,* adopted on 7 November 1952, BISD 1S/59, para. 3.

44. Panel Report on *EEC—Program of Minimum Import Prices, Licenses and Surety Deposits for Certain Processed Fruits and Vegetables,* adopted on 18 October 1978, BISD 25S/68.

45. Panel Report on *European Economic Community—Imports of Beef from Canada,* adopted on 10 March 1981, BISD 28S/92.

46. Panel Report on *Indonesia - Autos,* op. cit., paras. 14.143–14.148.

47. Working Party Report on *Accession of Hungary,* adopted on 30 July 1973, BISD 20S/34.

48. Article 2.3 of the SPS Agreement states that "Members shall ensure that their [SPS] measures do not arbitrary or unjustifiably discriminate between Members where identical or similar conditions prevail." Article 5.5, in turn, provides that "each Member shall avoid arbitrary or unjustifiable distinctions in the levels [of protection] it considers to be appropriate in different situations, if such distinctions result in discrimination or a disguised restriction on international trade." On the relationship between these two provisions the Appellate Body in its report on *EC – Measures Concerning Meat and Meat Products (Hormones)* (hereafter *"EC – Hormones"*), adopted on 13 February 1998, WT/DS26/AB/R, noted: "When read together with Article 2.3, Article 5.5 may be seen to be marking out and elaborating a particular route to the same destination set out in Article 2.3" (para. 212). Although the wording of these two provisions reminds one of the language used in the *chapeau* of Article XX, the Appellate Body in the same report (para. 239) stated that GATT/WTO jurisprudence on Article XX "cannot be casually imported into a case involving Article 5.5 of the SPS Agreement."

49. The rules for import licensing procedures are to be "neutral" in application. See Panel Report on *EC – Bananas,* op. cit., paras. 7.260 – 7.263. The Appellate Body in that case (op. cit., at para. 197) clarified, however, that "Article 1.3 of the *Licensing Agreement* clearly applies to the *application* and *administration* of import licensing procedures . . . [it] does not require the import licensing *rules,* as such, to be neutral, fair, and equitable."

50. It had been disputed as to whether safeguard measures taken under Article XIX of GATT were subject to an MFN requirement. The Panel Report on *Norway – Restrictions on Imports of Certain Textile Products,* adopted on 18 June 1980, 27S/BISD/119, found that quantitative restrictions imposed as emergency measures under Article XIX are subject to the non-discrimination provision of Article XIII. See, however, the EC position at a Council meeting in March 1978, invoking Article XIX with respect to measures on imports from Korea only (C/M/124). See also the discussion between Bronckers and Koulen quoted in John H. Jackson and William J. Davey, op. cit., 595 – 602.

51. Appellate Body Report on *EC –Bananas,* op. cit., para. 231.

52. Richard E. Gardner, STERLING-DOLLAR DIPLOMACY, 348 – 361 (1956).

53. The more general exceptions in Article XX (protection of human health, conservation of exhaustible natural resources, etc.) and Article XXI (security exceptions)53., the provisions allowing for anti-dumping and countervailing measures and the discriminatory quantitative restrictions provided for under Articles XIII and XIV, may in practice result in a legally justified less favorable treatment for certain WTO Members only. However, the introductory clause (chapeau) to Article XX precludes certain discriminatory treatment and, as noted above, the procedures by which antidumping and countervailing duties are imposed are subject to the

MFN obligation of Article I:1. See also the general exceptions in Articles XIV and XIV*bis* of GATS and Articles 17 and 30 of the TRIPS Agreement.

54. Article XXIV:8 of GATT.

55. In the case of customs unions, if the creation of a unified commercial policy leads to an increase in a rate of duty inconsistently with the provisions of Article II (i.e., in excess of bound tariff rates), Article XXVIII-like negotiations are required by Article XXIV:6.

56. In GATS, the provision corresponding to GATT Article XXIV is GATS Article V on economic integration.

57. See, in this respect, the recent Notes by the WTO Secretariat on certain systemic issues related to the concept of "substantially all the trade" in Article XXIV (WT/REG/W/21, 21a1 and 21r1).

58. In the first 45 years or so of GATT, 83 such agreements were notified. In the five years prior to 1998, 67 were notified.

59. In response, a new WTO Committee on Regional Trade Agreements has been established. See generally WTO SECRETARIAT, REGIONALISM AND THE WORLD TRADING SYSTEM (1995); REGIONALISM AND MULTILATERALISM AFTER THE URUGUAY ROUND: CONVERGENCE, DIVERGENCE AND INTERACTION (Paul Demaret, Jean-François Bellis & Gonzalo Garcia Jiménez, eds. 1997).

60. In practice, of course, MRA negotiations can take a long time, are expensive and may lack transparency for third countries wanting to participate, in particular developing countries. In this respect see The First Triennial Review of the Operation and Implementation of the TBT Agreement, Committee on Technical Barriers to Trade, G/TBT/5, 19 November 1997, paras. 27 – 29.

61. For a listing of these provisions and the extent to which they have been used, see WT/TCD/W35.

62. Decision of 28 November 1979 of the Contracting Parties on Differential and More Favorable Treatment, Reciprocity, and Fuller Participation of Developing Countries, BISD 23S/203.

63. In accordance with the so-called Generalized System of Preferences (GSP), described in the Decision of the Contracting Parties of 25 June 1971, relating to the establishment of "generalized, non-reciprocal and non-discriminatory preferences beneficial to the developing countries."

64. See, e.g., the Agreed Conclusions of the Special Committee on Preferences, 12 October 1970, 75, S-IV, respectively in Section IV on "Beneficiaries" and Appendix I "Statement on behalf of the Group of 77." The issue is unlikely to be resolved by means of dispute settlement procedures: In the event a discriminated developing country were to complain, the developed country granting the preference could simply withdraw it all together. The fact that such preference can unilaterally be withdrawn is not disputed. In this respect, however, see the request for consultations by Brazil in *European Communities – Measures Affecting Differential Treatment of Coffee*, WT/DS154/1, invoking *inter alia* the Enabling Clause.

65. The question of likeness also arises under the MFN principle contained in the GATS. There the problem is not to decide which products are like and should, therefore, obtain the

same advantages. Under GATS (Article II) one needs to determine whether services or service suppliers of WTO Members are "like" services or service suppliers of another country to which a more favorable treatment has been accorded. See Part III.C.5 infra. The concept of likeness does not appear in the TRIPS Agreement. Under TRIPS (Article 4), any advantage granted to nationals of any country needs to be accorded as well to nationals of all other WTO Members. There is no requirement that the nationals of these different countries be "like."

66. See the Panel Report on *US – Taxes on Automobiles,* unadopted, DS31/R, dated 11 October 1994, para. 5.15, where it was found that cars sold below and those sold above $30,000 are not like products under Article III:2, first sentence, because the threshold was not implemented so as to afford protection to the domestic production of automobiles.

67. See Panel and Appellate Body Reports on *Japan—Taxes on Alcoholic Beverages,* adopted on 2 November 1996, WT/DS8/R and WT/DS8/AB/R (*hereafter "Japan – Alcohol"*). There, Japan imposed the same taxes for both domestic and imported shochu (e.g. shochu from Korea); also vodka was taxed the same, irrespective of its origin. Nevertheless, it was found that under Article III:2, first sentence, vodka is like shochu and should for that reason be taxed the same.

68. For an alternative approach to likeness under Article III, based on economic principles of efficiency, see Aaditya Mattoo and Arvind Subramanian, *Regulatory Autonomy and Multilateral Disciplines,* JOURNAL OF INTERNATIONAL ECONOMIC LAW 1 (1998), 303 – 322.

69. Article I (MFN), Article III (National Treatment), Article VI (Anti-dumping and Countervailing Duties), Article VII (Valuation for Customs Purposes), Article IX (Marks of Origin), Articles XI and XIII (Quantitative Restrictions), Article XVI (Subsidies) and Article XIX (Safeguards).

70. During discussions at the London session of the Preparatory Committee, it was noted that "the expression had different meanings in different contexts of the Draft Charter" (EPCT/C.II/65, 2).

71. Appellate Body Report on *Japan - Alcohol,* op. cit., 21.

72. In its report on *Japan – Alcohol,* the Appellate Body, after having stated that the definition of "like products" in Article III:2, first sentence, should be construed narrowly, added the following (at page 20):

"How narrowly is a matter that should be determined separately for each tax measure in each case. We agree with the practice under the GATT 1947 of determining whether imported and domestic products are "like" on a case-by-case basis"

73. Article III:2, second sentence, does not contain the phrase "directly competitive or substitutable product," but the phrase is found in the Interpretative notes to Article III:2. The suggestion to interpret "like product" narrowly in Article III:2, first sentence, was confirmed by the Appellate Body in its report on *Japan - Alcohol,* op. cit., 19–20:

"Because the second sentence of Article III:2 provides for a separate and distinctive consideration of the protective aspect of a measure in examining its application to a broader category of products that are not "like products" as contemplated by the first sentence, we agree with the Panel that the first sentence of Article III:2 must be construed narrowly so as not to condemn measures that its strict terms are not meant to condemn. Consequently, we agree with the Panel also that the definition of "like products" in Article III:2, first sentence, should be construed narrowly."

In this respect, it may be noted that of all other GATT provisions referring to "like products," only Article XIX:1 (a) on safeguards also refers to "directly competitive products" when it deals with the requirement that imports are to "cause or threaten serious injury to domestic producers . . . of like or directly competitive products" before a safeguard measure can be imposed.

74. The Appellate Body referred to this approach (considering Articles III:2 and III:4 as having a different product coverage), without rejecting or accepting it, in footnote 44 of its report on *Japan – Alcohol,* op. cit., 20.

75. Working Party Report on *Border Tax Adjustments,* adopted on 2 December 1970, BISD 18S/97, para. 18. The Appellate Body relied extensively on this working party report on *Japan - Alcohol,* although it has since indicated that panels should not rely on working party reports even if adopted by the GATT contracting parties because, unlike adopted panel reports, they are not the result of a dispute settlement process. Appellate Body Report on *Argentina – Measures Affecting Imports of Footwear, Textiles, Apparel, and Other Items,* adopted on 22 April 1998, WT/DS56/AB/R, para. 43.

76. Analytical Index, 35.

77. Panel Report on *Germany—Tariff Treatment of Sardines,* adopted on 31 October 1952, BISD 1S/53.

78. Panel Report on *Spain – Tariff Treatment of Unroasted Coffee,* adopted on 11 June 1981, BISD 28S/102.

79. Panel Report on *Japan – Tariff Import of Spruce Pine Fir Dimension Lumber,* adopted on 19 July 1989, BISD 36S/167.

80. Appellate Body Report on *EC – Customs Classification of Certain Computer Equipment* (hereafter *"EC – LAN Equipment"*) adopted on 22 June 1998, WT/DS62/AB/R, para. 109.

81. Appellate Body Report on *EC – Poultry,* op. cit., paras. 98 – 99.

82. See GATT/WTO jurisprudence under Article II clarifying that a Member's schedule can qualify the *concessions* granted in that schedule, but not obligations under GATT provisions (e.g., Appellate Body Report on *EC – Bananas,* op. cit., paras. 153 – 158). One could also contend that classifications subdividing like products for tariff purposes (however that would be established) constitute a qualification of an obligation under Article I:1 and thus are contrary to Article I:1.

83. See Frieder Roessler, *The Concept of Nullification and Impairment in the Legal System of the World Trade Organization,* in INTERNATIONAL TRADE LAW AND THE GATT/WTO DISPUTE SETTLEMENT SYSTEM 133 (Ernst-Ulrich Petersmann ed. 1997).

84. Appellate Body Report on *EC – LAN Equipment,* op. cit. para. 80.

85. Panel Report on *Indonesia – Autos,* op. cit., paras. 14.137 ff.

86. The Appellate Body has provided an interesting discussion on this matter related, however, to the like product concept under Article III: "A uniform tariff classification of products can be relevant in determining what are "like products" . . . However, there is a major difference between tariff classification nomenclature and tariff bindings or concessions made by Members of the WTO under Article II of the GATT 1994. There are risks in using tariff bindings that are too broad as a measure of product "likeness." Many of the least-developed country Members of the WTO

submitted schedules of concessions and commitments as annexes to the GATT 1994 for the first time as required by Article XI of the *WTO Agreement*. Many of these least-developed countries, as well as other developing countries, have bindings in their schedules which include broad ranges of products that cut across several different HS tariff headings . . . This does not necessarily indicate similarity of the products covered by a binding. Rather, it represents the results of trade concessions negotiated among Members of the WTO. It is true that there are numerous tariff bindings which are in fact extremely precise with regard to product description and which, therefore, can provide significant guidance as to the identification of "like products." Clearly enough, these determinations need to be made on a case-by-case basis. However, tariff bindings that include a wide range of products are not a reliable criterion for determining or confirming product "likeness" under Article III:2." Appellate Body Report on *Japan—Alcohol,* op. cit., 21–22.

87. Op. cit., para. 14.113, footnotes omitted.

88. Ibid., para. 14.142.

89. Panel Report on *Canada – Certain Measures Concerning Periodicals,* adopted 30 July, 1997, WT/DS31/R (hereafter *"Canada – Periodicals"*).

90. A typical split-run edition is the Canadian regional edition of a magazine based in the US if, for each issue, the magazine has both a US edition and a Canadian (split-run) edition. The two editions are similar in editorial content, but do not carry identical advertising.

91. Panel Report on *Canada – Periodicals,* op. cit., paras. 5.20–5.30.

92. Appellate Body Report on *Canada –Periodicals,* op. cit., 21–22.

93. Ibid., 21

94. And this even though none of the parties appealed under Article III:2, second sentence. For a critique see Sydney M. Cone, *The Appellate Body and Harrowsmith Country Life,* JOURNAL OF WORLD TRADE 32 (1998), 103 – 117.

95. See generally id.

96. Panel Report on *United States – Denial of Most-Favoured-Nation Treatment as to Non-Rubber Footwear from Brazil,* adopted on 19 June 1992, BISD 39S/128.

97. Working Party Report on *The Australian Subsidy on Ammonium Sulphate,* adopted on 3 April 1950, BISD II/188, para. 8.

98. Panel Report on *Belgian Family Allowances,* adopted on 7 November 1952, BISD 1S/59, para. 3.

99. Panel Report on *EEC – Measures on Animal Feed Proteins,* adopted on 14 March 1978, BISD 25S/49, paras. 4.1 – 4.2.

100. This seems to be the view of the panel on *Indonesia – Autos*, which referred back to its like product examination under Article III:2, first sentence, to find that products were also like for Article I:1 purposes. Op. cit., paras. 14.140 – 14.142.

101. Op. cit., para. 7.346, referring to para. 7.322.

102. On the issue of likeness under GATS Article XVII (National Treatment) see Aaditya Mattoo, *National Treatment in the GATS -- Corner-Stone or Pandora's Box?* JOURNAL OF WORLD TRADE 31 (1997), 107 – 135, in particular at 127 – 129.

103. Panel Report on *United States – Measures Affecting Alcoholic and Malt Beverages,* adopted on 19 June 1992, BISD 39S/206.

104. Panel Report on *United States – Taxes on Automobiles,* op. cit.

105. Panel Report on *Japan—Alcohol,* op. cit.

106. Ibid., para. 6.16. On appeal, the Appellate Body (op. cit., at page 18) reiterated this as follows: "Article III:2, first sentence does not refer specifically to Article III:1. There is no specific invocation in this first sentence of the general principle in Article III:1 that admonishes Members of the WTO not to apply measures "so as to afford protection." This omission must have some meaning. We believe the meaning is simply that the presence of a protective application need not be established separately from the specific requirements that are included in the first sentence in order to show that a tax measure is inconsistent with the general principle set out in the first sentence."

107. Panel Report, op. cit., 6.17.

108. Appellate Body Report, op. cit., pages 18–23.

109. Appellate Body Report on *Japan – Alcohol,* op. cit., 23 and 24. See also Appellate Body Report on *Canada –Periodicals,* op. cit., 30–32.

110. The word "effect" is used here not in the sense of actual trade effects but in the sense of effect on the competitive relationship between imports and domestic products.

111. It could thus be argued that the aims-and-effect test more generally (i.e., delinked from the like product issue) was upheld under Article III:2, second sentence (which addresses the internal taxation of directly competing or substitutable products) since the challenged measure must be shown to be applied so as to afford protection. In the Appellate Body Report on *EC – Bananas,* op. cit., at para. 241, it was noted, however, that ." . . in our Report in *Japan - Alcoholic Beverages,* the Appellate Body rejected the "aims and effects" theory with respect to Article III:2 of the GATT 1994," without limiting this statement to the first sentence thereof.

112. Appellate Body Report on *EC –Bananas,* op. cit., paras. 215 and 216.

113. Ibid., at para. 241: "We see no specific authority either in Article II or in Article XVII of the GATS for the proposition that the "aims and effects" of a measure are in any way relevant in determining whether that measure is inconsistent with those provisions. In the GATT context, the "aims and effects" theory had its origins in the principle of Article III:1 that internal taxes or charges or other regulations "should not be applied to imported or domestic products so as to afford protection to domestic production." There is no comparable provision in the GATS."

114. It would seem to be difficult to transpose this approach to the GATS. Since most, if not all, features of services and service suppliers are intangible, none of them can really be said to be objectively linked to the service or service supplier itself. One way of solving this problem along the lines discussed in Part IV.B could be to adopt a wider definition of likeness under GATS, but then to restrict cases where a violation is found to those where proof of either *de jure* or *de facto* discrimination is established under the requirement of "treatment no less favorable." Following this approach, distinguishing, for example, service suppliers referring

only to a series of objective skills they need to have, would not to be in violation of either the MFN principle or national treatment (no *de facto* discrimination), even though the skills referred to would not make the service suppliers unlike.

115. See generally Peter Westen, *The Empty Idea of Equality,* 95 HARVARD LAW REVIEW 537 (1982).

116. As interpreted by the Appellate Body in *Japan - Alcohol,* the difference in wording between the first and second sentence of Article III:2, is relied upon to conclude that only under the second sentence is proof of protective application required. This analysis could be disputed. It is true that the first sentence does not refer back to Article III:1. However, the legally binding treaty language of the second sentence is in fact contained and exhausted in an *Ad* note to that sentence. The *Ad* note sets out an exhaustive definition of measures contrary to the second sentence. In that sense, it fills in and arguably even replaces the language of the second sentence. However, this *Ad* note does not refer back to Article III:1 either. Only the actual second sentence does. But it would seem to do so in a neutral way, arguably covering both the Ad note *and* the first sentence. The second sentence reads as follows: "Moreover, no contracting party shall otherwise apply internal taxes or other internal charges to imported or domestic products in a manner contrary to the principles set forth in paragraph 1" (underlining added). The words "moreover" and "otherwise" make a clear link between, on the one hand, both the first and second sentence of Article III:2 and, on the other hand, Article III:1. This was recognized by the Appellate Body in *Canada – Periodicals,* op. cit., 24. On these grounds, the second sentence itself could be considered as a legally binding confirmation of the general principle introduced in Article III:1 (this time using the word "shall" and not "should"), applying equally to the first sentence of Article III:2 and the *Ad* note to the second sentence. Following this line of reasoning, one could argue that there is not sufficient ground for distinguishing between the first and second sentence when it comes to proof of protective application. On this ground one could submit that also for a violation of Article III:2, first sentence, some proof of protective application or *de facto* discrimination is required.

117. It would not seem to be appropriate to set a fixed percentage of imports required to be within the higher taxed category. Under GATT not only actual trade flows count, but also competitive opportunities (thus also hypothetical or potential trade flows). The link between the higher taxed category and imports could be established on a case by case basis.

118. For example, if – because of the measure at issue – no actual imports are made.

119. This approach was followed to a degree in the Panel Report on *Japan –Alcohol,* op. cit., paras. 6.33 and 6.34. However, there the Panel reasoned the other way round. It set out the "so as to afford protection" concept in Article III:1 as a separate requirement for a finding of a violation and interpreted it in light of the "not similarly taxed" concept in the *Ad* note (which it did not consider to be a separate requirement), stating that "to conclude that dissimilar taxation afforded protection, it would be sufficient . . . to find that the dissimilarity in taxation is not *de minimis.*" The view outlined here would be to set out the "not similarly taxed" concept as the separate requirement, a requirement to be interpreted in light of the "so as to afford protection" concept (which itself would only be a guiding principle). One could argue that this is, in effect, what the Appellate Body has done to date: Even though it set up each of these two concepts as a separate requirement, in the specific cases it examined so far the "so as to afford protection" requirement was met each time because of the dissimilarity in tax. See Appellate Body Reports on *Japan – Alcohol,* op. cit., 29–31 and on *Canada – Certain Measures Concerning Periodicals,* op. cit., 30–32.

CHAPTER 2

# MFN and the GATS

*Aaditya Mattoo**

The GATS and its MFN obligation came into effect before WTO Members were willing to completely eliminate discriminatory measures in services trade. The Agreement therefore had to strike a difficult balance between creating meaningful multilateral disciplines and accommodating discriminatory trade practices. The challenge to multilateral disciplines posed by the explicit departures from the MFN obligation, such as the exceptions for regional integration agreements and the MFN exemptions listed by Members, are widely recognized. However, the difficulties arising from less visible, implicit discrimination have not been adequately appreciated. It is this second class of problems that this paper seeks to highlight, both from an economic and legal perspective.

The next three sections constitute the descriptive part of the paper. Section 2 contains a description of the basic MFN obligation in the GATS drawing upon recent jurisprudence. Section 3 briefly describes other GATS provisions which reiterate or extend the basic obligation, notably Articles XVI and XVII on market access and national treatment, and Article VIII dealing with monopolies and exclusive service suppliers, as well as provisions which allow for departures from the basic obligation, notably Article V dealing with regional integration and Article XIV with general exceptions. Article VII dealing with recognition receives special attention because the interpretation of this provision may well determine how GATS resolves the potential conflict between selective and multilateral liberalization. Then Section 4 describes the pattern of the MFN-exemptions listed by Members and assesses their potential impact.

---

* World Trade Organization, 154, Rue de Lausanne, CH-1211 Geneva 21, Switzerland. Email: aaditya.mattoo@WTO.ORG. Paper presented at the World Trade Forum Conference on "Most-Favored Nation (MFN): Past and Present," at Neuchâtel, August 28–29, 1998. The views expressed here are those of the author and should not be attributed to the WTO Secretariat. I would like to thank the conference participants, Antonia Carzeniga, Carlo Gamberale, David Hartridge, Robert Hudec, Patrick Low, Hamid Mamdouh, Petros Mavroidis, and André Sapir for stimulating discussions.

Section 5 contains an analysis of non-discrimination in services trade, from an economic and legal perspective. The implications of discrimination through domestic regulations, arguably the central issue in services trade, are analyzed in Section 5.1. It is argued that making distinctions between services and service suppliers in the pursuit of certain domestic policy objectives, such as to ensure the quality of professional services, financial stability, and competitive market conditions, is economically sensible. It would, therefore, be desirable to allow Members the legal freedom to pursue such objectives, but to discipline the exercise of such freedom by ensuring that the choice and level of instruments is not more burdensome than necessary—with economic efficiency considerations playing a role in this assessment. Section 5.2 addresses the other major form of protection in services, quantitative restrictions, and suggests that there may be need to clarify the rules governing the non-discriminatory allocation of quotas.

The next sub-sections examine three of the most important sources of tension between the MFN obligation and Members' desire to discriminate. Section 5.3 addresses the issue of reciprocity, the basis for several MFN exemptions and possibly the main reason for the failure of the maritime negotiations. Distinctions between services and service suppliers based on the openness of the home market raise complex economic questions, related, on the one hand, to avoiding adverse terms of trade movements and free-riding in bargaining, and on the other to preventing costly trade diversion and maintaining the security of concessions. This economic ambiguity is reflected in a compromise in the GATS: distinctions conditional on home-market openness are illegal, unless covered by an MFN exemption or the exception for regional integration agreements.

Section 5.4 discusses the scheduling "innovation" which played a crucial role in the financial services negotiations: grandfathering the superior conditions of operation for firms which were already established. It is argued that distinctions between service suppliers based on criteria such as time of entry into the market can only have a protectionist effect and are not economically desirable. Furthermore, there may be a conflict between the basic MFN obligation and the schedules of specific commitments containing grandfather provisions.

Finally, Section 5.5 addresses an issue which was particularly important in the context of the telecommunications negotiations: whether the MFN obligation in the GATS leaves Members adequate scope to take action against foreign anti-competitive practices. It is argued that if competition policy itself is based on non-discriminatory principles, then it would be acceptable for it to impact differentially on particular services or service suppliers in specific instances provided they themselves manifested the characteristics which aroused concern. However, any discrimination in treatment, based not on competition policy-related attributes of the service or the service supplier, but on unrelated attributes such as the fact of protection in the home market, would seem to violate the MFN obligation.

## 1. Article II: The Basic MFN Obligation

Article II of the GATS constitutes a general obligation which is, in principle, applicable across the board by all Members to all services sectors. Article II:1 of GATS states:

> With respect to any measure covered by this Agreement, each Member shall accord immediately and unconditionally to services and service suppliers of any other Member treatment no less favorable than that it accords to like services and service suppliers of any other country.

While the meaning of the basic MFN obligation is well understood, there remains scope for clarifying certain aspects in the services context – particularly in the light of the recent rulings of a WTO Panel and the Appellate body on the dispute concerning the European Communities' regime for the importation, sale, and distribution of bananas (henceforth, Bananas Case).[1] Consider each of the following terms:

*Any measure covered by this Agreement:* The scope of the GATS is defined in Article I:1 of the Agreement to encompass "measures by Members affecting trade in services." A closer look at the elements of this definition reveals the wide domain of the Agreement. First of all, the Agreement takes a view of "trade in services" that includes not only cross border supply, but also the supply of a service through consumption abroad, commercial presence and presence of natural persons. Hence, while the MFN obligation under GATT 1994 is concerned with measures affecting products per se, the domain of this obligation in the GATS includes also measures affecting service suppliers. Secondly, "measures by Members" are defined broadly to include measures taken by central, regional or local governments, as well as non-governmental bodies in the exercise of powers delegated by the government—even though the GATS only requires Members to take "such reasonable measures as may be available to it" to ensure compliance by sub-central entities.[2] Finally, the Bananas Case confirmed a broad interpretation of the term "affecting," i.e., measures concerned need not affect trade in services as such but could also be measures taken in other areas with repercussions on services—such as measures in respect of the purchase of goods.[3]

*Treatment no less favorable:* The key issue here is whether this should be interpreted to mean only *de jure,* or formal, discrimination or whether it also pertains to *de facto* discrimination. The Appellate Body in the Bananas Dispute upheld the Panel's conclusion that the provision prohibits both forms of discrimination, but differed on the basis for this conclusion.

The Panel argued that the basic requirement to accord "treatment no less favorable" was the same in GATS Article II:1 and GATS Article XVII:1, the national treatment provision. The standard of "no less favorable treatment" in paragraph 1 of Article XVII was meant to provide for no less favorable conditions of competition regardless of whether this was achieved through the application of formally identical or formally different measures. Paragraphs 2 and 3 of Article XVII served the purpose of codifying this interpretation, established in previous jurisprudence pertaining to the GATT national treatment provision, and did not impose new obligations on Members additional to those contained in paragraph 1. The absence of similar elaboration in Article II was not a justification for giving a different ordinary meaning to the words "treatment no less favorable," which were identical in both Articles II:1 and XVII:1. It could be legitimately inferred, therefore, that Article II, also proscribed both forms of discrimination—notwithstanding the absence of clarifying elaboration.

The Appellate Body found the Panel's reasoning on this issue to be "less than fully satisfactory."[4] It argued that the MFN obligation in GATS Article II should be interpreted, not in the light of the national treatment obligations in GATS Article XVII or GATT Article III, but in the light of the MFN obligation in GATT Article I. Article I of GATT 1994 had also been applied, in past practice, to measures involving de facto discrimination.[5] Significantly, the Appellate Body agreed with the Panel that if Article II were to be interpreted to require only formally identical treatment, "it would not be difficult—and, indeed, it would be a good deal easier in the case of trade in services, than in the case of trade in goods—to devise discriminatory measures aimed at circumventing the basic purpose of that Article" which was to ensure equality of competitive opportunities. For these reasons, it concluded that "treatment no less favorable" in Article II:1 of the GATS should be interpreted to include de facto, as well as de jure, discrimination. The Appellate Body went further than the Panel in clearly stating that its conclusion was not limited to the case under consideration.

*Like services and service suppliers:* In the Bananas Case, the question of how likeness of services and service suppliers should be established needed to be addressed to only a limited extent. First, and relatively straightforward, the Panel found that wholesale services of bananas are like, irrespective of the origin of the bananas supplied. Secondly, in the Panel's view, "to the extent that entities provide these like services, they are like service suppliers."[6]

It is relatively straightforward to apply the MFN provision to measures taken by governments that are overtly discriminatory, i.e., those that discriminate on the basis of the provenance of the good. The problem arises in relation to what might be termed as apparently origin-neutral (AON) measures; namely, those where the basis for applying a measure is not the provenance of the service or service supplier but some other characteristic or set of characteristics, such as the place of training. In such cases, a determination under Article II hinges on determining whether the imported products are "like" each other.[7] The wider the definition of "likeness," the greater will be the set of measures that are inconsistent with Article II. If a doctor is a doctor, a regulation which imposed greater qualification requirements on a doctor trained in Country A than on a doctor trained in Country B would violate Article II. On the other hand, the narrower the definition of "likeness" the more measures will conform with Article II. If a doctor trained in one country is not "like" a doctor trained in another country, then the treatment of the doctor trained in country A would have to be compared with the treatment of a doctor trained in a country with similar training standards, and the additional qualification requirement could then be found consistent with Article II. Similar questions also arise in establishing likeness of service suppliers. These are discussed in Section 5.1 below.

## Article II:2 of the GATS: MFN Exceptions

Certain sectoral sensitivities that emerged in the Uruguay Round raised the specter of wholesale sectoral exclusions from GATS as a means of avoiding the MFN rule. In order to prevent this, it was agreed to permit limited exemptions to MFN under GATS. Such exemptions, however, had to be taken at the time the negotiations were concluded. Any exception to this general obligation would have to be provided for explicitly in accordance with the terms of the GATS. Article II:2 states: "A Member may maintain a measure inconsistent with paragraph 1 provided that such a measure is listed in, and meets the conditions of, the Annex on Article II Exemptions."

The annex makes it clear that no new exemptions can be granted, at least by this route: any future requests to give non-MFN treatment can only be met through the WTO waiver procedures.[8] Some listed exemptions are subject to a stated time limit. For those that are not, the annex provides that in principle they should not last longer than ten years (that is, not beyond 2004), and that in any case they are subject to negotiation in future trade-liberalizing rounds. Meanwhile, all remaining exemptions will be reviewed in the Council for

Trade in Services before the end of 1999 to see whether they are still needed.[9]

A limited exception to the rule that no new exemptions could be listed after the entry into force of the WTO applied to financial services, maritime transport and basic telecommunications: GATS annexes providing for continuing negotiations on these subjects, allowed exemptions to be listed only at the end of the negotiations. Now that negotiations in basic telecommunications and financial services have been concluded, it is only in maritime transport services that it is still possible to take an MFN exemption.

## 2. The MFN Obligation and Related GATS Obligations

This Section discusses other GATS provisions which either extend/reiterate the scope of the basic MFN obligation or provide for departures from it.

### Articles XVI and XVII

While Article II applies across the board, Article XVI on market access and Article XVII on national treatment only apply to sectors included by a Member in its schedule of specific commitments. The liberalizing content of the GATS depends to a large extent on the nature of these specific commitments. Article XVI prohibits a range of measures (mostly quantitative restrictions) unless explicitly listed in a Member's schedule, and Article XVII prohibits measures which discriminate against foreign services or service suppliers, again unless listed in a Member's schedule.

The texts of Articles II, XVI, and XVII do not create an explicit hierarchy of obligations. Thus, it is not completely clear from the text itself whether a Member taking an MFN exemption would also be free to discriminate with respect to the commitments made under Articles XVI and XVII. However, the "Scheduling of Initial Commitments in Trade in Services: Explanatory Note" states that "where an MFN exemption has been granted for a measure, a Member is free to deviate from its Article II obligations, but not from its Article XVI and XVII commitments. Therefore, in such cases, a Member may accord treatment more favorable than the minimum standard to some Members, as long as all Members receive at least the that minimum standard of market access and national treatment appearing in its schedule."[10]

It follows that an MFN exemption would give a Member who had made no commitments in a sector considerable freedom to discriminate. However, an MFN exemption which coexists with fully liberal market access and national treatment commitments would have little meaning—unless a Member wished to provide more favorable treatment to certain foreign suppliers than it does to its own.

## Regional Integration

Apart from services specified in individual MFN exemption lists, the only permitted departure from Most-Favored-Nation treatment under the GATS covers preferential treatment among countries that are members of regional trading arrangements. The GATS rules on "Economic Integration," in Article V, are modeled on those in Article XXIV of the GATT. Article V:1 permits any WTO member to enter into an agreement to further liberalize trade in services with the other countries that are parties to the agreement, provided the agreement has "substantial sectoral coverage," eliminates measures that discriminate against service suppliers of other countries in the group, and prohibits new or more discriminatory measures. Recognizing that action to open up services markets may well form part of a wider process of economic integration, Article V:2 allows the liberalization achieved to be judged in this light.

The drafting of these rules improves on their GATT equivalents in some respects: for instance, "substantial sectoral coverage" is more carefully defined, since it disqualifies agreements that exclude any of the four modes of supply. Some other provisions are carried over from Article XXIV with little change. An approved agreement must be designed to help trade among its members, and must not result in an increase in the overall barriers faced by non-members in trading with the group within the respective sectors or sub-sectors (Article V:4). If the establishment of the agreement, or its subsequent enlargement, leads to the withdrawal of commitments made to non-members, there must be negotiations to provide appropriate compensation (Article V:5). No compensation, on the other hand, is due from non-members for any trade benefits they may gain from the agreement (Article V:8).

Article V:7 creates a transparency obligation, requiring Members who are party to regional agreements to notify promptly any such agreement and any enlargement or significant modification to it. The agreements which have been notified so far include the agreements establishing NAFTA, the European Communities and their Member States, as well as their agreements with the Slovak Republic, Hungary, Poland, the Czech Republic, Romania, Norway, Iceland, Liechtenstein, and Bulgaria, and agreements between Canada and Chile and between Australia and New Zealand.

A related exception from the MFN rule, for the movement of natural persons, is permitted by Article V bis of the GATS. This allows countries to take part in agreements which establish full integration of labor markets. The only such agreement notified so far is the one involving Denmark, Finland, Iceland, Norway, and Sweden.

## Recognition

Article VII of the GATS, dealing with recognition, attempts to strike a difficult balance. On the one hand, it is permissive. Thus, Article VII:1 states:

> For the purposes of the fulfillment, in whole or in part, of its standards or criteria for the authorization, licensing or certification of services suppliers, and subject to the requirements of paragraph 3, a member may recognize the education or experience obtained, requirements met, or licenses or certifications granted in a particular country. Such recognition, which may be achieved through harmonization or otherwise, may be based upon an agreement or arrangement with the country concerned or may be accorded autonomously.

This provision would seem to allow a Member at any point of time to recognize standards of one or more Members and not of others, without violating its GATS obligations—even though services and service suppliers of the former group have easier access than those of the latter group. The remaining paragraphs of Article VII seek to ensure that this freedom is not abused. Article VII:2 requires a Member who enters into a mutual recognition agreement (MRA) to afford adequate opportunity to other interested Members to negotiate their accession to such an agreement or to negotiate comparable ones. If a Member grants recognition autonomously, then it is obliged to give any other Member adequate opportunity to demonstrate that education, experience, licenses, or certifications obtained in that other Member's territory should be recognized. In this respect, Article VII mandates an openness vis-à-vis third countries in a way that Article V, dealing with economic integration agreements, does not.

Article VII:3 stipulates that a Member must not grant recognition in a manner which would constitute a means of discrimination between countries in the application of its standards or criteria for the authorization, licensing or certification of services suppliers, or a disguised restriction on trade in services. This raises the question of how it could be established whether selective recognition is discriminatory. This question we discuss more fully below. It is worth noting that Article VII:5 states that "wherever appropriate, recognition should be based on multilaterally agreed criteria" and requires Members to work towards the establishment and adoption of such criteria. The issue, of course, is how much discretion the phrase "wherever appropriate" gives Members in deciding whether to follow their own rather than internationally agreed criteria.

What is the empirical significance of MRAs? It is possible to provide a preliminary answer thanks to the transparency requirement created by Article VII:4: Members must inform the Council for Trade in Services about existing MRAs and of the opening of negotiations on any future ones. So far, 21 notifications have been received under Article VII:4, of which 10 are from Latin American countries, 4 from the United States, 3 from Switzerland, and 1 each from the European Commission, Australia, Norway, and Macau. Not surprisingly, all but one of these pertain to the recognition of educational degrees and professional qualifications obtained abroad.[11] The only other MRA is in the domain of financial services: owing to reciprocal recognition of the proof of solvency between the EU and Switzerland, foreign direct (other than life) insurance companies having their principal place of business in the territory of one of the contracting parties are not obliged to localize funds to a significant extent and are not obliged to furnish security.

Interestingly, mutual recognition of qualifications is also mentioned as an element of 11 regional integration agreements, notified under GATS Article V:7(a). These agreements include the one establishing the European Union, agreements between the European Union and neighboring countries, and the Closer Economic Relations Treaty between Australia and New Zealand. This raises the question of whether MRAs concluded in the context of a regional integration agreements are still subject to the disciplines in Article VII:2 and 3. One view may be that Article V provides an exception to the fundamental non-discrimination obligation in Article II and therefore an exemption also to similar obligations contained in other GATS provisions, including Article VII. Alternatively, it could be argued that all MRAs, regardless of whether they are concluded by parties to a regional integration agreement or other Members, are covered by Article VII and its disciplines cannot be circumvented by appealing to Article V.

## Monopolies and Exclusive Service Suppliers

Article VIII requires each Member to ensure that any monopoly supplier of a service does not "in the supply of the monopoly service in the relevant market" act in a manner inconsistent with the MFN obligation and the Member's specific commitments. A monopoly supplier of a service is defined in the GATS as any person, public or private, which in the relevant market of the territory of a Member is authorized or established formally or in effect by that Member as the sole supplier of that service (Article XXVIII(h)).

### Government Procurement

Article XIII of the GATS exempts government purchase of services for its own use from the MFN obligation (as well as from the market access and national treatment rules). However, the same provision mandates negotiations on government procurement in services which may lead to commitments to open up some government purchases to foreign service suppliers.

### General Exceptions

The GATS provisions on general and security exceptions resemble their GATT equivalents. The general exceptions are, as in the GATT, preceded by a headnote that makes the right of a member to adopt or enforce measures necessary for the purposes listed subject to the condition that they not be applied as a means of "arbitrary or unjustifiable discrimination between countries where like conditions prevail, or as a disguised restriction on trade in services." The list of purposes that follows includes the protection of public morals and maintenance of public order;[12] protection of human, animal or plant life or health; securing compliance with laws or regulations which are not inconsistent with the provisions of GATS including those relating to the prevention of deceptive and fraudulent practices, the protection of individual privacy in the handling of personal data, and safety; ensuring equitable and effective taxation and the avoidance of double taxation. A footnote spells out a number of ways in which a country's taxation practices may treat foreigners differently from its own nationals. The security exceptions are virtually identical with those in GATT 1994.[13]

### Sectoral Annexes and Decisions

The Annex on Air Transport specifically excludes the complex network of bilateral agreements on air traffic rights from GATS rules.[14] In consequence, the GATS applies at present only to aircraft repair and maintenance services, the selling and marketing of air transport services (a function defined as not including the pricing or conditions of transport services), and computer reservation systems.[15]

In the maritime transport sector, the failure to conclude negotiations successfully led to the June 1996 Decision to suspend the application of the

MFN obligation to the sector until the end of the next round of comprehensive services negotiations. The suspension was prompted by the difficulty in eliminating MFN-inconsistent measures in the maritime sector. Even though Members could have listed exemptions from the MFN obligations, the dominant view was that the continued suspension of the MFN obligation would avert the need for many countries to take MFN exemptions which may be more difficult to negotiate away once explicitly listed.

**Table 1. Examples of MFN Exemptions Listed by Members**

| Sector or Subsector | Description of Measure Indicating its Inconsistency with Article II | Countries to Which the Measure Applies | Intended Duration | Conditions Creating the Need for the Exemption |
|---|---|---|---|---|
| Audiovisual services | Measures which confer national treatment to audiovisual works for funding and distribution | Specific countries | Indefinite | Bilateral agreements to promote cultural exchange |
| Banking and other financial services | Licenses for establishment of foreign service suppliers on the basis of reciprocity | All countries | Conditional upon the level of commitments and exemptions of other WTO Members | To ensure access of domestic financial service suppliers to foreign financial markets on the basis of reciprocity |
| Road transport | National treatment is granted only to services and service suppliers of the parties to the regional convention on road transport | Specified regional countries | Indefinite | Promotion of regional integration |

## 3. MFN Exemptions Listed by Members

MFN exemptions have been listed by some 70 Members (Table 2). There are around 380 measures involved, with many Members listing several measures in the same sector.[16] Table 3 attempts to distinguish between measures according to the conditions specified by Members as creating the need for the exemption. The first category includes measures the reason for which is the existence of sector-specific preferential regional agreements; the second category consists of measures taken under other bilateral or plurilateral agreements—usually designed to preserve certain historical preferences; the third category includes measures based on a unilaterally imposed reciprocity condition and not an agreement with trading partners. These distinctions are sometimes fuzzy and Table 3 should be used to infer broad patterns rather than precise details.

**Table 2. Members with MFN Exemptions (by sector)**

| Sectors | Countries |
|---|---|
| 1. BUSINESS SERVICES | |
| A. Professional services | Brunei Darussalam, Bulgaria, Costa Rica, Dominican Republic, Honduras, New Zealand, Panama, Singapore, Thailand, Turkey, Venezuela |
| F. Other business services | Canada, Costa Rica, EU, Malaysia, Mexico, Poland, Thailand |
| 2. COMMUNICATION SERVICES<br>A. Postal services | Turkey |
| C. Telecommunication services | Antigua & Barbuda, Bangladesh, Brazil, Colombia, Honduras, India, Pakistan, Sri Lanka, Turkey, United States, Venezuela |
| D. Audiovisual services | Australia, Austria, Bolivia, Brazil, Brunei Darussalam, Bulgaria, Canada, Chile, Colombia, Cuba, Cyprus, Czech Republic, Ecuador, Egypt, European Union and its Member States, Finland, Hungary, Iceland, India, Israel, Liechtenstein, New Zealand, Norway, Panama, Poland, Singapore, Slovak Republic, Slovenia, Sweden, Switzerland, Tunisia, United States, Venezuela |
| 3. CONSTRUCTION SERVICES | EC + Member States, Indonesia, Liechtenstein |
| 4. DISTRIBUTION SERVICES | Liechtenstein, Switzerland, Venezuela |
| 7. FINANCIAL SERVICES | Brunei Darussalam, Canada, Colombia, Côte d'Ivoire, El Salvador, European Union and its Member States, Honduras, Hungary, Indonesia, Israel, Liechtenstein, Mauritius, Nicaragua, Pakistan, Peru, Philippines, Senegal, Singapore, Slovak Republic, South Africa, Swaziland, Switzerland, Turkey, United Arab Emirates, United States, Venezuela |
| 8. HEALTH RELATED SERVICES | Cyprus |
| 9. TOURISM & TRAVEL RELATED SERVICES | EC + Member States, Mexico |
| 10. RECREATIONAL SERVICES | EC + Member States, India, Peru |
| 11. TRANSPORT SERVICES | |
| A. Maritime transport service | Angola, Benin, Bolivia, Brazil, Bulgaria, Cameroon, Canada, Chile, Congo, Côte d'Ivoire, Cuba, EC + Member States (Germany), Finland, Gabon, India, Jamaica, Mali, New Zealand, Niger, Peru, Philippines, Senegal, Sweden, Thailand, Trinidad & Tobago, Tunisia, Turkey, Venezuela |

**Table 2—Continued**

| Sectors | Countries |
|---|---|
| B. Internal waterways transport | Austria, Bulgaria, Czech Republic, European Union and its Member States, Hungary, Poland, Romania, Slovak Republic, Switzerland, Turkey |
| C. Air transport services | Austria, Bulgaria, Canada, EC + Member States, Finland, Iceland, Korea, Kuwait, Liechtenstein, Norway, Poland, Romania, Singapore, Slovenia, Sweden, Switzerland, Thailand, Turkey, United States |
| D. Space transport | Turkey, United States |
| E. Rail transport services | Brazil, Bulgaria, Chile, Colombia, Costa Rica, Czech Republic, Honduras, Peru, Poland, Slovak, Turkey, Uruguay |
| F. Road transport services | Austria, Bolivia, Bulgaria, Brazil, Chile, Colombia, Costa Rica, Cyprus, Czech Republic, Egypt, European Union and its Member States, Finland, Honduras, Hungary, Liechtenstein, Mexico, Morocco, Norway, Peru, Poland, Romania, Sierra Leone, Slovak Republic, Slovenia, South Africa, Swaziland, Sweden, Switzerland, Thailand, Tunisia, Turkey, Uruguay, United States |
| G. Pipeline transport | United States |
| H. Auxiliary services | Bulgaria, Cameroon, Congo, Côte d'Ivoire, Gabon, Mali, Niger, Senegal, Singapore |
| ALL SECTORS | |
| Entry, visa or work permit requirements | Austria, Cyprus, Egypt, Portugal, France, Italy, United Kingdom, Member States of the European Union, Indonesia, Jamaica, Malaysia, Malta, New Zealand, Peru, Philippines, Singapore, Sweden, Switzerland, Liechtenstein, United States, Brunei Darussalam |
| Investment | Canada, Chile, Costa Rica, Cyprus, Guatemala, Kuwait, Malaysia, Poland, Singapore, Thailand, Turkey, United States, Brunei Darussalam |
| Social security | Cyprus, Tunisia, Turkey |
| Financial support | Denmark, Finland, Iceland, Norway, Sweden (Nordic cooperation) |
| Taxation | Singapore, Turkey, United States |
| Purchase of real estate | Italy, Turkey, United States |

*Source:* Adapted from Altinger and Enders 1996, table 9.

**Table 3. Distribution of MFN Exemptions (by Sector and Conditions)**

| Sector | Number of Members | Number of Measures | Conditions Creating the Need for Exemption | | | Other |
|---|---|---|---|---|---|---|
| | | | Regional Agree-ments | Other Bilateral or Plurilateral Agreements | Reciprocity | |
| 1. BUSINESS SERVICES | | | | | | |
| A. Professional services | 11 | 12 | 0 | 2 | 6 | 4 |
| B-F. Other business | 7 | 9 | 2 | 1 | 3 | 3 |
| 2. COMMUNICATION SERVICES | | | | | | |
| A. Postal services | 1 | 1 | 0 | 0 | 1 | 0 |
| B. Courier services | 0 | 0 | 0 | 0 | 0 | 0 |
| C. Telecommunication services | 11 | 17 | 18 | 8 | 1 | 0 |
| D. Audiovisual services | 33 | 69 | 37 | 26 | 4 | 2 |
| 3. CONSTRUCTION SERVICES | 3 | 3 | 1 | 0 | 1 | 1 |
| 4. DISTRIBUTION SERVICES | 3 | 4 | 3 | 1 | 0 | 0 |
| 5. EDUCATIONAL SERVICES | 0 | 0 | 0 | 0 | 0 | 0 |
| 6. ENVIRONMENTAL SERVICES | 0 | 0 | 0 | 0 | 0 | 0 |
| 7. FINANCIAL SERVICES | 25 | 36 | 10 | 7 | 15 | 4 |
| 8. HEALTH RELATED SERVICES | 1 | 1 | 0 | 1 | 0 | 0 |
| 9. TOURISM AND TRAVEL | 2 | 2 | 0 | 1 | 0 | 1 |
| 10. RECREATIONAL SERVICES | 3 | 4 | 1 | 1 | 2 | 0 |

Table 3—Continued

| Sector | Number of Members | Number of Measures | Conditions Creating the Need for Exemption | | | Other |
|---|---|---|---|---|---|---|
| | | | Regional Agree-ments | Other Bilateral or Plurilateral Agreements | Reciprocity | |
| 11. TRANSPORT SERVICES | | | | | | |
| A. Maritime transport services | 28 | 55 | 14 | 23 | 8 | 10 |
| B. Internal waterways transport | 10 | 11 | 1 | 1 | 0 | 9 |
| C. Air transport services[1] | 19 | 23 | 0 | 6 | 19 | 3 |
| D. Space transport | 2 | 2 | 0 | 2 | 0 | 0 |
| E. Rail transport services | 12 | 14 | 6 | 1 | 4 | 3 |
| F. Road transport services | 33 | 46 | 24 | 8 | 8 | 6 |
| G. Pipeline | 1 | 1 | 0 | 0 | 1 | 0 |
| H. Auxiliary | 9 | 16 | 7 | 0 | 2 | 7 |
| 12. OTHER SERVICES NOT INCLUDED ELSEWHERE | | | | | | |
| Entry/Visa | 23 | 26 | 4 | 18 | 0 | 4 |
| Investment | 15 | 17 | 1 | 13 | 0 | 3 |
| Financial support | 5 | 5 | 5 | 0 | 0 | 0 |
| Taxation | 3 | 3 | 0 | 3 | 0 | 0 |
| Real estate | 3 | 3 | 1 | 0 | 0 | 2 |
| Regional agreements | 7 | 7 | 7 | 0 | 0 | 0 |

*Source*: Compiled from GATS MFN Exemptions Lists.

[1] Pertaining to: Aircraft repair and maintenance services; the selling and marketing of air transport services; computer reservation system (CRS) services.

Nearly two-thirds of the exempted measures are to be found in communication services and in transport services. The largest number of MFN-inconsistent measures (69) were listed in the audiovisual sector. More than half of them mention promotion of common (regional) culture as a motive for limiting access to joint programs to finance and diffuse audiovisual works, while most of the others have been claimed for bilateral agreements on co-production of films and television programs. In maritime transport, many Members chose to maintain MFN exemptions despite the suspension of the obligation for the sector. Of the 55 measures listed, nearly half are exemptions by developing countries for measures implementing the provisions of the United Nations Convention on a Code of Conduct for Liner Conferences. These provisions, in principle, divide 80 per cent of the liner trade on a traffic route between the shipping companies of the two states at each end, leaving only 20 per cent for shipping companies of other nationalities, but full implementation of this rule is apparently rare. Many of the rest provide cover for existing and future measures for regional preferential treatment. In road, rail or inland waterways transport, governments have sought exemptions for preferential access granted to cross-border access to hauliers of passenger and freight transport of neighboring countries or regional partners, sometimes through bilateral agreements. More distant countries are probably not greatly affected by such preferences. It is worth noting that these sectors, which account for a substantial share of MFN exemptions, are also those in which Uruguay Round commitments were particularly limited.

Reciprocity conditions – which specify that a Member is willing to guarantee access to its market only to those Members who provide it with access to their markets—are particularly significant in air transport services and financial services. The exemptions listed for air transport services pertain to the services falling within the scope of the GATS, i.e., repair and maintenance, selling, and marketing of air transport services, and computer reservation system (CRS) services. In financial services, at the end of the first round of extended negotiations in April 1995, many countries followed the lead of the United States in listing MFN exemptions for the licensing of foreign service suppliers on the basis of reciprocity.[17] While several Members removed such exemptions at the end of the negotiations in December 1997, a number were maintained by countries, including Hungary, Pakistan, Peru, Philippines, and Venezuela – with the stated objective of obtaining equal access opportunities for domestic suppliers in foreign markets. It is notable that many of these countries made significant commitments in financial services, reducing significantly the discriminatory potential of the MFN exemption. The same is true of the United States, which narrowed the scope of its MFN exemption considerably, retaining the right to discriminate only against countries in which United States financial institutions were forced to disinvest on the basis of their nationality. In maritime transport, several Members have sought exemptions for MFN-inconsistent measures such as retaliatory action against trading partners who are perceived to restrict access to their markets. The most significant of such exemptions, for the United States retaliatory legislation in the maritime sector, was listed and then withdrawn when the application of the MFN obligation to the maritime sector was suspended.[18] Unlike in the case of financial services, only limited commitments have been made in maritime—primarily, as in the case of the United States, to retain the right to discriminate with respect to a broad class of measures.

In the case of basic telecommunications, relatively few MFN exemptions have been inscribed. Among them is the MFN exemption of the United States on one-way satellite transmission of DTH and DBS television services and of digital audio services, and a similar exemption by Brazil. A particular application of the MFN requirement in the basic telecommunications sector, however, concerns accounting rates—particularly through Article VIII dealing with monopolies and exclusive service suppliers.[19] Although there was general appreciation among most negotiators that competition resulting from liberalization would lead over time to the destruction of the accounting rate system, it was nevertheless decided to secure a shared understanding that Members would not challenge one another's accounting rate regimes under the WTO's dispute settlement provisions.[20] Despite the understanding, several countries, including Bangladesh, India, Pakistan, Sri Lanka and Turkey, listed exemptions to the MFN rule for their accounting rate systems.

Several MFN exemptions were claimed in professional services for bilateral agreements on the mutual recognition of qualifications – presumably because they did not wish such agreements to be subject to the disciplines of Article VII on recognition. But the number of countries claiming MFN exemptions for professional services is small in relation to the large number of WTO members which made specific commitments in this sector.

Measures for which MFN exemptions have been claimed affecting all sectors mainly concern bilateral agreements for the entry of workers or the protection of investments. Some Members have, however, claimed wide-ranging exemptions for preferential regional agreements – presumably because of uncertainty regarding whether they would fulfill the conditions of Article V dealing with regional integration agreements.

On the whole, MFN exemptions would seem to matter most in sectors like audiovisual services and maritime transport where few specific commitments have been made and discriminatory practices seem to be empirically important. In other cases, where the exemptions coexist with specific commitments (as in financial services) or legitimize preferences which do not greatly affect the pattern of trade (as in cross-border supply of land transport services), there is probably less cause for concern. Finally, the exemptions which cover retaliatory legislation need not lead to actual discrimination in trade policy though the credible threat itself may have real effects.

## 4. Analysis of Selected Issues

This Section begins with an analysis of the economic and legal implications of discrimination in services through domestic regulations and quantitative restrictions. It then examines, in turn, three instances of potential conflict between the MFN obligation and Members' objectives: reciprocity-based trade policy, grandfathering of the rights of existing suppliers, and the pursuit of competition policy.

### Discrimination through Domestic Regulations

In order to examine the implications of discrimination in services, we must first consider the instruments of protection that are usually employed. In general, governments rely more on domestic regulations, such as technical standards, licensing, and qualification requirements, and quantitative restrictions than on discriminatory taxes. The consequences of discrimination through taxation (or duties) are well understood. Does discrimination through alternative instruments raises new analytical issues from the legal and economic point of view?

#### *Economic Implications*

To begin with, consider domestic regulations pertaining to technical standards and qualification requirements. The requirement to meet a certain standard may involve a change in variable costs, fixed costs, or both. The requirement for financial institutions to maintain local reserves is an example of a standard that may increase variable costs of operation. The requirement for foreign professionals to requalify increases the fixed costs of entry for each individual, but if we define units so that each professional is assumed to provide a single unit of service, then even qualification requirements can be seen as affecting variable costs. The problem is that it would not usually be correct to treat all the additional costs imposed on foreign services or service suppliers as a form of protection. It is necessary to distinguish between the regulatory burden imposed on the foreign supplier which is necessary to ensure the desired quality of the service and that which is excessive.

This issue can be illustrated by considering the qualification requirements imposed on foreign professionals. Even though professionals obtain composite degrees and qualifications in each country, it should usually be possible to distinguish between a basic "universal" part of the training, consisting of u units, which is identical between countries, and country specific training (say in local law) equal to vi units. In some professions, like medicine and engineering, the universal component is likely to be high, whereas in other professions, like law and accountancy, the country-specific component is likely to be high. Outside of professional services, for instance in construction, financial, and transport services, it is reasonable to presume that there is a high universal component to standards though there is usually also a variable country specific elements.

Let us also assume that the cost per unit of training in country *i* is constant at *ci*. The variations in ci are meant to capture inherent advantages that certain countries have in certain areas. It would seem obvious that if a foreign lawyer wished to practice in country *i,* he would necessarily have to incur an entry cost equal to *civi*. But it is possible that the first country also refuses to acknowledge the equivalence of the universal part acquired in the home country, and insists on full requalification, implying entry *costs* $ci(u + vi)$. In this case, *ciu* would be a measure of the excessive regulatory burden. More subtle forms of protection could involve understatement of the universal element *u,* and exaggeration of the country specific element *vi.*

Recognition agreements may exempt certain suppliers from incurring whole or part of these costs.[21]

In situations where the impact of regulation is on variable costs, as is assumed here, the analysis of discriminatory regulation can proceed in a manner analogous to tariffs.[22] Assume that there are three countries: country X is an importing country, facing an upward sloping domestic supply of professionals (say because of increasing opportunity costs) and countries Y and Z are potential exporters. Let us say that $cx > cy > cz$, and that in the absence of any trade the prevailing price in country X is $p^*$. Assume now that country X recognizes the equivalence of the universal component of training obtained in country Y, but not in country Z. There are several possibilities, but we consider only two:

No trade prior to recognition: Prior to recognition, professionals from both countries Y and Z were required to obtain country-specific training in country 1 but neither found it worthwhile to do so, i.e., $cy(u + vy) + cx(u + vx) > p^*$ and $cz(u + vz) + cx(u + vx) > p^*$.[23] But $cy(u + vy) + cx\,vx < p^*$, i.e., when the universal component of training in country Y is recognized as equivalent to that in country X, then professionals from Y find it worthwhile to export to country X, and the price in X will fall. Hence, if all foreign professionals had been completely deterred from practicing in country X by the absence of recognition, then any recognition agreement is necessarily trade creating.

Country Z exports to country X prior to any recognition: In this case, $cz(u + vz) + cx(u + vx) < p^* < cy(u + vy) + cx(u + vx)$, i.e., when all foreign professionals were required to requalify, only those from the third country were willing to supply country 1. *But* $cy(u + vy) + cx\ vx < cz(u + vz) + cx(u + vx)$, i.e., once the second country professionals are exempted from the basic qualification requirement, they gain a competitive edge over the third country. That is, if lawyers from the third country were already present in the first country, then the recognition of second country professionals would put them at a competitive disadvantage and could lead to trade diversion.

This situation is depicted in Figure 1 (the following discussion resembles closely the discussion in Pelkmans and Winters, 1988). The pre-recognition situation involves domestic output $q2$, consumption $q3$, and imports from Z, $q3 - q2$. After country X recognizes qualifications in country Y, domestic output declines to $q1$, consumption increases to $q4$, and imports from Y, $q4 - q1$, displace imports from Z. So we are witnessing both trade creation and trade diversion. The welfare effects are straightforward. Consumer surplus rises by A + B + C + D as consumption expands from $q3$ to $q4$. The area A is a gain at the expense of domestic suppliers, whose surplus falls with their output. Area D is the gain from the better allocation of consumption expenditures; area B the gain from the resources released as inefficient domestic supply contracts; and area C the gain arising from the elimination of wasteful requalification.

The area C + E is of crucial significance, and can be interpreted in several different ways. It helps to recall the analysis of preferential arrangements when tariffs are the instruments of protection. In that case, area $C + E$ would be the loss in government revenue because preferential imports displace high tariff imports. While C is gained by consumers, E is completely lost because supply comes from the more expensive source, and is the loss due to trade diversion. The net gain to the country is only B + D – E, and could be positive or negative. In the example here, C + E were the costs of requalification for country Z professionals when they supplied country X. If these costs were completely dissipated, then they do not enter the welfare calculus of country X. That is, there is no cost of trade diversion for the importing country and the net gain to the importing country from the recognition agreement is B + C + D. If, however, part of these requalification costs (say a fraction a) were appropriated by country X, perhaps as the producer surplus of its training industry or as some form of regulatory rent, then they would be foregone with trade diversion and would need to be taken into account: the net gain to the importing country from the agreement would be B + C + D – a(C + E).

**Figure 1. Trade and Welfare Effects of a Recognition Agreement**

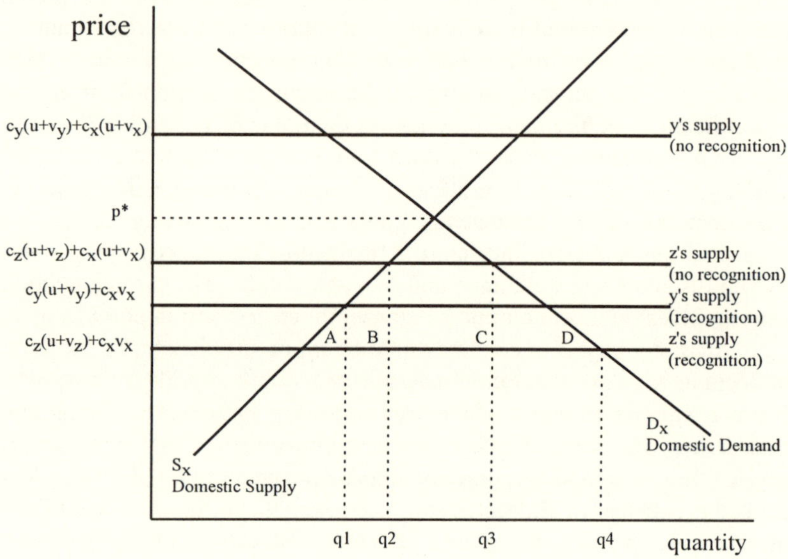


When tariffs are the instruments of protection, the costs of trade diversion for the importing country may be an important deterrent to preferential liberalization agreements. Despite the increase in consumers' surplus from any liberalization, governments may nevertheless be averse to such agreements because the displacement of high-tariff imports from third countries by low or no-tariff imports from preferential sources implies lost revenue. The same reasoning also applies to other regulations which imply a transfer from foreign suppliers to domestic interest groups. However, the situation is different when the protectionist instrument is a regulatory barrier which imposes a cost on the exporter without yielding a corresponding revenue for the importing government or other interest group. There is then no cost to granting preferential access because there is no revenue to lose. Therefore, preferential liberalization is necessarily welfare enhancing for the importing country.

In this simple model, trade diversion reduces the third country's sales to the first country. The simplest way of depicting the negative welfare effects on the third country is by assuming that its supply curve is upward sloping, so that lower sales imply lower prices and loss of producers' surplus. Interestingly, it is possible to show that recognition agreements may well increase global welfare even though suppliers who are left out of such agreements lose. In effect, a recognition agreement is like a positive cost shock to a certain class of suppliers leading to a reduction in price in the importing country. The gain to consumers from any decline in price is necessarily greater than the loss to a subset of suppliers. This makes intuitive sense: eliminating wasteful duplication of training should enhance global welfare. Though, of course, a non-preferential recognition agreement would enhance welfare even more because the service would be supplied by the most efficient locations.

*Legal Issues: Establishing Likeness*

In this Section, it is argued that there is a need to depart from the GATT precedent in examining consistency of measures with the MFN obligation.[24] First, the conventional criteria used to judge whether two products are like are not particularly useful in the services context and need to be replaced by a consideration of the end-uses of services. Secondly, the sequential procedure of first determining whether two products are like and then if one has been treated less favorably leads to a legal cul-de-sac, and needs to be replaced by a simultaneous consideration of the degree of unlikeness and differences in treatment. Thirdly, there is a need to read in the context of Article II a necessity test of the kind previously associated with the GATT exceptions provision. Finally, the necessity test itself needs to be refined to take into account the economic efficiency of instruments.

Consider, first, how the GATT precedents for defining "likeness" a priori would fare in the GATS context. In the GATT, likeness has been determined on a case-by-case basis in terms of criteria such as "the product's end-uses in a given market, consumers' tastes and habits, which change from country to country; the product's properties, nature, and quality, and the product's tariff classification."[25] In the context of Article I, considerable importance has been given to a country's tariff classification. Even though the Harmonized System has brought about a large degree of harmonization in the field of customs classification of goods, this system "did not entail any obligation as to the ultimate detail in the respective tariff classifications" and "a tariff classification going beyond the Harmonized System's structure is a legitimate means of adapting the tariff scheme to each contracting party's trade policy interests, comprising both its protection needs and its requirements for the purposes of tariff and trade negotiations..."[26] However, even though Members have significant discretion in the choice of classifications, the MFN obligation required "that the same tariff treatment be applied to *like products*" irrespective of the classification adopted.[27]

Corresponding to the tariff classification in the case of goods, commitments in services have generally followed a classification scheme based on the United Nations Central Product Classification, which is in the process of being revised.[28] The status of this classification, and the closeness with which it has been followed in scheduling commitments, do not compare favorably with the well-developed Harmonized System classification. However, in so far as the services classification was developed and used for negotiating commitments on both market access and national treatment, it could be argued that it represents mutually accepted product distinctions for regulatory purposes. Thus being classed in separate sub-sectors in the services classification may be regarded as a sufficient condition for "unlikeness." However, given the high level of aggregation of the services classification, being classed in even the finest sub-division can only be considered as at most creating a presumption that the services are like.[29]

In the goods context, the elevation of certain physical characteristics of the product to decisive status, regardless of consumer perception or behavior in the market-place, does not seen entirely persuasive nor is it capable of consistent application. In the case of services, physical characteristics are, perhaps fortunately, irrelevant. There may also be a need to consciously deviate from the narrow interpretation of the MFN obligation in the goods context based on the fact that the provision mentions "like products" but not the wider category of "directly competitive or substitutable products" as does the national treatment obligation.[30] It is the notion of "end uses" which offers the most appropriate basis for comparing services. This notion is related to the economically meaningful concepts of directly competitive or substitutable, and follows the logic of the market place. After all, what matters is whether consumers treat the services in question as substitutes.

But irrespective of the criteria chosen to arrive at an a priori notion of like services, it would be difficult to deny regulators the right to make further distinctions between services. Furthermore, the scope for making such distinctions is arguably greater in the case of services than in the case of goods. It may be useful to begin with an example which illustrates why these issues might be particularly difficult to tackle in the GATS context. Country X, imposes the requirement that only foreign doctors trained in country Y will be allowed to practice in X. It argues that the measure is not inconsistent with MFN because all foreigners have access to medical colleges in Y, and even citizens from Y trained elsewhere are not allowed to practice in X. Even though the measure is not de jure discriminatory, surely it is de facto discriminatory since the incidence of the measure is much greater on foreign doctors from countries other than Y? But X argues that a determination of de facto discrimination must be consequent upon a determination of likeness, and in its view the service provided by doctors trained in countries other than Y is unlike a service provided by a doctors trained in Y. Say country Z were to complain about the measure imposed by X. How would GATS disciplines deal with this problem?

The burden of proving likeness would fall on the complainant. County Z would argue that the services of doctors trained in Y and Z are indeed like products for the purpose of Article II. However, country X could argue could that training in Y is more suited to the needs of X (in terms of the earlier example, vx is similar to vy but not vz) or that the examination system in Y is more reliable (the u obtained in country Y can be trusted but not that in Z). Since standards and qualification requirements are unlikely to be exactly the same in any two countries, the question is how much difference justifies a pronouncement of unlikeness? A WTO panel would find it difficult to appropriate the right to make this judgment from the medical authorities of country X: if it did, and judged the services to be "like," it would be forced to recommend that X should provide access to doctors trained in Z on the same term as those trained in Y. If, on the other hand, it accepted that the services were "unlike" then no matter how great the difference in treatment, the disciplines of Article II would simply not apply.

In these circumstances, the most reasonable argument that a panel could advance would be that country X should subject doctors trained in countries other than Y to tests of competence (establish the authenticity of u) or to training only in country-specific areas (vx) rather than insist on their undergoing full retraining in Y. In other words, full requalification is not necessary to meet the objective of ensuring high quality medical services since the same objective could be met by the less trade-restrictive means. But here is the key question: can we read Article II to contain a necessity test which would enable a panel to pronounce judgment on the stringency of a measure? Of course Article XIV, dealing with general exceptions contains such a test, but to move to Article XIV would require the panel to establish first that the measure is inconsistent with Article II. It is only then that a country would need to invoke the general exceptions provision. Thus, it would be difficult for a panel to circumvent the need to pronounce judgment on "likeness."

*The "Temporary" Weakness of GATS Article VI*

There is, in principle, a more direct route under the GATS to address the problem of standards which are unduly trade-restrictive. This is through Article VI which deals with domestic regulation. Today Article VI primarily provides a mandate (in Article VI:4) to develop disciplines under the GATS to ensure "that measures relating to qualification requirements and procedures, technical standards and licensing requirements do not constitute unnecessary barriers to trade in services." Pending the entry into force of disciplines developed pursuant to Article VI:4, the only current disciplines are contained in Article VI:5, which requires that "the Member should not apply licensing and qualification requirements and technical standards that nullify or impair any existing sectoral commitments in a manner which:

1. does not comply with the criteria outlined in subparagraphs 4(a) [objectivity and transparency], 4(b) [not more burdensome than necessary to ensure the quality of the service], and 4(c) [in the case of licensing procedures, of not being in themselves a restriction on the supply of the service]; and
2. *could not reasonably have been expected of that Member at the time the specific commitments in those sectors were made.*" (emphasis added)

The requirements in 1. could have constituted a powerful discipline, but element 2. renders them toothless. In the extreme, it could be read as "grandfathering" all existing restrictive requirements. Thus country X could argue that training in medical schools in Y had always been a requirement to practice in X and it could, therefore, "reasonably have been expected" when the specific commitments were made. This provision seriously limits the scope for translating the commitments under GATS into non-discriminatory market access.

In this respect, it is worth comparing Article VI of the GATS with the newly strengthened Agreement on Technical Barriers to Trade (TBT). The key provision is Article 2. Article 2.2 states that:

> Members shall ensure that technical regulations are not prepared, adopted or applied with a view to or with the effect of creating unnecessary obstacles to international trade. For this purpose, *technical regulations shall not be more trade restrictive than necessary to fulfill a legitimate objective*, taking into account the risks non-fulfillment would create. . . (emphasis added)

Thus, not only does the TBT deter discriminatory measures, as does GATT Article III, it goes further in imposing additional disciplines on non-discriminatory measures. It makes possible a critical assessment of non-discriminatory standards (i.e., the choice of v1 itself) from the point of view of their impact on trade in a way that is not currently possible under GATS.[31]

It could be argued that Article VI will eventually contain a second line of defense against origin neutral measures which escape Article II. But there are two problems. First, even though the domain of Article VI is all domestic regulations, significant disciplines are to be developed under the Article VI:4 mandate only for qualification requirements and procedures, technical standards and licensing requirements. Secondly, there is an intertemporal problem. It is reasonable to assume that at some point in the future Article VI of GATS will be as strong as the TBT, and note furthermore, that its domain is wider than that of the latter. If this were to happen, then the escape of certain measures from Article II would indeed be less cause for concern. However, today, with Article VI not creating a strong discipline, reading Article II narrowly would mean an indefinite wait for meaningful disciplines.

*A Possible Solution*

One solution to the problem would be to take a stringent view of likeness in the context of Article II and then Members found to be acting inconsistently could invoke Article XIV, the exceptions provision in defense. However, the list of regulatory objectives in Article XIV as it currently stands is far too narrow, and cannot be taken as the universe of objectives that can be legitimately pursued by WTO Members.[32] Furthermore, the prospect that these objectives will be broadened in the near future through political negotiation does not appear very promising. The central problem is that on the one hand, it would be difficult to prevent Members from invoking objectives other than those listed in Article XIV (dealing with general exceptions) as a basis for taking measures which may have a discriminatory effect; on the other hand, allowing them to do so may make it possible to circumvent the disciplines of Article XIV and open the door to all manner of discrimination being justified as incidental to the pursuit of supposedly non-discriminatory aims.

There is a solution to this problem: to read disciplines in GATS Article II of the type previously associated only with GATT Article XX and GATS Article XIV, both of which deal with general exceptions. This implies, on the one hand, accepting the right of regulators to pursue a legitimate objective, but on the other hand, ensuring that the objective is not pursued in a manner which discriminates between foreigners. In effect, the question of whether two services or service suppliers are treated differently must not be separated from how they are treated differently. On this basis, a two stage test can be suggested:

1. Stipulate an a priori definition of like services based on similarity of end-uses, and a clear relationship of substitutability and direct competition based on market conditions. The criterion of end-uses serves to demarcate the class of services or service suppliers within which a particular measure may give rise to protectionist effect. For example, a higher regulatory burden on banks than on insurance companies would clearly not arouse concern in the same way that a higher burden on banks regulated in one country rather than another would. But, even within the class of similar end-use, a criterion is needed to distinguish between situations in which discriminatory effect is an incidental consequence of a domestic measure and those in which it is not.
2. If a Member takes measures which distinguish between what could be regarded as a priori like services or service suppliers, then that Member must assume the burden of proving that any resultant unfavorable treatment of foreigners is necessary. In other words, that the Member could not have achieved the stated objective through any other reasonably available measure which did not disadvantage foreign services or foreign suppliers, or did not disadvantage them as much.

There is no precedent of GATT panels applying a necessity test in the context of Article I (MFN).

There is a strong case that the GATT precedent of uncritical acceptance of the choice of instruments in the context of Article I needs to be disregarded. In the GATS context, since it will be difficult to resist the invocation of objectives in the context of II, it is imperative to apply a more stringent test. If such a test cannot already be read in Article II, then it would seem desirable that its explicit inclusion be considered in future negotiations.

Moreover, the necessity test, as interpreted by previous panels in the context of GATT Article XX, may itself may be in need of refinement.[33] In their exclusive concern with GATT-consistency, these interpretations do not explicitly address the issue of *efficiency* of measures. Economic principles can provide meaningful rules for the choice of instruments. Ideally, state intervention is meant to remedy distortions. The economic theory of optimal policy intervention provides an hierarchy of instruments to deal with the problem of domestic distortions. The "first-best" instrument is the one which attacks the divergence between the private and the social cost at the source. There is a case for interpreting the necessity test to create a presumption in favor of the choice of the economically optimal policy to achieve a legitimate objective. A Member choosing to pursue an objective by a measure other than the economically optimal policy would need to justify this choice.[34]

Thus, in ruling on the foreign doctor dispute, a Panel could argue: considerations of end-use and substitutability create a presumption that all foreign doctors provide like services. Country X, in the light of its objective of ensuring high quality medical services, does not consider the services provided by doctors trained in Y and those by doctors trained in Z like services. The objective is legitimate. But if the disciplines of Article II are not to be circumvented, *then the judgment of unlikeness itself and the manner in which supposedly unlike services are treated* must not be such as to accord less favorable treatment to some foreigners as compared with others. This implies that the instrument chosen, and the manner of its application, should not unnecessarily discriminate between foreign doctors. There are, in principle, a range of instruments which could achieve the objective of ensuring adequate quality of medical services. The optimal instrument would be one which achieved the objective of remedying the problem of asymmetric information about foreign suppliers' abilities at least cost: say through a test of competence. Even if Country X's distinction is accepted, the instrument chosen, full training in Y, modifies conditions of competition excessively even in the light of the objective, which could be attained by means less unfavorable to doctors from Z, such as tests of competence with regard to universal skills and additional training only in country-specific skills.[35]

The approach suggested here could be applied not only to establishing the likeness of services but also to the question of who can be regarded as like suppliers—a subject on which GATS offers little guidance. The logic of the MFN obligation would suggest beginning with the presumption that *suppliers of like services are like suppliers*. Any distinction made between suppliers presumed to be like would need to be justified. But there are indications that Members may wish to take a more flexible approach to this issue. First of all, by scheduling limitations under GATS Article XVI:2(e), a Member specifies the types of legal entity through which a supplier may supply a service. Thus a Member may allow the supply of a service through a subsidiary but not a branch. Secondly, the treatment of taxes under the GATS seems to suggest a willingness to accept that suppliers of like services located in different tax jurisdictions can be legitimately treated differently. Nevertheless, Section 5.5 illustrates how the suggested approach could be applied to the like supplier issue.

*The Implications for Mutual Recognition Agreements*

The previous reasoning can also be applied to resolve the difficulty of applying Article VII. An MRA essentially helps beneficiaries to circumvent the equivalence establishment process. The key question concerns the treatment of those with whom an MRA has not been concluded or to whom recognition has not been granted. Article VII:2 requires that an opportunity be afforded to other *Members* to conclude MRAs or to demonstrate equivalence, but says little about the rights of individual suppliers. The more powerful discipline is contained in Article VII:3 which prohibits the use of recognition as a means of discrimination. While recognition, unilateral or through an MRA, amounts to an acceptance of likeness vis-à-vis certain suppliers, it also defines a standard of treatment vis-à-vis other suppliers. In terms of the example, if X recognizes the universal element u obtained in Y, then an individual supplier from Z should have the possibility of demonstrating equivalent training obtained in Z. If X has legitimate doubts about the authenticity of the training, then the incremental burden imposed on such a supplier should be no greater than that necessary to achieve the regulatory objective. This would amount to a presumption in favor of a test of competence. Ideally, local qualification or training should only be used as a means of remedying differences in the country-specific element, $v_i$.

Such an interpretation of Article VII:3 would ensure that the liberalizing effect of MRAs can be generalized. At present, given the weakness of Article VI, if a Member has not made a commitment to grant national treatment, then the Member is free to impose uniformly burdensome regulations on all foreigners. However, if a Member concludes an MRA or grants recognition to one foreign country, then this provides all others with a potentially valuable foothold by defining a standard of treatment. The problem is that if it is rationally expected that extending recognition to one Member would eventually require extending it to many, then even the recognition of one may be deterred. This would be undesirable since even limited preferential liberalization through MRAs may be welfare enhancing in a second-best world, as the previous sub-section has demonstrated. The tendency of Members to notify MRAs under Article V rather than Article VII may reflect an attempt to share these gains on a limited reciprocal basis by avoiding the obligation to extend recognition more widely.

## Quantitative Restrictions and MFN

While quotas are an aberration in goods trade and have been more or less outlawed, they are a pervasive form of protection in services and are only inconsistent with the GATS in sectors where a Member has undertaken not to use them. Furthermore, quotas under the GATS restrict not only the quantity or value of services output, but, also the number of (foreign) service suppliers.

There is a huge economic literature examining almost every aspect of quotas so this section makes only a only a few brief remarks. The earlier analysis of discriminatory regulation is also relevant here. It could be argued that in services, since intermediation is difficult, rents are usually appropriated by exporters rather than domestic importers. As in the case of certain restrictive regulations where the protective instrument does not generate domestic revenue (or rents), there is no cost to granting preferential access because there is no revenue (or rents) to lose. Therefore, preferential liberalization is necessarily welfare enhancing for the importing country. However, we can conceive of certain situations, such as when there are quotas on workers from countries with low labor costs, where the rents accrue to the domestic employer/supplier. Such an employer/supplier would oppose a preferential allocation of the quota to countries with higher labor costs. It may also be the case that the importing country is not indifferent to the allocation of rents between foreign suppliers—as was the case in the European Union's régime for the distribution of bananas. In such cases, there may be welfare costs to preferential allocation of quotas as well as political economic opposition to such arrangements.

One central legal tension in the GATS, which has received surprisingly little attention, is between quotas on market access, particularly those specifically listed under Article XVI, and Article II concerning non-discrimination. Quantitative restrictions include those on the number of service suppliers, volume of output, value of output, and number of service suppliers. The problem concerns how these quotas are to be allocated in a manner consistent with the non-discrimination obligation. In the past, this was not a major issue because commitments reflected the status quo and the quotas, particularly with regard to service suppliers, were descriptions of the existing market structure. Thus when Bangladesh committed to "four licenses issued" in cellular telephony, the ambiguity in the choice of tense was not an accident: the licenses in question had already been issued. But in the future, as genuine liberalizing commitments are made, the non-discriminatory allocation of quotas is bound to be an important issue.

Does the goods precedent offer any guidance? GATT Article XIII, on the "non-discriminatory administration of quantitative restrictions," states in paragraph 2 that: "In applying import restrictions to any product, contracting parties shall aim at a distribution of trade in such a product approaching as closely as possible the shares which the various contracting parties might be expected to obtain in the absence of such restrictions. . ." It also stipulates that the country implementing a quota should ideally reach an agreement regarding its allocation with all countries which have a substantial interest in supplying the product. If this is not "reasonably practicable," then allocation should be based on proportions supplied by the countries during a previous representative period, "due account being taken of any special factors which may have affected or may be affecting trade in the product."

In the services context, the requirement to replicate historical shares may have no relevance if there was no previous foreign presence, or even perpetuate historical discrimination if previous quotas were allocated to Favored suppliers.[36] Furthermore, neither of the instinctive candidates for a non-discriminatory rule, first-come, first-served and a system of auctions to the highest bidder, would necessarily lead to distributions "which . . . might be expected to obtain in the absence of such restrictions." It is obvious that first-come, first-served favors the proximate. Auctions would give the relatively efficient producers larger shares than they would have obtained in the absence of quotas (when quotas are set at below unrestricted trade levels).[37] It would seem, therefore, that the rules for ensuring non-discriminatory allocation of quotas under GATS would need to look beyond the GATT-precedent. It is possible that a less elaborate variant of the disciplines in the Agreement on Government Procurement, designed to ensure competitive tendering on non-discriminatory basis, will need to be considered.

*Time and the Quota*

Once we introduce service suppliers and time into the picture, the picture gets more complicated. Consider the example of the several governments who have made market access commitments to issue an exclusive license to a telecommunications services provider and guaranteed no new entry for a fixed period, say ten years. This license may have been auctioned off in a non-discriminatory manner to a supplier at a price which reflects the future discounted monopoly profits over ten years. Now suppose a year later, the government decides to liberalize further and issues one more license.[38] The government is not prevented from doing so by Article XVI because limitations are minimum guarantees and not maximum limits. Say the new license is also issued through a non-discriminatory auction. The additional license is likely to be sold at a price lower than the previous price, because the expected profits of the new entrants are lower than those of the first entrant who believed that it would be a monopoly—first, because the new situation is a duopoly and the new entrant may build into its bid the expectation of more competition.[39] Quite apart from the first entrant's rights under the terms of its contract with the government, could it be claimed that the government's actions violated Article II because it had been charged a higher entry price than the new entrant? Would the fact that the government obeyed a non-discriminatory rule at each point of time be a sufficient defense or is it obliged to extend the same treatment across time after the GATS came into effect?

## Reciprocity

As described in Section 3, a number of Members have sought MFN exemptions on the grounds of reciprocity. Furthermore, initially in sectors like financial services and telecommunications and until now in maritime transport, MFN-based outcomes could not be attained because certain Members wished to retain the right to grant market access conditional on the treatment of their suppliers in other markets. It is important to distinguish between reciprocity as an aspect of the bargaining process and reciprocity as an aspect of the trade regime. In the former case, concessions are negotiated on a reciprocal basis and the results are multilateralized, so discrimination is not practiced in actual trade. In the latter case, reciprocity is the basis for the implementation of trade policy, so discrimination is a feature of actual trade policy.

*Economic and Bargaining Considerations*

Recently, Bagwell and Staiger (1997) have provided a rationalization of reciprocity-based negotiations which is independent of the national policy formulation process, i.e., of whether government policy is aimed at maximizing national welfare or promoting the interests of particular groups. They begin with the recognition that the spillover effects of policy in one country on other countries necessarily take place through changes in the terms-of-trade. They find, first in a two-country game, that a reciprocity rule in negotiations—in the sense, that I will reduce my protection if you will—can take the countries from an inefficient Nash equilibrium to the efficient policy locus. This result follows from the fact that reciprocity insulates each country from the terms-of-trade loss consequent upon unilateral liberalization and hence eliminates the negative externality which leads to the inefficient Nash equilibrium. Furthermore, if we include a rule for reciprocity-based renegotiation of concessions—in the sense, that if I increase my protection, so can you—then, the only renegotiation-proof equilibrium is, in fact, the Pareto optimum. If governments were welfare maximizing, then the Pareto optimum would be free trade. If they were not, then the Pareto optimum implies some positive level of protection.

In their model, given that reciprocity is the basis for negotiations, in a multi-country world, the MFN principle implements the efficient outcome. The intuition is that with discriminatory tariffs, countries have an incentive to import relatively more of a given volume of imports from countries on whom higher tariffs are imposed since this increases tariff revenue and hence welfare. The volume of imports from a particular source depends, of course, on the local price in the source country. Thus, under discriminatory tariffs both world and foreign local price externalities arise, whereas under the principle of non-discrimination, the only externality between government is the world-price externality. In the latter case, the principle of reciprocity works well to neutralize externalities and deliver efficient outcomes. However, in the former case, the principle of reciprocity neutralizes world price externalities but not local price externalities, and, therefore, no longer serves as a means to implement efficient trade-policy outcomes.

Bagwell and Staiger thus provide a useful rationalization of the non-discrimination principle as complementing reciprocity-based negotiations to deliver efficient outcomes. What they do not do is explore fully the incentive properties of the MFN rule when there is a possibility of strategic behavior in bargaining. For instance, how is the free-rider problem overcome when the results of reciprocity are immediately multilateralized? When do large countries have an incentive to play by such rules rather than do either bilateral deals or indulge in aggressive unilateralism? As noted above, these questions assume particular relevance in the context of services negotiations

The MFN principle is not simply a rule that constrains trade discrimination, but also a rule that influences the multilateral bargaining process (Schwartz and Sykes, 1996).[40] Acceptance of the MFN principle implies that ex ante the participants in the negotiations know that any concession negotiated with a single trading partner must be unconditionally extended to all other trading partners, regardless of their ability to extract a quid pro quo. At the same time, the benefit from any concession extended by others may be obtained without having to give a quid pro quo. Ex post, the participants know that the value of any concession that they obtain under MFN will not be impaired by subsequent more generous concessions to other countries – except, of course, in the context of a regional integration agreement.

The problem is that Members may try and free ride on each other during bargaining—as was alleged in the context of the financial services and telecommunications negotiations. Each of the beneficiaries of a concession from a trading partner may be tempted to understate their willingness to pay for it, hoping that offers of reciprocal concessions from other Members will be sufficient to induce the concession. If each Member behaves in this way, the result could be that mutually beneficial deals will not be struck. This was reflected in the unwillingness in some of the services negotiations of some Members to make binding commitments unless a certain "critical mass" of Members was willing to make significant liberalization commitments. But it is not clear how well-founded these fears of free-riding were. Table 4 presents estimates of how concentrated trade in services is on the basis of balance-of-payments statistics. These figures do not include trade through commercial presence, but such trade is probably even more concentrated than cross-border trade. It is evident that in most sectors, the top 10 exporters and importers account for a large part of total exports and imports, respectively, even taking into account the limitations in reporting. A more detailed analysis reveals that the major exporting and major importing countries tend to be the same. This degree of concentration does not provide strong support for the free-riding view.[41]

Nevertheless, in so far as free-riding is a real problem, two possible solutions exist: for beneficiaries to form a caucus to work out a collective offer for a desired concession—which may describe the European Union's efforts to form a package of offers in financial services and maritime negotiations. The second is to abandon product-by-product negotiations and agree instead that every Member will reduce barriers according to a mutually agreed formula—which may be difficult in services given the nature of the instruments of protections (see Sapir, 1998).

However, because there is no complete solution to the free-rider problem, it is likely that the MFN principle prevents the parties in large multilateral trade negotiations from exhausting all joint political gains and makes the first-best political optimum unattainable. In the absence of such a principle, a country that secured a discriminatory concession would realize the full benefit of it and seek no other concession from an alternative source to induce it. Ceteris paribus, the desirability of discriminatory arrangements would be greater, the more serious the free-rider problem for non-discriminatory arrangements, and the less the amount of trade diversion that

**Table 4. Share of Top Five and Top Ten Exporters and Importers of Commercial Services in 1995 (percentage)**

| Service Sector | Share of Top 5 Exporters in Total Reported | Share of Top 10 Exporters in Total Reported | Estimated Share of Total Reported in World Exports | Share of Top 5 Importers in Total Reported | Share of Top 10 Importers in Total Reported | Estimated Share of Total Reported in World Imports |
|---|---|---|---|---|---|---|
| Transportation | 44 | 66 | 100 | 43 | 60 | 100 |
| Travel | 45 | 61 | 100 | 49 | 66 | 100 |
| Communications | 49 | 67 | 83 | 67 | 81 | 81 |
| Construction | 61 | 91 | 73 | 69 | 93 | 71 |
| Insurance | 69 | 84 | 94 | 60 | 72 | 93 |
| Financial | 61 | 92 | 81 | 71 | 87 | 72 |
| Computer and Information | 70 | 98 | 49 | 71 | 96 | 50 |
| Royalties and Licence Fees | 89 | 97 | 83 | 60 | 81 | 84 |
| Other Business Services | 43 | 65 | 100 | 42 | 60 | 100 |
| Personal, Cultural, and Recreational Services | 82 | 93 | 76 | 61 | 88 | 75 |

*Source:* Estimated from IMF Balance-of-Payments Statistics.

results from discrimination. Under these circumstances, preferential trading arrangements may make some political sense as a second best alternative, even though such arrangements tend to dissipate political surplus through trade diversion, which affects producers and national treasuries; they also tend to undermine the security of trade concessions.

As Schwartz and Sykes argue, it is in averting this last cost that the MFN principle also brings benefits for the bargaining process. A trading regime without an MFN obligation creates an opportunity for a subset of Members to threaten to create a discriminatory arrangement to induce other nations to make concessions. The possibility of such threats may create an unstable trading regime. Furthermore, the MFN obligation protects the value of concessions against future erosion through discrimination. My willingness to pay for a concession may be undermined if I fear that you might subsequently grant preferred access to someone else. Faced with this possibility I would offer less for the concession in the first place and fewer mutually beneficial deals would be struck. A blanket MFN provision is of course not the only solution to the problem. Each party to a trade agreement could secure in conjunction with the concession additional promises limiting the future concessions that a trading partner could subsequently make in the same domain to other trading partners.[42] However, the transaction and information costs of proceeding in this fashion would be high. Alternatively, members could confine all concessions to well defined multilateral negotiating rounds—as is generally the case, with the exception of regional initiatives. No nation would commit to anything until it could review the entire schedule of proposed discriminatory concessions by each of its trading partners. Both these approaches would compare unfavorably with the simple MFN rule in terms of ease of administration and the maximization of joint surplus.

In the services context, the possibility of seeking MFN exemptions meant that ex ante bargaining often took place without the guarantee of the MFN principle. The United States and others held out against the acceptance of the principle until they were satisfied with the liberalization commitments obtained from others. The others in turn were unwilling to permanently bind these commitments unless the United States and others accepted adherence to the principle, i.e., guaranteed them a certain security of concessions. To an extent therefore the ex ante costs of the MFN principle were avoided while the ex post benefits were reaped—at least in areas where full MFN-based liberalization was achieved.

*Legal Limits to Discriminatory Action*

Is there any restriction on the type of measures for which an MFN exemption can be obtained? There is little doubt that a Member can list measures which grant discriminatory access in a particular sector. But can a Member, by taking an MFN exemption, maintain *the right to take retaliatory measures* on a discriminatory basis against, what it *unilaterally* judges to be, foreign restrictive trade practices? Examples of MFN exemptions of which reserve the right to do so are the European Union's exemption in audiovisual services states and the United States legislation in maritime transport for which an exemption was not listed because the MFN obligation was suspended for the sector.[43]

It would need to be examined whether an interpretation of Article II which allows this would be inconsistent with the Understanding on Rules and Procedures Governing the Settlement of Disputes (DSU), in particular, Article 23 which deals with strengthening of the multilateral system. This Article states that "when Members seek the redress of a violation of obligations or other nullification or impairment of benefits under the covered agreements or an impediment to the attainment of any objective of the covered agreements, they shall have recourse to, and abide by, the rules and procedures of this Understanding." To abide by the rules and procedures of the DSU would seem to preclude a unilateral determination of a violation.

Audiovisual services and maritime transport services are a part of GATS and thus covered by the DSU. Could it be argued that Article 23 of the DSU does not prevent a Member from taking unilateral action to obtain benefits beyond those accruing under the covered agreements? That is, could a Member unilaterally attempt to induce greater liberalization in another Member's market than is granted in its schedule of commitments? An argument could be made that this would imply seeking the redressal, without abiding by the rules and procedures of the DSU, of "an impediment to the attainment of any objective" of the GATS. The preamble to the GATS states that Members desire "the early achievement of progressively higher levels of liberalization of trade in services through successive rounds of multilateral negotiations." Thus, inducing further liberalization in all services sectors is an aim which has, in a sense, been appropriated by the GATS, and so Members are no longer free to pursue this aim by actions which are inconsistent with the DSU. This interpretation, however, needs closer examination.

## Grandfather Provisions

One of the central problems in the financial services negotiations was solved by a scheduling innovation. The conflict arose because certain countries were unwilling to make commitments which reflected the status quo with respect to commercial presence. Thus, they were either inclined to bind foreign ownership levels below those which currently prevailed, or insist on legal forms (local incorporation) other than those currently in the market (branches), or both. In some cases, the problem arose because domestic law had changed since the foreign firms first established commercial presence, e.g. in Malaysia, where the indigenisation policy was being implemented after the establishment of many foreign firms.

To see the nature of the problem, consider the following example. Say country A had allowed a firm from country B to establish a fully owned subsidiary in 1990. If it made a specific commitment under GATS to allow commercial presence through fully-owned foreign subsidiaries, then it would be obliged to allow firms from all Members to establish under similar conditions. The implied level of openness was apparently unacceptable for some Members in situations similar to country A. If, however, market access was bound only for, say, minority owned foreign firms, then the existing firm from country B would have no guarantee that it would not one day be asked to disinvest. Such an uncertain situation evoked significant concern in existing investors from countries in type B situations. The solution was to drive a wedge between the conditions facing firms which were already present and those which would enter when the commitments came into effect. In effect, the situation of existing firms was "grandfathered."

The three types of grandfather provisions, foreign equity-related, legal form-related and general, which are to be found in the financial services schedules are shown in Table 5. It is evident that grandfathering was primarily an Asian phenomenon, prompted either by the introduction of more restrictive regimes pertaining to foreign equity and legal form than had prevailed when the foreign firms first entered, or simply an unwillingness to guarantee what had previously been allowed ad hoc.

The grandfather provisions reflect the relative emphasis in these negotiations on guaranteeing the rights of incumbents. They provide the benefits of security to investors who are already present in the market rather than to new investors and thus do little to make markets more contestable. Furthermore, they may even place new entrants at a competitive disadvantage where differences in ownership and legal form affect firm performance. For instance, larger equity shares may make it easier to exercise effective control over the operations of a firm and ensure efficient production, and the marginal cost of providing a service through a branch may be lower than through a subsidiary. Thus, Members who incorporated such provisions into their schedules may have succeeded in using the GATS to discourage rather than encourage competition.

**Table 5. Grandfathering Provisions in GATS Schedules on Banking and Insurance Services**

| Country | Provision |
|---|---|
| *Foreign Equity-Related* | |
| Indonesia | *Banking and insurance*: Share ownership of foreign services suppliers is bound at the prevailing laws and regulations. The conditions of ownership and the percentage share of ownership as stipulated in the respective shareholder agreement establishing the existing individual joint venture shall be respected. No transfer of ownership shall take place without the consent of all parties in the joint venture concerned. |
| Malaysia | *Banking*: Entry is limited to equity participation by foreign banks in Malaysian-owned or controlled commercial and merchant banks with aggregate foreign shareholding not to exceed 30 per cent, but the thirteen wholly-foreign owned commercial banks are permitted to remain wholly-owned by their existing shareholders.<br>Insurance: New entry is limited to equity participation by foreign insurance companies in locally incorporated insurance companies with aggregate foreign shareholding not to exceed 30%. Foreign shareholding not exceeding 51% is also permitted when (i) existing branches of foreign insurance companies are locally incorporated, which they are required to be by 30 June 1998, and (ii) for the existing foreign shareholders of locally incorporated insurance companies which were the original owners of these companies. |
| Pakistan | *Insurance*: Foreign shareholding in new life insurance companies is limited to 51% and in existing to 25%, but the scope of operations and equity structure of existing foreign companies is guaranteed. |
| Philip-pines | *Insurance and banking*: New investments of up to 51% of the voting stock, but existing investments of foreign banks will be maintained at their existing levels. |

Table 5—Continued

| Country | Provision |
|---|---|
| *Legal Form-Related* | |
| Brazil | *Banking*: Banks established before 5 October 1988, are allowed to maintain the aggregate number of branches that existed on that date. However, for banks authorized to operate after that date, the number of branches is subject to the conditions set out, in each case, at the time authorization is granted. |
| Hong Kong | *Banking*: The condition that branches of foreign banks are allowed to maintain offices in one main building and no more than two additional offices in separate buildings, does not apply to banks incorporated outside HKSAR licensed before May 1978 in respect of fully licensed banks and before April 1990 in respect of restricted license banks. |
| Indonesia | *Banking*: Existing branches of foreign banks are exempted from the requirement imposed on new entrants to be in the form of locally incorporated joint venture banks. |
| Malaysia | *Insurance*: Branching is only permitted for direct insurance companies with aggregate foreign shareholding of less than 50 per cent but companies are permitted to maintain their existing network of branches. (See also foreign equity-related provision above.) |
| Pakistan | *Banking*: While new entrants are obliged to incorporate locally, the rights of existing branches of foreign banks are guaranteed. |
| Thailand | *Banking*: While the establishment of new branches is subject to discretionary licensing, existing foreign banks which already had the first branch office in Thailand prior to July 1995 will each be permitted to open no more than two additional branches. |
| *General* | |
| Philip-pines | *Insurance*: Limitations in market access listed in the specific insurance sub-sectors do not apply to existing wholly or majority foreign-owned authorized insurance/reinsurance companies as of the entry into force of the WTO Financial Services agreement. |

*Source:* Compiled from Schedules of Commitments in Financial Services

The legal question is of course the consistency of these provisions with Article II. This question can be posed in two forms: first, would it be consistent with MFN to allow new (post-GATS) foreign firms to operate under less favorable conditions than old (pre-GATS) foreign firms? Secondly, would it be consistent with MFN to provide a binding of such differences in treatment through the GATS schedules? The instinctive answer to both questions is probably negative. After all, the whole point of the GATS was to level the playing field and eliminate all forms of discriminatory treatment, historical or otherwise. However, regarding the first question, it could be argued that the GATS only applies to measures affecting trade in services after it came into affect. The conditions of operation of the old firms are governed by licenses issued before the Agreement came into effect and so are not covered by Article II of GATS. The question arises, of course, whether the continued operation of firms under such conditions does not in fact require continued measures to which the GATS applies. But regardless of how one treats the first question, a positive answer to the second question is difficult. For even if we accept that identical conditions of competition cannot be ensured because the inequity is caused by actions predating the GATS, to guarantee the perpetuation of the inequity under the GATS by scheduling different levels of commitments for old or new firms must surely raise questions of MFN-consistency. Or is the notion of likeness to be contingent on the time of a firm's entry into the market?

## The Exercise of Competition Policy

Even though it is evident that the GATS itself contains only limited obligations on Members to curtail anti-competitive practices, the question arises whether it leaves Members adequate scope to take action against the anti-competitive practices of the service suppliers of other Members.[44] An interesting issue arose in the context of the basic telecommunications negotiations pertaining to international services which illustrates this issue. Some Members were reluctant to grant unconditional MFN access to their liberalized markets to operators originating from non-liberalized markets. Apart from the desire to retain negotiating leverage, there were two main concerns. The first was the fear of anti-competitive cross-subsidization and the second was the problem of "one way monopoly by-pass." The first concern is relatively straightforward, and not unlike certain concerns about predatory pricing that have been raised about the dumping of goods. It was feared that the competitive structure of the liberalized market could be undermined if an operator from a closed home-market were to subsidize its activity in the liberalized market, using revenues generated in the closed home market, including revenue from excessively high accounting rates.[45] The second concern was that the operator from the closed market would be able to by-pass the accounting rate system by establishing commercial presence and its own facilities in the liberalized market and using this to terminate its own calls. Operators of the liberalized market would, meanwhile, still have to depend on the closed-market operator to terminate their calls. The imbalance in payments between the two would worsen, since the liberalized market operators would no longer be able to offset some of their payments for outgoing calls by receipts for incoming calls.

Several solutions were considered to the problem of achieving MFN-based liberalization while allowing Members the freedom to deal with possible anti-competitive practices by exclusive operators from closed markets. One was taking measures ex ante, consisting in limiting market access for operators capable of engaging in anti-competitive practices because their home-markets were closed. Second was taking measures ex post, after market access is granted, if there was evidence of actual anti-competitive practices. And finally, there was the possibility of commitments by non-liberalizing Members to restrain exclusive operators from engaging in anti-competitive practices in international services. The limited time available did not permit a full exploration of the alternatives, and eventually it was the second option which seems to have been adopted by default.

The ability to exercise national competition policy depends again on the interpretation of the notion of "likeness" in the MFN obligation. Is a long-distance call provided at a low price by the subsidiary of a protected monopolist like a long-distance call provided by any other supplier? And is the subsidiary of a protected monopolist like any other supplier? If the reply to these questions is in the affirmative, then the MFN obligation would preclude any discrimination between these services and service suppliers, including on the basis of competition policy considerations. Alternatively, it could be argued that if competition policy itself is based on non-discriminatory principles, then it would be acceptable for it to impact differentially on particular services or service suppliers in specific instances provided they themselves manifested the characteristics which aroused concern. For instance, if competition policy had general restrictions on cross-subsidization or on the expansion of dominant suppliers, then specific actions which happened to be directed against foreign services or service suppliers which had these attributes would not constitute infringements of MFN. However, it would be required, in line with the argument in Section 5.1, that the actions should not be more burdensome than necessary to achieve the relevant competition policy objective.

However, any discrimination in treatment, based not on competition policy-related attributes of the service or the service supplier, but on unrelated attributes such as the fact of protection in the home market, would seem to violate the MFN obligation. There would seem to be an acknowledgment of this distinction in the case of maritime transport. This time the concern was that anti-competitive practices in the provision of port services in certain countries hampered access of foreign maritime transport suppliers to their markets. How far these practices are facilitated by government action (or inaction) is subject to dispute. In this case, the MFN obligation was not a constraint on retaliatory action since the application of the obligation to the sector has been suspended. Indeed, one of the reasons the United States presented for seeking an MFN exemption when the application of the obligation was a possibility, was precisely to preserve its right to retaliate against foreign restrictive practices.[46]

## REFERENCES

Altinger, L. and Enders, A. 1996. The Scope and Depth of GATS Commitments. World Economy 19: 65–94.

Bagwell, K. and Staiger, R. 1997. GATT-Think. mimeo.

Farber, D. A. and Hudec, R. E. 1996. GATT Legal Restraints on Domestic Environmental Regulations, in Bhagwati, J. and Hudec, R. E. (eds.), Fair Trade and Harmonization: Prerequisites for Free Trade? Volume 2, Legal Analysis, MIT Press, Cambridge, Massachusetts, and London, England.

Hoekman, B. 1996. Tentative First Steps: An Assessment of the Uruguay Round Agreement on Services, in Martin, W. and Winters, L. A. (eds.). The Uruguay Round and the Developing Countries. Cambridge University Press, Cambridge.

Mattoo, A. 1997. National Treatment in the GATS—Corner Stone or Pandora's Box? Journal of World Trade 31: 107–135.

Mattoo, A. and Subramanian, A. 1998. Regulatory Autonomy and Multilateral Disciplines. Journal of International Economic Law 1: 303–322.

Pelkmans, J. and Winters, A. 1988. Europe's Domestic Market. Chatham House Papers 43, Royal Institute of International Affairs, Routledge, London.

Roessler, F. 1996. Diverging Domestic Policies and Multilateral Trade Integration, in: Bhagwati, J. and Hudec, R. E. (eds.) op. cit.

Sapir, A. 1998. GATS 1994–2000. mimeo.

Schwartz, W. F. and Sykes, A. O. 1996. Toward a Positive Theory of the Most Favored Nation Obligation and Its Exceptions in the WTO/GATT System. International Review of Law and Economics 16: 27–51.

## NOTES

1. See European Communities: Regime for the Importation, Sale and Distribution of Bananas, Report of the Panel, WT/DS27/R/USA, 22 May 1997, and European Communities: Regime for

the Importation, Sale and Distribution of Bananas, Report of the Appellate Body, WT/DS27/AB/R, 9 September 1997.

2. The language in Article I:3(a) of GATS is less detailed and possible weaker than that in Article XXIV:12 of GATT 1994, which is also concerned with ensuring compliance by sub-central entities. Moreover, completely excluded from the scope of the GATS are services supplied in the exercise of governmental authority, defined as services supplied neither on a commercial basis, nor in competition with one or more service suppliers.

3. See paragraphs 7.277–7.286 of the Panel Report and paragraphs 217–222 of the Report of the Appellate Body. It was also confirmed that GATT 1994 and GATS may overlap in application to a particular measure.

4. See paragraphs 231–234 of the Report of the Appellate Body.

5. The Appellate Body referred, in particular, to the panel report in *European Economic Community - Imports of Beef from Canada* (Adopted 10 March 1981, BISD 28S/92, paras. 4.2–4.3) which examined the consistency of EEC regulations implementing a levy-free tariff quota for high quality grain-fed beef with Article I of the GATT 1947. Those regulations made suspension of the import levy for such beef conditional on production of a certificate of authenticity. The only certifying agency authorized to produce a certificate of authenticity was a United States agency. The panel, therefore, found that the EEC regulations were inconsistent with the MFN principle in Article I of the GATT 1947 as they had the effect of denying access to the EEC market to exports of products of any origin other than that of the United States.

6. Paragraph 7.322 of the Panel Report

7. The modal approach to scheduling commitments in the GATS reflects an acceptance that services supplied through different modes need not be treated as like. For a discussion of this issue, see Mattoo (1997).

8. As the Annex on Article II exemptions states, "Any new exemptions applied for after the date of entry into force of the WTO Agreements shall be dealt with under paragraph 3 of Article IX of that Agreement." The relevant paragraph stipulates that "In exceptional circumstances, the Ministerial Conference may decide to waive an obligation imposed on a Member by this Agreement or any of the Multilateral Trade Agreements, provided that any such decision shall be taken by three fourths of the Members unless otherwise provided for in this paragraph."

9. The individual lists of exemptions are legally part of the GATS agreement, in the same way as the national schedules of concessions. They have been issued as separate GATS documents in the series GATS/EL/. . . They are described more fully in Section 3, below.

10. MTN.GNS/W/164, 3 September 1993. The document warns that "the answers should not be considered as an authoritative legal interpretation of the GATS."

11. The Latin American countries have notified agreements on the recognition of educational degrees and professional qualifications obtained in other (mostly Latin American) countries. Switzerland too has notified measures pertaining to qualifications of auditors (EU) and professional representation in respect of patents (Liechtenstein). The United States has notified four agreements covering different types of professionals: two, with Australia and Canada, eliminate the need for chartered accountants trained in the these countries to duplicate all steps in the licensing process, and provide for abbreviated examination requirements; another, with Canada, facilitates the movement of architects from the two countries, particularly through the

use of a uniform written examination; the third with a group of countries recognizes the substantial equivalency of the accreditation processes leading to a basic engineering degree. Norway's notification concerns permission for lawyers to provide legal aid in foreign and international law, as well as the recognition of diplomas and higher professional education obtained in other EEA countries. Macau's notification describes licensing requirements and procedures for a range of different professions, medical, accounting, auditing, and legal

12. The maintenance of public order is not an objective listed in the general exceptions provision of GATT 1994, and may be invoked "only where a genuine an sufficiently serious threat is posed to one of the fundamental interests of society" (footnote 5 to Article XIV).

13. Nothing in the GATS requires a member to give information, or take action, against its essential security interests concerning services for a military establishment, related to fissionable or fissionable materials, or in time of war or international emergency or in pursuit of obligations under the United Nations Charter for peace and security.

14. International air transport services are for the most part governed by arrangements negotiated under the Chicago Convention (i.e., the International Air Services Transit Agreement, done at Chicago, 7 December 1944).

15. The WTO dispute settlement procedures can be invoked only in respect of obligations specifically assumed by members, and even then only after any bilateral or other procedures have been exhausted. A provision for periodic reviews of developments in the air transport sector, to be undertaken at least once in every five years, leaves the door open for a possible future extension of GATS commitments in the sectors.

16. See also Altinger and Enders (1996) and Hoekman (1996).

17. The MFN exemption of the United States reserved the right to discriminate between trading partners with respect to new entry or the expansion of existing activities, in order to "protect existing activities of United States service suppliers abroad and to ensure substantially full market access and national treatment in international financial markets."

18. The three relevant pieces of legislation are: Section 19 of the Merchant Marine Act of 1920, Section 13(b)(5) of the Shipping Act of 1984, and the Foreign Shipping Practices Act of 1988. Even though specific action has rarely been taken, it is claimed that the credible threat of doing so has induced an opening of foreign markets in some instances.

19. To the extent that accounting rates may be deemed government measures, the significant degree of price discrimination typically encountered in the rates applying between pairs of countries would be hard to justify on MFN grounds. But to the extent that accounting rates are considered non-governmental measures, then differences in rates that cannot be defended in terms of cost differentials could be challenged under GATS Article VIII, which extends the MFN obligation to monopolies and exclusive service suppliers. Thus, accounting rate regimes might be challenged on the grounds that by maintaining monopolistic structures "formally or in effect," governments were permitting suppliers to practice price discrimination.

20. It was further agreed that the understanding would be reviewed no later than the commencement of new services negotiations, foreseen to begin by 1 January 2000 at the latest

21. For instance, owing to the reciprocal recognition of the proof of solvency between the EU and Switzerland, foreign direct (other than life) insurance companies which have their principal place of business in the territory of one of the contracting parties are not obliged to localize funds to a significant extent. The United States agreement with Canada eliminates the need for

chartered accountants trained in these countries to duplicate all steps in the licensing process, and provides for abbreviated examination requirements.

22. Where the impact of the regulation is on fixed costs, the effects are likely to be seen in terms of entry and exit of suppliers from different countries depending on the regulatory burden.

23. It may be asked why some individuals from countries Y and Z do not directly qualify as professionals in country X instead of first obtaining qualifications at home. One reason is that professionals are often allowed to enter foreign markets only on a temporary basis (as under the GATS), so they need to be qualified also to serve the home market. Where longer term movement of professionals is allowed, we need to assume that the individual elements of qualifications are not separable, and that there is a part, say w, which is universally recognized as equivalent. The incentive to obtain the qualification at home arises as long as cyw and czw are sufficiently smaller than cxw. The w element is suppressed here to keep the notation simple. Non-separability is indeed an aspect of many qualifications: a student can usually not switch institutions after doing only part of a course.

24. This Section draws upon the discussion in Mattoo (1997). Related issues are also discussed in Farber and Hudec (1996) and Roessler (1996).

25. See Japan - Taxes on Alcoholic Beverages, Report of the Appellate Body.

26. See the 1989 Panel Report on "Canada/Japan: Tariff on Imports of Spruce, Pine, Fir (SPF) Dimension Lumber (Analytical Index of the GATT, 38)

27. See the 1981 Panel Report on "Spain – Tariff Treatment of Unroasted Coffee," (Analytical Index of the GATT, 37).

28. This classification scheme is given in GATT Document MTN.GNS/W/120.

29. There are only 160 non-overlapping services sectors in the services classification list (GATT Document MTN.GNS/W/120) compared to 5019 at the 6-digit level in the Harmonized System 1992 classification.

30. For the implications of this see the 1978 Panel Report on "EEC – Measures on Animal Feed Proteins," (Analytical Index of the GATT, 37)

31. There is at least one other difference between the two Agreements which may be important. The TBT creates a strong presumption in favor of harmonized international standards. Thus Article 2.5 of the TBT states:

." . . Whenever a technical regulation is prepared for one of the legitimate objectives explicitly mentioned in paragraphs 2 to 4 [national security, protection of human health, environment, etc.], and is in accordance with relevant international standards, it shall be rebuttably presumed not to create an unnecessary obstacle to international trade."

The corresponding provision in GATS (Article VI:5(b)) would seem to be somewhat weaker. It states:

"In determining whether a Member is in conformity with the obligation under paragraph 5(a), account shall be taken of international standards of relevant international organizations applied by that Member."

32. Some may argue, on the basis of the experience of the European Union, that the "maintenance of public order" provision in Article XIV could be read to cover a range of objectives but the requirement that this provision only be invoked when there is a "genuine and sufficiently serious threat is posed to one of the fundamental interests of society" would seem to preclude a wide interpretation.

33. This argument has been more fully developed in Mattoo and Subramanian (1998).

34. Is there any textual basis for the test that is being proposed? There is, of course, no precedent of GATT/WTO panels applying a necessity test in the context of Article III, and certainly no precedent of economic efficiency being a criteria for determining the legitimacy of domestic regulation. However, even though the test does not find clear support in existing jurisprudence, certain aspects of the Appellate Body Report on Alcoholic Beverages Panel imply that the suggested interpretation is not unduly radical. In determining whether a measure is applied so as to afford protection, the Report prescribes a comprehensive and objective analysis of "the design, the architecture, and the revealing structure of a measure." In this analysis, it would seem important to consider whether the measure in question was the economically optimal means of achieving the particular objective. The creation of such a hierarchy is not without precedent in the WTO. In general, WTO law accepts the legitimacy of tariff while seeking to eliminate quantitative restrictions, reflecting the broad consensus in economic thinking that in most situations the former are to be preferred to the latter. There is also an analogy in the new Agreement on Technical Barriers to Trade, which creates a presumption in favor of international standards but does not oblige Members to use these standards.

35. How, it may be asked is the proposed criterion of economic efficiency different from the traditional GATT necessity test? Consider, for instance, a situation in which doctors in Z can demonstrate superior training to those in Y. Say a Member imposed a uniform qualification requirement not related to prior training on all foreign doctors. The measure could not be challenged under conventional approaches because there would seem to be no discriminatory effect on which to base a case. It is, however, lower on the hierarchy of instruments which serve a medical safety objective than a requirement which distinguishes between doctors on the basis of prior training, and impacts more adversely on better-trained doctors than a superior economic instrument would have. It could, therefore, be challenged on efficiency grounds and only exonerated if the non-feasibility of economically superior instruments was convincingly demonstrated.

36. In the Bananas Case, the European Union's method of allocating import licenses for bananas from certain sources was found to be inconsistent with Article II because it reallocated quotas and quota rents away from the importers who traditionally imported from these sources (see paragraphs 7.350–7.353 of the Panel Report). In a sense, the Panel's reasoning followed the logic of GATT Article XIII.

37. Jackson (1991, 140) notes that first-come, first served and auctions would seem to fulfill the MFN obligation, and refers to the Article XIII reliance on historical patterns as a "quasi" MFN principle.

38. This is precisely what certain Caribbean countries, locked into monopoly contracts with Cable and Wireless, are considering doing.

39. There is an analogy here with the time-inconsistency problem which arises in the case of a durable goods monopoly.

40. This Section draws upon Schwartz and Sykes (1996).

41. A notable feature of the WTO negotiations in financial services is that they did not take place in the usual context of a multi-sectoral and multi-issue round of negotiations. Although this had, of course, been the original intention, failure to complete the negotiations before the end of the Uruguay Round effectively turned financial services into a single-sector negotiation. This tended to divide countries into those that looked for export gains and those whose focus could only be the conditions of competition in the domestic market. Despite the absence of any possibility for cross-sectoral trade-offs, or for improvements in the policy environment facing exports for those without export potential in financial services, many governments made significant new commitments—which reflected unilateral liberalization (in the hope of attracting inward investment), and probably promised gains in other areas or political pressure.

42. For instance, Guatemala's MFN exemption states that "The Central American Exemption Clause does not allow the extension to third countries of the bilateral or multilateral concessions made among the Central American countries themselves.

43. The original US MFN exemption for maritime transport services reserved the "right to investigate and take action against foreign carriers to address adverse or unfavorable actions affecting US shipping or US carriers in US oceanborne commerce and the cross trades between foreign ports." Note this exemption goes beyond the reciprocity provisions in the Chilean, Columbian, and Mexican MFN exemption lists. Only Tunisia has maintained a similar open-ended exemption. The US, Columbia, and Mexico withdrew their MFN exemptions at the end of the Uruguay Round when it was decided that the operation of Article II would be suspended for the duration of the extended negotiations.

44. Apart from GATS Article VIII, the only other article which deals with anticompetitive practices is Article IX. The scope of Article IX is wider, dealing as it does with "certain business practices of service suppliers, other than those falling under Article VIII, [which] may restrain competition and thereby restrict trade in services," but its disciplines are much weaker. In effect, the only obligations imposed relate to consultation and information sharing.

45. This problem highlighted the limitations of Article VIII:2 since it only requires that a Member shall ensure that a monopoly supplier "does not abuse its monopoly position to act *in its territory* in a manner inconsistent with [a Member's *specific*] *commitments*." (italics added) The behavior at issue is not taking place in a Member's territory and is not inconsistent with its specific commitments.

46. Recently, the United States imposed discriminatory penalties on Japanese ships visiting United States ports because of the perceived persistence of anti-competitive practices in Japanese ports, but the dispute was eventually resolved.

CHAPTER 3

# "Like Product": The Differences in Meaning in GATT Articles I and III

*Robert E. Hudec*

A commonplace usually recited at the beginning of every discussion of the term "like product" is the observation that the term appears in several different GATT provisions,[1] and that its meaning is likely to vary from one GATT provision to another.

This statement must be distinguished from the equally common statement that "like product" must be defined on a "case by case" basis—a statement that suggests that the concept itself cannot be reduced to definable criteria, and thus that individual applications of the concept, even under the same provision, will differ for reasons cannot be explained. The former statement suggests that, notwithstanding the lack of a precise definition, there may be identifiable and describable differences in the policy contexts of the various GATT Articles in which the term "like product" is used, and that these policy differences may yield identifiable differences in the meaning, or at least the range of meaning, accorded to that term from one Article to another.

The purpose of this paper is to examine one setting in which such a difference of meaning might be expected to occur. The paper asks whether such a policy-based difference in meaning can be found between (1) the meaning accorded to the "like product" concept in the Most Favored Nation obligation of GATT Article I:1, and (2) the meaning accorded to "like product" concept in the National Treatment obligations of paragraphs 2 and 4 of GATT Article III.

During the past decade, an effort was made to launch a new definition of "like product" as that term is used in Article III of GATT. Basing their ruling on the policy statement in Paragraph 1 of Article III stating that internal taxes and internal regulatory measures should not be used "to afford protection to domestic production," two GATT panel decisions ruled that "like product" was to be defined in terms of two questions that were only indirectly connected to the issue of "likeness"—the question whether the product distinction in question had the "aim" of protecting domestic industry, and the question whether that product distinction had the "effect" of protecting the domestic industry.[2] In 1996, the WTO Appellate Body rejected this "aim and effects" interpretation of the "like product" concept as contrary to the text of Article III:2, and indicated that GATT dispute settlement panels should to return to the more traditional definitions in terms of "likeness."[3]

This paper is not a further discussion of the "aim and effects" definition of "like product." Instead, it sets aside that definition and examines policy-based differences in the definition of "like product" within the traditional concepts of "likeness" called for by the Appellate Body. It asks how more traditional interpretations of the "like product" concept have been, or should be, impacted by the difference between that policies underlying GATT Articles I:1 and III respectively.

The thesis of the paper is that, in certain cases, there should be a difference between the meanings given to the "like product" concept under Articles I and III. Specifically, it will be argued that the term "like product" in Article I:1 should be interpreted to allow rather fine distinctions between products when it is applied to product distinctions made by tariffs, but that the "like product" term should not allow such fine distinctions when it is being applied to product distinctions made by internal taxes and internal regulations. The latter, more demanding standard for product distinctions made by internal measures would apply not only under Article III:2 (taxes) and Article III:4 (regulations), but also to that part of the Article I:1 MFN obligation that applies to "all matters referred to in paragraphs 2 and 4 of Article III." Because of the rather unusual two-sentence architecture of Article III:2, however, it will be necessary to make a further qualification about how the term "like product" should be interpreted under that particular GATT provision.

The paper finds that present GATT/WTO tariff practice does reflect this distinction to a significant degree, but that GATT/WTO legal precedents for the most part do not. It finds that governments generally do employ a quite permissive interpretation of "like product" with regard to the product distinctions they make in their own national tariffs, and that this permissive interpretation has been given general support in at least one GATT dispute settlement ruling. The paper also finds, however, that no such distinction between tariffs and internal measures has as yet been recognized by the small group of other dispute settlement rulings that have treated this issue to date. Whatever the policy merits of the distinction argued for in this paper, it would appear to be quite far from being recognized.

## 1. The Policy Dimension

### Differences in Definitions of Likeness

It is often said that one cannot apply the concept of "likeness" without specifying the characteristics by which likeness is to be measured. The usual illustration of this point is to say that it is impossible to tell whether one apple is "like" another apple without specifying whether or not characteristics such as edible quality, taste, color, size, or other features are relevant. In fact, however, it is quite common to compare different definitions of "like product" according to what looks like a single scale of "likeness." For example, if we see two legal rulings, one ruling saying that the only product "like" an apple is another apple, and the other ruling saying that any edible fruit is "like" an apple, we have no difficulty in saying that the standard applied in the former decision requires a greater degree of likeness than the standard applied in the latter—meaning, of course, that by any criteria one can imagine being applied as relevant, the former standard requires a closer degree of "likeness" than the other. The one-dimensional "likeness" scale works best, of course, the closer one of the two standards being compared is a standard requiring nearly identical qualities.

For most purposes, however, meaningful comparisons of "like product" definitions requires specifying the criteria by which likeness to be measured. One must describe the individual criteria with some care, and after that it is possible to talk about degrees of likeness within the boundaries of those criteria or characteristics.

The first criterion of likeness that comes to mind is physical characteristics—the more two products have the same physical characteristics, the more "like" they can be said to be. Taken individually, physical characteristics would appear to be a sterile concept in a policy sense. That is, it is usually difficult to understand why a difference in this or that physical characteristic, as such, should dictate that two products need not be treated the same. To be sure, a high degree of physical likeness can be a reliable proxy for many other criteria that do have policy content—criteria such as commercial interchangeability. The greater the physical identity of two products the more likely it is that they are interchangeable. That is probably why similarity of physical characteristics is so often the first criterion that legal decisions look to. As soon as any difference of physical characteristics is found, however, one has to resort to other criteria to determine whether the difference is relevant to the question of "like" treatment.

Since GATT is a commercial agreement, it seems reasonable to start with the assumption that "likeness" is (or should be) a commercial concept, meant to describe one or more market phenomena. The central commercial concept that comes to mind is competitiveness. The two most important articles in which the "like product" concept is used—Articles I and III—involve rules prohibiting differences in treatment between certain products. The obvious reason for preventing differences in treatment is to prevent distortions in competition between otherwise competitive goods. The other main "like product" rules are Articles VI and XIX, in which GATT tries to define the producers who are to be protected from unfair or harmful imports. Once again, the logical candidates for protection are those producers whose goods are competitive with the harmful imports.

Many of the criteria of likeness that have been offered in GATT legal discussions of the "like product" concept can be viewed as overlapping variations on the idea of competitiveness. First, there is substitutability—the extent to which consumers perceive two products as functionally equivalent, measured by the consumer's willingness to substitute one for the other, a willingness which in turn is usually measured by the extent to which relatively small changes in price affect consumer preferences for one or the other. Next, there is concept of functional likeness, the extent to which the two products do in fact perform the same function, like sweeping dirt. Finally, although the producer-oriented provisions sometimes do employ "likeness" criteria that do not, strictly speaking, relate to the competitiveness of the goods in question—e.g., the extent to which two products are made from the same raw materials, in the same establishments, by the same capital goods, or by the same workers—the competitiveness criteria are still the first and most important factor in the "like product" decisions in those areas as well.[4]

It is not the purpose of this paper to explore all the criteria that have been suggested to date. In keeping with our purpose of comparing the application of the "like product" concept under Articles I and III, we turn to the more particular policy goals that can be identified in those two legal settings.

## The Policy Goals of GATT Article III:2 and III:4

The general policy behind paragraphs 2 and 4 of Article III is fairly simple.

The starting point is the policy stated in Paragraph 1 of Article III: Governments should not employ "internal" measures—internal taxes or internal regulations—to give protection to domestic industry. A rule that internal measures must not give less favorable treatment to "like" foreign products, will achieve this anti-protection goal if "like [foreign] products" is defined to mean competitive foreign products. Less favorable treatment will tend to protect domestic products whenever it imposes a commercial disadvantage on those foreign products with which the domestic product competes for sales. "Competitiveness" in this sense is best measured by the substitutability of the foreign product—the extent to which consumers are willing to choose the foreign product in substitution for the domestic product.

By the same token, the basic policy of Article III would not be served by a definition of "like product" which limited that concept to products that had nearly identical physical characteristics. Such a narrow definition of "like product" would allow governments to give less favorable treatment to a foreign product that, although competitive with the relevant domestic product, had some different physical characteristics.

If one were re-writing Paragraphs 2 and 4 of Article III, and wanted to be clearer about where to draw the line, there would be a temptation to substitute the word "competitive" for "like." Upon further reflection, however, one would realize that the word "competitive" would probably need to be narrowed a bit, for political rather than economic reasons. The range of foreign products that would feel at least some negative competitive impact from being taxed or regulated more heavily than a particular domestic product could be fairly wide. To avoid undue interference with the tax and regulatory policy of the importing country, one would probably want to draw a line that separates those foreign products that suffer a major competitive disadvantage from those upon whom the negative effect will be milder.

Looking for a way to narrow the concept of "competitive," we would see that GATT itself usually frequently uses the term "directly competitive" when it wishes to narrow the scope of the word "competitive" to some extent.[5] For purposes of analysis, we can adopt "directly competitive" as the next, less intrusive concept for defining the scope of protection given to foreign products.

At this point, however, we confront the fact that the drafters of Article III:2 seemed to regard "like product" as a term defining an even narrower relationship than the term "directly competitive." The second sentence of Article III:2, as explained by its Ad Note, makes it clear that "directly competitive" products include a range of products that are not "like" the product in question. Thus, it would appear that the concept of "like product" in Article III:2 may in fact be referring to similarity of physical characteristics, contrary to the idea that such a standard would be too narrow to prevent the kinds of product discrimination that one would need to prevent in order to achieve Article III's general policy against protectionism described above. The answer, of course, is that Article III:2 does not in fact allow such protective product distinctions, because the second sentence of

Article III:2 goes on to prohibit those other kinds of product discrimination as well—the less favorable treatment of "not-like-but-directly-competitive" products—if the protective effects of such discrimination can be shown.[6] Thus, the overall policy of Article III:2 is consistent with the policy goals of Article III described above. In this particular setting, the drafters of Article III:2 have simply used a narrow definition of "like product" to define a subgroup of the competitive products that were to receive protection from less favorable treatment—a subgroup that could receive that protection without having to prove anything more than their "likeness," rather narrowly defined. In other words, a narrow concept of "likeness" is used in Article III:2 as the basis of a per se rule. Because of this rather limited function accorded to the "like product" concept in the two-sentence architecture of Article III:2, t seems clear that one should treat the narrow definition of "like product" in that section as a definition that should not necessarily be generalized to other parts of Article III, where the same legal architecture does not appear. The need for a "like product" definition based on competitiveness is not otherwise altered by the peculiar structure of Article III:2.

As all students of GATT will already know, the main problem with this explanation of GATT Article III:2 is the fact that Paragraph 4 of Article III—the other pivotal rule of Article III that deals with internal non-tax regulations—is not constructed the same way as Paragraph 2. Paragraph 4 does not contain a second sentence prohibiting differential treatment of not-like-but-directly-competitive products. The rule for all internal regulation is a simple per se rule and nothing else—one that states that less favorable treatment must not be given to "like" foreign products, period. If the foreign product is not "like" the relevant domestic product, the government may treat it less favorably, even if such differential regulation has a protective effect (or purpose).

There would seem to be two possible ways to reconcile the apparent conflict between the wording of Paragraphs 2 and 4 of Article III:

1. It may be that the term "like product" simply has a different meaning in Paragraph 4. Given that recent WTO legal rulings tend to give the "like product" test of Article III:2 a very narrow reading,[7] a different meaning is quite likely to be adopted if, as one assumes, it is thought necessary to give Article III:4 a broad enough scope to make it effective. It must be noted, however, that this answer would create a reverse kind of mismatch with Paragraph 2—that is, if Paragraph 4's "like product" concept includes some or all of Paragraph 2's "directly competitive" products, it will be giving "directly competitive" products the benefit of a per se rule whereas Paragraph 2 requires

that all but nearly identical products must prove adverse competitive effects (and possibly discriminatory purpose).

2. It may be that the term "like product" is really a lot broader than we have assumed, that it includes a lot of what we would normally call "not-like-but-directly-competitive" products, and that the second sentence of Paragraph 2 is meant to cover only quite dissimilar goods—goods like bananas and apples that are so dissimilar that one would not be inclined to assume meaningful competitive impact unless it were proved. Such a broader definition of "like product" would take us back to the idea of directly competitive products—a category that might be defined in market terms as a competitive relationship, or degree of substitutability, sufficiently strong to make it likely that differential treatment would have protective effects. Although this explanation leaves us with an unusually restricted interpretation of the words "directly competitive" in Paragraph 2, it is the most logical way to make Paragraphs 2 and 4 at least roughly consistent despite their quite different structures. The second sentence of Paragraph 2 would still result in somewhat broader protection for foreign products from tax discrimination than from other regulatory discrimination, but one could possibly justify that difference with two arguments: **(a)** Differences in tax rates are inherently arbitrary, and thus should be harder to justify than regulatory distinctions. **(b)** It is easier to trace the competitive effects of tax differences (money charges) on dissimilar but competitively related products than it is to trace the effects of regulatory distinctions on such products.

Before examining what GATT legal rulings and other sources have to say about the puzzle of the Article III concept of "like product," we must look at how the "like product" concept relates to the somewhat different policy context of GATT Article I:1.

## The Policy Goals of GATT Article I:1

The anti-discrimination rule of Article I:1 covers a variety of measures. It covers tariffs, it covers most other measures taken in connection with border charges, it covers payments restrictions, and it covers all internal measures covered by Paragraphs 2 and 4 of Article III (i.e., essentially all internal measures). Although the words of Article I:1 appear to apply the same MFN principle to each of these different subject areas, defined in terms of what appears to be the same "like product" concept, the fact that the provision covers so many different measures raises the possibility that the content of the MFN rule may not be the same for each area. Instead, it may be that the different policies applicable to different subject areas will call for a different type of MFN rule, expressed by a different definition of "like product" for at least some of the different subject areas. This section of the paper focuses on one such difference of meaning within Article I:1.

From an economic point of view, the non-discrimination policy behind the MFN rule of Article I:1 should be quite similar to the anti-protection policy behind the National Treatment rule of Article III. In terms of its economic effects, "discrimination" (less favorable treatment of goods from one foreign country vis a vis the goods of another foreign country) is no different than breach of the National Treatment obligation (less favorable treatment of foreign goods vis a vis domestic goods). The economic effect of discrimination is to "protect" the goods of the advantaged country from competition with the goods of the disadvantaged country, just as denial of national treatment protects local goods against all foreign goods. Both kinds of protection equally distort the market, equally distort the allocation of resources, and thus equally diminish global wealth.[8] Consequently, it would seem that the range of goods protected by Article I's MFN obligation should be same as the range of goods protected by Article III's National Treatment obligation. In each case, the goods to be protected against less favorable treatment should be those goods that are directly competitive with goods receiving more favorable treatment. The same "like product" definition should do for both obligations.

With regard to the internal measures covered by Article III, there really is no reason to distinguish between the Article I definition of "like product" and the Article III definition of "like product." The basic policy of Article III is the economic policy to eliminate market distortions caused by internal measures, and that economic policy is just as compelling with respect to National-Treatment-type discrimination as it is to MFN-type discrimination.[9]

If we look at the non-discrimination policy with regard to tariffs, however, the policy picture becomes clouded by countervailing considerations. In the first place, we must be careful not to miss the obvious. The GATT policy of allowing governments to maintain tariffs is a policy to allow a market distortion. There is thus no overall, "no-distortions" policy that one can appeal to for guidance in the way we treat tariffs. The overall goal of Article I here is not chastity. It is merely the orderly management of protection in order to contain its effects and remove its unnecessary evils.

The fact that Article I accepts the business of tariff protection means, among other things, that it must also accept the tools of tariff protection. Specifically, governments managing a policy of tariff protection need to be able to draw lines between products in order to confine protection to those imports which do in fact threaten domestic producers, and also to confine tariff liberalization to those products for which the removal of protection will be found acceptable to domestic interests. The policy being served by such product distinctions is thus something different from, and potentially more complex than, the Article III goal of eliminating market distortions.

A second and more important policy difference between the Article I policy toward tariffs and the Article III policy toward internal measures is the fact that GATT policy toward tariffs must include an added objective of promoting negotiation to lower tariffs. For political reasons, it has been considered necessary to conduct such negotiations on the basis of a reciprocity principle—the principle that governments are expected to pay for the market opportunities created when other governments lower their tariffs, by lowering their own tariffs in return. As long as everyone contributes equally, a reciprocity policy can be consistent with anti-discrimination policy. But in the case where reciprocal payment is not made, a reciprocity policy requires that the non-paying party be denied the benefit of the tariff concessions for which it is unwilling to pay. A reciprocity policy requires being able to discriminate against "free riders." In sum, the reciprocity dimension of tariff negotiations is in conflict with the non-discrimination rules of Article I:1.

The GATT has reconciled these conflicting policy preferences in two ways. The first way has been to avoid the conflict by management of negotiations. Tariff negotiations usually do not proceed until there is a general political agreement that the important parties will make a roughly equal contribution, thereby eliminating the largest part of the free-rider problem by advance agreement. Advance agreement cannot eliminate the free rider problem entirely, however, and so there is need for some further lever to solve the reciprocity problem at the margin. The second answer has been to allow a limited type of discrimination against countries that decline to offer reciprocal payment. Although the terms of the Article I:1 MFN obligation preclude explicit discrimination against other countries by name, governments have agreed, tacitly, that they may discriminate against free riders by making fine product distinctions in their tariffs—product distinctions that are calculated to limit the benefit of tariff reductions to the countries that have granted equivalent concessions in return.

Everyone has heard the story of the 1904 German tariff concession to Switzerland lowering the tariff on "Large dapple[d] mountain cattle reared at a spot at least 300 meters above sea level and having at least one month's grazing each year at a spot at least 800 meters above sea level."[10] The example is primarily used today as an illustration of something that would not be allowed under Article I:1. Probably so. To the author, however, the more important message conveyed by this story is the fineness of tariff differentiation that must have been considered acceptable practice in 1904 in order for the German government, bound by MFN clauses with all its European trading partners, to have even considered trying to get away with such a finely wrought product distinction. Ultra-fine tariff distinctions were a well established tradition among the trade negotiators who, forty-three years later, wrote the GATT.

What rules apply to this traditional tolerance for fine product distinctions? The rules are defined only by established practice. According to the author's perception of the practice followed by GATT governments, the guiding principle appears to be a tolerance for any distinction based on an objective characteristic of the products in question. The types of characteristics that have been used in practice suggest a very broad range of possibilities. The following is merely a sample of the kinds of product characteristics that have been used in tariff distinctions:

1. Differences in materials of construction.
2. Differences in method of manufacture.
3. Scientifically recognized distinctions between plant or animal species.
4. Differences in value ("value brackets").[11]
5. Differences in shape, size or dimension.
6. Quality distinctions, e.g., differences in the thread count of textiles.

Practice indicates that the validity of such distinctions does not depend on the competitive significance of such characteristics. Nor, indeed, does the purpose of such distinctions matter. Although the reason for most tariff distinctions can be found in the trade-neutral taxonomic motivations of the ordinary tariff writer, with some contribution from the frequent non-discriminatory desire to limit concessions to products that will not threaten domestic producers, a significant number of the very finest product distinctions are an unconcealed effort to discriminate against non-contributing third parties, imposed without objection.

Most observers have their own anecdotal evidence to support this generalization about tariff practice. The author's is the United States "Chicken War" retaliation against the European Community in 1963, an action in which the author served as very junior member of the legal team acting as counsel to the United States.[12] The United States had a right to retaliate under Article XXVIII:3 due to a prior withdrawal of a tariff concession on poultry by the Community. It was decided that Article

XXVIII:3 retaliation must be imposed on an MFN basis. Wishing to strike only the Community, and France in particular, the United States examined its import data to find existing tariff lines under which all imports had been supplied only by the Community, and by France in particular. Nothing suitable was found for France, and so the United States looked for a more general tariff line that could be subdivided to accomplish this objective. The product chosen was brandy. Although many countries supplied the United States with brandy, none sold brandy as expensive French Cognac and Armagnac, and the expensive brandy imports from France were large enough to supply the volume of retaliation desired. So, the United States subdivided the brandy tariff into two parts—"brandy at more than $9.00 per gallon" and "other brandy"—and then withdrew the GATT tariff concession on the former. All this was done openly, the purpose acknowledged. To the author's knowledge, neither the EC nor France uttered a word about the discriminatory purpose of the tariff subdivision.[13] It was something that every GATT member had done hundreds of times before in trade negotiations.

Where is the limit? The author's sense of actual practice is that it would take something like the 1904 German cattle concession to set off a legal alarm. What was wrong with that concession? As understood by the author, the sense of the objection is that the particular combination of objective characteristics used to limit that concession was so unique that it could not have had any conceivable taxonomic function—in other words, that its only conceivable function was to identify goods from a particular country. Stated differently, a product distinction will be objected to when it is closer to an explicit distinction between countries than it is to a distinction between products according to their objective characteristics. So viewed, the 1904 German cattle concession essentially falls within the Article I:1 prohibition of "origin-specific" discrimination—discrimination that distinguishes between goods explicitly by country of origin.

Why would GATT permit governments to do indirectly ( discrimination-by-product-distinction) what it prohibits them from doing directly (origin-specific discrimination)? The technique is the familiar one of seeking compromise between conflicting objectives by bending the rules on one side while appearing to honor them. Although product distinctions are a clumsy tool that often fails to produce the desired kind of discrimination, their clumsiness is part of the eventual balance. This is not a sophisticated attempt to balance conflicting policies by sorting out winners or losers according to their proximity to one policy objective or the other. Rather, it is simply an attempt to create a limited opportunity to discriminate against free riders by allowing governments to use a rather weak and ineffective tool. The fact that it doesn't work very well is what makes it a tolerable compromise.

It may be easier to understand this compromise if one understands that a country's need for "reciprocity" in tariff negotiations is primarily a political need rather than an economic one. It is more important that the government appear to be achieving reciprocity than it is that the government actually achieve it. Consequently, product distinctions serve their primary purpose as long as they look like they punish non-paying parties, satisfying the political need for reciprocity, while the fact that they work rather badly in practice actually helps to satisfy the conflicting economic goal of non-distortion.

To sum up, it is suggested that the GATT policy toward tariffs and tariff negotiations would justify a quite narrow interpretation of the "like product" concept with reference to claims of tariff discrimination under Article I:1—an interpretation in which any objective difference between products would justify a separate tariff classification, and thus a different tariff rate. In contrast, we suggest, the "like product" concept should be given a to a broader interpretation—one that would prohibit product distinctions between directly competitive products—when applied to product distinctions made by internal measures. We suggest that such a broader definition be applied both under Article III and under that part of Article I:1 that applies to internal measures which discriminate between foreign countries. Such a broader interpretation would best be achieved by defining "likeness" in terms of the competitive relationship between the products in question, rather than requiring near identity of physical characteristics.

## 2. The Legal Rulings

In this section of the paper, we assess whether GATT/WTO legal rulings reflect the suggested differences in the definitions of "like product" with respect to tariffs, on the one hand, and with respect to internal measures, on the other.

### The 1970 Working Party Report

There are only a few GATT/WTO legal rulings on the meaning of "like product," and a significant number of those have been seriously questioned. Perhaps for that reason, most GATT and WTO panel rulings on "like product" issue start their analysis by quoting a comment on (but hardly a definition of) the term "like or similar products" from a 1970 report of a Working Party on Border Taxes. After noting that the term appears sixteen times in the 1947 GATT agreement, the working party concluded that the term caused uncertainty, needed improvement, and should be interpreted on a case-by-case basis (i.e., without any fixed criteria specific enough to govern its application). The Working Party went on to say:

> Some criteria were *suggested* for determining, on a case-by-case basis, whether a product is "similar": the product's end-uses in a given market; consumers' tastes and habits, which change from country to country; the product's properties, nature, and quality.[14]

It is difficult to understand why so much respect is accorded to this passage, given that it is discussing the term "like or similar" and "similar," whereas the key words of Article I, III:2 and III:4 are "like product"—period. Moreover, the criteria listed in the report were just "suggestions" from one or more members of the Working Party, and even at that are merely an illustrative list of "some" criteria that might be applied. The suggestions are merely *reported* by the Working Party, but in no way officially recommended by it. Although the subject before the Working Party—border tax adjustments—fell under GATT Article III, the Working Party's discussion of "likeness" says nothing to indicate it is speaking of Article III in particular. For all one can tell, the Working party is referring to all sixteen provisions where the "like product" concept appears.

Read as a definition, the quotation from the 1970 Working Party report calls for analysis of both competitive factors and physical characteristics. Although the reference to competitive factors would seem to lead toward a broader interpretation, the list of factors can just as easily be used as a list of individual factors that can be used to justify a rather fine product distinction. Panels have not settled on either inference. On the whole, the principal legal value of the quotations seems to be its legitimization of the case-by-case approach

## The Article I:1 Tariff Cases

As of July 1998, there were only five panel decisions that said anything substantive about the "like product" concept in Article I:1. The cases are *Australian Subsidy on Ammonium Sulfate,*[15] *Germany—Treatment of Imports of Sardines,*[16] *EC Measures on Animal Feed Proteins,*[17] *Spain—Tariff Treatment of Unroasted Coffee,*[18] and *Japan—Imports of SPF Dimension Lumber.*[19] Of these, only the *Sardines*, *Coffee,* and *SPF Lumber* decisions involve claims of tariff discrimination (as opposed to internal measures). Only the latter two decisions actually rule on such a claim.

***SPF Lumber.*** The most recent panel ruling, the *SPF Lumber* decision, comes close to affirming this paper's effort to distinguish tariff treatment under Article I. The case involved a quite well documented claim by Canada that certain types of softwood lumber were competitively equivalent regardless of the particular species of evergreen tree form which they were made. The background to the claim appears to have been a typical case of reciprocity discrimination—the classification of lumber by species of tree, resulting in more favorable treatment of United States origin lumber, in response to a tariff concession granted by Japan to the United States in a trade agreement bargain in which Canada did not participate. The panel's reason for rejecting of the Canadian claim was clouded to some extent by the peculiar type of ruling Canada had sought.[20] But in the course of its general analysis, the panel report states that the General Agreement leaves members wide discretion in tariff classification, even after HTS. The panel goes on to state that tariff differentiation is a legitimate tool to serve a party's trade policy interests, "comprising both its protection needs and its requirements for the purposes of tariff- and trade-negotiations." The fact that the panel limited itself to these rather opaque references to the needs of tariff negotiations is not surprising, for it was no doubt awkward for the panel to acknowledge, in the face of all the fanfare proclaiming the MFN obligation to be a "cornerstone" of GATT policy, that governments do need a bit of freedom to discriminate in tariff negotiations.

***Coffee.*** The *Coffee* case, decided eight years before the *SPF Lumber* case, comes to a quite different conclusion. The case involve a tariff classification that distinguished between five different types of unroasted coffee beans. The different types were recognized as distinct types of coffee by coffee merchants, and by processors who made the final product for consumers. The basis of the commercial distinction between these types of coffee seems to have been a difference in taste, due partly to botanical differences and partly to cultivation and processing. The final product sold to consumers was a blend of the various types, each blend assembled in order to achieve the desired taste. Viewed objectively, the product distinctions involved in the *Coffee* case appeared to have a far stronger commercial foundation than the product distinctions in the *SPF Lumber* case. The panel ruled all five types of coffee to be "like products."

The *Coffee* panel relied on the fact that the coffee was always sold to consumers in blended form, where it was impossible to distinguish between the various types of coffee in the blend. This was a *non sequitur*, however, because the views of consumers had nothing to do with the market for this product. The market was the coffee merchants and processors to whom the unroasted beans were sold. Indeed, once the proper market was identified, the practice of blending tended to prove quite the contrary conclusion. The practice of blending meant that each component of the blend was regarded as a commercially separate product, one that could not be substituted for by other types of coffee.

The other main argument advanced by the panel was that the product distinctions made by Spain did not appear in the coffee tariffs of other countries. In the face of this evidence of commercial non-substitutability, however, the fact that this product distinction did not appear in the tariffs of other countries hardly seems weighty enough to call for a classification of "like product." Nor, indeed, is it supported by GATT's general practice with regard to this issue. Based on the author's observation of GATT tariff practice in general, there should be a large number of cases in which nations have made unique product distinctions to deal with unique negotiating needs, and have never been challenged on them despite the fact that they are not made in other national tariffs. For example, it is highly unlikely that any other GATT member had a sub-item in its tariff equivalent to the "brandy-valued-at-more-than-$9.00-per-gallon" sub-item created by the United States in its Chicken War retaliation, but the uniqueness of that tariff distinction seems to have never mattered.

If one looks for an explanation for the disparity between the decision in the *Coffee* case and what we can see of customary GATT tariff practice, the answer can probably be found in two related factors. First, it was generally believed there was a different sort of discriminatory purpose behind the Spanish tariff classification in this case. It was believed that Spain had been pursuing a policy of favoring the coffee exports of certain developing countries, originally through the purchasing policy of a state coffee monopoly, and that the differential tariff classification had been adopted to preserve the favored market position of those countries when the state monopoly had been abolished. This was not, in short, discrimination incident to the reciprocity demands of tariff negotiation. The suggestion is that less desirable types of tariff discrimination elicit different types of legal response on the issue of "like product."

Second, Brazil conducted a rather vigorous campaign to enlist developing country support for its complaint, apparently persuading many developing countries that Spain's effort to distinguish between developing country coffee producers was a kind of discrimination offensive to developing countries. Judging by the response when the panel report was adopted, the campaign was successful. Twenty-two other developing countries rose to speak in favor of the report, most of whom usually have nothing to say about panel reports.[21]

In sum, the *Coffee* case has to be viewed as a very strained reading of the "like product" concept as it is normally applied to tariffs—inconsistent with normal GATT practice toward tariff distinctions and quite possibly even inconsistent with the broader sort of interpretation one could hope to see under a more general, competition-oriented interpretation. One might be justified in dismissing the decision simply as wrong. Alternatively, one could view it as a distinctive response to a distinctive set of policy concerns peculiar to the specific type of discrimination involved in that case.

Because it is one of the few decisions interpreting the "like product" concept, the *Coffee* case has invariably been cited by the "like product" cases that followed, whether or not they involve tariffs. Its main legal impact has been to give general support for the idea that panels can overlook fine distinctions when they analyze the "likeness" of two products. The point is more appropriate for application of the "like product" concept to internal measures rather than tariffs. Most of the subsequent citations have in fact been in cases involving non-tariff measures, leading to a kind of two-wrongs-sometimes-make-a-right result.

***Sardines.*** The Article I claim in the *Sardines* case related to a tariff distinction between three types of sardine, according to the species of fish from which the sardine was made—pilchard, herring, or sprat. The tariff distinction was a classic example of an objectively-based distinction of virtually no commercial significance.[22] As such, the case provides another good illustration of the type of tariff distinction that the author has suggested is common practice among GATT member countries—a practice that would support a uniquely narrow concept of "like product" for product distinctions made in tariffs.

The panel in the *Sardines* case chose not to decide the Article I claim, resolving the case in Norway's favor on the ground that the specific facts of the negotiations between Norway and Germany had created "reasonable expectations" of equal treatment that gave Norway a claim of non-violation nullification and impairment when those expectations were not met. The disposition of the case precludes drawing any firm conclusions about the Article I claim. Nonetheless, two speculations can be offered. First, if the Article I claim had been considered clearly valid, there would have been no need to rely upon the considerably less solid legal concept of non-violation nullification and impairment. The surmise that the Article I claim was not valid—that these three types of sardines were *not* "like products"—would be consistent with the thesis that GATT tariff practice treats such fine product distinctions as perfectly normal, and legal, tariff behavior.

Second, it could not have escaped the panel's notice that the complainant, Norway, had negotiated with Germany on the basis of these tariff distinctions in the Torquay negotiations, and had actually benefited from the product distinctions in the German tariff, because at Torquay it had been able to bargain for a tariff concession limited to the sardines it produced (herring and sprats ) while leaving a higher tariff rate on the sardines produced elsewhere (pilchards). It would have been especially difficult for a panel to sustain a claim of illegality on behalf of a party that had actually taken advantage of the same distinction at a previous negotiation. It is reasonable to assume that a similar "unclean hands" factor accounts for the lack of challenges to the product distinctions make by national tariffs.

## Internal Measures under Articles I:1 and Article III:4

The thesis of this paper is that product distinctions involving internal measures—internal taxes, subsidies, and various other regulations affecting internal sale—should be judged under a broader standard that focuses on the competitive relationship between the affected products and pays less attention to physical characteristics. As noted earlier, the particular two-sentence architecture of Article III:2 leads to a *result* consistent with this standard, but because of that architecture the "like product" concept has been relegated to a subordinate role in achieving that policy. Thus, it is only in Articles I:1 and III:4 in which the "like product" concept is employed to define the governing standard, and it is to these cases that one must look for broader interpretations of "like product" needed to carry out this anti-protection policy.

Only two Article I cases contain meaningful discussions of the "like product" concept with regard to internal measures: *Australia—Subsidy on Ammonium Sulfate*[23] and *European Community—Measures on Animal Fee Proteins*.[24] Only four Article III:4 cases have involved meaningful discussions of "like product" claims pertaining to internal measures: *Animal Feed Proteins* again, *Spain—Measures Concerning Domestic Sale of Soyabean Oil,*[25] *United States—Measures Affecting Alcoholic and Malt Beverages*,[26] and *United States—Taxes on Automobiles*.[27] Of these, the last three decisions contain rulings that cannot be considered authoritative. *Soyabean Oil* was not adopted, and the "aim and effects" definition developed in *Malt Beverages*, and *Autos* was explicitly rejected in the 1996 Appellate Body decision in *Japan Alcoholic Beverages*.[28]

The first three cases—*Australian Subsidy, Animal Feed Proteins* and *Soyabean Oil*— involved "like product" claims that provided a good test of the concept—claims based on the competitiveness of physically dissimilar products. The cases involved, respectively, two types of chemically distinct fertilizers (one natural, one artificial), different types of animal feed proteins (from both animal and vegetable sources), and different types of vegetable oil (made from different kinds of oilseeds).

***Australian Subsidy and Animal Feed Proteins.*** Both *Australian Subsidy* and *Animal Feed Proteins* begin by calling attention to the Article III texts that indicate that "like product" is a distinct and narrower concept than "directly competitive." Having said that, the panels seem content to ignore any further consideration of the extent to which the products in question are competitive. This can hardly be regarded as giving serious attention to the competitive dimensions of the "like product" concept.

The analysis of "like product" in *Australian Subsidy* and *Animal Feed Proteins* tends to focus on other rather limited criteria. Physical differences are obviously in the forefront of the analysis, most explicitly in *Animal Feeds Proteins.* Equally important is tariff classifications in other countries. Both cases also rely heavily on the fact that tariffs in other countries make the same product distinctions. The tendency to cite tariff practice would seem to be quite inconsistent with the thesis of this paper that product distinctions made by internal measures should be judged more rigorously than product distinctions made by tariffs. One is tempted to think that something else may be involved here—for example, the idea that the appearance of the same distinctions in other places indicates that the distinction does have an objective basis, making it less likely that its *purpose* is discriminatory or protective.[29]

***Soyabean Oil.*** In the *Soyabean Oil* case the panel rejected the claim of "likeness" on the ground that "like product" meant "more or less the same product"—a definition that was so narrow that it drew a protest from the United States, which in connection with another more serious error,[30] led the GATT Contracting Parties to "note" the panel report rather than adopting it—a decision tantamount to rejection. Except for making clear that "like product" at least means something broader than near identity, the final outcome of the *Soyabean Oil* case is of relatively little value.

***The "aim and effects"* cases.** The two other "like product" cases involving Article III:4 were the two 1990s cases in which GATT panels suggested abandoning the traditional definitions of "like product" and replacing them with what became called the "aim and effects" test—*Malt Beverages* and *Auto Taxes.* These cases represented an effort, *inter alia,* to establish a definition of like product that would require analysis of market effects in every case. These two decisions were rejected by the WTO Appellate Body as an incorrect application of the "like product" concept under Article III:2. Shortly thereafter, the aim and effects test was rather summarily rejected as an incorrect application of the "like product" test under Article III:4 as well.[31]

In sum, except for the two now-repudiated "aim and effects" cases, the scanty body of panel decisions interpreting the "like product" concept with regard to internal measures covered by Articles I:1 and III:4 shows little sign of adopting an interpretation that would focus on the competitive relationship between the products. Indeed, there is little evidence of any interest in distinguishing in any way between cases involving internal measures from those involving tariffs. Oddly enough, the broadest definition of "like product" to date appears to be the *Coffee* decision—a case involving tariff distinctions. However good the policy reasons for a broader "like product" test with regard to product distinctions in internal measures, GATT and WTO legal decisions have not so far accepted it.

## The Article III:2 Cases

Although it is possible to set aside Article III:2 definitions of "like product" as *sui generis* due to the two-sentence architecture of Article III: 2, the tendency to cross cite all manner of "like product" cases makes it relevant to examine the contribution of such cases to the "like product" literature. The cases of particular importance are (1) the two *Japan Alcoholic Beverages* cases—the 1987 GATT panel report in the first case,[32] and the 1996 Appellate Body report in the second case[33]—and (2) the recent Appellate Body report in *the Periodicals* case.[34]

***Japan Alcoholic Beverages I and II.*** In the first, 1987 *Japan Alcoholic Beverages* case, the panel made an interesting series of "like product" rulings. It ruled that standard distilled spirit classifications were "like products"—gin, vodka, whiskey, grape brandy—as well as classic liqueurs, still wine and sparkling wine. The functional effect of the holding was to rule that Japan could not impose different internal taxes on different quality grades within these product categories—in other words, that it was impossible to subdivide these product categories according to quality.

Arguably the rejection of distinctions based on quality offered a broader and more rigorous definition of "like product" than one would expect to find applied to product distinctions made in tariffs, where similar distinctions appear routinely. The panel did nothing, however, to suggest that Article III requires a more stringent test. The panel said that its "likeness" conclusions had relied upon the criteria listed in the 1970 working party report, plus a variety of tariff and statistical reporting categories that subdivided alcoholic beverages into these categories without further breakdown—the same kind of reasoning involved in all other "like product" cases. The panel also relied on the broader definition applied in the *Coffee* case, citing that decision for the proposition that minor differences in taste, color, and other properties would not affect the "likeness" of products.

The panel in the first *Japan Alcoholic Beverages* case indicated that it would not have had a problem with tax differences based on alcohol content, which it viewed as an "objective" basis for product distinctions. The remark indicates that the determining issue in its "like product" analysis, whether consciously or not, may have been the question of protective purpose. The quality distinctions involved in that Japanese tax law apparently struck the panel as protective in purpose, partly because their arbitrary and subjective character, and partly because of their manifestly protective results.

In the second *Japan Alcoholic Beverages* case, the main "like product" issue involved an internal tax on shochu that was lower than the comparable tax on several Western varieties of distilled spirits. Under the first sentence of Article III:2, the question was whether any of Western-type distilled spirits were "like" shochu. The initial panel decision had followed the first panel's "like product." classification in which only vodka, which is almost identical to shochu in all respects except filtration, was found to be "like" shochu. In distinguishing other types of distilled spirits, the panel in the second *Japan Alcoholic Beverages* case claimed to be applying market principles, but in fact the panel did do so. Instead of relying on market-based characteristics such as consumer preferences, the panel relied on physical characteristics reminiscent of those employed to make very fine tariff distinctions—color, raw materials, presence of additives. The Appellate Body confirmed the narrowness of the criteria applied by the panel, stating that the juxtaposition of "like" products in the first sentence of Article III:2 with "directly competitive" products in the second sentence of III:2 requires giving "like product" a very narrow reading in this particular context.

***Periodicals.*** The narrow view of "like product" taken in the second *Japan Alcoholic Beverages* case was implicitly confirmed by the outcome in the subsequent *Periodicals* case. The initial issue was whether certain foreign periodicals were "like" more favorably treated domestic periodicals. Although the two kinds of periodicals were clearly competitive, the panel apparently had great difficulty in finding a plausible rationale to explain why such periodicals were "like," in the face of an argument that the content of the two groups of periodicals was an important distinction. The panel eventually issued a difficult-to-follow rationale that the Appellate Body could not accept. But rather than try its hand a better "like product" rationale—the usual Appellate Body practice in such cases—the Appellate Body proclaimed the record inadequate to make such a judgment, and so decided the case under the "directly competitive and substitutable" standard of the second sentence of Article III:2—an issue as to which there was even less information in the record. The tortured course of the "like product" issue strongly suggests that both panel and Appellate Body were operating within a quite narrow view of "like product" in which different characteristics carried more weight than competitiveness.

Given the tendency of GATT/WTO tribunals to treat all "like product" decisions as fungible, these two most recent Appellate Body decisions on the "like product" issue will probably direct subsequent decisions toward a narrower rather an a broader interpretation of "like product," policy context notwithstanding. If so, it may well be a long time before the policy distinctions argued for in this paper are accepted by WTO legal decisions. And that is where the issue stands.

NOTES

1. Professor Jackson lists 10 GATT provisions" I:1, II:2(a), III:2, III:4, VI:1(a,b), IX:1, XI:2(c), XIII:1, XVI:4, JACKSON, WORLD TRADE AND THE LAW OF GATT (1968) at 259n1. The 1970 Working Party on Border Tax Adjustments reported that the phrase "like or similar products" appears 16 times in the text of the General Agreement. GATT, BISD, 18th Supp. 97, 101 (1972). In his comprehensive study of the texts, negotiating history and dispute settlement rulings on the "like product" concept and similar expressions in GATT, Professor Zedalis counts 17 GATT provisions that use the term "like." Zedalis, *The Theory of GATT "Like" Product Common Language Cases,* 27 VANDERBILT JOURNAL OF TRANSNATIONAL LAW 33, 36 (1994).

In addition to the above-listed sources, other studies of the "like product" concept include: Berg, *Dividing the Like-Product: Economics, the Law and the International Trade Commission,* 20 WORLD COMPETITION LAW AND ECONOMICS Review 73 (1997); Berg, An Economic Interpretation of "Like Product," 30 JOURNAL OF WORLD TRADE 195 (1996); Steen, *Economically Meaningful Markets: An Alternative Approach to Defining "Like Product" and "Domestic Industry" under the Trade Agreements Act of 1979,* 73 VIRGINIA LAW REVIEW 1459 (1987); Langer, *The Concepts of Like Product and Domestic Industry under the Trade Agreements Act of 1979,* 17 GEORGE WASHINGTON JOURNAL OF INTERNATIONAL LAW AND ECONOMICS 524 (1983).

Finally, the paper by Marco Bronkers and Natalie McNelis in this volume contains a lengthy study of the "like product" concept as it applies to GATT/WTO antidumping law and to the GATT/WTO law pertaining to environmental measures.

2. *United States — Measures Affecting Alcoholic and Malt Beverages,* BISD, 39th Supp. 206 (1993); *United States — Taxes on Automobiles, GATT,* GATT Doc. DS.31/R (11 October 1994).

3. *Japan — Taxes on Alcoholic Beverages,* WT/DS8, -10, -11/AB/R (4 October 1996).

4. For an essay in this volume that argues in favor of a "like product" definition in terms of competitiveness for the producer-oriented rules, see the paper by Marco Bronkers and Natalie McNelis.

5. To be accurate, the Ad Note to Article III:2 which introduces this term uses the longer term "directly competitive or substitutable." Notwithstanding the rule that every word of a treaty must have a meaning and purpose, the author views the two terms as essentially synonymous, and for convenience this paper will omit reference to "substitutable."

6. There is some disagreement at present about the exact meaning of the policy statement contained in closing words of Article III:1. The authors of the "aim and effects" test found that the language contained a prohibition of *purposeful* protection. The Appellate Body ruled that no such "aim" was not to be considered in applying this policy statement, but when the Appellate Body itself applied this policy statement, it came up with an analysis that looked quite like the "aim" analysis put forward by the panel decisions it was rejecting. The point is beyond the scope of our "like product" analysis. Further discussion can be found in Hudec, *GATT/WTO Constraints on National Regulation: Requiem for an "Aim and Effects" Test,* 32.

7. See, e.g., *Japan — Taxes on Alcoholic Beverages, supra note 3,* at page 21 ("We believe that, in Article III:2, first sentence of the GATT 1994, the accordion of "likeness" is meant to be narrowly squeezed.")

8. To be sure, the effects are not exactly symmetrical. "Discrimination" that consists of lowering barriers to goods from favored countries can also involve a little trade creation.

9. Article III is often explained in terms of the practical value of confining protection to the border—the value of removing the difficulty that traders have in identifying the multiple sources of internal protection, and also the value of removing the difficulty that trade negotiators have in dealing with multiple political authorities when internal measures are used as instruments of protection. The use of internal measures for third-country discrimination would be equally objectionable on this score as well.

10. CURZON, MULTILATERAL COMMERCIAL DIPLOMACY (1965) at page 60n1. Curzon provides the original German text of the concession.

11. Unlike ad valorem tariffs which apply the same percentage rate to the value of a product, value brackets have different rates for different ranges of value.

12. See Walker, *Dispute Settlement: The Chicken War,* 58 AMERICAN JOURNAL OF INT'L LAW 671 (1964); Lowenfeld, *"Doing Unto Others . . .," The Chicken War Ten Years After,* 4 JOURNAL OF MARITIME LAW & COMMERCE 599 (1973).

13. The one legal consequence of the brandy retaliation was a lawsuit in the U.S. courts by an importer of expensive Spanish brandy, arguing that the domestic US legislation relied upon for authority to increase the tariff did not allow MFN tariff increases that punished innocent countries. *United States v. Star Industries,* 462 F.2d 558 (C.C.P.A.), cert. denied 409 U.S. 1076 (1972). The MFN scope of the retaliation was upheld as authorized by U.S. law.

14. BISD, 18th Supp. at 101–102. (1972) (Emphasis added)

15. II BISD 188 (1952).

16. BISD, 1st Supp. 53 (1953).

17. BISD. 25th Supp. 49 (1979).

18. BISD, 28th Supp. 102 (1982).

19. BISD, 36th Supp. 167 (1990). The list does not include *United States — Denial of Most-Favored-Nation Treatment as to Non-rubber Footwear from Brazil,* BISD, 39th Supp. 128

(1993), because a specific "like product" determination was rendered unnecessary in that case by a statutory provision requiring adverse treatment of all products from disfavored countries.

20. Rather than attacking the validity of tariff distinctions based on the species of tree from which the lumber came, Canada asked the panel to rule that all "dimension lumber" was a like product. By arguing the case in this way, Canada never called upon the panel to rule specifically on the validity of distinguishing lumber products according to the type of tree. The panel's general comments made it clear, however, that the panel was prepared to sustain a product distinction on those grounds.

21. See GATT Doc. C/M/148 (meeting of 11 June 1981).

22. The author is informed that persons with a well-educated palate for fish products can tell the difference between pilchards and the other two, and would never consider them substitutable. Most of the ordinary mortals to whom the author have spoken are surprised to learn that different types of fish are used, and taste tests conducted with the author's International Trade Law classes (admittedly not the most educated palates) invariably support the latter view.

23. BISD, vol. 2, 188 (1952).

24. BISD, 25th Supp. 49 (1979).

25. GATT Docs. L/5142 & L/5142/Corr.1 (17 & 22 June 1981) (not adopted).

26. BISD, 39th Supp. 206 (1993).

27. GATT Doc. DS31/R (11 October 1994) (not adopted).

28. *Japan — Taxes on Alcoholic Beverages, supra note 3.*

29. The *Australian Subsidy* case also relies on the fact that the Australian tariff distinguished between the two products, using the practice of the same government in another, unrelated area to demonstrate that the product distinction with regard to fertilizer was objectively justified, and thus not protective in purpose.

30. The panel also took the position which appeared to say that Article III complaints require proof of trade damage. Both that position and the "like product" ruling were the basis of the decision to merely note the report.

31. *European Community — Regime for the Importation, Sale and Distribution of Bananas,* WT/DS27/AB/R (9 September 1997) at paragraphs 215–16.

32. BISD, 34th Supp. 83 (1988).

33. *Japan—Taxes on Alcoholic Beverages,* supra note 3.

34. *Canada — Certain Measures Concerning Periodicals,* WT/DS31/R (panel decision, 14 March 1997) and WT/DS31/AB/R (Appellate Body decision, 30 June 1997).

CHAPTER 4

# "Like Products": Some Thoughts at the Positive and Normative Level

*Petros C. Mavroidis**

## 1. Introductory Remarks

The definition of the term "like products" is an issue debated in a number of integration schemes. There is no need therefore, to re-invent the wheel, unless one ends up concluding that all definitions that have seen the light of day are inadequate or inappropriate. This is hardly the case though. As the contributions by Hudec and Mattoo in this volume amply show, there are no agreed definitions of the term at the domestic level. Instead, competent authorities in both sides of the Atlantic have tried to come up with a list of relevant criteria that would help define the term.

It is submitted that such efforts (essentially by the judiciary) are, in principle, relevant for the interpretation of the term as it appears in the WTO contract (both in the GATT and in the GATS). On the other hand however, one has to take into account the particularities of the WTO contract before proposing that interpretative efforts in the WTO should be inspired by experience in other fora; a lock, stock, and barrel approach is almost never recommendable.

What are the WTO specificities? First, the mandate of the WTO. The WTO is, at the present stage of integration, an instrument for trade liberalization. It does not aim at establishing a unified market where all factors of production circulate without any restriction. Admittedly, this could be the case in the future. For the time being though, it has to take care of a much less ambitious agenda. It is only logical therefore that, with some notable exceptions (TRIPs, Telecoms, PSI), the WTO contract imposes on its parties negative integration-type obligations ("thou shall not"). The inference from the mandate is that the WTO is an instrument prescribing non-discrimination and not an instrument for deregulation, since, with the

* I would like to thank Henrik Horn af Rantzien for helpful discussions and comments on a previous draft.

exceptions mentioned above, no common policies are established. In fact, this point is reflected black on white in Art. III GATT.

Second, the GATT and the GATS are based on exchange of concessions. This explains the distinction between "like" and "directly competitive or substitutable" (DCS) products in the GATT context: since concessions are exchanged on an item by item basis, they are reflected as such in the schedule of commitments: country A binds its tariff for bananas at 5% against a promise by country B to bind its tariff for cars at 5%. The original promise however, can be completely annihilated if country A, through an internal regulation, imposes a VAT (value added tax) of 0% on apples and oranges (that it happens to produce domestically) and 50% on bananas (that it happens to import). Although the tax differential is not imposed on two "like" (in the strict sense of the term) products, it does affect, in all likelihood, the value of the original promise to bind tariffs for bananas at 5%. This is so, because arguably in A's market, bananas, apples, and oranges are directly competitive products and consumers will switch to the cheaper product.

It is standing GATT/WTO case law that the purpose of Art. III is to maintain, through tax neutrality at the internal level, the value of promises given through tariff bindings.

The remaining part of the paper builds on what has been mentioned above. In Section 1, we briefly present the two notions, that is "like" and "directly competitive or substitutable products," as they appear in the GATT/WTO contract. In Section 2, we turn to the question whether the term "like" product has a mere transitional value. In Section 3, we focus on the implications on the interpretation of the terms "like" and "directly competitive" products stemming from the reading and understanding the WTO not as an instrument for deregulation but rather as an instrument disallowing discrimination. Section 4 contains the conclusions of our analysis.

## 2. Section 1

The term "like" product appears in various parts of the WTO treaty. In the GATT, for example, the term appears, among other places, in Arts. I, III, VI. For the purposes of this paper we will focus on the term as used in Arts. I and III. The term is not further interpreted in the GATT (the opposite is the case though in the WTO Antidumping Agreement). The term "DCS" products appears in the Interpretative Note ad Art. III without any further clarification.

In the GATS, no distinction is made between like and DCS services; throughout the GATS, the drafters of the treaty use only the term "like" services and services suppliers. As Mattoo however correctly, to our mind points out, the term "like" services and services suppliers should be understood as covering DCS services and services suppliers as well.[1]

As such the terms are vague. Legitimate questions could *a priori* be asked as to their precise ambit. Does the term "like" cover only cases of absolute identity, mere similarity? How should substitutability be measured? The terms in other words invite interpretation.

For the sake of consistency, it is highly recommendable that interpreters have a theory of interpretation.[2] Such theory is in fact facilitated by the general rule of interpretation laid down in Art. 31 of the Vienna Convention on the Law of Treaties (VCLT). The VCLT system requests from the interpreter to place the terms about to be interpreted in their proper context. And the context is of course, trade liberalization under the auspices of the WTO.

## 3. Section 2

As mentioned above, Art. III GATT reflects both the term "like" and the term "DCS" products. The argument could be made that Art. III GATT "inherited" the term "like" products from Art. I GATT which requests, *inter alia*, WTO Members to grant MFN treatment with respect to customs duties to all like products. In some sense, "likeness" is there to guarantee equality of treatment at the border, whereas "DCS" relationship is there to ensure that promises of tariff reductions (bindings) at the border with respect to like products will not be reduced meaningless by favoring domestic DCS products.

Does trade liberalization amount to establishment of one integrated world market where all factors of production will circulate without any restriction? Following this logic, Art. II GATT and GATS negotiations would have to vanish in a free trade world. Consequently, no concessions would need to be exchanged anymore. The starting question in this Section would therefore read as follows: does the term "like" products have a mere transitional value? In this line of argument, when we reach the world free trade area, all we will need to check when a country intervenes through regulatory means would be the effect on the relevant market properly defined so as to include all competition affected by the regulatory intervention (in the field of goods or services as the case may be).

And this is the first area where experience from other integration schemes can be useful. In the EC, goods circulate almost freely and, in the last years, substantial progress has been made in the liberalization of services as well. Still Art. 95 ECT (Treaty Establishing the European Community) distinguishes between like and DCS products. The ECJ (European Court of

Justice) case law though, has so far failed to establish a clear dividing line between like and DCS products. An excellent illustration of this point is offered by the *Beer and Wine* case,[3] where the Court failed to establish whether beer and wine should be qualified as like or DCS products. The analysis starts by examining whether the two products are DCS products, since in this way, one can be sure about the ambit of a regulatory intervention in the wider relevant product area.

In this context, one can only welcome the recent WTO Appellate Body (AB) report on *Korea – Taxes on Alcoholic Beverages* which holds for the proposition that:

"Like products are a subset of directly competitive or substitutable products: all like products are, by definition, directly competitive or substitutable products, whereas not all directly competitive or substitutable products are like."[4]

This approach, which covers the wider product area (both like and DCS products), leads to a meaningful scrutiny of regulatory interventions. However, the distinction between like and DCS products will not disappear in the immediate future. First, because we are still far from establishing a world free-trade area that would at least put into question the usefulness of the distinction. Second because, as the EC experience shows, even if the WTO does establish a world free-trade area, the distinction will not be automatically eliminated. This is so maybe because of the fact that with respect to the inner circle (like products) the legal test to establish violation is easier to meet: in both 95 ECT and III:2 first sentence GATT, all the plaintiff needs to show after having established likeness of the domestic and the foreign product at hand is a tax differential even at a *de minimis* level.[5] With respect to DCS on the other hand, one has to show that the tax differential amounts to protection of the domestic good over the foreign (again, same test in both the EC and the WTO legal order).

The distinction (in a post- exchanges of concessions world) is essentially mandated by procedural concerns (burden and quantum of proof). For substantive reasons, one could very well imagine a WTO contract putting into question regulatory interventions in the context of DCS products: after all, since such interventions are purely internal, they should be placed in their appropriate context, that is internal relevant markets where various products (not only the like products) compete. No matter however the intellectual merit of such an approach, if the EC experience is an indication, the distinction will stay around for some time.

## 4. Section 3

With respect to both like and DCS products, the WTO contract requests from its Members to ensure that, when they intervene, they ensure that they do not disfavor foreign products. This is the case for both goods (Art. III:1 GATT) and services (Art. XVII:1 GATS). On its face therefore, all that WTO imposes on its Members is an obligation not to discriminate against foreign products through regulatory means. This obligation, as we saw earlier, covers both like and DCS products. With respect to goods only (since the GATS does not know of this distinction), the plaintiff has an easier task to establish violation of the non-discrimination obligation when it comes to like products (see Section 2 *supra*). Does this conclusion however, change if the relevant Articles (III GATT and XVII GATS) are put into their appropriate context?

### The Role of Art. XX GATT: Is it Really Necessary?

The working hypothesis is that the GATT (and the GATS) is not an instrument for deregulation. This means that, in principle, WTO Members can make any regulatory distinction among products to the extent that, as a result of their intervention, they do not confer an advantage to domestic products (like or DCS). Why then do we need an Art. XX GATT which stipulates that WTO Members can intervene (and make regulatory distinctions between two otherwise like or DCS products) in the areas mentioned in the body of the Article? If Art. XX GATT contained an indicative list of grounds where regulatory intervention was permitted, then its existence would not put into question the non deregulatory function of the GATT. But doctrine and GATT/WTO case law conclude that the list in Art. XX GATT is exhaustive. What is the inference then? One tenable reading would be to exclude regulatory intervention on grounds not mentioned in Art. XX GATT, even if no discrimination in favor of domestic products results from such intervention.

Conceivably, if the list of Art. XX GATT could cover all potential areas of regulatory intervention, this would be the end of the discussion. This is not the case though. Precisely because some areas are not covered (i.e., consumer protection) a strain is imposed on WTO Members. This strain has led Hudec for example, to question the well-founded of the GATT – test (as laid down in the *Japan – Taxes on Alcoholic Be*verages jurisprudence, see Section 4) to establish whether two products are like in the context of Art. III by focusing only on the marketplace. Hudec essentially believes that Art. XX GATT cannot capture all of the areas for legitimate non discriminatory regulatory intervention and consequently, that some breathing space has to be created in the context of Art. III GATT that will allow governments to intervene in order to pursue goals not mentioned in Art. XX GATT.[6]

Is this exclusively a WTO problem? Not at all. The ECT knows of a very comparable problem. Art. 36 ECT is an exhaustive list and covers essentially comparable to Art. XX GATT grounds. EC Members felt the need and did intervene in areas beyond those mentioned in Art. 36 ECT. The choice, from a legal point of view, would be to either proceed in a formal amendment of the ECT in this respect (and add grounds, or simply declare that the list is of indicative character) or allow the judiciary to come up with an imaginative interpretation that will make room for governmental intervention beyond the grounds mentioned in Art. 36 ECT, without putting into question the objectives of the ECT.

From a principal/agent angle, it is a very interesting question. The answer largely depends on the legitimacy of the agent (the judiciary in this case), on the trust that it enjoys by the principal (the EC Member States).

The ECJ has already established its credibility in an intense integration scheme like the EC, and Member States felt comfortable enough with its case law; they did not proceed to a formal amendment of Art. 36 ECT. Instead, the ECJ every time it confronted a regulatory intervention on grounds beyond those mentioned in Art. 36 ECT, the pursuance of which however did not discriminate between foreign and domestic products, accepted it as legitimate. It even found a name for such grounds: mandatory requirements. The ECJ kept the exclusive privilege to declare a grounds invoked by a Member State as mandatory requirements.

Although they have a function comparable to that of Art. 36 ECT, the ECJ preferred to examine them under Art. 30 ECT (the equivalent to Art. III:4 GATT) and declare that mandatory requirements are not covered by the prohibition not to discriminate as laid down in the body of Art. 30 ECT.[7]

## Mandatory Requirements in the WTO Law?

Could one imagine a comparable solution for the WTO? I am afraid not. The principals (WTO Members) are constantly opposed to any sort of judicial activism exercised by the agents (panels). If at all, the coming into being of the Appellate Body marks a shift by the WTO judiciary towards deference in favor of the WTO Members.[8]

The only realistically feasible way to remove the described strain would be a formal amendment of Art. XX GATT. And WTO Members, assuming they take such a decision, do not have to look very far for inspiration: Art. XIV GATS differs from its GATT counterpart, Art. XX, in one important respect; it includes in paragraph (a) a mention to public order. WTO

Members can distinguish between two otherwise like services or services suppliers in order to protect their public order.

It is submitted that this is a notion, which if transplanted in the GATT, will prove sufficiently wide to remove the strain. An alternative would be to declare that the Art. XX GATT list is of indicative character. Two problems are associated with such an approach however: first, it *de facto* amounts to recognizing to the WTO judiciary the competence to pick and choose from the invoked grounds (a function not that far from giving them the possibility to accept some grounds as mandatory requirements); second, it would mean a drastic departure from previous GATT case law which time and again has proclaimed the exhaustive character of the Art. XX GATT list.

## The Japan Taxes on Alcoholic Beverages and Korea Taxes on Alcoholic Beverages Test

Against this background, one can better appreciate the test laid down in the panel and AB reports on *Japan – Taxes on Alcoholic Beverages*[9] and *Korea-Taxes on Alcoholic Beverages.* These reports hold for the following proposition:

1. The test to establish whether two products are like / DCS is in the marketplace.
2. The inner circle contains the like products whereas the outer circle contains the DCS products. Since any item in the inner circle must be at least a DCS product, one will have to establish first whether two products are in a DCS relationship. And since the test is in the marketplace, DCS relationship can only be established by using substitutability of demand as the relevant criterion. Economic theory suggests that any two products are, in principle, substitutable. If for example, price of oranges rises dramatically, consumers can switch to cheaper apples but will have more available income to eventually buy (at least some of them) a second newspaper. This would not mean that oranges and newspapers are substitutable products in the Art. III GATT sense of the term. A high degree of substitutability is required. Perhaps this is the role that the adjective "direct" in the term "directly competitive or substitutable" products is called to play. An analysis inspired by the antitrust definition of the relevant market could prove very useful in this context.[10] This approach could lead to some *prima facie* odd results. Take the case of apples in the north and southern hemisphere. Assume that they are produced in different seasons. If costs of stockage and transportation are high enough to

exclude that both categories of apples can time wise coincide in a given market, then, notwithstanding their quasi identity in every respect, they should never be considered DCS products. Such outcomes however should not shock anybody. At the end of the day, the purpose of Art. III GATT (and XVII GATS) is to avoid discrimination against foreign products (protectionism). This can hardly be the case in the case of our example for northern and southern hemisphere apples.

3. Since however the WTO is not an instrument for deregulation (indeed, all Art. III GATT and XVII GATS disallow is discrimination without putting into question at all, as we saw above, the right of WTO Members to intervene), WTO Members can of course intervene and operate distinctions between two otherwise like/DCS products. The legitimacy of any such intervention will be judged against the background of Art. XX GATT (for goods) and XIV GATS (for services and services suppliers). With the caveat that a "public order" exception is read into Art. XX GATT as well, the currently applied test seems adequate to take care of the need to guarantee a proper balance between trade liberalization and the will by Members to pursue their revealed preferences.

## Three Issues of Concern

### *The Relationship between GATT Art. III:2 First and Second Sentence*

So far the GATT/WTO case law has not dealt with this issue. Imagine the following scenario: country A produces bananas and other fruits. Out of a total production of 100 items, bananas account for 1 unit of production whereas other fruits for 99. Country B also produces bananas and other fruits, but the ratio there is 90 to 10. Country A imposes a VAT of 100% for bananas and 0% for other fruits. Country B complains. A's defense would be that like products are treated alike (domestic and foreign bananas, domestic, and foreign fruits).

In a very similar case, the ECJ established the principle that compatibility of a national measure with Art. 95.1 ECT (the equivalent to GATT Art. III:2 first sentence) does not *ipso facto* amount to compatibility with Art. 95.2 ECT (the equivalent to GATT Art. III:2 second sentence).[11] The Court went on to examine compatibility of the national measure with the obligation to treat similarly DCS products and found that cases of substantial tax differential do not meet this obligation.

The same law should be good law for the WTO context as well. Indeed the very purpose of Art. III GATT (as reflected in its first paragraph) "not to afford protection to domestic production" would be defeated otherwise. At any rate, since, according to the currently applied test, one has first to establish a DCS relationship before moving to examine whether likeness also exists, one should expect that it is only a matter of time before such case law finds its way in the WTO context as well.

*The Relationship between Art. III:2 GATT and Art. XI GATT*

What in case where a huge VAT is imposed on products where no domestic production (either like or DCS) exists? Country A does not produce any vehicle. It imposes a 500% VAT on cars and as a result imports of cars into its market are substantially reduced. In a similar case, the ECJ found that compatibility with Art. 95 ECT does not exonerate EC Members States from their obligations with respect to Art. 30 ECT (which covers both Art. III:4 and Art. XI GATT).[12]

Such case law however is not recommendable for the WTO, at least not at the current stage of integration. For a start, the WTO aims at trade liberalization and not at the establishment of a unified market. Only in the latter case one could potentially raise such arguments. In the WTO if at all, establishment of a unified market will be established by using non-discrimination as a tool and not by disciplining taxation to low levels.

*"Like" in Art. III:2 GATT and "Like" in Art. III:4 GATT: Like or Unlike?*

Art. III:2 GATT deal with the "charge" elements of internal regulation (i.e., taxation) whereas Art. III:4 GATT deals with the "non charge" elements (i.e., distribution). The former distinguishes between like and DCS products, the latter does not. Does it mean that with respect to Art. III:4 GATT WTO Members have a much more limited in scope obligation?

This question should be answered in the negative. Both sub-paragraphs are informed by the first paragraph of Art. III GATT which contains the objective function of the Article ("not to afford protection to domestic production"). A narrow reading (that is a reading which excludes DCS products from its scope) of the obligation laid down in Art. III:4 GATT is an a-contextual interpretation of the term which ends up defeating the very purpose of Art. III GATT.

The only interpretation of the term "like" products in the body of Art. III:4 GATT which takes care of the context (in conformity with Art. 31

VCLT) and which is in line with the purpose of Art. III GATT is the one that brings under this term both like and DCS products.

## 5. Section 4

The GATT/WTO case law with respect to the definition of like/DCS products is on the right track. However, this is partly due to the fact that so far difficult cases have been avoided in this context: absence of direct effect of WTO law can sometimes operate as a blessing as well.

A legislative change in the GATT (inspired by the GATS) which would include the "public order" exception in the body of Art. XX GATT is recommended in order to avoid future turbulences.

REFERENCES

Dworkin, Roland. 1986. The Law's Empire. Harvard University Press: Cambridge, Mass.

Oliver, Peter. 1996. Free Movement of Goods in the EC. Sweet & Maxwell: London.

Possner, Richard. 1995. Overcoming Law. Harvard University Press: Cambridge, Mass.

Roessler, Frieder. 1996. Divergent Domestic Policies and Multilateral Trade Integration, 21–56 in Jagdish Bhagwati and Robert E. Hudec (eds.), Fair Trade and Harmonization. MIT Press: Cambridge, Mass.

Vermulst, Edwin, Petros C. Mavroidis, and Paul Waer. 1999. The Functioning of the Appellate Body After Four Years: Towards Rule Integrity. Journal of World Trade, April.

NOTES

1. See the very convincing arguments he puts forward in favor of this position in his contribution to this volume.

2. See on this issue Possner (1995) and for counter arguments Dworkin (1986).

3. See Commission v. United Kingdom and the Republic of Ireland, 170/78, Judgment of 27 February 1980, Rep. 1980 at 417 ff.

4. See WTO Doc. WT/DS75/AB/R, WT/DS84/AB/R of 18 January 1999 at §118.

5. See the 1987 panel report on *United States – Taxes on Petroleum and Certain Imported Substances,* adopted on 17 June 1987, BISD 34S/136.

6. It must be pointed out here, that Hudec does not espouse the "aims and effect" test as laid down in the panel report *US-Taxes on Automobiles,* GATT Doc. DS31/R of 11 October 1994 which holds for the proposition that likeness of the product depends on whether it was the intended effect of the regulating WTO Member to discriminate against foreign products. To the extent that this was not the case, two otherwise like or DCS products (in the case at hand, light

tracks and passenger vehicles) will be deemed to be unlike. For a defense of this point of view, see Roessler (1996).

7. Similar grounds have been invoked and been accepted as legitimate exceptions to Art. 95 ECT which, contrary to Art. III GATT, knows of no exceptions. For a comprehensive presentation of this issue, see Oliver (1996). See in the same book the discussion on non-discrimination – deregulation as a result of the *Keck and Mithouard* and the *Bosman* jurisprudence.

8. See on this issue, Vermulst et al. (1999).

9. See WTO Doc. WT/DS/8–11 and WT/DS/8/AB/R of 4 October 1996.

10. On this issue, see the contribution by Damien J. Neven in this volume.

11. See Commission v. Italian Republic, 184/85, Judgment of 7 May 1987, Rep., 1987, 2013ff.

12. At stake was the internal taxation of automobiles in Denmark, a country which does not produce cars. Allegedly the high level taxation could operate as a measure having an equivalent effect to a quantitative restriction. Since no such claim was raised however, the ECJ limited its remarks to an *obiter dictum* that compatibility with Art. 95 ECT does not *ipso facto* amount to compatibility with Art. 30 ECT, see Commission v. Denmark, C-47/88, Judgment of 11 December 1990, Rep. 1990, I-4509 ff.

# Part III: Empirical Analysis

CHAPTER 5

# Managing the Interface between International Trade Law and the Regulatory State: What Lessons Should (and Should Not) Be Drawn from the Jurisprudence of the United States Dormant Commerce Clause

*Robert Howse**

Increasingly, the application and interpretation of international trade law engages the dispute settlement organs of the World Trade Organization with the contemporary regulatory state in its full complexity. Whether in determining if required risk assessment procedures for health and safety regulations have been followed in interpreting the TBT and SPS codes, or deciding if a Member has respected the criteria for compulsory licensing of patents in the TRIPs Agreement, including "adequate remuneration" to the patent holder, or in the application of Art. XX of the GATT to environmentally-based trade measures, WTO panels cannot avoid making complex trade offs between free trade and other public values.

This raises fundamental issues of democratic legitimacy, far beyond those implicit in what might have appeared to be the character of the multilateral trading order in the past—a bargain about tariff reductions, with a code of conduct to help ferret out cheating on the bargain. From the perspective of the traditional trade policy elites, under the GATT domestic regulation tended to fall on one side or the other of a bright line, dividing entirely evil "cheating" from entirely benign "normal" domestic regulations. Not entirely surprisingly, the difficulty with such an approach became apparent once GATT panels were faced with determining whether measures that violated trade rules could be justified on the basis of other objectives and values, as provided for in Art. XX of the GATT. In the *Tuna*/Dolphin[1]

---

* I am grateful to Julie Soloway for excellent research assistance and to both Julie Soloway and Stevan Pepa for insightful discussions about these issues. A number of participants in the forum provided helpful comments and criticisms, especially Thomas Cottier, Meinhard Hilf, Gary Horlick, Petros Mavroidis, Kalypso Nicolaidis, and David Palmeter. I owe a very large debt of gratitude to Don Regan, my colleague while I was visiting at the University of Michigan Law School in the fall of 1998, who read a revised draft of the original paper and through several lengthy discussions, helped me to better understand the dormant commerce clause. I of course am alone responsible for all remaining errors and omissions.

disputes, GATT panels, somehow intuitively sure that unilateral measures to protect the global environmental commons didn't fit within their image of the "normal" regulatory state, resorted to a number of spurious distinctions, unsupported by the text of the General Agreement, to avoid directly facing a conflict of values.[2] In the *Thai Cigarette* case,[3] shortly before the *Tuna/Dolphin* decisions, a panel had applied a least restrictive means test in order to find that Thai measures targeted at foreign cigarettes could not be justified as "necessary" for the protection of human life and health under Art. XX(b) of the GATT: the panel dreamed up a range of hypothetical less trade-restrictive measures that could have been chosen (such as anti-smoking advertising campaigns), with no sensitivity to and little interest in the real policy world in which the Thai regulators lived.[4] A legal economist can always imagine a hypothetical welfare-maximizing regulatory instrument that achieves a public purpose without resort to trade restrictions; the logical conclusion is that the choice of any other instrument is due to protectionist pressures.[5] It is easy to see why such a construct would be attractive to trade diplomat panelists, for it avoids the impression that there is any need to adjudicate competing values at all. Yet in the real world, the "first best" instrument may create serious compliance problems; cultural norms may make Western-style ad campaigns ineffective; a tax may be more efficient than command-and-control regulation but may face constitutional problems or may skew more general fiscal policies. In the real world of regulation, policy makers face hard choices, and need to address difficult normative trade-offs.

With the WTO Appellate Body now requiring rigor and consistency in the interpretation of WTO legal instruments,[6] the free manipulation of legal concepts and texts by trade diplomats to produce results that correspond to their own intuitions about what is protectionism and what is normal regulation is increasingly less viable. In any case, where dispute settlement rulings fail to take into account legitimate public values other than trade liberalization itself, this will risk provoking even more severe legitimacy crises than those provoked by the *Tuna/Dolphin* rulings—more severe at least in part because under the negative-consensus rule of the WTO DSU, the safety valve of non-adoption through a veto of the losing party is no longer available.[7]

Where then to turn in order to educate WTO panelists (and to some extent the Appellate Body, too) in the kind of institutional sensitivity appropriate to review of domestic regulation in the context of adjudicating potentially competing values? One rather obvious place might be to the internal economic integration jurisprudence of federal states. The courts in the United States, for example, have passed through, as it were, their era of

"Lochnerism," where they acted as protectors of some kind of natural, laissez-faire baseline against what were viewed as the intrusions of a growing regulatory state.[8] They have developed a set of techniques for engaging in constitutional and administrative law review of regulatory action, which show a degree of appreciation for the need for democratically legitimate institutions to trade off competing values. In addition, there is a body of sophisticated legal scholarship which addresses itself to the institutional strengths and weaknesses of courts in relation to other agencies, in addressing the various empirical and conceptual questions that surround the rationality of and justification for regulatory action.[9]

Of course, this has all largely occurred in contexts other than the interpretation of constitutional rules on free trade between federal sub-units. Nevertheless, one would expect that the sensitivity to the regulatory state and its democratic demands acquired through the post-Lochner juridical revolution would inform the economic integration jurisprudence of the courts. The jurisprudence in question is based on the so-called "dormant" Commerce Clause (DCC); from the constitutional mandate of the U.S. federal Government to regulate interstate commerce, the U.S. courts have crafted constitutional limitations on the ability of the states to interfere with interstate economic mobility, even where Congress has not regulated.

The prospect that those involved in WTO dispute settlement could learn to do their job better by studying the U.S. Commerce clause jurisprudence is, however, put in question by the main existing comparative article on the DCC and the GATT, by Daniel Farber and Robert Hudec.[10] This article purports to show that the U.S. courts' jurisprudence on the dormant Commerce Clause is really as "diplomatic" and results-oriented, and indeed lacking in doctrinal principle, as that of GATT panels on analogous issues, particularly the dividing line between protectionism and benign or normal regulation.[11] There is the implication that Americans should be more tolerant of apparently unprincipled decisionmaking of GATT panels in dealing with the trade law/regulatory state interface, since their own courts have been doing much the same kind of job. Indeed, Farber and Hudec even appear to suggest that the GATT is more deferential to non-free trade regulatory goals than the DCC: "The carefully stated exceptions found in GATT Article XX represent an acknowledgment by the GATT's drafters that certain national regulatory goals have a high enough priority to override GATT's free trade goals in case of true conflict."[12]

However, to properly assess the implications of the dormant Commerce Clause jurisprudence requires serious attention to the jurisprudential techniques of the U.S. courts and to constitutional and regulatory context. Once one pays such attention, a striking contrast emerges, almost opposite in character to the thrust of the Farber and Hudec article: while GATT panels have been given an explicit mandate to manage the potential conflict between free trade and other values with a degree of deference to the regulatory state, they have virtually never accepted an Art. XX justification for an otherwise GATT-inconsistent measure, the U.S. courts—even without need of such a mandate—have worked their way to an approach that gives the regulatory state a legitimate place, not simply to be trumped by the requirements of free trade. In some respects then this paper is a challenge to, and hopefully a corrective to the Farber and Hudec article. It also reflects jurisprudence—both WTO and DCC—subsequent to that article, which of course (in fairness) could not have been dealt with by its authors.

My intent is to open up the real possibility of learning something important from the jurisprudence of internal economic integration in federal states like the U.S. I shall argue that in a number of respects DCC doctrine reflects useful insights for defining the proper role for a tribunal in managing the interface between free trade norms and the regulatory state. These are insights that WTO panels could well learn something from, especially with respect to the institutional sensitivity required when scrutinizing democratically legitimate domestic regulatory outcomes.

## 1. Regulation, Deregulation, and the Commerce Clause

Under the DCC, regulation that negatively affects interstate commerce is subject to constitutional scrutiny. Measures that discriminate on their face against interstate commerce, or in "practical effect"[13] will be found unconstitutional, unless it can be shown that no other means is available to achieve a legitimate state objective.[14] By contrast, non-discriminatory measures which incidentally affect interstate commerce will only be struck down where the burden on such commerce is significant or substantial, and the measures fail to provide *any* plausible regulatory benefit. Indeed, it has been persuasively argued that, in the case of non-discriminatory measures, only those that create real or potential multiple and/or conflicting requirements for businesses operating across state lines, or impose unjustified burdens on the interstate transportation or communications network, or constitute extraterritorial exercises of jurisdiction are actually invalidated by the Supreme Court.[15]

As Farber and Hudec acknowledge, "DCC law and GATT law operate in two quite different institutional settings. . ."[16] Foremost among these is that the restrictions on state government interference with interstate commerce in the "dormant" Commerce Clause do not derive from the concept of market freedom and laissez faire at all—they derive from the explicit mandate of the U.S. Congress to *regulate* interstate commerce, i.e., from the non-dormant Commerce Clause.[17]

Implicit in the mandate of Congress to deal with interstate commerce, is the notion that parochial or protectionist interference with interstate commerce by *state* governments is presumptively unconstitutional, and this is what is referred to as the dormant Commerce Clause. However, because this notion is derived from the powers of Congress, Congress can pre-empt its operation, authorizing any protectionist measure it so chooses as long as this is done explicitly. Thus, in many cases involving the dormant Commerce clause a major legal issue is whether Congress has provided a sufficiently clear mandate to the states to enact the kind of regulation in question. In sum, the dormant Commerce clause does not constitutionalize the ideology of free trade.[18]

As Ann-Marie Slaughter has pointed out in an important article on the origins of the Bretton Woods institutions, the free trade guarantees that became the GATT were originally part of a package of institutions for global economic *regulation*.[19] The design of these institutions, as she shows, was closely related to New Deal thinking about the regulatory state. With the failure, however, to launch the International Trade Organization, which would among other things have dealt with workers' rights and competition policy, a regime for free, or freer, trade came into being (the GATT), which was removed from its intended context of global social and economic regulation. From the perspective of this (stunted) regime, regulation came to be primarily viewed as something *domestic*, either irrelevant to free trade (if "normal" or non-protectionist) or threatening to it, if suspected to be protectionist.

There is a basic difference between the impact of a U.S. court decision that a state regulatory measure violates the Commerce clause and a decision by the WTO dispute settlement organs that a Member's regulatory measure is a violation of a WTO Agreement. In the former case, there is always a democratic safety valve—if there is sufficient public discontent with the way that the court has adjudicated conflicting values (say, free trade and environmental protection), another level of democratic governance exists (the federal level), where the balance can be re-struck. In the case of measures impugned by a WTO ruling, however, there is no real democratic escape from the result.[20] Farber and Hudec blunt this difference by suggesting: "In the DCC context, Congress can implement the policy itself or authorize the state to do so. Under GATT, political negotiation or outright disobedience are like alternatives to compliance."[21] But this is hardly a relevant comparison. First of all, disobedience to the law is always a *factually* possible response to a democratically unacceptable legal ruling, but obviously often has a very high price.[22] Secondly, political negotiation—which presumably means getting the party that won to forbear, perhaps in return for compensation—depends on the agreement of others who do not form part of a common democratic community with those whose regulatory choices have been constrained.

Thus, on the basis of a misleading analogy, Farber and Hudec are able to largely discount the special role of Congressional regulation of interstate commerce in the functioning of the dormant Commerce clause. Accordingly, they do not consider the crucial possibility that WTO panels might well need to operate with a higher level of deference to democratic regulatory choices than a U.S. court in a comparable DCC case, because there is no higher level of democratic community that is able to intervene to reinstate those regulatory choices, or—more likely—to provide a general transboundary regulatory scheme that takes into account the interests of both the importing and exporting jurisdiction, indeed of all relevant jurisdictions. What is striking once this possibility comes into view is that the U.S. Supreme Court is so much more sensitive to the demands of democratic regulation than GATT/WTO panels have been, even though there is a democratic safety valve in the form of federal regulatory authority.

## 2. Institutional Sensitivity in the Scrutiny of Regulatory Choices

A good example of institutional sensitivity with which to begin is the application of the dormant Commerce clause is the case of *Maine v. Taylor*.[23] In this case, the prohibition by the state of Maine of all imports of a bait fish was challenged under the dormant Commerce Clause. Since the state did not prohibit *intra*state commerce in bait fish, this measure was regarded under established Commerce Clause doctrine as a measure that discriminates on its face against interstate trade, thus requiring strict justification as the least restrictive means available to achieve the state's legitimate objective.[24]

Here, the legitimate objective was the protection of the state's wildlife populations from parasites. At trial, expert testimony was heard from the prosecution to the effect that parasites specific to other jurisdictions could have harmful impacts on Maine's fisheries, while the expert for the importer challenging the ban claimed that there was no scientific evidence of harm. The prosecution established that no existing method was available less restrictive of trade to deal with the risk, since inspection techniques of proven effectiveness did not exist. The importer's expert claimed that such techniques could be developed for bait fish, as had been done for salmonids, but had not been developed precisely because of lack of scientific evidence that they posed a risk.

In approaching the problem, the Supreme Court displayed how strict scrutiny under a least restrictive means test may undertaken in a manner compatible with sensitivity to the real world of democratic regulation. The Court upheld the trial judgment which found that the Maine ban passed strict scrutiny as a least-restrictive means, reversing the Appeal Court which had overruled the trial judgment.

First of all, in addressing the possibility that inspection techniques could be developed to detect parasites in bait fish, the Court noted that the standard against which less restrictive alternatives are to be assessed is the real world, not the best of all possible worlds: "we agree with the District Court that the "abstract possibility" . . ., particularly when there is no assurance as to their effectiveness, does not make these procedures [an available non-discriminatory alternative]."[25] Secondly, one of the reasons why the Court was unwilling to impose a burden on the state of developing a currently unavailable least-restrictive alternative was its "uncertain cost." The Court noted that exporters, or would- be exporters of bait fish were free to develop or invest in the development of inspection procedures, and once such procedures were developed, Maine's ban might no longer qualify as a least restrictive alternative.

I believe this is finding of considerable interest and importance. If the ideal first-best alternative is inspection—i.e., the alternative that best reconciles free trade with the regulatory goal of protecting wildlife—then the question still remains: who should bear the additional costs of that alternative? The Court's suggestion that exporters and by implication consumers of bait fish should bear these costs, not the democratic community as a whole, reflects what one might call an anti-Lochnerist perspective on the relationship between free trade and the regulatory state—regulation isn't an imposition on a "laissez-faire" norm for which the democratic community must pay the full price of assuring that it is the least possible interference with free markets. The idea developed by the Court of the state being held only to "reasonable efforts" to adopt the least restrictive means thus suggests a balance of rights and responsibilities between democratic communities and the trading interests of outsiders.

Third, in considering the way in which the lower courts handled the conflicting scientific evidence, the court affirmed the trial court's application of what is known in international environmental law as the Precautionary Principle: "we agree with the District Court that Maine has a legitimate interest in guarding against imperfectly understood environmental risks, despite the possibility that they may ultimately prove to be negligible . . .

[quoting the district court judgment] the constitutional principles underlying the commerce clause cannot be read as requiring the State of Maine to sit idly by and wait until potentially irreversible environmental damage has occurred or until the scientific community agrees on what disease organisms are or are not dangerous before it acts to avoid such consequences."[26] Again here, the Court recognized the nature of the real world of democracy, where legislatures have a mandate to act to protect the interests of citizens, and where effectively so doing requires complex judgments, including about real world constraints on compliance, and possible perverse or secondary effects of a given regulatory instrument. In accepting the legitimacy of democratic action, as opposed to inaction, in the presence of uncertainty about risk, the Court again rejected the idea of laissez-faire as a natural baseline not to be lightly disturbed. Likewise, the Court recognized that science cannot replace practical judgment, what Aristotle calls *phroneis*, in the regulatory process.[27] Finally, and concomitantly, the Court recognized its own institutional limitations in second-guessing the practical judgments that legislators make in the presence of uncertainty.

A fourth dimension of this decision of importance in understanding the nature of institutional sensitivity to the process of democratic regulation arises from the Court's treatment of a statement by officials of the Main Department of Inland Fisheries, concerning the possible desirability of repealing the ban on importation of bait fish. The statement was relied on by the appeal court to find protectionist intent. It read in part "We can't help asking why we should spend our money in Arkansas when it is far better spent at home? It is very clear that much more can be done here in Maine to provide our sportsmen with safe, home-grown bait. There is also the possibility that such an industry could develop a lucrative export market in neighboring states."

In rejecting the finding of protectionist intent at the appeal court level, the Supreme Court made several observations about this statement. First of all, the Department was strictly speaking only dealing with the choice between increasing the safe intra-state bait supply or expending resources to ensure that imports are safe. The Court understood that "protectionism" does not exist simply because a jurisdiction fails to adopt a regulatory alternative that *prefers* imports over support of the domestic industry. Secondly, the Court observed that the context of statements of this nature must be carefully examined before inferring from them an overall protectionist purpose. Here, for example, the statement did not come from legislators themselves but from an *ex post* justification of the law by officials.

Opportunism is an inescapable dimension of liberal democratic politics—governments and politicians will not refrain from attempting to justify policies by any means that garners votes from diverse constituencies. As David Vogel notes, "[b]aptist-bootlegger alliances have long been a staple of domestic regulatory policy-making."[28]

In the presence of such coalitions, Farber and Hudec suggest that "what we really mean [by protectionist motivation] is that protectionist effect played a stronger causative role in the passage of legislation than its purported regulatory benefits."[29] Because, however, liberal democratic politics is complex, and the minds of legislators often hard to read, such a judgment is almost impossible to make—and indeed a court or tribunal would be stepping into a place in the political realm inconsistent with its institutional role in deciding as it were which interest groups really won in a regulatory outcome.[30] Farber and Hudec are relatively complacent about the idea that judgments concerning protectionist motivation will fundamentally influence the decisions both of courts and trade tribunals; because the latter are, however, so removed from the real world of regulation and regulatory politics, inferences about motive may often be little more than an intuition that a "normal" regulatory state would never have bothered about this or that risk, or saving this or that species, but for protectionism. In these circumstances, it is all too easy for the tribunal to seize on the kind of statement rightly discounted by the Court in *Maine v. Taylor*, as the "smoking gun" that proves its intuition.[31] As Farber and Hudec suggest, diplomatic sensitivities have led trade panels to largely conceal the influence of this kind of factor behind "objective" analysis of the rationales of the measures in question; in a recent case, the responding party to complain—at the stage of interim review of the panel report—about the possibility of just such covert influences on the panel's decision.[32]

An examination of the use of the least restrictive means test in scrutinizing GATT-illegal measures in *Thai Cigarette*, already alluded to, provides an instructive contrast with the institutional sensitivity of the U.S. Supreme Court in *Maine v. Taylor.*

In *Thai Cigarette*, Thailand sought to defend import restrictions and discriminatory tax treatment with respect to American cigarettes as justifiable under Art. XX(b) of the GATT as "necessary" for public health reasons.[33] Thailand argued that American cigarettes posed a particular health risk, because of their attractiveness to young people who might otherwise not take up the habit—an attractiveness in part due to advertising and marketing campaigns carefully targeted at youthful populations in developing countries. Thailand had sought to deal with the problem by a variety of measures, which included advertising bans, public information campaigns, and health warnings on cigarette packages, as well as the prima facie GATT-inconsistent measures at issue.[34] In finding that these less-restrictive alternatives were adequate to Thailand's public health purpose, the panel simple ignored evidence by the World Health Organization that opening up markets to American cigarettes in a number of Latin American and Asian countries has led to increased smoking. The WHO had found that in the real world regulatory context faced by these developing countries, U.S. multinationals had the resources to circumvent advertising bans, either finding loopholes in the laws or evading compliance efforts.[35] The panel completely ignored this real world context—it simply assumed that a regulatory state of the level of development, and under the constraints, that characterized Thailand would have the capacity to bring U.S. multinationals effectively under its regulatory control. Of course, the panel was right to point out the less-restrictive alternatives were not a completely abstract possibility, and indeed were being tried in Thailand itself: what was abstract (and simplistic) was the assumption that they would be adequately effective to achieve the Thai government's goal of preventing young people from starting to smoke, given the real world of the Thai regulatory state, and the real power imbalances that often exist between developing country regulators and large multinational firms.

### 3. Managing the Environmental Commons

In light of the controversy that has surrounded such GATT panel decisions as *Tuna/Dolphin I* and *II*, and more recently the *Turtles* case, the approach to environmentally based import and export restrictions in Commerce clause jurisprudence merits close attention. In a series of cases, beginning with *City of Philadelphia* v. *New Jersey*,[36] the U.S. Supreme Court has invalidated under the dormant Commerce Clause restrictions on the importation of toxic waste for disposal in the importing state.[37] On the other hand, the Court has sustained restrictions on exports of water for conservation purposes.[38]

In understanding how the water export restrictions were able to withstand strict scrutiny as a conservation measure, but not the waste import restrictions, it is important to pay careful attention as to how the Court characterized the environmental challenge at issue, and its view of the level—local, state, inter-state, federal—of regulation appropriate to the solution. In the waste disposal cases, the Court understood the environmental problem as national in scope: it viewed the various flow control restrictions as a "parochial" approach to a common problem, i.e., problem generated by the operation of the U.S. economy as a whole. As the Court put it in *Chemical Waste Management Inc.* v. *Hunt*, "No state may attempt to isolate itself from a problem common to the several States by raising barriers to the free flow of interstate trade."[39] Behind most of these decisions was the regulatory context of a comprehensive federal regulatory scheme which emphasized construction and operation of environmentally sound waste disposal facilities,[40] but within parameters set at the national level and under the supervision of the federal Environmental Protection Agency. In the absence of explicit authorization of border controls in the statute, the Court was prepared to view import restrictions as a beggar-thy-neighbor measure at odds with a national approach. In her concurring judgment in *Carbone v. Clarkstown*, Justice O'Connor noted, for example, that flow control measures at the state and local level were proliferating and more were being contemplated, resulting in "the type of balkanization" that the Commerce Clause "is primarily intended to prevent."[41]

In *Sporhase*, while the Court found that there was enough of a transboundary dimension to allow Congress to regulate if it so chose, the approach that had emerged to the problem throughout the country was rationally based on state and local management, with the commons dimension managed through interstate agreements or compacts.[42] Interestingly though, the Court rejected reciprocity as a basis for such interstate agreements—thus the one aspect of the scheme that was struck down in *Sporhase* was a ban on exports to states that did not grant to Nebraska reciprocal rights. The Court rightly noted that in this context such reciprocity requirements could force a state with scarce water to allow exports to one with abundant water resources. The former would have a legitimate conservation basis under the DCC to withhold exports, but not the latter.

On the whole, this jurisprudence displays some real awareness about the nature of environmental commons problems and the possible impact of trade restrictions on those problems in different contexts. After the panels in *Tuna/Dolphin* and *Turtles*[43] it is clear that WTO panels have something to learn in this respect. Once an environmental problem has been identified as having a genuine commons dimension, one would want—in determining whether trade restrictions can be justified under Art. XX for example—to understand, *given the specific context*, whether these kinds of unilateral measures are an appropriate part of the solution to that commons dimension, or whether they might even aggravate the commons problem, (which would be the case if they resulted in "beggar-thy-neighbor" effects). The crude dichotomy between unilateralism and cooperation employed in rejecting out of hand unilateral measures by panels in *Tuna/Dolphin* and *Turtles* would then be replaced by a much more subtle analysis, sensitive to the context. This is, in effect, what the Appellate Body did, in reversing the legal analysis of the *Turtles* panel and holding that there is nothing in principle that excludes unilateral measures from justification under Art. XX: "It is not necessary to assume that requiring from exporting countries compliance with, or adoption of, certain policies (although covered in principle by one or another of the exceptions) prescribed by the importing country, renders a measure *a priori* incapable of justification under Article XX. Such an interpretation renders, most, if not all, of the specific exceptions of Article XX inutile, a result abhorrent to the principles of interpretation we are bound to apply."[44]

Let us take, first of all, the case where the trade restrictions are specifically authorized, even if not required, by a multilateral environmental agreement. Whether or not one or both parties to the dispute have signed the agreement, it nevertheless represents an indication of a policy shared by a range of legitimate actors that such measures are part of an appropriate solution to the commons problem at issue.

A second case would be unilateral measures to deal with a commons problem that are neither authorized nor required by any mulitlateral agreement, such as the ban on imports of turtle-unfriendly shrimp at issue in the *Turtles* case. In the case of *National Solid Wastes Management Ass'n. v. Meyer*,[45] the U.S. Court of Appeals, Seventh Circuit invalidated a Wisconsin law that conditioned access of solid waste to Wisconsin facilities on the community where the waste originated out-of-state having recycling standards comparable to Wisconsin's. The basis for this decision was that, because the condition did not apply only to the waste accepted by Wisconsin but all waste produced in the other state, it regulated commerce *wholly* outside the boundaries of Wisconsin. This was not unlike the judicial interpretation (now reversed by the Court of Appeals) of the scheme which confronted the panel in *Turtles*, which had been held by the U.S. Court of International Trade to entail banning all shrimp from countries that had not adopted a requirement of Turtle-Excluding Device (T.E.D.) technology, regardless of whether the actual shrimp imported had been caught with such technology. Unlike the WTO panel, the Court of Appeals, following the Supreme Court in the early case of *Healy*,[46] did not simply conflate two different normative issues: the first is whether such a measure is a discriminatory trade restriction and invalid because it cannot be justified as the least restrictive alternative to achieve the environmental objectives; the second is whether it is *per se* invalid because it violates some rule against extraterritoriality.

The prohibition on extraterritorial regulation by U.S. states is of course concomitant with the main thrust of the Commerce clause—the authority of *Congress* to regulate interstate commerce. Reading such a prohibition into a international trade regime, in the absence of a world government, or international regulatory authority with the capacity to address commons problems, is quite a different proposition. And apart from such a norm, which is connected with a *federal* system of regulatory power, whether such extraterritorial regulation can be justified as a trade restriction should depend on the context, and the regulatory alternatives available. Unlike the panel in *Turtles*, the Appellate Body, instead of simply assuming or reading into the GATT a presumed absolute rule against extraterritoriality, explored the actual state of international law on this issue in the course of interpreting Art. XX, and was careful not to collapse the issue of extraterritoriality into the issue of discrimination or protectionism. Thus, having found that under international environmental law unilateral extraterritorial action is regarded as acceptable only where serious efforts at a cooperative solution, e.g. through a negotiated agreement, have failed, the AB applied the wording of the chapeau of Art. XX on "arbitrary discrimination" against this baseline; the United States had made serious efforts to negotiate a solution with some countries in the Western hemisphere, which had resulted in a resolution of the problem through a treaty. Based upon (the arguably suspect) finding of fact of the panel below that similarly vigorous efforts had not been extended to the complainant countries, the AB found that this constituted "arbitrary discrimination" under the *chapeau.*

On this approach, if the first-best solution is transboundary regulation, then under Art. XX a fundamental issue will be the interaction of the unilateral measures in question with such a solution. Let us alter the facts in *Turtles* for a moment. Assume that an international regulatory regime existed, support by a significant number of states, that dealt with turtle mortality through a technology called XYZ. Dissatisfied with that regime, the United States decided to break out of the regime and instead unilaterally require T.E.D. technology as a condition of imports. In such an instance, the U.S. unilateral measure would seem to undermine the first-best solution to the commons problem. Of course, if the international regime were a sham, or never enforced, that would be a different matter. But to the extent that functional transboundary regulation exists to deal with a commons problem one should be very reluctant to conclude that unilateral measures are permissible under Art. XX, where they conflict with the transboundary regulatory scheme.

One factor that should influence an assessment of the place of unilateral trade measures in addressing a commons problem is whether these measures have "beggar-thy-neighbor" or contagion affects such as those the Court identified with waste import restrictions in *Carbone*. In *Turtles*, the general *kind* of measure adopted by the United States was speculated by the panel to, hypothetically, have exactly such effects, potential leading to a chaos of conflicting attempts at unilateral regulation. Yet the *Carbone* court was surely right in considering this as dependent on the context, not an inherent property of unilateralism as such. In the case of waste, it is easy to understand why lack of access to disposal facilities in other states would lead a state to guard its own facilities for itself. It is much harder in *Turtles* to see how the U.S. measures would provoke a spiral of conflicting unilateral measures by other countries.

The fundamental issue is determining whether unilateral measures are part of a beggar-thy-neighbor strategy, as opposed to a positive contribution to the solution of a commons problems, is whether the measures purport to shift the environmental costs onto others, while retaining the gains from exploitation of the environment for oneself. Thus, in considering the water export restrictions as justified in *Sporhase*, the Court placed considerable emphasis on the fact that the restricting state imposed a significant conservation burden on its own residents; it noted that the "State imposes severe withdrawal and use restrictions on its own citizens . . ."[47] Conversely, in the non-environmental case of *Kassel*, which concerned length limitations on trucks, a factor in impugning the law in question—even though not discriminatory on its face—was that it allowed certain exceptions that reduced the burden on in-state truckers but did not apply to those from out-of-state.[48] It noted: "Iowa's scheme, although generally banning large doubles from the State, nevertheless has several exemptions that secure to Iowans many of the benefits of large trucks while shunting to neighboring States many of the costs associated with their use."[49] This is precisely the kind of analysis that is appropriate under the "arbitrary and unjustified restriction on trade" rubric of the chapeau of Art. XX. This is illustrated by the WTO Appellate Body ruling in *Reformulated Gasoline*, where the AB placed emphasis on the fact that in designing its regulatory scheme, the United States had been attentive to the costs of regulatory compliance faced by domestic refiners but not those faced by foreign refiners.[50]

In its arbitrary approach of excluding per se from justification under Art. XX measures such as those at issue in *Turtles*, the panel of course ignored these considerations (as well as misapplying the jurisprudence of the AB). But it is significant that the record of the case shows that such matters were very much on the minds of the parties. Was the United States imposing an unreasonable amount of the costs of the commons problem on other countries? The developing country complainants argued that the economic position of their shrimp industries was such that a significant burden would be involved in the acquisition of TED technology, relative to that which the industry in a rich country like the United States faced. The U.S. responded that it had provided considerable technical assistance to a number of developing countries, allowing shrimpers to adopt the technology at very low cost. The U.S. also pointed out (to my mind a very telling consideration) that a various developing countries had adopted the technology without an apparently undue burden on their shrimping industries.

Rightly, at the appellate level, there was a rejection of the *Turtles* panel's view that hypothetical "spiral" effects do not simply remove whole generic classes of measures from the possibility of justification under Art. XX. Instead, the Appellate Body engaged precisely in a more contextual analysis of whether the application of the U.S. measures constituted "unjustified discrimination" between countries "where similar conditions prevail" within the meaning of the *chapeau* of Art. XX. The AB held that the rigid application of the U.S. regulatory standard—the use of T.E.D. devices—as a condition for access of imports constituted "unjustified" discrimination of a "disparate impact" character, since other countries, with different circumstances, might more appropriately achieve the same regulatory objective (reduction of turtle mortality) through other, comparable means. Indeed, the AB noted that the U.S. statute itself had wording that allowed access for shrimp caught with other methods that achieved similar positive environmental results.

## 4. Non-Discriminatory Regulatory Measures

As was noted at the outset of this paper, a fundamental characteristic of DCC analysis is a sharp distinction between measures that discriminate on their face against interstate commerce or in "their practical effect" and those that merely affect interstate commerce incidentally. The former, as noted, must survive strict scrutiny under a least-restrictive-means test to be upheld as constitutional. The latter are subject to a much more deferential standard of review. One criterion for distinguishing between these two categories is the degree of "evenhandedness" of the regulation—if a measure affects interstate commerce, for example by imposing a distinctive regulatory requirement that is different from what is standard in other jurisdictions, but doesn't as such impose greater costs on out-of-state actors, it may be considered to only incidentally affect interstate commerce, and therefore be upheld as long as there is at least some genuine regulatory benefit and the burden on interstate commerce is not extraordinarily severe. The distinction between these two categories is of course often not clear-cut—at what point a burden is no longer "incidental" to a evenhanded scheme and constitutes instead de facto discrimination is often difficult to determine. As noted above, it would seem to be the case that non-discriminatory measures are only thus invalidated if they fall into one of several specific categories, namely conflicting or potentially conflicting requirements on actors engaged in inter-state commerce, burdens on inter-state transportation and communication infrastructure, or extraterritorial measures.

Yet the idea that a different approach may be appropriate for measures the trade impact of which is simply intrinsic to the existence of regulatory diversity, and those that are discriminatory, may be useful to consider in respect of some of the difficult interpretive issues posed by the WTO Technical Barriers to Trade (TBT) and Sanitary and Phytosanitary)(SPS) codes, and their relationship to Art. III, Art. XI, and XX of the GATT. Traditionally the issue of justification of domestic regulation has arisen under the GATT where a measure has been found to be discriminatory (i.e., a violation of Art. III and or Art. I) or a direct barrier to trade (Art. XI), and where the enacting state seeks to justify it under one of the heads in Art. XX. This parallels the category of measures that attract strict scrutiny under the U.S. Commerce clause. Superimposed on this tradition is now an SPS Agreement that both alters and refines the process of strict scrutiny of these kinds of measures (violations of articles of the GATT such as III and XI), but also creates a basis for scrutinizing measures that are not violations, but which may place an incidental burden on international trade by virtue of their divergence from international standards, which can lead to conflicting or multiple requirements that increase the transaction costs of international transactions (this category of non-discriminatory measures, as noted above, may run afoul of the DCC, as well).

Thus, Art. 3 of the SPS Agreement creates a qualified obligation to base *all* measures on international standards, whether they would otherwise be violations of National Treatment or some other anti-protectionist GATT rule, as well as supplementing Art. XX by creating a new justification for GATT-inconsistent measures, i.e., that they conform to international standards (Art. 3.3). At the same time, the SPS Agreement lays out a set of criteria to which all SPS measures not based on international standards must conform regardless of whether these measures are violations of any anti-protectionist rule in the GATT.

The manner in which the panel in the *Beef Hormone*[51] case read the SPS Agreement reflects the tradition of dealing with GATT-inconsistent measures that a member is seeking to justify under Art. XX—the tradition of strict scrutiny. Had the panel's ruling on issues like burden of proof stood, it would have converted the SPS Agreement into a strict scrutiny regime even for non-discriminatory measures, which have not been shown to violate provisions of the GATT. This would have placed WTO panels in a role of close oversight with respect to the general regulatory process that the U.S. courts have refused to play even within the context of a single federal state. The WTO Appellate Body, on a range of issues, including burden of proof, interpreted the SPS Agreement as providing for a more deferential examination of SPS regulations than the panel had undertaken. The AB was, in part, considering provisions that left open to some extent the degree of fit required between an assessed risk and the measure in question. These provisions required that SPS measures be "based on an assessment, as appropriate to the circumstances, of the risks to human, animal or plant life or health, . . ."[52] It viewed "based on" as implying the existence of *some* rational basis for a measure in assessed risks—a measure could still be based on a risk assessment even if scientific opinion were divided or uncertain. All that was required in the evidence represented by a risk assessment was some support for the connection being drawn by the government between the measure in question and the reduction or elimination of the identified risks. It is worth citing the AB's analysis in full: "We do not believe that a risk assessment has to come to a monolithic conclusion that coincides with the scientific conclusion or view implicit in the SPS measure. The risk assessment could set out both the prevailing view representing the "mainstream" of scientific opinion, as well as the opinions of scientists taking a divergent view. Article 5.1 does not require that the risk assessment must necessarily embody only the view of a majority of the scientific community. In some cases, the very existence of divergent views presented by qualified scientists who have investigated the particular issue at hand may indicate a state of scientific uncertainty. Sometimes the divergence may indicate a roughly equal balance of scientific opinion. In most cases, responsible, and representative governments tend to base their legislative and administrative measures on "mainstream" scientific opinion. In other cases, equally responsible and representative governments may act in good faith on the basis of what, at a given time, may be a divergent opinion coming from qualified and respected sources. By itself, this does not necessarily signal the absence of a reasonable relationship between the SPS measure and the risk assessment, especially where the risk involved is life-threatening in character and is perceived to constitute a clear and imminent threat to public health and safety. Determination of the presence or absence of that relationship can only be done on a case-to-case basis, after account is taken of all considerations rationally bearing upon the issue of potential health effects."[53]

This notion of rational basis or rational connection obviously provides regulators with much more leeway to reflect democratic preferences than would the imposition of some rigid conception of a balance of costs and benefits, or proportionality.[54] This is similar to the leeway that the DCC jurisprudence affords regulators in the case of measures that are non-discriminatory within the meaning of the jurisprudence, only incidentally affecting interstate trade. Thus, unless the Court can conclude on the whole record that "the total effect of the law as a safety measures in reducing accidents and casualties is so slight or problematical as not to outweigh the national interest in keeping interstate commerce free from interferences which seriously impede it" the statute will be upheld.[55] The Court's concern is that there be some legitimate, reasonable basis, that the "safety benefits not be illusory"; if this is the case, "the Court will not second-guess legislative judgment about [the importance of the safety justifications] in comparison with related burdens on interstate commerce."[56] As Justice Brennan states in his concurring judgment in *Kassel,* "[I]t is not the function of the court to decide whether *in fact* the regulation promotes its promotes its intended purpose, so long as an examination of the evidence before or available to the lawmaker indicates the regulation is not wholly irrational in light of its purposes."[57]

This analysis, consistent with the approach taken by the AB in *Hormones*, reflects a sensible and sensitive view of the appropriate role of a court or tribunal in overseeing general regulatory processes from a free trade perspective. Regulation of risks is a norm in the modern regulatory state, not an exceptional, and inherently suspicious intervention in free markets; free trade rules and norms should not be interpreted so as to countenance massive and relentless interference in this process of by courts or tribunals, second-guessing the justification for regulatory outcomes. Such bodies have several comparative disadvantages in playing such a role—they are removed from the regulatory context (*a fortiori* for international trade tribunals); they are not directly accountable to the democratic community in question; and they lack any special expertise to rewrite or redo the kind of analysis and trade-offs that occurs in the domestic regulatory process.[58] As judicial or quasi-judicial bodies they can of course claim to have a role in assessing evidence for its existence, testing whether it is fraudulent or biased, and scrutinizing the rationality of policy conclusions drawn from a particular empirical premise. But they have very little legitimacy to re-work judgment calls made in the domestic democratic regulatory process under conditions of scientific controversy, limited information, etc.—i.e., all the real world constraints on democratic regulation.[59]

Yet old habits die hard in Geneva—in a recent panel decision also based on the SPS Code,[60] a panel misapplied the reasonableness standard articulated by the Appellate Body in *Hormones*, replacing its own inferences from a risk assessment as to the extent to which the regulatory measure in question would serve the disease-prevention goals of the Australian government. The regulatory measure was a heat-treatment requirement for importation of almost all uncanned salmon into Australia, which effectively barred access to the market for fresh, uncooked salmon. Australia sought to base its measure on a 1996 document, "Salmon Import Risk Analysis, Final

Report." The Report clearly suggested that there was some rational basis for heat treatment as a means of destroying agents of disease in the fish, but noted that there might be some agents resistant such treatment, and that comprehensive data on the effects of heat treatment were not yet available. Indeed, the Report concluded: "Most fish pathogens would be expected to be readily inactivated by heat. . .,"[61] i.e., on the basis of normal scientific principles. Ignoring this judgment, the panel zeroed in on the qualifications and limitations in scientific evidence in the 1996 study, coming to the conclusion that it provided no rational basis for heat treatment. The panel used the study's own caution to simply invalidate its recommendation that, given the kind of risk involved, and even considering the limits of the empirical evidence on heat treatment, maintaining such precautions was desirable. In defense of this manipulation of the 1996 risk assessment, the panel cited a 1995 document, the BRS Report, which endorsed the panel's view that the uncertainty and ambiguity of the existing empirical evidence deprived heat treatment of a rational basis.[62] The panel considered that this raised a presumption of no rational basis that Australia would have to rebut. Of course, Australia could not provide such a rebuttal, at least without considerable new empirical work. But nor did it need to under the terms of Art. 5—as the AB stated clearly in *Hormones*, in precisely such a situation of divided scientific opinion, a "responsible and representative government" has the prerogative to make its own judgment about the existence of a rational basis, as long as there is some scientific support for the choice it makes. Australia, following the "bottom line" in the 1996 Report exercised this prerogative, and decided that the uncertainties of the empirical evidence with respect to heat treatment, did not justify as yet removing measures based on the general scientific principle of the effectiveness of heat treatment in killing pathogens, a principle which the 1996 Report had obviously found not to have been refuted by the empirical evidence to date, even if some of this evidence might point to limited effectiveness in the case of certain particular pathogens. These are precisely the kinds of judgment calls that the U.S. Supreme Court has understood itself as not well-positioned to second-guess. And as the AB grasped in *Hormones*, panels don't have the qualifications and institutional legitimacy to do so, either.

Upon appeal, the panel in *Salmon* was found to have erred in identifying the measure under scrutiny as heat treatment rather than an import ban (which was really what Canada had complained about), and also in finding that the Australian document was an adequate risk assessment.[63] On this last issue, the Appellate Body relied upon the panel's own characterization of the Australian risk analysis as vague or imprecise in a number of respects, in overruling the panel's judgment that despite these defects the document qualified as a scientific assessment of risk within the meaning of the SPS Agreement. This result is not entirely unreasonable—Australia failed entirely to explain its use of a risk analysis that was less precise and specific than the 1995 document.

The protection of animal and human life and health in most liberal democracies generates many thousands of legitimate regulatory initiatives; the *Salmon* panel found that the risk assessment provided by Australia was defective in various respects as against the standards in the SPS Agreement as interpreted by *scientific experts*. But the panel was right not to come to an automatic finding that the risk assessment was inadequate for purposes of trade law. As the U.S. Supreme Court recognized in *Maine v. Taylor*, there are limits to the resources that real-world governments can spend to investigate all possible individual risks and alternative risk responses prior to enacting regulations. Too high a threshold for a "risk assessment" under the SPS Agreement would result in de facto substantive constraints on the ability to regulate to which Members never agreed. In *Salmon*, Australia produced a document of several hundred pages with extensive scientific and regulatory analysis of the problem.

It is frightening to contemplate the implication of the AB Report that even more is required as a pre-condition for *every* SPS regulation a Member chooses to enact, or has enacted.

This does not mean that SPS measures should never be subject to the kind of (nevertheless context-specific) strict scrutiny that is reserved for discriminatory measures in DCC jurisprudence. As the panel in *Salmon* correctly found, the GATT 1994 and the SPS Agreement operate co-terminously; this means that, to the extent not based on international standards, if found to violate Art. III or XI of the GATT, these measures would still have to be justified under the least restrictive means test of Art. XX, as "necessary" for health and safety purposes.[64]

There is a relaxed version of this test built into the SPS Code itself, in Art. 5.6 which requires that "Members shall ensure that [SPS] measures are not more trade-restrictive than required to achieve their appropriate level of sanitary or phytosanitary protection, taking into account technical and economic feasibility." The less-restrictive alternative must be "reasonably available" and must be "significantly less restrictive to trade" (fn. 3).[65]

In *Salmon*, there was clearly some empirical evidence that put in question the effectiveness of heat treatment in some cases, and the possibility that exhaustive empirical work might show that less restrictive alternatives would offer a comparable level of safety. Nevertheless, there was a rational basis for Australia to choose heat treatment, as I have argued. Part of the issue here, then, is who should bear the cost of undertaking the comprehensive empirical work that might justify or finally show a lack of justification for the regulation in question. The panel's approach suggests that the responsibility is Australia's, not that of those who seek to gain access for their imports to Australia, once the complainant has raised a "presumption" that less-restrictive alternatives exist in the abstract. Thus, in significant measure the panel based its judgment that less-restrictive alternatives existed on a statement of an international regulatory organization that eviscerated fish present a minimal health risk, without even considering whether an evisceration requirement would be an economically and technically feasible alternative in the Australian context, or for that matter, whether the level of risk which that organization considered "minimal" was accorded with Australia's own chosen appropriate level of protection.[66]

This is a clearly erroneous interpretation of the SPS Agreement taken as a whole. If the regulatory judgments of an international organization that less-restrictive alternatives exist to achieve a level of protection that the *organization* deems appropriate were to result in a presumption that the SPS agreement had been violated, as the panel seems to be saying, then the right of Members under 3.3. to "introduce or maintain sanitary or phytosanitary measures which result in a *higher* level of protection than would be achieved by measures based on the relevant *international* standards, guidelines or recommendations" (emphasis added) would effectively be eviscerated.

This brings us back to the issue of balance of rights and responsibilities between the democratic community and free trade interests. In *Maine* v. *Taylor,* it will be recalled, the U.S. Supreme Court, dealing with a case of strict scrutiny of a discriminatory measure, limited the responsibility of the regulating jurisdiction to the adoption of less restrictive alternatives, where there feasibility and effectiveness had already been established; if importing interests wanted such alternatives to be chosen, they were free to establish the feasibility and effectiveness of such alternatives, at their own expense. In the case of measures that simply incidentally affect interstate commerce, the requirement that there be *some* rational basis for the measure, if anything implies a balance of rights and responsibilities even more favorable to democratic communities.

## 5. Conclusion

The jurisprudence of the dormant Commerce Clause can provide a useful reference point for critical reflection on the way the WTO panels have managed the interface between free trade rules and the regulatory state. The constraints on state regulation imposed by the dormant Commerce Clause occur in a context where the balance between state and market can always be re-struck by a higher democratic authority, the U.S. Congress. Nevertheless, despite a far more obvious and effective democratic safety valve, the U.S. Supreme Court in many respects proves more cautious in disrupting putatively legitimate regulatory outcomes than do WTO panels.

Perhaps this is because the U.S. Court has self-consciously reflected on its more general role within the modern regulatory state, and also because the U.S. Commerce Clause itself is not a laissez-faire charter, but a scheme for organizing the division of regulatory authority over commerce in a manner consistent with the federal principle. If WTO dispute settlement is to retain and enhance its legitimacy, a better understanding and appreciation is needed of the multi-layer regulatory world in which the multilateral trading regime functions. Regulatory economists and lawyers need to devote more attention to the multilateral trading regime, and conversely trade policy analysts need to go back to school with the public philosophers and jurists of the modern regulatory state—the school in which, as Anne Marie Slaughter[67] has shown, the architects of Bretton Woods were themselves educated, the cosmopolitan offspring of the New Deal. Consideration of the DCC jurisprudence of the U.S. Supreme Court is merely an adumbration of some of the changes in perspective and approach to which such an education might lead.

## NOTES

1. *United States—Restrictions on Imports of Tuna,* 30 I.L.M. 1594; *United States—Restrictions on Imports of Tuna,* (1994) 33 I.L.M. 936.

2. For a critique of the unadopted reports along these lines, see Michael J. Trebilcock and Robert Howse, *The Regulation of International Trade* (London and New York: Routledge, 1995), 2nd ed. Forthcoming, 1998, "Ch. 15: Trade and the Environment"; see also H. Chang, "An Economic Analysis of Trade Measures to Protect the Global Environment" (1995) 83 *Georgetown Law Journal* 4; B. Kingsbury, "The Tuna-Dolphin Controversy, The World Trade Organization, and the Liberal Project to Reconceptualize International Law, *Yearbook of International Environmental Law 1995* (Oxford: Oxford University Press, 1995). But for a defense of the general approach in these panel reports, see Thomas Schoenbaum, "International Trade and the Environment: The Continuing Search for Reconciliation,"(1997) 91 *American Journal of International Law* 268.

3. *Thailand-Restrictions on Importation of and Internal Taxes on Cigarettes,* Report of the Panel (1990).

4. See Michael Trebilcock and Robert Howse, "Trade Liberalization and Regulatory Diversity: Reconciling Competitive Markets with Competitive Politics," *European Journal of Law and Economics,* July 1998, at 33.

5. This is the view to which E-U. Petersmann tends. See "Trade Policy as a Constitutional Problem. On the "Domestic Policy Functions" of International Trade Rules," (1986) 41 *Aussenwirtschaft* 405. I actually support the notion that in domestic policy debate it is always important to pose the issue of how policy objectives can best be obtained with the least loss to the welfare gains from free trade, and to move the constraints that limit the adoption of such

first-best alternatives. But because of the issue of democratic legitimacy, I do not think the application of this abstract approach by the WTO dispute settlement organs is appropriate in evaluating actual outcomes of the democratic process. This is in part due to a disagreement with Petersmann that trade law should be viewed as a means of saving democracy from its own imperfections (interest group capture, etc.)

6. See, for example, *United States-Standards for Reformulated and Conventional Gasoline,* Report of the Appellate Body (1996), 16–18; *Japan-Taxes on Alcoholic Beverages,* Report of the Appellate Body (1996).

7. See P. Nichols, "Comments on Ch. 5," in J. S. Bhandari and A. O. Sykes, eds., *Economic Dimensions in international law: comparative and empirical perspectives* (Cambridge: Cambridge University Press, 1997), at 238–239.

8. Cass R. Sunstein, "Lochner"s Legacy," (1987) Colum. L. Rev. 875.

9. As an understanding and analysis of these techniques and approaches, Cass R. Sunstein, *After the Rights Revolution: Reconceiving the Regulatory State* (Cambridge: Harvard University Press, 1990) is a work of central importance, and has enormously influenced my view of these matters.

10. D. Farber and R. E. Hudec, "Free Trade and the Regulatory State: A GATT's Eye View of the Dormant Commerce Clause" (1994) 47 Vand. L.Rev. 1401 [Hereinafter, "Free Trade and the Regulatory State"].

11. See especially the conclusion at 1440: "Despite the great conceptual difficulties posed by regulatory trade barriers, both U.S. and international tribunals seem largely to have struggled their way to defensible results. Because of the difficulty of constructing a clear doctrinal solution, the quality of the process, and that of the decision makers, is and will remain crucial."

12. Ibid, at 1421.

13. *Healy et al.* v. *Beer Institute et al.*, 491 U.S. 324 at 336.

14. *Maine* v. *Taylor,* 477 U.S. 131 (1986).

15. D. Regan, "The Supreme Court and State Protectionism: Making Sense of the Dormant Commerce Clause," 84 *Michigan Law Review* 1091 (1986); D. Regan, "Movement of Goods Under the Dormant Commerce Clause and the European Community Treaty," forthcoming, Kluwer, 1999, 9.

16. Ibid, 1403.

17. The clause states that "[the] Congress shall have Power . . . To regulate Commerce among the several States." U.S. Const. Art I, 8, cl. 3.

18. See Julian N. Eule, "Laying the Dormant Commerce Clause to Rest" (1982) 91 *Yale L.J.* 425.

19. A. M. Burley-Slaughter, "Regulating the World: Multilateralism, International Law, and the Projection of the New Deal Regulatory State" in J. Ruggie, ed., *Multilateralism Matters: The Theory and Praxis of an Institutional Form* (New York: Columbia University Press, 1993).

20. Trebilcock and Howse, "Trade Liberalization and Regulatory Diversity: Reconciling Competitive Markets with Competitive Politics," supra n. 1, at 33: "In adopting approaches that rely upon negative Commerce Clause type jurisprudence in the United States, or European

Court jurisprudence, trade panels must remember a key difference between the WTO and these regimes—the latter provide institutional mechanisms for positive harmonization which can be availed of where negative integration through judicial or quasi-judicial enforcement proves inadequate, or does undue damage to non-trade policy objectives. There are no equivalent political or regulatory institutions available to provide a safety valve within the WTO, . . ."

21. "Free Trade and the Regulatory State," at 1407.

22. See John H. Jackson, "The WTO Dispute Settlement Understanding—Misunderstandings on the Nature of Legal Obligation," (1997) 91 *American Journal of International Law* 60.

23. 477 U.S. 131.

24. *Hughes v. Oklahoma,* 441 U.S. 322 (1979).

25. 477 U.S. 131, at 147.

26. 477 U.S. 131, at 148.

27. A similar recognition of the importance of practical judgment is to be found in the way the Court rejects the imposition of "scientific" or technocratic cost-benefit analysis on non-discriminatory state regulation that has incidental effects on inter-state commerce.

28. David Vogel, *Trading Up: Consumer and Environmental Protection in A Global Economy* Cambridge, MA: Harvard University Press, 1995.

29. "Free Trade and the Regulatory State."

30. Indeed, in a pluralistic society, there may be important reasons of principle for courts not to pronounce on what rationale for a particular law or policy is predominate or decisive. Preserving a diversity of rationales for an outcome may be part of preserving the possibility of legitimate regulation in a society characterized by diverse legitimate interests and values. See in general Cass Sunstein, *Legal Reasoning and Political Conflict* (Oxford: Oxford University Press, 1996), especially the Introduction, "Law Amid Diversity." This argument would not apply to rationales that are per se illegitimate, for example racist rationales for racial classifications in legislation; but at least in the WTO context, unless a specific provision of a WTO treaty is violated, the rationale of protection is not per se illegitimate—hence the permissibility of tariffs up to the bound rate, as well as safeguard measures. One reason that Regan, as noted in the next footnote is, more favorable to legislative intent inquiries, at least in the DCC context, is that he seems to understand protectionism as a per se illegitimate rationale for state legislation under the U.S. constitution.

31. Regan defends the use of intent analysis based on legislative history, "The Supreme Court and State Protectionism: Making Sense of the Dormant Commerce Clause," 1143–1160. However, this defense appears largely based on the track record of US courts in interpreting US statutes. The dispute settlement organs of the WTO are much further removed from day to day interaction with the legislative processes of the various Members than are US courts from US legislatures. I am not at all certain that Regan, had he put his mind to it, would have been so dismissive of objections to the institutional competence of tribunals in these respects, had he been reflected on the international context. In any case, what Regan has in mind is clearly a sensitive and thorough consideration of the legislative record, and elsewhere in the article he cautions against taking casual protectionist-sounding statements of an individual legislator as a decisive evidence of legislative intent, see 1169.

32. *Australia-Measures Affecting the Importation of Salmon,* Report of the Panel (1998). Not surprisingly the panel, in its final report, denied being so influenced. For a discussion of its misapplication of certain provisions of the SPS Code, and related misreading of its institutional role in scrutinizing regulatory outcomes not *prima facie* discriminatory or GATT-illegal, see below.

33. Although in the case of XX(b) the word "necessary" provides a textual basis for strict scrutiny of otherwise illegal GATT measures, as Feddersen notes, some commentators (and I would add GATT panels as well) have read into all the provisions of Art. XX the notion of strict scrutiny. Christoph Feddersen, "Focusing on Substantive Law in International Economic Relations: The *Public Morals* of GATT's Article XX(a) and "Conventional" Rules of Interpretation," (1998) 7 *Minnesota Journal of Global Trade* 75, at 95–96. With, however, the AB ruling in *Reformulated Gasoline,* this tendency has been arrested: the AB held that the difference of wording between the individual head of Art. XX mattered, and one could not import a least restrictive means test based on the language "necessary" into a provision that used the expression "relating to" to express the required relationship between the GATT-illegal measure and the non-trade regulatory purpose at issue, in this case conservation of exhaustible natural resources. However, the AB in this case also held that something like strict scrutiny will apply to any discriminatory elements in the *application* of a measure that a Member is seeking to sustain under Art. XX, this by virtue of the language "arbitrary and unjustified discrimination" in the chapeau of Art. XX. This actually brings Art. XX analysis in line with the approach of the Supreme Court in the DCC cases, namely that strict scrutiny is, as a general principle, warranted only where discrimination is present in the measure. However, as I am suggesting, the DCC jurisprudence suggests a much more institutionally sensitive view of what strict scrutiny entails.

34. Report of the Panel, para. 24.

35. "The WHO representatives stated that the experience in Latin America and Asia showed that the opening of closed cigarette markets dominated by a state tobacco monopoly resulted in an increase in smoking. Multinational tobacco companies had routinely circumvented national restrictions on advertising through indirect advertising and a variety of other techniques." Report of the Panel, para. 55.

36. 437 U.S. 617 (1978)

37. *C & A Carbone Inc. v. Town of Clarkstown* 511 U.S. 383 (1994); *Chemical Waste Management, Inc. v. Hunt, et al.* 504 U.S. 334 (1992); *Fort Gratiot Sanitary Landfill, Inc. v. Michigan Department of Natural Resources, et al.* 504 U.S. 353 (1992).

38. *Sporhase et al. v Nebraska ex rel. Douglas, Attorney General* 458 U.S. 941 (1982).

39. 504 U.S. 334 (1992) at 339–340.

40. *Resource Conservation and Recovery Act of 1976 as amended.*

41. 511 U.S. 383 (1994) at 406.

42. 458 U.S. 941 at 952, 956.

43. *United States-Import Prohibition of certain Shrimp and Shrimp Products,* Report of the Panel, WT/DS/58/R, 15 May 1998 [hereinafter, *Turtles*]. The *Turtles* case concerns a U.S. embargo on shrimp imported from countries not certified by U.S. authorities as having a regulatory program to reduce incidental deaths of endangered species of sea turtles that is comparable to that of the Unites States. As with the *Tuna-Dolphin* rulings, unilateral trade

measures for environmental purposes were found to be excluded *per se* from justification under Art. XX, but again without textual basis. This time the panel read into the words "unjustified discrimination in the chapeau of Art. XX an absolute rule against the justification of measures that condition import access on adoption of certain laws or policies by the country of origin—whether discriminatory or not in the ordinary sense of the word. See my discussion of this panel ruling, "The *Turtles* panel—Another Environmental Disaster in Geneva," *Journal of World Trade,* October 1998.

44. *United States-Import Prohibition of Certain Shrimp and Shrimp Products,* Report of the Appellate Body, WT/DS58/AB/R (1998), para. II.18.

45. 63 F.3d 652 (7th Cir. 1995).

46. *Healy et al. v. The Beer Institute et al.*(1989) 491 U.S.324.

47. 458 U.S. 941 at 955–956.

48. *Kassel v. Consolidated Freightways Corp.* 450 U.S. 662.

49. Ibid, at 676.

50. *United States—Standards for Reformulated and Conventional Gasoline,* Report of the Appellate Body (1996), 28: "Clearly, the United States did not feel it feasible to require its domestic refiners to incur the physical and financial costs and burdens entailed by immediate compliance with a statutory baseline. The United States wished to give domestic refiners time to restructure their operations and adjust to the requirements of the Gasoline Rule. This may very well have constituted sound domestic policy from the viewpoint of the EPA and U.S. refiners. At the same time we are bound to note that, while the United States counted the costs for its domestic refiners of statutory baselines, there is nothing in the record to indicate that it did other than disregard that kind of consideration when it came to foreign refiners."

51. *EC Measures Concerning Meat and Meat Products,* Report of the Panel (1997).

52. WTO, *Agreement on the Application of Sanitary and Phytosanitary Measures,* Art. 5.1.

53. *EC Measures Concerning Meat and Meat Products,* Report of the Appellate Body (1997), para. 194.

54. Obviously, in some semantically minimalist sense, a judgment that there is some regulatory benefit of a measure with trade restrictive impact implies a kind of balancing or tallying of two effects, the regulatory effect and the trade-restrictive effect. But in a strict balancing or proportionality approach, the reviewing tribunal will actually substitute its own weighing of the one against the other for that of the legislature. Here, as long as some regulatory benefit can be identified, a measure will not be invalidated, unless the burden it imposes is one of the specific types discussed above.

55. *Southern Pacific Co. v. Arizona,* 325 U.S. 761 at 775–776; followed in *Bibb* v. *Navajo Freight Lines,* 359 U.S. 520 (1958) at 524.

56. *Raymond Motor Transportation, Inc., et al.* v. *Rice,* 434 U.S. 429 (1977) at 449.

57. *Kassel* v. *Consolidated Freightways Corp.*450 U.S. 662 at 680–681.

58. To their credit, Farber and Hudec, at 1438, acknowledge a legitimacy problem with "second-guessing." But they wrongly characterize the answer in DCC jurisprudence to the problem as unclear or plagued with difficulties. This comes from viewing the plurality of the

Court in *Kassel,* discussed above, as having employed "balancing," i.e., a kind of recalculation of regulatory costs and benefits. But the plurality did not balance—it found that the "State failed to present *any* persuasive evidence"(at 662: emphasis added) of a safety benefit from the length requirement and sustained the conclusion at trial that "there is *no* valid safety reason" for the measure in question (at 667; emphasis added) and it made an independent finding of a serious burden on interstate commerce. There was no balancing here, because there was zero credible evidence of regulatory benefit. Farber and Hudec are suggest that the concurring judgment would have resolved the matter by an analysis of legislative intent. This, however, is too crude a reading of Brennan's opinion—he views the existence of a rational basis for regulation as a kind of surrogate for a inquiry by the Court into actual intent, stating the issue as "whether the lawmakers could rationally have believed that the challenged regulation would foster those purposes"(at 680). Brennan is as cautious as the plurality about the appropriateness of the Court making a *judgment* about legislative intent: what he seized upon in this case was what he viewed as the *admission* by the state's own lawyers at trial of a protectionist intent. According to Brennan, "Iowa's attorneys forthrightly defended the regulation in part on the basis of the State's interest in discouraging interstate truck traffic through Iowa."(at 682, fn. 2). In a GATT/WTO proceeding as well, there would be no legitimacy issue surely involved in impugning a measure, for example, as a "disguised restriction on international trade" within the meaning of the chapeau of Art. XX, or the relevant provision of the SPS code, if the responding party makes an admission in the proceedings of a protectionist intent. In fairness to Farber and Hudec, occasionally the U.S. Supreme Court *has* articulated the inquiry in a way that suggests balancing, suggesting for example in *Healy* v. *Beer Institute* that the Court has examined in cases of non-discriminatory measures "whether the burden on interstate commerce clearly exceeds the local benefits" (491 U.S. 324 at 327). However, precisely the interesting lesson is that the only way the Court actually finds itself able to avoid simply second guessing a judgment call of democratic authorities is by understanding a clear excess to exist only in a case where there is a burden on interstate commerce of some significance and *no* identifiable, defensible regulatory benefit. For a comprehensive analysis and explanation of the fallacy that the Court is "balancing" in dormant Commerce clause cases, see D. Regan, "The Supreme Court and State Protectionism: Making Sense of the Dormant Commerce Clause," 1092–1108.

59. See, generally, J. Fraiberg and M. J. Trebilcock, "Risk Regulation: Technocratic and Democratic Tools for Regulatory Reform," forthcoming, *McGill Law Journal.* John Jackson identifies a further consideration that weighs against this sort of fact finding being engaged in by WTO panels: "A serious and prolonged fact-type hearing could easily bankrupt the resource allocation to the WTO dispute settlement system. For example in a personal communication one party gave an account of a hearing on environmental matters in Canada that lasted nearly 120 days! This would exceed all the hearing days of all the procedures in a typical GATT (sic) dispute settlement year, and would probably involve budgetary allocation exceeding all the normal procedures combined for a year." J. H. Jackson, *The World Trade Organization: Constitution and Jurisprudence* (London: RIIA/Pinter, 1998), 92.

60. *Australia-Measures Affecting the Importation of Salmon,* Report of the Panel (1998)(Appealed).

61. Quoted in the panel report at para. 8.98.

62. Report of the Panel, paras. 8.98–8.99.

63. *Australia-Measures Affecting Importation of Salmon,* Report of the Appellate Body, WT/DS18/AB/R (1998).

64. And see above the argument as to how one could learn from the DCC jurisprudence about how to make this test more institutionally sensitive.

65. In *Salmon,* the panel misapplied this provision as well: even though the 1996 Report had identified heat-treatment as providing a level of security or protection higher than that of other options, the panel decided to draw its own conclusions about whether heat treatment would in fact afford the appropriate level of protection, in comparison to less-trade restrictive options, thereby making its own scientific and technical inferences from uncertainty and ambiguity in the empirical evidence. Report of the Panel, paras. 8.174–8.178. At the same time, the AB was right to be concerned about defects in the *risk assessment* in the 1996 report, judged against the earlier study, even if the *policy conclusions* of the 1996 report were reasonable, measured against Australia's choice for maximum protection.

66. *Salmon,* Report of the Panel, para. 8.180. The Panel here relied on the supposed emphasis of the SPS Agreement on "harmonization." However, as the AB noted in *Hormones,* para. 165, (in response to a similar misreading by that panel), harmonization is only stated in the SPS Agreement as a future goal or aspiration—the SPS Agreement must not be read so as to transform international "standards, guidelines and recommendations into binding *norms.*"(emphasis in original).

67. "Regulating the World," supra.

CHAPTER 6

# Comment on "Managing the Interface between International Trade Law and the Regulatory State: What Lessons Should (and Should Not) Be Drawn from the Jurisprudence of the United States Dormant Commerce Clause"

*Gary N. Horlick*

Rob Howse in his excellent paper for this conference raises important questions about WTO review of national regulation, and the very important implications for democracy of that review. He also demonstrates the useful insights provided by the similar review which arises within one large single-market federal state, the United States, often dealt with under the "dormant Commerce Clause" in U.S. jurisprudence.

Jurisprudence in integrating economies may well offer very useful insights for the relatively young WTO dispute settlement system (which is either 51 years old or 4 years old, depending on your count). I am less sanguine than Professor Howse about using recent U.S. Commerce Clause jurisprudence in that regard. Viewed in context, the U.S. is at least 209 years into its market integration process. U.S. courts today operate within the framework of a fully integrated single U.S. market and, as such, may not need to show the same unifying fervor as did courts in the earlier years[1] of the endeavor (but perhaps I betray my legal-realist leanings). Indeed, at this stage, one would not necessarily expect to find a consistent doctrine either for or against efficient economic integration as long as the issues remain somewhat marginal.[2] Further, the dormant Commerce Clause is not the determination of permissible federal/sub-federal regulation in the United States. Rather, it is permission given by federal courts to sub-federal units to regulate only in the absence of federal regulation. There are few – if any – dormant Commerce Clause cases where the federal government could not have overruled state regulation under the Commerce Clause. Thus, Congress could certainly impose GATT 94 on the states, and in some sense has done so in the GATT services agreements by grandfathering but "freezing" state laws.

It will be interesting to explore similar jurisprudence of innovative integration efforts such as Mercosur (if it is able to maintain its surprising progress in light of the current financial crises), and the rather haphazard NAFTA dispute resolution processes (including Chapter 11 for investor-state disputes, Chapter 19 for antidumping and countervailing duty disputes, Chapter 20 in general, and several other specialized dispute resolution mechanisms). The more mature EU "market integration' jurisprudence of the ECJ has much to offer in this regard.

The questions Professor Howse raises concerning democracy and decision-making are quite timely. The debate so far frequently reflects more passion than is justified by the number of cases and their rather unusual fact patterns. The first Tuna/Dolphin cases[3] and the Shrimp/Turtle case,[4] whatever the merits of the cases and the various GATT/WTO decisions, are not a clear arena for analysis of democracy in the GATT/WTO system. Both factual situations represent fairly explicit attempts by (democratic) citizens of one country to force (democratic) citizens of other countries to change their behavior. Thus, democracy advocates could logically be found on either side of the case.[5] For a time global commons, citizens of Country A may decry attempts by citizens of Country B (unilaterally) to tell Country A how to deal with the relevant commons – and citizens of Country B can equally express concern about citizens of Country A exploiting Country B's interest in that commons! Note that this is a different question than whether Country B can unilaterally act inconsistently with its binding obligations to Country A under, e.g., the WTO.

The Thai Cigarettes,[6] Australian Salmon,[7] and, especially, the Beef Hormones[8] cases offer more food for thought. As Professor Howse points out, in the "real policy world in which the Thai regulators lived," banning advertising may not have been a realistic option (presumably because of the ability of foreign advertisers to continue to impact Thai consumers from outside of Thailand, or because the established value of foreign brand names was already so large that an impartial ban on advertising would leave the foreign brands better off). By the same token, however, the regulators, who presumably are in a better position that WTO panel members to "fine-tune" the regulations, did not ban only those foreign cigarettes which would benefit from advertising, but banned all of them. Similarly, the national regulators had not made a reasoned finding (which probably would have been impossible) that Thai cigarettes posed less health hazard than imported cigarettes. Professor Howse poses the question of whether "there is *any* need to adjudicate computing values at all" (emphasis added) as compared to trade values, yet, at the same time, the opposite question is also valid.

*Beef Hormones* represents a far more challenging case—a sovereign entity (the EU for these purposes) banning both the local *and* the imported product, on the claims of protecting its population from allegedly unhealthy food products, albeit with no scientific evidence. As Professor Howse correctly points out, the WTO goes well beyond the GATT in this area. Where the GATT focused on discrimination, and possible exceptions to the non-discrimination rule, the SPS and TBT Agreements create obligations to rely on sound science, with an express preference for international standards.

While a WTO panel [which was formed with the agreement and participation of all the parties] may not be directly accountable to the democratic community in the importing country, neither is the importing country directly accountable to democratic communities elsewhere. As Professor Howse points out, the Appellate Body in Beef Hormones was quite extremely deferential, apparently permitting a national authority to base an import ban on the opinion of "a reputable scientist." While Professor Howse's paper assumes that responsible and representative governments will act in good faith where there are divergences of opinion, one cannot blame WTO panels facing overt examples of discrimination such as *Reformulated Gas* (or Australia choosing a method of treating fish imports that destroys their value) to suspect the worst. Indeed, in a democratic legislative process, one will frequently find "political" factors – including special interest lobbying – in much trade legislation (*Bananas* in the U.S. *and* EU, perhaps).

Thus, the argument goes beyond democracy, and even beyond the right of democracies to agree to "precommit" not to restrict trade, to the market liberalizing dynamic. The success of European integration has shown (through the very large gains possible from the abolition of borders),[9] why a world of markets segmented by individually justifiable barriers may not be a good idea. That said, economic efficiency is not the only value [although, from a development perspective, richer countries which already clear cut their forests and destroyed local species should be wary of taking this position too easily against poorer countries]. We want efficiency, but we also want local responsibility and control of our lives. Which one of the two do we want? Both! And thus the debate advanced by Professor Howse's paper is likely to continue for the foreseeable future.

NOTES

1. The dormant Commerce Clause was invented in 1851, Cooley v. Board of Wardens, 53 U.S. (12 How.) 299 (1851).

2. While a state tariff on goods from another state would certainly be struck down in ringing terms, the Supreme Court in recent years has affirmed a state's right to discriminate in giving trade-distorting positive subsidies (*Hughes v. Alexandria Scrap Corp., 426 U.S. 794 (1976),* 1976, but rejected a state's ability to apply negative subsidies to out-of-staters, *West Lynn Creamery, Inc. v. Healy, 512 U.S. 186 (1993)*. The "market participant" doctrine looks more like a label than consistent analysis if, as many economists believe, subsidies can be equivalent

to tariffs, and government procurement at an above-market price is a subsidy. The application of U.S. Commerce Clause jurisprudence in the subsidy area is well described in an excellent recent article, Mathew Schaefer, State Investment attraction Subsidy Wars Resulting from a Prisoner's Dilemma: The Inadequacy of State Constitutional Solutions and the Appropriateness of a Federal Legislative Response, 28 New Mexico L. Rev. 303 (1998).

3. *U.S. – Prohibition of Imports of Tuna and Tuna Products From Canada* (Panel Report), GATT BISD 29S/91 (22 February 1982).

4. *See United States - Import Prohibition of Certain Shrimp and Shrimp Products* (Appellate Body Report), WTO DOC. WT/DS58/AB/R (12 October 1998*); see also United States - Import Prohibition of Certain Shrimp and Shrimp Products* (Panel Report), WTO DOC. WT/DS58/R (15 May 1998).

5. While Professor Howse gives prominence to the fact that a policy might be preferred by "a range of legitimate actors" as a solution to a common problem, it is unclear why one range of legitimate actors has more right to appeal to values of democracy than another range of legitimate actors (or, in the Shrimp/Turtles case, a "significant number of states" but not all). Careful readers will not become excited by the absence of emphasis on either the environmental aspects of protecting species specified by citizens of the first country, or by the moral aspects of richer people telling poorer people how to act.

6.Thailand *Restrictions on Importation of and Internal Taxes On Cigarettes,* GATT BISD 37S/200 (November 7, 1990).

7. *See Australia – Measures Affecting Importation of Salmon* (Panel Report), WTO DOC. WT/DS18/R (4 February 1998); *see also. Australia – Measures Affecting Importation of Salmon* (Appellate Body Report), WTO DOC. WT/DS18/AB/R (20 October 1998).

8. *See EC Measures Concerning Meat and Meat Products (Hormones) – Complaint by Canada* (Panel Report), WTO DOC. WT/DS48/R/CAN (18 August 1997); *see also EC – Measures Concerning Meat and Meat Products (Hormones) – Complaint by the United States* (Panel Report), WTO DOC. WT/DS26/R/USA, (18 August 1997); *); see also EC – Measures Concerning Meat and Meat Products (Hormones),* (Appellate Body Report), WTO DOC. WT/DS26/AB/R, WT/DS48/AB/R (16 January 1998).

9. The gains may be more than economic. As one drives from Maastricht to Liege—territory which was unified in 800 AD—one passes some exceptionally bloody battlefields of 1914, 1940 and 1944–45, but now no border posts, only a single sign saying "Bienvenue a Wallonia."

CHAPTER 7

# The Non-Discrimination Principle and the Removal of Fiscal Barriers to Intra-Community Trade

*Paul Demaret*

The Neuchâtel Conference is dedicated to the principle of non-discrimination in international trade. The topic assigned to my colleague Piet Eeckhout and I by the conference organizers is entitled "From Dassonville to Keck & Mithouard and Beyond." The Dassonville and Keck judgments of the EC Court of Justice concern the interpretation of Article 30 of the EC Treaty, a provision which applies to national regulations restricting the free flow of goods between Member States. Actually, Article 30, like several other provisions of the Treaty (Article 48, 52, 59 most notably), has been interpreted by the Court of Justice as going quite beyond the prohibition of discrimination. Even though the Keck judgment may have somewhat reduced the scope of Article 30, the precise boundaries of this provision remain a subject of debate. This issue is discussed in Piet Eeckhout's paper.

My paper concerns a sector of EC law where the non-discrimination principle is given the leading role: the removal of fiscal barriers to intra-Community trade. The main focus of the paper is on Article 95 of the EC Treaty, which is an implementation of the non-discrimination principle in the field of internal taxes. The wording of Article 95 is directly borrowed from Article III § 2 of GATT. However, there are other provisions of the EC Treaty which deal with fiscal barriers to trade: Articles 12, 13, and 16 of the Treaty, which forbid charges having an equivalent effect to customs duties. How to distinguish internal taxes from taxes which qualify as charges having an equivalent effect has been a perennial problem for the European Court of Justice. The prohibition of taxes having an equivalent effect, although covering mainly discriminatory taxes on imports, has been construed by the Court as going somewhat beyond the non-discrimination principle.

The paper is divided into four sections. The first presents the general context in which the prohibition of fiscal barriers to intra-Community trade applies. The second section deals with the case law of the Court of Justice regarding charges having an equivalent effect to customs duties. The third section identifies the scope which the Court has given to the non-discrimination principle in the framework of Article 95. In the fourth and last section, some general remarks are made in relation to the case law of the Court of Justice regarding fiscal barriers.

In the course of the paper, I will refer to discriminatory and to protective taxes. To avoid any ambiguity, I should say that protective taxes are, in my view, taxes that discriminate against foreign products in the economic sense.

## 1. The General Context

The general context in which the prohibition of taxes having an equivalent effect to customs duties and internal discriminatory taxes applies is defined by the EC rules on border tax adjustments (BTAs). In the main, these rules are the same as the rules on BTAs applicable under the General Agreement on Tariffs and Trade. Direct taxes and indirect taxes are respectively subject to the country of origin and the country of destination principles. The adoption of the V.A.T. system by all the Member States has introduced transparency with respect to the computation of indirect tax rebates (in the case of exports) and indirect compensatory taxes (in the case of imports) and had removed the risk that border tax adjustments be manipulated in order to facilitate exports and limit imports.

In a true internal market, indirect taxes should be paid at the place of purchase and BTA would become irrelevant. This, however, requires not only that V.A.T. and excise duties rates be harmonized throughout the Community, but also that a mechanism be established in order to compensate Member States who are net importers and who stand to lose tax revenues as a result of the abolition of the country of destination principle. Neither of these two conditions has yet been achieved. Even though in 1993, fiscal border controls were eliminated between Member States, the country of destination principle still applies: indirect taxes are levied in the country of the buyer. The elimination of BTAs is not envisaged in the immediate future. However, since January 1, 1993, the private consumer is permitted to buy goods in any Member State, pay the required indirect taxes at the place of purchase and bring back the goods in question to his or her home country. But this does not apply to the purchase of cars or to purchases by mail.

Today, the most blatant fiscal barriers to intra-Community trade in goods have probably disappeared as a result of the vigorous enforcement of Articles 12, 13, and 95 of the EC Treaty. The Court has rendered more than 200 judgments with respect to charges having an equivalent effect to customs duties and internal discriminatory taxes.

In the future, the elimination of indirect tax adjustments in intra-Community trade would further reduce the potential for Member States to discriminate against products from other Member States through indirect taxes.

## 2. The Prohibition of Customs Duties and Charges Having an Equivalent Effect (Articles 12, 13, and 16 of the EC Treaty)

Customs duties have all been removed in intra-Community trade. However, the prohibition of charges having an equivalent effect has not yet lost its relevance.

### The Criterion: Taxes Which Formally or Materially Apply Only to Imports

As interpreted by the Court of Justice, the notion of charges or taxes having an equivalent effect to customs duties extends to all kinds of charges or taxes which are specifically aimed at imports, or which, although imposed on both imports and domestic products, are in reality only borne by imports.

Before the removal of border controls in intra-Community trade, there were many examples of such charges in the form of taxes levied on imports in conjunction with sanitary controls or other types of controls or formalities at the border. The qualification of charges having an equivalent effect could be avoided only if a similar tax was levied on domestic products at exactly the same commercial stage. Other typical examples are provided by taxes which prima facie apply in an identical manner to imported and domestic products, but whose proceeds are used to subsidize activities directly beneficial to the domestic industry, such as industrial research activities.[1] As a result of the broad interpretation given by the Court of Justice to the notion of "charges having an equivalent effect to customs duties," taxes which are legitimate under Article III § 8 (b) of GATT are squarely forbidden under Articles 12 and 13 of the EC Treaty.

The Gingerbread judgment of 1962[2] still stands out as one of the most important pronouncements of the Court of Justice regarding charges having an equivalent effect to customs duties. There the Court ruled that Belgium was precluded from taxing imported gingerbread. No similar tax was imposed on Belgian gingerbread. Belgium claimed that the tax on imported gingerbread was justified because it was intended to equalize Belgian and foreign production costs, since as a result of public intervention, Belgian producers of gingerbread had to pay a higher price for an essential input, rye, than their foreign competitors. The Court of Justice rejected the Belgian argument on the ground that taxes on imports were justifiable only if they served to compensate for similar taxes on domestic products.

### Beyond Discriminatory or Protective Taxes

In Gingerbread, the Court had stressed the discriminatory and protective character of the Belgian tax. Indeed the great bulk of taxes which have fallen under the prohibition of charges having an equivalent effect consist of taxes which either formally or materially discriminated against imports. However, in Fonds des diamantaires,[3] the Court extended the scope of the prohibition to a charge which Belgium had imposed on imports of diamonds. Belgium did not produce anything which could qualify even remotely as "like" or "competing" products. The purpose of the tax was to finance a social fund operating for the benefit of workers in the diamond industry. Despite the fact that the tax in question was in no way discriminatory or protectionist, the Court concluded that it was a charge having an equivalent effect to customs duties because it only applied to imported products. The Court reasoned that since customs duties had to be removed even in those cases where they did not protect a domestic industry, the same had to hold for taxes on imports.

Actually, there have been very few cases where taxes levied on imported products and devoid of any protectionist character were deemed to be in violation of Articles 12 and 13 of the EC Treaty.[4] This is so because if the same type of tax which is imposed on an imported product is also imposed on a domestic—even non-competing—product, the tax is not treated as a "charge having an equivalent effect to a custom duty," but as an "internal tax."[5] VAT, excise duties or taxes on cars have always been treated as internal taxes, which are legal under the Treaty except if they have a discriminatory or protectionist character (see infra concerning Article 95 of the EC Treaty).

### Taxes of Equivalent Effect on Exports

Although not numerous, there have been cases of "charges of equivalent effect" on exports. Here too the typical example is that of a tax which is collected only in relation to some kind of export control.[6] A tax levied on a domestic product for the purpose of financing promotional activities on the domestic market is also to be treated as a "charge having an equivalent effect" on exports since those products which are exported do not benefit from these activities.[7]

## The Absence of Exceptions

As mentioned above, the EC Treaty does not explicitly provide for exceptions to the prohibition of "charges of equivalent effect"[8] and overall the prohibition has been vigorously enforced by the Court of Justice.[9] However, the Court has in fact allowed exceptions in some cases but without saying so explicitly. The most notorious example is that of the so-called Monetary Compensatory Amounts (MCM) which applied to a great number of agricultural products for almost twenty years.[10] MCM were intended to limit the consequences of currency fluctuations on agricultural exchanges within the common market. They acted as trade barriers or as export subsidies depending on the Member States. In a sense, MCM provided the best—and economically most significant—illustration of a "charge having an equivalent effect to a customs duty." However, if MCM had not been put in place, the common market might have fallen apart altogether. The Court understood thus. It ruled that MCM were not "charges of equivalent effect" since they had been adopted by the Council in the interest of the Community and in order to maintain normal trade flows between the Member States under exceptional and temporary circumstances.

## 3. The Prohibition of Internal Taxes of a Discriminatory Nature or with a Protective Effect

Article 95 of the EC Treaty forbids Member States to tax imports more than similar domestic products as well as to tax imports in a manner that would afford indirect protection to other products, i.e., competing domestic products.

The abundant case law of the Court of Justice relating to Article 95 can be summarized in three points. First, the Court recognizes that the existence of formal or material fiscal discrimination or, at least, the existence of fiscal protectionism is required for the prohibition to apply. Second, this being said, the Court has given a broad scope to Article 95 and under the guise of tracking down discrimination has in some cases extended the prohibition to taxes devoid of a protectionist character. Third, the EC Treaty does not provide for an exception to the prohibition. However, in some ways, this has been compensated by the flexibility which the Court has introduced in the framework of Article 95 by allowing tax differentiations based on "sound justifications" among like or competing products.

The interpretation of Article 95 of the EC Treaty by the Court of Justice is, in some respects, broader and, in other respects, more flexible than the interpretation of III § 2 of GATT by GATT and WTO panels.

## The Criterion: Tax Discrimination or Tax Protection

As seen supra, the prohibition of charges having an equivalent effect to customs duties has been construed by the Court of Justice as extending to taxes on imports which were neither discriminatory nor had the effect of protecting a domestic industry. Regarding internal taxes, a similar extension of the prohibition seemed precluded by the very wording of Article 95. The Commission nevertheless challenged the received interpretation of Article 95, but without success, in a case concerning Danish taxes on cars.[11]

The factual situation was the following. Denmark does not produce cars. All cars sold in Denmark are imported. For various social and economic reasons, Denmark imposes very high taxes on cars. Taxes on cars in Denmark exceed the level of taxes on cars in most other Member States. For large cars, they amount to much more than 100 % of the price of vehicles before taxes. Since Denmark does not produce goods which could be reasonably thought to be even in a distant competitive relationship with cars, the Danish taxes have no protective effect. However, the Commission contended that Article 95 had to be construed as prohibiting those internal taxes which were unduly restricting trade between Member States even if they were devoid of a protective effect. In the Commission's opinion, the very high level of the Danish taxes had the effect of reducing the volume of cars imported in Denmark from other Member States. The Court of Justice, with reason, in my opinion, refused to follow the Commission on this point. The Court confirmed that Article 95 only applied to taxes of a discriminatory nature or affording protection to domestic products. However, the Court, in an obiter dictum, stated:

> . . . the only possibility of appraising an adverse effect of that kind on the free movement of goods is by reference to the general rules contained in Article 30 et seq. of the Treaty, and the Commission's action is based exclusively on infringement of Article 95 of the Treaty.

The Court's remark is of course consonant with the interpretation it has given to Article 30 since Dassonville, (now limited by Keck), according to which restrictive trade measures are within the compass of Article 30, even in the absence of any protective effect. Taken literally, the remark means that, had the Commission brought the case on the basis of Article 30, rather than on the basis of Article 95, it then might have succeeded. To this issue, I shall return infra (section IV).

## The Broad Interpretation of Article 95

If the Court of Justice, constrained by the wording of Article 95, has not accepted to interpret the prohibition of Article 95 as extensively as the prohibition of measures of equivalent effect, it has nevertheless given a very broad scope to the prohibition. This will be illustrated first by comparing the internal case law and the external case law of the Court of Justice; second, by examining the market definitions which the Court uses in relation to Article 95; third, by showing how far the concept of discrimination has been extended in certain cases; fourth, by the extension of the prohibition to exports.

### *The Interpretation of the Prohibition of Internal Discriminatory Taxes in the Context of Agreements between the EC and Third Countries*

The Court of Justice interprets more broadly the prohibition of internal discriminatory taxes when it applies to the Community internal trade than when it applies to the Community external trade. In the context of free trade agreements between the EC and EFTA countries, which provided for the prohibition of fiscal discrimination between similar products, the Court twice refused to give the prohibition the same extensive and "integrationist" interpretation as under the EC Treaty.

In Kupferberg,[12] the Court implied that the interpretation of the words "similar products" was not necessarily the same under Article 95 § 1 and under a similarly worded provision contained in the free trade agreement between the EC and Portugal.

Metalsa[13] concerned the interpretation of a similar free trade agreement between the EC and Austria. The facts were the same as in Drexl,[14] an Article 95 case. In Drexl, the Court had ruled that a Member State violated Article 95 of the EC Treaty if, under its laws, a tax offense was much more severely punished when it was committed in the course of intra-Community trade than in the course of domestic trade. In Metalsa, it stated that the Drexl interpretation of the prohibition of discriminatory taxes could not be transposed in the context of a free trade agreement.

It is only in the context of the association agreement between the EC and Greece, which led to the entry of Greece in the Community, that the Court of Justice was willing to interpret the prohibition of internal discriminatory taxes as broadly as under the EC Treaty.[15]

How the Court will interpret Article III § 2 of GATT is a question which has not received an answer. Up until now, the Court has denied direct effect to GATT provisions, including to Article III § 2.[16]

### *The Definition of the Relevant Product Market*

#### *Article 95 and Article 86*

Under Article 95, the Court of Justice adopts broader product market definitions than under the EC competition rules. This can be explained by the fact that Article 95 concerns the behavior of Member States, whereas competition rules concern the behavior (and structure) of undertakings. Particularly under Article 86, market definitions are, at times, tailored to the behavior which the Commission and/or the Court of Justice find offensive.

A good example of the different market definitions used by the Court of Justice under respectively Articles 86 and 95 comes from two banana cases. In United Brands,[17] an Article 86 case, bananas were deemed to constitute a market of their own. Both the Commission and the Court of Justice rejected the argument made by United Brands that the relevant product market consisted of bananas and other table fruits. By contrast in Commission v. Italy,[18] bananas imported in Italy from other Member States and table fruits grown in Italy were treated as competing products for the purpose of Article 95.

Under Article 95, the decisive factor is whether internal taxes may have the effect of protecting domestic products against competition (even partial or potential) from products of other Member States. The British Beer and Wine case[19] provides probably the best example. In that case, beer, a typical British product, was eventually found in a competitive relationship with table wines imported from Southern Member States.

#### *The Relationship between Domestic and Imported Products: Similarity, Direct Competition and Less Direct Competition*

Assuming that, for the purpose of Article 95, domestic and imported products belong to the same market, any tax differential will not necessarily amount to a violation of Article 95. This will depend on whether the relationship between domestic and imported products is a close one or a more distant one.

Here it is worth stressing that the Court of Justice does not seem to attach practical consequences to the distinction between respectively similar and competitive products. The important distinction is rather between what I would call directly competitive products (including similar products) on the one hand and products which are in a more distant competitive relationship on the other hand. Any difference in taxation will amount to a violation of Article 95 in the first case. In the second case, the existence of a significant difference in taxation is required in order to demonstrate a violation of Article 95. Two set of examples will illustrate the point just made.

In the Sparkling wine case[20] and in the three Alcohol cases of 1980,[21] the Court of Justice did not bother to actually determine which products did qualify as "similar" and which as "competitive" products. It simply stated that the products in question, sparkling wines and champagne in the first instance, various types of alcohols, such as cognac and whiskies in the second instance, were to be viewed as being similar or, if not, then as competing products. The Court apparently considered that, because of their characteristics, all the products involved were rather close substitutes. As a result, any tax differential entailed a violation of Article 95.

By contrast, in the Beer and wine cases,[22] one involving the United Kingdom, the other Belgium, the products involved were quite different in their physical composition and shared a looser competitive relationship. There a higher tax rate on wines (all imported) did not automatically amount to a tax affording protection to domestic beer. More had to be demonstrated. First only table wines and beer were considered to be in a competitive relationship. Second, the tax differential had to be quite large for the Court to be convinced that the differential could influence consumer choice. In other words, outside the circle of similar and directly competitive products, the demonstration that a tax affords protection to domestic products is subject to a higher burden of proof.

### *The Extensive Interpretation of the Concept of Tax Discrimination*

The Outokumpu[23] and Schul judgments[24] will serve to illustrate how far the prohibition of discrimination is, at times, extended and how this may affect the fiscal autonomy of the Member States.

#### *The Outokumpu Judgment and the Taxation of Electricity According to the Environmental "Cleanliness" of the Production Source*

The prohibition of Article 95 applies even though imported products may suffer a small disadvantage in only a few instances.[25] More importantly, it applies even though the disadvantage suffered by imported products may be exactly offset by the fact that, in other instances, domestic products in turn suffer a disadvantage.

The Outokumpu case concerned the taxation of electricity in Finland. Finland was taxing domestically produced electricity according to the environmental "cleanliness" of the energy source. The sources of electricity produced in Finland could be identified without difficulty. However, for technical reasons, the precise sources of electricity imported from Sweden could not be identified. In consequence, Finland was taxing imported electricity at an average rate, calculated on the basis of the shares taken by the different energy sources in the production of electricity in Finland. The manner in which Finland taxed electricity could not qualify as protectionist since it did not restrict the volume of imports. Nevertheless, the Court of Justice, contrary to the opinion of Advocate General F. Jacobs, found the Finnish system of taxing imported electricity in violation of Article 95. It gave decisive importance to the fact that imported electricity produced with hydraulic power was not as well treated as Finnish electricity from a similar source. Imported electricity from other sources was—to the same extent—better treated than electricity produced in Finland. However, this was not deemed relevant.

The Outokumpu judgment is somewhat troublesome. It implies that, if indeed the sources of imported electricity cannot be precisely identified, Finland may have to modify its system of taxing the production of electricity with the consequence that its environment would be less protected. This indicates that, as construed by the Court of Justice, Article 95 may significantly reduce the fiscal autonomy of the Member States. In the Finnish electricity case, I submit that it might have been enough to require Finland to allow importers to prove the source of imported electricity if this were ever to become technically feasible.

*The Schul Judgments and Double Taxation*

To the extent that VAT and excise duties are subject to adjustments in the case of exports and imports, double taxation may not occur. Double taxation may, however, occur with respect to indirect taxes which are not subject to adjustment mechanisms in intra-Community trade. The Court of Justice normally considers that cases of double taxation do not fall within the scope of Article 95 and that double taxation is a matter for the Community legislator to resolve.[26] However, in Schul, the Court did not hesitate to apply Article 95 to a case of double taxation.

The case concerned the imposition of VAT on second-hand goods imported by private consumers. This was the only situation where VAT was not rebated on exports. Again the Court of Justice extended the concept of discrimination quite far. Indeed, from an economic standpoint, the importing country was taxing in the same manner any added value, whether of domestic or foreign origin. Domestic second-hand goods had been subject to VAT when they had been first marketed. Double taxation arose only because, in the exporting country, no rebate mechanism existed with respect to second-hand goods exported by non-traders.

The avowed motive for the Court to apply Article 95 in Schul was that the private consumer ought to benefit from the internal market as much as trade operators did as a result of BTAs. The Court was here performing a task pertaining to the Community legislator, but which the latter, at the time, had been unable to perform. Actually, the Court recognized that it might be better if the Community legislator were to subsequently intervene to deal with the matter and were to replace the somewhat awkward solution devised by the Court on the basis of Article 95 by a more elegant and permanent solution.

Eventually, the 6$^{th}$ VAT directive was modified. Since 1995, second-hand goods acquired by private consumers may circulate throughout the Member States without being subject to VAT.

*The Prohibition of Discriminatory Taxes on Exports*

Article 95 of the EC Treaty, as Article III § 2 of GATT, refers only to taxes on imports. Discrimination against exports is indeed seldom encountered in developed economies. However, in Staatenskontrol,[27] the Court of Justice stated, by way of an obiter dictum, that internal taxes that would discriminate against exports would also fall under the prohibition of Article 95. The Court pointed out that the system of Articles 95 to 98 of the EC Treaty aimed at achieving tax neutrality in trade between Member States. Therefore, Article 95 had to forbid tax discrimination not only in respect of imports, but also in respect of exports.

## The Flexible Interpretation of Article 95

*The Absence of Exceptions*

The Treaty provides an exception to the prohibition of quantitative restrictions and measures having an equivalent effect in the form of Article 36, which, in practice, has been supplemented by the Court of Justice by means of its so-called mandatory requirements doctrine. This has enabled the Court to allow, in some rare instances, national measures which were of a truly discriminatory and protectionist nature, but which allegedly were justified by some reasons of general interest. The Campus Oil[28] and the Walloon Waste[29] cases are probably the best examples.

The prohibition of internal discriminatory taxes, like the prohibition of charges having an equivalent effect, is not subject to general exceptions of the kind provided by Article 36 (or, for that matter, Article XX of GATT) or the doctrine on mandatory requirements. The Court seems to take the view that taxes which do discriminate against imports and protect a domestic industry are hardly justifiable. However, once the prohibition of internal discriminatory taxes, as construed by the Court, reaches taxes, like the Finnish tax on imported electricity, one might feel a need for an exception to the prohibition.

*Tax Differentiations among Identical, Similar or Competing Products*

The Court of Justice has, however, brought a measure of flexibility in the implementation of Article 95 by allowing Member States to make tax differentiations among identical, like or competing products. The differentiations may be based on characteristics relating to either:

1. The final products, for example the power of different models of car.
2. The producers, for example their volume of output in the case of breweries or distilleries.
3. Or the production process, for example the kind of raw material used to manufacture gasoline or denatured alcohol.

Differentiations such as these are legitimate under Article 95 provided they are indistinctly applicable to domestic and imported products. In addition, they may not be designed to protect a domestic industry. What matters most is whether, in the opinion of the Court, there is some sound justification for the tax differentiation. If this is the case, there will be no violation of Article 95 even though the fiscally disfavored category happens to consist entirely of imported products.

Hereafter are illustrations of tax differentiation which were respectively found incompatible and compatible with Article 95.

*Tax Differentiations Incompatible with Article 95*

A Member State may not define the fiscally favored category by reference to a criterion which only domestic products can satisfy. Such was the case in Essevi & Salengo,[30] where the favored category referred to spirits which could be controlled in Italy at the production stage.

Italy was also found in violation of Article 95 in a case where alcohols protected by a geographical indication were treated as luxury goods, and accordingly taxed more heavily, at a time when no alcohol produced in Italy was so protected.[31] Similarly, the Court found inconsistent with Article 95 the fact that Italy was applying a higher VAT rate to sparkling wines which had naturally fermented in their bottles, but only when rules governing the use of a designation of origin made such process compulsory.[32] Only certain foreign products, most notably French Champagne, were subject to such a requirement in their country of origin.

France was found in breach of Article 95 because it taxed alcohols made from grain more than alcohols made from wine or from fruits.[33] In this case, the bulk of French alcohols consisted of the latter, whereas the bulk of imported alcohol was made up of the former. Denmark and Italy had similar systems of taxation which were also found to contravene Article 95.

In the Humblot case,[34] the manner in which annual taxes on cars were set in France was also declared incompatible with Article 95. The level of taxation increased gradually in direct relation with the power of the car engine, expressed in fiscal HP, up to 16 HP. This kind of tax differentiation was consistent with Article 95. There may indeed be good environmental, social, and economic reasons to tax cars on the basis of engine power. However, what was inconsistent with Article 95 was the fivefold increase which the tax underwent when moving up 16 to 17 HP. The attention of the Court of Justice was caught by the fact that no French producer was manufacturing cars with engines exceeding 16 HP.

It is important to stress that France could have consistently with Article 95 taxed powerful cars more heavily than less powerful ones, even if the former were all produced in other Member States. In Humblot, the violation resulted from the disproportionate increase affecting the tax scale at the very point where the only cars subject to taxation were all foreign made. Such disproportionate increase made a mere pretence of any attempt to justify the tax differentiation by a reason other than the protection of the French car industry.

*Tax Differentiations Compatible with Article 95*

In several cases the Court of Justice recognized the compatibility with Article 95 of tax differentiations destined to favor small producers of beer or spirits provided that identical, similar or competing products coming from small producers located in other Member States could benefit from the same favorable tax treatment. For example, when Germany taxed at a reduced rate alcohol made from certain fruits and produced by small German distilleries, the same tax reductions had to be extended to rum produced by small distilleries in the French Antilles.[35] Similarly, when Italy taxed gasoline made from regenerated oil at a much lower rate than conventional gasoline, the same tax reduction had to apply to imports.[36]

The Member State of importation may make the granting of the fiscal advantage dependent on the importer proving that the imported products satisfy the conditions with which domestic products have to comply. This may not always be easy and may require the cooperation of administrative authorities in the exporting country.

In two cases, the Court of Justice has allowed tax differentiations which, in light of Article 95, might have been questioned.

The Natural sweet wines case[37] concerned the more favorable tax treatment granted by French law to "natural sweet wines" compared to other liquor wines. The denomination in question was reserved to "wines the production of which is traditional and customary," and which must comply with a series of very precise oenological rules and practices which codify what is fair and traditional. The Commission held that such conditions would in fact only be satisfied by French products and that the concept of "traditional and customary production" left the door open to arbitrariness. Indeed, it meant secular (emphasis added) production inseparable from a given region, their long standing being an element of fame. The Court of Justice found the French tax scheme nevertheless consistent with Article 95 since at least a foreign product, wine from Samos, could meet the very strict conditions required in order to enjoy the more favorable tax treatment.

It is submitted that the French scheme had a protective effect as natural sweet wines of more recent origin, produced in other Member States, suffered a disadvantage on the French market. The judgment of the Court in Natural sweet wines is somewhat at odds with the dynamic view the Court often takes of the common or internal market, as illustrated by its judgment in the British Beer and Wine case.[38]

In Chemial Farmaceutici,[39] the Court dealt with the taxation of denatured alcohol in Italy. If made from agricultural surpluses, through a fermentation process, denatured alcohol was only lightly taxed. By contrast, denatured alcohol of synthetic origin, made from ethylene, a petroleum derivative, was so heavily taxed that it could not be sold on the Italian market. As a result there was no Italian production of denatured alcohol of synthetic origin and no imports. The Court found the tax differentiation in conformity with Article 95. It was satisfied with the fact it was equally uneconomical to produce or to import in Italy denatured alcohol of synthetic origin.

It is submitted that, in Chemial Farmaceutici, the Court should have verified whether denatured alcohol produced in other Member States was not mostly of synthetic origin. If this had been so, the tax differentiation could have been viewed as affording protection to Italian products.

*The Permissible Difference Regarding the Payment of VAT on Imports before 1993*

The prohibition of internal discriminatory taxes normally implies that domestic and imported goods be treated equally not only with respect to the rate of taxation, but also with respect to the base on which taxes are assessed or the way taxes are collected. This was confirmed in the Irish Alcoholic Beverages case.[40] There, the Court decided that Ireland was in breach of Article 95 because, by comparison with domestic products, imported alcoholic beverages were subject to excise duties at an earlier commercial stage.

Later, in Dansk Denkavit,[41] the Court had to deal with facts somewhat similar to the Irish case, but this time in a much broader context, that of the VAT system. A Danish firm pointed out that VAT on domestic transactions was paid only at the end of a reference period and in the form of a balance (VAT received minus VAT paid). This meant that on the Danish market on average, a 95 day delay separated the moment goods were invoiced from the moment VAT had to be paid. By contrast, on average, VAT on imports had to be paid 45 days after the imported goods had cleared through customs. Danish Denkavit argued that, as a result, it was financially more advantageous to buy domestic goods and that the way VAT was imposed on imports was thus discriminatory. In fact, at the time, imports in the other Member States were subject to the same type of system, distinct from the VAT system applicable to domestic transactions.

As could be foreseen, the Court of Justice rejected Dansk Denkavit's argument which, if accepted, could have meant that all the Member States had to change their VAT system on imports. The Court distinguished the Irish case relating to the payment of excise duties on alcoholic beverages stating:

"imported products are, as regards tax periods, in a position which cannot be compared with that of products subject to the internal system, since their tax position is net as from the time of importation.

"Consequently, . . . such tax periods need not, as Community legislation stands at the present time, be taken into consideration in the comparison of the payment and collection periods granted in respect of imports and in respect of domestic transactions."

Obviously the Dansk Denkavit judgment was influenced by the fact that earlier, the Council had been unable to unify the manner in which VAT on imports and VAT on domestic transactions was collected. The Court realized that this was a question for the Community legislator, and not for the Community judge, to decide in view of its important financial implications for the Member States and its administrative complexity.

Since 1993, VAT on imports is collected in the same manner as VAT on domestic transactions.

## 4. A Few General Remarks to Conclude

1. The prohibition of charges having an equivalent effect to customs duties extends beyond the realm of discriminatory or protective taxes. However, cases where national taxes of a non-discriminatory or protective character have been forbidden by the Court of Justice have been few and of no great economic import. Today, insofar as intra-Community trade is concerned, one may wish to simplify EC law and bring all cases regarding domestic taxes bearing on goods within the scope of Article 95. They would all be examined in the light of the non-discrimination principle (understood as encompassing the prohibition of taxes with a protective effect). Those which discriminate completely against products from other Member States would be completely forbidden. Those which discriminate in part would be partially forbidden. This would save the Court of Justice and domestic courts the time they continue to spend on the sometimes arcane distinction between taxes having an equivalent effect and internal taxes. Actually, today, the distinction is of no practical consequence in the context of intra-Community trade.

2. It is only in the external trade of the Community that the distinction between the two types of taxes remains important. The Court of Justice has decided that, under the Treaty, Member States have been forbidden to establish new taxes having an equivalent effect to customs duties, bearing on trade with third countries, from the moment the Common Customs Tariff was in place.[42] By contrast, the Court has continuously refused to extend the prohibition of internal discriminatory taxes (in the sense of Article 95) to trade between Member States and third countries,[43] at least in the absence of an international agreement between the EC and a third country that would explicitly prohibit internal discriminatory taxes. However, even when internal discriminatory taxes are forbidden under an agreement between the EC and a third country, the prohibition is then not necessarily construed as broadly as under Article 95 of the EC Treaty.[44] By contrast, the Court of Justice is apparently ready to give the notion of taxes having effect to customs duties the same scope under a free trade agreement between the EC and a third country as under the EC Treaty.[45]

In the Community external trade, important practical consequences remain thus attached to the distinction between the two categories of taxes, particularly in view of the fact that taxes illegal under EC law are not only forbidden for the future, but are also subject to refunds.

3. In the context of Article 95, the concept of discrimination has received a broad, but also a flexible interpretation. As pointed out in the course of the paper, at times the interpretation may have been too broad or too strictly enforced, at other times, it may have been too flexible or too leniently

enforced. However, the main point, in view of the theme of the conference, is that the Court of Justice has refused to explicitly extend the prohibition beyond discriminatory or protective taxes. Actually, the Court was, in this regard, constrained by the very explicit wording of Article 95. The same constraint did not apply in the interpretation of the prohibition of "charges having an equivalent effect to customs duties," measures having an equivalent effect to quantitative restrictions," restrictions on freedom to supply services or restrictions on the freedom of establishment. These prohibitions have been given a scope which reaches beyond discriminatory or protective measures.

The difference in the interpretation of respectively Article 95 and Article 30 may explain the observation made by the Court of Justice in Danish Taxes on Cars. There, the Court left the door open for dealing with non-discriminatory taxes under Article 30. In my view, the door should not be left open, but should be closed. I submit that, for political as well as for technical reasons, the Court of Justice is not qualified—neither on the basis of Article 95 nor on the basis of Article 30—to pass judgment on the proper level of national taxes which do not discriminate against foreign-made products nor protect a domestic industry. The proper level of taxation is something which only Member States individually, through their respective political organs, or the Community legislator may determine on the basis of social and economic preferences expressed by their respective constituencies. The Treaty does not provide any criterion on the basis of which a judge could decide that a tax restricts intra-Community trade unduly. For instance, in the Danish case, how could the Court have determined the acceptable level of taxes on cars: by reference to the next most taxing Member State or by reference to some kind of European average? It is obvious that these are not acceptable criteria since their implementation would lead to very bizarre results.

I should add that, even in the framework of Article 30, the Court of Justice, when it deals with national price regulations, is usually careful to avoid discussing their economic or social merits. It essentially examines the possible discriminatory features or the possible protective effect of such regulations. Prices regulations which are neither discriminatory nor protective are, as such, deemed consistent with Article 30. Their justification is not discussed on the basis of either Article 36 or the doctrine of mandatory requirements. The same should apply to internal taxes if they were to be dealt with under Article 30.

Admittedly, in a price regulation case predating Keck, the Court had indicated, in an obiter dictum, that a price regulation indistinctly applicable to domestic and imported products would nevertheless violate Article 30 if it were to prevent importers from getting access to the market.[46] However, I think that the doctrine relating to market access impediments, developed in the context of Article 30 and then implemented in the Alpine Investments[47] and Bosman[48] cases, should be used with great care. It should be limited to cases where at least some protective effect can be shown.

NOTES

1. See the Capolongo judgment, 19 June 1973, ECR 611.

2. 14 December 1962, ECR 813.

3. 1 July 1969, ECR 211.

4. In addition to Fonds des diamantaires, cited supra, see Commission v. Denmark (Aflatoxin), 9 Nov. 1983, ECR 3573.

5. See Steinike, 22 March 1977, ECR 595.

6. See Cadsky, 26 February 1975, ECR 281.

7. See Van der Hulst, 23 January 1975, ECR 79.

8. Except Article 46 of the EC Treaty with respect to agricultural goods.

9. The Court has refused to incorporate the Article 36 exception in the field of taxes, see Commission v. Italy (Works of art), 10 December 1968, ECR 618.

10. See Rewe, 24 October 1973, ECR 1175.

11. 11 Dec. 1990, ECR I, 4509.

12. 26 October 1982, ECR 3641.

13. 1st July 1993, ECR 3751.

14. 25 Febr. 1988, ECR 1213.

15. See Pabst & Richarz, 29 April 1982, ECR 1331.

16. See Chiquita, 12 Dec. 1995, ECR 4533.

17. 14 Febr. 1978, ECR 207.

18. 7 May 1987, ECR 2013.

19. 27 Febr. 1980, ECR 417 and 12 July 1983, ECR 2265.

20. 11 July 1985, ECR 2503.

21. 27 Febr. 1980, ECR 347 (France), 385 (Italy), 447 (Denmark).

22. See the British Wine & Beer case, cited supra, together with Commission v. Belgium, 9 July 1987, ECR 3299.

23. 2 April 1998, as yet unreported.

24. 5 May 1982, ECR 140 and 21 May 1985, ECR 1491.

25. See for instance Bobie, 16 February 1977, ECR 247 or Commission v. Italy, 21 June 1988, ECR 3249.

26. See Statenskontrol, 29 June 1978, ECR 1543, confirmed by Scharbatke, 27 October 1993, ECR I, 5509.

27. Cited supra.

28. 17 July 1984, ECR 2727.

29. 9 July 1992, ECR I, 4431.

30. 27 May 1981, ECR 1413.

31. Commission v. Italy, 15 March 1983, ECR 601.

32. Commission v. Italy (Sparkling wines), 11 July 1985, ECR 2503.

33. Commission v. France, 27 February 1980, ECR 347.

34. 9 May 1985, ECR 1367.

35. See Hansen III, 7 May 1981, ECR 1165.

36. 8 January 1980, ECR 1.

37. 7 April 1987, ECR 1583.

38. Cited supra.

39. 14 January 1981, ECR 1.

40. Commission v. Ireland, 27 February 1980, ECR 481.

41. 14 January 1981, ECR 1.

42. See Fonds des diamantaires II, 13 December 1973, ECR 1609, and April, 5 October 1995, ECR 2919.

43. See Hansen, 10 October 1995, ECR 1787 and OTO, 13 July 1994, ECR 3281.

44. See Kupferberg and Metalsa, cited supra.

45. See Legros, 16 July 1992, ECR I, 4625.

46. Commission v. Belgium (Program contracts), 19 March 1991, ECR I-1275.

47. 10 May 1995, ECR I-114.

48. 15 December 1995, ECR I-4921.

CHAPTER 8

# After Keck and Mithouard: Free Movement of Goods in the EC, Market Access, and Non-Discrimination

*Piet Eeckhout*

The distinction which the European Court of Justice drew between product regulations and selling arrangements in the famous case of *Keck and Mithouard* is well known.[1] The Court decided to re-examine and clarify its case-law on Article 30 EC Treaty, the basic provision concerning free movement of goods, in the light of the increasing tendency of traders to invoke Article 30 as a means of challenging any rules whose effect is to limit their commercial freedom even where such rules are not aimed at products from other Member States.[2] The Court then referred to its established 'Cassis de Dijon' case law, according to which obstacles to free movement of goods which are the consequence of applying, to goods coming from other Member States where they are lawfully manufactured and marketed, rules that lay down requirements to be met by such goods constitute measures of equivalent effect prohibited by Article 30. This is so even if those rules apply without distinction to all products, unless their application can be justified by a public-interest objective taking precedence over the free movement of goods.[3] This is the test for product regulations, and the Court refers as examples to provisions relating to designation, form, size, weight, composition, presentation, labeling, packaging. For product regulations the test remains restriction-based, and not discrimination-based. Even measures which do not discriminate against imported products can be caught by Article 30. What matters is whether the measures restrict trade between Member States. The result of that approach is mutual recognition: a product lawfully produced and marketed in one Member State is in principle entitled to free circulation, and the importing Member State cannot impose its own product regulations unless justified by overriding public interest requirements.

By contrast, a different approach is adopted for selling arrangements. Contrary to what has previously been decided, the Court states, the application to products from other Member States of national provisions restricting or prohibiting certain selling arrangements is not such as to hinder trade so long as those provisions apply to all relevant traders operating within the national territory and so long as they affect in the same manner, in law and in fact, the marketing of domestic products and of those from other

Member States.[4] Thus, measures concerning selling arrangements remain outside the scope of Article 30, provided they are non-discriminatory. The Court takes the view that such measures, as applied to imported products, are not by nature such as to prevent the access of those products to the market or to impede access any more than it impedes the access of domestic products.[5]

The judgment has drawn a lot of criticism, one of the most recurring objections being that the different treatment of product regulations and selling arrangements is artificial, and that it is very difficult, if not impossible, to draw a clear line between the two. That is particularly true for advertising, as was emphasized by Advocate General Jacobs in his Opinion in *Leclerc-Siplec*.[6] There the Advocate General proposed an alternative test, focusing on the concept of market access. In his view, national measures are caught by Article 30 where there is a substantial restriction on market access. However, the Court did not at the time follow the Opinion and decided the case—which was on restrictions on television advertising—by applying *Keck*: the restrictions were considered to be selling arrangements, and since they were not discriminatory they fell outside the scope of Article 30.

A second general criticism was that the Court appeared to revert to a discrimination-based analysis under Article 30, and there was apprehension that this might produce an undesirable regression in the construction of the EC internal market—*Keck* could be a deconstruction of the internal market.[7]

Despite this criticism the Court in the first few years after *Keck* seemed to stick rigorously to the distinction between product regulations and selling arrangements. If anything, that seemed to suggest that *Keck* at least created some degree of legal certainty. However, a number of judgments which came out more recently appear to throw up new questions. The purpose of this paper is to discuss some recent cases which develop the test laid down in *Keck*, and which increasingly focus on the concept of market access. The paper first sets out the relevant cases. It subsequently analyses the market access test which those cases seem to lay down. It then concludes by briefly reconsidering non-discrimination, and by attempting to identify the parameters for a comparison between the EC law test for trade barriers and the approach within the WTO, which combines the notions of market access and non-discrimination.

Before we move into the analysis of the recent cases on free movement of goods, however, it may be noted that the concept of market access played a vital role in two judgments concerning other EC internal market freedoms. In *Alpine Investments*, which concerned the freedom to provide services, both the Advocate General and the Court emphasized that a prohibition of cold-calling in connection with offering certain investment services—a prohibition which was also applied to "exports" of those services—directly affected access to the market of other Member States.[8] There was thus no scope for applying the *Keck* principle in relation to those services and the restriction was in need of justification. Similarly, and with an explicit reference to *Alpine Investments*, the Court in *Bosman* decided that restrictions on transfers of football players, even if non-discriminatory, directly affected the free movement of workers (and thus access to the employment market of other Member States). Those restrictions were therefore not comparable to the rules on selling arrangements in issue in *Keck*.[9]

## 1. The Cases

The first cases which will be discussed are *Pistre and Others*[10] and *Familiapress* v *Bauer Verlag*.[11] *Pistre* concerned French legislation on the use of indications of "mountain" provenance for agricultural products and foodstuffs. The legislation protected those designations and instituted a system of authorizations. Pistre and Others were French producers prosecuted for failing to comply with the rules, on the grounds of having marketed in 1991 cooked meat products under a label on which appeared "montagne" or "Monts de Lacaune" without proper authorization. The Court examined the legislation under Article 30, despite the fact that the case appeared to be purely internal: French legislation was applied to French products produced by French producers. The Court said that the legislation might have effects on trade, in particular where it facilitates the marketing of goods of domestic origin to the detriment of imported goods. The French defense that the legislation was never applied against imported products was discarded because such products were not expressly excluded from its scope. Further, the legislation clearly discriminated against imports because it reserved use of the description "mountain" to products manufactured on national territory and made from domestic raw materials. Thus there was a discriminatory obstacle, which could not be justified under Article 36 because the description "mountain" cannot be characterized as an indication of provenance coming within the concept of industrial and commercial property.

The Court did not refer to the distinction between product regulations and selling arrangements, nor was there any need for doing so since the legislation was discriminatory and therefore in any event caught by Article 30. However, if the question had arisen, arguably the Court would have followed its rulings in *Clinique*[12] and *Mars*[13] and would have classified the regulation as a product regulation, since it concerned designations borne by the product. It is none the less obvious that the use of such designations will often be a component of a company's advertising or, more broadly, marketing strategy. Those designations are therefore likely to be used not only on the product but also in advertising relating to the product, and indeed the French provisions in issue in *Pistre* could be construed as also prohibiting such advertising in the absence of a proper authorization. Suppose that the French rules were used against television commercials for imported products, would they then be classified as a selling arrangement?

*Familiapress* again illustrated the difficulties associated with advertising. The case concerned Austrian legislation prohibiting, in effect, price puzzle competitions or games in periodicals. The aim of the legislation was to prevent cut-throat competition against small publishers, in order to maintain press diversity in what is already a highly concentrated press market. The legislation was invoked against the German magazine "Laura," which contained crossword puzzles offering readers the chance to take part in games for prizes.

Advocate General Tesauro carefully examined whether Article 30 applied. His starting-point was that, since the measure prevented the access to the Austrian market of magazines lawfully manufactured and marketed in the Member State of origin, it appeared at first sight capable of hindering intra-Community trade. He then considered the Austrian argument that the measure, relating to a mere method of sales promotion, concerned a selling arrangement in the meaning of *Keck*. Mr. Tesauro emphasized that the competitions in question formed part of the magazine's content and thus related directly to the product. He referred to *Mars* and pointed out that in *Keck* the Court stated that, where selling arrangements apply to all traders and are non-discriminatory, "the application of such rules to the sale of products from another Member State meeting the requirements laid down by that State is not by nature such as to prevent their access to the market or to impede access any more than it impedes the access of domestic products." It was clear in this case that the measure in question, by preventing the access to the market of the product in question, did not fall within the scope of the *Keck* principle.[14]

The Court was much shorter, but basically confirmed the approach of the Advocate General. It found that, even though the legislation was directed against a method of sales promotion, it bore on the actual content of the products and was thus not concerned with a selling arrangement. Moreover, the Court added, since it required traders established in other Member States to alter the contents of the periodical, the prohibition impaired access of the product concerned to the market of the Member State of importation and consequently hindered the free movement of goods.[15] That statement is interesting. Here the Court emphasizes the concept of market access, and seems to be giving it some degree of autonomy. There are two possible interpretations. Either the Court simply used the concept to corroborate its conclusion that the rules constituted a product regulation, and not a selling arrangement. Or, and that is a further step, the concept of market access is given more weight, and might in some cases actually determine whether a measure is subject to a *Cassis de Dijon* or a *Keck* type examination. Under the second interpretation one could envisage measures which would be classified as selling arrangements but for the impact on market access. Such measures, even if non-discriminatory, would need to be justified under the mandatory requirements or under Article 36. That interpretation would put some flesh on the reference in *Keck* to "certain" selling arrangements: only those selling arrangements which do not impair access to the market fall outside the scope of Article 30 (subject to the conditions imposed by *Keck*).

It may be noted that the remainder of the judgment in *Familiapress* perfectly illustrates the main advantage of the Court's ruling in *Keck*, which is to bring certain types of legislation out with the scope of Article 30 altogether, thus discharging from the often difficult task of examining the justification for the legislation in issue under the public interest requirements or under Article 36. In many cases that task will to a large extent fall on the referring court, like in *Familiapress*: the Court of Justice accepted the prohibition in issue, provided it was proportionate to maintenance of press diversity and that that objective could not be achieved by less restrictive means. That assumed, *inter alia*, that the newspapers offering the chance of winning a prize in games, puzzles or competitions were in competition with small newspaper publishers who were deemed to be unable to offer comparable prizes and the prospect of winning was liable to bring about a shift in demand. Furthermore, the national prohibition was not to constitute an obstacle to the marketing of newspapers which, albeit containing prize games, puzzles or competitions, did not give readers residing in the Member State concerned the opportunity to win a prize. It was for the national court to determine whether those conditions were satisfied on the basis of a study of the national press market concerned.[16] Clearly a daunting task.

The next judgment is *KO* v *De Agostini and TV-Shop*.[17] That case concerned Swedish restrictions on television advertising, examined under the EC television directive and under Articles 30 and 59 of the Treaty. Advocate General Jacobs referred to *Leclerc-Siplec*, thus accepting that the restrictions concerned selling arrangements. However, he expressed doubts on whether the *Keck* condition of non-discrimination was fulfilled. The Advocate General reverted to his Opinion in *Leclerc-Siplec*, arguing that "it would be inconsistent with the objectives of the Treaty to interpret *Keck* so as to exclude from the scope of Article 30 a total ban on the advertising of a product which may be lawfully sold in the Member State where the ban is applied and in other Member States: the effect of such a ban would be that manufacturers in other Member States would find it virtually impossible to penetrate the market in which the ban was imposed, so that the measure would be tantamount to a quantitative restriction on trade between Member States." However the discrimination test was interpreted, it was difficult to resist the conclusion that in practice such a ban would almost certainly have a perceptible effect on imports. A fortiori the same concern arose with regard to a total ban on the television advertising of any product to a particular sector of consumers—as in the case of the Swedish ban on advertising to children. Therefore such a ban had to satisfy imperative requirements relating to the general interest.[18]

The Court was not as outspoken as the Advocate General. It classified the restrictions on advertising as selling arrangements, and then referred to the conditions which *Keck* imposes. On non-discrimination the Court stated that it could not be excluded "that an outright ban, applying in one Member State, of a type of promotion for a product which is lawfully sold there might have a greater impact on products from other Member States." It then referred to De Agostini's argument that television advertising was the only effective form of promotion enabling it to penetrate the Swedish market since it had no other advertising methods for reaching children and their parents (De Agostini sells a children's magazine about dinosaurs). The Court only noted that argument, however, taking the view that the efficacy of the various types of promotion was a question of fact to be determined by the national court.[19]

Thus the Court again made a reference to market access, albeit in a somewhat veiled manner. If restrictions on advertising are such as to impair market penetration for new entrants from other Member States then there is factual discrimination in the sense of *Keck*, and the restriction will have to be justifiable on the basis of imperative requirements or on the basis of Article 36. There is of course considerable merit in such an approach, on condition that the test is further refined so as to permit national courts to assess whether market access is actually impaired.

There are two further judgments which, although the Court did not even mention *Keck*, are arguably highly relevant. *Harry Franzén*[20] concerned the Swedish alcohol monopoly. In his Opinion Advocate General Elmer made an interesting analysis of post-*Keck* case-law. Like Advocate General Tesauro he laid stress on the passage in *Keck* where the Court stated that non-discriminatory selling arrangements were not such as to prevent access to the market or to impede access any more than they impede the access of domestic products. Mr. Elmer also took the view that the reference to "certain" selling arrangements confirms that some selling arrangements, even if non-discriminatory, would be caught by Article 30 because of their effect on trade (the second interpretation mentioned above). He further referred to *Commission* v *Greece*[21] on processed milk for infants and *Banchero*[22] on retail distribution of tobacco in Italy. In both cases the Court stated that the measures did not impede market access, and in the latter case the Court stressed that retailers were free to purchase their products and thus purchases were not centralized. According to Advocate General Elmer, that suggests that if there had been centralization the Court would have examined the legislation under Article 30. He subsequently also referred to *Bosman* and *Alpine Investments*.

The Advocate General took the view that commercial monopolies are subject to both Article 30 and Article 37 (the specific EC Treaty provision on commercial monopolies), and examined the alcohol monopoly on that basis. The Court did not follow his Opinion in that respect, as it distinguished between the rules relating to the existence and operation of the monopoly as such, which were to be tested against the non-discrimination rule of Article 37 only, and the other provisions of the Swedish legislation (mainly on the production and wholesale licensing system for alcoholic drinks), which had to be examined with reference to Article 30. The Court accepted that the monopoly was not discriminatory against imports. The licensing system, however, constituted an obstacle to importation in that it imposed additional costs on imported beverages (there were restrictive conditions as well as fees and charges), and the Swedish Government's own evidence showed that few licenses were issued and almost all of them went to traders established in Sweden. The Court concluded that such legislation was contrary to Article 30, and the Swedish Government had been unable to show that the licensing system was proportionate to the public health aim or that that aim could not have been achieved by measures less restrictive of intra-Community trade.[23]

It is striking that the Court did not refer to *Keck*, although arguably the licensing system could be regarded as a selling arrangement. Perhaps the view was taken that, where there is a commercial monopoly which is, by its nature, restrictive of trade, but which is subject only to the non-discrimination rule of Article 37, any further restrictions have to be made subject to the broader *Cassis de Dijon*-type test. Alternatively, it might have been thought that, as the licensing system entailed discrimination in fact, it fell outside the scope of *Keck* in any event.

The last case discussed here is *Christian Dior* v *Evora*,[24] on the attempted use of trade mark rights and copyright to stop a reseller outside the selective distribution system advertising the perfumes which it markets. It is worth noting, before looking at the case, that the use of intellectual property rights has appeared to fall outside the product regulations—selling arrangements dichotomy. In the past most cases on the relationship between intellectual property rights and intra-Community trade concerned parallel imports,[25] and it was always assumed, also after *Keck*, that in those circumstances there is a breach of Article 30, the discussion concentrating on Article 36. In *Evora*, however, the question was raised whether Dior's reliance on its trade mark rights and copyright was indeed contrary to Article 30, and the reply to that question was obviously not a foregone conclusion since Dior did not object to the parallel imports as such, but only to their advertising by Evora, which allegedly damaged Dior's luxurious and prestigious image. However, the Court brushed aside all doubts about the applicability of Article 30 by stating that it was sufficient that the main proceedings concerned goods which the reseller had procured through parallel imports and that a prohibition of advertising such as that sought in the main proceedings would render commercialization, and consequently access to the market for those goods, appreciably more difficult.[26] Thus the market access concept was again used, centering apparently on the right of a parallel importer to freely import, market, and advertise his imports.

## 2. Market Access

It is clear from the above cases that the Court gives at least some weight to the concept of market access which in Advocate General Jacobs' view is central to determining the scope of Article 30. Two questions follow. First, how much weight is actually given to the market access concept, how does it affect the analysis under Article 30? And secondly, what does the concept imply, what does it add to the so well-developed case-law on Article 30 (perhaps in some respects too developed)?

There appears to be some shift of emphasis in the judgments. In *Familiapress* the Court referred to market access as a secondary, corroborating point, after having concluded that the Austrian legislation bore on the actual content of imported periodicals and was thus not concerned with a selling arrangement. In *De Agostini* the reference to market access was more veiled: the Court first classified the restrictions on advertising as a selling arrangement, and then accepted that those restrictions might impede market penetration and thus have a discriminatory effect on imports. Here market access becomes relevant in examining whether national provisions on selling arrangements comply with the non-discrimination condition imposed by *Keck*. However, in *Franzén* and *Evora* market access appears to occupy a more dominant position. There is no reference to *Keck*, despite the fact that the cases related to, respectively, the licensing of traders and advertising, both arguably some form of selling arrangements. In *Franzén* the Court simply stated that the licensing system constituted an obstacle to trade, and in *Evora* that it was sufficient that the case concerned parallel imports and that a prohibition of advertising would render access to the market for those parallel imports appreciably more difficult. In those cases, therefore, the fact that the national measures impede market access appears to pre-empt the classification as a product regulation or selling arrangement. That does not necessarily imply that the Court seeks to abandon that classification. One could well read the judgments as saying that, since market access is impeded, there is in any event discrimination against imports and thus the *Keck* conditions are not fulfilled and the measures are caught by Article 30. Moreover, both cases are to some degree particular. *Franzén* concerned the interplay of Articles 30 and 37, and *Evora* concerned intellectual property rights and parallel imports. Yet the least one can say about the analyzed cases is that, where market access is impeded, the Court will examine a measure under Article 30, looking at its justification under the "imperative requirements" or under Article 36. One step further, one could say that the concept of market access informed *Keck*, and thus explains it to some extent. As Advocate General Tesauro pointed out, in *Keck* the Court referred to the fact that non-discriminatory selling arrangements are not such as to prevent market access or to impede market access more than in the case of domestic products. Thus it would be the concern with market access which explains the distinction between product regulations and selling arrangements.

But what is meant by market access? What does the concept connote, and what does it add to the well-known tests which were previously developed in the case-law: discrimination against imported products, the *Dassonville*-formula of measures capable of hindering intra-Community trade, the *Cassis de Dijon*-test of mandatory requirements and mutual recognition, and the principle of proportionality? Of course products from one Member State have to be granted access to the market of another Member State. That is inherent to the concept of an internal market, and measures impeding access to the market are naturally suspect under Article 30. And what is the difference between a measure restricting market access and a measure capable of hindering intra-Community trade?

In this author's view the concept of market access does draw attention to one particular aspect of the Court's case-law on Article 30 which deserves some clarification. By referring to market access the Court appears to focus on the position of specific products imported from other Member States, or on the position of producers or traders engaging in intra-Community trade, perhaps more than in the past. That is not as self-evident as it may seem. It is arguable that at least some of the problems of the Article 30 case-law stem from what one could call the abstract character of that case-law. Cases on

Article 30 reach the Court in two ways: on a reference by a national court or in an action by the Commission against a Member State under Article 169 of the Treaty. In the case of a reference the Court has no jurisdiction over the facts of the case, nor is it able to apply Article 30 to the facts of that case. The Court can only interpret Article 30. Of course we all know that the Court often attempts to do that in a very specific manner, in order to be as helpful as possible. None the less, it is not possible for the Court to take the final step and say: in the case of *Christian Dior* v *Evora* Article 30 prohibits Christian Dior from relying on its trade mark rights against the advertising by Evora; or, in *De Agostini* the Konsumentombudsmannen cannot apply Swedish legislation on advertising against De Agostini because that would amount to a breach of Article 30. In Article 169 actions, on the other hand, the Court is of course entitled to look at the facts, but these actions almost invariably concern general legislation or other types of general action by the authorities of a Member State.

In contrast it is clear that Article 30 of the Treaty creates directly effective rights for Community citizens and companies engaging in intra-Community trade.[27] In legal terms the internal market is not merely an abstract notion referring to a set of economic transactions, but also a concrete asset to which citizens and companies are entitled.[28] Hence rulings on Article 30 should also have a concrete dimension, concentrating on the specific position in which traders and consumers find themselves and examining whether they are faced with unjustified hurdles when attempting to benefit from intra-Community trade—i.e., to have access to the market of another Member State. Thus understood the concept of market access may include what one could describe as the concrete, or personal, or rights-based dimension of the free movement of goods. It is submitted that such a concrete approach explains and justifies the different (or potentially different) outcome of cases such as, on the one hand, *Keck and Mithouard* and *Leclerc-Siplec*, and, on the other hand, *De Agostini*, *Franzén* and *Evora*. *Keck* involved French supermarkets re-selling what were apparently French products ("Sati rouge" coffee and "Picon bière") at a loss. Those supermarkets could not point to any link between their case and intra-Community trade other than the fact that they were established near the border with Germany and that the French legislation in issue might also be applied in the case of sales of imported products. *Leclerc-Siplec* concerned a prohibition on television advertising by the distribution sector; the case was brought on a refusal by TF1 to broadcast a commercial for Leclerc-Siplec's gas stations. The only link with intra-Community trade was that the products sold at those stations could have been imported from other Member States. There was however no indication in the case that the prohibition in issue constituted a noticeable restriction on imports. *De Agostini* is different. Here we have an Italian company selling on the Swedish market and facing restrictions on advertising which could affect its competitive position on that market. *Franzén* is also clearly concerned with companies aiming to export to another Member State: the Swedish licensing requirements are an obvious barrier to selling alcohol products on the Swedish market. And *Evora* involved a parallel importer, as the Court pointed out, one of a breed which obviously needs some protection if the internal market is to become more integrated.

The suggested concrete approach was touched upon by Advocate General Cosmas in *Belgapom* v *ITM and Vocarex*.[29] That case concerned Belgian legislation prohibiting sales at a loss, and it was not clear whether the case related to imports. Advocate General Cosmas considered the point whether Article 30 could apply to a purely internal situation. In his view it could be argued that "the connecting factor bringing a given situation within the ambit of Article 30 of the Treaty should be sought in the provenance of the goods allegedly affected, in the specific case, by a given national measure. The application of Article 30 would thus be excluded if the situation which gave rise to the proceedings before the national court exclusively and solely concerned goods produced or manufactured in the Member State in which they were marketed and in which the dispute at issue arose."[30] The Court did not reply to that suggestion and simply applied *Keck and Mithouard*. It is none the less submitted that, although the above statement may be somewhat too strong in that there might be internal situations where Article 30 should be considered, it does bring home an important point for the further development of the Article 30 case-law.[31]

In that respect one should also not lose sight of the fact that the result of an Article 177 reference is never to invalidate national legislation as such. Where such legislation is contrary to Article 30 it cannot be applied—that is all.[32] For some national provisions the result of a ruling by the Court may be that they can no longer be applied at all, but in most cases the result will only be that the provisions cannot be applied against imports. It is thus perfectly apposite for a national court to consider whether national legislation operates as a barrier to trade on the facts of the case before it, rather than in the abstract; indeed that is what Community law requires the national court to do. The 1997 cases clarify that, when doing so, the national court should in particular investigate whether there is a restriction on market access. From that perspective, the Court's judgment in *Keck and Mithouard* makes more sense than many commentators are willing to concede: where selling arrangements are in issue, and there is no de iure or de facto discrimination against imports, market access is unlikely to be impaired. Perhaps one can add, in the light of the recent cases, that where provisions on selling arrangements do affect market access the *Keck* exemption will not apply and the provisions will need to be justified.

This leads to some comments on the potential extension of *Keck* to other freedoms, in particular the freedom to provide services, which is closest to the free circulation of goods. The above concrete approach brings out a fundamental reason for great caution towards such an extension. Goods are tangible, and as such the object of a range of transactions. At any stage of those transactions the question may be raised whether certain restrictions on those transactions affect intra-Community trade—the import (or market access) transaction. It is none the less clear that the effect will be more or less direct, visible, and ascertainable, depending on the transaction stage involved. Thus in *Keck* the effect on imports of the rules on sales at a loss was considered insufficient for bringing those rules within the scope of Article 30. However, services are intangible, they are basically a legal fiction denoting certain types of transactions between economic operators—individuals and companies. Therefore a restriction on the provision of services will by definition affect the service providers themselves, and where those service providers operate across borders the restriction will have to be examined under Articles 59 and 60 of the Treaty. Again, if one looks at the fundamental freedoms from a personal, rights-based perspective, it is obvious that it is difficult to transpose *Keck* to services—as indeed to freedom of establishment and the freedom of movement for workers.

## 3. Non-Discrimination and WTO Law

The recent case-law demonstrates that *Keck* is part of a natural dialectic process. As a reaction to cases stretching the free movement of goods principle beyond its inherent elasticity of a principle concerned with trade between Member States (cases where it is argued that an internal restriction on the marketing of goods has an automatic knock-on effect on trade between Member States), *Keck* was proclaimed as a stop-sign which may have appeared fundamental and revolutionary. However, the subsequent case-law very much softens its impact by making increased reference to market access, thus qualifying the alleged return to a non-discrimination principle. In this author's view, *Keck* does not at all jeopardize the construction of the internal market, since it deals with the approach to borderline cases in terms of integrating the European market. It may be worth noting, in that respect, that there are far more significant issues for the internal market in other areas, such as the scope of intellectual property protection, issues of competition policy, and elements of the EC's trade policy like anti-dumping.

As the present volume deals with the non-discrimination principle, however, it may be useful to take a further look at elements of non-discrimination in the application of Article 30, notwithstanding the fact that *Keck* is certainly not a general "return" to non-discrimination. We may then try to contrast that with the approach to non-discrimination at WTO level.

Non-discrimination is part of the *Keck* test, in that measures concerning selling arrangements fall outside the scope of Article 30 on the condition of being non-discriminatory, in law and in fact. *De Agostini* illustrates that a broad view may be taken of this condition. There the Court acknowledged that an outright ban of a type of promotion for a product lawfully sold in a Member State might have a greater impact on products from other Member States. That is clearly connected with the important role of advertising in obtaining access to new markets, and thus in achieving greater market integration. The judgment clarifies, if that was necessary, that so-called indistinctly applicable selling arrangements (selling arrangements which do not on their face treat imported products differently) may none the less be caught by Article 30, and made subject to the *Cassis de Dijon* test of justification under public interest requirements.

Arguably, the broader the approach to non-discrimination under *Keck*, the less difference there will be between the approach to selling arrangements and classic *Cassis de Dijon* cases. Although in relation to the latter the language of discrimination is no longer used in the Court's case-law, there remains scope for identifying elements of discrimination against imported products also in those cases. One could say that where a Member State applies its legislation to an imported product lawfully produced and marketed in another Member State it is in fact treating in an identical manner products which are not in a comparable position: in archetypal terms, the home product has been produced in accordance with that legislation, whereas the imported product has been produced in accordance with the legislation of the Member State of production. And to treat identically products in a different position amounts to discrimination. That is not to say that Article 30 as a whole boils down to non-discrimination—the case-law shows that it is more than that, and that it is not helpful to try and cast the Court's approach to non-tariff barriers in non-discrimination terms. The point is that, the broader the reach of non-discrimination, the further one moves in the direction of market integration.

There is another non-discrimination element in *Keck* which is worth mentioning. In *Keck* the Court has it that, where selling arrangements are non-discriminatory, they do not prevent access to the market, or impede access of imported products any more than they impede the access of domestic products.[33] Where access to the market is not prevented, but only impeded, the overall test for the application of Article 30 seems to be that market access of imported products must not be more impeded than market access of domestic products. Article 30 is not about general deregulation, it is about integrating markets.

How does that compare to WTO law? It is striking that both in relation to goods (GATT) and in relation to services (GATS) the concepts of non-discrimination (in the form of MFN and national treatment) and market access also play a vital role. It is none the less clear that the strong EC imperative of market integration is not as such present in the WTO setting. This would suggest that in WTO law market access and non-discrimination are tools which are not capable of cutting as deep into the regulatory autonomy of States as the prohibitions on trade restrictions in the EC. The question can be raised, however, whether at present the difference is not rather one of quantum than of quality. It is clear that in the EC there is a much more developed body of case-law, complemented by a high level of harmonization of legislation. The quantity of intervention is therefore much higher than in the WTO. But, as was noted, the basic concepts are similar, and when one looks at the approach to the interpretation of those concepts in WTO law, one discovers great potential for the development of far-reaching case-law. The GATT panel process has established that both Article III, on national treatment, and Article XI, on import and export restrictions, aim to protect expectations of the Contracting Parties as to the competitive relationship between their products and those of the other Contracting Parties.[34] Those provisions therefore oblige WTO members to establish and maintain equality in the conditions of competition affecting trade in goods. That principle is also incorporated in GATS Article XVII on national treatment, which refers in paragraph 3 to conditions of competition. A moment's thought will make it clear that this test of equality in the conditions of competition may have just as much potential as the tests developed by the European Court of Justice analyzed in the preceding sections.

One would therefore hope that a dialogue could develop, at academic level and in practice, between EC law experts and WTO law experts, on how the basic principles are developing and on the lessons to be drawn from each other's experiences in finding a balance between liberalizing trade and integrating markets, on the one hand, and safeguarding essential national policies, on the other.

NOTES

1. Joined Cases C-267/91 and C-268/91 *Keck and Mithouard* [1993] ECR I-6097.

2. See paragraph 14 of the judgment.

3. See paragraph 15.

4. See paragraph 16.

5. See paragraph 17.

6. Case C-412/93 *Leclerc-Siplec* v *TF1 Publicité and M6 Publicité* [1995] ECR I-179.

7. Compare with D. Chalmers, "Repackaging the Internal Market—The Ramifications of the *Keck* Judgment," *ELR* (1994), 385–403 and M. Ross, "*Keck*—Grasping the Wrong Nettle," in Caiger and Floudas (eds), *1996 Onwards: Lowering the Barriers Further* (John Wiley & Sons 1996) 45–62.

8. Case C-384/93 *Alpine Investments* [1995] ECR I-1141, paragraphs 58 to 61 of the Opinion and paragraph 38 of the judgment.

9. Case C-415/93 *Union Royale Belge des Sociétés de Football Association and Others* v *Bosman and Others* [1995] ECR I-4921, paragraph 103 of the judgment. See also paragraph 206 of the Opinion of Advocate General Lenz.

10. Joined Cases C-321/94, C-322/94, C-323/94 and C-324/94 *Pistre and Others* [1997] ECR I-2343.

11. Case C-368/95 *Familiapress* v *Bauer Verlag* [1997] ECR I-3689. For a general and excellent discussion of the state of play as regards *Keck* before the cases discussed here see S. Weatherill, "After *Keck*: Some thoughts on how to clarify the clarification," 33 *CMLRev.* (1996) 885–906, with further references to literature.

12. Case C-315/92 *Verband Sozialer Wettbewerb* v *Clinique Laboratories and Estée Lauder* [1994] ECR I-317.

13. Case C-470/93 *Verein gegen Unwesen in Handel und Gewerbe Köln* v *Mars* [1995] ECR I-1923.

14. See paragraphs 5 to 10 of the Opinion.

15. Paragraphs 11 and 12 of the judgment.

16. See the Court's ruling.

17. Joined Cases C-34/95, C-35/95 and C-36/95 *KO* v *De Agostini and TV-Shop* [1997] ECR I-3843.

18. Paragraphs 95 to 101 of the Opinion.

19. Paragraphs 39 to 44 of the judgment.

20. Case C-189/95 *Harry Franzén* [1997] ECR I-5909.

21. Case C-391/92 *Commission* v *Greece* [1995] ECR I-1621.

22. Case C-387/93 *Banchero* [1995] ECR I-4663.

23. See paragraphs 67 to 77 of the judgment.

24. Case C-337/95 *Christian Dior* v *Evora* [1997] ECR I-6013.

25. See for an overview P. Oliver, *Free Movement of Goods in the European Community,* 3rd ed. (Sweet and Maxwell 1996), 247–300.

26. Paragraph 51 of the judgment.

27. Compare with the Opinion of Advocate General Jacobs in *Leclerc-Siplec,* where he states that the guiding principle should be that all undertakings which engage in a legitimate economic activity in a Member State should have unfettered access to the whole of the Community market (paragraph 41).

28. Compare with Chalmers, cited above, at 392–396, where he develops arguments concerning an individual right to trade, but along different lines.

29. Case C-63/94 *Belgapom* v *ITM and Vocarex* [1995] ECR I-2467.

30. Paragraph 14 of the Opinion.

31. For another example of the concrete approach compare the two Opinions by Advocate General Van Gerven in *Keck.* Compare also with the theory developed by Sascha Oliver Hödl, *Die Beurteilung von verkaufsbehindernden Massnahmen im Europäischen Binnenmarkt* (Nomos 1997).

32. See Joined Cases 314 to 316/81 and 83/82 *Procureur de la République* v *Waterkeyn* [1982] ECR 4337.

33. See paragraph 17 of *Keck.*

34. See e.g. United States - Taxes on Petroleum and Certain Imported Substances, *BISD* 34S/136.

CHAPTER 9

# Comments on Papers Presented by Paul Demaret and Piet Eeckout

*Jacques Bourgeois*

The discussant has the easy part. The main theme and the variations are written by the rapporteur(s). The discussant is there like a pianist in a jazz band to fill gaps, if there are any, without having to do his bit of improvisation.

Both papers are clear and concise. They also complement each other. Unlike on the US Federal system where there is one single main inter-State commerce clause, in the EC legal system there are several "inter-State commerce" clauses relating to goods (Article 12 on customs duties and import charges having equivalent effect to customs duties; Article 30 on quantitative restrictions and measures having equivalent effect to quantitative restrictions; Article 95 on discriminatory and protective internal indirect taxes) as well as "inter-State commerce" clauses relating to capital movements, establishment, persons, and services. Fortunately, Paul Demaret and Piet Eeckhout entered into a market sharing agreement avoiding overlaps on subject matter.

## 1. EC Aspects

This does not mean that they agree on their assessment of the case-law of the Court of Justice of the European Communities (hereinafter: the ECJ). More precisely, and being aware of the risk inherent in simplifying, I would say that Piet Eeckhout appears to support the broad interpretation of the prohibition on Member States regulatory action, while Paul Demaret advocates an interpretation that takes the interests protected by Member States regulation more into account. In so doing, they echo a debate that is maybe not new but was bound to become more robust. As traditional barriers to trade disappear and economic integration proceeds, the effect of non-traditional barriers is increasingly felt and objected to by those most interested in carrying on business across Member State lines. From their perspective, whether or not Member State regulation has the object to impede trade does not matter, the effect counts.

Paul Demaret criticizes the overly broad interpretations of the ECJ. In his introduction and in his concluding remarks he takes the view that the ECJ in its case law or the EC "commerce clauses" does not leave enough room to protect legitimate interests served by Member States regulation. This is a criticism often heard. However, a critical analysis is not complete if it does not include a review of the end-result of the case-law, i.e., the proportion of cases in which the judgments of the ECJ resulted in the impossibility for Member States to protect any longer the legitimate interests which their regulations were meant to safeguard.[1]

There is an interesting difference between the ECJ's approach of the EC "commerce clauses" on trade in goods and that of the EC "commerce clauses" on capital movement, or movement of persons and trade in services. Under the Keck/Mithouard doctrine product regulations are caught by Article 30 EC, regulations on "selling arrangements" are not, unless they are discriminatory. The ECJ does not make such distinction when interpreting the other EC "commerce clauses." Piet Eeckhout refers to the most recurring objections being that the distinction is artificial and that it is very difficult, if not impossible, to draw a clear line between the two. And he demonstrates this well in his paper. Following the path opened by certain Advocates general of the ECJ, Piet Eeckhout suggests replacing the distinction between "product regulations" and regulations on "selling arrangements" by the concept of "substantial restriction on market access." This raises the question of whether this should be quantified and how.

In a truly Hegelian fashion Paul Demaret presents then a sort of anti-thesis. This leads almost inevitably to another, more fundamental, issue: is the decisive criterion "discrimination" or is it the broader criterion of access to (other Member States') markets? This too is an old debate in legal literature. It is echoed by Paul Demaret and Piet Eeckhout. Paul Demaret acknowledges that the case law on EC "commerce clauses," other than Article 95 EC, goes beyond prohibiting discriminatory features of Member State regulations but considers that the "market impediments" test "should be used with great care." Commenting on his paper as an "agent provocateur" on could say that at least implicitly he is in favor of the theory that only discriminatory measures should be caught. Piet Eeckhout takes the view that "the concept of market access may include the concrete, or personal, or rights based dimension of the free movement of goods."

It seems fair to say that the tendency of the ECJ is indeed to structure the various EC "commerce clauses" also as rights of the EC citizens and not only as the right of EC citizens not to be discriminated against but also the right of these citizens to access the EC market as a whole. The ECJ defines that the EC should operate as a market under conditions as close as possible to the conditions occurring in a genuine internal market (Schul [1982] ECR 1490 para 33).

The ECJ approach may be illustrated by the well-known case of the Belgian soccer player who was prevented from joining a French club because this club refused to pay a high transfer fee to the Belgian club as required by the rules of the European Soccer Federation (Bosman [1995] ECR I-4921). What this effectively amounts to is the right for Mr. Bosman derived from EC law to take up employment in another Member State without having to obtain the agreement of his club or of the European Soccer Federation. Nationality had nothing to do with it. One should, however, not overstate the significance of this development of EC law. It remains within the scope ratione materiae of the EC Treaty, i.e., relating to matters covered by this Treaty, and it arises when a citizen of a Member State wants to take up employment in another Member State.

As I see it, this is not an issue of the ECJ shifting the boundary between EC law and Member State law. The only genuine issue is one of the relationship between the judiciary and the legislative bodies of the EC.

## 2. WTO Aspects

The legal developments in the EC in relation to trade in goods and services, to the right of establishment, to movement of persons and capital may have a WTO aspects. E.g. under the Cassis de Dijon doctrine EC Member State A is bound to accept goods from EC Member State B, that do not comply with technical rules of EC Member State A, provided that these goods were produced and marketed in Member State B in compliance with the technical rules of that Member State, except for mandatory requirements in Member State. A. Under EC law, the problem whether a good marketed in EC Member State B in compliance with that Member State's technical rules but produced in a third country must be accepted by Member State A has, to my knowledge, not been formally resolved.

In WTO terms, the issue whether, if Member State A were to refuse the goods originating in the third country, that third country could successfully rely on the national treatment clause to claim the same treatment in Member State A on goods originating in Member State B does not appear to have been settled so far. Paul Demaret referred to the EC's schizophrenic attitude in this respect. One could read Cassis de Dijon as applying only to goods originating in Member States. Nevertheless, if the third country good marketed in Member State B complies with that Member State's technical regulation, there does not seem to be a rationale to allow Member State A to prohibit its sale. From a WTO perspective the EC cannot present itself as one entity with common internal trade rules on the one hand, and deny national (EC) treatment to goods originating in third countries on the other. One cannot have one's cake and eat it.

NOTES

1. In the discussion on his report Paul Demaret offered a list of cases.

CHAPTER 10

# Market Integration in a Small Federal State (Switzerland): The Role of Public Health

*Olivier Guillod*

Switzerland provides an interesting case for studying the process of market integration. It is a federal State made of 26 "cantons" enjoying broad legislating powers which have formed as many local markets for more than a century. It has a long tradition of direct democracy, with tools such as the right of initiative and the referendum on federal Acts. Even though it is not a member of the European Union, not even of the European Economic Area, it nevertheless plays a prominent role in international trade and finance. It is a small country in geographic (circa 40'000 square kilometers) as well as demographic terms (about 7 millions people), but a diverse one in terms of culture, nationality (20% of the population does not hold the Swiss citizenship) and language (there are three official languages, used for all federal legal texts: German, French, and Italian).

The Swiss judiciary is made of 26 cantonal systems of civil, criminal, and administrative courts of first and second instance, plus one Federal Court, as a court of last instance. It has shown a striking political stability for the last fifty years or more, due mainly to a profound taste for coalition and compromise.[1]

Finally, Switzerland has probably been the country in Europe with the softest antitrust legislation.[2] As a result, there has been for a long time a rather soft economic competition within the country, illustrated by the numerous domestic "cartels,"[3] by contrast with the growing international competition.

If the choice of Switzerland was appropriate for studying the process of market integration, the limited scope of this contribution did not allow to report on all aspects of such a broad issue. Since my specific field of research is health law, I was asked to explore how the notion of "health of the public" has been construed and used by cantons to restrict trade and obstruct market integration. Such a perspective is different from the usual focus of health law specialists who tend to study the dynamics of the health care system or of the health professional-patient relationship, in order to find the best ways to promote the health of the population while protecting fundamental individual rights. At the same time, the specificities of health have usually not been considered by the specialists of constitutional law or competition law. In other words, the topic is at the junction between two areas of the law. That may explain why it is almost unexplored territory, at least in Switzerland,[4] but perhaps also beyond Swiss borders.

The issue, obviously, is not limited to Switzerland. It is known in European law (especially article 36,[5] but also articles 48, 56, and 66 of the Treaty of Rome) as well as to specialists of the World Trade Organization. The scope of the present paper is, however, restricted to an analysis of the Swiss legal situation and does not encompass any comparison with European law or WTO rules. Lack of space and time as well as this author's insufficient knowledge of international economic law explain what might be perceived as a shortcoming of this paper. I believe, however, that most of the theoretical issues pertaining to the definition and use of the concept of public health are similar, whether we speak of intercantonal trade within Switzerland or of international trade at the world level.

My paper will be divided in three parts. In the first, I shall briefly recall the main features and peculiarities of the process of market integration in Switzerland. In the second part, I shall survey under what circumstances and within which boundaries cantons have adopted or may adopt trade restrictions for the sake of protecting public health. Special weight will be given to the decisions from the Federal Court. Finally, in the third part of the paper, I shall make a few personal, more analytical, comments on the notion of public health and its use by cantons to restrict trade and access to the market.

## 1. Market Integration in Switzerland: an Outline

### The Bear

Historically, the first important step towards market integration in Switzerland goes back to 1874 when the (second) federal Constitution [Cst] was adopted in a popular referendum. Article 31 Cst provides that: "*La liberté du commerce et de l'industrie est garantie sur tout le territoire de la Confédération . . . Les prescriptions cantonales sur l'exercice du commerce et de l'industrie ainsi que sur leur imposition sont réservées . . .*"[6]

Article 31 Cst has been construed[7] as fulfilling three main functions:

1. Guaranteeing the right of an individual to chose any lucrative economic activity (individual right function).

2. Ensuring an economic system based on competition and a free market (constitutive function).
3. Achieving a "Swiss single market" (what has been called the federative, or unifying, function).

The first function has played a dominant role for a long time. The second function was repeatedly affirmed (although more in words than in deeds) and then was taken as granted. The third function deserves a closer look.

Indeed, the federative function, i.e., the progressive deconstruction of intercantonal trade barriers, had been neglected for a long time. One had to wait more than one hundred years, until the European integration had enormously progressed and until the Swiss people had rejected joining the European Economic Area in December of 1992 to witness a resurrection of the idea of a Swiss common market. Such a long delay can partly be explained[8] by the Swiss political climate that had been favorable to the many cartels existing in the country as well as to the strong compartmentalization in cantonal markets.[9]

Cantons and municipalities alike had actually erected all kind of local walls and hurdles (technical barriers, non-recognition of cantonal diplomas, *marchés publics*, etc.) that had hindered access to the market by outsiders. The situation was assessed by a federal commission of experts who warned in a 1994 report[10] that: *"Un marché intérieur protégé de la concurrence internationale et fragmenté en marchés partiels fermés ne réduit pas seulement la marge de manoeuvre de la politique économique extérieure; il met aussi inéluctablement en danger, par l'imbrication des secteurs économiques, les parties de l'économie à orientation internationale."*

## The Bull

The Swiss people's refusal to join the European Economic Area in December 1992 was a shock for many people within political and economic circles. The Federal Council (i.e., the Swiss government) quickly developed a program of regeneration of the Swiss economy. Part of the program were three laws: the federal Act on technical barriers to trade,[11] the reform of the federal Act on cartels[12] and the federal Act on the internal market [AIM].[13] All three were passed in a very short time by Swiss standards: the federal Parliament adopted the three bills on October 6, 1995.[14] While the first two laws address issues within the power of the federal State, AIM aims at suppressing the provisions and measures of a protectionnist nature that have been adopted by cantons and municipalities.[15]

The federal Act on the internal market went into force on July 1, 1996. Article 11 para 1 AIM provides that cantons, municipalities, and other organs executing public tasks must adapt their own legal provisions and take the necessary organizational measures within two years, i.e., until June 30, 1998. In many cantons, the feeling apparently prevailed at first that AIM would have no real impact as long as cantonal provisions were not adapted. A number of cantonal public bodies remained initially in a state of inertia: very little was actually achieved to make cantonal and municipal provisions compatible with AIM. The cantons' sleepiness was however shaken in 1997 when the Federal Court held quite logically that cantons had to apply the material rules contained in AIM, quite independently from the two-year respite they enjoyed to bring their legislation in conformity with AIM.[16]

The Act on the internal market is basically the materialization of the federative function of article 31 Cst. It applies as much to wares as to services. It seeks to implement the principle of free access to market for all economic agents within Switzerland.[17] Article 2 AIM provides indeed that: *"Toute personne a le droit d'offrir des marchandises, des services et des prestations de travail sur tout le territoire suisse pour autant que l'exercice de l'activité lucrative en question soit licite dans le canton ou la commune où elle a son siège ou son établissement. . . . L'offre de marchandises, de services et de prestations de travail est régie par les prescriptions du canton ou de la commune où l'offreur a son siège ou son établissement."*

In addition, article 4 AIM states that cantonal diplomas entitling their holders to pursue an economic activity are recognized in the whole country. AIM, therefore, does not harmonize or unify the law in Switzerland but compels cantons and municipalities to adapt their legal provisions and decisions to its requirements, in order to ensure the materiality of a Swiss single market.

The drafters of the Act on the internal market were clearly influenced by European and international law.[18] Indeed, the basic underlying principles of AIM are, on the one hand, the *Cassis-de-Dijon* rule set forth by the European Court of Justice in 1979[19] and, on the other hand, the principle of non-discrimination (including the most-Favored nation and the national treatment clauses) which is at the core of WTO trade rules.

## 2. Trade Restrictions for the Sake of Public Health

The freedom of commerce and industry guaranteed by article 31 Cst can be restricted by cantons, provided the restriction be spelled out in a legal provision, be justified by an overwhelming public interest and be proportionate to its aim. In other words, a restriction must meet three requirements (that are systematically scrutinized by the courts): to have a statutory basis, to pursue a legitimate public interest[20] and to respect the principle of proportionality.

The protection of essential common goods is a legitimate public interest. The Federal Court has repeatedly stated that public safety, health, morality, and quietness[21] belonged to the fundamental goods that the State may safeguard even through limitations to individual rights. The State may adopt measures aiming at protecting the public good from serious dangers, what German-speaking scholars call "*Gefahrenabwehr*."[22] Protecting the health of the public has therefore long been recognized as a legitimate public interest allowing a canton or a municipality to restrict trade or economic freedom.[23]

Since the federal Act on the internal market materializes one of the functions of article 31 Cst, it tolerates the same kind of restrictions to the principle of free access to the market. Indeed article 3 AIM provides:

> 1 La liberté d'accès au marché d'offreurs externes ne peut être restreinte en fonction des prescriptions applicables au lieu de destination que si ces restrictions:
> a) s'appliquent de la même façon aux offreurs locaux;
> b) sont indispensables à la préservation d'intérêts publics prépondérants, et
> c) répondent au principe de la proportionnalité.
>
> 2 Par intérêts publics prépondérants, on entend en particulier:
> a) la protection de la vie et de la santé de l'être humain, des animaux et des végétaux;
> b) la protection de l'environnement; . . .

As to the recognition of diplomas, article 4 AIM provides for the same restrictions through an explicit reference to article 3.

To the best of my knowledge,[24] the Federal Court has not (one should probably say not yet) applied or discussed the notion of "protection of the life and health of human beings" in the context of article 3 para 2 litt. a AIM. Similarly, the 1994 report from the Federal Council did not elaborate the definition of the public interests that may allow one canton to restrict free access to the market.[25] For the time being, it is therefore impossible to conduct an empirical analysis of the implementation of AIM by the judiciary.

Proportionality is another vague concept. Article 3 para 3 AIM provides some general guideline, though, by spelling out criteria to assess proportionality largely borrowed from the European Court of Justice. It states that a restriction is not proportionate when the protection that is sought can be achieved through the implementation of legal provisions in force in the canton of origin or when proofs of security or certificates ("attestations de sécurité ou certificats) produced in the canton of origin are not taken into account.[26] Moreover, the general meaning of proportionality, as developed by the Federal court,[27] remains applicable: any cantonal measure must not go beyond what is necessary to reach its protective aim, must be the appropriate means to achieve this aim and must be in a reasonable relation to it. For instance, the risk that a product entering the market creates for the health of the public must be balanced with the usefulness of this product. A life-saving drug may rightly be allowed to enter the market even if it entails a high risk of injuries to human health.

In the absence of judicial decisions on article 3 AIM, one can try to build on the Federal Court rulings on restrictions to article 31 Cst.[28] In that context, the health of the public has consistently been recognized as a legitimate public interest for restricting economic freedom. In order to give a hint of the wide range of trade restrictions based on public health, here are a few instances where it was a decisive argument:[29]

1. To require a diploma from anyone who intends to work as mountain guide, beautician, midwife or numerous other health professionals (in order to protect the health of clients or patients);[30]
2. To limit working hours or opening hours for shops (in order to protect the health of workers);
3. To restrict the sale of certain products (e.g. drugs or vitamins) to specific stores or to forbid altogether the sale of a product (in order to protect the health of citizens);
4. To require preventive measures (against fire, accidents, contamination, etc.), including warnings printed on products, in all kind of economic activities (in order to protect the health of consumers).[31]

One interesting aspect of the Federal Court decisions related to article 31 Cst is the acceptance, since a famous decision of 1971,[32] of restrictions not intended to protect essential public interests against dangers, but to promote social policy goals. The purpose of such measures is to "provide well-being to all or a majority of citizens, or to increase their well-being by improving life and health conditions or leisure."[33] To be justified, the measures must be "felt by a large part of the population as legitimate" and must satisfy "a need so widely recognized as to empower the State to fulfill it."[34] A similar widening of the public interest is expressly recognized in article 3 para 2 litt. d AIM: the pursuit of social policy goals may actually constitute an overwhelming public interest in the sense of article 3 para 1 AIM. When applied to health and pushed to its farthest point, that idea could potentially justify a whole range of restrictive measures.

As to public health, the Federal court distinguished between, on the one side, restrictions to economic freedom aiming directly at protecting public health from dangers and, on the other side, measures taken within the larger framework of the State's health policy.[35] Both, however, are considered valid since they are based on legitimate public interests within the *Griessen* line of reasoning. The question remains open to know whether a canton could argue that in pursuing its health policy goals, it may validly restrict for instance the sale of goods in order to promote the health of the population, even in the absence of any substantial, direct danger.

The reading of dozens of Federal court decisions has proved disappointing. It is, I submit, impossible within the scope of the present contribution[36] to see some clear principles or criteria behind the Federal court's numerous decisions accepting that the protection of public health is a valid argument to restrict constitutional rights. It seems to me that the Federal court has followed a case-by-case approach, without trying to develop a theory on the meaning and limits of public health as a restriction to individual rights. My impression is consistent with more general assessments pertaining to the notion of "legitimate public interest." Many writers, and occasionally the Federal court itself,[37] have indeed stated that one cannot identify theoretically a legitimate public interest without making reference to the specific circumstances of the case.

The legal writings do not bring much to the determination of what "public health" means. Few authors have ventured on proposing a definition. For instance, Grisel first states that "la santé publique se définit d'elle-même"(!); he then adds that the State "protects people against injuries to life, bodily integrity and physical well-being."[38] Junod writes that it is a vague notion and that it is impossible to assess *a priori* its precise scope.[39]

Reinhard makes some more pointed comments. He starts from a wide definition of health (physical, mental, and psychological well-being) and asserts that the State should not limit itself to protect the health of the public from serious dangers. According to him, the State may legitimately pursue "a wide health agenda that takes rightly into account the psychological, social, and environmental causes of diseases."[40]

By contrast, Saladin wrote (but it was before the *Griessen* decision) that when protecting public health, the State may only act for the purpose of preventing the onset of illnesses and of preserving people from a variety of disease-causing hazards, as long as its intervention seems necessary to protect public order.[41]

## 3. Analytical Comments

### The Main Issues

After surveying what courts and legal writers have said about trade restrictions based on the protection of public health, no clear picture or trend emerges. The notion of "health of the public" as well as the assessment of the "legitimate level of protection" seem to elude precise material definitions.

The notion of health of the public must perhaps remain vague if one wants it to be operational. More recent writings seem to accept a wider notion of public health that allows a canton to intervene not only for protecting the public against serious dangers, but also for furthering its wider health agenda. As to the legitimate level of protection, it cannot be defined *per se*: any tentative description of it has to include political, economic, moral, and cultural aspects. In other words, it rests on a broad value judgment.

At this point, we are left, it is submitted, with many open questions and few definite answers. Among the issues that should be discussed further, I would like to mention at least the following ones:

1. Which definition of "*health*" should be adopted?
2. What exactly means the health "*of the public*"?
3. Can it be argued that the "health of the public" is endangered only through contagious diseases? If not, when is it imperiled?
4. Should/may local conditions be considered?
5. Who must prove that the health of the public is endangered and what kind of evidence should be presented?
6. Isn't a warning always an appropriate alternative to more restrictive measures?

### The Notion of "Health"

The first point is to try and determine what "health" is. The definitions of health are as numerous as the definitions of the law! They cover the whole spectrum from the broadest definition ("health is a state of complete physical, mental, and social well-being," according to the preamble of the World Health Organization Constitution[42]) to the narrowest ones ("health is the absence of illness"; "health is the ability to work"; etc.).

I think it is reasonable to include in the notion of health the physical as well as the mental and psychological well-being of individuals. But health remains a very complex and highly variable condition: it is the result in any given individual of numerous internal and external influences. Health has an objective side (the condition that can be assessed by a health professional according to a number of scientifically verifiable parameters) and a subjective side (how one feels at a given time).[43] It is, therefore, impossible to find a definition satisfying everybody; each society has to develop its own definition, coming as close as possible to the most widely perceived notion of health among its population. It means that the notion of health is largely cultural and can, therefore, legitimately vary from one country to the other.

In addition, it is in most cases difficult to assess what exactly caused an illness and, therefore, which measures taken from the State have really the effect of maximizing the protection of health. External agents (not only viruses, bacteria, and prions but also the contact with chemicals or the ingestion of foods, etc.) are usually a contributing factor rather than the sole cause of an illness. This situation makes it all the more difficult to develop a coherent view on the legitimate level of health protection one wants to achieve. Very differing opinions on this point (from the maximalist to the minimalist) are not uncommon, even among self-proclaimed health experts. Here again it belongs eventually to each country to set the level of health protection it wants to assure to its population. One should also recognize that no country has developed a globally coherent policy in this respect!

## "Public" Health

A second point is to circumscribe who exactly "the public" is when one speaks of the health of the public. Should it be the whole population, large segments in it, small groups, a few individuals or even one individual alone?

It is difficult to find any guidance in the Federal court decisions. In one decision, it wrote that "a public interest must be common to at least a large part of the population."[44] The health of children or of women was obviously accepted as part of the health of the public. So was the health of dependent workers, but not the health of independent workers (about the limitation of working hours). The health of small groups of consumers (e.g. haemophiliacs in need of Factor VIII, a medicine made from blood) is also clearly accepted as part of the health of the public.

But what about the health of one or only a few individuals? As Reinhard points out, protecting the health of one person can justify the State intervention because the protection awarded serves directly the interest of the whole community, by acknowledging the value of each member in it. Reinhard concludes that it is impossible to find reliable criteria to ascertain when protecting the health of one individual amounts simultaneously to protecting public health.[45]

A good example of the Federal court's uneasiness in defining the health of the public is given in a 1992 decision:[46] "It is difficult, in this field, to distinguish between public and private goods. Protecting the health of an individual means protecting his own interest in the first place. But a global perspective is needed: it is also in the interest of the whole population that every individual stay in good health, especially where there is a risk of propagating a communicable disease. . . . Because of the social cost of illness, everybody has an interest in the fact that the highest possible number of his fellow citizens be in good health." That decision seems to confirm that the health of one individual may be equated under certain circumstances with "the health of the public." This would be true especially where it is commonly felt that the State "should do something."

### Public Health as Prevention of Communicable Diseases

Historically, the concept of health was first used in the legislation as a justification for restrictive, or even repressive, State measures against people suffering, or suspected of suffering, from a contagious disease. It is certainly the narrowest view of the concept of protecting public health. But is it still defensible today?

Adopting such a standard would mean that free access to the market could only be restricted for the sake of public health where contagious or may be communicable[47] diseases were involved. The State could restrict the sale of contaminated blood (to prevent AIDS), but not of cigarettes or asbestos (to prevent lung cancer), alcohol (to prevent cirrhosis), English beef (to prevent Creutzfeld-Jakob disease) or Swiss Mont d'Or cheese (to prevent listeria)! Obviously, such a position would make little, if any, sense. Not all contagious diseases are dangerous; by contrast non-contagious or non-communicable diseases may be lethal. The criterion, therefore, is a poor one to distinguish legitimate State measures from illegitimate ones.

The communicability of the disease should, however, be used as a valid criterion in one field: that of restricting the free movement of people. When the "source" of the danger lies not in the carrying of any economic activity but within a person, the argument of protecting public health should be used to prevent somebody from entering the country only if he or she suffers from a contagious disease. Indeed, it is the only way a person can, by herself, endanger the health of others (though it should be admitted that the distinction between the protection of public health and the protection of public safety is not always easy). Such is for instance the view adopted in EC Directive 64/221 of February 25, 1964:[48] article 4 provides that only the diseases or disabilities listed in an annex may justify an exception to the free movement of persons. The annex includes only contagious diseases, to the notable exception of syphilis (which is merely communicable). Where, on the contrary, the health of the public argument is used to prevent goods from entering the market or to limit health-hazardous activities, the notion of health of the public should be broader and encompass any serious harm to the health of a certain number of people.

### Nature and Intensity of the Dangers for Public Health

Another point, related to the previous one, is to circumscribe which health hazards may legitimately be taken into account by the State to restrict trade. Is any injury to health a sufficient reason or should there exist a risk for life, or at least a risk of permanent injury to essential human mental or bodily functions?

The Federal Court has usually not spelled out specifically the health risks involved in a case and seems to accept that a wide range of health hazards may qualify. I can give here only a small sample of court decisions where the protection of public health was, according to the judges, at stake.

A series of decisions involved the requirement of a professional degree for granting a State license to practice various activities. For instance, in a 1977 decision about the cantonal requirement that beauticians be in possession of a professional diploma to get the license to practice, the Federal Court argued that the professional activity of beautician threatened the health of clients in many (not very convincing in my view) ways.[49] It decided that a cantonal monopoly for ramonage was justified for the protection of public health (to better fight against air pollution).[50] It also ruled that the activity of physiotherapist, of optician or of dental hygienist entailed dangers for patients that are serious enough to justify the requirement of holding a professional diploma.[51]

Several cases dealt with the sale of medicines. In a 1997 case, the Federal court ruled that a canton could restrict advertisements for medicines because public health dictated to fight against the excessive or abusive consumption of medicines.[52] It had decided long ago that the sale of prescription drugs could be limited to pharmacies because of the dangers associated with the taking of medicines.[53] According to another decision, a canton could legitimately forbid physicians to sell medicines because a sound health policy required that a region be equipped with a sufficient number of pharmacies which have in stock a wider range of products than physicians can have, and which may provide a useful assistance to patients.[54]

All those decisions have again followed a case-by-case approach. They do not show any coherent position as to a generally required minimum intensity of the danger for public health that would justify the restrictions imposed on economic freedom.

More than twenty years ago, the Zürich administrative court[55] made an attempt to delineate which kind of dangers could justify restrictions to economic freedom. The question was to know whether a high intake of vitamin C could be dangerous for health, which would justify to restrict the sale of vitamin C to pharmacies and drugstores. The Zürich court held that a theoretical danger for public health could not justify such a restrictive measure unless it would result, in a majority of cases according to ordinary life experience, in an actual danger for health. This distinction of "abstract dangers" and "concrete dangers" was quashed by the Federal court. The latter stated that "one may doubt that such a distinction, which is difficult to implement, could apply in the field of public health, where the importance of the protected good should lead to take into account any danger whatsoever."[56] The Federal court went on saying that even if the danger was merely abstract, restricting the sale to specific stores "was a measure intended to promote and safeguard the health of the population as part of the general well-being."[57]

## Weighing Local Conditions

A further point has to do with the legitimate level of health protection. In assessing it, one should determine, among other factors, whether and up to which point local conditions can be taken into account.[58] It is well documented that dietary habits[59] for instance, or ethnic origin, or working conditions, influence to a great deal the prevalence of specific illnesses in the population. The geographical environment, including climatic conditions, has also a measurable impact on population health. The same could be said of the availability, quality, and remoteness of health care services.

Speaking in general terms about the notion of "public interest," Swiss writers have stressed that it must always be assessed *in concreto* and that, therefore, it may vary from one local community to the other, as well as through time.[60] If the point is accepted as relevant between cantons of a small and economically homogeneous country like Switzerland, it should have even greater relevance at the European or world level, where economic and cultural diversity is much higher. However, the burden should rightly be placed on States to show that peculiar local circumstances justify trade restrictions that would not stand scrutiny elsewhere.

## Evidentiary Problems

It is commonly accepted that it belongs to the canton restricting access to the market to present evidence supporting its claim that a product, an activity or a person would endanger the health of the public. Such a claim would almost invariably be based on some kind of "scientific" opinion or, in most obvious cases that I shall not deal with here, on common sense. The Federal court occasionally recognized that assessing the danger of a product or activity for the health of the public was indeed an issue to be resolved by expert opinion.[61] For instance, in the already mentioned case of 1973 about the possible danger of letting supermarkets sell vitamin C in high dosage, the court relied on scientific opinions (contradicted by expert opinion produced by the appellant!) that "a durable intake of high doses of vitamin C may have deleterious effects on health, especially by forming kidney stones"[62]

Relying on expert opinion or scientific evidence is, however, not unproblematic and may even be used by the court to conceal what are merely value choices. First of all, the word "scientific" should be taken cautiously and in any case not as a synonym of "true and objective." Take for instance the danger of second-hand (or passive) smoking. A recent meta-analysis of studies on the danger of passive smoking, published in one of the most famous medical journals,[63] reveals that 94% of scientific studies written by somebody who is affiliated with, or has other links with a tobacco company conclude that passive smoking is innocuous, while only 13% of studies by people without any link to tobacco companies reach the same conclusion!

Secondly, it is the rarest case where one can find a whole body of converging evidence on the dangers associated with a specific product or activity. Few products go through extensive clinical trials before reaching the market, like medicines and medical devices. In a number of other cases, still rather easy to solve, standards set by the World Health Organization [WHO] or another recognized professional or scientific organization may exist. However, it will not be always easy to define which standards (when they exist at all) will be used to assess the reality and extent of the danger for the health of the public. In addition, one can wonder whether this assessment should be left to specific State agencies or international organizations (e.g. in Switzerland the Federal Office for Public Health, at the European level perhaps the Health Committee of the Council of Europe or at the international level WHO) or whether private firms should be entrusted with the task. One can also wonder whether standards should be set only by so-called "experts" or whether the State should elicit the opinion of the population at large?

Thirdly, most of the time, there is to date no evidence, because a health hazard is only suspected. The possible communication of mad cow disease to human beings as a form of Creutzfeld-Jakob disease provides a good example. In such cases, I would personally argue that each canton or State should be allowed to determine very freely the level of health protection it wants for its population. It has become usual to call that attitude the "principe de précaution."[64] But I would simultaneously argue that the canton or State has the duty to investigate the matter in order to clarify within a reasonable time span whether the danger is real or not.

I would adopt the same position when there is conflicting "scientific" evidence. In such cases, every State should be recognized the right to follow what appears as the safest way or, in other words, the "principe de précaution." The Federal court alluded to this view once: "Faced with conflicting evidence, the canton could in any case retain that the possibility of deleterious effects of a durable consumption of high doses of vitamin C was not excluded."[65] But the court regrettably did not ask the canton to bring further evidence in support of its position. The ruling thus amounts to a reversal of the burden of proof: it is up to the individual or to the firm whose economic activity has been limited by the State to prove that the economic activity at stake is, in fact, not dangerous for the health of people.

## Warning as the Least Restrictive Alternative

A last issue I want to address is related to the principle of proportionality. More specifically, I'd like to briefly discuss whether the health of the public is not protected enough through some kind of public warnings, for instance a notice written on the product. As everyone knows, this has been the basic strategy for a long time for medicinal products which are all (or almost all) hazardous to our health.[66] The same could be said of certain foods or of pleasure-providing products like alcohol and cigarettes.

The European Court of Justice has stated in many cases that consumers could be sufficiently protected through a compulsory system of written notice.[67] In Switzerland, this argument was used to no avail in the vitamin C case. Appellant indeed submitted that instead of restricting the sale of vitamin C to specific stores, the State should merely ask for a compulsory notice on the boxes of vitamin C which would spell out the indications as well as the necessary warnings. In light of the principle of proportionality, the argument seemed a valid one. The Federal court nevertheless rejected it bluntly: " Generally, consumers do not read much of the notices; they would undoubtedly read them even less if the product was available in supermarkets."[68]

It is far from certain that the Federal court would decide the case today as it decided it in 1973. In many cases, warnings would indeed be the least trade-restrictive alternative and other, more restrictive, measures would therefore be unwarranted. But beyond any discussion about warnings and trade restrictions, the fundamental issue that should be addressed in this context is the right balance to be found between individual and State responsibility in preserving the health of people.

## 4. Concluding Remarks

"Health may not, in the absolute, be the ultimate personal good, but it tends to become it as soon as one loses it."[69] Everybody would probably agree with that statement. The State has therefore a strong interest in protecting health, especially in preventing diseases and accidents. At the same time, the State intervention should not be too paternalistic and rob individuals of their primary responsibility in that area.

Now, if the State wants to act with any positive and durable impact on the health of people, it cannot limit its interventions to the sector of health-care. The State must indeed integrate the concern for health protection in all its policies. This has been increasingly recognized lately, for instance by the Council of Europe that recently declared that health should be a primary concern of the State and that the latter had a duty to protect and promote health in all its sectorial policies.[70] One could expect, therefore, that cantons (or countries) will in the future use more extensively the notion of health to restrict access to their market.

It is still unclear in Switzerland whether the Federal Court would accept an extensive notion of "health of the public" that would allow each canton to pursue its own health agenda, including health promotion goals. The many controversies surrounding the assessment of health hazards make it difficult to reach solid conclusions on the reality and intensity of the dangers for health. Such uncertainties could be a justification for an active health promotion policy. At the same time, they could make it relatively easy for cantons (or countries in international trade) to hide protectionnist measures[71] behind the veil of health protection.

A deciding factor will, of course, be the attitude of the courts in all the cases where there is as yet no clear evidence supporting the reality or intensity of a health hazard or where there is conflicting evidence about them. I would plead for granting States large elbow room in such occurrences but at the same time for imposing them a duty to investigate impartially and, as far as possible, to make a good-faith effort to clear up the uncertainties.

NOTES

1. To get a more detailed picture of Swiss political institutions, see F. Dessemontet, T. Ansay (Eds), Introduction to Swiss *law,* 2nd ed., The Hague-Boston-London, 1995, especially chapters 1 to 3, 1ff, 15ff, 27ff.

2. For an introduction, see Dessemontet/Ansay, note 1, Chapter 10, 162ff.

3. The notion of "cartel" encompasses "all contracts and agreements or gentlemen's agreements that may influence the market of certain wares and services through a collective limitation of competition, especially by means of regulating the output, the sale or the purchase of wares and the prices and other terms and conditions": Dessemontet/Ansay, note 1, 166.

4. I couldn't find any contribution in the Swiss legal literature specifically dealing with the topic. A number of scholars have written a few pages on the issue within the framework of more general works on constitutional law, economic law or competition law. See, e.g. R. Rhinow, G. Schmid, G. Biaggini, *Öffentliches Wirtschaftsrecht,* Basel, 1998; H. Reinhard, *Allgemeines Polizeirecht,* Bern, 1993.

5. See for instance P.-Chr. Müller-Graff, Artikel 36, *Kommentar zum EU/EG-Vertrag,* von der Groeben et al. (eds), 5th ed., Baden-Baden, 1997.

6. "Freedom of trade and industry is guaranteed on the whole territory of the Swiss Confederation . . . Cantonal legal provisions on the exercise of trade and industry as well as on their taxation are reserved."

7. For developments, see especially R. Rhinow, *Commentaire de la Constitution,* article 31, Basel/Bern/Zürich, 1988, N° 27ff with numerous further références; see also Rhinow/ Schmid/Biaggini, note 4.

8. According to Th. Cottier, B. Merkt, La fonction fédérative de la liberté du commerce et de l'industrie et la loi sur le marché intérieur suisse: l'influence du droit européen et du droit international économique, *De la Constitution. Etudes en l'honneur de Jean-François Aubert,* Basel, 1996, 449, 456ff.

9. The compartmentalization should not, however, be exagerated because it varied vastly from one market to the other. In some fields, there had been for a long time a unified market in Switzerland. See for instance V. Martenet, C. Rapin, *Le marché intérieur suisse. Les mesures restrictives du droit suisse à la lumière du droit européen,* Swiss Papers on European Integration 19, Bern-Zürich, 1999, 39ff.

10. Commission d'experts, *Rapport explicatif concernant l'avant-projet de loi sur le marché intérieur (LMI),* from January 21, 1994, Bern, 10. Similar views are expressed by the Office fédéral des affaires conjoncturelles (OFAC), *Le marché intérieur suisse,* Berne, 1993 and by the Federal Council in its *Message concernant la loi fédérale sur le marché intérieur (LMI),* from November 23, 1994, Feuille Fédérale [FF] 1995 I 1193. See also R. Senti, J. Baltensberger, *Binnenmarkt Schweiz,* Zurich, 1991.

11. See FF 1995 II 489.

12. See FF 1995 I 472.

13. See FF 1995 I 1193.

14. Recueil officiel des lois fédérales [RO] 1996, 1725, 1996, 546, and 1996, 1738.

15. Message, note 10, FF 1995 I 1193, 1216.

16. Recueil officiel des arrêts du Tribunal fédéral [ATF] 123 I 313, 318f.

17. See, among others, P. Richli, K. Wunder, Über die Möglichkeiten zur Beschränkung des freien Warenverkehrs nach dem Binnenmarktgesetz, *Aktuelle Juristische Praxis* 7/1996, 908; Weber K., Das neue Binnenmarktgesetz, *Schweizerische Zeitschrift für Wirtschaftsrecht* 4/1996, 164; Th. Cottier, M. Wagner, Das neue Bundesgesetz über den Binnenmarkt, *Aktuelle Juristische Praxis* 12/1995, 1582.

18. See Message, note 10, FF 1995 I 1193, 1219f.

19. Recueil des arrêts de la Cour de justice des Communautés européennes [Rec.] 1979, 662.

20. This is, of course, the crucial, but elusive, notion. Interesting thoughts on it are provided by Reinhard, note 4, 96ff; P. Moor, Intérêts publics et intérêts privés, *La pesée globale des intérêts,* Ch.-A. Morand (ed.), Basel/Frankfurt, 1996, 22ff.

21. The list is not exhaustive: see Reinhard, note 4, 68; I. Coveris, *Certificat de capacité et liberté du commerce et de l'industrie,* thèse Lausanne, 1988, 121; H. Marti, *Die Wirtschaftsfreiheit der schweizerischen Bundesverfassung,* Basel/Stuttgart, 1976, n° 153; *contra*: E. Grisel, *Liberté du commerce et de l'industrie,* vol. II, Bern, 1995, n° 462.

22. See, among others, L. Schürmann, *Wirtschaftsverwaltungsrecht,* Bern, 1994, 49. The State may not, therefore, limit individual rights in order to protect adult, competent individuals against themselves: Schürmann, 54f; A. Jost, *Die neueste Entwicklung des Polizeibegriffs im schweizerischen Recht,* Bern, 1975, 50ff.

23. Rhinow, note 7, n° 192.

24. See also Martenet/ Rapin, note 9, 39ff.

25. Message, note 10, FF 1995 I 1193, 1245.

26. For more substantial explanations, see Message, note 10, FF 1995 I 1193, 1245. For critical comments, see Martenet/Rapin, note 9, 63ff.

27. See for instance ATF 109 Ia 37.

28. Same view: Richli/Wunder, note 17, 910.

29. See Rhinow, note 7, N° 192ff; Richli/Wunder, note 17, 910f; Marti, note 21, n° 212ff, all with further references.

30. See, e.g. ATF 103 Ia 259, ATF 112 Ia 325.

31. See further examples in B. Stauder, Warenverkehrsfreiheit und Sicherheit von Konsumgütern, *Jahrbuch des Schweizerischen Konsumentenrechts* 1996, 79ff.

32. Known as the *Griessen* decision: ATF 97 I 499.

33. ATF 97 I 499, 505; see also Semaine Judiciaire [SJ] 1997, 421, 428.

34. ATF 97 I 499, 505f.

35. See for instance ATF 112 Ia 322, cons. 4d; Revue jurassienne de jurisprudence [RJJ] 1996, 308.

36. It would be interesting to undertake a more extensive research on this topic. I am not sure, however, that it would bring much more clarity on the basis of court decisions. But at least, we would be sure that the courts take a purely casuistic approach.

37. Conveniently quoted by Moor, note 20, 17ff. For an attempt to provide an analytical framework for assessing legitimate public interests, see Moor, note 20, 24ff.

38. Grisel, note 21, 19. One can wonder why mental and psychological well-being are not included. At least one writer, Reinhard, note 4, 70, includes the latter aspect within the notion of public health.

39. Ch.-A. Junod, Libertés économiques, ordre public et politique sociale, Louis Dallèves (ed.), *XIVe journée juridique,* Genève 1975, 77. A similar position is found by Jost, note 22, 64.

40. Reinhard, note 4, 70.

41. P. Saladin, *Das Recht auf Werbung und seine öffentlich-rechtlichen Schranken,* St-Gall 1969, 189.

42. The WHO Constitution is published in the Recueil systématique du droit suisse [RS] 0.810.1. For a discussion, see O. Guillod, D. Sprumont, Le droit à la santé: un droit en émergence, *De la Constitution. Etudes en l'honneur de Jean-François Aubert,* Bâle, 1996, 337ff.

43. Various studies have shown that this subjective assessment is highly individual and can be based on very different criteria. For instance, surveys have indicated that a number of handicapped people or of people suffering from cancer consider themselves to be in good health. Maybe health should only be defined as "one's ability to cope with life": see the works of A. Antonovsky, *Health, Stress and Coping: New Perspectives on Mental and Physical Well-Being,* San Francisco, 1979; *Unraveling the Mystery of Health, San Francisco,* 1987.

44. Quoted by Moor, note 20, 22. The court went on to say: "There is no public interest by nature: each historical era, each political system gives to the concept its own content."

45. Reinhard, note 4, 94ff. He writes that, in the end, it is always a value judgment.

46. ATF 118 Ia 427.

47. Both terms are not synonymous. AIDS or syphilis are communicable diseases but not contagious diseases because they cannot be caught simply by staying near somebody already infected. The flu is both communicable and contagious, as is tuberculosis.

48. JOCE 56, 850 (April 4, 1964).

49. ATF 103 Ia 259: "The beautician is in close contact with the face and other parts of a woman's body where the skin may be most sensitive; she must, therefore, work under strict hygienic conditions . . . It appears that the treatment with electrical, ultraviolet or infrared devices may have positive or deleterious effects according to the type of skin . . . A beautician uses also creams, milks, lotions, and other cosmetics that may cause allergies to certain types of skin. A beautician may therefore endanger the health of her clients if she has no professional qualifications."

50. ATF 109 Ia 193. See also RJJ 1991 115.

51. SJ 1995, 713 (physiotherapist); the court added that foreign qualifications had to be considered. ATF 112 Ia 322 (optician). ATF 116 Ia 118 (where the court spoke of the risk of

injuries, even lethal ones (!) for specific patient like those suffering from cardiac disease, associated with the activity of a dental hygienist).

52. ATF 123 I 201.

53. ATF 99 Ia 370.

54. ATF 118 Ia 175. This policy, it is submitted, is directed more towards health promotion than health protection.

55. Zentralblatt [ZBl.] 1973, 361.

56. ATF 99 Ia 370, 378: "l'importance du bien juridique à protéger devrait inciter à tenir compte de tout danger quelconque."

57. ATF 99 Ia 370, 379.

58. Local conditions are taken into account in European law, for instance concerning the withdrawal of drugs from one national market: see e.g. Müller-Graff, note 5, N° 102.

59. They differ much even within tiny Switzerland! As the Administrative Court of Geneva wrote in a decision from March 4, 1998 published in Plädoyer 6/1998, 59: "The "saucisson vaudois," as the "longeole genevoise" belong to the cultural sphere of the French-speaking part of Switzerland whereas the "Schüblig" is part of the dietary habits in the German-speaking part of the country."

60. See e.g. Jost, note 22, 24; Reinhard, note 4, 96.

61. See e.g. ATF 110 Ia 99, 104 (requirement of a medical prescription for adjusting contact lenses).

62. ATF 99 Ia 370, 377.

63. 316 British Medical Journal 1554 (1998).

64. See for instance J.-S. Cayla, Le principe de précaution, fondement de la sécurité sanitaire, *Revue trimestrielle de droit sanitaire et social* 1998, 491ff. In environmental matter, the "principle of caution" is defined as follows in French law: "l'absence de certitude, compte tenu des connaissances scientifiques du moment, ne doit pas retarder l'adoption de mesures effectives et proportionnées, visant à prévenir le risque de dommages grave et irreversibles . . . à un coût économiquement acceptable. . . Son objectif est de satisfaire le besoin de développement et la santé des générations présentes, sans compromettre la capacité des générations futures à répondre aux leurs."

65. ATF 99 Ia 370, 377.

66. A recent study published in the Journal of the American Medical Association showed that more than 2 million Americans become seriously ill every year because of toxic reactions to correctly prescribed medicines taken properly, and 106,000 die from those reactions: J. Lazarou, B. H. Pomeranz, P. N. Corey, Incidence of adverse drug reactions in hospitalized patients: a meta-analysis of prospective studies, 279 (15) *JAMA* 1200 (April 15, 1998).

67. See e.g. the decisions quoted by Martenet/Rapin, note 9, 60f.

68. ATF 99 Ia 370, 380.

69. M. Vannotti, La pratique médicale à l'épreuve d'une approche complexe de la santé et de la maladie, *La santé, Bulletin de l'Université de Neuchâtel* n° 132, 1999, 7.

70. A similar declaration was issued within the European Union: see the Resolution of the Council of the European Union of December 20, 1995 on the integration of requirements of health protection in EU policies, JOCE 350, 2 (December 30, 1995).

71. An example was provided by a recent expert opinion claiming that the protection of public health justified the non-recognition by one canton of health-care professional diplomas obtained in another canton.

CHAPTER 11

# Comment on: "Market Integration in a Small Federal State: The Case of Switzerland" by Olivier Guillod

*Antonios Haniotis*

Olivier Guillod analyses the restrictions to the freedom of commerce foreseen—for reasons of public health policy—in the Swiss Federal Act on the Internal Market (AIM) which was adopted in 1995. He addresses a number of normative questions, such as: How is "the health of the public" to be defined? Which measures are legitimate for the sake of health promotion? Which health hazards may legitimately be taken into account? Is product information sufficient for protecting public health? To what extent should each canton be allowed to pursue its own health policy goals?

Policy measures can, in principle, either take the form of non-discriminatory, purely domestic policies in accordance with the principle of national treatment, or of trade-restrictive and discriminatory policies. Unfortunately, Guillod does not emphasize this fundamental distinction sufficiently. In my view, it would have been helpful to separate these two cases more clearly. From an economic perspective at least, it is much easier to find justifications for domestic state interventions than for trade-restrictive policies. While various forms of market failures can justify domestic state interventions, they are not sufficient as a justification of trade-restrictions. In the context of public health policy, for example, it is not difficult to argue that public goods considerations and the existence of information asymmetries require restrictions on the freedom of (domestic) commerce, e.g., regulations on the sale of antibiotics. The more interesting question, though, is whether public health considerations can serve as a justification of trade-restrictive policies. My comments developed below, focus on this latter question.

For answers to the questions stated above in the first paragraph, one can, as Guillod does, look in the rulings of the Federal Court. Naturally, as an economist, I am used to study such normative questions in the light of efficiency considerations. In this perspective, one can ask whether restrictions on the intercantonal (or international) mobility of persons and goods can improve economic efficiency, or not.

A simple answer to this question would be to state that restrictions on the movement of persons and goods can never be optimal, unless public health is directly affected by the border-crossing *per se,* as in the case of contagious diseases, or of explosive or hazardous goods. In other words, as long as the mobility *as such* of persons and goods has no direct effect on public health, mobility should not be restricted. Public health policies should be domestic policies, targeted to the actual health hazards, thereby avoiding unnecessary distortions in other areas of the economy. This view is clearly in line with the basic theorems of the traditional theory of international trade.

The reasoning outlined in the preceding paragraph, implicitly assumes, however, that no significant *indirect* effects of cross-border movement of goods or persons on public health policies exist either. This is a crucial point. In what follows, I argue that—in cases other than contagious diseases or hazardous goods—trade restrictions can be justified on efficiency grounds, if:

1. Sufficiently important *indirect* effects of cross-border mobility exist, *and*
2. Interjurisdictional policy coordination and redistribution policies are ineffective.

Indirect effects[1] are likely to arise when cross-border mobility of persons and goods is associated with interjurisdictional spillovers (or external effects). Interjurisdictional spillovers exist when part, or all, of the benefits or costs of a particular policy accrue outside the jurisdiction of that political authority. For example, if a government which subsidizes the hospitals in its jurisdiction cannot—or does not want to—exclude non-residents from being treated there, then a positive spillover to other jurisdictions occurs because residents of other jurisdictions may enjoy some of the benefits of the subsidy (e.g., in the form of lower prices for medical treatment). Another example of an interjurisdictional spillover is an investment in industrial air cleaning filters which affects air quality also beyond jurisdictional borders.

Interjurisdictional spillovers may also operate through the market. This is the case, for example, when a government requires all nuclear power stations producing under its jurisdiction to respect relatively high safety standards. Although designed as a purely domestic policy for the protection of public health, such a measure may have a distortive effect on international trade. Due to a possible increase in production costs of domestic producers, it may convey a benefit (in the form of a production cost advantage) to competitors located in other jurisdictions where production standards remained unchanged. Similar examples of interjurisdictional spillovers in the area of public health policy, which operate through their impact on production costs may be associated with: compulsory health insurance, limitations of working hours, hygienic, environmental, social or safety standards, professional qualification requirements etc. In all these cases, increased regulatory standards in one jurisdiction may convey a competitive advantage—on both, domestic, and foreign markets—to producers based in other jurisdictions.

Yet another type of interjurisdictional spillovers is associated with interdependent public finance decisions. Take, for example, the case of capital taxation. If one government raises its capital tax rate, then some capital may move to another jurisdiction. Increasing the tax rate on a mobile tax base exerts, therefore, a (positive) interjurisdictional fiscal externality since other jurisdictions will experience a rise in their tax revenues, without having increased their tax rates. This type of interjurisdictional spillover is the basis for the phenomenon of tax competition which has been a prominent issue in the recent literature on local public finance.[2]

All types of jurisdictional spillovers imply that external costs and benefits of national (or cantonal) policies are not taken into account by governments in their unilateral policy decisions. As a result, too many activities associated with external costs, and too few activities associated with external benefits are undertaken. With respect to regulatory standards, interjurisdictional competition implies that they tend to be inefficiently high (low), when they are associated with external costs (benefits). The existence of interjurisdictional spillovers, therefore, requires policy coordination. For example, governments can agree on minimum regulatory standards or minimum tax rates. Or, more generally, they can engage in multilateral negotiations on country-specific reductions of external costs and on increases of external benefits. Optimal coordination would induce efficient policy outcomes with all types of interjurisdictional spillovers. Where effective policy coordination works, the basic statement that trade restrictions cannot be optimal will still be valid, because any market failures could be remedied with coordinated (first-best) domestic policies.

Very often, however, interjurisdictional policy coordination is ineffective or inexistent.[3] In this case, a second-best policy for a government may consist of imposing restrictions on the movement of persons or goods. For example, in the case of capital taxation, it may be optimal to restrict the movement of capital in order to limit the negative effects of fiscal competition. Similarly, in the case of production standards, it may be optimal to restrict the movement of goods across jurisdictions. In many instances of interjurisdictional spillovers, however, restrictions on cross-border mobility may turn out to be useless or even counter-productive. A careful examination of all costs and benefits of trade restrictions is therefore necessary in each particular case.

The arguments developed above, illustrate that interjurisdictional spillovers, together with the absence of effective policy coordination, can justify the use of trade-restrictions, although such restrictions will never be first-best. This insight is not only reflected in the Swiss AIM, but also in many international trade agreements, including the WTO Agreements. The latter implicitly acknowledge the fact that, in certain areas in which international policy coordination is not sufficiently developed, trade restrictions may be a second-best solution. This is probably the essence of the General Exceptions, in Art. XX of GATT 1994.[4]

Applied to the case of market integration in Switzerland, the considerations developed above suggest that, intercantonal spillovers may justify intercantonal trade restrictions on efficiency grounds, but only if federal public health policy coordination is not sufficiently developed. In the case of Switzerland, I would say that political and cultural integration is sufficiently well-developed (allowing for both, inter-cantonal policy coordination and compensations) that no trade restrictions should be maintained and professional qualifications should be recognized in all cantons.

The reading of Guillod's article might convey the impression that the Swiss economy had not been fully integrated before the entry into force of the AIM. Such an impression would, in my view, be wrong. Switzerland has already had a well-integrated economic and political system for many years.[5] The most important role of the AIM was, essentially, to eliminate certain remaining discriminations in the areas of government procurement and professional qualifications.

## NOTES

1. The issue of indirect - as opposed to direct - effects is also touched upon in section III of Guillod's paper where he states that "the Federal Court distinguished between, on the one side, restrictions to economic freedom aiming directly at protecting public health from dangers and, on the other side, measures taken within the larger framework of the State's health policy."

2. For a survey of the literature on local public finance, see, e.g., David Wildasin (1987) "Theoretical Analysis of Local Public Finance," in Edwin S. Mills (ed.) *Handbook of Regional and Urban Economics,* Vol. II, Amsterdam. The issue of tax competition is also studied in OECD (1998), *Harmful Tax Competition: An Emerging Global Issue,* Paris.

3. One reason for this is that, under policy coordination, some jurisdictions may have to be compensated for their losses relative to the situation without coordination. If no compensating transfers from the net beneficiaries to the net losers of the policy coordination are possible, then the latter might not be feasible (see, e.g., Peter Klibanoff and Jonathan Morduch (1995), "Decentralization, Externalities, and Efficiency"; *Review of Economic Studies* 62 (2), 223–47).

4. At their Ministerial Meeting in Singapore, Trade Ministers of WTO Members have recognized, moreover, that further trade liberalization should be related to the process of

multilateral policy coordination in the area of core labor standards, i.e., that the WTO and the ILO should closely cooperate. In the area of public health, though, no particular cooperation between the WTO and the WHO is foreseen.

5. Jürg Baltensberger and Richard Senti (1991) *Binnenmarkt Schweiz, Wettbewerbsverzerrende Bestimmungen im öffentlichrechtlichen Bereich,* Strukturberichterstattung, BFK, gives an overview of regulations which were in place before the entry into force of the AIM and which may have had a trade-distortive effect within Switzerland. That study shows that a very high degree of market integration existed in Switzerland already before the entry into force of the AIM. The essential innovations of the AIM are analyzed in Thomas Cottier and Manfred Wagner (1995) "Das neue Bundesgesetz über den Binnenmarkt (BGBM), Übersicht und kurzer Kommentar," *Aktuelle Juristische Praxis 4,* Vol. 12, 1582–90.

CHAPTER 12

# Comments on Olivier Guillod's Paper

*Jean-Marie Grether*

In this provocative paper, Olivier Guillod questions the degree of market integration across the 26 cantons of Switzerland. He notes first that it was not until the Swiss turned down membership in the European Economic Area (EEA) that the Federal Council proposed three laws that would help integrate markets (in a way similar to the four liberties in the European Union and the Single Market Program[1]). These laws involved a tightening of antitrust policies, harmonizing standards to remove technical barriers to trade and the Federal Act on the Internal Market (AIM) whose main purpose was the liberalization of public procurement policies. He then goes on to examine trade restrictions in the public health area, thereby offering a case study of the extent of market integration.

I am not an expert of the health sector so it is difficult for me to judge the extent to which integration in this area trails behind that achieved in other federal countries like the US for instance. I therefore comment on two general issues raised by the paper: the degree and nature of market segmentation in Switzerland, and the relationship between trade and internal policies.

## 1. International Segmentation of Swiss Markets

References to market segmentation usually mean segmentation between national and foreign markets. This is the most common form of market segmentation, occurring when governments use tariff and non-tariff barriers to protect domestic producers. However, it turns out that Switzerland is fairly open in this field, whatever the choice of the protection index (see table below, which compares Switzerland with its main trading partners, the US and the EU).

**Table 1. Indicators of international market segmentation (1993)**

| | Switzerland | US | EU |
|---|---|---|---|
| Non-weighted average tariff (%) | 4.2 | 6.8 | 7.6 |
| Coefficient of variation | 2.8 | 1.4 | 0.8 |
| Import-weighted average tariff(%) | 4.5 | 4.2 | 6.1 |
| Frequency of non-tariff barriers [1] | 13.5 | 22.9 | 23.1 |
| Coverage of non-tariff barriers [2] | 13.2 | 17.1 | 10.4 |

***Source***: **CNUCED (1995)**

[1] Percentage of tariff lines subject to one or more non-tariff barriers.

[2] Percentage of the value of imports subject to one or more non-tariff barriers.

The first line shows that Switzerland has by far the lowest tariff protection as measured by the simple average across all tariff lines. This applies mostly for industrial goods, but not for agricultural and food products, whose tariffs are significantly higher. This explains the higher dispersion of the Swiss tariff structure (second line) and why the import-weighted average tariff of Switzerland (third line) becomes comparable to the US level (but still significantly under the EU level). A similar outcome is obtained for non-tariff barriers (quotas, import licenses, etc.), illustrated by the last two lines of the table.

Up to this point, it seems that the level of integration of Switzerland, even before the enforcement of the recent reforms, was quite comparable to, if not higher than the one achieved by economies considered as substantially integrated. In fairness, Guillod is not referring to market segmentation with the rest of the world; he is rather referring to internal market segmentation. Why then do I mention external market segmentation? Because in the absence of external market segmentation, it is difficult to imagine how internal segmentation could stand up.

## 2. Relationship between Internal and External Integration

However, even if tariff and quantitative restrictions are low, there are other ways to segment markets. Differences in standards and regulation may limit foreign competitive pressure. Public procurement policies may restrict market access to local providers. Last but not least, even if trade policy is liberal, competition policy still provides some scope for protecting domestic producers.

All these factors probably account for the relatively high domestic prices with respect to European levels (more than 50% for food and medical products, as reported by the OECD (1990)). Nevertheless, it is precisely in these domains that the array of recent Federal Acts are expected to enforce competition and market integration. And the striking feature of these internal adjustments is that they all contribute to the international integration of the Swiss market.

With respect to technical barriers to trade, Swiss reforms have basically to be understood as a unilateral and gradual process of harmonization with EU rules. The "Swisslex program" adopted in 1994 included most of the adaptation package provided by EEA law. The 1996 Federal Act set down the bottom-line requirement that Swiss standards must conform to the rules and practices of the EU. Should they be implemented, the recent "bilateral agreements" negotiated with the EU would push harmonization further, through the mutual recognition of conformity procedures (although Switzerland would still not benefit from the "Cassis de Dijon" principle in the non-harmonized domain).

A signatory of the 1994 WTO agreement in the field, Switzerland was due to reform its public procurement policies. For any project whose value is above the threshold, Swiss cantons must now respect the principles of transparency and non-discrimination, as well as giving providers the opportunity to appeal to an independent court. Regarding domestic providers, the AIM extended these obligations to all public projects, taking one of the last necessary steps to ensure the completion of the Swiss internal market. Finally, the corresponding chapter in the bilateral agreement implies the application of the WTO principles at the municipal level.

So far, so good, but what about competition policy? Switzerland has long been presented as "cartel paradise," where restrictive practices through explicit understandings, gentlemen's agreements and professional associations were flourishing. Its competition policy was indeed basically driven by the protection of economic freedom (art. 31 al. 3 of the Federal Constitution) rather than by the protection of competition *per se*. Moreover, the old Cartels' Commission had only limited powers, issuing recommendations that could be either accepted or refused by the parties.

Things have changed since 1996. Under the new law, the re-named and better-endowed Competition Commission takes enforceable decisions which can be appealed up to the Federal Supreme Court. Although cartels are still not prohibited as such, their lawfulness is subject to harsher restrictions, mostly inspired by European law. Dominant position criteria are those used in the EU, and have positively contributed to the liberalization of the telecommunications sector. In principle, control of mergers is also based on the European system and has led in recent years to more frequent examination procedures. This strengthening of antitrust authority raises hopes that Swiss competition policy is becoming more similar to current European practice as far as results are concerned (e.g. Mercier et al., 1998).

However, the debate is not over. Unlike its European counterpart, the Commission's sanctions are subject to the prior examination of the illicit character of the agreement. Mergers, whose notification thresholds are quite high, are prohibited if they eliminate "effective competition," a requirement which is less transparent and probably more demanding than the usual concepts used in OECD countries (substantial lessening of competition or the creation or strengthening of a dominant position). Moreover, the accountability of the Commission is less clearly established than in other European countries (see Neven and von Ungern, 1998).

## 3. Convergence between Cantons

An indirect way to test the degree of market integration between regions is to analyze the disparities of income per capita. Economic growth models predict a "catching-up" process through which the initially more backward regions experiment faster growth. Broadly speaking, this leads to a convergence of regional income per capita levels, the speed of the process being larger the deeper market integration in terms of factor mobility. A number of empirical analyses confirm the convergence between States of the American Federation during this century.

Applied to Switzerland, this methodology should reveal a reduction of differences in income per capita between cantons over time, with an acceleration of the trend following the international and internal integration process. But it does not. A careful and recent survey by Zürcher (1998) shows on the contrary that disparities between cantons' per capita incomes have remained fairly stable over the 1965–1994 period. The variance of income per capita levels decreases between 1965 and 1975, but then picks up again, reaching at the end the same level as at the beginning of the time period. Moreover, there is a strong dynamic inertia in the relative ranking of cantons, with very small probabilities of moving to a higher income class.

Does this mean that Switzerland stands as a surprising case of deeply segmented internal markets in spite of a strong international openness? Not really, and for several reasons. First, when the tax-haven canton of Zug is excluded from the sample, convergence is stronger, at least until 1992. Second, available data do not permit to capture the effects of the recent reforms described above. Third, Zürcher's study relies on factor incomes, excluding federal taxes and transfers, which are precisely meant to reduce inter-regional income disparities, and constitute a fundamental instrument of Swiss fiscal federalism.

Fourth and perhaps more fundamentally, convergence does not depend only on factor mobility; it is also highly, and negatively, dependent on inter-regional differences in terms of technology, preferences, and institutions. Although Swiss cantons have a fairly similar access to technology, they do not share a common linguistic and cultural background and keep their sovereignty in important aspects of public policy such as health and education. Therefore, it is not surprising that they remain different in spite of their market integration efforts.

In a sense, this may simply reveal a "voting with the feet process," as it is well-known in the public choice literature. In this framework, individuals reveal their preferences for public goods, not through the ballot vote, but by locating in the community that best suits their tastes in terms of tax/expenditure policy. This leads to a sorting of the whole population into homogenous subgroups, of which the suburbs of Los Angeles are an often-quoted example.

However, this model does not suit Swiss cantons very well. On the one hand, the nature and level of local services offered by the different cantons is not strikingly different, and differences are smoothed through federal efforts in terms of road and communication system, and easier access to health care and higher education services. But for a few exceptions, like the Zug case, intercantonal differences in tax burden remain moderate, and in any case must be compared with intracantonal differences between municipalities. There remain linguistic and cultural differences, but whose impact on locational choice is difficult to assert, and which are mostly inherited from the past rather than resulting from a within-life sorting process.

On the other hand, inter-regional labor mobility in Switzerland is not particularly high by international standards, a result that calls for two final comments. First, this may indeed reflect internal barriers through imperfect inter-cantonal recognition of professional titles and authorizations to practice, thus providing a clear justification of the recent reforms. Second, one should remember that the voting with the feet process is considered as an alternative to the "voice" process, in which individuals express their preferences through some form of written or verbal communication. Switzerland, where direct democracy instruments are available at the three basic institutional levels (municipality, canton, and confederation), provides its citizens with a unique and effective way of expressing opinions. With the power to influence directly the level of public expenditure and the tax burden, one can expect that most Swiss people will not consider these issues as decisive motives to relocate in another canton. In other words, an explanation of why Swiss people do not vote frequently with their feet is plainly that they vote very often—at the ballot box.

## REFERENCES

Mercier, P., A. Raas, M. Wagner and P. Zurkinden. 1998. "Politique de la concurrence de la Suisse dans un contexte international." *La Vie Economique* 2: 12–18.

Neven, D. and T. von Ungern. 1998. "Competition Policy in Switzerland." *Antitrust Bulletin.*

Zürcher, B. 1998. "Income Distribution Dynamics across Swiss Cantons." *Swiss Journal of Economics and Statistics*, 159–173.

## NOTES

1. The four "liberties" in the European Common Market were relative to the free movement of (i) goods, (ii) people, (iii) capital and (iv) services; the Single Market Program pursues further integration through the harmonization of standards and regulations.

# Part IV: Issues For the Future; Mutual Recognition

CHAPTER 13

# Technical Regulations and Industry Standards (TRIS)

*Patrick A. Messerlin and David Palmeter*

"Technical regulations and industry standards" (TRIS) are a well-known issue in trade policy because they can easily generate barriers to trade and domestic distortions.[1] The 1979 Tokyo Round and the 1994 Uruguay Round have seen the adoption of two successive Codes on "technical barriers to trade" (TBT) by GATT Parties. Ideally (simplistically) there are two possible major ways of dealing with TRIS. First, one can rely on mandatory public norms (the "TR" side of TRIS). Until 1989, this approach had been used on a large scale by centrally-planned economies. In market economies, it has been largely abandoned in the industrial sector (except for health and safety related norms) because its slow pace of development did not fit well the rapid pace of technical progress. At the other end of the spectrum, TRIS can rely exclusively on a firm's reputation (the "IS" side of TRIS). Firms are seen as the only economic operators knowledgeable enough for mastering adequately the problems raised by technical progress: they are induced to develop appropriate voluntary standards, to monitor them with the necessary disciplines, and to invest their own credibility since loose standards would damage the firm's reputation and profits.

These two alternative ways of handling TRIS have a different impact on trade. The working hypothesis adopted in this paper is that the deeper the involvement of public authorities, the more likely the protectionist and discriminatory *impact* of TRIS will be. This hypothesis does not imply that firms-based standards have no protectionist or discriminatory *content*: they do –one could even easily argue that they can have a higher protectionist or discriminatory content than mandatory standards designed by public authorities. However, firms have a high capacity to lobby on technical issues in the short run, but a small capacity to enforce trade barriers in the long run.[2] By contrast, public authorities have a small degree of resistance to lobbying on technical issues, and a high capacity to enforce trade barriers in the long run. These trade-offs between the TRIS protectionist content and impact constitute the rationale for the adopted hypothesis.

The paper examines the following questions. How have the two major economies, the EC and the U.S., dealt with this issue? What lessons for the world economy could be drawn from these two contrasted experiences? In particular, could the WTO "multilateral" trade regime benefit from the EC "plurilateral" experience?

The EC and the U.S. deserve special attention for several reasons. First, from the start the EC devoted considerable efforts to TRIS, which were perceived as severe barriers in intra-EC trade in such key sectors as food, pharmaceuticals or automobiles. The first EC TRIS Directive was adopted in 1965, only seven years after the beginning of the implementation of the Treaty, although it has been mostly under the Single Market Program (1985) that the European Community (EC) began to develop a general doctrine and to build a large body of procedures and rules in TRIS matters. As of December 1997, the EC TRIS regime consists in 503 Directives –36 percent of the 1381 Directives constituting the *acquis communautaire* [Annual Report to the Parliament on Community Law, 1998], by far the most important source of EC legislation.[3] Second, the EC regime is a "compromise" (a mix) of the two possible above-mentioned approaches to the TRIS issue, with a tilt towards a substantial role to the public authorities: Member States and (increasingly) the Commission impose basic standards ("essential requirements"); they can have a strong influence in the detailed regulations generated by the European Standard Bodies; they can impose a tight framework for conformity assessment (test, certification, and marking) operations; and they are the dominant (often unique) operator in "market surveillance" actions.

All of these reasons have induced observers [Pelkmans, 1992; Nicolaidis, 1996; Neven, 1996; The Single Market Review, 1998] to look at the EC TRIS regime as a potential blue-print for a multilateral approach. At a first glance, this view seems in line with the recent negotiations and signatures of 58 MRAs between the EC and its major industrial trading partners [WTO TPR, 1997, p.139]. However, our view is that the EC could hardly be a model for the multilateral trade regime.

The situation in the United States is very different from that in the EC, no doubt because the "single market" in the United States was formed in the late 18$^{th}$ Century by a group of small, pre-industrial agricultural economies that had no TRIS of their own. The Member States of the European Union, by contrast, were highly industrialized economies when they formed their single market in the latter half of the 20$^{th}$ Century. Unlike their U.S. counterparts, they had developed, along with their industrial economies, their own TRIS. Thus, the "commerce clause" of the United States constitution gives the federal Congress complete power to regulate interstate commerce. Even when Congress has not exercised its power to pre-empt the regulatory field (as it largely has, for example, with food and drug regulation) the authority of the states even to impose standards is limited. The judicially-developed doctrine of the "dormant" commerce clause limits the power of individual states to regulate, even in the absence of federal action. Without the showing of a compelling need, they may not enact their own trade regulations if those regulations interfere with interstate commerce. For similar historical reasons, when industries in the United States began to develop industry standards, for the most part they did so as national industries, not as industries confined to particular states.

The paper is organized as follows. The first section considers harmonization of TRIS, while the second treats mutual recognition of TRIS. The third section reviews enforcement issues.

## 1. The "Harmonization" Approach

The first natural approach to TRIS issues is harmonization. Before examining this approach, it is useful to have a broad view of the five different types of TRIS issues, as perceived today, that is after a long process of trial and error for fully understanding the complete range of issues raised by TRIS. These five types are: notification of existing TRIS by trading partners, harmonization of standards by trading partners, mutual recognition of standards, mutual recognition of conformity assessment and market surveillance.

The adoption of the harmonization approach by the EC induced it to focus on the three first kinds of issues: the so-called "Old Approach" consisted (still consists) in a complete harmonization of pre-existing Member State TRIS at the EC level. On the basis of Article 100 of the Treaty of Rome, it was envisaged to create European standards ("ENs") in lieu of Member State (national) standards. ENs were to be based on proposals by the Commission and on negotiations between the Commission and Member States. Between 1958 and 1985, 225 Directives have been adopted, mostly for motor vehicles, equipment goods, and food.[4] However, this apparent success hides several failures.

### The Failure of the EC "Old" Approach

First, in 1968 (at the end of the transition period of the elimination of the intra-EC tariffs), there were only 3 EC TRIS Directives adopted, despite the growing number of cases where intra-EC trade was hampered by Member States TRIS. In 1969, the Commission launched a pharaonic "General Program for the Elimination of Technical Barriers to Trade" of 124 Directives (one fifth of the current number) to be adopted in eighteen months which failed miserably: at the end of this deadline, only one Directive was adopted by the Council. On average, it took two to three years for the Directives adopted within the framework of the General Program –up to eleven years in the case of the "Mineral water" Directive.

Second, the high number (222) of Directives adopted between 1969 and 1986 (the last year of systematic use of Article 100) flows from the very narrow scope in terms of products and TRIS covered of these Directives. All these Directives are estimated to cover only 29 percent of the Community's industrial value-added [Single Market Review, Sub-series III, volume 1, 1998].[5] Moreover, because they are drafted in detailed manner, many Old Approach Directives require frequent substantial redrafting (that is why the Old Approach is surviving until today and why there has been as many Old Approach Directives adopted between 1986 and 1997 than before 1986).

Two reasons were invoked for the Old Approach impasse: Article 100 imposed the unanimity rule in the Council of Ministers; and the technical work (devoted to the Commission by Article 100) was too complex to be easily handled by the Commission officials. The Commission could only try to address the second issue. It did it by reducing the scope of harmonization through *optional* harmonization (a producer has the choice between EC harmonized rules or national rules, but goods traded across borders will have to meet EC harmonized standards or the standards of the destination country), *partial* harmonization (harmonized rules apply only for cross-border transactions), *minimal* harmonization (Member states may add more stringent rules to the EC harmonized rules), *alternative* harmonization (the Directives provide alternative harmonization schemes for achieving the objective pursued) or lastly *piecemeal* harmonization (each aspect or input of a product is harmonized separately: for instance, car tires, manometers for car tires and auto glass are subject to separate Directives of harmonization).

Beyond all the legal and political problems, there is a more profound economic problem: is the harmonization approach an efficient mean for reducing the *protectionist* component of TRIS? The EC Old Approach provides a mix answer to this key question. A study done for the EC Commission [Single Market Review, op. cited, 1998] suggests that despite the huge reglementary effort, barriers to intra-EC trade are still serious in all the industries concerned (except for cars) –leading to the conclusion that harmonization does not really bite.

All these observations suggest that the harmonization approach is very unlikely to be developed at the world level. However, exceptions to this general conclusion can exist. Certain regulatory bodies can develop enough competence and prestige that they could nurture a *de facto* harmonization approach at the world level in their narrow sector of competence. An example to look at would be the U.S. Federal Aviation Authority and aircraft safety during the 1970s and the 1980s.[6]

## Harmonization and Monitoring

However, the lesson from the Old Approach experience is not entirely negative. The increasing recognition of the failure of the Old Approach led the Commission to take an initiative which proved to be very valuable: the implementation of a notification process (under Directive 83/189 the coverage of which was expanded by Directive 88/182 to key sectors, such as food products, pharmaceuticals, and cosmetics) whenever a Member state was considering the adoption of new technical regulations. In addition to a purely monitoring function, this Directive allows for standstill arrangements and for proposals of an EC TRIS (instead of the domestic TRIS) whenever the Commission believed that the proposed national legislation would generate new technical barriers.

Member states notify their new TRIS laws and regulations which are then examined by the Committee 83/189, formed of high level officials from Member states and the Commission. Notifications revealing possible conflicts between EC and national TRIS are sent for comments to the concerned bodies of each Member state (Ministries and Member State Standard Bodies) and of the Community (the Commission and the European Standard Bodies described below). Comments can eventually lead to "observations" and (in case of possible infringement to Community law) to "detailed opinions" (*avis circonstanciés*) suggesting Community measures in order to eliminate conflicts.

How efficient has been the EC notification process? Since the early 1990s, the 83/189 Committee examines between 430 and 470 new regulations each year (covering the EC-15 before 1995 because the Committee covers EFTA countries). Many of these notifications have been effectively done by the Member states; the others have been the outcome of cross-notifications or firms' complaints. Out of these 430–470 annual regulations, 75 percent have raised observations and 40 percent detailed opinions. Despite the fact that action has been taken in a very small number of cases (2 percent) these figures suggest that the net put in place by Directive 83/189 seems to be relatively tight.

This monitoring system could be extended to the world level (maybe, by expanding it to larger geographical zones, such as the Transatlantic zone, the Quad zone, the OECD zone, etc.). In this respect, it is interesting to note that since 1990, the Directive 83/189 notification mechanism covers EFTA countries (a particularly important point because EFTA countries are large producers of pharmaceuticals and other TRIS-intensive goods).

## 2. The "Mutual Recognition" Approach

The impasse of the harmonization approach led the EC to look for an alternative approach, the so-called "New Approach," based on the mutual recognition of the TRIS of each country by its trading partners. According this concept, countries harmonize a minimum number of technical aspects involved in a TRIS, and they recognize the regulations of the trade partners for all the remaining aspects. If the harmonization element is nil, then mutual recognition is unconditional. If there is some harmonization, mutual recognition is conditional. What follows discusses only conditional mutual recognition.

The mutual recognition concept looks very attractive because it seems to impose the minimum level of pre-requirements (from a diplomatic, legal, and technical point of view). However, its enforcement within the EC shows that this first impression is somewhat misleading: the EC New Approach has required several pre-conditions suggesting that its implementation at the multilateral level will not far to be easy.

### Mutual Recognition: Substantial Legal Conditions

The EC New Approach could not have been possible without the existence of the European Court of Justice, and the full legal order established by the European Treaties, in particular, Article 30 of the Treaty of Rome. Article 30 bans quantitative restrictions "*and all measures having equivalent effects.*" What the European Court did was to consider TRIS as such measures having equivalent effects to quantitative restrictions (they ban the imports of the product in question, or are equivalent to some "tariff").

In 1974 and 1979, the Court of Justice used Article 30 in two rulings raising TRIS issues. In the 1974 *Dassonville* ruling, the Court stated the so-called Dassonville formula: "*all trading rules which are capable of hindering, directly or indirectly, actually or potentially, intra-EC trade are to be considered as measures having an effect equivalent to quantitative restrictions.*" In the 1979 *Cassis de Dijon* ruling, the Court added—almost incidentally—that "*any product imported from another Member state must in principle be admitted to the territory of the importing Member state if it has been lawfully produced, that is, conforms to rules and processes that are customarily applied and traditionally applied in the exporting country, and is marketed in the territory of the latter.*" In sum, the Court considered that, by virtue of Article 30, to be lawfully produced and marketed in a Member state was a sufficient condition for selling the product in question in other Member states.

The basic legal requirements for a wide use of the mutual recognition approach are thus high: the existence of a wide prohibition of restrictions to trade (as Article 30), and the existence of a Court able to make effective the enforcement of such a provision., These legal pre-conditions are not currently fulfilled by the multilateral trade system and, realistically, are not likely to be fulfilled in the foreseeable future. There is no international counterpart to the European Court of Justice, or the federal courts in countries such as the United States. The jurisdiction of the International Court of Justice in the Hague could enforce mutual recognition agreements between the parties to those agreements, but only if the agreements themselves gave the Court jurisdiction to do so. Many of the nations of the world, including the United States, have been quite reluctant to bestow jurisdiction on the International Court of Justice, and it seems unlikely that these attitudes would change in the short term.

The key role of the European Court is underlined by the following observations. First, the EC Commission could have tried to get out of the problems raised by the harmonization approach by invoking itself Article 30. However, the Commission did not feel empowered to take such an initiative, mirroring the necessary role of the European Court. Second, it took time for the Commission to engulf the EC in the new track prepared by the Court. In 1985, almost ten years after the *Dassonville* formula and six years after the *Cassis de Dijon* ruling,[7] the Commission issued the White Paper on the Single Market and a Notice on technical harmonization. Both texts introduced explicitly the concept of mutual recognition as a solution to TRIS issues. Council Resolution (May 1985) provided the official guidelines of the New Approach. Lastly, a few more years were necessary to introduce directly all these elements in the Treaty of Rome: the Maastricht version of the Treaty of Rome added to Article 100 two Articles, Article 100A and Article 100B, in order to take into account the wider ambit of Article 30 and the mutual recognition principle in the field of the "approximation of laws." In addition to the implicit wide definition of measures having equivalent effects, Article 100A introduced another innovation: the qualified majority vote (instead of the unanimity of Article 100) in TRIS matters, except for fiscal and labor-related issues. As of today, Article 100B remains a legal curiosity: so far, it has never been used. In sum, the early 1980s witnessed the building of a consistent and systematic EC legal regime for TRIS. Articles 30 and 100A are the backbone of the regime –closely related and interdependent: a wider coverage of Article 30 increases the capacity of the EC to launch European standards based on Article 100A.

There were more basic requirements to be met that the Court's use of Article 30. As usually in international trade matters, no liberalization can be introduced without some kind of safeguards. The mutual recognition approach does not escape this general rule: hence it requires additional disciplines. In the EC case, there are three "safeguard" clauses: Article 36 of the Treaty, the "mandatory requirements" (sometimes mentioned as the "rule of reason") included in the Cassis de Dijon ruling, and Article 100A:4 (recital 4). However, the Court has strictly limited the use of these safeguards.

Concerning Article 36, the Court imposed three conditions which also prevail for the other safeguards: (a) *causality* (for being preferred to EC TRIS, national TRIS must contribute directly to the policy objective); (b) *proportionality* (national TRIS should not be more trade-restrictive that it is necessary for achieving the policy goals); and (c) the choice of the *least trade-distorting instrument* (the Member State shall choose the least trade-distorting instrument for achieving its fixed goals). In the "mandatory requirements" accompanying the *Cassis de Dijon* ruling, the Court recognizes the right to enforce Member State TRIS in a few limited cases: fiscal effectiveness, fairness of commercial transactions, public health and consumer protection. Lastly, Article 100A:4 offers the possibility of applying Member states provisions "*on grounds of major needs referred to Article 36, or relating to protection of the environmental or the working environment.*" However, this safeguard provision is limited by the fact that the Commission is part of the safeguard process: it shall verify that this safeguard is not "*a means of arbitrary discrimination or a disguised restriction on trade between Member states.*" Moreover, the one or few Member states which would like to invoke Article 100A:4 are likely to be penalized by their marginal position with respect to the rest of the EC (the other Member states can go ahead, and benefit from the harmonization process). Indeed, so far, Article 100A:4 has been invoked in a handful of cases.

## The Enforcement of the New Approach: Emerging Frustration

The New Approach was expected to enhance considerably the process of solving TRIS issues. However, there have been increasing signs of frustration. This disappointment is not related to the capacity to "produce" Directives: 28 New Approach Directives have been adopted. This figure may look small, but the product coverage of the New Approach Directives is often large. For instance, the Directive 89/392 (machines and lift machines) alone is estimated to cover roughly 55,000 types of machines [Pelkmans and Egan, 1992]. The 28 New Approach Directives are estimated to cover 27 percent of the EC industrial value-added (almost as much as the 475 Old Approach Directives), and 16 percent of EC industrial value-added operates under a regime of complete mutual recognition [Single Market Review, 1998].

Why, then, such a disappointment? First, "producing" Directives is only one aspect of a complete EC TRIS regime: it leaves (and exacerbates) many pending problems at the enforcement (conformity assessment and market surveillance) level, as examined in section 3. Second, the New Approach does not completely eliminate the harmonization element, but it limits it to key technical aspects (the essential requirements in EC parlance). As a result, the New Approach allows to achieve a higher flexibility in producing EC TRIS, but at the cost of "disintegrating" the definition of these TRIS between two operators –the Commission and the European Standards Bodies (ESBs). This raised two problems which became rapidly visible.

The first problem is that, being no more the exclusive source of TRIS definition, the Commission issues "mandates" to the European Standard Bodies (ESBs) by which it invites them to prepare "European Standards" (ENs) complying with the "essential requirements" the Commission defines in the Directives. In order to allow for maximum flexibility, these essential requirements have often been too vague to be useful –leading to unclear mandates for the technical work to be done by the ESBs. For instance, in the "Machine safety" and "Construction products" Directives, the Commission has been obliged to draft "interpretative documents" of its own essential requirements –making the process of defining EC TRIS again very slow and frustrating.

The second problem was more circonstancial: the ESBs were not initially conceived for fulfilling the role of providers of ENs devolved to them by the New Approach. The three major ESBs are CEN (Comité européen de normalisation) CENELEC (Comité européen de normalisation électrotechnique) and ETSI (European Telecommunications Standards Institute). Until the mid-1980s, CEN and CENELEC were mere fora where Member state standards bodies (MSSBs), such as DIN in Germany or AFNOR in France, could gather for implementing international standards drawn up by the international standard organizations (ISO) in an uniform manner in the EC. After the adoption of the New Approach, CEN and CENELEC were induced by the Commission to develop "autonomously" ENs with a funding from the EC.[8] ETSI is more closely related to the New Approach: it has been created in 1988 (following a 1987 proposal by the Commission) exclusively for dealing with TRIS related to telecommunications, with a membership of EC Member states (plus EFTA countries, Cyprus, Malta, and Turkey) and of Europe-based Telephone Operators.

## A Preliminary Conclusion about the Mutual Recognition Approach

The EC New Approach is not the panacea people thought it was: it is the uneasy (unholy?) alliance of government-based and market-based forces, the difficult compromise between regulatory costs and market-based trust. This ambiguity leads to the following preliminary comment.

There are four major ways for dealing with TRIS-based barriers: complete harmonization, the conditional mutual recognition of the existing TRIS, their unconditional mutual recognition, and no regulation at all (eliminating all existing TRIS is rarely possible because regulations may have other goals than protecting the producers). These four options can be ranked by decreasing order of trust and by increasing order of regulatory costs. Under the no regulation option, the country trusts (distrust) the regulations existing in its trading partners as much as its own, and there is no (or minimal) regulatory costs. Harmonization implies the absence of trust between trading partners, and it is likely to impose high regulatory costs, both *ex ante* (to write down the rules) and *ex post* (to enforce them). Conditional and unconditional mutual recognitions correspond to intermediate situations—conditional being closer to harmonization, unconditional to no regulation.

The EC TRIS experience suggests that the trade-off between trust and regulatory costs varies over time. In the 1970s, the EC was looking for complete harmonization because trust was low. As the regulatory costs imposed by the unanimity voting rule were also high, the failure was severe. The *Cassis de Dijon* ruling "imposed" a higher level of trust within the EC—hence led to the intensive use of conditional mutual recognition in the Single Market Program. However, as shown below, conditional MRAs can have heavy *ex post* costs related to the correct enforcement of the new regulations. The recent years have brought a better awareness of these costs to the EC Member states: as a result, MRA equilibria may look increasingly unstable—with Member states induced to go back to harmonization or to go further towards unconditional recognition or no regulation.

In the world forum, many of the ingredients described above are simply missing: no Court of Justice (again the real force behind the New Approach) preparing the field for conditional mutual recognition, no political power and will for harmonization, and limited trust between trading partners. Paradoxically, trust may be the least rare factor: trading partners with the same legal framework and a similar set of firms could be tempted to go towards unconditional recognition. However, this approach (which expands the market-based component of MRAs at the detriment of its government-based element) may be difficult with countries such as the U.S. or the EC—too large and complex to feel in confidence with each other (the U.S. with the EC loose rule of law, and the EC with the U.S. federalist syndrome). This remark suggests that MRAs may be easier to negotiate and enforce between sub-entities (US States or EC Member States). In fact, bilateral or plurilateral intra-EC efforts of unconditional mutual recognition have preceded or accompanied the New Approach (which has been a way of extending to "communitarize" these efforts).

### 3. Enforcement Issues

Any TRIS regime requires two *enforcement* processes: (i) "conformity assessment" which comprises testing, certifying, and marketing (hereafter TCM) activities undertaken to ensure that, before being sold, products comply with the specifications laid down;[9] (ii) "market surveillance" consisting in monitoring the markets in order to be sure that all the products sold are conform to the adopted technical standards.

In the EC, the New Approach focuses on the mutual recognition of *standards* by the EC Member states.[10] Almost no attention was initially given to the these two other levels of conformity assessment and market surveillance. It is only later on, and quite recently, that these two levels have been dealt with the so-called "Global" and "Common" Approaches. Again, rulings by the Court of Justice have been necessary in order to make a breakthrough in these domains. For instance, the Court considered as having equivalent effect under Article 30 the following measures: (a) the obligation to produce certificates, (b) the obligation to impose import inspections and customs controls, (c) the obligation to make a declaration of origin or of origin marking, (d) the obligation to type approval before sale or use, (e) the obligation to appoint a representative in the importing Member State, (f) the imposition of liabilities on the importer, (g) the requirement that goods shall be sold by qualified persons, (h) the existence of discriminatory restrictions on advertising and promotion, (i) the obligation of references to the law of the exporting Member State, (j) the abusive reservation of "appelations d'origine" or indications of source, (k) the requirements as to the presentation of products, and language requirements.

## Conformity Assessment: The "Global" Approach

Conformity assessment requires specialized TCM units of all kinds (laboratories, public agencies, private firms). By its traditional reluctance to build a TRIS regime based on manufacturers' reputation, the EC relies largely on TCM units not vertically integrated to producers, but often related to Member state governments. This TRIS "industry" is large: it involves 100,000 separate TRIS, relies on 10,000 independent TCM units, is employing 200,000 workers and has a turnover of ECU 10–11 billion (these estimates date from the early 1990s).

The type and degree of regulation of the TCM units is thus a crucial component of the EC TRIS policy, and this leads to the following (somewhat ironical) main questions: is it necessary to "harmonize" the EC TCM units in order to make sure that intra-EC mutual recognition works, and if yes, to which extent? The importance of these questions flows from the fact that the TCM stage raises two broad types of difficulties –hence generates two sources of trade barriers and costs:

1. Mutually recognized TRIS can still impose a burden on trade if TCM activities require additional costs when the product is exported to another Member state (for instance, when it requires additional tests in the importing country).
2. The voluntary use of the "CE" marking by manufacturers do not solve all these issues. Of course, Member states cannot exclude products under CE marking from their domestic markets, nor can they impose additional certification requirements: the "CE" marking provides unhindered access to all EC markets for the producer in question. However, the CE marking makes more acute the problems related to the certification of the CE marking process because a manufacturer under CE marking benefits from a presumption of conformity with the essential requirements of the EC Directive in question.

All these problems converge to one point: the level of technical competence of the TCM units. The ongoing EC-CEC discussions underline the importance of this point because they nurture the EC fear that the CECs will not be able to meet the level of competence seen as desirable for the TCM units without drastic measures.

In 1989, a Council Resolution on conformity assessment was adopted. It introduced the so-called "New and Global" approach: "New" because it relies on the mutual recognition of standards, "Global" because it relies on mutual recognition in terms of conformity assessment. This Council Resolution led to Directive 90/683 on the CE marking amended by the Council Decision of July 1993 which tried to encompass all the possible configurations about conformity assessment by spelling out fourteen "modules" taking into account the nature of the product, the stage and type of the production process, the kinds of risks involved.

These fourteen modules cover the "conception" level as well as the "production" level of a product.[11] For each of these modules, the Decision defines the tasks to be done, the operators (manufacturer or TCM units) who can be in charge and the sharing of their responsibilities. For instance, under module "A-A," it is up to the manufacturer to declare the conformity of its product to the essential requirements listed in the appropriate Directive(s) and to the ENs established by the appropriate ESB. By contrast, the procedure under the module "B-F" is more complex: it is a TCM unit which declares the conformity at the conception level of the product (with the necessary tests, if any) whereas, at the production level, the manufacturer is also involved for declaring the conformity of its product to its "type." It should be underlined that the 1993 Council Decision defines only "general" rules: each of the New Approach Directives selects the modules effectively open to the manufacturer (or importer) and to the TCM units.

In such a framework, the TCM units are crucial. As a result, each Directive requires that Member States "notify" the TCM units that they declare competent to carry out the TCM activities required: the chosen TCM units are called the "Notified Bodies" (NBs) for the group of products covered by the Directive in question. The New and Global Approach relies on roughly 600 NBs (compared to the 10,000 TCM units existing in the EC).

As mentioned above, the EC TRIS regime is a mixed system—though less market-based than government-based. Nowadays, the balance between these two aspects is under stress precisely at the way TCM units are notified. The Commission is arguing that more harmonization is needed. In a recent survey (1996), it found that picking up NBs—or, in EC parlance, "accrediting" NBs—obeys to a wide range of rules, methods, and procedures among EC Member States. I perceived this high variance as a threat to the whole EC TRIS regime—and, in particular, to the CE marking which is the vault stone of the New Approach. As a result, the Commission has tabled several proposals in order to "harmonize" these accreditation procedures.

It should be added that, if there is no harmonization of Member State TRIS, the TCM problems remain similar in nature, but that they are made more difficult because there is a wider range of TCM activities (not "merely" fourteen modules) a larger number of available TCM units (10,000 units, compared to the 600 NBs for the New and Global Approach) and allegedly wider discrepancies between these units (which range from the large organizations, such as SGS or Veritas, to small in-house private units or to large government laboratories). In this context, the key issue remains the recognition of the TCM unit chosen by a given manufacturer (often in its own country) or by its business partners (other producers, large retailers or distributors, or even consumers). Initially, this recognition has relied on bilateral MRAs (such as those signed by France, the Netherlands and Sweden in the early 1980s). Since then, a successful process of "plurilateralization" has been going on in the EC –leading to the European Accreditation of Certification Bodies (EAC) in 1990 and to the European Cooperation for Accreditation of Laboratories (EAL) in 1994. These agreements have ramifications external to the EC (including with APEC countries).

### Market Surveillance: the "Common" Approach

The credibility of any TRIS regime depends on its impact on the markets. There are two views –one focusing on reputation and *ex post* penalties, the other one on *ex ante* surveillance of the markets by public agencies. An efficient functioning of TCM and market surveillance requires a delicate balance between reliance on manufacturers' reputation and credible actions from *ad hoc* quasi-public agencies. As mentioned above, the EC TRIS regime tends to discount the disciplines of the private reputation of the firms. As a result, it requires the action of public authorities for monitoring markets.

There is a wide variety of "market surveillance operators" (MSOs) in the EC. As of today, there are no specific EC regulations related to the MSOs. However, the Commission and certain Member States would again like to reinforce the regulatory framework in this domain. The CEC accessions are perceived as an additional reason for moving in this direction because the CEC weakness in this domain is perceived as a threat to the whole EC TRIS regime.

### First Comments on the Global and Common Approaches

These Approaches are where currently the action is in the international fora: as said in the previous sections, the EC experience for *determining* TRIS is unlikely to be matched at the world level: the Old and New Approaches seem to remain EC specialties. Mutual recognition of TCM activities (and, to a lesser extent, market surveillance) is the core of the problem in a multilateral framework.

In this perspective, the future evolution of the EC will certainly be interesting. As said above, the EC has abandoned its negotiations of MRAs (about standards and enforcement) with Central European countries and shifted (two years ago) towards the full acceptance of the *acquis communautaire* in TRIS matters by the Central European countries. In turn, this move has generated worries in the EC about the candidates' ability to enforce the *acquis* –and proposals to reinforce the "communitarization" of the EC TRIS regime, in particular its enforcement. All this flows from a mix of factors: the Commission wants to be more involved in key aspects of the current regime (the accreditation of the NBs and TCM units, market surveillance); EC Member States with "higher" TRIS push for higher "credentials" of the involved bodies, as a price for their consent to mutual recognition; the bodies involved in the EC TRIS regime have often a long tradition of public firms –hence are afraid of the potential competition that new bodies (which could emerge in the Central European countries) could represent; the old bodies involved in Central European TRIS regimes want to maintain their traditional grip on their domestic economy.

All this suggests that the EC TRIS policy is at a crossroad in terms of the balance between a market-based and a government-based TRIS regime. An alternative to increased communitarization –which, it must be said *en passant*, goes against the popular view in the EC according to which MRAs are a way to promote competition between rules and between regulators– could be the emergence of a healthy competition between European agencies currently involved in TCM and market surveillance activities. For instance, an agency located in a Member state could decide to provide the "best" services in terms of TCM activities only for a limited range of goods (for which this agency believes to have the best expertise). If successful, the "specialized" agency would attract manufacturers from the *whole* EC –and not only those of its Member state of origin (as today).

## 4. Concluding Remarks

Two final remarks may be useful. First, the EC TRIS dilemma may be another example of the risks of confusion –illusion?– between deeper integration and deeper regulation: the communitarization of the EC trade policy (the EC trade barriers) in the late 1980s and early 1990s has led to an *increased* –not a decreased– range of rates of protection of the Member States' economies.

Second, the fundamental issues raised by the TCM activities and market surveillance are close to those examined by the economic analysis of crime initiated by Becker [1968]. What is at stake is the optimal trade-off between *ex ante* inhibition and *ex post* penalties: indeed, this aspect is underlined by EC officials who argue for a deeper involvement of the EC authorities because of lack of technical competence and legal framework.

NOTES

1. An industry standard is "a document, established by consensus and approved by a recognized body, that provides, for common and repeated use, rules, guidelines or characteristics for activities or their results, aimed at the achievement of the optimum degree of order in a given context" [ISO Guide, 1991]. Industry standards are thus voluntary by nature. By contrast, public regulations are mandatory.

2. This is why protectionist-minded firms always look for public support.

3. The two next largest packages of Directives are agriculture (383, to be compared to the 201 TRIS Directives on automotives only) and environment (144 Directives, some of which being very close from the TRIS field).

4. The EC legal body consists in the following legal sources: Treaties, Rulings of the European Court of Justice, Directives, Regulations, Resolutions, and Decisions of the EC Council of Ministers, Recommendations, and Communications of the European Commission.

5. And an additional coverage of 4 percent if one takes into account the Old Approach Directives with some elements of mutual recognition.

6. Today, firms' reputation in these matters may be dominant (see the ValueJet case).

7. Other Court's rulings have confirmed the Dassonville and Cassis de Dijon cases, such as, for instance, Buet (1989), GB-Inno (1990), SARRP (1990), Aragonesa de Publicidad (1991), Schutzverband (1993), Delattre (1993).

8. CEN "produced" 124 ENs in 1985, 224 in 1992, 350 in 1994, whereas CENELEC "produced" 200 ENs in 1992 and 350 in 1994 [WTO TPR, 1993, 111] and Aftalion [1998] quoting Egan [1997]. ESTI is credited of 68 ENs in 1992 [WTO TPR, 1993, op. cited].

9. Conformity assessment focuses generally on products. As a result, it may be required on all the inputs (or on all the key inputs) of a given final product—as was best illustrated by the air-brakes in tractors or tires in cars.

10. For a legal analysis, see, for example, Eeckhout [1994] or Oliver [1996] on which this paper relies.

11. At the product conception level, conformity is defined with respect to the product (modules A and Abis), to the "type" (module B), to the product with unitary test (module G), and to the "complete quality-insurance" (module H) requiring a substantial amount of additional information on the procedures ensuring a defined level of quality. Concerning the production level, conformity is defined with respect to the same references, except for module B which leads to four possible modules: conformity to the "type" (module C), production-quality insurance (module D), products-insurance quality (module E), and tests on products (module F).

CHAPTER 14

# Comments on Messerlin and Palmeter's Paper

*Thomas Cottier*

The papers by David Palmeter and Patrick Messerlin discuss regulatory approaches to the elimination of discrimination, inherently produced by diverging regulatory standards in the field of technical prescriptions and norms, but also of sanitary and phytosanitary measures. I was intrigued to listen to two different philosophies in addressing comparable problems both in the United States and the European Community. The papers clearly shows that these philosophies are formally different, and difficulties encountered in negotiating mutual recognition between the U.S. and Europe may well be understood from that perspective. Yet, it is interesting to ask whether the two approaches nevertheless show comparable traits and commonalities, at least to some extent. First it would perhaps be useful to seek a clarification on terminology. David points to the fact that Mutual Recognition Agreements (MRA's), as they developed in Europe, are unknown in the U.S. I would submit that they are equally unknown as a matter of internal EC law and regulation. MRA's should be understood to comprise international *agreements* in international law between nations or customs territories, but not be used within such constituencies. Thus, while it inspired the European policy of seeking MRA's with third countries, the principle of Cassis-de-Dijon does not amount to an MRA's in a legal and technical sense, but rather establishes a fundamental principle of EC internal market law within the ambit of Article 30 ECT.

David, rightly so, recalls that within U.S. constitutional law, no principle similar to Cassis-de-Dijon emerged. Under the interstate commerce clause, and the judicially developed dormant commerce clause, there is no general obligation to mutually recognize marketing standards established by the other States of the Union. David is certainly right that there is no counterpart to this phenomenon in a formal sense. In substance, however, it would be of interest to study in depth to what extent constitutional case law does not amount, to some extent, to a comparable concept which assumes the functions of interfacing legal regimes of the different States of the Union with different techniques. Comparison is facilitated if it is recalled that the Cassis-de-Dijon principle, or the regulatory principle of origin, is by no means absolute but leaves Member States rights to deviate to the extent that they can demonstrate that this is *necessary* to protect the public good, such as the environment or consumers, all in addition to the exceptions enshrined within Article 36 ECT. Thus, *Maine v. Taylor* may also be upheld before the European Court of Justice to the extent that – absent a Community wide regulation of the matter—a Member State can show necessity of applying its own rules and regulation in order to secure health protection of the respective fish stock. Equally, *Balwin v. Selig* may produce similar results in EC law as the measure applied involved what typically amounts to a protectionist scheme to the economic benefit of domestic producers. The differences between U.S. and EC case law therefore may not be that fundamental in the end. Perhaps, one explanation for the absence of an open Cassis-de-Dijon principle in the U.S. might be that federal powers to regulate interstate commerce have been used more widely and that harmonization by way of federal law is much more advanced than within the EC. David's finding that there are virtually no state standards of mutual recognition or full harmonization and that, instead, regulations are enacted by the federal government, support this view. In Europe, instead, the failure to bring about successfully full harmonization under the so called Old Approach caused the European Court to compensate a weak constitutional structure by judicial activism and by introducing a far reaching principle of mutual recognition within the bounds of Article 30 ECT in order to promote free movement of goods within the EC.

The absence of a philosophy of mutual recognition in the U.S. may well explain some of the conceptual difficulties encountered in negotiating sectoral approval of foreign product standards. Yet, such problems would arise at any rate, even between two partners fully applying mutual recognition domestically. Switzerland is an example in point. The paper by Olivier Guillod shows that the Swiss today are fully applying Cassis-de-Dijon internally in inter-cantonal commerce and dream to expand this to community trade. Yet, bilateral MRA negotiations with the EC resulted far from extending the scope of Article EC to Swiss relations (as this is the case with the EEA Agreement). Nor can it be expected to construe the Swiss-EC free trade agreement of 1972 in such a manner. The fact that the Swiss and other European partners fully adopt EC standards does not change this. The level of mutual integration simply is not high enough. The more so this is true in EC - U.S. relations. While in the European theater, the EC is in a dominant and hegemonic position to have others adopt EC standards and regulation in bilateral treaties (e.g. Eastern European States), this is not the case in negotiations with the United States. The paper submitted by Kalypso Nicolaidis provides ample evidence that this is a business of mutual political concessions and an exercise of long-term building of mutual confidence and experience. This, as it is with other third countries, necessarily leaves the matter to piece-meal and gradual progress over time, as David aptly described the situation. Mutual recognition in the sense of the Cassis-de-Dijon principle requires a very high level of legal, social, and economic integration. And this brings me to the Patrick's paper.

Patrick gives an interesting historical account of the history of the different approaches to bring about abolishment of unnecessary technical barriers to trade within the European Community in the form of "technical public regulations and industry standards" (TRIS). The paper seeks to describe the historical process in three stages: the Old Approach (1960–1985), The New Approach (1985 onwards) and Global or Common Approaches under way. From a legal point of the view, the following comments should be made.

First, while the two approaches mentioned first are alternatives to standard setting, the Global or Common approach relates to implementation of standards, and should not be dealt with on the same level as standard setting. Implementation policies are required under any of the standard setting procedures, and may vary. Efforts to harmonize testing, certifying, and marketing (TCM) and bring about comparable quality in this field of work within the many institutions involved is a task on is own and should be distinguished from standards setting.

Second, I would not agree in the way the new approach has been described. Patrick argues that the new approach essentially relies upon mutual recognition by the Member States, essentially based upon the principle of Cassis-de-Dijon. From a legal perspective, the New Approach is based upon Council Resolution of May 7, 1985 (OJ 85/C136/01). It addresses the process of formulating community-wide and thus EC-wide *common* standards. The New Approach, as opposed to full harmonization by the Old Approach, consists of bringing about a division of labor between setting governmental standards (essential requirements) by the EC and their specification by private norms (technical specifications), elaborated by private standard organizations, in particular CEN, CENELEC, and ETSI. While these norms are voluntary, they are nevertheless legally relevant as the observance of such norms by the industry triggers a *presumption* of compliance with the set of corresponding essential EC standards. This is a major incentive to comply with voluntary private norms, as the burden of proof shifts to the government challenging the safety of a product. The principle of Cassis-de-Dijon, on the other hand, applies to all areas still within the jurisdiction of the Member States, absent harmonization either under the Old or the New Approach. I would therefore suggest to deal with Cassis-de-Dijon under quite a separate heading. It is not legally part of the

New Approach. This, of course, does not mean that the two do not interact. The somewhat surprising findings that the new approach did not result, as expected, in a high number of harmonized standards may well be explained by the fact that additional harmonization no longer is a pressing need, thanks to the Cassis-de-Dijon principle. Matters can be left without much harm to the common market to national governments, subject to mandatory notification procedures and rights of the Commission to take up the matter if need be. In constitutional terms, the New Approach is an expression of policies of subsidiarity. Also, I do not see a close relationship between Cassis-de-Dijon and Keck and Mithouard. The latter case brought about a restriction of Dassonville as the scope of restrictions having equivalent effect were legally limited to product related measures, exempting non-discriminatory marketing and price regulation from the scope of Article 30 ECT, and thus from scrutiny by the Court. As TRIS standards per se relate to the quality and safety of the product, I fail to see how this affected the operation of Cassis-de-Dijon principle in the present field.

Let me also comment on the application of Cassis-de-Dijon to third country trade. It is said that a vast majority of legal commentators consider that the principle of equivalence also applies to non-EC imports. From my comments on David's paper, a qualification may be helpful. The principle does apply, once a product has been lawfully put on the market in one of the Member States, in accordance with Art. 9:2 ECT. However, the principle does not apply short of treaty provisions with regard to the same product put on the market abroad. This means, in practical terms, that certification and marketing approval must be obtain both on the domestic and on the EC market. The very core of Cassis-de-Dijon thus, does not apply even if the product has been produced in conformity with EC standards abroad. Again, the level of integration is not high enough for such effects.

Patrick states at the outset the working hypothesis that the more public authorities are involved in standard setting, the more likely the protectionist and discriminatory effect of TRIS will be. This could imply that standards should be abolished and the matter essentially left to product liability which in effect amounts to ex post standard setting by Courts and which implies heavy insurance costs and legal uncertainty. It is not likely to protect the well-being of citizens and consumers to a sufficient degree. It could also imply that standards should be set by private bodies alone. I am not sure whether the paper supports such an approach, as private norms developed by national industries would seem to be much more prone to segmenting markets, short of government involvement. It should be recalled that governmental standards are heavily influenced by private sector interests and lobbies. The answer, in my view, to prevent predominance of local interests would be in promoting New Approach rules on the EC level. Courts could promote this, paradoxically, by construing national exceptions to the Cassis-de-Dijon principle more leniently, thus creating a necessary momentum to bring the matter on the level of EC regulation (as this can be observed in legal areas, such as copyright harmonization) and thus improve the record of the New Approach in the future. I would fully agree, however, that mutual recognition of TCM institutions is a prime key in order to avoid unnecessary red tape in transnational business transactions and bring about enhanced market access of competing products. These problems of administrating and applying standards need to be dealt with in parallel with the problem of standard setting.

Finally, what can be learned for the global level and the WTO? Is it possible to go beyond the principle of necessity and proportionality of national standards in accordance with the TBT Agreement? The evidence relating to the Cassis-de-Dijon principle and mutual recognition in general shows that the approach requires a high level of integration and mutual trust and confidence. It requires a common culture and philosophy, to some extent. The experience of negotiating MRA's shows that mutual recognition may be achieved on a piece-meal basis, in sectors where such confidence is building. Inherently, it is a bilateral approach, taking into account the particular situations of two jurisdictions. Results cannot be readily extended to third parties short of detailed examination and thus a full further negotiation. In my view, this leaves us with little hope for comprehensive approaches in the multilateral system with its 134 WTO Member States. Members should pursue MRA policies on a bilateral basis, and procedural obligations to negotiate recognition based upon conditional MFN modeled after Article VII:2 GATS should be examined. An approach encompassing all Members, however, inherently needs to be based on piece-meal, sectoral, and limited harmonization, difficult as this may be to be achieved within or without the WTO. Yet, the experience of the TRIPs Agreement shows that such sectoral harmonization and positive integration can be achieved and implemented over a longer period of time, provided that a majority of governments and the private sector see this to be in their mutual advantage. Similarly, reference of the SPS Agreement to standards of Codex Alimentarius demonstrates that harmonization is not entirely new and possible, and will be further possible if we succeed in finding legitimate procedures of decision-making to bring about global safety standards.

CHAPTER 15

# Non-Discriminatory Mutual Recognition: An Oxymoron in the New WTO Lexicon?

*Kalypso Nicolaïdis*

Is non-discriminatory mutual recognition a contradiction in terms? What is the meaning of "non discrimination" in international trade? First and foremost, it is the obligation to treat "like" products, firms or people similarly, be it non-nationals among themselves (MFN) or non-nationals relative to nationals (national treatment). As an obvious corollary, treating different products, firms or people differently is therefore perfectly compatible with non-discrimination. So why should Mutual Recognition Agreements (MRAs) be considered as antithetical to the principle of non-discrimination? MRAs are agreements based on such a diagnosis of "unlikeness" between parties inside and outside the agreement: they should pass the national treatment and MFN test. At the same time, their *prima face* effect is to discriminate between foreign laws, regulations, and standards that are "recognized" as valid domestically and those that are not. This is done through an exclusionary negotiation process akin to (or as part of) regional agreements, which constitute exceptions to MFN under GATS. This paper explores the relationship between mutual recognition and non discrimination and suggests what could be the conditions for a more harmonious coexistence between the two. Non-discriminatory mutual recognition needs not be an oxymoron in the WTO lexicon.

Section 1 presents some basic definitions and typologies that lay out the range of phenomena captured by the label of "recognition." Specifically, it is difficult to speak of mutual recognition of laws and regulations between countries without specifying first and foremost *what* is being recognized. Three fundamental distinctions need to be drawn, between the recognition of the standards or laws themselves and of the enforcement or conformity assessment procedures; between certification and accreditation levels for mutual recognition; and between the recognition of entry requirements and of on-going regulatory supervision.

We then need to understand mutual recognition agreements for what they are in practice. In section 2, I provide a quick overview of the genesis of Mutual Recognition, I then highlight the main features of MRAs and show that they constitute a complex set of political deals that should be understood under the rubric of "managed" mutual recognition. In short, MRAs should be seen not so much as establishing a static standard of equivalence but rather as a process, a process of institutionalized regulatory cooperation. In this process, there continues to be some discrimination between the parties to the agreement itself. I then turn to the external impact of MRAs and assess their discriminatory effect on third parties. MRAs create what could be called new "mutual recognition zones" within which free movement is based on the principle of home country jurisdiction. In this context, we need to distinguish between two separate effects: on one hand, the impact of MRAs on the initial conditions of entry of "outsiders" within such mutual recognition zones; on the other hand, the impact of MRAs on the conditions of circulation of "outsiders" within the zone.

In section 3, I draw the consequences of this diagnosis for analyzing the basic inter-relation between mutual recognition on one hand and the classic hallmark principles of non-discrimination in the GATT/WTO, namely MFN and national treatment. I argue that mutual recognition agreements can be understood in two ways, e.g. under a "weak" and a "strong" interpretation of mutual recognition. While we can find examples of either form, the latter one is much more prevalent. Under the first interpretation, mutual recognition is simply a codification of national treatment and is more vulnerable to findings of violation of MFN. Under the second interpretation, mutual recognition is a covenant to move *beyond* national treatment and less vulnerable to findings of violation of MFN.

The section 4 examines the current WTO approach to non-discrimination and MRAs and suggests possible improvements. I argue that MRAs - understood as the "strong" version of the principle- should be subject to a form of "conditional MFN" that needs to be both more lenient than unconditional MFN in terms of threshold of "likeness" (substantive MFN) but more constraining than currently envisaged in terms of bargaining rules and processes (procedural MFN).

## 1. Definitions and Typologies

### Mutual Recognition: Principle, Contract and Agreement

Mutual recognition establishes the general principle that if a product or a service can be sold lawfully in one jurisdiction, it can be sold freely in any other participating jurisdiction, without having to comply with the regulations of these other jurisdictions.[1] In order to give effect to this general principle, governments need to adopt mutual recognition as a contractual norm whereby they agree to the transfer of regulatory authority from the host country—or jurisdiction—where a transaction takes place, to the home country—or jurisdiction—from which a product, a person, a service or a firm originate (jurisdictions are generally sovereign states but they can also be sub-national units in federal entities). The "recognition" involved here is of the "equivalence," "compatibility" or at least "acceptability" of the counterpart's regulatory system; the "mutual" part indicates that the reallocation of authority is reciprocal and simultaneous. Finally, mutual recognition agreements (MRAs) are specific instances of application of this general principle, between specific parties, applying to specific goods and services and including more or less restrictive constraints and caveats.

## Legal Standard or Political Rule? Recognition of Equivalence vs. MRAs

As will be illustrated in the historical section of this chapter, recognition can come about through two routes: judicial or political. The judicial route reaches recognition by inference: from broader legal standards or principles that attempt to push the limit of negative integration commitments (e.g., variants on national treatment and more stringent tests). The political route reaches recognition by deference: national representatives decide that can defer their regulatory jurisdiction to their counterpart.

Whether analysts approach the issue of recognition from one route or the other has a strong influence on their assessment of its import. What rubric does mutual recognition fall into when it is reached as a political agreement? Since regulatory control formally shifts from one regulation to the other, we should view it as an issue of allocation of jurisdiction; in political terms there is an actual transfer of sovereignty. But many analysts are reluctant to view mutual recognition as an issue of jurisdictional allocation and would rather characterize it as a mutually agreed "waiver."[2] This position can be motivated by strategic reasons, that is to underplay the importance of the concessions involved; or it can stem from a conceptual framework focusing on classical trade law rather than the political economy of deeper integration. This chapter falls squarely in the first school of thought. We will come back to the tension between the legal and political route in section III of this paper. We now turn to the second route and a quick typology of MRAs.

## Categories of MRAs: Three Fundamental Distinctions

There is of course a wide difference in terms of sectorial and regulatory scope between the kind of regulatory environment created through mutual recognition in different contexts, especially between the European Union and the rest of the world. At a most general level, we can identify categories of mutual recognition agreements according to three fundamental distinctions.

### *Mutual Recognition of Standards vs. Enforcement Procedures*

One fundamental distinction is between recognition of actual substantive standards and regulations and the recognition of regulatory control, or what is often called "conformity assessment systems."[3] In addition to mandating substantive regulations, governments require that exporters comply with certification (e.g. goods), licensing (e.g. professionals), control (e.g. manufacturing processes) or supervision (e.g. banks) procedures; these procedures are meant to assess conformity with underlying standards and are enforced by the regulatory authorities of the host country or increasingly by quasi-public or private entities operating on their behalf. When it comes to underlying standards, harmonization is an alternative for eliminating barriers to access. But on the enforcement side, mutual recognition is the *only* mechanism for liberalization. Unless we envisage the creation of supranational agencies responsible for conformity assessment, mutual recognition of home country jurisdiction is the only alternative to host country control. Even in cases where countries adopt the same rules or both rely on international rules, such mutual recognition of conformity assessment is generally not extended as a matter of course.[4] In other words, "harmonization" as an alternative to either home or host country jurisdiction is not available along this second dimension. As a result, when we say that harmonization of the standards themselves provides a single rule from the economic actors' viewpoint, it does not necessarily follow that it provides a single point of control. Mutual recognition is thus the only path to market access.[5]

Observers differ on the import of this distinction. The prevailing view is that "merely" recognizing conformity assessment procedures is much less significant that recognizing underlying standards. It is the differences in these underlying standards that reflect differences in regulatory choices between countries and recognizing the possibility for another country to check the conformity of their products to one's own standards ought not to be very controversial. But indeed, it has been. Which gives credence to the view that recognition of conformity assessment is indeed as significant as that of the standards and regulations themselves: the more general the latter the higher the regulatory burden put on the testing or conformity stage. A European and US pharmaceutical standard might both state that drug must be safe and exhibit no harmful side effect; the difference will be in how thoroughly and for what length of time.

*Certification Bodies vs. Accreditation System*

Within mutual recognition of conformity assessment one must establish a further distinction. In many, if not all, national systems and/or sectors, the bodies which certify that products or professionals "conform" must themselves be accredited, that is entrusted for their task by a public authority. In short, conformity assessment systems operate at two levels. Mutual recognition agreements generally have to do with the recognition of the accreditation procedure itself. To be sure, country X can decide to accredit/recognize given labs or universities in country Y on a one shot basis. This will have the same effect as recognition for a subset of professionals or products from Y; but unless there is recognition of the accreditation system as a whole, we cannot speak of recognition of conformity assessment *between countries* but only of access to a given national accreditation system. In some cases, such limited access is really what is at stake Indeed, a lab in country Y may prefer this option if it gives him a competitive advantage vis a vis home competitors.

*Mutual Recognition of Entry Requirements vs. On-Going Supervision*

A third fundamental distinction that needs to be kept in mind is that between recognition of entry requirements and on-going supervision. The notion of home country control implemented in the EU reflects this further distinction: banks and insurance were granted a single European passport allowing them to operate on the basis of a single initial authorization as well as under a single authority of control (with caveats as we will see below). Similarly, professional service providers whose professional credentials may be recognized as equivalent for the purpose of entering a professional market in the host country may then be subject to host country control for professional rule of conduct. Or it may be the case that a bank be allowed to set up a branch and sell products on the basis of home country authorization but then become subject to host country control for its operations.

### Unilateral vs. Mutual Recognition: MRAs as Reciprocal Commitments

The Final question is whether recognition needs to be based on reciprocal commitments. Strictly speaking, the principle of mutual recognition does not require that the recognition in question be "mutual." Country X can decide that a product lawfully manufactured in country Y shall be sold freely in its territorial jurisdiction without added regulatory requirements even when country Y does not reciprocate. This would presumably be based on a diagnosis that the standards and regulations applicable in Y are equivalent to its own. Such a diagnosis is generally facilitated by the fact that country X and Y might both conform to the standard of a third jurisdiction, such as an "international standards" adopted under the umbrella of an international organization. Note that recognition based on an assessment that the standards of the two countries are the same, implies that the recognition in question is of conformity assessment.

While there is no reason to rule out such a scenario, it is based on three assumptions: a) that national regulators view their regulations on a quantitative scale relative to each other -making it plausible for a country with least "stringent" regulations to recognize an other's more stringent one without reciprocity; b) that recognition of conformity assessment can occur short of a process of regulatory cooperation which by definition is mutual; c) that recognition is about trade liberalization (deemed beneficial, even if unilateral) more that about economic integration (reciprocal by definition); d) and relatedly, that recognition is devoid of commercial considerations and only based on criteria of regulatory acceptability. I hope to make clear in the discussion below that these assumptions are relatively implausible.

## 2. Mutual Recognition in Practice

### From "Mutual Recognition Directives" in the EU to "Mutual Recognition Agreements" under WTO

The story has often been told as to how mutual recognition appeared and was institutionalized in the EU context.[6] The concept itself was included in the 1957 Treaty of Rome, contrary to the often-stated claim that it was "invented" by the European Court of Justice in 1979 in its famous *Cassis de Dijon* judgment. The Treaty called for the adoption of mutual recognition between member states in the field of professional diploma; in other words, mutual recognition was to be operationalized through a set of political "contracts." There is something ironic in recalling these historical roots. First because mutual recognition came to the fore two decades later as a legal principle rather than a political contract; second because the notion had to migrate to the field of goods before eventually being applied wholesale to services (including professional services) through the single market program.

Indeed mutual recognition became the main paradigm for trade liberalization within the EU in the mid 1980s. Conceptually, there are three alternative approaches to trade liberalization which can each be considered as alternative paradigms, even if, in practice, these approaches can be combined in a given case: policed national treatment, harmonization, and mutual recognition. National treatment and harmonization are the operative norms which correspond respectively, to negative and positive integration, that is the *removal of discrimination* in national economic rules and policies under joint and authoritative surveillance on one hand and the *transfer* of public market-rule-making and policy-making powers from the participating polities to the union level on the other.[7] Under the so called "old approach" that prevailed until the early 1980s, approximation of laws was seen as requiring detailed harmonization and, "pending" such harmonization, national treatment was policed by the Commission and the European Court of Justice in an increasingly constraining manner. Historically, mutual recognition came about as a "residual" alternative to either of the other two, a *hybrid* between negative and positive integration, promoted by the European Court of Justice as an extreme version of the former and introduced in EU harmonization legislation as a relaxation of the later.

The idea of mutual recognition was refined over more than a decade through a fascinating interplay between European institutions. The ECJ's *Cassis de Dijon* ruling and the Court's subsequent jurisprudence forced a reappraisal of the "harmonization method" in the Community and effectively prepared the grounds for Europe 1992. But rightly acknowledging the importance of *Cassis de Dijon*—as most commentators have- should not lead into the trap of *a posteriori* biased assessment. The Court's jurisprudence, especially for trade in services, generally shied away from enforcing mutual recognition as a legal obligation in the cases that came under its purview, including in the areas of professional services, insurance, and food safety. The Court's jurisprudence had a dual character both limiting and expanding states' regulatory discretion: some national measures were deemed to be "recognizable" as a direct implication of the principle of proportionality; at the same time an increasingly broad array of regulatory objectives were deemed legitimate by the Court and therefore not subject to recognition obligations. Paradoxically, the influence of the Court must be measured not so much according to the extent to which it could threaten to apply mutual recognition by *judicial fiat*, but by its role in suggesting the outlines of what was to become "managed" mutual recognition and providing a roadmap for the complex political deals that were to make possible the implementation of the set of European directives agreed upon under the "Europe 1992" program.

There is no denying the contagious effect of the mutual recognition principle.[8] First, these effects stem directly from the "natural" extension of intra-EU to extra-EU mutual recognition with selected trade partners. By the mid 1990s, the EU initiated bilateral talks not only with the US but also with Australia, New Zealand, Canada, Switzerland, and Japan. Moreover, MRAs were started to be negotiated outside the purview of the EU especially in the professions and for certain products. There is no evidence however of unilateral recognition.

These regional or bilateral deals might have occurred anyway but have come to be sanctioned multilaterally. Since the signing of the Uruguay round agreement, the practice and legal basis for MRAs is progressively being incorporated in the WTO framework. Mutual recognition has become embedded in the international trade regime through three WTO codes: the Phitosanitary Code (SPS), the Non-Tariff Barriers Code (TBT) and the General Agreement on Trade in Services (GATS). All of them not only allow but also encourage mutual recognition among contracting parties as well as unilateral recognition on the part of individual parties. The TBT includes a relatively strong injunction obligation regarding unilateral recognition of equivalence: "Members *shall* ensure, whenever possible, that results of conformity assessment in other Members are accepted, even when those procedures differ from their own . . . (article 6.1)."

Article VII.1. of GATS encourages signatories to enter mutual recognition agreements. It states: "For the purpose of the fulfillment, in whole or in part, of its standards or criteria for the authorization, licensing or certification of service suppliers . . . a member may recognize the education or experience obtained, requirements met, or licenses or certification obtained in a particular country." Recognition under the TBT agreement for products is not as far reaching as it does not include recognition of substantive regulations: "Members are encouraged, at the request of other members, to be willing to enter into negotiations for the conclusion of agreement for the mutual recognition of results of each other's conformity assessment procedures. . .(article 6.3)." This clause serves as the legal basis for the span of MRAs currently negotiated around the world and in particular for the US-EU MRAs signed in 1997.

The scope of MRAs under the TBT leads us back to the first distinction put forth in section 1. The kind of recognition initially negotiated between the EU and the US or other bilateral MRAs is certainly less ambitious than that inside the EU since it does not apply to underlying standards. But as discussed above, MR of conformity assessment can be where the crux of regulatory sovereignty lies. Moreover, the current Transatlantic Partnership is extending recognition discussion to services where the distinction is much less operational.

**Table 1. EU vs. Transatlantic: Standardization vs. Conformity Assessment**

| | | Standards | | |
|---|---|---|---|---|
| | | **Host Country** | **Home Country** | **Harmonized** |
| **Conformity Assessment (Enforcement** | **Home Country** | US-EU MRAs & rest of the world | EU global approach & Transatlantic Market place | US-EU recreational & Ex-post EU |
| | **Host Country** | National Treatment | EU new approach | Traditional ISO |

## From the "Principle" to the Actual Bargains: Managed Mutual Recognition

Agreements between countries—whether in the EU or under currently negotiated bilateral MRAs—do not generally apply mutual recognition in its "pure" form: full unhindered rights of access reflecting full reallocation of authority from the host to the home country jurisdiction. Instead mutual recognition agreements vary in their regulatory scope and usually leave residual powers to the host state; they are not based on blind trust but involve mutual monitoring between regulatory authorities; they require pre-conditions to ensure some degree of mutual convergence before the implementation of mutual recognition and they involve reversibility clauses whereby the host country can take back regulatory power if it is not satisfied by home country regulations.

This set of characteristics is what I refer to as "managed mutual recognition." As an outcome, managed mutual recognition can be contrasted with "pure" mutual recognition in the same sense as managed trade can be contrasted with total free trade. Pure mutual recognition implies granting fully unconditional and open-ended rights of access. In contrast, mutual recognition in operational terms actually involves complex sets of rules and procedures, that may serve to reduce, if not eliminate, the open-endedness of mutual recognition. Thus, managed mutual recognition refers to a process whereby transfers of sovereignty are partial and progressive, conflicts are managed in a manner acceptable to the majority of the population, and the adoption of the norm is only the beginning of a dynamic of regulatory, sectoral, and geographic expansion.

Judging from the prevailing conditions in the world economy, "managed mutual recognition" is going to be the name of the game of globalization in the 21st century. It is a way to ensure that national regulatory sovereignty is transferred only gradually between countries and that domestic regulators are provided with reassurances that such transfer is not unconditional. By striking a creative compromise between regulatory diversity and free trade it is a policy option that is usually superior to policed national treatment and full harmonization.

Managed mutual recognition also means that even within an MRA zone, some degree of discrimination between players is sustained. In order to assess the discriminatory character of mutual recognition deals we need to analyze the regulatory bargains that have served to bridge the gap between the pure form of mutual recognition that would institutionalized unchecked regulatory competition and the threshold of such competition acceptable to regulators. Drawing on the European experience as well as that of NAFTA, Australia-New Zealand and WTO—and extrapolating from these examples—it is possible to define and describe more precisely what I mean by managed mutual recognition and which of its features may be most appropriate in different contexts. Examples provided her are drawn both from services (professional and financial services) and from products. This is to help show that beyond differences in labels and constraints goods and services are subject to the same fundamental principles.[9]

There are four main dimensions along which mutual recognition can be managed or fine-tuned as summarized in table 2.

**Table 2. The Main Features of "Managed Mutual Recognition"**

| *Variation in:* | **Professional Services** | **Financial Services** | **Products** |
|---|---|---|---|
| **Prior Conditions** for Equivalence between National Systems | a. Equivalence of accreditation and licensing procedures<br>b. Inter-recognition between competent bodies | a. Equivalence of prudential standards<br>b. Equivalence of licensing & authorization procedures | a. Equivalence of technical standards<br>b. Equivalence of testing and certification procedures, including ex-ante confidence building measures<br>c. Mutual recognition of certification bodies |
| **Automaticity:** What is Recognized at the Individual Level? What Are the Residual Entry Requirements? | | a. Notification by home state<br>b. Proof of licensing | a. Test data & inspection report vs. final approval<br>b. Additional tests & approval procedures |
| | | a. Consumer type | Usually full scope except for market characteristics including distribution channels. |
| Alternatives to Host Country Control. | d. Case-by-case safeguards and general reversibility | | |

*Prior Conditions for Equivalence between National Systems*

First and most visibly, national authorities need too agree on conditions for equivalence. How similar must qualification (for professionals), licensing (for banks) or certification (for factories or universities) is before we can consider engaging in mutual recognition? How is such equivalence determined?

Earlier I distinguished between substantive requirements and conformity assessment procedures. Prior conditions of equivalence for the former, e.g. "professional standards," "technical standards, consumer safety laws etc., involves on agreeing on more or less specific criteria for adequate product characteristics or adequate professional qualification and for accrediting training institutions, including the content of studies and licensing examinations. Prior conditions of equivalence for the latter involves mutual examination of the procedures by which individuals are made to conform and comply with requirements, including through examination, and the process by which the institutions that certify them are themselves accredited.

Mutual recognition in the professions for instance technically applies to the second category: it is the process by which a professional acquires a stamp (whether of qualification or license to practice) that is recognized as equivalent. Such recognition is in turn conditional on assessing whether the underlying requirements or criteria for qualification should themselves be unilaterally or mutually recognized or harmonized (and if the later to what extent). The GATS and TBT state explicitly that recognition may or may not be achieved through prior harmonization of the content of the relevant measures. Thus mutual recognition and harmonization are neither mutually exclusive nor necessarily corollaries.

*Variation in Automaticity: Regulatory Scope as the Benchmark for What is Recognized at the Individual Level*

Thus, mutual recognition is necessarily based on an "equivalence test" between national systems. But the question arises whether only national systems as a whole must pass such an equivalence test or whether, given some broad equivalence at the macro-level, incoming foods and services providers still ought to be subjected to some residual equivalence test at the individual level. Given that equivalence is so hard to establish at the macro level, most MRAs are unlikely to automatically extend *fully automatic* rights of access—from the rights to sell drugs certified in the home country too the right of professionals from one country to practice in another. This is true whether or not agreement has been reached on common minimal standards. Thus MRAs need to establish procedures to deal with variations and gaps between qualification, licensing or certification systems and must design means to bridge these differences.

MRAs vary according to the degree of automaticity of recognition, which they afford and as a result, the ease with which access will be granted to applicants. Automaticity in turn depends on *regulatory scope* or what part of the regulatory chain or process recognition extends to. Mutual recognition—like the regulations recognized—can apply to *input* (relied upon by the regulatory body to make its decision), *determinations* (agency decisions regarding the application of regulatory standards in particular instances) and *legal results* (ultimate decision resting on input or determination).

For product conformity assessment, this means that recognition can applied to the tests applied to the products (input), the foreign determination of safety level (determination) or the final approval stamp (result). In the professions, this means that recognition can be limited to the whole or part of the education and diploma obtained (input), the license or certification granted on this and other basis (determination), or the right to practice granted by the home country whatever the input and determination. Only under this third recognition of results, is there direct effect of the home country rules on the territory of the host country and right to practice follows not only from positive regulation but also from a failure to regulate in the home country.

In almost all cases, MRAs fall short of granting automatic access, beyond even minimal interface requirements like proofs of testing. Rather, they constitute agreed mechanisms whereby the host country "*takes into account*" the tests undergone in the home country. Under the US-EU1997 MRA, the FDA retains the final authority for approving drugs tested in the EU according to FDA standards. Even inside the EU, foreign professionals are granted only "adequate opportunity for recognition," an approach referred to as "semi-automatic" recognition.[10] Such lack of automaticity implies lack of predictability and remaining room for arbitrary behavior of the part of the host country. Nevertheless, MRAs provide greater transparency and above all standardized criteria for building bridges across product certification or professional licensing systems.

Finally, it is important to underscore that, automaticity depends on *two sets of factors*: the first has to do with conditions for migrants to be eligible for recognition in the first place; the second has to with compensatory requirements that the host country can impose on migrants as a condition for granting recognition (such as facilitated examination and aptitude test, local professional experience and adaptation period for the professions). Crafters of MRAs may choose to cast a broad net through generous clauses on eligibility if they need to accommodate very different systems; this may in turn call for greater compensatory allowance; or they may choose to narrow down eligibility and leave little room for compensation if they do not have enough resources to manage the recognition mechanisms.

*Variation in Scope: Access to What?*

Mutual recognition can also be characterized in terms of the scope access granted e.g. what is the market range too which financial firms have access or the mode and object of practice accessible by professionals benefiting from recognition. Scope of access can be a most controversial issue simply because modalities of access to a given market can vary from one country to the next for the local firms or the locally qualified professionals themselves. Even when this is not the case, limiting scope during the initial phase of a mutual recognition process can be seen as an opportunity to create a laboratory to test the impact of liberalization. Steps towards full mutual recognition can be achieved through the progressive expansion of scope. In the meanwhile, some beneficiaries of recognition might be satisfied with performing only some activities, for some period of time, as reduction in scope calls for.

There are six ways in which the scope of access falling under mutual recognition can be circumscribed. Some of these distinctions may overlap or even be redundant but they nevertheless reflect alternative rationales that may or may not be relevant in different contexts. First recognition can simply imply a *right to practice or* it can also include access to the local *title*, which in some cases may be an invaluable signaling device vis-à-vis potential clients; Second, access is a function of *scope of permissible activities* and/or products -which may not include all the activities permitted in the home countries, and in some cases may even not include all those allowed in the host countries; Third, one of the least common domains where home country modes of practice is likely to apply concerns *rules of conduct and enforcement,* including codes of ethics, privacy issues, and advertising rules. Fourth, it is possible to limit the scope of mutual recognition by limiting the choice between mode of delivery in the case of services, especially the choice between *cross-border supply vs. establishment;* Fifth, recognition can be granted *temporarily* rather than on a permanent basis in order to allow for the provision of a specific service at or until a given point in time. Finally, the scope of access granted through mutual recognition may be reduced through *consumer type*, using criteria that distinguish consumers on the basis of their investigative capacity or "sophistication."

*Variation in Ex Post Guarantees: Alternatives to Host Country Control*

Finally, in addition to the degree of automaticity of the recognition extended or its scope, MRAs may give different emphasis to the setting up of cooperative mechanisms between parties in order to compensate for loss of host country control. The aim is to increase the confidence that parties have in the mutual recognition process and therefore the legitimacy and sustainability of the agreement.[11] But control mechanisms are not costless, and their development is therefore itself an object of negotiation. These mechanisms include:

1. Rights of regulatory oversight and mutual monitoring that allow for the continued assessment of technical competence, capabilities, and efficiency of the counterpart's system;
2. Collaboration mechanisms that allow for supporting the upgrading of standards where they are lagging and ensure that the signatories of the MRA agreement are accountable for the quality of regulatory control in their jurisdiction. In the professions, this can also include collaboration on accreditation procedures and support for inspection and evaluation. In financial services, this may mean collaboration in investigating misconduct as well as in upgrading standards relevant for instance to "e-money;" In all cases, regulatory authorities need to set up ways of specifying their respective accountability and collaborating to ensure that such accountability is credible;
3. Case-by-case safeguard clauses and overall reversibility of the agreement, acknowledging the character of MRAs, as contingent agreements that can be terminated should a jurisdiction fail to produce the required standards. These are in effect measures against regulatory dumping. MRAs could include trial periods, periodic reviews, safeguard provisions for the temporary lifting of obligations vis-à-vis one or several parties, and reversibility clauses allowing parties to nullify the agreement altogether.
4. Finally, parties must invest resources in dealing with external factors that might emerge and would unduly nullify the agreement. For example, the access provided by mutual recognition may be incomplete as private anti-competitive behavior replaces previous requirements.

## The Evolutionary Character of MRAs

Managed mutual recognition can be viewed in a static or a dynamic manner. At a given point in time, variations along each of these dimensions can be seen to indicate how far parties have traveled down the road to full recognition. Dynamically, mutual recognition can be viewed as a process, involving trade-offs between these dimensions that may change over time. Every MRA needs to include provisions that pertain to the licensing, certification, and accreditation system on one hand and to the individual professionals, firms or product manufacturers seeking to be recognized on the other hand. At the level of the systems, MRAs are based on prior harmonization and/or criteria for equivalence and cooperative mechanisms to make up for loss of host country control once the agreement is in place. The individual candidate for recognition will be affected by the provisions on how automatically and on what basis the recognition is granted, and the scope of recognition set out in the MRA. These various dimensions are obviously connected. How confident the parties are on the degree of equivalence between their systems will determine how automatically they are ready to grant recognition. Scope for access might be inversely related to automaticity. The need for spelling out prior conditions of equivalence may be reduced if there are good prospect for sustaining a high level of *ex-post* cooperation after the agreement and if reversibility is a plausible option of last resort.

In short, whether implicitly or explicitly, trade-offs can be exploited among the features of an MRA. The more parties are aware of these potential trade-offs, the higher the likelihood that they will reach agreement and devise solutions acceptable to all. In some cases, it may be more appropriate to relax prior conditions of equivalence and concentrate on fine-tuning automaticity (EU). In others, reducing initial scope may be considered as a way to test the grounds (NAFTA). From a dynamic viewpoint, scope, and automaticity can be reduced initially to accommodate insufficient prior equivalence and expanded later on in light of ex-post cooperation. Overall, however, these complex tradeoffs demonstrate that mutual recognition is not easily amenable to simple "up or down" findings by dispute resolution panels. Mutual recognition deals are political bargains that need to be managed initially and overtime through the appropriate transnational institutions. This in turn will have an impact on their discriminatory nature vis a vis third parties to which we will now turn to.

**Figure 1. Tradeoffs between Features of Mutual Recognition**

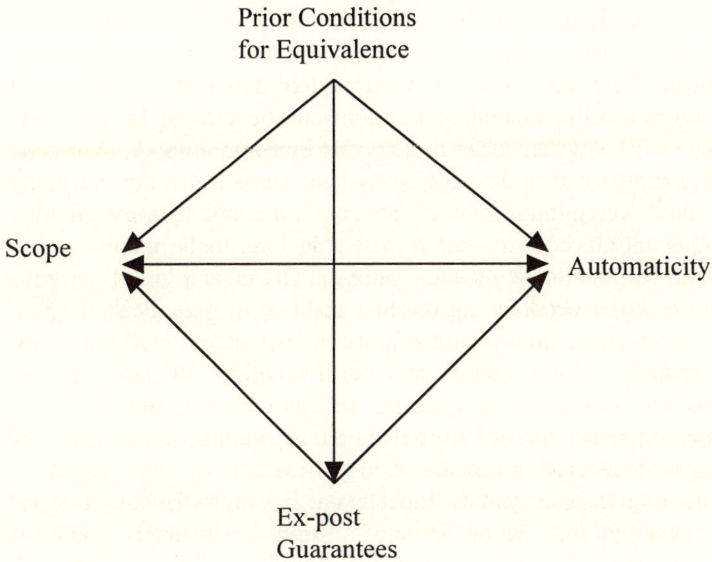


## The External Impact of Regional Mutual Recognition: The EU / US Example

Mutual recognition is the last frontier of regional trade liberalization. As such its external impact must be assessed by comparing its trade creation and trade diversion effect. Clearly foreign products benefit from trade creation to the extent that mutual recognition is usually transitive. If a product, a firm or a professional have fulfilled initial conditions of entry they benefit from the internal economies of scale available inside a given mutual recognition zone. At the same time, the very creation of such a mutual recognition zone usually changes the conditions of entry in the different jurisdictions pertaining to the zone. The controversial external impact of regional mutual recognition in the EU is a case in point.

During the first phase of the single market exercise, the issue of market access for third country products and services was often treated as an afterthought and third countries were not consulted in this regard. Even applicant countries were not granted more than the option to buy into the existing rules of the game. The tensions and misunderstanding around "fortress Europe" seemed to have been as much a byproduct of neglect as a result of intent protectionist biases in the new European laws. Indeed, halfway through the process, European authorities sought to reassure their trading partners that "any product, which is introduced on the Community territory, as long as it satisfies the legislation of the importing member country, and is admitted on its markets, will be entitled, as a matter of principle, to the benefits of free circulation in the Community."[12] In effect, foreigners would have access to the new mutual recognition zone. This overall principle was set forth against the wishes of the most highly regulated member states who feared the effects of regulatory competition among ports of entry.[13] But it also had to be read in light of the new requirements for participating in the single market incumbent upon member states. Under the so called "global approach" instituted in the EU in 1989, only bodies *notified* by member state governments to the Commission had the authority to grant a CE mark -e.g. to certify products for the EC market (this was a way to assert the delegated character of non-governmental certification). In turn, and most importantly, member states could only notify bodies located on their territory. Thus, discrimination was introduced on the basis of the second distinction stressed at the outset between the certification process itself and the accreditation process (or "notification" in this case).

The notification clause was the proximate cause for the EU external MRA negotiations: external MRAs would be a precondition for entry into the single market for products short of EU-based certification.[14]

The 1989 Directive on the new global approach duly addressed the issue of market access by third country parties. It provided that the EU would endeavor to promote its relations with third countries, in particular by concluding MRAs on the basis of article 113 of the Treaty.[15] Presumably, the conceptual rationale for the locational limitation was that European governments could only delegate regulatory authority with confidence to bodies within their geographical reach. The need to "communitarize" external trade policy with the advent of the single market meant that if things were to be otherwise that would have to be a collective decision. A concurrent rationale -albeit implicit- was that if individual EU members were allowed to notify foreign bodies, their requirement would naturally vary and they could be tempted to enter into port of entry competition. Conceptual consistency required that foreign certification bodies providing the same regulatory guaranties as their European counterpart be allowed "into" the system. From a European viewpoint, the announcement of the EU's intention to allow third country conformity assessment bodies to participate in the new European system on the same basis as European bodies was allegedly "a small conceptual step."[16] The Europeans had found a method to accelerate trade liberalization and were willing to extend it to the rest of the world. Indeed, trustworthy partners such as the EFTA countries were immediately offered extended MR (Tempere meeting, 1988).

Underscoring the assumption that regulatory compatibility ought to be the core condition for the extension of mutual recognition to third party, the 1989 Directive laid down the conditions to be fulfilled in order for third country operators to be considered on a par with their EU counterparts and for MRAs to be concluded: 1) testing and certification was to be done on the basis of European standards; 2) parties to the agreement [e.g. governments] were required to have an agency with the necessary authority and competence to notify the competent bodies [e.g. accredit labs or recognize accreditors]; 3) the notifying authorities were required to have the power to withdraw notification where the notified bodies would cease to meet the relevant criteria. Two years later, the EU Commission put forward a Communication to the Council of Ministers which discussed in greater detail the softer conditions for entering into MRA discussions, including the fact that negotiations could only be opened with countries that held technical and industrial competence comparable with that of the EU.[17] The Commission also emphasized the need to create mechanisms to inspire mutual confidence between parties that would enter into MRAs. Recognition of foreign regulatory authority was to be based on the same principles of trust and cooperation as had been the case internally. On this basis, on 26 September 1992, the Council of Ministers issued a decision authorizing the negotiation of MRAs with a number of countries, including the United States.[18]

In normative terms, MRAs can thus be seen as a typical instance of proselytizing on the part of EU regulators and Commission officials; mutual recognition is a European normative export, a natural extension of its internal process of trial-and-error integration. Even American officials will concede that "MRAs are a European invention unlike anything before."[19] Most importantly, the proximate reason for negotiating external MRAs was the logically discriminatory nature of the internal MRA system.

This is not the place to recount the negotiation process that led to the final MRA agreement between the US and EU in May 1997. Let me only indicate the final feature of the agreement that:

*Prior Conditions and Harmonization of Procedures*

While both parties required confidence in the other's technical competence as a pre-condition to negotiations, they disagreed on how to determine such competence. The US side insisted on prior harmonization of the detailed conformity assessment procedures rather than merely accepting the results of such assessment as demanded by the EU. The FDA and EPA actually worked with some of their foreign counterparts to reach agreement on equivalency of assessment standards as a precondition for the MRAs in parallel with the negotiation process over MRAs. Some US agencies, like the FAA argued from the outset that prior conditions would not likely be fulfilled and could be worked out better in the long run through regulatory cooperation (in the FD case, Bilateral Aviation Safety Agreements). They were able to bail out of the MRAs altogether.

*Automaticity and Regulatory Scope*

Agencies like the FDA sought to reduce the scope of MR to recognition of test data or inspection reports (the first three steps in a 12 step conformity assessment procedure), thus ensuring that they retain the ultimate authority of approval and significantly reducing the automaticity of access for EU exporters.[20] While EU negotiators argued that such a truncated agreement would leave intact arbitrary decision power in the host country it finally became clear that they would have to settle for an incremental approach where full MR would be attained at a later stage through progressive regulatory scope expansion.

*Scope of Access*

Negotiations over product liberalization as opposed to services are much less amenable to "managing" variations in scope of access to market. The crucial issue in this regard was whether access to the US actually meant access to each of its state jurisdiction. Some commitments were made in this regard but would need to be tested.

*Ex-post Guarantees*

A great deal of the negotiations were spent on this dimension. Maybe the most fundamental difference between the US and the EU laid in the link between automaticity and ex-post guarantees. US agencies insisted on the importance of a lengthy period of confidence-building after the signing of the agreement that would condition increases in automaticity through agreed upon flexibility as to the timing of implementation of actual recognition (whether confidence building is branded as ex-post or ex-ante depends on the reference point adopted; "ex-post" refers to the actual signing of the MRA, ex-ante refers to the actual implementation of recognition). Europeans have long insisted on a short term deadline for implementing MRAs along with a firm commitment to action at that point, without allowance for further review. Here again, the EU accepted to compromise, acknowledging implicitly that its own strategy of setting quasi-automatic deadlines for completion of the single market was predicated on two decades of prior discussions and familiarization between regulators, something that is not true across the Atlantic. As a fallback, the EU did insist that the FDA show its good faith by stopping to inspect on a routine basis firms located in Europe.

Joint inspections were to be implemented and their frequency progressively decreased. Compromise on the big picture has meant small reassurances that US regulators are moving in the "right" direction.

On their part EU negotiators had insisted from the outset of the negotiations that a most important requisite for establishing their confidence in US conformity assessment would be a marked increase in the US government involvement in such conformity assessment conducted by US private bodies. If US certifyers were to be granted a status equivalent to "notified" bodies in the EU, the US government would need to guarantee their competence. The Department of Commerce came up with a creative answer: it asked the National Institute of Standards & Technology to create the National Voluntary Conformity Assessment Program (NVCASE) as a mechanism for addressing this European demand.[21] This was in effect a way of "selling" the EU notification/accreditation system to the United States with regards to products aimed at the European market.[22] In short, this institutional innovation clearly established the regulatory accountability of the US government.

## 3. National Treatment, MFN, and Mutual Recognition in the WTO

I have argued that mutual recognition agreements are complex deals that are better understood as "managed mutual recognition." In this context, fined tuned discrimination is institutionalized both inside and outside the mutual recognition zones thus created. Inside the zone, mutual recognition is usually neither full and complete not given once and for all. The access granted my still be customized as a function of the characteristics of the entrant (professionals in the EU). Parties that stop fulfilling initial conditions may lose access privileges. Outside parties may face more or less stringent conditions to enter the mutual recognition zone. In effect MRAs do not necessarily establish a sharp contrast between "ins" and "outs" but rather and continuum along a spectrum of discrimination vis a vis firms, people, and products subject to domestic regulations.

In light of the existing practice of mutual recognition, we can now turn to an evaluation of the WTO framework under which such agreements are to take place. How constraining is this framework? and how are the principles and procedures of WTO adapted to dealing with managed mutual recognition?

## Mutual Recognition vs. National Treatment and MFN

Unconditional most-favored-nation treatment and diffuse reciprocity, the core tenants of multilateralism imply that broadly equivalent concessions are expected of all WTO signatories but not on a quid pro quo basis. But bilateral or plurilateral mutual recognition deals cannot be "multilateralized" automatically as provided by MFN, simply because concessions based on assessing current and future equivalence of regulatory systems are not fungible. Hence, under MR, MFN treatment is indeed conditional, not on some symmetrical lowering of trade barriers, but on actual compatibility of rules or equivalence of procedures. This fundamental contradiction between mutual recognition and non-discrimination raises a number of questions that have not been fully clarified.

One of the core mission of the Uruguay Round was to lay out more detailed rules to address so called non-discriminatory barriers to trade, be it with regards to food products, industrial goods or financial and professional services. Several chapters in this volume assess the criteria for enforcing international disciplines upon such national measures both under the MFN and national treatment headings. These have to do with the discrimination test (de facto and de jure), the likeness test (does likeness depend on regulatory or physical characteristics?), and the necessity test (are regulations necessary/proportionate to enforce legitimate national objectives). If a (non de jure discriminatory) national measure passes the national treatment test at any of these levels it is cleared from international scrutiny.

How much more access does mutual recognition buy relative to the access obligations embedded in MFN and national treatment? The answer depends on the way in which these obligations are construed, a subject well beyond the scope of this chapter.

### *Likeness, Necessity and Recognition*

Let us only restate the basic criteria. In GATS for instance, MFN reads: "each member shall accord immediately and unconditionally to services and service providers of any other Member treatment no less favorable than that it accords to *like* services and service suppliers of any other country." Similarly, national treatment in GATS calls for "treatment no less favorable" than *like* domestic products or services.[23] If we consider that mutual recognition is formally a recognition of equivalence, then the difference in access obligations between traditional non-discrimination principles and mutual recognition lies in the difference in the mechanisms and criteria for establishing "likeness" on the one hand and "equivalence" on the other.

The necessity test goes one step further than national treatment and likeness. Even when domestic measures may be deemed unlike it asks whether these measures are not "more burdensome than necessary." In its extreme variant, it asks of a measure if it is the "least restrictive" possible. It is still sparingly used in the WTO context, including for testing the legality of grounds for exceptions (article XX for GATT and XIV for GATS).

How do these mechanisms and criteria differ then? First, and most obviously, the national treatment-related notion of "likeness" pertains to services and/or services providers directly and only indirectly to the national regulations relevant to them; "equivalence" as a basis for MR on the other hand compares the regulatory measures per se; "necessity" is a direct assessment of domestic regulations but not necessarily comparative. Second, if contested, the scope of national treatment obligations is adjudicated by dispute resolution panels, while the scope and form of mutual recognition is negotiated through a political process. As a result, mutual recognition has a higher political legitimacy than "far reaching" national treatment which implies both that it can be bolder in terms of sovereignty transfers but at the same time the object of capture by national and transnational interest groups. Second, a dispute resolution panel can only suggest what a "proportional" treatment would be (such as imposing only an aptitude test to an incoming professional); but its ruling on access is black or white. Conversely, an MRA will actually set in place detailed criteria and institutional mechanisms for implementing such proportional treatment; It will "fine-tune" extent and modes of market access. For instance, the elements of the testing procedures recognized as equivalent, the extent to which a professional needs to be tested upon entry, or the list of activities or products that can be sold by a bank or a professional benefiting from recognition. Third, an MRA is also about establishing institutional mechanisms -customized access and ex-post guarantees to *compensate for the lack of equivalence* between regulatory system. This is why it can be more far reaching than national treatment even given the same regulations in question. Finally and maybe most importantly, because managed mutual recognition is a dynamic process whereby the degree of automaticity, scope of access and ex-post guarantees can be traded off against one another in time, the adaptation of market access conditions to regulatory convergence can be embedded in the clauses of the agreement itself. Thus managed mutual recognition is a dynamic concept whereby policed national treatment is a static one.

Beyond these broad elements for a comparison, we need to take into account variations in what national treatment may mean since the significance of mutual recognition is inversely correlated to that of national treatment as interpreted at one moment in time by dispute resolution panels.

For one, the scope of access granted by alternative understandings of national treatment is itself subject to interpretation. National treatment can apply to conditions of entry/establishment or post-entry conditions (supervision), or both.[24] The greater the scope, the less mutual recognition is *a priori* needed to allow for access. More importantly, the extent to which national treatment requires to forego host country jurisdiction is obviously one of the most highly contested issue in current international trade debates. Under extreme versions of strict scrutiny of national measures national treatment can be construed as implying a necessity test, which itself can result in an obligation of recognition—this is what the European Court of Justice does in many cases, as discussed above. Against this interpretation of the reach of legal standard, others would argue that domestic regulatory sovereignty should prevail short of blatant discrimination.[25]

*Weak vs. Strong MRAs and Implications for MFN*

As a result, there are two prevailing notions of what mutual recognition agreements are about. Under what I would call the "weak MRA principle," MRAs are to be seen only as a means to codify and ease out determinations of equivalence between national regulations (or indirectly of the "likeness" of the regulated services/services providers) that would in any case eventually fall under the sword of national treatment, at least under an expansive interpretation of national treatment.[26] MRAs constitute stop-gap mechanisms. Such an interpretation in turn makes MRAs highly vulnerable to challenges by third parties on the basis of MFN since recognition lowers the benchmark for discrimination (see discussion in the next section).

Under the alternative "strong MRA principle," mutual recognition becomes relevant where traditional national treatment clauses stop representing a constraint on national measures. It is a way for contracting parties to say, "we commit to opening up our markets to each other in spite of the unlikeness of our regulatory oversight." In this case, mutual recognition is functionally equivalent to a selective expansion of the reach of national treatment—construed as a necessity test—at the expense of MFN. More foreign products, people or firms will be treated de facto like nationals, but such a treatment is a signal that home jurisdictions thus selected are indeed "unlike" other home jurisdictions. The very implementation of managed mutual recognition sets up an institutional framework that renders such discrimination between trading parties more legitimate.

## Legal Obligation vs. Political Agreement: The Argument in Favor of MRAs

What should be the legal obligations of countries short of mutual recognition? I have discussed above how the answer to this question obviously changes the incentives for negotiating over MR in the first place. The more one gets out of national treatment and necessity, the less mutual recognition is needed. Let me further make the case in favor of the MRA route to market access over policed national treatment. To be sure there is a strong case for putting the burden of liberalization on the "national treatment principle." At a broad legal level, some have argued that it is fruitful to let courts and panels explore the acceptability of new norms and obligations (thus creating standards of interpretation), before engaging in a political process that fleshes out these interpretation. The European Court of Justice judgments mandating unilateral recognition (or not) provided a "roadmap" for the drafting of EU directives on mutual recognition. Moreover, from a bargaining viewpoint, a broad interpretation and strict enforcement of policed national treatment (even to the point of enforcing unilateral recognition) ensure a minimal level of liberalization and may constitute an incentive for MRAs. Given their purely voluntary nature countries may simply refuse to negotiate MRAs with countries that approach them for fear that their product or services will not be competitive once mutual recognition is in place. It is not even clear that signatories are obliged to give reason for refusing to respond to demands for MRA negotiations. In such cases, the stringency of alternative obligations must make it clear that the country cannot simply get away with it. This is obviously the goal of the TBT embellishments on national treatment that are also included in GATS' article 6 regarding non-discriminatory regulations. They include familiar obligations to use least restrictive means, proportionality criteria, etc. But the question of whether given domestic standards and regulations conform to these obligation is likely to be extremely difficult to answer, especially for services where they are more vague and less tested. The current task of "article 6.4" working groups to establish disciplines on standards and regulations beyond the accounting sector needs to be pursued even while some members already resort to the more ambitious MRA approach.

But such attempts at strengthening unilateral obligations should not overlook the fact that recognition is above all a process of mutual adaptation. Granting too much ground for imposing recognition by judicial *fiat* at the multilateral level endangers the legitimacy of the system as a whole and foregoes the benefits of regulatory cooperation that go along with mutual recognition. Even when unilateral recognition is voluntary, the prospect of falling under MFN obligations enforceable by dispute settlement bodies may discourage parties to extend unilateral recognition in the first place. This is true for GATS where the granting of national treatment is voluntary but could theoretically result in unilateral recognition. The very fact that MFN was not made conditional on the compatibility between regulatory regimes for concessions made in national schedules has greatly decreased their utility as mechanisms for addressing regulatory barriers to trade; this is also why MFN exemptions have abounded. In short, while disciplines on national regulations ought to be strengthened to withstand multilateral scrutiny, they ought not to be strengthened to the point of making MRAs redundant. The MRA route, if well supervised and if generalized, may prove to be the optimal one.

## 4. Mutual Recognition Under Multilateral Scrutiny

### Substantive vs. Procedural MFN

Having just explored the boundary between MFN, national treatment and mutual recognition, we can ask now ask what is the role of non-discrimination principles *given* mutual recognition. How can the broad notion of non-discrimination be salvaged while MRAs are exempt from MFN? How can MRAS be "policed" under WTO?

Let us use services trade as an example. Under GATS, mutual recognition is policed in two ways. First of all, the general MFN requirement applies to all services trade benefiting or not from mutual recognition. Second, the GATS spells out under article VII.2 and VII.3 what such requirements ought to mean in the specific context of MRAs. We will examine these clauses in greater detail in the next section.

MRAs can be exempt from the above requirement in two ways. If a national measure included under the MRAs is part of a national list of MFN exemptions (a Member has the option of listing national measures in its "exceptions" annex). In this case, "a member may accord treatment more favorable than the minimum standards of market access to some members as long as all members receive at least the minimum standard of market access and national treatment appearing in its schedule." Presumably, this clause would allow for MRAs to be exempted from scrutiny. Indeed, the MFN exemption has been claimed for a number of bilateral MRAs in professional services.

The second way is less straightforward than the first. It appears that MRAs would not be subject to non discrimination requirements if they are part of a regional trading arrangement (GATT-article XXIV and GATS article V), e.g. an agreement with "substantial sectoral coverage" that is not overtly aimed at targeted trade diversion. GATS includes a corollary exception (article V bis) allowing countries to take part in agreements that establish full integration in labor markets. Thus, the question is raised whether by filing an MRA under Article V, contracting parties can escape basic non-discrimination constraints.

While the signatories of the Uruguay Round have sought to ensure procedural if not actual non-discrimination in the wording of their recognition clauses, these attempts may be viewed at best as insufficient to ensure that customized rights of access granted through recognition do not become a means of discrimination between countries based on non-regulatory criteria.

## MRA Specific "MFN Requirements"

Three types of guarantees have been introduced but need to be reinforced:

*Third Party Awareness of MRAs: Transparency*

Under GATS, the Council must be informed "as far in advance as possible" of recognition negotiations before they enter a substantive phase. In addition and to the extent possible, the criteria for recognition should be multilaterally agreed upon and based on cooperation with relevant intergovernmental and non-governmental organizations. In practice, however, the degree of transparency of MRA discussions is hard to ensure when involving highly sensitive sectors, where multilateral criteria do not preexist and when there is great asymmetry between regulatory practices and cultures involved.

For the moment, the best that might be hoped for is greater post-hoc transparency. Indeed, since the entry into force of the GATS, 21 MRA agreements have been notified to the Council. One of these agreements is that between Switzerland and the EU on the recognition of proof of solvency in the insurance sectors. The other 20 MRAs are all in the area of professional services. But the most fundamental question is whether it might be eventually possible to require transparency of process rather than simply the content of the agreement at the end of the day. If third parties are to understand how a new MRA affects their relative rights of access, they need to be able to understand what has been done by the parties in order to assess each other's standards and regulations and accommodate their practices to their mutual needs.

*Third Party Access to Market: Equitable Treatment*

The second set of obligations has to do with the treatment of economic actors originating from non member countries and their opportunity to access a mutual recognition zone. Presumably, this concerns countries that have been given the opportunity but did not pass the test, as well as those that have not yet entered MRA negotiations. The GATS specifies that a Member must not use recognition as a means of discrimination between countries in the application of its standards or criteria or constitute, or as a "disguised restriction on trade in services."

Such an obligation is possibly fraught with more interpretative ambiguity than any other concerning MRAs. Let us imagine an MRA on the medical profession between the US and the EU. The MRA grants doctors from both sides the right to practice in the other jurisdiction. With "managed mutual recognition" remaining national measures applied to MRA-originating parties still imply less than fully automatic access in the host country. Moreover, the scope of access may be limited, also as a function of the degree and types of differences in certification requirements between the parties. Thus we have three category of access requirements to the practice of medicine in the US (notwithstanding sub-national differences): that for domestically trained and certified doctors, that for doctors trained in the EU (with some additional residual requirements) and that for doctors trained in other countries (presumably with full requirements for non-US certified doctors). How does the MRA change the conditions of entry for the later group? let us call the US, country A, the EU country B, and say, Japan, country C.

Without recognition, country C need to demonstrate likeness to A (e.g. equivalent regulation) in order to gain access to its market. But if country A extends recognition to country B (or rather to certain regulations for certain products in country B), it could be argued that C would need to demonstrate likeness to B and not to A in order to benefit from recognition. The very act of recognition shifts the standard of appraisal of national measures from national treatment to MFN and in doing so changes the benchmark of appraisal of national regulations for all WTO parties. On this ground, country C could easily claim that countries A and B are using their MRA "as a means of discrimination." By definition, host country requirements discriminate between MRA-originating and non-MRA originating parties. Discrimination is measured by the difference in conditions of entry for professionals originating from B or C. So the aggrieved party will have little difficulty showing discrimination. The burden of proof will then be on the MRA members to show that such discrimination is justified. But instead of having to prove non-equivalence with its own regulation, the defendant will logically have to prove non-equivalence with its partner's regulations. This may be more difficult since recognition between countries A and B (the US and the EU in this example) may be based on a host of other factors that simple training requirements, especially provisions for ex-post cooperation as described among the features of "managed recognition." Thus the evaluation of "legitimate discrimination" will ultimately depend on an understanding of MRAs beyond *static equivalence between national regulatory systems*.

It is important to note that the so-called "measures" that must not be discriminatory include those taken by sub-central entities as well as non-governmental bodies in the exercise of powers delegated by governments. This is especially important when it comes to the enforcement dimension (whether through university diploma or laboratory safety stamps). In effect, if a lax enforcement body can be shown to have been the ultimate beneficiary of recognition, this party's standard becomes the benchmark for equivalence with the partner in the recognition deal.

In short, MRAs have a double effect on non-MRA parties. First, they shift the benchmark of discrimination for a given national regulation from national treatment (all the more optional for services) to MFN. Second, assuming "likeness" includes regulatory characteristics, MRA will have shifted the base standard of liberalization against which MFN will be tested to the smallest common denominator agreed upon in the MRA.

If the very open interpretation sketched out above was to prevail it, the actual result would be that non-MRA parties could be granted more favorable treatment than MRA parties in that they would only need to prove "equivalence" with one party to the MRA without having to undergo the other complex obligations linked to managed MRAs. Such a prospect in turn might be part of the reason why so many parties have chosen to register their MRAs under article 5 (regional agreement) which allows escaping the untested constraints of article 7 altogether. I argue that there must be a presumption that the very process of negotiating an MRA grants a presumption of regulatory convergence absent with non partners. Substantive MFN must be narrowly circumscribed. In exchange, the openness of the process, and thus procedural MFN, should be greatly enhanced.

*Third Party Access to the Agreement itself: Openness*

What type of legitimate constraint can be imposed on contracting parties to open their agreement to other potential members? Under GATS, members who grant recognition must "afford adequate opportunity" for other interested members "to negotiate their accession" to existing or future bilateral or plurilateral MRAs; or, if recognition is granted unilaterally, "to demonstrate that education, experience, licenses, or certification obtained in their territories should also be recognized." The TBT simply "encourages" members to permit participation of conformity assessment bodies of other members on their own territory under conditions "no less favorable" than those accorded to their own bodies or those of other members (a voluntary recognition and a voluntary MFN clause in one). It is still unclear whether such obligations are formal or substantive. Will signatories simply be asked to show that the "opportunity" was indeed given (when? how?); or will they be obliged to give substantive reason for refusing to consider incorporation of an applicant in a preexisting MRA or an MRA negotiation. This is where the WTO constraints put upon MRAs need to be made stronger and more explicit.

For one thing, contracting parties need to confront the fact that the obligation of openness can be seen as an unfounded mandate. National "accreditors" who accredit lab for certifying products or accredit university diplomas do not have infinite resources. Negotiating an MRA with foreign partners involves mutual contacts and assessment, initial, and continued familiarization. What exactly does the obligation to make such a process "open" involve? Will such accreditors be obliged to evaluate their counterparts' systems around the world in order to sort out those that should and should not be recognized and incorporated into the MRA. This is obviously unrealistic.

Three prescriptions can be put forth here. At a minimum however, foreign bodies that are potential candidates should be allowed to witness the negotiation themselves when possible, an approach that is less costly for MRA members than ex-post openness. Internet technology makes such transparency much more plausible. Second, if a panel was to rule on procedural MFN, the burden of proof of regulatory equivalence should be on the third party not on the MRA parties. Only if the later claim an exception after the former has won should the burden of proof be shifted. Thirdly, there is also a more proactive role here for the WTO that could engineer a data base of accreditors and its own system for accrediting accreditors.

But such an approach is made harder by a second consideration. Even when regulatory systems are deemed equivalent under an MRA negotiation, there can be grounds for discrimination beyond regulatory equivalence. Let us assume that a party is given "adequate opportunity" to demonstrate the equivalence of its regulations, diplomas, and the likes and passes the test. Does this guarantee membership in the MRA? What are the conditions that parties to an MRA ought to be allowed to demand in addition to assurances regarding regulatory equivalence? In other words, what can such agreements be conditional on?

Since they are voluntary, the answer could simply be that this is up to the parties themselves. But such openhandedness might leave MRAs vulnerable to the bargaining leverage of the strongest parties and the imposition of lopsided deals. Thus, the TBT specifies that Members may require that such agreements, "give mutual satisfaction regarding their potential for facilitating trade in the products concerned." This is in part what the EU has been demanding through its requirement of "balanced agreements" with the US, whereby actual gains in market access need to be considered in addition to the symmetrical lifting of regulatory requirements. While the intent is legitimate, such broadening of conditionality to encompass actual market access does increase the closed nature of MRAs and their potential trade distorting effects. "Mutual recognition areas" become closer to article 24 exemptions. So the WTO should certainly police the creeping introduction of balance in market access as an additional criterion for entering an MRA. Regulatory compatibility is demanding enough!

## 5. Conclusion: Multilateral Mutual Recognition as the New WTO Frontier

The current so-called MRAs negotiated as sectorial stand alone are likely to become building blocks for what should be seen as a set of interconnected regional mutual recognition zones that are likely eventually to lead to a global mutual recognition regime. If the prospect for world wide application of mutual recognition is to be enhanced, the mission of the WTO should be seen as threefold: ensuring the transparency and openness of individual bilateral agreements, helping to maximize the geographical reach of plurilateral MRAs, and providing an umbrella for the eventual integration of these disparate agreements under a global and decentralized framework.

Under the first rubrique, the WTO must first and foremost set constraints on the discriminatory nature of MRAs as discussed in the previous section, but it also needs to encourage a more proactive approach to non-discrimination. This can be done for instance through the support of plurilateral programs for regulatory assistance and "regulatory upgrading" in developing countries in order to increase their potential acceptability as members of mutual recognition regimes. WTO can also encourage the development of regulatory databases, of a worldwide system for accreditation of laboratories or the coordination of a global system for the accreditation or recognition of accreditors themselves. The OECD can support this process through its program on globalization and regulatory reform.[27]

In order to maximize the geographical reach of MRAs, the WTO should establish presumption of transitivity across MRAs. The question is: if the US negotiates an MRA with the EU and with some APEC countries, to what extent are the EU and the concerned APEC countries obliged to recognize each other's regulations? Transitivity would preclude the need for "rules of origin" in mutual recognition zones and increase the consistency between such zones. Parties might be tempted to object to transitivity because the actual trade benefits may not be balanced; but this argument should be rejected unless asymmetries in trade benefits could easily be remedied by the inclusion of new products that are *prima facie* good candidates for recognition. Parties may also make a more serious argument that the compounded regulatory differentials through "chain recognition" may pass over their threshold of "acceptable" differences. But in this case, regulatory divergence must be significant and the burden of proof should be born by opponents of transitivity. This should not preclude the use of safeguards and ex-post guarantees as outlined in the section II and the allowance for generous confidence-building periods to allow regulators to set up networks for mutual monitoring. By enforcing such transitivity the WTO could help decrease the closed nature of MRAs, "plurilateralize" bilateral agreements, and thus prepare the grounds for eventual worldwide mutual recognition.

Finally, the WTO may preside over the multilateralization of recognition obligations when agreement over essential requirements have been reached at the multilateral level, including by private bodies as in the field of professional services. This would involve setting up "MRA multilateralization" conference after a given trial period for the original MRAs. Surely, a future worldwide reach of mutual recognition is likely to magnify both the potential conflicts inherent in the adoption of mutual recognition and the regulatory benefits that can be reaped. If mutual recognition is well managed at the world level, trade liberalization and regulatory goals need not be seen as two conflicting objectives that need to be somehow weighted against one another. Mutual recognition agreements can serve as instruments to improve regulatory quality, by allowing for a better division of labor between overburdened regulators around the world, by allowing for more effective control at the source in the country of origin, by giving impetus to the transfer of "regulatory technology," and by fostering regulatory cooperation as well as competition between regulators, quasi-public and private bodies and governments around the world. All these worthy goals become more than mere ideals in a world were information can be exchanged with the ease provided by the Internet and the World Wide Web. Managed mutual recognition is a more realistic proposition in the information age. But what if the Web in turn, by making regulatory bypass much easier, leads to a world where consumers really become able to choose between national regulations and thus renders mutual recognition compulsory? Managing access, identity, and regulatory territory in the information age constitute the new frontier for WTO.

NOTES

1. Although this was not the first articulation of the principle, the European Court of Justice in its *Cassis de Dijon* ruling of 1979 is usually the reference used for defining mutual recognition. See for instance, *A proposal for the Trans-Tasman mutual recognition of standards for goods and occupation,* 1995. The term "mutual recognition agreements" was not actually used in the internal EU context for government-to-government agreements, where the principle of mutual recognition was embedded in directives and regulations agreed by governments or judgments by the European Court of Justice. It was introduced to describe contracts between private conformity assessment bodies and then transferred to the external bilateral context.

2. See for instance the chapter by Zampetti in this volume.

3. For goods we refer to standards versus conformity assessment, for services to regulation vs. home country control.

4. This point is often overlooked by those who present harmonization as a complete alternative to mutual recognition. See for instance Sykes, *Products standards and international integrated goods market,* Brookings, 1996

5. When we navigate between goods and services or among services, semantics matter. In the realm of goods, mutual recognition is used to refer to both: mutual recognition of standards, and mutual recognition of testing and certification procedures. In the realm of professional qualifications, mutual recognition is also used to refer to both the recognition of equivalence of the *content* of training, and the recognition of the home country's authority to sanction such training through the granting of diplomas or other evidence of qualification. When we come to financial services or more generally services provided by firms and requiring supervision of these firms, mutual recognition alone the second dimension is usually referred to as home country control

6. See for instance Simon Bulmer, "The Governance of the Single Market," 1998; Kalypso Nicolaïdis, "Mutual Recognition of Regulatoy Regimes: Some Lessons and Prospects," in Regulatory Reform and International Market Openness, OECD Publications, November 1996

7. The distinction was introduced by Tinbergen, J. International Economic Integration, Amsterdam: North Holland, 1954 and developed by Pinder, H., *Positive Integration and Negative Integration: Some problems of Economic Union in the EEC,* 24 World Today 88, 1968.

8. For an early discussion, see Kalypso Nicolaïdis, "Mutual Recognition: The Next Frontier of Multilateralism?" Project Promethee Perspectives, July 1989

9. For an extended treatment of managed mutual recognition see Kalypso Nicoolaidis, "Promising Approaches and Principal Obstacles to Mutual recognition" in International Trade in Professional Services: Advancing Liberalization through Regulatory Reform, OECD, 1997

10. Jean-Eric de Cockborne, OECD Documents, 1985.

11. This line of thinking can be presented under the general category of "securing insecure contracts." For a discussion, see Nicolaïdis, op cit. OECD, 1996, p18–20. Section IV.4 draws heavily on this chapter.

12. "Europe 1992: Europe World Partner" Communiqué of the European Commission, Brussels, 19 October 1988, p3.

13. Some member states argued early on that they should be allowed to apply article 115 in cases when third country merchandise was introduced through a member state with lower levels of consumer or environmental protection. But others argued that if article 115 was to apply in areas pertaining to article 30–36 and 100a (e.g. remedies to trade barriers inside the EU) this would implicitly give technical regulations a commercial dimension which they are not supposes to have and/or to base the application of article 115 on considerations other than economic. In other words, if the low level of regulation in a member state justifies the application of article 36 for goods or 56 for services (e.g. exceptions to free movement), the application of host country control must be done *erga omnes,* against both foreign products having entered the Community through that state and products originating form that state. The second view prevailed in Commission-Council debates.

14. It is important to stress that consideration of external mutual recognition by the EU was limited from the start to recognition of conformity assessment in the field of goods whereby bodies accredited in the country of origin are to be allowed to certify to rules of the country of destination. MRAs have not involved (at least formally) the recognition of underlying standards.

15. Council Resolution of 21 December 1989 (OJ 1990 C10/1).

16. See John Clarke (1996), "Mutual Recognition Agreements," Journal of International Trade Law, Oxford, April, 1996

17. Commission Communication to the Council on the Negotiation of Agreements between the European Economic Community and Certain Third Parties on Mutual Recognition in relation to Conformity Assessment, June 1992.

18. The list of countries was the following: United States, Canada, Japan, New Zealand, Australia, Hong Kong, Israel, Singapore, Korea, Philippines. In addition, Turkey, South Africa, Thailand, China, Malaysia, and Indonesia were referred to n the assumption that these countries would sign the GATT TBT code. In addition other countries had expressed interest in MRAs: Taiwan Czechoslovakia, Hungary, Yugoslavia, Poland, Romania, Brazil, Mexico, and India Cited in Sebastian Farr, op cit., 1992.

19. See Charles Ludolph, "Mutual recognition Agreements: Access to the European Union," The European Report on Industry, Quality, and Standards, 1994.

20. In the pharmaceutical field, the scope of regulation to be recognized was already narrowed at an early stage of the negotiations to cover only Good Manufacturing Practices (GMPs) not Good Clinical Practices (GCPs) and Good Laboratory Practices (GLPs) regulations. The latter two were simply too sensitive from the point of view of the FDA.

21. NVCASE will officially recognize the competence of US accreditors to check the capacity of to work with EU requirements and may temporarily fill in the gap and accredit certifiers where accreditation programs are still lacking.

22. For a repudiation of this view, see "Mutual Recognition Agreements: Some Key issues for Consideration," John A. Clarke, Regulatory reform and International Market Openness, OECD Publications, 1996. The author states: "All the Community demands in an MRA is that the US government ensure that the bodies it appoints under and MRA be competent to test and certify

products to European requirements: no more, no less." For the initial defense of this view see, Kalypso Nicolaidis, OECD, 1996, op cit.

23. Since such national treatment is non compulsory and selective, article 6.5 provides for some degree of constraint -a national treatment minus.

24. Aaditya Mattoo, "National Treatment in the GATS: Corner-Stone or Pandora's Box?" Journal of World Trade Law, February 1997,

25. For illustrations of these two views see the chapters by Matto and Howse in this volume.

26. See for instance Mattoo in this volume.

27. For a synthetic analysis of the overall issue of regulation and globalization as explored in the last three years by the OECD Secretariat, see OECD Report on Regulatory Reform, Paris: OECD Publications, 1997. See also regulatory Cooperation for an Interdependent World, OECD Publications 1994.

CHAPTER 16

# Mutual Recognition in the Transatlantic Context: Some Reflections on Future Negotiations

*Americo Beviglia Zampetti**

The EU and US economies are growing ever more integrated and interdependent. However, despite successive rounds of substantial trade liberalization, the transatlantic marketplace remains hampered by a significant array of non-tariff barriers. This is the inevitable result of expanding transatlantic trade in sophisticated, and often technology-intensive manufactured goods, services, as well as growing investment links. All these products and business activities are increasingly subject to a variety of domestic regulations, standards, licensing, and other requirements, as well as conformity assessment procedures.[1] These often reflect largely shared, but in a number of cases very sensitive, public policy concerns, such as that of ensuring a high level of protection for public health and safety, consumers, and the environment. By accident, and at times by design, these standards and regulations use different and in certain cases incompatible instruments and approaches which hinder, instead of facilitate,[2] trade and investment flows. Hence, it has become apparent that new and innovative efforts are needed to increase the compatibility of the regulatory frameworks and to eliminate unnecessary regulatory obstacles in order to further ease and liberalize the conduct of transatlantic business. This would provide significant benefits to consumers on both sides of the Atlantic.

Until now, liberalization efforts have been mainly pursued through successive rounds of multilateral trade negotiations, spearheaded by both the EU and the US. But for the complicated and highly sensitive regulatory issues that now preoccupy businesses on both sides of the Atlantic, the traditional multilateral route may not offer early and effective solutions. The EU and the US share the responsibility to trail-blaze in these new areas in order to respond to the need of their firms and consumers, as well as their economies as a whole. However, by pursuing the "best liberalizing practice" in these areas, which third countries may find attractive to converge, the EU and the US will also pave the way for the future development of the multilateral trading system.

---

* The views expressed are personal.

It is the realization of the importance of regulatory issues that has fed an intense debate in the last months and years. In this field in particular, the protracted Mutual Recognition Agreement (MRA) negotiations between the EC and the US, which lasted over four years, have shown the limits of a step-by-step, "building block" approach in transatlantic liberalization. This suggests that it is necessary to pursue a "bolder" approach, sufficiently visible and economically significant to achieve enough momentum and public support. A large package of liberalization and cooperation initiatives may also engender a positive dynamic, allowing both sides to address some highly sensitive and entrenched regulatory obstacles that at present appear difficult to solve in isolation. The construction of a broad package is also highly desirable since regulatory impediments tend to permeate the vast majority of economic sectors with large economic interest at stake for the two transatlantic partners, their businesses, and their consumers. This is the key rationale behind the *Transatlantic Economic Partnership* (TEP)[3] initiative, which was launched at the EU-US London Summit of 18 May 1998.

The paper first describes this new initiative and the economic considerations that underpin it. A number of reflections follow on how to structure a bilateral agreement based on the principle of mutual recognition as foreshadowed in the TEP. The discussion generally refers to the area of industrial goods, although some aspects may be relevant for negotiations in the area of services as well. The paper then reviews the WTO consistency of this approach, while concluding with some considerations on future prospects in this area of trade relations.

## 1. The Transatlantic Economic Partnership

The TEP initiative is set out in a joint EU-US statement issued at the 1998 London Summit. This is a wide-ranging declaration of political intent, which does not introduce any legally binding obligations on the parties.[4] The comprehensive approach of this partnership involves a broad array of immediate, as well as more long-term actions and negotiations, which also go beyond the regulatory field, both at the multilateral and at the bilateral level. This is further combined with the strengthening of transparency and dialogue with societal actors. The basic aims underpinning this new initiative are twofold: firstly, to cover those trade issues which really matter for transatlantic business and which, if effectively tackled, promise substantial new economic opportunities and benefits for transatlantic firms and consumers. Secondly, to lead the way forward, and stimulate further multilateral liberalization through deeper integration at the bilateral level, and closer EU-US cooperation in multilateral trading fora, in particular the WTO. A political dimension may also be detected in the background. The TEP should not be seen purely in economic terms as a collection of specific liberalization and trade facilitation actions and negotiations. In fact, it is obvious that the strengthening of transatlantic economic relations will also improve and place on a firmer footing the wider EU-US political relationship in the post-Cold War era, helping to overcome the strains that periodically and inevitably arise between the two partners.

The TEP Summit statement includes a clear reference to the general priority given to pursuing EU and US trade policy objectives through the WTO and, collectively with other WTO Members. This is reflected, in particular, in a strong commitment to work together towards further broad-based liberalization in the WTO. The core bilateral element of the partnership lies, as mentioned, in the goal of achieving a widespread removal of regulatory barriers, both for goods (including agricultural and biotechnological products), and services. The emphasis on regulatory issues was confirmed in the TEP Action Plan that has been established in order to implement the objectives contained in the TEP statement.[5] Other important bilateral liberalization and trade facilitation objectives extend to the areas of government procurement, intellectual property and electronic commerce. The Partnership also foresees cooperative actions in the labor and environment areas.

## 2. Economic Considerations

The US and EU markets have now reached a stage of considerable integration. Through the successive rounds of multilateral trade negotiations, traditional border restrictions and particularly industrial tariffs are now far less important than the remaining host of non-tariff barriers. The latter, which include divergent regulatory policies and rules, are emerging as the most important barriers to transatlantic trade for both goods and services. Despite the shared objectives, in particular the protection of health and safety, consumers, and the environment, regulatory requirements often diverge widely and thus act as barriers to trade and investment, which add to higher costs for European and American businesses and consumers. They may lead to delays in realizing new economic and technological opportunities and may also hinder the creation of new jobs. These are among the issues that now matter the most in transatlantic trade and investment, as is frequently stressed by the transatlantic business community. This is confirmed by the emphasis that both EU and US business have placed on these barriers: for instance, the Transatlantic Business Dialogue (TABD)[6] has repeatedly called for the elimination of non-tariff obstacles as one of the elements of an efficient transatlantic marketplace.

In the last few years, a number of studies have analyzed the economic effects of further transatlantic trade and investment liberalization.[7] These studies vary in terms of depth of the analysis and methodologies used. However, the results in all cases indicate that there is a positive economic impact resulting from possible EU-US trade and investment liberalization initiatives. Furthermore, macroeconomics assessments of such an impact tend to confirm that large economic benefits begin to accrue only once non-tariff barriers have been addressed.

Regulatory barriers are among the most important non-tariff obstacles to trade in a wide range of sectors. Diverging technical regulations and standards, which require product adaptations or separate production lines for different national markets, significantly increase research and development, production, inventory, and distribution costs.[8] Technical specifications agreed by standards bodies, or that arise *de facto* from the practices of major market players, are also potential sources of trade barriers, where voluntary compliance with them brings marketing advantages and increased market acceptability.

Barriers typically arise from a divergence in norms concerning: information and labeling of goods, technical specifications or performance requirements relating to goods and their packaging, test specifications and procedures with which goods must comply, declarations or certificates that have to be provided, accreditation of bodies entitled to carry out tests or issue certificates, and the marking of goods to indicate their conformity with requirements. Such divergence, whether it arises at the regulatory or another level, may reflect different positions as regards, *inter alia*, the desirable level of safety, the means used to achieve that level, and the method chosen to demonstrate conformity with the requirements. Nevertheless, there is no reason why such legitimate differences should act as barriers to trade.

With regard to testing and certification in particular, it is estimated that redundant procedures increase the base cost of export by up to 15 percent depending on the sector.[9] By way of example, in the electrical appliance sector (including various types of equipment from washing machines to computers), the existence of different standards and certification procedures in the US (also at sub-federal level), make it very difficult to market a product there without undergoing an additional certification. In the sector of veterinary biologicals (vaccines for use in animals), although the EU is an important producer, virtually no product is authorized for sale in the US. The mutual recognition currently being negotiated in this area concerns the surveillance of the manufacturing conditions of these products, and would have no effect on the ability to market these vaccines, which requires individual authorizations. In the sector of fasteners, the British accreditation body is still the only European authority recognized in the US. Since fasteners are vital parts of planes and cars, excessive regulatory compliance costs have an impact on sectors as important as aircraft and vehicle manufacturing. Similar grievances are voiced on the US side.

## 3. An Agreement to Free Transatlantic Trade of Technical Barriers

Against this background, the TEP initiative, in its bilateral dimension, has been mainly aimed at removing regulatory barriers that still hamper transatlantic business relations as well as preventing new ones from arising.[10] The notion of regulatory barriers, while not precisely defined, is broad and includes technical and other requirements, whether set by government regulation, or contained in standards developed by private standardization bodies and product conformity assessment systems. In order to address regulatory barriers, there are three main instruments indicated in the statement. Firstly, mutual recognition going beyond the level of conformity assessment to achieve the mutual acceptance of equivalent regulatory requirements.[11] Secondly, regulatory cooperation[12] between regulatory agencies and other standard setting bodies, and finally, the alignment[13] of, or the adoption of identical,[14] regulatory requirements and standards. This approach appears broadly in line with business expectations[15] and with the need for regulators to share ideas and experiences with a view to converging towards the best regulatory practice for the benefit of consumers on both sides of the Atlantic. While these instruments are clearly mutually reinforcing, they fulfill different tasks. From a trade policy perspective, regulatory cooperation aims at making regulators more aware of the trade and investment consequences of their decisions and to discourage the development of divergent regulations. This is in order that issues, which might otherwise become the source of a future trade dispute, may be addressed at an early stage. It is thus mainly a preventive instrument which is to be carried out through dialogue, whether accompanied or not by specific procedural, transparency, and other information obligations. On the other hand, both harmonization and mutual recognition directly affect the existing regulatory framework by introducing new rules, modifying existing rules or waving their application. But, at the same time, they generally require extensive cooperation between regulators. Furthermore, since the acceptance of these instruments is predicated upon the building of significant trust between the parties, the use of them in any one sector contributes incrementally to the creation of such trust in related areas. However, from a negotiating viewpoint, it is the mutual recognition instrument, supported by regulatory cooperation and harmonization, that will—hopefully—drive the process launched by the TEP initiative.

In the next few months and years, experts and negotiators will have to give substance and effect to the approach agreed at the London Summit. This includes selecting products or sectors (or issue areas with broader product application[16]) for initial negotiations of mutual recognition.[17] The recently agreed TEP action plan provides a detailed schedule for the various initiatives that need to be taken. The inherent difficulty and novelty of this endeavor suggests an incremental approach, whereby further mutual recognition commitments and new sectors will be added over time. Looking back at the Community's internal experience, which has very much inspired the TEP initiative, the prospect is nonetheless daunting. The policy aimed at eliminating technical barriers to trade goes back to the early 1960s.[18] It took well over two decades to fine-tune the harmonization and mutual recognition instruments that have allowed the vigorous advancement of the Internal Market. While this experience was very much shaped by the institutional structure specific to the Community, with its powerful regulatory and judiciary competencies, some of the broad lessons learned can be usefully applied to the international context.[19] As far as the mutual recognition of conformity assessments is concerned, this has already happened with the negotiation of the EU-US Mutual Recognition Agreement (MRA) and its sectoral annexes.[20] However, the approach now chosen in the TEP is more challenging, and is predicated upon the recognition that the fragmentation of markets resulting from different and inconsistent technical requirements remains a powerful barrier to trade in an international (and transatlantic) context as it was between the Member States of the Community. Hence, it aims at going beyond the level of conformity assessment recognition, in order to achieve the mutual recognition—or, perhaps more precisely, the mutual acceptance of "equivalence"—of technical and other requirements both in the area of goods and services. A similar approach has been adopted in the sanitary area with the recently negotiated EC-US Veterinary Agreement,[21] and to an extent, as part of the Sectoral Annex for Pharmaceutical Good Manufacturing Practices of the EC-US MRA.[22] The mutual acceptance of "equivalence" is indeed the core commitment that the two parties will have to make on a reciprocal basis. In general, equivalence entails that the parties agree that the respective technical regulations are interchangeable since they are satisfied that the objectives sought by domestic regulation are also fulfilled, in a different but equivalent way, by the other party's regulation.[23] This means that the latter can be applied in lieu of the domestic regulation that is effectively waived with respect to products originating from the partner jurisdiction.

Following the example of the existing EC-US MRA, the agreement which the EU and the US may negotiate in order to realize the broad liberalization objectives set out in the TEP statement in the regulatory area (hereinafter the Agreement or the framework Agreement) should be composed of horizontal, framework principles, rules, and sectoral annexes including specific commitments. Such an approach would allow for the necessary flexibility required by the inherent differences and varying degree of complexity existing across sectors. At the same time, it would ensure a measure of consistency in approach, and some useful economy of scale in what promises to be very time-consuming and labor-intensive negotiations. The definition of the general obligations and objectives, the various instruments to pursue the latter, the key notion of equivalence of technical regulations, the mechanisms to ensure that the acceptance of such equivalence would translate into effective facilitation of trade, the necessary (emergency) safeguards and dispute settlement rules could be agreed upon in a framework, umbrella Agreement. Similarly, provisions relating to definitions, entry into force, institutions, and management, amendment, accession, termination, and the like, could be included therein. The specific commitments should be set out in sectoral annexes to be extended and added over time. Any necessary adaptation of the framework rules to the specificities of any particular sector could also be included in the relevant annex.[24]

In general, the envisaged Agreement should aim at ensuring that goods can be traded across the Atlantic without being subject to duplicate and redundant technical requirements in the market of destination. The objective should be to bring about a situation where, as far as technical regulations are concerned, a product that is legally marketed in the territory of one party, having met the requirements applicable there, would be accepted without further formality in the market of the other.[25] This approach appears feasible and desirable between two of the world's most sophisticated economies sharing, as they do, similar public policy concerns as regards, inter alia, the protection of public health, safety, consumers, and the environment. However, it is clear that since the existing regulatory situation is very different across sectors, the degree and speed of realization of such an objective will vary significantly.

One of the crucial tasks of the Agreement will be to define the functioning of the various instruments that can be used, with a mix specific to each product or sector, in order to attain, or to move in the direction of realizing, the Agreement's general goal. In doing so, the issue of diverging regulatory requirements as well as of duplicative conformity assessments, need to be tackled, since both remain important obstacles and sources of additional costs for companies, often devoid of any significant public policy justification.

In the area of diverging regulations, the full achievement of the objective enunciated above would require either the complete harmonization of, or – alternatively—the mutual acceptance (recognition) of "equivalence" between, the relevant requirements on both sides. In the first instance, different regulations on the two sides would be replaced by a uniform regulation, preferably, but perhaps not exclusively, using standards developed at the international level. In the second case existing regulations would not in any way be altered but deemed equivalent. A decision to accept equivalence will be based on an in-depth comparison of the domestic technical regulation and the one proposed as being equivalent by the other party. A determination to this effect will rest solely with the accepting party and will be taken only when the accepting party is satisfied that the other party's regulation adequately fulfills the public policy objectives of its own technical regulation.[26] In this way each party's sovereign regulatory autonomy is preserved. These two polar approaches may not be practical for a large number of products or sectors. In effect, widely diverging technical requirements would make mutual recognition impossible and harmonization extremely time consuming as well as not cost-efficient. Alternatively, a middle course approach could be devised coupling only partial harmonization with mutual recognition. In this case, partial harmonization or at least a measure of convergence in technical regulations would function as the necessary prerequisite of mutual recognition.[27]

As the Community's experience demonstrates, the (full) harmonization route is rather difficult and best left only to specific situations.[28] It is, in particular, to be pursued through the appropriate international fora.[29] As a general principle, the Agreement could aim at strengthening the commitment of the parties to pursue the harmonization work in international organizations, such as the ICH[30] for medicinal products, or the UN-ECE[31] for motor vehicles and tires, and to ensure the effective implementation of the results of this work. However, it should not be excluded that, if the action at the international level proves unsatisfactory, the two parties may decide to work together with the view to adopting common or similar—and thus equivalent—regulatory requirements. Depending on the specificities of individual products or sectors, commitments to either adopt international or jointly-developed standards, or to pursue regulatory convergence may be included in the sectoral annexes. This alignment effort, that may well be limited to what in EC parlance would be termed "essential safety requirements," could also pave the way towards accepting the "equivalence" of the specific regulatory requirements that are constructed around them. Hence, the use of the harmonization instrument in the Agreement would give rise either to an obligation to adopt an international or otherwise common standard through the Agreement implementing legislation, or to pursue convergence work (perhaps within an agreed timeframe) with a view to allowing for the mutual recognition of the ensuing regulatory requirements.

With regard to mutual acceptance (recognition) of "equivalence" between the relevant requirements the challenge is to devise ways to apply it in a context that is rather different from the deep economic and institutional integration which characterizes the Community. In the EC mutual recognition is compulsory across the board.[32] Such a situation, if not for technical then certainly for political reasons, would be virtually impossible to achieve through a bilateral EC-US agreement.

However, for parties such as the EC and the US who largely share many public policy objectives, including health, safety, consumer, and environmental protection, and which also have highly sophisticated but rather different regulatory systems, mutual recognition of regulatory requirements can certainly be pursued on an incremental basis: product by product, or groups of product by groups of products, or even more meaningfully, sector by sector. As mentioned earlier, this implies the negotiation of annexes to the framework Agreement including the specific commitments that were agreed. Such commitments would take the form of lists of regulatory requirements, applicable to the product, group of products or sector in question, which were deemed to be equivalent. As any list of commitment, it can be drawn up in a negative or positive fashion.

A negative list would mean that all regulatory requirements applicable to the product, group of products, or sector in question, are deemed equivalent, except those listed. A positive list would instead include the regulatory requirements that the two parties consider as being equivalent.[33] Leaving aside the issue of the conformity assessment to the technical regulations, it is clear that a manageable negative listing, namely, a list containing a limited number of exceptions, would more closely approximate the general objective of the Agreement, i.e., to eliminate the obligation to meet duplicate technical requirements in the market of destination. A positive list of commitments would eliminate such an obligation only with regard to the technical requirements listed, thus ensuring trade facilitation and cost reduction effects commensurate to the significance and number of the equivalence commitments undertaken. Clearly, it is envisaged that, after the conclusion of the negotiation on the Agreement and its initial set of sectoral annexes, further commitments may be scheduled (or exemptions withdrawn, as the case may be), and further sectoral annexes may be added.

Depending on whether positive or negative listing is considered appropriate for the specific products/sectors, different legal consequences arise. Positive listing commitments would give rise to the obligation for either party to deem its regulatory requirements (listed in the specific sectoral annex) as fulfilled when a product has been produced following the respective regulatory requirements listed by the other party and accepted as equivalent. As for mutual recognition through negative listing, a product meeting the excepted (listed) regulatory requirements of the country of destination, in addition to the mutual recognition partner's requirements, would be deemed to have fulfilled all mandatory requirements as far as the country of destination is concerned. This would also entail a presumption that such a product, duly certified, can be put on the market of the country of destination.

The Agreement would thus lead to a situation whereby the parties agree to waive either the application of the listed regulatory requirements, if a positive list approach has been chosen, or, alternatively, the application of all the requirements except the listed ones, if negative listing is used. This waiver could only be invoked if assurance is given (through third party- or self-certification, as specified by the sectoral annex) that the corresponding domestic requirements have been met. In principle, since what is being accepted as equivalent are the regulatory requirements, products which are actually manufactured in a third country, to meet the regulatory requirement of mutual recognition partner A, and certified accordingly, should enjoy the same treatment in mutual recognition partner B, as the goods physically produced in party A.[34] Furthermore, the person responsible for putting a specific product on the market who has fulfilled the mutual recognition partner's mandatory requirements will be able to avail himself of a defense against prosecution for non-compliance with the listed—or all but the listed (depending on whether a positive or negative list applies)—mandatory requirements of the country of destination of the product. Such a defense will also be important in product liability suits, since a manufacturer's non-compliance with regulatory requirements is always quite useful to a plaintiff trying to establish liability. At the same time, in a product liability action involving foreign products that were produced following foreign regulatory requirements deemed equivalent, the judge will have to use and interpret them in order to adjudicate the dispute. In this regard it may be helpful to include in the Agreement specific conflict of law provisions to deal with the issue.

Any commitment both to adopt an international (or common) standard and/or to accept as equivalent the majority of, or specific, regulatory requirements would freeze the situation at the time when they are undertaken. Obviously such a constraint on the sovereign regulatory authority would not be—at least totally—acceptable by either the EC or the US. The two parties would want to preserve the possibility of altering their regulatory requirements for various reasons including the advancement of science and technology, as well as possible shifts in environmental and consumer safety preferences.[35] A substantial modification of the applicable regulatory requirements, including a departure from a previously adopted international (or common) standard by one party, would entail the withdrawal of the equivalence recognition in the case of positive listing, or the scheduling of further exceptions in the case of negative listing.

An important issue would be to consider ways to deal with this eventuality which has the potential of affecting the balance of trade facilitation benefits originally negotiated. One possibility would be for the parties to allow themselves a complete free hand obviously subject to some form of reciprocity. If a party decides to change its existing technical regulation and, as a consequence, to withdraw a mutual recognition commitment, or does so in response to the other party's change in its technical regulation (which is no longer deemed as equivalent), the other party would be free to withdraw all other commitments pertaining to the specific product or sector.[36] This approach appears undesirable, and could only be partially corrected by a strong procedural commitment to regulatory cooperation, as much upstream in the regulatory rule-making process as possible, in order to try and minimize the possibility of diverging requirements being developed. Preferably, parties may decide to make this change in the original commitments subject to consultation and conciliation procedures to be carried out by, or under the auspices of, the joint management body of the Agreement and failing that to dispute settlement review. The framework Agreement would need to include provisions to this effect including the standard of review. Relevant principles such as those included in Art. 2 of the TBT Agreement and in particular a general proportionality requirement, would need to be, at least, inserted by reference and perhaps clarified and elaborated on.[37]

Although the advantages for transatlantic business of harmonization, convergence or mutual recognition of technical regulations would remain significant, their trade facilitation and cost reduction impact would be significantly curtailed if the commitments in this area would not be matched by mutual recognition of conformity assessment systems, broadly along the line of the present EC-US MRA, or by commitments to accept as sufficient for the particular product, group of products or sector, the "supplier's declaration of conformity."[38] The main difference with current MRA would be that, for product and sectors where harmonization and/or equivalence commitments have been entered into, each party will have to accept the results of the conformity assessment carried out in the other party not only to its requirements, but also to the other party's requirements (deemed equivalent), as set out in the relevant sectoral annex. For products which do not present particular risks and for which third party certification is not necessary, the "supplier's declaration of conformity" could be accepted. The commitment to accept "supplier's declaration of conformity" to its requirements and/or the other party's requirements, as listed would be included in the relevant sectoral annex.

The instruments described above, given that they may be combined and applied in a flexible and incremental fashion, appear to have the potential for a significantly broad product and sectoral coverage over time. However, for a number of particular products or product groups involving high risks, or for which regulatory objectives and requirements are genuinely different, the parties may feel the need to maintain the full applicability of their own specific regulations and product conformity assessment. In these cases harmonization cannot be sought, equivalence cannot be accepted, and no such commitments can be entered into. In this case, more limited obligations, such as the exchange of test data, or the recognition of production site inspection results should also be contemplated by the Agreement and sought for those products or sectors where the more ambitious instruments are considered inappropriate. The mechanisms for regulatory cooperation should also be exploited to the fullest.

If clearly most needed where regulatory objectives and requirements diverge, regulatory cooperation should apply across the board, thus also covering new areas where no technical regulations yet exist. Such a mechanism seeks to ensure cooperation and dialogue between regulators as well as effective participation of all interested parties as early as possible in the regulatory process and to promote the exchange of technical and scientific knowledge as a basis for regulatory activities. This should foster the identification of the best regulatory solutions, prevent the development of divergent regulations and reduce the scope for future trade disputes. Ideally, through cooperation, regulators could arrive at a shared analysis of the problem at hand, leading to similar or compatible policy responses and regulatory decisions. Procedural obligations in this regard, covering issues such as transparency, information, consultation, and modalities for effective dialogue (starting at a very early stage in the drafting of technical regulations), should be included in the framework Agreement.

Another issue that is sometimes of crucial importance to achieve the objective of the Agreement, namely avoiding compliance with duplicate and redundant technical regulations, relates to the need to include specific commitments covering those regulatory requirements that are imposed at the sub-central (or sub-federal) level. Both in the EC and in the US, federal (Community in the EC) as well as State, regional, and local public agencies and institutions set technical regulations on products and processes in order to protect health, safety, consumers, and the environment. In the US, state regulation has proliferated in many policy areas and often coexists with federal regulation, imposing a double layer of regulatory requirements with significant economic impact on business.[39] Hence, in a sector where federal pre-emption has not been (fully) exercised, it may be difficult to achieve mutual recognition without involvement and consent at the state level.[40] A similar situation applies in the EC where national regulations are not excluded, provided they do not constitute unjustified barriers to intra-Community trade, and in particular, with regard to so-called "non-harmonized" sectors, namely those sectors where no harmonization directive has (yet) been enacted.[41]

Finally, the Agreement will have to deal with the problems posed by voluntary standards developed by private standard-setting organizations. Mandatory technical regulations often refer to privately developed, voluntary standards, by inserting or citing them.[42] Voluntary standards play a critical role in the Community, since in general, products manufactured in accordance with harmonized European standards[43] whose use is not mandatory, are nonetheless presumed to meet the essential requirements set out in the so-called "new approach" directives. Depending on the specificities of each sector's regulatory framework, the mutual acceptance of "equivalence" of technical regulations may imply deeming such voluntary standards as equivalent. Such an evaluation may require the close involvement of the organizations responsible for developing the standards, thus rendering the process more burdensome.

Furthermore, it is clear that existing differences in the regulatory approaches on either side, and, in particular, the extent to which voluntary standards (as opposed to mandatory technical requirements) are used, may curtail the number of products or sectors for which specific commitments could be negotiated. In the EC mandatory requirements are often the rule, while in the US market-driven voluntary standards are more widespread and producer's liability is often relayed on in order to induce compliance. A specific approach should be devised for those instances in which a particular product or sector is governed by a mandatory technical regulation on one side, and where only a voluntary standard exists on the other. In such cases, an acceptance of equivalence will give rise to different consequences on the two parties. A product having fulfilled a voluntary standard deemed equivalent to a mandatory one, can be put on the market without further formalities in that respect. Conversely, as no specific mandatory technical regulation had to be met in any case, the advantage would mainly come from the recognition by consumers and users in the marketplace, which arises from being considered as having attained the same levels of safety, quality, environmental friendliness and so on, as those resulting from the respect of the prevailing voluntary standards. In this last case, the key issue would be to provide for mutual recognition of conformity assessments. At the same time, it would be crucial to ensure that certification organizations (public and accredited private ones) would be able and ready to issue certification marks for the products having been evaluated as conforming to a mandatory technical regulation of one mutual recognition partner that has been deemed equivalent to the voluntary standard prevailing in the other party's marketplace.[44] Again the close involvement of the organizations concerned would be essential. Furthermore, the party whose voluntary standard has been deemed as equivalent to a mandatory one of the other party, should also ensure that in as far as any legal consequence arises from the fulfilling of a voluntary standard, such a consequence be valid also for products having fulfilled the mandatory technical regulation (deemed equivalent) and for the person responsible for putting a such product on the market. This aspect may be particularly relevant in case of product liability suits.

A similar approach could be envisaged when voluntary standards apply to a product or sector on both sides. Since voluntary standards play a very important role both as a trade facilitator and, sometimes when diverging, as a trade hindrance, the Agreement should try to foster contacts and cooperation between private standards developers. Incentives to set up technical working groups bringing together the experts of the two sides' private standard setting organizations could be foreseen in the sectoral annexes. In this context the equivalence of voluntary standards could be evaluated and/or convergence be pursued.

## 4. WTO Compatibility

Any bilateral trade agreement between the EC and the US is bound to stir controversy and preoccupation in terms of WTO compatibility. The latter should be looked at both from a political economy and a legal viewpoint. From a political economy perspective, it seems fair to say that, for the sort of regulatory issues which an Agreement as outlined in this paper would address, initiating action via the multilateral or plurilateral route may not be the quickest for achieving effective results. Bilateral action in this area thus seems indispensable. A successful pioneering initiative by the EU and the US would also encourage timely action and progress in the WTO and in its Member on these sensitive issues and serve as a model for future WTO rule-making.

From a legal point of view, a bilateral agreement of the kind described above appears to be WTO compatible. In general, the non-discrimination principle, including MFN and national treatment, applies also in the area of regulatory requirements (technical regulations and procedures for the assessment of conformity).[45] With regard to full harmonization or convergence, all WTO Members are free to determine the standards they require products to meet, as long as they respect certain substantive and procedural rules. Of particular importance is the requirement that technical regulations shall not be more trade restrictive than necessary to fulfill a legitimate objective.[46] Nothing prevents two countries from harmonizing their standards, provided that their harmonized standards are drafted in a non-discriminatory manner, and are applied to domestic products as well as to other Members' products in the same fashion. All Members need to be afforded the possibility of commenting and discussing any proposed, new technical regulation. Adoption of, or alignment with, international standards is actually strongly encouraged by the TBT Agreement.[47] Regulatory cooperation commitments going beyond the transparency and consultation obligations of the TBT Agreement would also be WTO compatible. Again this is conditional upon the resulting drafting of new, or the application of existing, technical regulation being non-discriminatory.[48]

With respect to mutual recognition of technical regulations and conformity assessment procedures, the application of the non-discrimination principle needs to be qualified. When two parties accept the "equivalence" of any regulatory requirement, they are in effect mutually waiving the application of otherwise mandatory requirements that would need to be fulfilled in order to market a specific product or group of products. While regulatory requirements for domestic products remain unaltered (the treatment applied to nationals and national products), the mutual recognition partner receives a more favorable treatment. Since third countries' products would still have to fulfill the same requirements as domestic like products, the national treatment obligation is respected. However, on a MFN ground, such a more favorable treatment, accorded to the mutual recognition partner, would have to be extended.[49] However, in light of the very technical work that needs to precede and underpin the decision to accept the "equivalence" of any regulatory requirement, the unconditional application of the MFN treatment would render mutual recognition virtually impossible. Recognizing this reality, the TBT agreement provides a specific legal basis for proceeding with bilateral or plurilateral mutual recognition.

With regard to technical regulations, the TBT Agreement encourages Members to accept as equivalent differing regulations: "provided they are satisfied that these regulations adequately fulfill the objectives of their own regulations."[50] While it could be done unilaterally, such a process of evaluation appears technically feasible (and politically acceptable) only on a bilateral, country-by-country, basis. But obviously, it need not be limited to a bilateral basis. Once a bilateral agreement has been reached, the same approach applies, and Members are again required to "give positive consideration" to accepting the "equivalence" of other Members' technical regulations, presumably on their request.[51] As far as the mutual recognition of conformity assessment procedures is concerned, the TBT Agreement is even more explicit. WTO Members may require an independent verification of a product, mandate a government agency to verify compliance, or be satisfied with a "supplier's declaration of conformity." In any of these cases Members may unilaterally or bilaterally recognize the results of such conformity assessment procedures: "provided they are satisfied that these procedures offer an assurance of conformity with applicable technical regulations or standards equivalent to their own procedures."[52] The same would apply to the recognition that a particular assessment procedure, the supplier's declaration, is sufficient to certify conformity.[53] Not only from a political economy, but also from a practical point of view, it is rather unlikely that mutual recognition be granted unilaterally. Such recognition requires a rather intense technical relationship between the parties, including specific consultations,[54] or—more realistically—a specific mutual recognition agreement.

The TBT Agreement explicitly recognizes the acceptability of pursuing these kinds of bilateral agreements and encourages Members "to be willing to enter into negotiations" at the request of other Members. In turn, third party Members may then request to accede to an existing bilateral mutual recognition agreement, or to negotiate a similar one. A process of mutual examination will have to be started and pursued in good faith by the mutual recognition partners and the requesting Member, in order to ascertain whether accession or a new agreement are possible. This is a procedural obligation, similar to the "positive consideration" requirement for the acceptance of "equivalence" of other Members' technical regulations.[55]

Agreements of these kind are predicated upon the existence of sufficient and reciprocal confidence, that the other party's regulatory requirements can achieve the relevant national public policy objectives, and that firms on the two sides are able to reap similar trade facilitation benefits. In the absence of these elements, it would seem difficult for any third party to challenge a refusal to accede to an existing mutual recognition agreement or to conclude a new one. However, a blatant refusal to discuss the issue would appear objectionable. On the other hand, a stronger case would present itself if a third party asks for the extension of a specific "equivalence" commitment entered into by one mutual recognition partner, reasoning, for instance, that the particular requirement in its statute books is identical[56] to—or more stringent then—the one of the other mutual recognition partner (which has been accepted as equivalent). Nevertheless, the isolation of an individual commitment from the general context of a bilateral agreement, and its extension to a third party, would appear problematic. At least the requesting party would have to accede to the bilateral agreement's framework rules. While it should not be required that the acceding country matches all the commitments of the original parties (nor would that be technically possible in most cases), the overall trade facilitation objective may also need to be considered.

Moreover, otherwise like products which are produced in a third country to meet the requirements of one of the two mutual recognition partners, should be considered as like to the ones manufactured in the mutual recognition partner whose requirements they meet and thus accorded "treatment no less favorable" in the other mutual recognition partner.[57] Furthermore, in case of mutual recognition of conformity assessment, a further complication arises for like products which are produced in a third party to the requirements of one of the two mutual recognition partners but tested and certified in the other mutual recognition partner. Such a conformity assessment although performed on a third country product, would need to be accepted as equivalent to certification executed domestically. This would not mean extending mutual recognition to the third party, but to treat all like products alike with regard to conformity assessment procedures.[58] This would also allow certification bodies and laboratories of the mutual recognition partners the full range of business opportunities.

While bilateral agreements such as the one outlined in the previous paragraph appear WTO compatible, the clear direction indicated in the TBT Agreement is to move beyond the bilateral level. Such a preference is made evident by the need to foresee the possibility of accession by third parties.[59] Furthermore, while the Agreement envisaged above would not involve the creation of any new barriers with the rest of the world, it is clear that many third countries would be keen to allow their own businesses to enjoy the same trade facilitation and cost reduction benefits which are expected from any EC-US Agreement. At the same time, the geographical spreading of the convergence and mutual recognition commitments would be of economic interest to all participants.

Along with a systemic preference to insert the envisaged EC-US Agreement into the fold of the WTO, the potential larger economic benefits and business opportunities to be had from a broader participation suggests that the negotiation initiative undertaken under the Transatlantic Economic Partnership should not necessarily remain exclusive to the Community and the US. These initiatives and in particular an Agreement such as the one described above, should be designed to permit extension to those third countries that are willing and able to match commitments entered into by the EU and the US.

An avenue to facilitate this result would be to couch the framework Agreement as a WTO Plurilateral Agreement, or at least to draft it in a way that would make the transformation easier. The sectoral annexes containing the lists of commitments, in light of their individualized and technical nature, would however remain bilateral. This set-up would thus be similar to that of the WTO Agreement on Government Procurement (GPA). The accession clause could also mirror that of the GPA.[60] The inclusion of any trade agreement in Annex 4 of the WTO Agreement needs to be approved by WTO Members by consensus.[61] While a number of adaptation may prove necessary, the possibility of bringing into the WTO remit an agreement reached by two major trading countries should be welcome by other WTO Members and allay their fears of the EU and US going solo in this area. More specifically, as far as dispute settlement is concerned, this approach would also have the significant advantage that, as provided by Appendix 1 of the Dispute Settlement Understanding (DSU), the WTO dispute settlement system, including its deterrent power, could be used to enforce such an agreement. "Special and additional" provisions could be introduced to supersede the normal DSU provisions as appropriate to the specific case.

## 5. Conclusion

Replicating the wide use of the mutual recognition instrument in a purely international, as opposed to a supranational and regional integration context, is certainly challenging. The TEP initiative has taken up this challenge. The observations offered above have tried to highlight some of the main difficulties that will need to be overcome in future negotiations.

It is nonetheless encouraging to note that the use of such an instrument is already spreading.[62] This is probably due to the understanding that mutual recognition represents a flexible instrument of regulation which does not entail a necessary loss of sovereignty and delegation of regulatory authority, but it is based on the existence, or the progressive building, of enough mutual trust between the participating nations.[63] In line with subsidiarity,[64] it allows mutual recognition partners to preserve intact their national regulations, while achieving—through a much more decentralized and flexible approach—the same trade facilitation benefits that full harmonization could bring about. At the same time, it requires enhanced contacts and cooperation between regulators and some limited amount of regulatory competition,[65] which may facilitate the emergence of the most cost-effective regulation. Mutual recognition thus partakes of an approach to international trade relations that attempts to foster comity and to reduce conflicts. It will be a very significant achievement indeed, if the Transatlantic Economic Partnership is able to help push such an approach forward in EU-US relations. However, while experimentation at the bilateral level remains essential, it would still be desirable to extend mutual recognition on a plurilateral basis, and firmly ground it in the multilateral trading system so as to allow a growing number of countries to enjoy the benefits it can bring.

## NOTES

1. For a generally accepted definition of these terms with regard to goods, see Annex 1 of the WTO Agreement on Technical Barriers to Trade (TBT Agreement). A *technical regulation* is a document which lays down product characteristics or their related processes with which compliance is mandatory. A *standard* is a document approved by a recognized body that provides for rules or characteristics for products or related processes with which compliance is not mandatory. Both may refer to terminology, symbols, packaging, marking or labeling requirements. A *conformity assessment procedure* is defined as, any procedure used, directly or indirectly, to determine that relevant requirements in technical regulations or standards are fulfilled. This means that conformity assessment procedures include *inter alia* procedures for sampling, testing, and inspection; evaluation, verification, and assurance of conformity; registration, accreditation, and approval as well as their combination.

2. For an interesting account of the positive functions performed by standards, see C. Kindleberger, "Standards as Public, Collective and Private Goods," in *Kyklos,* Vol. 36, 1983, 377–396.

3. The Transatlantic Economic Partnership statement is reproduced in UK Presidency of the European Union, Press Release of 18 May 1998 and also in the US Federal Register of June 9, 1998, Vol. 63, No. 110, 31546–31548. The genesis of this initiative goes back to the idea of the New Transatlantic Marketplace, as originally sketched out in the EU-US New Transatlantic Agenda of December 1995 (see H. Krenzler, A. Schomaker, "A New Transatlantic Agenda," in *European Foreign Affairs Review,* July 1996, 9–27 and 135–141 for the text of the document), and subsequently developed conceptually in the Commission's Communication of 11 March 1998 on "The New Transatlantic Marketplace" (COM(1998) 125 final). This document has played a catalytic role in the recent discussions both in the EU and in the US on the need to improve the framework for transatlantic trade and investment, and its possible future shape leading to the launch of the TEP initiative.

4. Both the Council of Ministers of 25 May 1998 and the European Council of 15 and 16 June 1998 "took note" of the statement.

5. The Action Plan was drafted by the European Commission and the US Administration as requested by the London Summit statement. The EC Council at its meeting of 9 November 1998 endorsed the Plan. The Council also decided that the Commission is authorized to enter into negotiations in four areas including technical barriers to trade and services. The annexed negotiating directives make clear that in both cases the focus is on the removal of regulatory barriers through mutual recognition. See EU Press Release of 9 November 1998, IP/98/974 and US Trade Representative Press Release of 11 November 1998. The text of the Plan is reproduced in *International Trade Reporter,* Vol. 15, No. 44, November 11, 1998, 1897–1904.

6. The TABD was launched in Seville, Spain in November 1995 with the aim of boosting transatlantic trade and investment opportunities through the removal of costly inefficiencies caused by excessive regulation, duplication, and differences in the EU and US regulatory systems and procedures. The TABD offers an effective framework for enhanced cooperation between the transatlantic business community and the governments of the EU and US. It is an informal process whereby European and American companies and business associations develop joint EU-US trade policy recommendations, working together with the European Commission and US Administration. In the communiqué issued at the end of its 1997 meeting in Rome, the TABD emphasized that "in order to achieve our goals, EU and U.S. business needs an efficient regulatory framework, which maintains high levels of consumer protection without unnecessary, and wasteful duplication. As globalisation progresses, our regulatory agencies can no longer continue to function solely on the basis of national considerations. In particular, we urge the governments to establish a solid basis on which to build transatlantic cooperation between agencies aimed at achieving regulatory harmonization." On TABD activities see P. Stern, "The Transatlantic Business Dialogue: New Paradigm for Trade Expansion and Regulatory Harmonization," mimeo, 1997; On regulatory issues and disputes in the transatlantic context, see D. Vogel, *Barriers or Benefits? Regulation in Transatlantic Trade,* Brookings Institution Press, Washington, D.C., 1997.

7. See, *inter alia,* The Transatlantic Policy Network, "Towards a Transatlantic Partnership: A European Strategy," Brussels, 1994; Brookings Institution, "Perspectives on Transatlantic Relations," a Report for the Forward Studies Unit of the European Commission, 1995; K. Frankena, "Transatlantic Ties to Be Strengthened," USITC International Economic Review, August 1995; Prestowitz C. and L. Chimerine, "The case for a Transatlantic Free Trade Agreement," Economic Strategy Institute, Washington, 1995; P. Rashish (ed.), "Building Blocks for a Transatlantic Economic Area," the European Institute, Washington, D.C, 1996.; C. Bail, W. H. Reinicke, R. Rummel, "Toward a Balanced Partnership? A mid-term Perspective on EU-US relations," Nomos Verlag, 1996 and in particular, S. Woolcock, "US-EU Commercial Relations" therein; Canzoneri, Ethier, Grilli (eds.),"The New Transatlantic Economy," CEPR, London, 1996; CEPR, "The New Transatlantic Marketplace," a CEPR/FCO Workshop, 27 March 1996, mimeo; W. H. Reinicke, "Deepening the Atlantic. Toward a New Transatlantic Marketplace?" Bertelsmann Foundation Publishers, Gütersloh, 1996; B. Stokes, (ed.), "Open for Business. Creating a Transatlantic Marketplace," Council on Foreign Relations, New York, 1996; R. Baldwin and J. F. Francois, "Preferential Trade Liberalization in the North Atlantic," CEPR discussion paper No. 1611, 1997.

8. See *European Economy,* No. 35, March 1988; on the standards *problematique* see, in general, A. Sykes, *Product Standards for Internationally Integrated Goods Markets,* The Brookings Institution, Washington, D.C., 1995.

9. This figure is also quoted by P. Stern, cit. *supra* note 6, at 2.

10. The TEP statement reads in relevant part:

"*Bilateral action*

9. The EU and the US will intensify their efforts to reduce or eliminate barriers to trade and investment between them. This will be done in ways which are in full conformity with their international and, in particular, WTO obligations and supportive of the primary goal of multilateral liberalization making as much progress as possible before 2000. Such efforts will expand transatlantic commerce and reduce frictions, benefiting both our peoples. We will maintain high standards of safety and protection for health, consumers, and the environment. Our partnership will not create new barriers to third countries.

10. We will focus on those barriers that really matter to transatlantic trade and investment and to this end we will aim in particular at the removal of those regulatory barriers that hinder market opportunities, both for goods and for services. We will concentrate specifically on the following:

a) technical barriers to trade in goods, reinforcing our efforts for the elimination or substantial lowering of the remaining barriers, while further pursuing our commitment to high health, safety, and environmental standards;

b) services, with the aim of substantially improving opportunities for market opening to the benefit of consumers and small, medium, and larger enterprises;

c) agriculture, with the objective of strengthening our regulatory cooperation in the field of human, plant, and animal health issues, including biotechnology, while recognizing the importance of continuing to improve our respective regulatory processes and of improving our scientific cooperation. [...]

11. We will build on efforts already underway for goods but extending to services, to cover as wide a range of barriers and sectors as possible identifying the priorities both for the near and longer term. Instruments to achieve this will be:

a) The mutual recognition of testing and approval procedures, of equivalence of technical and other requirements and, in certain areas, where appropriate, the progressive alignment or, where possible, the adoption of the same standards, regulatory requirements and procedures adopting internationally agreed standards where possible;

b) The intensification of the dialogue between scientific and other expert advisers, standard setting bodies, and regulatory agencies;

c) A high degree of transparency and consultation with all interested parties."

11. The instrument of mutual recognition has been one of the main contributing factors to the success of the 1992 program. In a nutshell it establishes that, once a product meets the technical requirements in one EC Member State, it cannot be denied access to another market. While this principle appears simple, its implementation has proved far more complex.

12. On regulatory cooperation and beyond, see OECD, *Regulatory Co-operation for an Independent World,* Paris, 1994.

13. The notion of alignment is not clear-cut nor defined in the TEP statement. In this paper it is taken to be tantamount to partial harmonization. Other practically equivalent concepts are convergence and approximation.

14. This notion appears tantamount to full harmonization.

15. See, for instance, *Seville Conference: Overall Conclusions* of 1995 where is stated that "the ultimate aim of any reform efforts should be the adoption of harmonized standards,

certification, and regulatory policies around the world that will enable products to be approved once and accepted everywhere." See also *supra* note 6.

16. As is the case in the US-EC MRA for the electrical safety and electromagnetic compatibility annexes. The Harmonized System classification could be used to define groups of products or sectors, although it may not be the most appropriate for the purpose of isolating coherent groups or sectors to which particular regulatory requirements apply.

17. A number of broad sectors are already being explored, including elevators, calibration, cosmetics, telecommunication, and road safety equipment.

18. For a detailed analysis, see A. Mattera, *Le marché unique européen; ses règles, son fonctionnement,* Ed. Jupiter, Paris, 1990; see also P. Messerlin's contribution to this volume and bibliography quoted therein. For a description of a different experience in another regional economic integration context, see Q. Hay, M Taylor and D. Webb, "Trans-Tasman Mutual Recognition: A New Dimension in Australia-New Zealand Legal Relations," in *International Trade Law and Regulation,* No 1, 1997, 6–13. See also J. Wilson, *Standards and APEC: An Action Agenda,* Institute for International Economics, Washington, D.C., 1995.

19. Indeed some of these lessons may be useful for federal states which still experience some problems in integrating their internal markets, see R. Chaitoo and M. Hart, *Reducing Regulatory Barriers to Trade: Lessons for Canada from the European Experience,* Occasional Paper No. 18, Feb. 1998, Industry Canada, Ottawa.

20. The Agreement has entered into force on 1 December 1998 and is reproduced in OJEC L 31/3 of 4 February 1999. On this experience see J. Clarke, "Mutual Recognition Agreements," in *International Trade Law and Regulation,* No 2, 1996, 31–36 and K. Nicolaidïs, "Negotiating Mutual Recognition Regimes: A Comparative Analysis," *Working Paper 6,* Center for International Affairs, Harvard University, Spring 1998. The EC has also negotiated – or is negotiating – mutual recognition agreements with other countries including Australia, Canada, Israel, Japan, and New Zealand.

21. See OJEC L 118 of 21 April 1998, corrigendum OJEC L 130 of 1 May 1998 and C 136 of 1 May 1998. The agreement has not yet entered into force.

22. This annex establishes mutual recognition of each party's inspections of pharmaceutical sites carried out according to the other party's inspection procedures and good manufacturing practices (GMP) requirements, once they have been declared as"equivalent," i.e., capable of producing the same level of confidence as to a manufacturer's ability to properly and safely produce drugs. Such a determination will take place during a three-year transition period.

23. This approach is positively embodied in Art 2.7 of the TBT Agreement.

24. A question that may deserve further thoughts is to consider whether the framework principles to be used to reduce or eliminate barriers and regulatory obstacles to trade in industrial goods could also be used to tackle regulatory barriers affecting services trade.

25. This remains a general objective and not an obligation. It is thus different from what is the case in the EC contest where, in particular after the Cassis de Dijon jurisprudence consolidated, Member States are obliged to accept goods lawfully produced and/or marketed in another Member States, in so far as the goods in question meet, to an equivalent extent, the legitimate objective which its legislation is designed to achieve (see also below note 32).

26. Any broader trade facilitation objective will have to yield in any specific case although an overall balance of commercial benefit needs to be ensured in order to justify the negotiating effort.

27. This approach is the one that most closely resembles the Community's "new approach" where harmonization limited to the essential requirements of health and safety is linked to the mutual recognition of national technical regulations.

28. In the words of the Commission "experience has shown that the alternative of relying on a strategy based totally on harmonization would be over-regulatory, would take a long time to implement, would be inflexible and could stifle innovation." The policy of seeking full harmonization is generally referred to as the "old approach" in Community parlance. See Commission of the European Communities, *Completing the Internal Market,* COM (90) 283 final, 1985, 18.

29. Both the WTO Agreement on the Application of Sanitary and Phitosanitary Measures (SPS Agreement) and the TBT Agreement, promote the use of international standards by encouraging Members to use them as the basis for their technical regulation unless this would be inappropriate for the fulfillment of their legitimate policy objectives, see Art. 2.4 TBT and Art. 3 SPS.

30. International Conference on Harmonization of Technical Requirements for the Registration of Pharmaceuticals for Human Use.

31. United Nations Economic Commission for Europe.

32. In the EC context, mutual recognition needs to be seen as part of the policy aimed at establishing the Internal Market and ensuring the free movement of goods. This policy is based on key provisions of the EC Treaty, in particular Articles 30–36 EC; the role of the European Court of Justice and its case-law (see, in particular, Rewe-Zentral AG v. Bundesmonopolverwaltung fur Branntwein (Case 120/78, ECR, 1979p. 649, CMLR, 1979, 494, generally referred to as the Cassis de Dijon case); a number of preventive mechanisms which aim to prevent barriers between Member States from arising, and which include the Information Directive 83/189 and Council Decision 3052/95. With regard to technical requirements for products, free movement is achieved through a wide range of harmonization measures (such as those laid down in the "Old Approach" Directives, e.g. motor vehicles, chemicals, pharmaceuticals, foodstuffs, etc.; and the "New Approach" Directives, covering a variety of products such as appliances operating on low voltage, toys, etc.; and a number of risks such as electromagnetic compatibility), combined with mutual recognition of products legally produced and marketed in other Member States. This is based on the assumption that their respective national requirements provide equivalent protection of public policy objectives such as health, the environment, etc. See Mattera, cit. *supra* note 18; J. Pelkmans, "The New Approach to Technical Harmonization and Standardization," in *Journal of Common Market Studies,* March 1987; D. Waelbroeck, "L'harmonisation des règles et normes techniques dans la CEE," in *Cahiers de Droit Européen,* Vol. 24, No. 3, 243–275.

33. A similar instrument was envisaged by Art.100b of the EC Treaty (never actually used and now repealed by the Treaty of Amsterdam) which provided that: "[d]uring 1992, the Commission shall, together with each member States, draw up an inventory of national laws, regulations, and administrative provisions which fall under Article 100a and which have not been harmonized pursuant to that Article.

The Council, acting in accordance with the provisions of Article 100a, may decide that the provisions in force in a Member State must be recognized as being equivalent to those applied by another Member State." See P. Eeckhout, *The European Internal Market and International Trade – A Legal Analysis,* Clarendon Press, Oxford 1994, 285.

34. This aspect appears particularly important for firms that delocalize (transplant) some of their production in third countries while maintaining production, safety, and quality specifications unaltered. In these instances the conformity assessment (certification) aspect would assume critical importance.

35. The debate surrounding Art. 100(a)(4) of the EC Treaty may be instructive in connection, see for instance, E. L. M. Völker, *Barriers to External and Internal Community Trade,* Deventer, 1993, 180–81.

36. By way of simplification, two cases could present themselves. Firstly, one of the mutual recognition partners may decide to make its own technical regulation "more stringent" and thus consider that the regulation of the other party originally deemed equivalent is no longer so. In such a case protectionist motives could also be alleged. Otherwise, one partner may decide to make its own technical regulation "less stringent," leading the other party to consider that the new version of the regulation is no longer equivalent. A form of competitive deregulation could be alleged in this case. Here the possibility of withdrawing mutual recognition commitment would neutralize any "race to the bottom" pressure, allowing for the preservation of high levels of safety and protection.

37. The key issue here would be how deferential the standard of review should be vis-à-vis the sovereign autonomy of national legislators and regulators. See Sykes, *cit. supra* note 8, at 126–27 and R. Hudec, "GATT/WTO Constraints on National Regulation: Requiem for an "Aim and Effect" Test," in *The International Lawyer,* Fall 1998, 619–49.

38. The "supplier's declaration of conformity" is a declaration by a manufacturers certifying that its product meets certain regulations or standards. Less precisely, it is sometimes referred to as self-certification.

39. Take, for instance, the case of the toy sector. At federal level, toys are regulated mainly by the Federal Hazardous Substance Act, 15 U.S.C. §§ 1261–77; the Consumer Product Safety Act, 15 U.S.C. §§ 2051–84; and the Flammable Fabrics Act, 15 U.S.C. §§ 1191–1204. However, due in large measure to lax enforcement at the federal level, states have become significantly active in the regulation of consumer products, including toys. Nineteen states have adopted hazardous substances acts that include specific reference to toys; four states have statutes dealing specifically with hazardous toys; five states have statutes that regulates stuffed toys; and ten states regulate lead paint in toys (Hogan & Hartson, "Study of Market Certification Procedures in the United States and Related Market Access Problems," 1994, mimeo).

40. The US Constitution mandates Congress to regulate inter-state commerce. However, federal law totally pre-empts state laws in only a few areas. Partial pre-emption prevails in a broad range of areas including health, safety, and environmental protection that nonetheless affect interstate commerce. Important areas, such as product liability, are entirely governed by state laws.

41. Technical regulations represent a very significant part of EC legislation. As mentioned (*supra* note 32), a wide range of products are covered by the so-called "new approach" directives, including the directive on machines, electromagnetic compatibility, medical devices

and pressure equipment. For other products, such as pharmaceuticals, dangerous chemicals and cars, regulations are still based upon the "old approach," detailed harmonization directives. However, the volume of technical regulation at national level far exceeds that at the EC level.

42. For example, in the US, many of the regulations applied in state and local building codes require that electrical materials meet parts of the National Electrical Code, a voluntary standard developed by the private National Fire Prevention Association. For an overview of the US standardization system, see US National Research Council, *Standards Conformity Assessment and Trade: Into the 21st Century,* National Academy Press, Washington, D.C., 1995.

43. European standards are considered those developed by the European standardization organizations: CEN (the European Committee for Standardization), CENELEC (the European Committee for Electrotechnical Standardization) and ETSI (the European Telecommunications Standards Institute).

44. Specific certification marks to this effect may need to be introduced. There are already examples of specific marks, such as the Underwriters Laboratories (UL) Mark for Canada. UL is a non-profit organization incorporated under the laws of the State of Delaware to establish, maintain, and operate laboratories for the investigation of devices, systems, and materials with respect to hazards affecting life and property. UL was established in 1894 and its principal business is safety investigation of electrical and electronic equipment, products, and components, mechanical products, building materials, construction systems, fire protection equipment, burglary protection systems and equipment, and marine products. The UL mark, signaling product safety certification, is one of the leading certification marks for consumer safety in the US. By virtue of accreditation by the Standards Council of Canada, UL can evaluate products intended for the Canadian marketplace to Canadian National Standards and Codes, and authorize clients to label those products with the UL Mark for Canada.

45. See Artt.2.1 and 5.1.1 of the TBT Agreement.

46. Art. 2.2 TBT.

47. Art. 2.4 TBT.

48. Art. 2.9 and 2.11 TBT. The non-discrimination obligation (contained in Art. 2.1) with respect to the preparation, adoption, and application of technical regulation remains unaffected.

49. Art. 2.1 TBT. See J. Mathis, Mathis "Mutual Recognition Agreements, Transatlantic Parties and the Limits to Non-tariff Barrier Regionalism in the WTO," Journal of World Trade, Vol 32 No. 6, 1998 at 13.

50. Art. 2.7 TBT.

51. Ibid.

52. Art. 6.1 TBT. The applicable technical regulations would be (partly) those of the other party in as far as any regulatory requirement has been deemed equivalent and included in a sectoral list of commitments.

53. The acceptance of supplier's declarations of conformity can generally only happen if either party is satisfied with the quality assurance systems used by the other party's firms. On quality assurance, see A. Zuckerman, *International Standards Desk Reference,* American Management Association, New York, 1997, 93–145 and J. McMillan, "Une politique Européenne pour la

promotion de la qualité," in *Revue du Marché commun et de l'Union européenne,* September-October 1997, pp. 520–26.

54. Art. 6.1 TBT.

55. Art. 6.3 and 2.7 TBT.

56. This could happen, for instance, when both regulations are based on the adoption of internationally developed standards.

57. As required by Art. 2.1 TBT. By way of example, this would be the case of a Canadian product, manufactured (and duly certified) to meet the US technical regulations deemed equivalent to the EC ones. Such a product should be treated in the EC as a US product with respect to the non-application of the EC technical regulations deemed as equivalent to the US ones and already met by the Canadian product in question.

58. As required by Art. 5.1.1 TBT. By way of example, this would be the case of a Canadian product, manufactured to meet the EC technical regulations and then assessed for conformity by an agreed US conformity assessment body. Since it is the ability of the conformity assessment procedures that are recognized as equivalent with respect to the objectives pursued, it is immaterial whether the assessment is performed on products originating in the mutual recognition partner or elsewhere.

59. The same should be said for mutual recognition in the services area, where article VII of the GATS specifically provides for the conclusion of agreements for the mutual recognition of education, qualifications, ability to provide services or other requirements. Similarly, the Annex on Financial Services allows mutual recognition of prudential measures, facilitating the establishment and provision of financial services. Article VII (and a similar requirement in the Annex on Financial Services) requires Members which are party to a mutual recognition agreement to give "adequate opportunity" for accession to other Members or for the negotiation of similar agreements with them.

60. Art. XXIV.2 of the GPA.

61. Art. X.9 of the Marrakesh Agreement Establishing the World Trade Organization.

62. As it has been rightly pointed out MRAs "constitute the building blocks of European economic integration and are likely to represent the hallmark of trade diplomacy in the decade to come," see K. Nicolaidïs, cit. *supra* note 20 at 1.

63. See G. Majone, "Mutual Recognition in Federal Type Systems," European University Institute Working Paper No. 93/1, 1993.

64. See A. Mattera, "Le principe de la reconnaissance mutuelle: instrument de préservation des traditions et des diversités nationales, régionales et locales," in *Revue du Marché Unique Européen,* No. 2, 1998, 5–17.

65. On regulatory competition see, for example, J.-M. Sun and J. Pelkmans, "Regulatory Competition and the Single Market," in *Journal of Common Market Studies,* March 1995, 67–89.

# Part V: Trade and Competition Interlinkage

CHAPTER 17

# The Economic Evaluation of Protection under Art III: Some Principles and Suggestions for the Definition of a Trade Relevant Market

*Damien J. Neven**

This paper starts from a puzzling observation; whereas antitrust investigations conducted by experienced agencies follow a structured set of principles in their economic analysis, in particular through the delineation of a relevant market, investigations for trade cases often fail to do so. Yet, few would dispute that a rigorous and systematic approach greatly contributes to the clarity and ultimate quality of antitrust decisions.

This paper attempts to clarify some principles underlying the economic analysis to be undertaken in trade case under art III GATT. It also outlines an approach for handling the investigation through the delineation of a relevant market.

We argue that discriminatory measures against foreign firms can in general be seen as a relative increase in their marginal cost and that the domestic price distortion associated with such discrimination is an adequate measure of the extent to which domestic firms are protected and one which can be implemented in practice. We find that the ability to raise price for domestic firms will be determined both by the extent of substitution between foreign and domestic products and the intensity of competition between them. A strong similarity between domestic and foreign products will thus not be a sufficient condition for the former to obtain protection from a differential treatment.

At the same time, art III of the GATT draws a distinction between "like" and "directly competitive and substitutable" products and the case law seems to have established a presumption that the extent of protection is always higher when domestic and foreign products belong to the former category. This presumption is thus not supported by economic principles.

---

* Paper prepared for presentation at the second World Trade Forum, in Neuchâtel (August 1998). I would like to thank Thomas von Ungern-Sternberg for useful discussions, Petros C. Mavroidis for comments on previous draft of the paper and M. Waelbroeck for an insightful discussion of the paper at the conference.

We further argue that since protection is a matter of degree, a benchmark on protection, i.e., on the ability for domestic firms to raise price should be specified in order to determine whether there is a violation of art III. For instance, protection could be deemed unlawful if domestic firms have the ability to raise price by x %.

The question then arises of how to evaluate the protection in practice. It is of course difficult to evaluate substitution and rivalry at the same time. So, it may useful to disentangle the two effects, and first consider protection when one factor is absent. In this respect, there is an interesting parallel to draw between the evaluation of market power and the evaluation of protection.

In antitrust cases, the definition of a relevant market is meant to "calibrate" a concentration. The relevant market is one in which a market share of 100% (that of the hypothetical monopolist) has "serious" consequences in terms of market power (would lead to a significant non transitory increase in price). The market share of the firms under review can then be assessed against this benchmark.

As mentioned above, the ability of domestic firms to raise price when the cost of foreign firms is increased is directly related, for a given degree of demand substitutability across products, to the extent of competition across these products. That is, if domestic firms collude, they should be able to benefit more from a increase in the cost of foreign firms,

Accordingly, if we want to separate the evaluation of substitution from the evaluation of rivalry, an appropriate calibration of protective effects should be made by reference to a hypothetical situation with no rivalry (that is with a hypothetical monopolist or full collusion).

The economic evaluation of protection could thus be undertaken in two steps. First, the relevant market would be defined very much in the same way as in antitrust cases, by asking what is the scope of products over which a hypothetical monopolist could permanently increase price by some percentage. In the second step, one would evaluate the extent of rivalry in the domestic market. If is found that rivalry is intense, the likelihood of a significant protection would be reduced and the case may be dismissed. In antitrust cases, what would be evaluated in the second step is both the market share of the parties and the ease of entry, and likelihood of a competition problem would be reduced if it found that the market share is low or that entry is easy. Hence, the essential difference between procedures in antitrust and trade cases would be associated with the evaluation of the second stage – the criteria for the evaluation being different.

Section 1 reviews the practice of recent GATT and WTO panels for selected trade cases focusing on investigations under art III. Section 2 considers some principles for the economic evaluation of protection under art III. Section 3 outlines a possible definition of the relevant market for trade cases. Section 4 concludes.

## 1. Protection under Art. III of GATT

The issue of protection arises in trade cases both at the level of individual jurisdictions and at the level of the WTO. For instance, anti-dumping investigations require the evaluation of the harm suffered by the domestic parties as a result of dumping. At the level of the WTO, any case dealing with discrimination against foreign firm will need to identify the parties affected by the alleged discriminatory measure.

In what follows, we will focus on the application of art III of the GATT, even though a similar analysis could be undertaken for other provisions including anti-dumping provisions.

Art III is concerned with situations where domestic regulations including taxes are applied in such a way as to discriminate in favor of domestic firms. This provision establishes two important references. First, the article emphasizes the protection that is granted to domestic firms and makes no reference to the cost imposed on foreign firms. Accordingly, an investigation of a possible violation of art III will focus on the effect of domestic regulation on domestic firms. Second, art III is concerned with facts and not intent. What matters is not whether member governments designed their domestic regulation in order to favor domestic firms but only whether domestic regulation do actually grant protection. Admittedly, this interpretation of art III has been a matter of debate. But the panel decision on Japanese Alcoholic beverages has clarified the matter and this position has been confirmed by the Appellate body. Not to require evidence of intent seems highly welcome since evidence on such a lose matter as intent would naturally be extremely difficult to obtain and this would potentially make art III rather void. A contrario, the sole concern of art III for facts makes it potentially very powerful and underlies the need for a rigorous and systematic approach to evaluate whether domestic firms are effectively protected by the implementation of a domestic regulation. In the absence of a consistent and rigorous approach, members countries will be naturally very reluctant to initiate proceedings under art III, as the outcome will be difficult to predict. Such a powerful instrument as art III will only be used if it can be implemented in such a way as to offer guarantees in terms of adequate legal certainty and economic consistency. This in turn requires an analysis of the protection of domestic firms grounded in sound economic and legal principles.

Art III provides some structure for the investigation of domestic protection. It draws a distinction between domestic products which can be qualified as "like" products relative to those imported (first sentence of para 2) and domestic products that are "directly competitive and substitutable " for imported ones (second sentence of para 2). These two sets of products are subject to different legal standards.

As clarified by various panel decisions, "like" products form a subset of "directly competitive and substitutable" ones. Imported and like domestic products are supposed to share most physical characteristics and should normally be subject to the same HS tariff heading. The legal standard for the treatment of imported and like products is also particularly strict as it admits no difference of treatment across products. This standard has been affirmed without ambiguity by the Appellate body in the case of Japanese alcoholic beverages; according to the Appellate body, "even the smallest amount of excess is too much... The prohibition under article III2, first sentence, is not conditional on a trade effects test nor is it qualified by a de minimis standard."

With respect to "competitive and substitutable products," the legal standard is less clear cut. First, it appears that differences in the treatment of domestic and foreign products is subject to a de minimis standard. Hence, in order to find a prohibition, it will necessary to show that the treatment of domestic and foreign products is not similar. Second, since the second sentence of art III.2 makes explicit reference to the first paragraph of the same article,[1] it appears that in order to find a prohibition, it will also be necessary to show that differences in the treatment of foreign and domestic products do effectively grant protection to the latter.

The distinction between "like" and "directly competitive and substitutable" products and the very strict standard applied to the former relative to the latter seems to be associated with the presumption that if two products are very similar, any difference in the treatment applied to them will translate into a significant protection for the product which benefit from more favorable conditions. In such case, it can simply be presumed that the protective effect exists and is significant. By contrast, when products are more differentiated, the significance of the protective effect has to be established.

The practical significance of the distinction between the different legal standards applied to "like" and "directly competitive and substitutable" products could be questioned. First, the distinction between the two types of products is in practice not easily drawn. According to various panel decisions, the distinction has to be made on case by case basis and there is not single criteria that should be used in all cases. As indicated above, there is an apparent consensus that "like" products should share most physical characteristics. With respect to the assessment of whether products are directly competitive and substitutable, there is repeated suggestion in panels that it should be determined in the market place and that similarity in end-use (as measured possibly by the elasticity of substitution across products or the cross-price elasticity of demand) is an important factor to take into account. Beyond this, little systematic guidance is offered by the panel decisions. The (unusually lyrical) comment by the Appellate body on Japanese alcoholic beverages (p 23) that the "concept of likeness is one that evokes the image of an accordion… (which) stretches and squeezes in different places as different provisions of the WTO agreements are applied" also offers little comfort that the distinction between the two types of products can be established on a sound and systematic basis.

Second, the distinction between the legal standards applied to the two types of products seems (at least so far) largely immaterial. The case of Japanese alcoholic beverages is particularly telling in this respect: the panel decided (p120) that "for it to conclude that dissimilar taxation afforded protection, it would be sufficient for it to find that the dissimilarity is not de minimis." In other words, if the difference of treatment is large enough the protective effect can simply be presumed (as in the case of "like" products). Hence, the only difference between the standard applied to "like" and "directly competitive and substitutable" products relates to the importance of the dissimilarity in treatment. Admittedly, the Appellate body disagreed with this approach and insisted that the issue of whether protection was granted should be handled separately from the issue of whether the treatment was dissimilar. Unfortunately, however, the Appellate body only provide vague guidance on how to assess protection. It merely referred to the fact that beyond the importance of the dissimilarity in treatment, there will be "other factors to be considered." What these factors should be has unfortunately not been clarified by the Appellate body.

Overall, the approach followed in trade cases to evaluate protection is thus markedly less sophisticated than the approach that would be followed in antitrust cases. As indicated above, given that provisions like article III are potentially quite powerful, a structured approach to the evaluation of protection which offers adequate guarantees for legal security and consistency with economic principles would be greatly valuable.

The next section will outline such an approach. In light of this framework, it will also become clear that the distinction between two different degrees of substitution between products and the associated differences in legal standards can hardly be justified in terms of economic principles.

## 2. Some Principles for the Evaluation of Protection

As discussed above, a trade investigation will involve two sets of firms which either allegedly behave differently (as in the case of dumping) or are subject to different rules. In the latter case, associated with investigation under art III of the GATT, the effect of differential rules (like differential taxation, different product standards and whatever non tariff barrier) is best thought of as in increase in the marginal cost of the foreign firm.

To the extent that the measures concerned do indeed raise the cost of foreign rivals, the evaluation of protective effects thus requires to identify the extent to which domestic firms are protected by a change in the marginal cost of a subset of their competitors.

The first question which arises is then how to measure the protection granted to domestic firms. One natural candidate would be the rents accruing to domestic firms (relative to what they would earn in the absence of a measure raising the marginal cost of the foreign firms). This is however not realistic. Profits and rents are notoriously difficult to measure (because of accounting conventions which blur economic profits but more fundamentally because much of the rent accruing to firms is likely to translate into higher cost rather than higher profit). To evaluate changes in profits relative a counterfactual which is not observed is of course even harder and this can only be undertaken at great cost – and with a substantial degree of imprecision. Profits and rents are thus hardly used even in antitrust investigations and it would equally inadequate to use them in trade investigations. One alternative candidate to measure protection would the importance of the price distortion associated with protection, namely the price that domestic firms are able to charge relative to the level that would prevail without the increase of the marginal cost of foreign firms. Such measure has clear advantages. First, it is well associated with the profits and rents accruing to domestic firms. Indeed, the ability to raise price is a sufficient condition for domestic firms to benefit from protection (which enables them to exercise market power). In most circumstances, an increase in price will also be a necessary condition for domestic firms to benefit from protection.[2] Price distortions will thus be a reliable indicator of the rents associated with protection. Second, counterfactuals over prices are routinely used in antitrust investigations and there is presumably a benefit associated with a common approach in antitrust and trade case. The use of prices in antitrust cases also confirms that the approach can be implemented from a practical point of view. Third, the focus on price distortions is also well in line with the stated objective of the GATT agreements, whose preamble emphasizes an efficient allocation of ressources.[3]

Let us thus assume that protection can be adequately measured by the extent to which domestic firms can raise price. In principle, the ability of domestic firms to raise price is determined by the demand substitution between domestic and foreign products but also by the rivalry between foreign and domestic firms and between domestic firms. Clearly, if domestic and products hardly differentiated, domestic firms will benefit from an increase in the cost of their foreign competitors; in those circumstances, the cross price elasticity of demand for the domestic product with respect to the foreign price will be high so that when the foreign firm raises it price following its rise in cost, it will lose a substantial proportion of its customers to the domestic firms. In turn, domestic firms will also tend to have a strong incentive to raise their own price.

If the demand substitution between foreign and domestic products will be an important determinant of protection, the type of rivalry which prevails between firms will also matter a great deal. For instance, consider an extreme case where there is perfect competition between firms (see figure 1). Assume that domestic firms operate with a constant marginal cost so that the supply curve of the domestic industry (DS) is horizontal. Foreign firms have an upward sloping supply curve (FS). As their supply curve is shifted to the left by the discriminatory measure (to FS'), the equilibrium price in the domestic market does not change. All what happens is that the market share of the domestic firms increase at the expense of foreign firms and domestic firms do not earn additional rents (in perfect competition and constant marginal cost, producer surplus is anyway zero). Admittedly, this example is a bit constricted but it illustrates that even if substitution is perfect, protection can be absent. At the opposite, consider a situation where domestic firms co-ordinate price and set a limit price just below that of their foreign competitors. In those circumstances, an increase in the marginal cost an price and foreign firm will be fully translated into an additional protection of domestic firms.

**Figure 1. Product Differentiation and Protection**

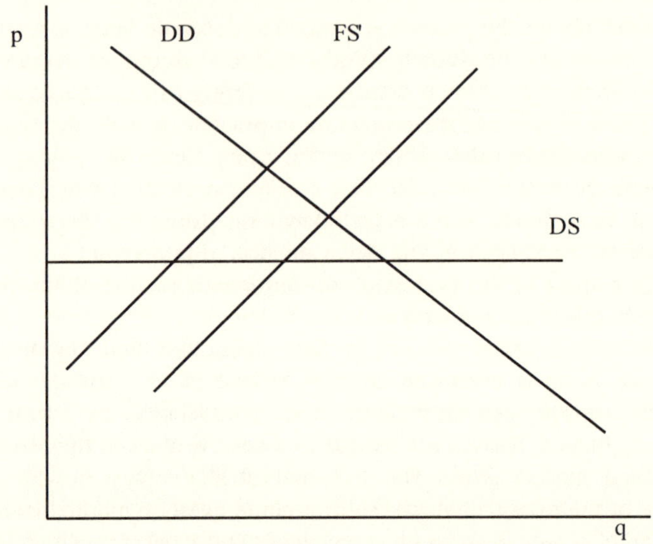


In general, the substitution between products is thus not the sole determinant of protection. The higher is the number of competitors and the stronger is the rivalry between them, the lower will be the protection granted by a discriminatory measure against foreign firm.[4] Importantly, this suggests that the distinction drawn by article III of the GATT between "like" and "directly competitive and substitutable" products is unlikely to be very useful. The presumption that "like" products will always be protected is simply not supported by economic principles.

Holding the competitive interactions constant, the higher is the substitutability between foreign and domestic products, the higher is the protection granted to the latter, as mentioned above. That is also to say that firms selling highly substitutable domestic products will be able to raise price by more than firms selling more differentiated items. As the market is enlarged to include less substitutable items, the ability to raise price at the margin will decline.

The extent to which firms are protected is also a matter of degree. Hence, in order to determine whether there is a violation of art III, it will thus be necessary to set a benchmark for what is considered a significant protection. For instance, protection could be deemed unlawful if domestic firms have the ability to raise price by x %.

## 3. How to Evaluate Protection?

As indicated above, the protection granted to domestic firms is determined by the substitutability between products and the extent of rivalry between domestic firms and between domestic and foreign firms. The question then arises of how to evaluate the protection in practice. It is of course difficult to evaluate substitution and rivalry at the same time. So, it may useful to disentangle the two effects, and first consider protection when one factor is absent. In this respect, there is an interesting parallel to draw between the evaluation of market power and the evaluation of protection.

With respect to the evaluation of dominance (or the ability to exercise market power), there is a well established approach in antitrust investigation such that the relevant market is first delineated and the prospect for dominance is then evaluated in that market. The rationale behind this approach is simply that the volume of sales undertaken by a firm has to be calibrated. Indeed, if sales are related to a narrow market, they will translate into a high market share. But this market share may not be a reliable indicator of the extent to which the firm could exercise market power if there is no market power that can be exercised in that market anyhow. Hence, the relevant market is first computed as a market where a significant degree of market power could be exercised if there was no competition. A share of sales computed in that market will then take some significance as by construction a share of 100% would confer significant market power. The share of the firm under review in that market will be a meaningful indicator of its ability to exercise market power (under the presumption supported by economic theory that increased market shares translate into enhanced market power).

With respect to the evaluation of protection, there is, as mentioned above, a direct link between the ability of domestic firms to raise price when the cost of foreign firms is increased and to extent of rivalry across firms (for a given degree of substitutability across products). That is, if domestic firms collude, they should be able to benefit more from a increase in the cost of foreign firms.

Accordingly, if we want to separate the evaluation of substitution from the evaluation of rivalry, an appropriate calibration of protective effects should be made by reference to a hypothetical situation with no rivalry (that is with a hypothetical monopolist or full collusion).

Hence, the economic evaluation of protection could be undertaken in two steps. First, the relevant market would be defined very much in the same way as in antitrust cases, by asking what is the scope of products over which a hypothetical monopolist could permanently increase price by some percentage. In the second step, one would evaluate the extent of rivalry in the domestic market. If it is found that rivalry is intense, the likelihood of a significant protection would be reduced and the case may be dismissed. In antitrust cases, what would be evaluated in the second step is both the market share of the parties and the ease of entry, and likelihood of a competition problem would be reduced if it found that the market share is low or that entry is easy. Hence, the essential difference between procedures in antitrust and trade cases would be associated with the evaluation of the second stage – the criteria for the evaluation being different. For antitrust cases, the evaluation focuses on market shares and the extent of potential competition from outside the relevant market. For trade case, the evaluation would focus on the extent of rivalry and competition within the relevant market.

## 4. Conclusion

Overall, it seems that the legal certainty and the consistency of proceeding under art III would be greatly enhanced if a clear benchmark was formulated in terms of unlawful protection. We have argued that such benchmark could be formulated in terms of the increase in price that domestic firms can afford because of the differential treatment between domestic and foreign firms. In turn, we suggested that protection could evaluated in two steps. First, it would be assumed that there is no competition and a relevant would be delineated very much in the same way as in antitrust cases. In a second step, the extent of rivalry within the relevant market would be estimated. If it is found that rivalry is intense, protection granted to domestic firms would be considered insignificant and the case could be dismissed.

One can wonder whether the approach outlined here is at all practical. With respect to the first step, market delineation, it is routinely and effectively implemented in antitrust case so that there is a prior that the delineation of the trade relevant market may be equally feasible. However, the second step involves a rather more intricate counterfactual than in antitrust cases, to the extent that it requires an evaluation of supply substitution within the candidate market. A number of quantitative techniques can be used for that purpose. The observation of competitive conduct around particular market events like the introduction of new products or a sudden shift in cost or demand will also often be revealing. This question is further discussed in a companion paper.[5]

APPENDIX

## Article III[6]

*National Treatment on Internal Taxation and Regulation*

1. The contracting parties recognize that internal taxes and other internal charges, and laws, regulations, and requirements affecting the internal sale, offering for sale, purchase, transportation, distribution or use of products, and internal quantitative regulations requiring the mixture, processing or use of products in specified amounts or proportions, should not be applied to imported or domestic products so as to afford protection to domestic production.*

2. The products of the territory of any contracting party imported into the territory of any other contracting party shall not be subject, directly or indirectly, to internal taxes or other internal charges of any kind in excess of those applied, directly or indirectly, to like domestic products. Moreover, no contracting party shall otherwise apply internal taxes or other internal charges to imported or domestic products in a manner contrary to the principles set forth in paragraph 1.*

Ad Article III

Any internal tax or other internal charge, or any law, regulation or requirement of the kind referred to in paragraph 1 which applies to an imported product and to the like domestic product and is collected or enforced in the case of the imported product at the time or point of importation, is nevertheless to be regarded as an internal tax or other internal charge, or a law, regulation or requirement of the kind referred to in paragraph 1, and is accordingly subject to the provisions of Article III.

*Paragraph 1*

The application of paragraph 1 to internal taxes imposed by local governments and authorities with the territory of a contracting party is subject to the provisions of the final paragraph of Article XXIV. The term "reasonable measures" in the last-mentioned paragraph would not require, for example, the repeal of existing national legislation authorizing local governments to impose internal taxes which, although technically inconsistent with the letter of Article III, are not in fact inconsistent with its spirit, if such repeal would result in a serious financial hardship for the local governments or authorities concerned. With regard to taxation by local governments or authorities which is inconsistent with both the letter and spirit of Article III, the term "reasonable measures" would permit a contracting party to eliminate the inconsistent taxation gradually over a transition period, if abrupt action would create serious administrative and financial difficulties.

*Paragraph 2*

A tax conforming to the requirements of the first sentence of paragraph 2 would be considered to be inconsistent with the provisions of the second sentence only in cases where competition was.

NOTES

1. See appendix.

2. It is only for unrealistic demand and cost conditions that profits could raise without an increase in price following a change in the marginal cost of a subset of firms. In general, prices will thus rise following an increase in cost.

3. At least, abstracting from second best considerations.

4. This is shown formally in a companion paper, Neven (1999), Market definition for trade cases, mimeo.

5. Neven, 1999, op cit.

6. This Protocol entered into force on 14 December 1948.

CHAPTER 18

# Comments on Damien Neven's Paper

*Michel Waelbroeck*

I would like to make two comments concerning Damien Neven's very interesting paper. The first comment concerns the issue whether the methodology for defining the relevant market is fundamentally different in competition cases and in trade cases. In my opinion, the answer is no. As I see things, the basic question in both cases is whether there exists a sufficiently direct competitive relationship between two products for an increase in the price of one of the products to bring about a switch in demand towards the other product. This is the well-known "cross elasticity of demand" test.

I would like to give a concrete example. Let us suppose that the United Kingdom authorities have been alerted to the fact that imports of Greek ouzo have been increasing massively, provoking a switch in demand away from domestically produced drinks such as whisky and gin. To protect the latter, they decide to impose a 20 percent charge on ouzo and other anise-flavored drinks.

It seems to me that the compatibility of such a measure with GATT (let us forget for a while that both Greece and the UK are members of the EU) will depend on the extent to which ouzo, whisky, and gin are, if not "like," at least "directly competitive and substitutable," in other words, whether the increase in the price of ouzo caused by the additional charge will bring about a switch in demand to whisky and gin. If there is no sufficient cross-elasticity, the products will be deemed to belong to separate products markets and the measure will be deemed not to produce protective effects.

Let us now imagine that, instead of lobbying the government in order to obtain the adoption of a protective trade measure, the main producer of whisky and gin decides to take over the main producer of ouzo—thus eliminating the source of the increased competition to which it had been exposed. In examining such a merger, the competition authorities will look at exactly the same issue as the trade authorities had to examine in the preceding hypothesis, i.e., whether there is sufficient cross-elasticity of demand between ouzo, on the one hand, and whisky and gin, on the other, for these products to be treated as belonging to the same market.

I must add, however, that in practice the antitrust authorities have a tendency to define markets more narrowly than in trade cases. Paul Demaret gave us the example of bananas, on which the Court of Justice adopted conflicting positions in the United Brands judgment of February 14, 1978 and in the Commission v. Italy judgment of May 7, 1987. The reason for this, according to me, is that the antitrust authorities use an excessively strict standard as to what constitutes "sufficient" cross-elasticity. According to them, if as a result of an increase of as little as 5 percent in the price of a product, consumers switch to another product, the two products cannot be considered as being in the same market. This has led to extremely narrow market definitions. However, this is not necessarily a problem to the extent the authorities recognize the need to take into consideration indirect competition arising from products belonging to neighboring markets to see if there is any need to broaden the initially defined market, trade authorities use a single stage method, adopting a broad view of substitutability from the start. However, this does not mean that their methodology is fundamentally different from that of the antitrust authorities, only that the facts they have to examine generally involve grosser distortions of competition.

My second observation concerns Damien Neven's interesting remark about the need to take into account the intensity of competition between domestic producers. I would have liked him to take his reasoning a bit further. Indeed, what conclusions does he draw from the fact that, even if they are theoretically "protected," it is possible that domestic producers will not be able to take advantage of this protection because of the intensity of competition between them? He seems to imply that, in such a case, there would be no GATT violation. However I doubt that this is correct.

Let me revert to my alcoholic example to illustrate my point. Let us imagine that ouzo was selling at 10 percent below the price of whisky and gin before the adoption of the 20 percent surcharge and that, after the adoption of the charge, importers find it necessary to increase prices of ouzo to a level higher than the prices of whisky and gin if they wish to remain profitable. Let us also imagine that whisky and gin producers in the UK are engaged in such fierce competition that they do not increase their prices after the adoption of the charge. Under such conditions, it is possible that those UK consumers who had been enticed by the charms of ouzo will all switch back to whisky and gin. Can it be said that the surcharge does not have a protective effect and that it is compatible with GATT, simply because the UK producers of whisky and gin keep their prices unchanged? This would mean forgetting that the measure has effectively excluded ouzo from the market. I confess that I find it hard to believe that this result can be correct.

CHAPTER 19

# Rethinking the "Like Product" Definition in GATT 1994: Anti-Dumping and Environmental Protection

*Marco Bronckers and Natalie McNelis**

"Like product" is a central concept in the GATT Agreement. It appears in numerous provisions, and then defines to which products the rights and obligations of the GATT Agreement apply. For instance, according to Article I GATT (the Most-Favored Nation principle), once a WTO Member grants a benefit at customs to a particular imported product, the same benefit must be given to any "like product" imported from every WTO Member. Accordingly, the interpretation of "like products" defines the scope of the GATT's MFN principle.

Although it is a central concept, and has been around since the origins of GATT in 1947, the definition of "like" products is not settled.

One GATT provision where the interpretation of "like" product has been especially difficult is Article III:2, prohibiting tax discrimination between imported and domestic products. As a result, this interpretation has shifted over the years. Recently, the Appellate Body has confirmed a new approach, which explicitly emphasizes the importance of the "marketplace" in the determination of "like" products. A mere reference, for example, to similarities in physical characteristics is not enough. Crucial is whether, from a consumer perspective, "like" products are sufficiently competitive or substitutable. As the Appellate Body explained, the WTO is concerned, after all, with markets.

The Appellate Body, being a cautious tribunal, pointed out that its interpretation of "like" products was limited to the GATT provision in dispute (Article III:2).

Nevertheless, the rationale of the Appellate Body's approach, that the WTO is about markets and improving competitive conditions in those markets, suggests that the test it approved for Article III:2 is capable of broader application. In fact, we consider that a market-place based analysis of the competitive relationships between products should be a central feature of any inquiry into GATT provisions that use the "like product" language,

---

* We would like to thank Reinhard Quick for helpful comments on this paper, although any errors or omissions are solely those of the authors.

where it can be said that the purpose is to protect or improve competitive conditions. Already, there are indications of a broader application of these concepts.[1] However, such a market-based analysis is not always a part of current "like product" determinations. Further, when competition is discussed, conclusions drawn therefrom are not always given the primary importance they deserve.

With this paper we seek to analyze whether this market-based interpretation of "like" products could help resolve some current controversies in other GATT fields. We will look at two instances: anti-dumping and environmental protection.

## 1. The Market Based Approach in Article III:2

The starting point of our discussion is the recent interpretation of the terms "like product" provided by the Panel and the Appellate Body in the second Japanese Liquor Taxes case, in the context of Article III:2 GATT 1994.[2] This approach was followed in the subsequent Korean Liquor Taxes case.[3]

Article III:2 states that:

> The products of the territory of any contracting party imported into the territory of any other contracting party shall not be subject, directly or indirectly, to internal taxes or other internal charges of any kind in excess of those applied, directly or indirectly, to *like domestic products*. [emphasis ours]

In the Japanese Liquor Taxes II case, the Panel was called upon to determine whether Japan's system of alcohol taxation, which taxed spirits such as whisky and vodka more highly than the largely domestically-produced "shochu," was in violation of these GATT rules on non-discriminatory taxation.

In that case, the Panel took much guidance from the way that Article III:2 had been interpreted in the past, but it also added some innovative perspectives. For one thing, the Panel stressed that:

> . . . in the Panel's view, the wording makes it clear that the appropriate test to define whether two products are "like" or "directly competitive or substitutable products" is the marketplace. The Panel recalled in this respect that the words used in the Interpretative Note ad Article III, paragraph 2, namely "where competition exists": competition exists by definition in markets.[4]

The Panel also made another interesting comment:

> In the view of the Panel, like products should be viewed as a subset of directly competitive or substitutable products. The wording ("like products" as opposed to "directly competitive or substitutable products") confirmed this point, in the sense that all like products are, by definition, directly competitive or substitutable products, whereas all directly competitive or substitutable products are not necessarily like products.[5]

The Appellate Body, in reviewing the case, had the following remarks on the Panel's approach:

> The Panel emphasized the need to look not only at such matters as physical characteristics, common end uses, and tariff classifications, but also at the "market place." This seems appropriate. The GATT 1994 is a commercial agreement, and the WTO is concerned, after all, with markets.[6]

This approach was subsequently followed by the Panel and the Appellate Body in the Korean Liquor Taxes case, which also involved an Article III:2 determination. There, among other things, the Appellate Body said "[t]he context of the competitive relationship is necessarily the marketplace since this is the forum where consumers choose between different products."[7]

What the Liquor Taxes cases have done is emphasize that what counts in defining "like" or "directly competitive or substitutable products" is competition in the marketplace, which is determined from the consumer's perspective. This approach ties together the different and disparate elements of the "like" product determination (such as physical characteristics, end use, price, channels of distribution), and allows them to be given their proper weight in a coherent analysis. This approach is attractive in that it ensures that the determination of the class of products subject to the GATT rule is made with an eye to the purpose of that rule, which is ultimately about ensuring fair competitive conditions between imported and domestic products.

In some instances, the market-based approach may mean that a "like product" definition in one field is the same as that in another. Indeed, in the 1998 Indonesia - Certain Measures Affecting The Automobile Industry case,[8] the Panel took note of this development in the interpretation of Article III:2, and stated that its analysis of "like products" in that case should be the same under Article III:2 GATT 1994 and the Agreement on Subsidies and Countervailing Measures. That analysis included market-oriented considerations such as that "there would not appear to be any relevant differences in respect of consumers" tastes and habits sufficient to render these products unlike." It ultimately held that "in the present case the same facts which support a finding of likeness for the purpose of the SCM Agreement also support a finding of likeness for the purpose of the first sentence of Article III:2 of GATT."[9]

However, this is not to say that what is a "like product" under one WTO provision must be a "like product" in another domain. For example, in the Japanese Liquor Taxes II case, shochu was found to be a "like product" to vodka—this does not necessarily mean that these two products also must be considered "like products" under other WTO provisions, such as Article I or Article VI, or that they ought to be found to fall in the same "relevant product markets" under domestic competition law, for example. While different provisions may use the same words, they serve different purposes. However, when coming to "like product" determinations, analyses of competitive relationships that have already taken place in other domains are relevant. Accordingly, where authorities arrive at different conclusions, they should explain why that different conclusion is merited in their domain. To date, this overall view is rarely taken by authorities, and we call for change.

## 2. Applying the Market Based Approach to Anti-Dumping Cases

The determination of "like products" has long been a controversial issue in the anti-dumping field. This is because defining the category of "like products" is a critical preliminary step that will set the stage for the rest of the investigation and which will, if measures are imposed, govern the scope of their application.

Article VI and the WTO Anti-dumping Agreement employ the phrase "like product" at numerous points, and so its establishment has by its very nature a broad-reaching impact. At the same time, the determination of "like products" is necessarily carried out on a case-by-case basis and involves a degree of discretion. Because the determination of "like products" is at the same moment flexible and crucial, there is both the incentive and the opportunity to manipulate the category of "like products" in order to achieve specific goals.

In the interest of legal certainty, the latitude for that manipulation should be as limited as possible. In that regard, the market-based approach taken by the Panels and the Appellate Body in Liquor Taxes cases to the determination of "like products" in the context of Article III:2 could add an overarching guideline for the determination of "like product" in the anti-dumping field.

Indeed, anti-dumping is designed to correct an injurious situation on the Community market. Therefore, the "market-based" approach taken in the Liquor Taxes cases could help to ensure that anti-dumping measures are tailored to that objective, and lose some of their reputation for arbitrariness.

## The Legal Texts

The rules applying to anti-dumping mention several instances in which it is necessary to delineate "like products."

First, from the start of an anti-dumping case, it is critical to determine which products are at issue, especially because the investigation cannot normally be initiated if the complaint is not sufficiently supported by the "domestic industry."[10] The domestic industry is defined in relation to the "like product," as it is made up of those companies producing the "like product" in the importing country:

> For the purposes of this Agreement, the term "domestic industry" shall be interpreted as referring to the domestic producers as a whole of the like products or to those of them whose collective output of the products constitutes a major proportion of the total domestic production of those products, except that . . . when producers are related to the exporters or importers or are themselves importers of the allegedly dumped product, the term "domestic industry" may be interpreted as referring to the rest of the producers . . .[11]

Aside from this standing requirement, the group of companies making up the domestic industry will also be important later on, in the examination of the existence of injury. Under Article VI, in order to impose anti-dumping measures, the anti-dumping authority must determine whether the dumping "causes or threatens material injury to an established industry in the territory of a contracting party or materially retards the establishment of a domestic industry."[12] In this regard, it should be noted that the Anti-dumping Agreement does not require that material injury be proven for every domestic producer of the "like product"—it can be limited to those producers that constitute a "major proportion of the total domestic production of those products . . ."[13]

The determination of the "like product" is also important to the calculation of dumping. In determining whether products are sold abroad for less than they are sold at home, and are therefore "dumped," anti-dumping authorities will try to compare sales abroad to sales of a "like product" at home. In other words, the authorities will try to compare, for example, the prices charged by Japanese Company A for Product B in the EC to the prices charged by Company A for Product B in Japan. The aim here is for the "like products" to be the same products manufactured and sold by the same company in the two markets.[14] Because the point of departure in the dumping comparison is that "like" means physically as close as possible to "identical," there is less room for discretion in this instance of determining "like products" as there is in the determination of the Community industry and injury.

Last but not least, at the end of the day, the determination of which products are "like" will have an impact upon the scope of application of any anti-dumping measures imposed.

## Strategy and the "Like Product" Definition

From the very inception of an anti-dumping action, the determination of "like products" can be a critical strategic choice.

Complainants are faced with conflicting interests in this regard: there is a strong incentive to define the category of "like products" broadly, because in that way one can sweep a larger group of products into the scope of the investigation and any eventual anti-dumping duties.

On the other hand, by drawing too broad a category of "like products," complainants can make it more difficult to meet the standing criteria and to prove injury. These two concepts make reference to the "domestic industry," and the domestic industry is defined by reference to the producers of the "like product."

First, as to standing, while the group of complainants might be representative of a sufficient proportion of domestic producers of product A, in the larger group of producers of products A, B, C, and so on, the complainants may not be able to garner enough support for their action.

This problem can reappear even if the complainants do manage to pass the standing threshold: it is still necessary to prove injury to a major proportion of domestic producers, a task which may be more difficult the wider the category of "like products." While the producers of Product A may be doing poorly, those of B and C might be thriving. By defining the category of "like products" as including A, B, and C, the A-producers might find that they have sacrificed a solid case of injury in trying to achieve a broad application of anti-dumping duties.

In the same way, it might be that by defining the category of "like products" too broadly, complainants may water down the calculation of dumping, if the percentage of dumping for product A is very high, while that for B and C is lower. The same can be said for the de minimis threshold, which provides that "dumped imports shall normally be regarded as negligible if the volume of dumped imports from a particular country is found to account for less than 3 per cent of imports of the like product in the importing Member . . ."[15] It is perhaps easier to avoid falling foul of this provision with a narrower "like product" definition. However, as noted above, narrowing the "like product" definition means that eventual anti-dumping measures will apply to a smaller class of products.

## The Guidelines of the GATT

Following an evolution in which the term "like product" in the anti-dumping context has been defined as "the same product,"[16] as "a product which is identical in physical characteristics subject, however, to such variations in presentation which are due to the need to adapt the product to special conditions in the market of the importing country,"[17] Article 2.6 of the current Anti-dumping Agreement provides the following definition of "like product":

> Throughout this Agreement the term "like product" ("produit similaire") shall be interpreted to mean a product which is identical, i.e., alike in all respects to the product under consideration, or in the absence of such a product, another product which, although not alike in all respects, has characteristics closely resembling those of the product under consideration.

This definition obviously leaves much room for interpretation. While at first the "identical" and "alike in all respects" language seems strict, that standard is perhaps softened by the "characteristics closely resembling" qualification. It is not clear whether, if one has an "identical" product, one is entitled to also look at products which have "characteristics closely resembling" that product. According to the wording of this provision, it would seem that one can only look further "in the absence of" an identical product, but this issue has not been definitively decided.

One GATT anti-dumping case in which the concept of "like product" was examined was the New Zealand - Imports of Electrical Transformers from Finland case. There, the Panel stated:

> In its examination whether the New Zealand transformer industry had suffered injury from the imports in question, the Panel subsequently dealt with the argument put forward by New Zealand that this industry was structured in such a way that there existed four distinguishable

> ranges of transformers. . . which for purposes of injury determination had to be considered separately. The Panel was of the view that this was not a valid argument, especially in light of the fact that the complaining company. . . produced the whole range of transformers, most of which in a range. . . which was not at all affected by the imports from Finland. . . . It was thus, in the Panel's view, the overall state of health of the New Zealand transformer industry which must provide the basis for a judgment whether injury was caused by dumped imports. To decide otherwise would allow the possibility to grant relief through anti-dumping duties to individual lines of production of a particular industry or company—a notion which would clearly be at variance with the concept of industry in Article VI. . .

This case speaks to the problem of "like product" definitions that are too narrow, so as to carve out a pocket of injury in an otherwise healthy industry. On the other hand, the Panel on United States - Definition of Industry Concerning Wine and Grape Products speaks rather to the problem of "like product" definitions that are too broad. In that case, the Panel considered amendments the US had made to its anti-dumping and countervailing duty laws to the effect that wine and grapes would be considered to be "like products." The Panel rejected that interpretation, holding that,

> because of different physical characteristics, wine and grapes were not "like products" in the sense of the Code. In view of the precise definition of "domestic industry," the Panel considered that producers of the like products could be interpreted to comprise only producers of wine.

In between "too narrow" and "too broad" lies a gulf of uncertainty as to the constraints the GATT places on the proper delineation of the category of "like products" in anti-dumping cases. This definition of "like product" obviously leaves much to the discretion of the implementing authorities, and in looking at the decisional practice of those authorities, one sees that its interpretation has not always been consistent.

### An Example: the EC Practice

Let us take the EC anti-dumping practice with regard to "like products" as an example. There, one sees that "like product" determinations have been made in many different, often irreconcilable, ways. In the beginning, more emphasis was placed on physical and technical characteristics.[18] In recent years, however, end use and consumers' perceptions have become more important, although they are not treated as controlling. The 1988 Serial-impact dot-matrix printer case provided a useful summary of the elements evaluated:

> In order to determine the like product . . . the Commission had first to examine the physical and technical characteristics of the printers. Secondly, when assessing the closeness to and resemblance of the different products, it had also to take into account their application and use. Thirdly, the Commission took the view that in these proceedings the like product determination cannot be separated from the particularities of the printer market in question and the consumers' perceptions of these products. Finally, with regard to the different types of printer models, the Commission thought it should also consider other factors[19] in order to find whether a clear dividing line exists.[20]

As to physical and technical differences, the Commission considered that such differences "should not be interpreted in such a narrow way as to render products not like each other unless these differences have the effect that the application, use or customer's perception of the products in question are fundamentally different."[21]

Therefore, the guidelines that the EC has built up as to the "like product" definition are geared toward an overall appreciation that leaves a great deal of discretion to the implementing authorities. In that regard, the European Court of First Instance, which is charged with judicial review of EC anti-dumping determinations, has deferred to the discretion of the Community institutions, rather than providing further clarification of the proper confines of that determination. It reiterated in a recent case: "[t]he institutions enjoy a wide discretion in analyzing complex economic situations . . . and the determination of "like products" falls within that context."[22]

One can see the consequence of the lack of clear guidelines in some of the recent EC anti-dumping cases, which have sometimes seen a hodgepodge of different types of products grouped together as "like products," while other seemingly similar products were excluded. Examples that will be discussed below are the Footwear case and the Ring Binder Mechanism case. In that regard, the EC "like product" determination seems to lack rigor and could benefit from a market-based approach.

Some cases (such as the Bicycles case, also discussed below) do show that the role of market-based factors, in particular competition and substitutability, in the "like product" determination is increasing. However, it is our thesis that consideration of market place factors should assume pride of place in the determination of like products in an anti-dumping case, and ought to be analyzed with the same level of care and detail as, for example, in similar competition law cases.

*Footwear*

A recent case in which there was an interesting exchange over the right like product definition was the Footwear with textile uppers case.[23] There, the Commission initially included in the category of like products a variety of indoor and outdoor slippers and shoes with rubber or plastic soles and textile uppers for children and adults. The Commission admitted that:

> Although the footwear falling within any of the above categories can cover a wide range of styles and types, as well as different production methods, their essential characteristics, their uses and consumer perception thereof remain basically the same. Therefore, for the purposes of the present proceeding and in accordance with the consistent Community practice, they are regarded as one single product.[24]

Meanwhile, the Commission excluded from the proceeding tennis shoes, basketball shoes, gym shoes, training shoes and espadrilles.

It is difficult to understand how the Commission could have initially grouped products such as indoor slippers and outdoor shoes. On the one hand, one can point to physical differences between these products, but more important seems their end uses and competitive relationship. On its face, it would seem comical to argue that a customer looking for shoes to wear outside would be willing to accept house slippers as a substitute, or vice versa. In any event, it seems inconsistent to consider it appropriate to group slippers and certain outdoor shoes, while concluding that those outdoor shoes (with rubber or plastic soles and textile uppers) should not be associated with tennis shoes, basketball shoes, gym shoes, training shoes and espadrilles.

Indeed, in response to such arguments, the Community institutions changed their approach, as was reflected in the definitive regulation:

> . . . slippers, due to their usual flimsiness, do not appear to be suitable for most outdoor uses. This also appears to be confirmed by the consumers' perception of both products. It has therefore to be concluded that the second "interchangeability test," i.e., whether an indoor shoe can replace an outdoor shoes, is not satisfied and accordingly that slippers and outdoor footwear of the kind under consideration cannot be regarded as one single category of products. Such a conclusion also mean that the results of the investigation would have to distinguish between slippers and outdoor footwear.

Slippers were subsequently withdrawn from the proceedings. However, all the like product issues were not resolved. In particular, certain interested parties had argued that "vulcanized" footwear could not be grouped with footwear made through a process of "injection molding." That issue, among others, has been taken to the European Court of First Instance in pending actions for annulment of these provisional and definitive regulations.[25]

This Footwear case shows that the Community institutions have not yet defined a coherent approach to the like product definition that automatically incorporates a consideration of market-place factors. However, it also shows that the Community will on occasion be persuaded by arguments based upon market factors such as interchangeability and consumer perceptions.

*Ring Binder Mechanisms*

Another recent case of interest is the Ring Binder Mechanism case. There, one sees that "several hundred different types of RBM" varying by "size, shape, and number of rings, the size of the base plate and the system to open the rings (pull open or opening trigger)" were considered as one "like product."[26] However, excluded from the proceeding was a product which is at least as close, both physically and in terms of end use, as any of the other ring binder mechanisms, the lever-arch mechanisms,[27] which incidentally fall into the same CN code as the other ring binder mechanisms.

In the definitive ring binder mechanism regulation, the Commission noted that it had been argued that lever arch mechanisms were more similar to two-ring mechanisms than other types of mechanisms that were included in the proceeding, such as those with 17- and 23-rings. However, the Commission rather tersely responded that "In this respect, the physical characteristics and the market for lever arch mechanisms were found to be sufficiently distinct from those of ring mechanisms to justify these lever arch mechanisms being excluded from the complaint and from the scope of the proceeding."[28]

The decision to exclude lever-arch mechanisms was apparently motivated primarily by the fact that the complainants asked for them to be excluded in their complaint. It is a question whether complainants should have the power to so circumscribe an anti-dumping complainant, and whether that circumscription should, or can, be carried over in the anti-dumping investigation and eventual measures.

*Bicycles*

There have been some recent cases in which market-based factors such as competition and substitutability from the consumer's perspective were discussed at length—although it should be noted from the start that the outcome of that discussion was often a grouping of rather heterogeneous products.[29] An example is the Bicycles from China case.[30]

There, exporters had argued that it was incorrect for the Community institutions to group all types of bicycles together as a single "like product," instead of distinguishing five separate categories, namely mountain bicycles, sports/racing bicycles, touring bicycles, children's bicycles and the residual category of other bicycles. Exporters argued that each of these categories, but in particular mountain bicycles, should be considered separately because there were "clear physical and technical differences as well as differences in the use, manufacturing processes, materials used, marketing, and development of each segment."[31] In the definitive regulation, it was reported that exporters made explicit reference to market-based factors, arguing that these types of bicycle could not be grouped:

> On the grounds that the specific applications and the use of the bicycles in the various categories are *perceived by the market* as being different . . . [in particular] they argued that the mountain bicycle was clearly a separate product in terms of components used, price, and the *perception of the average buyer*.[32] [emphasis ours]

However, the Commission had a different view of the market, and considered in particular that "There is a high degree of interchangeability and, consequently, of competition between models classified in different categories."[33] This position was confirmed in the definitive regulation, where the Community institutions concluded:

> as far as the consumers' perception of the bicycles is concerned, it is true that the different categories are, in principle, intended to meet different end-user requirements. However, end users will regularly put a bicycle in a particular category to a variety of uses and applications.[[34]] Moreover, there is the trend of using bicycles which are designed for more than one specific application. . . . This trend even increases the interchangeability between various categories of bicycles and thus increases the competition between the overlapping areas. There is consequently no clear dividing line based on end-users' application and consumers' perception of different categories.[35]

One exporter took this matter to the European Court of First Instance, asking for annulment of the regulation on this and other grounds.[36] The applicant continued to maintain that these different types of bicycles were not "like products," in part because they were not in competition. In particular, the exporter argued that the Commission should not have concentrated on how the product was actually used once it was purchased, but should have focused on the criteria on which the purchaser bases his choice, since that is the stage at which competition takes place.

However, the Court held that the Community institutions had not exceeded their "wide discretion" in grouping the products concerned in this way. In particular, the Court noted that:

> There is competition both between bicycles in adjoining sub-categories and between those classified in the various sub-categories. . . . [and that the differences the exporter had cited] are not sufficient to establish that all those models have different functions or answer different needs. As is apparent, moreover, from the eighth recital in the preamble to the contested regulation, the fact that consumers tend to use multi-purpose bicycles and that it is possible to alter models by adding various components weakens, even eliminates entirely, the relevance of any distinction drawn between various categories of bicycles for the purposes of an anti-dumping procedure.[37]

In sum, one can see the Bicycles case as an example of a procedure in which much discussion was devoted to the importance of market-based factors in determining the category of "like products." Even so, the outcome of this case failed to reflect what were ostensibly meaningful market place distinctions. Further, in considering these arguments, the Court seems to grant the anti-dumping authorities a wider margin of discretion than it would competition law authorities considering similar questions arise about market definition.

## How Could the Market Based Approach Help?

As we have noted above, what was made clear in the Liquor Taxes cases, both by the Panels and by the Appellate Body, was that a market-based approach to the definition of a category of "like products" is appropriate, the GATT, after all, being concerned with markets.[38] Further, the Liquor Taxes cases stand for the proposition that "like products" are a "subset" of "directly competitive or substitutable products."[39] Therefore, according to that definition, products that do not compete simply cannot be "like products." Within that category of directly competitive or substitutable products, "like products" must have an especially close competitive relationship.

A market-based approach certainly is appropriate in anti-dumping, as anti-dumping measures are specifically meant to correct an injurious situation on a Member's market. The assumption of anti-dumping is that an exporter, by selling products at a lower price abroad than at home, is engaging in unfair competition. His low prices are causing injury to domestic producers, in other words, domestic producers cannot compete against said low-priced imports. The only way that an exporter's behavior can have this impact is if his products are actually in competition with domestically-produced products. If dumped products are not competing with domestic products, then that dumping would have no consequence for domestic producers.

Therefore, showing that products are directly competitive or substitutable would be a logical starting point for the "like product" determination in anti-dumping. It is true that Article VI does not use the term of art "directly competitive or substitutable products" that we find in the Interpretive Note to Article III:2. However, at some level, all products are "in competition" for a consumer's budget, so the starting point to define "like products" must be in some way restricted. The fact that the drafters have chosen not to include the "directly competitive or substitutable" language in Article VI but preferred the "like" language (and have defined that term as "identical" or with "closely resembling") is an indication that their intention was to very strictly limit the category of competitive products in the anti-dumping context.

In other words, in the anti-dumping field, by starting with a determination of directly competitive or substitutable products, at the very least, products that were decidedly *not* in direct competition would be excluded from the definition of "like products," even though they might be physically similar.[40]

Having established that a competitive analysis is necessary to arrive at a "like product" determination, our second point is that there is no reason why the analysis of the competitive relationships between products should be any less serious than that carried out in other domains, such as antitrust. It is in fact disturbing to see that this is not currently the case, as was stated in the European context in the Saint-Gobain+Wacker-Chemie/NOM merger decision. In that case, the competition authorities of the European Commission dismissed the relevance of conclusions about the silicon carbide market made in European anti-dumping proceedings, stating that:

> In an investigation under the Merger Regulation, a detailed assessment of, among other things, the applications of a product in the Community, customer groups or substitute products is given more attention. This can, therefore, lead to a wider or narrower definition of the relevant product

market than would be the case under the assessment of the anti-dumping legislation.[41]

In our view, a market-based analysis of competitive relationships ought to be carried out in anti-dumping cases, and that analysis ought to be conducted in the same way as it would be in other domains, such as competition law. A market is a market, and consumers do not consider two products to be in competition for antitrust purposes, and not in competition for anti-dumping purposes.

It is a somewhat larger question, and one which merits more discussion than the confines of this paper permit, whether the *conclusion* of that analysis ought to be the same in every domain. Competitive relationships differ in degree. We could imagine that one could conclude that in light of the purpose of different provisions, a different degree of competition is of concern in different domains (e.g., anti-dumping might be limited to products in a closer competitive relationship than mergers). However, that does not mean that the market analysis itself should be different. Furthermore, the links between different domains ought to be recognized and distinctions ought to made according to some logic—it is unacceptable for authorities to disregard as irrelevant a competitive analysis simply because it was carried out in a different domain.

At first glance, it may appear that a more rigorous process for determining "like products" is a pro-exporter proposition, in that it might have the effect of limiting the reach of anti-dumping investigations and measures. In fact, the suggestion is rather more neutral than that, because honing in only on those products that meet all the "like product" criteria, that is, are directly competitive or substitutable and physically similar, etc., would not be likely to drastically change the status quo in every case. Furthermore, in certain cases a more tailored "like product" definition could be positive for the domestic industry. As noted above, too broad a definition of "like product" could make proving injury much more difficult. A narrow view could make it easier for the domestic industry to launch and "win" an anti-dumping case. For example, too broad a "like product" definition might have been the downfall of the EC proceedings brought against Luggage and Travel Goods and Briefcases and Schoolbags from China.[42]

Furthermore, the fact that two products are not "like" does not mean that they cannot be separately subject to dumping investigations, which might even be carried out concurrently.[43] Greater precision in the definition of "like products" would simply mean greater surety that "like" is compared to "like," which is after all the overarching intention of the GATT anti-dumping rules. First of all, only domestic producers of that "like product" would be eligible to bring a complaint and would have to be representative of all the producers of that specific product. On the one hand, this might make it easier for a group of producers to meet the representativeness requirements. At the same time, it might mean a greater voice for domestic producers of that particular product who do not wish to lodge a complaint, for whatever reason. Next, the calculation of dumping and injury would be focused on that carefully-defined "like product," which might lead to results that are less of an average and more accurate. Finally, final dumping measures would be directly related to that strictly-defined product category, rather than covering a broad range of products. This would at least partly alleviate the problem that anti-dumping measures that cover a broad range of products inevitably penalize some products that were not dumped, or not as dumped as others.

Authorities would likely argue that so dividing categories of products would render their task of investigating and calculating dumping unworkable. Imagine, they might say, that the "hundreds" of ring binder mechanisms mentioned in the ring binder case had to be separately investigated. However, these kinds of administrative convenience arguments are not very compelling. First of all, it is unlikely that some categories of competing products could not be defined. For example, with the ring binder mechanisms, it might have meant grouping 2-, 3- and 4-ring mechanisms, but considering 6-, 17- and 23-ring mechanisms separately. In an anti-dumping investigation, the European Commission already requires the submission of detailed computerized information. It is not convincing to say that that information could not be, for example, analyzed in a different way.

Using the market as the guide could also reduce the possibility for complainants to piece together a case of injury in an otherwise healthy industry, or to circumscribe their complaint in such a way specifically to avoid hitting their own foreign production. One can imagine a scenario in which domestic producers make 3 products that are all competing and otherwise similar. Few of those producers are succeeding with Product 1, and there is a suspicion that a foreign country is dumping that product on the domestic market. However, most of the producers are having great success with Product 2, so much so that if Product 1 and 2 were considered together, it would be difficult to prove injury. Finally, one of the largest domestic producers has a production facility for Product 3 in the foreign country concerned and will refuse to support the complaint if there is a chance that his own production facility would be included in the duties. In that scenario, there is an incentive to define the complaint in such a way as to include only Product 1. However, if the starting point is that all three products are directly competitive or substitutable and even "like," this kind of manipulation would be more difficult to pull off.

What could be the impact of a more market-based approach in specific cases? Let us look back at the examples discussed above from the EC anti-dumping realm. There, we noted that market factors such as competition and substitutability already sometimes figure in the EC authorities' determinations. However, there is no formal requirement to consider whether products are in direct competition in drawing up the category of "like products," and some recent cases have clearly emphasized physical characteristics and administrative convenience over the indices of the market.

If one looks at the examples from the EC practice cited above, one can imagine that the existence of a threshold requirement to show that products were directly competitive or substitutable could have been of some assistance in arriving at a proper "like product" definition. For example, we noted above that the EC's Footwear and Ring Binder Mechanism cases were characterized by "like product" definitions that seemed too broad.

The Footwear case is an example of how consideration of market-based factors can change the course of an anti-dumping proceeding. There, using its traditional methods, the Commission first took the stance in the provisional regulation that house slippers and some kinds of rubber-soled outdoor shoes were "like." After all, they were both types of shoes with rubber soles and fabric uppers. However, that conclusion became untenable when market factors came to the fore. We see in the definitive regulation that the Community institutions withdrew house slippers from the proceeding due to a lack of "interchangeability" in the eyes of consumers.

The same kind of approach could have been taken in the Ring Binder Mechanism case, where hundreds of styles of mechanisms were considered to be "like products," while the 2-ring lever arch mechanisms were excluded from the "like product" definition. First of all, one may have doubts about the competitive relationship between mechanisms that have 2-rings and those that have 23. In that regard, it seems that some physical characteristics and potential end uses (it has metal rings; it holds paper) took precedence over market factors.[44] On the other hand, it would seem difficult to argue that there is a lack of a competitive relationship between the lever arch mechanism, which is a popular type of 2-ring binder mechanism, and other types of 2-ring mechanisms. Approaching this case on the basis of market-based factors would have been likely to lead to a very different like product definition.

One can imagine in both these examples that if the Community institutions were bound to begin their examination by determining products that are directly competitive or substitutable, the findings of these cases would have been more logical and more strictly tailored to the injury found by the Community institutions. The same can be said for the above-mentioned Bicycles case, where perhaps if the standard had been "directly competitive or substitutable," the class of products concerned would have been more limited. However, in that case, market factors and competitive relationships were discussed at some length—and the Community institutions still defined a class of "like products" that would seem broader than those that are truly "in competition."

On the other hand, treating market factors as the starting line could also provide a way for anti-dumping authorities to address what has so far been the intractable problem of high-quality, high-priced imports that find themselves falling into the same category as dumped imports. This has often been a problem in anti-dumping cases where the intention is to affect low-priced imports, but high priced imports are also swept into the measures. One such example arose in the EC in the recent Bed Linen case,[45] where an Indian exporter of luxury bed linen called "Shades of India" was subject to anti-dumping duties even though the bed linen he imported was sold at the top of the range, bearing brand names such as Cartier.[46] One's first thought could be that if the exporter concerned had cooperated in the investigation, he would have been subject to his own (0%) dumping margin. However, in that case, the Commission found that there were too many companies concerned for it to be feasible to investigate all of them. Therefore, it carried out its dumping calculations by means of sampling—meaning that the dumping duties imposed were an average of different companies' dumping margins.[47] Thus, it is altogether possible that a company such as Shades of India could be hit by dumping duties even though the products it imports were never dumped.

However, the Commission has thus far resisted excluding products from the "like product" definition on the basis of quality differences:

> It should be recalled that it is the standard practice of the Commission that quality differences between the product manufactured in the Community and that manufactured in the third country under investigation does not prevent the imported product from being considered a like product to the extent that the basic physical characteristics and the intended use of the product are not affected by these differences.[48]

However, when quality differences translate to large price differences, it will be possible to argue that two products are not in direct competition with each other. For example, an importer such as Shades of India could argue that its products, being many times more expensive than standard bed sheets, were not in the same league as the other products at issue in that case. Being so much more expensive, consumers could not easily substitute between them. Furthermore, the fact that a consumer is willing to pay several times more for one product than another is already an indication that the products are different. This is not to say that high-quality, high-priced imports cannot be dumped. There may very well be price discrimination between markets for these products. However, drawing such distinctions would ensure that products are judged on their own terms, and bear the consequences of their own market behavior.

## Anti-Dumping Conclusion

As we have demonstrated above, the determination of the category of "like product" is a critical moment in any anti-dumping investigation, one whose effects will reverberate throughout the proceeding and ultimately color its results. Yet the GATT provides few guidelines as to the proper determination of a category of "like products," and that, coupled with the broad discretion traditionally granted the Member authorities, sometimes leads to irreconcilable results.

At the same time, the GATT is peppered with instances in which a "like product" determination is required—not only in anti-dumping have Members tried to grapple with this concept. Although one must always be cognizant that the same terms may have different meanings in different contexts, it is worthwhile to consider whether the results of that struggle in other domains can be of use in another.

Recently, we have seen a few instances, notably in the Liquor Taxes cases, where Panels and the Appellate Body were called upon to analyze the proper determination of "like products" in the context of Article III:2 GATT, the discriminatory tax provision. In that case, the Panels and the Appellate Body emphasized the importance of a market-based approach to the determination of "like products," and in particular, the Panels insisted that "like products" are, of necessity, a "subset" of those products that are directly competitive with and substitutable for each other.

In the Liquor Taxes cases, the Panels and the Appellate Body stressed that "The GATT, after all, is concerned with markets." That logic would also seem appropriate and applicable to the anti-dumping field, as anti-dumping is, after all, about correcting an injurious situation on the market. Already, the competitive relationship between products sometimes figures in the determinations of some Member authorities; an example would be the EC's Bicycles case. However, the Liquor Taxes cases" approach would go further: in particular, market-based factors would not simply be one of many factors considered; they would be an essential threshold consideration, which could be an important preliminary constraint on the "like product" determination. Adding this element of control to the determination of "like products" in the anti-dumping field would be a welcome precision that would, as noted above, have repercussions throughout the proceeding. That being said, more precision in determining "like products" would not prevent anti-dumping authorities from addressing the same products as before, through separate, even concurrent, investigations. However, approaching anti-dumping from the perspective of the market would be a further step toward comparing "like" to "like," and avoiding arbitrary comparisons between apples and oranges in anti-dumping proceedings.

## 3. Applying the Market Based Approach to Environmental Protection

Reconciling environmental protection with liberal trade principles has proven to be difficult. One controversial issue has been to what extent a WTO Member can make its treatment of imported products dependent on processes used in their production, particularly when these processes and production methods (PPMs) leave no trace in the final imported product.[49]

For example, can a WTO Member limit or tax the imports of products that are produced in factories which use production methods that cause damage to the global environment (e.g., without regard to environmentally harmful emissions)? Can a WTO member impose restrictions on imports of animal products, when the animals have been caught in ways that it finds unusually cruel or dangerous (e.g., can the EU ban imports of furs from furry animals caught in leg hold traps; can the US ban imports of tuna or shrimp from countries using fishing methods which unintentionally kill off large number of dolphins or sea turtles)?

As is well-known, when such issues have been litigated in the GATT and WTO to date, the measures taken by importing countries addressing such environmental concerns have been condemned, for various reasons, as being inconsistent with the liberal trade principles of the GATT and the WTO. We are referring in particular to the two Tuna - Dolphin cases, adjudged by the GATT in the early 1990s, and the Shrimp - Turtle case, adjudged by the WTO in 1998.[50] These rulings are of concern to those who worry about the protection of the environment.

Environmentalists have often suggested that a reconsideration of the "like" product definition in the GATT could have changed the outcome of these cases, and would make the GATT (and WTO) more environmentally friendly. For example, in the run up to the 50th anniversary of the GATT in May 1998 the European Parliament passed a resolution in which it:

> Urges the Commission to advocate at the WTO ministerial conference due to meet in Geneva in May that the WTO should draw up a Statement of Understanding concerning the application of the principle of "like products" which enables otherwise identical products to be differentiated where the production or processing of such products have different impacts on the environment, this Statement of Understanding should elaborate on the findings of the Panel on the US tax treatment of automobiles (the so-called "Gas Guzzlers" ruling).[51]

To understand how the "like" product definition came to play such an important role in the trade and environment debate we first have to go back to the Tuna -Dolphin cases.

## The Tuna / Dolphin Cases

The measure at issue here was the US Marine Mammal Protection Act. This Act required US fishermen to use fishing techniques that reduced the taking of dolphin incidental to the harvesting of tuna. Furthermore, the Act also required the US Government to ban the importation of tuna caught with commercial fishing technology that resulted in the incidental killing of dolphins (i.e., yellow fin tuna caught in the Eastern Tropical Pacific Ocean with so-called purse-seine nets, in which large numbers of dolphins were inadvertently caught and so died). The Act also provided that imports of tuna from "intermediary" nations, that did not catch but traded in tuna products, would be prohibited in the US, unless these intermediary nations proved that they, too, banned tuna imports from those countries that were subject to the US import embargo. Finally, the Act provided that whenever tuna was sold in the United States with the optional label "Dolphin Safe," that this indication should be backed up by documentary evidence, showing that such tuna was not caught with purse seine nets or other techniques harmful to dolphins.

In the first Tuna - Dolphin case, decided in August 1991, Mexico attacked these different elements of the Act. Mexico argued, first of all, that the US import embargo violated the GATT's prohibition on quantitative trade restrictions (Article XI:1). Furthermore, Mexico said that the Act was also contrary to the national treatment obligations of Article III, as the Act introduced distinctions between domestic and imported tuna based on the way they were caught. Yet these tuna products were "like" products, and according to Mexico, non-product related PPMs violated Article III.

The United States responded that the import embargo could not be reviewed in isolation, and was therefore not covered by the prohibition of Article XI:1. Rather, the Act contained fishing regulations, applying to tuna caught by US vessels and by foreign vessels, and these internal regulations were compatible with Article III:4 GATT. According to the US, domestic, and foreign tuna were effectively subject to the same fishing requirements, limiting the number of dolphins accidentally caught.

The panel first addressed the complaint about national treatment. It reasoned that the fishing regulations did not constitute internal regulations within the meaning of Article III:4 GATT, as they were not applied to the tuna as such. According to the panel, the fishing regulations "would not directly regulate the sale of tuna and could not possibly affect tuna as a product."[52] For this interpretation the panel relied heavily on the text of Article III:1 and the general Interpretive Note to Article III, by underlining the use of the words "product." Furthermore, the panel referred to an interpretation of Article III:2 relating to border tax adjustment, where a GATT working party had stated in 1970 that taxes that were not directly levied on products were not eligible for adjustment.

To be precise: The panel did not rule that the fishing regulations introduced impermissible distinctions (i.e., discriminated) between "like" products.[53] Rather, the panel ruled that the fishing regulations were not covered at all by Article III:4 GATT.

The panel then went on to find, without much ado, that the US import embargo did constitute a quantitative import restriction in violation of Article XI:1 GATT.[54] That import restriction was not justified under any of the public policy exceptions of Article XX GATT according to the panel.

In the second Tuna - Dolphin case, decided in May 1994, the ban on imports from "intermediary nations" was the object of contention. Again, the panel found that this import ban did not constitute an internal regulation within the meaning of Article III:4 GATT. The panel followed the same reasoning as the first Tuna - Dolphin case.[55]

Instead, the panel reviewed this import ban under Article XI:1 as well, found a violation, and for different reasons than the previous panel rejected the US attempts at justification under Article XX.[56]

Much of the analysis of these two cases has focused on the panels' interpretation of the public policy exceptions in Article XX, notably on such questions as to whether and to what extent the GATT allows its Members to take into account environmental events that take place outside their jurisdiction or territory. In addition, the panels' refusal to consider the fishing regulations under Article III:4 has also come under attack. It has been argued that if only these panels had taken a different view of "like" products, and had allowed distinctions in treatment on the basis of PPMs, the outcome would have been different. However, the recent Shrimp - Turtle case shows that might not necessarily be the case.

## The Shrimp / Turtle Case

This case pitted India, Malaysia, Pakistan, and Thailand against the United States. These four countries attacked a US ban on the importation of shrimps that have been caught with nets without so-called "turtle excluder devices." Again, the United States was concerned about the incidental killing of another sea animal (sea turtles) in the harvesting of fish (this time, shrimp).

The four complainants, as well as a number of intervening countries, argued that the Act violated both the non-discrimination obligations of Article I and XIII as well as Article XI. Interestingly, the United States now changed its defense. Contrary to the Tuna - Dolphin cases, it no longer argued that the conservation measures were internal regulations compatible with Article III:4, which could not be reviewed under Article XI. This time around the United States concentrated its defense on the public policy exceptions of Article XX, having virtually conceded that the import ban constituted a violation of Article XI without mentioning Article III:4.

The panel did not address the complaints about discrimination under Article I and XIII. Having found that the US conservation measure banning shrimp imports constituted a violation of Article XI, the panel considered it was not necessary to review whether the import ban also violated other GATT provisions. The panel went on to consider whether the violation of Article XI was justified under Article XX, and did not think so.[57]

On appeal, the debate centered on the Panel's interpretation of Article XX. Accordingly, the Appellate Body did not have occasion to review the "like product" definition in Article III, I or XIII.

In light of this Shrimp - Turtle case, and other recent WTO case law, notably the Liquor Taxes cases, we offer the following comments on the "like" product definition in the trade and environment debate. We focus on provisions in the GATT Agreement itself, and do not address any of the implementing agreements, such as the Agreements on Technical Barriers to Trade, or on Sanitary and Phytosanitary Measures.

## Preliminary Remark

It will be recalled that the definition of "like" products becomes an issue particularly when a WTO member complains that its exports are being discriminated against.

One such complaint could be that its exports receive less favorable treatment in an importing country than the exports of another WTO member. This complaint could be framed under the general MFN obligation of Article I GATT, or under Article XIII GATT if the complaining member believes that its exports are not receiving equal treatment in the administration of a (lawful) quantitative restriction by the importing country. In such cases the complaining country compares the treatment its exports receive to the treatment received by the products by other exporting countries.

Another complaint could be that regulations of the importing country treat imported products less favorably than domestic products. That would be a complaint under the national treatment obligation of Article III:4 (or, in a complaint about discriminatory taxes, under Article III:2 GATT).

Environmental measures by definition mete out different treatment to products that are considered environmentally-friendly as opposed to products that are considered detrimental to the environment. Understandably, therefore, in the trade and environment debate the question is often raised whether environmental measures amount to illegal discrimination between "like" products under the GATT, or whether the differences in treatment are GATT-legal because the distinction between environmentally-unfriendly and friendly products can legally be made by the importing country.

However, discrimination is not the only concern raised by environmental measures under the GATT.

*Comment I:* The "like" product definition has been circumvented in the evaluation of environmentally inspired trade restrictions under the GATT

The Shrimp - Turtle case shows that one should be careful not to overemphasize the importance of the "like" product definition in the trade and environment debate.

The complaining party may simply choose not to attack an environmental regulation as a discriminatory measure under Article III:4 (I or XIII), or the panel (or Appellate Body) may not reach the issue of discrimination. As in the Shrimp - Turtle case, the dispute may focus on Article XI, the classic prohibition on quantitative trade restrictions. It does not matter then whether the measure affects a larger or smaller group of imports (e.g., all tuna, or only tuna caught with purse-seine nets; all shrimps, or only shrimps caught with turtle excluder devices). The definition of "like" products is irrelevant to Article XI:1. This provision prohibits any quantitative import restriction.

In this connection, one ought to consider as well that once a panel (or the Appellate Body) has found that a particular measure violates one particular GATT obligation, it need not investigate whether the same measure violates other GATT obligations as well.[58] For example, in the Shrimp - Turtle case, the panel declined to decide whether the US measure amounted to discrimination under Article I or XIII GATT. Thus, the "like" product issue did not arise. From the perspective of judicial economy this could be acceptable,[59] albeit that in WTO dispute settlement proceedings this is currently problematic given the way the appellate process is structured.[60]

Furthermore, if the defendant party chooses not to invoke a particular defense (e.g., Article III:4 in the Shrimp - Turtle case), then the panel or the Appellate Body are not at liberty to consider it. WTO dispute settlement is an adversarial, not an inquisitorial system. Panels, and the Appellate Body are impartial and passive.[61]

The interesting question, of course, is why the United States chose not to defend the ban on shrimp imports as a domestic regulation that was compatible with Article III:4 GATT, as it had done in the Tuna - Dolphin cases. There is no official explanation, but it may be that the United States did not feel very confident that this argument could prevail, in light of the Tuna - Dolphin reports (which stated that measures, applied at the border, and distinguishing between products on the basis of requirements that did not affect the product as such, were not covered by Article III:4). Then again, the Tuna - Dolphin reports were never adopted by the GATT Council, and the United States might have reargued the point before a WTO panel. After all, the relationship between Article III and Article XI is a difficult one, and could be clarified further.

Indeed, in our opinion the Tuna - Dolphin rulings are not compelling on this point. This is illustrated by the US Section 337 case. The case was triggered by an order issued by the US International Trade Commission (ITC) pursuant to section 337, banning all imports of a high-strength chemical fiber produced by the Dutch company Akzo. The ITC found, among other things, that Akzo manufactured this fiber in the Netherlands according to a process which was patented in the United States by the US chemical producer DuPont.

At the request of Akzo, the EC Commission complained before a GATT panel that the patent infringement proceedings conducted by the ITC were discriminatory in a number of respects, violating the national treatment principle of Article III:4 GATT. The EC compared administrative litigation before the US International Trade Commission, establishing whether imported products violated a US patent, to regular patent infringement proceedings before a US federal court. For example, one EC complaint was that a defendant before the ITC could not bring a counterclaim, stating that the US industry requesting an import ban violated a US patent of the defendant as well, whereas such counterclaims were admissible in US federal courts of the defendant.

The US ban was imposed in response to a production process used abroad. Furthermore, the availability or not of a counterclaim to litigating parties before the ITC in no way affected the imports "as a product" either. None of these points was raised as an objection against the application of Article III GATT.

The panel found that these administrative proceedings under Section 337 treated imported products less favorably within the meaning of Article III:4 GATT. The panel emphasized that Article III:4 covered all rules and regulations "affecting" the internal sale of imported products. Recalling an earlier precedent,[62] the panel stated that:

> The selection of the word "affecting" would imply . . . that the drafters of the Article intended to cover in paragraph 4 not only the laws or regulations which directly governed the conditions of sale or purchase but also any laws or regulations which might adversely modify the conditions of competition between the domestic and imported products on the internal market.[63]

Accordingly, the panel found that procedural provisions regarding the enforcement of patent rights were covered by Article III:4 GATT. This GATT panel report was adopted by the GATT Council. Furthermore, this broad coverage of Article III was subsequently endorsed by the WTO Appellate Body.[64]

In sum, we submit that the Tuna - Dolphin cases neglected to squarely address the "like" product definition in Article III:4.[65] We see no reason why an environmental regulation, distinguishing between products (both imported and domestic) on the basis of environmental concerns, could not be tested against Article III:4. However, whether such a distinction would be justified is a different matter.

*Comment 2:* The environmental "aims and effects" of domestic regulation or taxes are no longer relevant to the definition of "like" products

After the set-backs of the Tuna - Dolphin cases, environmentalists took some heart from two other GATT cases, decided in the early 1990s. In these cases, a different approach to defining "like" products in Article III:4 GATT was outlined.

First, in the US - Malt Beverages case, a panel decided that marketing regulations of several US states, distinguishing between low alcohol and high alcohol beer, did not violate Article III:4 GATT. While the complainant, Canada, had argued that these regulations discriminated against high alcohol beer, a product "like" low alcohol beer, the panel disagreed. The distinction was not introduced for protectionist motives, but out of public health concerns (and for revenue maximization purposes), according to the panel.[66] This panel report was adopted by the GATT Council in 1993.

Second, in the Gas Guzzler case the EC attacked a number of US measures which it believed adversely affected its car exports to the United States. For instance, the EC argued that an extra sales tax on cars with relatively low fuel economy introduced a distinction between "like" products, and therefore was inconsistent with Article III:2 GATT. The panel disagreed. The tax was not shown to have protectionist aims and effects, but rather served a laudable environmental motive: increased conservation of fossil fuels.[67] This time, however, the GATT Council did not approve the report.

One can appreciate that environmentalists were encouraged by these two reports. Apparently, environmental objectives could justify a distinction in treatment between similar products. From this perspective, only one hurdle still needed to be overcome: in both these cases the public health or environmental concerns related to the territory of the importing country: essentially, discouraging intoxication of US beer drinkers, and reducing fuel consumption in the United States. Could also environmental concerns relating to events outside the territory or jurisdiction of an importing country justify a difference in treatment of otherwise "like" products under Article III:4 (e.g., could the incidental killing of dolphins or sea turtles by foreign fishermen outside US territorial waters justify import bans on tuna or shrimp?).

Building on these two GATT reports several environmentally concerned scholars answered this question affirmatively. They argued that the objections to extraterritorial and extrajurisdictional measures, expressed in the Tuna - Dolphin cases in connection with Article XX GATT, could be overcome.[68]

However welcome the Malt Beverages and Gas Guzzler reports may have been from an environmental perspective, they met with strong resistance in other circles. One observation was that the "aims and effect test" test rendered the regulatory justifications of Article XX superfluous,[69] and was not based on the text of Article III GATT. Furthermore, this test risked imposing an impossible burden of proof on WTO members who felt that their products were being discriminated against by the domestic regulations or internal taxes of another member. "Protectionist intent can always be hidden by smart lawyers who recite the recitals of legislation in order to give it a respectable purpose and by cautious legislators which are careful in their choice of words. . ."[70] In other words, trade lawyers felt that the "aims and effects" test jeopardized a fundamental objective of the GATT: to counter protectionist measures unrelated to any environmental concerns.

The "aims and effects test" was never adopted in WTO. In the Japanese Liquor Taxes II case the panel explicitly rejected this test in defining "like" products within the meaning of Article III:2 GATT. The panel emphasized textual arguments to reject this test.[71] The Appellate Body accepted this reasoning.[72]

The Liquor Taxes cases concerned only an interpretation of Article III:2, and can thus be distinguished from the interpretation of other GATT provisions, such as Article III:4, I or XIII. The text of these provisions differs from Article III:2. Yet any attempt to apply the "aims and effect" test to discrimination claims under another GATT provision would have to contend with the concerns raised by this test (such as burden of proof).

*Comment 3:* The current market-based approach to defining "like" products in Article III will permit some, but not all distinctions in regulatory treatment that may be desirable from an environmental perspective

Having rejected the "aims and effects" test, the Japanese Liquor Taxes II case introduced a new approach. To appreciate this new approach, it will be recalled that the GATT provision at issue in this case, Article III:2 GATT, establishes two prohibitions on tax discrimination: a stringent prohibition on tax discrimination of "like" products, and a somewhat looser prohibition of tax discrimination regarding so-called "directly competitive or substitutable" products.

*The Test of Japanese Liquor Taxes II*

For the panel the appropriate test to define whether two products are "like" or "directly competitive or substitutable" was the marketplace, not just physical characteristics, tariff classification, etc. taken in isolation. According to the panel, "what is at issue is the responsiveness of consumers to the various products offered in the market."[73] The Appellate Body confirmed: "The GATT 1994 is a commercial agreement, and the WTO is concerned, after all, with markets."[74]

Another important holding of the panel was its clarification of the relationship between "like" and "directly competitive or substitutable" products. According to the panel, as confirmed by the Appellate Body, "like" products are a "subset" of "directly competitive or substitutable" products.[75] In other words, from a demand or consumer perspective the relationship between "like" products must be even closer than between "directly competitive or substitutable." The importance of this holding has not always been understood. Some have mistakenly argued that, according to Japanese

Liquor Taxes II, consumer perceptions were not relevant to a "like" product finding.[76]

Individual factors like tariff bindings, that were traditionally associated with a finding of likeness, are no longer decisive. According to the panel, tariff bindings might "confirm" whether products are "like," especially when the tariff bindings are sufficiently detailed.[77]

Various factors may influence consumer demand. In Japanese Liquor Taxes II, common end uses and physical characteristics of products received particular attention. This led some commentators to conclude that this precedent had again struck a blow to the environmental cause, by refusing to consider non-physical characteristics or attributes.[78] However, such comments placed too much emphasis on the facts of this particular dispute, while ignoring the overarching approach announced by the panel.

For instance, it was noted that the panel in Japanese Liquor Taxes II found the fact of vodka being put through a different filtration process than shochu insufficient grounds to conclude that they were not "like" products. From this finding it was concluded that the panel rejected non-physical characteristics (such as PPMs) as a basis for distinguishing "like products" in Article III.[79] However, the panel's reasoning was different. The panel found that the difference in filtration processes did not contradict the "likeness" of vodka and shochu, because this difference was not shown to have affected consumer preferences.[80]

In the wake of the Tuna - Dolphin cases, environmentalists argued that many problems in the trade and environment debate could be resolved if "like" products were defined from the consumer perspective. Thus, it was argued that American consumers did make a distinction between tuna that was harvested in a dolphin-safe manner and tuna that was not.[81] As one author stated, the Marine Mammal Protection Act was the result of "grass-roots consumer movement."[82]

Can one conclude then that, with the approach of Japanese Liquor Taxes II, environmental concerns could finally be done justice; notably, that PPMs would become lawful under Article III:4 GATT? The short answer is: the market-based approach will solve some, perhaps many, but not all environmental concerns.

*The Implications of Japanese Liquor Taxes II*

Let us first acknowledge that, because of a textual difference, like products may be defined more or less broadly in Article III:4 than in Article III:2.[83] This is still an open question.[84] However, it seems fair to assume that the market-based approach adopted in Japanese Liquor Taxes II could also apply in relation to Article III:4. Furthermore, let us also recall our view that the

Tuna - Dolphin cases wrongly decided that regulations must affect products as such, in order to be covered by Article III.[85] In other words, PPMs, like procedural rules on patent litigation, can be tested against Article III:4 GATT.

According to Japanese Liquor Taxes II one must conduct a market analysis. If two products are recognized to be different in the marketplace, in that consumers do not consider them to be close substitutes, then they are not "like" and governments can subject them, for instance, to different sales regulations without running afoul of Article III:4, or to different taxes without infringing Article III:2.

It is not sufficient for a WTO Member to make a political statement that consumers want, or should want, to make a distinction between different products out of environmental or other concerns. "Like" products are not determined by legislative command; they are created by market perceptions. A market-based approach, envisaged by Japanese Liquor Taxes II, requires an economic analysis, case-by-case, country-by country, of consumer responses.[86] Factors such as physical characteristics, end use and price will usually determine whether two products are in a sufficiently close competitive relationship to be considered "like" products.

With this new approach, a number of environmental concerns can be addressed, notably when consumers perceive a difference between environmentally friendly and environmentally unfriendly products. The point to be stressed here is that the difference consumers perceive between two products may well be unrelated to environmental concerns; yet such difference in consumer perception could allow the government to subject these products to different regulations out of environmental concern.

*Physically Identical and Non-Identical Products*

To begin with, one should not too easily assume that products are physically identical. Different production processes can easily lead to some variations in the final product, however small these may be. Taken by themselves, such small distinctions in physical characteristics may seem negligible. Under the old test of "like" products, where physical characteristics tended to be analyzed in isolation, such small distinctions might not have prevented the conclusion that these various products were "like."

Small variations, however, can be very important to consumers, and influence the use to which they put a product (consider, e.g., tap water v. bottled water). Consumers may also be willing to pay a lot for a small difference.[87] From the market-based perspective of the Japanese Liquor Taxes II case, these would be good reasons to conclude that such products are "unlike." In those circumstances, governments can tax and regulate these products differently too.[88]

In other cases the distinctions between environmentally friendly and unfriendly products may be quite important. For example, large gas guzzling cars (e.g. a Rolls Royce) normally do not compete directly with small, fuel-efficient compacts (e.g. a Volkswagen Polo). Their technical specifications and price, to mention two obvious factors, will usually put them in separate consumer markets. Changes in the price of a Polo (say a 10% price increase) presumably will have very little effect on the demand for Rolls Royces. In the market-based approach towards interpreting Article III:2 and 4 GATT, Volkswagen Polos and Rolls Royces are not "like" products. Countries would therefore be free to subject gas guzzlers to higher sales taxes, or different domestic regulations generally, compared to compact cars.

Let us also consider, however, products from different manufacturers or origin that are physically identical (a very small group of products indeed). Their end use will be the same and one would normally expect that consumers will not be willing to pay much more for one as opposed to the other product. In other words, consumers will supposedly not have a strong preference either way. From a demand perspective, these products would then be substitutable. In such cases, non-physical characteristics related to their production process do not influence the consumer's choice for one or the other product, and regulatory distinctions or tax differences between such products would easily run afoul of Article III GATT.[89]

Nevertheless, it is conceivable that consumers do perceive a difference between physically identical products. For instance, when faced with a choice between dolphin-safe tuna and other tuna, consumers in an environmentally-conscious country might show a strong preference for dolphin-safe tuna. Their preference for dolphin-safe tuna might be reflected in their willingness to pay a higher price for such tuna; prices of dolphin-safe tuna might remain relatively impervious to price changes of other tuna (Presumably, consumers would need to have information, such as labeling, to make an informed decision). In those circumstances, it would be possible to argue that dolphin-safe tuna is "unlike" other tuna. The country involved might then lawfully distinguish between these two types of tuna in sales regulations and taxes.

On the other hand, if despite being informed about the production characteristics of a particular product, consumers as a whole (rather than specific interest groups) do not differentiate between environmentally "safe" and "unsafe" products, the market-based approach of the Japanese Liquor Taxes II case does not help the government to make regulatory distinctions between these products. These distinctions will then be vulnerable to attack under one of the GATT's prohibitions on discrimination (such as Article III:4).

In other words, market perception comes first; government regulation comes second. When assessing market conditions under Article III, government regulation cannot be deemed to anticipate or guide consumer perceptions. One may have certain reservations to accept this approach when trying to shield each and every environmental regulation from attack. Yet one has to take into account the origins and driving force of the GATT, which has no sympathy for planned economies and state intervention. Experience of the past ten years shows a general consensus that this is what governments want for their economies. If governments want something else to take care of the environment, then they should negotiate an international framework to deal with that.

In sum, it is expected that a good many environmental regulations, which distinguish environmentally friendly from unfriendly products, will not violate the national treatment principle of Article III GATT. After all, small and large differences in physical characteristics will easily make a difference from the consumer perspective. Once the consumer has recognized a difference between products, the market-based approach towards interpreting Article III GATT should permit regulatory distinctions between these products that address environmental concerns.

One can even think of cases where the market-based approach to defining like products might shield particular PPMs, which impose distinctions between physically identical products, against GATT attacks about discrimination between "like" products. This is conceivable in those countries where the product distinctions made in these PPMs reflect strong and broadly shared consumer preferences.

However, it is also clear that not all PPMs can be so immunized in all WTO Member countries. Anticipating or guiding consumer preferences through PPMs does not fit well into a market-based approach. If this were admitted, one easily ends up inquiring again about the aims and effect of regulations, trying to distinguish laudable ("save dolphins") from objectionable ("buy national") guidance of consumers. The Japanese Liquor Taxes II case has rejected that approach.

Therefore, the market-based approach to "like" product definitions may well be helpful to the evaluation of environmental measures under Article III GATT. But it does not offer a general solution to the problems posed by PPMs under the GATT.

## Environmental Conclusion

Before taking any further positions in the trade versus environment debate, it makes sense to clarify where the problems in GATT 1994 lie.

One would first need to assess in more detail whether the new market-based approach to interpreting Article III:2 exposes environmental regulations to more or fewer legal challenges. Our guess is that quite a few product distinctions environmentalists like to make are already recognized by consumers, though perhaps for other reasons; this would need to be verified. Once product distinctions are recognized in the marketplace, governments are free, in principle, to regulate and tax these products differently. From this perspective then, it may not even be necessary to change the "like" product definition in order to save environmental regulation.

Second, as far as PPMs are concerned, one first has to realize that they concern a relatively small group of internationally traded products, i.e., physically identical products. As we have seen, so far the problem with PPMs has not been caused so much by the definition of "like" product, but rather by the relationship between Article XI and Article III GATT. We have submitted that the Tuna - Dolphin panels have wrongly ruled that regulations relating to non-physical characteristics of products are not covered by Article III. There is precedent for the opposite view, which we believe to be better.

Assuming then that such regulations are covered by Article III GATT, it is conceivable that some PPMs would be GATT-legal. Again, the critical question would be whether consumers recognize the difference between the products concerned. However, it also seems safe to assume that some PPMs introduce distinctions between products, which the market still treats as interchangeable (e.g., because consumers do not have all the relevant information to make the distinction, or are unwilling to pay a higher price for a seemingly similar product because they are not deterred by the environmental risks of the cheaper substitute).

If indeed the current market-based approach to defining "like" products is not the panacea to render all desirable environmental regulations (notably, all PPMs) invulnerable to attack under the GATT, one might consider the approach suggested by the European Parliament in the above-cited resolution: legislate.

One can think of different forms: a formal amendment of the GATT 1994, requiring consensus by the WTO membership,[90] or the adoption of an authoritative interpretation of the "like" product concept, requiring a three fourth majority of the WTO membership.[91] On substance, one might consider reinstating the "aims and effects" test, which was rejected in the Japanese Liquor Taxes II; or one could think of a different test, more explicitly allowing non-physical characteristics to differentiate between "unlike" products.

One practical objection to this approach is that it is very difficult to obtain the requisite votes amongst the WTO Members to either amend or "interpret" a WTO Agreement. One could also observe that to date the WTO membership never adopted a formal interpretation.

We have a substantive concern with the suggestion of the European Parliament. The liberalization of trade and the protection of the environment are both laudable policies. As far as we are concerned, neither one of these policies is necessarily superior to the other, nor are they mutually exclusive. However, the implementation of these policies is quite different.

Trade liberalization, as contemplated in the GATT, seeks to minimize government intervention, and to allow the market mechanism, and private initiative, as much as possible free reign. Environmental protection seeks to curb wasteful private or undesirable action; the method of choice is government regulation.

There is a serious risk that, by changing a key concept such as "like" product in the GATT, one may protect environmental objectives better, but at a considerable cost to the trade liberalization framework. One spill-over was already mentioned above: the "aims and effect" test may look attractive from an environmental perspective, but it probably creates considerable obstacles to attack potentially protectionist taxes and regulations. By allowing countries to differentiate the treatment of products on the basis of non-physical characteristics only, one not only allows them to differentiate on the basis of presumably desirable environmental standards, but also on the basis of social and other conditions in the exporting country. Instead of creating a panacea, one may well end up opening Pandora's box.[92]

On the other hand, if the "like" product definition is not changed, some laudable environmental measures (notably, PPMs) may remain vulnerable to attack under Article III GATT, even under the new market-based approach. The current exceptions listed in Article XX may not provide a way out. For instance, being exceptions to basic rules, they will be narrowly interpreted.[93]

For those cases we believe the better approach would be to negotiate a dedicated WTO agreement, while recognizing the practical difficulties of obtaining sufficient support (and trade offs) in WTO. This agreement may be limited to immunizing particular PPMs against GATT attack. Other specific issues (e.g. restrictions on trade in waste) could be tackled as well. Again, however, we would recommend to verify carefully whether the GATT (and WTO) framework does indeed present a problem for particular types of environmental regulation, and to limit solutions to those problems.

NOTES

1. See the Panel Report of 2 July 1998 (WT/DS54/R, WT/DS55/R, WT/DS59/R, WT/DS64/R) in the *Indonesia - Certain Measures Affecting The Automobile Industry* case.

2. Panel Report of 11 July 1996 (WT/DS8/R, WT/DS10/R, WT/DS11/R) and Appellate Body Report of 4 October 1996 (WT/DS8/AB/R, WT/DS10/AB/R, WT/DS11/AB/R) in the case *Japan - Taxes on Alcoholic Beverages* (the "*Japanese Liquor Taxes II*" case).
As mentioned above, we take note of the fact that the Panel in the *Japanese Liquor Taxes II* case took care to qualify its remarks by stating that its findings were *"relevant only for the interpretation of the term "like product" as it appears in Article III:2."* (at para. 6.20).

3. Panel Report of 17 September 1998 (WT/DS75/R WT/DS84/R) and Appellate Body Report of 18 January 1999 (WT/DS75/AB/R, WT/DS84/AB/R) in the case *Korea - Taxes on Alcoholic Beverages* (the "*Korean Liquor Taxes*" case).

4. *Japanese Liquor Taxes II* Panel Report, at para. 6.22.

5. *Id.*

6. *Japanese Liquor Taxes II* Appellate Body Report, at 25.

7. *Korean Liquor Taxes* Appellate Body Report, at para. 114.

8. Cited above at note 1.

9. *Id,* at para. 14.111.

10. See Article 5.4 of the Anti-dumping Agreement.

11. See the definition of "domestic industry" under Article 4 of the Agreement on Implementation of Article VI of the GATT 1994.

12. See para. 1 of Article VI.

13. See Article 4.1 of the Anti-dumping Agreement.

14. Where the same product exists, the determination of a "like product" is uncontroversial. On the other hand, difficulties can arise when there is no identical product sold at home or where the Commission uses an analogue country for the calculation of normal value.

15. See Article 5.8 of the Anti-dumping Agreement.

16. At the Havana Conference, as noted by GATT, ANALYTICAL INDEX: GUIDE TO GATT LAW AND PRACTICE, UPDATED 6TH EDITION (1995), at 227.

17. By the 1959 Group of Experts on "Anti-dumping and Countervailing Duties." That Group also *"pointed out that the meaning of 'like product' as agreed by them should not be interpreted either too broadly so as to cover products of a different kind with higher prices on the internal market, nor too stringently so as to elude the application of paragraph 1(a) of Article VI." (Id.)*

18. See Vermulst & Waer, E.C. ANTI-DUMPING LAW AND PRACTICE, Sweet & Maxwell, 1996, at 282.

19. In that case, the "other factors" considered were the impact of technical progress, the fact that producers themselves make no distinction between the products classified in different market segments with regard to production, distribution or accounting.

20. Commission Regulation No 1418/88 of 17 May 1988 imposing a provisional anti-dumping duty on imports of serial-impact dot-matrix printers originating in Japan, OJ L 130, 26/05/88 12, at point 11. The definition of the like product in this case was challenged and upheld by the European Court of Justice in Case C-69/89, *Nakajima All Precision Co. Ltd v Council of the European Communities* [1991] ECR I-2069.
The Commission's reasoning has recently been reiterated in Commission Regulation 165/97 of 28 January 1997 imposing a provisional anti-dumping duty on imports of certain footwear with textile uppers originating in the People's Republic of China and Indonesia: *"It should be recalled that the main criteria to be applied in the determination of the 'like product` are based on the general technical or physical characteristics, the use or functions and finally, the consumer's perception of products. . .,"* OJ L 29, 31/01/1997 3, at point 18.

21. *Id,* at point 12.

22. Judgment of the Court of First Instance of 15 October 1998, case T-2/95, *Industrie des Poudres Sphériques v Council of the European Union,* not yet reported, at recital 204. See also Judgment of the Court of First Instance of 25 September 1997, case T-170/94, *Shanghai Bicycle Corporation v. Council,* 1997 ECR II-1383. Important past Court cases that treated like product issues were the numerous *Photocopiers* cases, such as Case C-171/87 *Canon v Council* [1992] ECR I-1237; Case C-174/87 *Ricoh v Council* [1992] ECR I-1335; and Case C-179/87 *Sharp Corporation v Council* [1992] ECR I-1635.

23. This case was initiated by Commission Notice of Initiation of an anti-dumping proceeding concerning imports of certain footwear originating in the People's Republic of China and Indonesia, OJ C45 of 22/02/95, 2. The provisional regulation was Commission Regulation 165/97, OJ L 29, 31/01/1997 3, and the definitive regulation was Council Regulation 2155/97, OJ L 298 of 01/11/97, 1.

24. *Id,* to provisional regulation, at point 16.

25. Action brought on 19 December 1997 by BSC Footwear Supplies and Others against the Council of the European Union, Case T-598/97, OJ C 55, 20/02/98, 30, and Action brought on 28 March 1997 by British Shoe Company and others against the Commission of the European Communities, OJ C 166, 31/05/97, 17.

26. According to the Commission, because *"all RBM have the same basic physical characteristics and that the types of RBM can, within a certain range, replace each other."* See Commission Regulation 1465/96 of 25 July 1996 imposing a provisional anti-dumping duty on imports of certain ring binder mechanisms originating in Malaysia and the People's Republic of China, OJ L 187, 26/07/1996, 47 at point 12 and 13.

27. *Id.,* at point 12. Lever arch mechanisms are a common type of 2-ring binder mechanism in which the rings are opened by means of a lever.

28. Council Regulation 119/97 of 20 January 1997 imposing definitive anti-dumping duties on imports of certain ring binder mechanisms originating in Malaysia and the People's Republic of China and collecting definitively the provisional duties imposed, OJ L 22, 24/01/1997 1 at point 14. Note that the Court of First Instance recently dismissed an action for annulment that was brought against this regulation, based not on "like product" but on procedural issues

(judgment of the Court of First Instance of 19 November 1998, Case T-147/97, *Champion Stationery Mfg Co. Ltd., et al v. Council of the European Union*, not yet reported.)

29. See, for example, the *Photocopiers* cases, cited above.

30. See Commission Regulation 550/93 of 5 March 1993 imposing a provisional anti-dumping duty on imports of bicycles originating in the People's Republic of China (OJ 1993 L 58, 12) and Council Regulation 2474/93 of 8 September 1993 imposing a definitive anti-dumping duty on imports into the Community of bicycles originating in the People's Republic of China and collecting definitively the provisional anti-dumping duty (OJ 1993 L 228, 1). These categories of bicycles were also grouped together in the more recent *Bicycles from Indonesia, Malaysia, and Thailand* case, Council Regulation 648/96 of 28 March 1996, OJ 1996 L 91, 1. This regulation was recently upheld by a judgment of the Court of First Instance of 17 July 1998, Case T-118/96, *Thai Bicycle Industry & Co. Ltd v Council of the European Union*, not yet reported.

31. See the provisional regulation in the *Bicycles from China* case, at recital 10.

32. See the definitive regulation in the *Bicycles from China* case, at recital 7.

33. *Ibid.*

34. One might query whether, if the *Footwear* case had been subject to the same approach, would the Commission have not found that many persons buy tennis shoes, not to play tennis, but to wear around town? It could be said that basketball shoes, like mountain bikes, have become fashion statements. That would bring these products into a closer relationship with the rubber-soled outdoor shoes that were subject to that proceeding.

35. See the provisional regulation in the *Bicycles from China* case, at recital 8.

36. Judgment of the Court of First Instance of 25 September 1997, case T-170/94, *Shanghai Bicycle Corporation v. Council of the European Union,* 1997 ECR II-1383.

37. *Id.,* at recital 69.

38. See, *supra,* text at note 4.

39. *Japanese Liquor Taxes II* Panel Report, at para. 6.22, *Korean Liquor Taxes* Appellate Body report at para. 118.

40. Arguably, dumped imports that simply compete with domestic products could cause injury. However, in that regard we are inclined to agree with the position taken by Vermulst and Waer, who state:

*"the definition of like product is an independent, separate decision that has to be made on the basis of the definition of Article 2(12)* [now Article 1(4)]. *In a case like this it is indeed possible that a product* [in their example, which was not produced in the Community] *can nevertheless cause injury, but that does not make it a like product. The like product issue operates on its own terms as a limit on the injury determination and should not be viewed as a function of injury."* See Vermulst and Waer, *supra,* at 285.

41. OJ 1997 L247, 1, at recital 47.

42. See Commission Decision of 1 July 1997 terminating the anti-dumping proceeding concerning imports of certain luggage and travel goods originating in the People's Republic of

China, OJ 1997 L 174, 53, and Commission Decision of 9 June 1997 terminating the anti-dumping proceeding concerning imports of certain briefcases and schoolbags originating in the People's Republic of China, OJ 1997 L 151, 44.

43. For example, the above-mentioned cases were based on complaints that were simultaneous and investigated concurrently with the procedure against *Handbags from China,* the only one of the three that resulted in definitive duties, see Council Regulation 1567/97 of 1 August 1997 imposing a definitive anti-dumping duty on imports of leather handbags originating in the People's Republic of China and terminating the proceeding concerning imports of plastic and textile handbags originating in the People's Republic of China, OJ 1997 L 208, 31.

44. If physical similarities and end uses are permitted such a decisive role, then one can imagine that Fiat Unos and Rolls Royces could be "like products," because they both have 4-wheels, an engine, etc., and are used for personal transportation. However, in competition-type analysis these two products would never find themselves in the same relevant product market.

45. Commission Regulation 1069/97 of 12 June 1997 imposing a provisional anti-dumping duty on imports of cotton-type bed linen originating in Egypt, India, and Pakistan, OJ 1997 L 156, 11, and Council Regulation (EC) No 2398/97 of 28 November 1997 imposing a definitive anti-dumping duty on imports of cotton-type bed linen originating in Egypt, India, and Pakistan, OJ 1997 L 332, 1. Note that Shades of India, *inter alia,* was granted the "cooperating companies" duty rate of 11.6% subsequent to Council Regulation 1508/98 of 13 July 1998 amending Regulation 2398/97, OJ L 200, 16/07/1998, 9.

46. See for example "EC anti-dumping rules trap Indian high-quality exports," FINANCIAL TIMES of 3 February 1998.

47. The same is true when the Community institutions treat a country as being "non-market." Then, barring individual treatment for particular companies, all companies bear an average dumping rate.

48. See the provisional regulation in the *Handbags from China* case, cited above, at recital 20.

49. On PPMs, and their relation to liberal trade principles, see generally Stevens, *Trade and the Environment: The PPMs Debate* in SUSTAINABLE DEVELOPMENT AND INTERNATIONAL LAW 239–247 (Lang ed., Graham & Trotman/Martinus Nijhoff, London, 1995).

50. Panel Report of 15 May 1998 (WT/DS58/R) and Appellate Body Report of 12 October 1998 (WT/DS58/AB/R) in the case *United States - Import Prohibition Of Certain Shrimp And Shrimp Products.*

51. See European Parliament Resolution A4–0125/98 on environmental, health, and consumer protection aspects of world trade, adopted on 30 April 1998, available on http:/wwwdb.europarl.eu.int.

52. See first *Tuna - Dolphin* Report, *US - Restrictions on Imports of Tuna from Mexico*, BISD, 39th Supp. 155 (1993), at para. 5.14 (unadopted).

53. A finding of discrimination was read into the panel report by, e.g. Esty & Geradin, *Environmental Protection and International Competitiveness: A Conceptual Approach,* 32 JOURNAL OF WORLD TRADE 7, 24 (No 3, 1998); Snape & Lefkovitz, *Searching for GATT's Environmental* Miranda*: Are "Process Standards" Getting "Due Process"* 27 CORNELL INTERNATIONAL LAW JOURNAL 777, 790 (1994).

54. Thus, the United States made no attempt to justify its disputed measures under the exception to Article XI:1, which is set forth in Article XI:2(c)(i). According to this exception, import restrictions on fisheries products are tolerated, if they are necessary to the enforcement of measures restricting the marketing or production of like domestic products, or of domestic products for which the imported product can be "directly substituted." This exception was originally designed to immunize certain US agricultural stabilization programs designed to protect domestic farmers and fishermen. See Jackson, WORLD TRADE AND THE LAW OF GATT 317–320 (1969). Yet, on the face of it, the text of this exception allows application to other circumstances, such as environmental protection programs, as well. One difficulty could be the requirement that, in order to benefit from this exception, a restriction shall not "reduce the total of imports relative to the total of domestic production, as compared with the proportion which might reasonably be expected to rule between the two in the absence of restrictions."

55. See second *Tuna - Dolphin* Report (unadopted), at paras. 5.8–5.9 (1994).

56. For a fuller discussion see Petersmann, INTERNATIONAL AND EUROPEAN TRADE AND ENVIRONMENTAL LAW AFTER THE URUGUAY ROUND 27–28, 31–35 (Kluwer, London etc., 1997).

57. See *Shrimp - Turtle* Panel Report, at para. 7.23.

58. See WTO Appellate Body Report of 25 April 1997 (WT/DS33/AB/R) in the case *India - Measure Affecting Imports of Woven Wool Shirts and Blouses,* at 18–20, or the WTO Appellate Body Report of 13 July 1998 (WT/DS69/AB/R) in the case *EC - Measures Affecting the Importation of Certain Poultry Products,* at 52–55.

59. For critical views about the judicial economy principle in the context of WTO litigation see the (as yet unpublished) remarks of Judge Pescatore at the Trier conference, on WTO and EC (11–12 June 1998).

60. Because the Appellate Body lacks remand authority, it may venture into issues that were left undecided by the panel. This is problematic, as the Appellate Body may then give a final decision, within extremely short deadlines, on an issue that has not been fully explored at the panel stage. See Palmeter, *The WTO Appellate Body Needs Remand Authority,* 32 JOURNAL OF WORLD TRADE 41–44 (No 1, 1998).

61. Although this has been standard practice, there are instances where panels or the Appellate Body have been more activist. See, e.g., WTO Appellate Body Report of 5 June 1998 (WT/DS62/AB/R, WT/DS67/AB/R, WT/DS68/AB/R) in the case *EC - Customs Classification of Certain Computer Equipment,* at para. 89 (where the Appellate Body itself raised an argument, while explicitly mentioning that it had never been made by one of the parties during the panel proceedings or on appeal). Nevertheless, no instance is known of a case where a panel or the Appellate Body added a legal claim or defense.

62. See GATT Panel Report, *Italy - Discrimination against Imported Agricultural Machinery,* BISD, 7th Supp., 60 (1958).

63. See GATT Panel Report, *US - Section 337 of the Tariff Act of 1930,* BISD, 36th Supp., 345, 385 (1990).

64. See WTO Appellate Body Report, *Japanese Liquor Taxes II,* at 16.

65. The legal reasoning of the first *Tuna - Dolphin* report, and notably its reliance on the *Border Tax Adjustment* Report, has also been criticized elsewhere. See Thaggert, *A Closer Look*

*at the Tuna Dolphin Case: "Like Products" and Extrajurisdictionality in the Trade and Environment Context* in TRADE & THE ENVIRONMENT: THE SEARCH FOR BALANCE 68–95 (Cameron, Demaret & Geradin eds., Cameron & May, London, 1994).

66. See GATT Panel Report *United States - Measures Affecting Alcoholic and Malt Beverages,* adopted on 19 June 1992, BISD 39th Supp., 206 (1993) at paras. 5.70–5.77.

67. See *Gas Guzzler* Report (1994 GATT Doc. DS31/R September 29, 1994), at para. 5.17 and following.

68. See, e.g., Diem, FREIHANDEL UND UMWELTSCHUTZ IN GATT UND WTO 93–110 (Nomos Verlaggesellschaft, Baden-Baden 1996).

69. See Farber & Hudec, *GATT Legal Restraints on Domestic Environmental Regulations* in 2 FAIR TRADE AND HARMONIZATION 59, 73 (Bhagwati & Hudec eds., MIT Press, Cambridge, 1996).

70. See Kuyper, *Booze and Fast Cars: Tax Discrimination under GATT and the EC,* LEGAL ISSUES OF EUROPEAN INTEGRATION 129, 136 (1996/1).

71. See *Japanese Liquor Taxes II* Panel Report, at para. 6.16.

72. See Appellate Body Report, at 20 and following (though statements at 18 may suggest that while a complainant need not prove protectionist intent or effect in order to establish his tax discrimination case in relation to like products, the complaint might still be rejected in the event a defendant can show the absence of protectionist "application"—the Appellate Body did not explain what exactly a defendant would have to show to succeed).

73. See *Japanese Liquor Taxes II* Panel Report, at para. 6.21 and following.

74. See *Japanese Liquor Taxes II* Appellate Body Report, at 25. The Appellate Body confirmed this approach in the *Korean Liquor Taxes* case, at its para. 114.

75. See *Japanese Liquor Taxes II* Panel Report, at para. 6.22; *Korean Liquor Taxes* case at para. 118.

76. See, e.g., Canada's argument in the *Hormones* case, WTO Panel Report of 18 August 1997 (WT/DS48/R) in the case *EC - Measures concerning Meat and Meat Products,* at section IV.349. Canada seemed to confuse here a fact-specific finding in *Japanese Liquor Taxes II* (that vodka and shochu were "like" products), with the general market-based approach towards defining "like" products which, being a subset of "directly competitive or substitutable" products, does involve an evaluation of consumer demand and preferences.

77. *Id.*

78. See Zedalis, *Product v. Non-Product Based Distinctions in GATT Article III Trade and Environment Jurisprudence: Recent Developments,* EUROPEAN ENVIRONMENTAL LAW REVIEW 108, 110 (April 1997).

79. See Zedalis, *id.*

80. See *Japanese Liquor Taxes II* Panel Report, at para. 6.23.

81. See Snape & Lefkovitz, *supra* note 53, at 793–794.

82. See Thaggert, *supra* note 65, at 72.

83. While Article III:2 (at issue in *Japanese Liquor Taxes II*) refers to "like" products and to "directly competitive or substitutable" products, Article III:4 (at issue in the *Tuna - Dolphin* cases) only refers to "like" products.

84. See *Japanese Liquor Taxes II* Appellate Body Report, 20, n. 44. The *Korean Liquor Taxes* case shows that this need not be a quantitative analysis and that evidence from other markets can be admitted, see Appellate Body Report in this case at paras. 129–130, 134, and 137.

85. See, *supra*, text at note 63.

86. See *Japanese Liquor Taxes II* Appellate Body Report, at 20

87. Consider as well that many traded products are not consumer products, but are only traded between manufacturing industries. The market-based demand test would then have to be undertaken from the perspective of the purchasing industry.

88. In Belgium, for instance, tap water is subject to 6% VAT, whereas bottled water is subject to 21%.

89. Though one could still think of exceptional situations. One possibly lawful border tax adjustment under Article III:2 GATT might have been the case where the US had decided to tax heavily US tuna fishing activities detrimental to dolphins and to levy an offsetting tax on imported tuna caught under similar detrimental conditions. This hypothetical was mentioned in Demaret, *Trems, Multilateralism and the GATT* in TRADE & THE ENVIRONMENT: THE SEARCH FOR BALANCE 52, 64 (Cameron, Demaret & Geradin eds., Cameron & May, London, 1994).

90. See Article X WTO Agreement.

91. See Article IX:2 WTO Agreement.

92. See also Schoenbaum, *International Trade and the Environment: The Continuing Search for Balance,* 91 AMERICAN JOURNAL OF INTERNATIONAL LAW 268, 291 (No 2, 1997) ("[T]here simply is no principled way to permit 'good' PPM regulations without opening the door to unacceptable abuses").

93. This is true, even if one takes a broader interpretation of the individual clauses of Article XX, which has been the Appellate Body's approach. See e.g., the *US - Standards for Reformulated and Conventional Gasoline* Appellate Body Report (WT/DS2/AB/R), adopted 20 May 1996. After all, the Appellate Body in this same case has given quite a strict interpretation of the headnote of Article XX.

# Part VI: Conclusions

CHAPTER 20

# Conclusions

*Thomas Cottier and Petros C. Mavroidis*

The Westphalian system of nation states has been built upon discrimination. The very purpose of the State consisted in protecting its own nationals and to provide privileges and advantages to them over those coming from foreign jurisdictions. Distinctions between nationals (citizens) and foreigners, domestic, and foreign product and productions are at the core of the identity of nation states for Centuries. Indeed, the very essence and purpose of statehood consisted in providing privileges by way of discrimination to inhabitants of its territory and thus to provide protection of livelihood and well-being of its populace and taxpayers. Sovereign equality of States, by no means, did not imply any limitations to that. States, while formally equal, were free to chose and discriminate among other nations. As of today, no general principles of non-discrimination or equal treatment oblige to act in fair and equitable manner exist in general international law.

The gradual emergence and development of international law, setting forth some limitations to crude system and the exercise of unfettered sovereignty and a rights to go to war, did not get very far in general or customary international law. This is particularly true in the field of trade relations. Yet, Discriminations were increasingly addressed by way of treaty law, first bilateral, later on regional and multilateral, culminating in the post-World War II Order of the GATT, and today the World Trade Organization. These treaties affirmed or introduced fundamental concepts of non-discrimination, in particular Most favored nation treatment and National Treatment as may have before bilateral agreements many years before. These principles emerged as the indispensable, necessary cornerstones of an open international trading system, Market access and the creation of competitive relationship between domestic and foreign products essentially depends on the effectiveness of non-discrimination principles. Enshrined in treaty law, and thus in mutually agreed restrictions of sovereign rights, they countervail the discriminatory nature of the nation state.

These principles, for a long time, were limited to trade in goods. They have been gradually expanded. They now cover, in principle trade in services, and may further expand in the future into walks of life affecting human even more directly. All this is well known. Yet, we state this at the outset in order to recall that the second World Trade Forum and this book are dealing what amounts to the most fundamental problem of the contemporary and future trading system. We are dealing here with a very difficult question of balance. We are dealing, on the one hand, with the precepts, traditions, and functions of the nation state in and outside regional integration. And on the other hand, we seek to define the role and function of the international system. We are seeking to define how much and how far the international trading system can and should, by means of international law, limit the powers of States to distinguish different products and treat them differently for policy purposes. We are dealing with sensitive issues of national identity and power and democratic rule, as much as we are dealing with economic and legal issues of trade regulation. We are, as a corollary, dealing with fundamental precepts and issues of international law and the international system, as it moved from coexistence to cooperation and into integration, both negative and positive.

It is evident that the subject of non-discrimination is not open to clear cut conclusions. The papers, comments, and discussion offer a large variety of viewpoints and approaches. There are no easy answers to fundamental questions, even if the concepts themselves look quite straightforward at first sight. Moreover, we face the problem that all these questions need to be addressed in a changing landscape. Technologies fundamentally alter the parameters of the game, and traditional perceptions of statehood and international law, still persisting in education and mentalities, no longer are in a position to solve basic problems. Increasingly, the basic concept of territoriality, a foundation of the nation state, no longer serves as a useful concept in an increasing number of policy areas. At the same time, the international system has not been in a position to substitute for these deficiencies, and states have remained the principled actors on the scene. The old does not work any longer, and the new is not there. Nevertheless, it would seem that a number of elements for the interpretation of current WTO law and further construing the international system and its relationship to statehood federal type Unions with own international personality) may be addressed in this final part.

The main theme of this book is product differentiation for policy purposes. Non-discrimination has long passed the stage when it aimed at preventing and remedying merely de jure discrimination of imported products. Today, we are mainly confronted with formally non-discriminatory measures which, however, may have an negative impact on conditions of competition of imported products. Generally, the motivation for product differentiation does not rest with foreign trade, but relies upon domestic policy goals. To what extent does and should the trading system channel such decisions in one way or the other by imposing disciplines how legislators should treat imported products? This is at the core of the like product issue which has been dominating much of the debates. Answers to this question vary in the different contributions to this volume. It is fair to say that no consensus emerged among the participants of the conference as to who precisely specific provisions of the GATT and GATS should be construed. Nevertheless, the debates allow to discern some common ground upon which future work could rely upon. Perhaps, two basic considerations can and should be distinguished.

From a functional, trade policy perspective, it is evident that goals of market access and equal conditions of competition for imported products requires no less favorable treatment of all competing products. Substitution on a market is the constitutive concept and approach. From this angle, the concept of like products is too narrow. Limitations of non-discrimination to physically identical products, or those conceived similar by the consumer, would fail to bring about equal conditions of competition in many markets. Comparisons with approaches in competition law confirm such a finding. At the same time, there is a price to pay for creating equal conditions. Product differentiation by governments for purposes other than protection are inherently limited to create tensions with other policy goals to be pursued under the constitution. The concept of substitution, on its own, is a highly intrusive concept and therefore raises questions of legitimacy if fully applied by the trading system.

From a constitutional perspective, things look somewhat different. The angle here is not on trade policy and conditions of competition exclusively, but in finding an overall balance of different, and equally legitimate policy goals of governments under their respective constitutions. Market access and conditions of competition in international trade are being recognized as an important and crucial task which, however, needs reconciliation with other policy objectives. These objectives often are being pursued by means of product differentiation, in particular for incentive tax purposes. The constitutional school of thought therefore is inclined to explore the limitations of non-discrimination of substitutable or like products in order to bring an overall balance of different policy objectives. Whether or not such limitations should be sought by way of interpretation of the concept of likeness and substitution, or by reference to exceptions, or by recourse to the very purposes of a particular provision has been controversial. But whatever the tools, it would seem fair to say that the requirement of balancing policy interests strikes a common cord among the conference participants.

It is difficult to conclude where current interpretation of the GATT stands with respect to these schools. The notion of likeness is construed differently in different contexts. Product differentiation of like products in tariff schedules leaves Member States ample room, both in state practice and adjudication. The Chaumont Conference, taking place at a spot of 1087 meters beyond sea level in the Neuchâtel Jura and grazing pastures, was well suited to look at the example of the 1904 German Swiss tariff concession which was limited to "Large dapple[d] mountain cattle reared at a spot at least 300 meters above sea level and having at least one month's grazing each year at a spot at least 800 meters above see level." Bad luck for cattle staying at home in the summer. Today, the WTO probably would and should remedy such discrimination, as the concession sought to privilege a very succinct group of cattle of one country at the expense of trading partners. This concession clearly seeks exclusion of MFN obligations. Yet, apart from such excessiveness, Art. I and II GATT hardly impair the pursuit of other policy goals as protection of domestic industry by means of tariffs inherently allows not only for such policies, but even protection in itself.

Article III GATT, on the other hand, leaves much less leeway. With regard to taxation, the basic rule can be found in Article III:2 second sentence and the interpretative note ad Article III. Imported substitutable products must not be treated no less favorable provided that such treatment serves the purpose of protecting domestic industry. The treatment of like products in Article III:2 first sentence is a subset of this rule and excludes, at present interpretation, a test of protectionist effect. The category of physically identical products per se requires treatment no less favorable. With regard to general regulations affecting the sale of like products, Article III:4, emanating the most general in Article III, limits obligations to like products and currently does not allow for a discriminatory effects test.

Upon rejecting the aims and effect test interpretation of Article III, it would seem that current practice of WTO dispute settlement bodies is closer to a functionalist, than a constitutional way of thinking. This becomes clear if WTO practice is compared with similar issues raised in a constitutional context. In the United States and in the European Union, it is interesting to observe that Courts allow for more discretion and room in the field of product differentiation, including for tax purposes, to the extent that such differentiation do not have a protective effect. It is interesting to observe that the global system, at its present stage of development, is more stringent on limitation on governmental policy options than federal and regional constitutional structures. Similarly, it is interesting to observe that the Swiss experience required a particular boost to reinforce equal conditions of competition by way of the internal market bill of 1995 in order to remedy constitutional practices which had been too lenient on scope and legislative discretion of the Cantons. Unlike the U.S. or Switzerland, and even unlike the European Union, the WTO still is in its first phase of integration which explains a preference to functionalist approaches.

This, however, should change. While functionalism was suitable under GATT and its weak mechanism of implementation, interpretation needs to shifts towards constitutional thinking. This is necessary in comparison to federal and regional experience, but also due to enlarged scope of the WTO, including in particular services, and due to the fact that implementation of obligations has become more powerful due to the absence of veto powers by which, formerly, excessive functionalism was controlled.

The papers, comments, and discussion of the conference point in this direction as they suggest that some sort of protectionist effect test should be applied in assessing product differentiation. While the aims-and-effect test was a bold, and for many too bold an approach, other avenues might be reasonably pursued to achieve this goal. At the same time, this also allows to leave artificial distinctions between like and substitutable products behind, and work on the basis of substitution. This will both serve the goal of equal conditions of competition and of protecting other legitimate policy goals. It allows the WTO to keep in mind its room of action and limits intrusion to areas where the core mandate of the organization is well established; It is about combating economic protectionism and not other legitimate policy goals which may result in trade restrictions of need be. It allows of an approach, in other words, which causes less headache in terms of legitimacy and democratic accountancy. Also, it would assist in working towards a common understanding of likeness in different provisions of the WTO, including the GATS for which, evidently, criteria of physical characteristics of a product are not very helpful. While differences may exist in context, a basic common reading should be able to cover goods and services alike, as much as products involved in countervailing and anti-dumping procedures. Whether or not these goals can be achieved by interpretation, or require treaty adaptations and authentic interpretation require further studies.

Problems relating to technical barriers to trade, a major source of discrimination and distortion of market access and equal conditions of competition were given ample attention at the Conference. Again, it is difficult to draw specific conclusions. There has been some confusion about the notion of Mutual Recognition Agreements (MRA's). There is no consensus on further strategies to be pursued. While some believe that old fashioned harmonization is the path for the global system, other seek more potential for MRA's in the multilateral system. Perhaps both avenues need to be followed wherever possible, creating windows of opportunity and competition among different approaches and philosophies. The linkage of bilateral MRA's and the global system remains a challenge. At any rate, it is necessary to further work on Conditional MFN, a field which has not been sufficiently dealt with by this Conference. Similarly, the Conference did not focus on MFN in terms of regional exceptions. It rather focuses on the mutual relationship of MFN and National Treatment. While extensive problems relating to regional integration and its relation to the global systems remain to be pursued elsewhere, and must not be understated, the Chaumont conference shows that in today's complex World, reconciliation of market access and conditions of competition and other legitimate policy goals more than ever depend on a new interpretation of the core concept of National Treatment in the WTO.

Annex

# Transcript of Roundtable Discussion

*August 28 and 29, 1998, Chaumont, Switzerland*

## 1. Friday Afternoon

### Crawford Falconer (Chairman)

The discussions have not been so long ago that you need to be reminded what went into them. I do not intend to try to sum up the detail of what people had to say. Two or three things occurred to me which might be useful when we come to the discussion, to try to distinguish the themes which I saw in the comments which have been made.

First is the more general question, which I think is worth maintaining throughout all the discussion, why does MFN matter? Why is it such a big deal? Or indeed is it such a big deal? I am sure Patrick Low has the figures in hand but as far as goods trade is concerned I think the majority of international trade takes place on the basis of preferential tariffs rather than on the basis of MFN tariffs. That brings us to the question what is the rationale for being concerned about the MFN issue when in fact the system has been very tolerant as far as goods trade is concerned of preferential departures from it.

The other thing is that a lot of the discussion seemed to be about MFN as far as goods was concerned and the case law that was cited tended to be about tariffs. Of course, as tariffs have come down the question of the importance of MFN tends to fall into the background. Because if you have no tariffs, or very low tariffs, the question of discrimination at the border becomes less and less of a political issue. The consequence of that would be the national treatment question, to what extent are the conditions of competition behind the border. I think perhaps one thing I would identify as what is the real importance of it in the classic sense of goods trade as an issue, has it diminished in importance? Is it really of historical importance on the assumption that current trade liberalization is here to stay on goods? Have we moved away from that question, as far as MFN is concerned, to the question of regulation, vis-à-vis the goods trade as it effects discrimination between countries and also at the national treatment level?

This was the second theme which was derived largely from Bill Davey's paper. That covered a large number of issues but I think it significant when you discuss MFN as it affects conditions of competition you find yourself discussing, almost inevitably, like products. This has become the fulcrum on which the MFN turns, rather than pure discrimination per se. There will be a lot of discussion about these but it is worth reflecting in more detail about some of the ways that issue might be dealt with. Is an approach based on aims and effects something that should be discarded as part of the dustbin of history? Is that now in light of the accordion-playing Appellate Body something we no longer need to worry about? Or is there going to be a return to the world of aims and effects? Is there, what Bill was alluding to, a soft core protective effects? This is not the full blown aims and effects but something that is basically implicit in Article III and has an impact on competition in order to get rid of frivolous, unimportant, inadvertent discriminatory themes. Maybe there are some other alternatives? I think Petros alluded to that in the role of Article XX in conjunction with Article III, playing possible a role to resolve matters in a way that deals with the same set of problems.

If the state of jurisprudence and debate as far as like products has been so fraught to what extent do we avoid the same difficulties in Services? This was the theme coming from Aaditya's paper. At one point we had the view that maybe in the case of services we have a completely clean sheet to work off. Therefore, a possibility of clarifying the matter much better than goods. Aaditya thought the concept of end-use may well be something that should be used as a basis for making this determination in a way that has not been the case as far as goods trade is concerned. A number of other ideas were put on the table there, to do with providing some kind of rationale or defense of whatever decision has been made, whether it has been stretched or elaborated or has been reached an agreement by Petros by going to the extent of challenge procedures as a means of enforcing MFN obligations. How you would have those challenge procedures would be another question.

From my point of view I see those three papers neatly falling into different categories. I would not want to dictate that the discussion be compartmentalized but it might be useful to deal with them.

## Bob Stern

Most of what I have to say is drawn from papers that have been presented and commented upon. Let me start with the points that André Sapir made when he was discussing the paper by Bagwell/Staiger. First of all, the presentation focused on how to interpret the terms of trade improvement that countries may seek to obtain. Joining this with the point that Patrick Messerlin made, I think the diagram André presented is misleading because, in a technical sense, it depicts a small country that does not really have the market power that is required to realize a terms of trade improvement.

I agree generally with the criticism that was made by both André and Patrick about the importance of the terms of trade that is emphasized in the Bagwell/Staiger analysis. If you look at the reasons why countries engage in multilateral trade negotiations, in my view, terms of trade considerations are not very significant. There are all kinds of other economic and especially foreign policy and political objectives involved in negotiations that provide a much better explanation of what we have seen in the multilateral trading system in the past half century. When one considers how countries engaging in negotiations view the extent of their negotiating offers, most of the time they focus on the depth of the tariff cuts or the extent of trade coverage, or things of that sort. Under these circumstances, it is unlikely that terms of trade considerations play any significant role.

The next point is that the major departure from MFN has come about in the form of preferential trading arrangements. This is something that the GATT originally condoned, and, if you look at the course of development of the trading system, we have seen major changes in preferential trading arrangements. These started with the arrangements in Western Europe, going on—although not very successfully especially in the 60s—in a number of developing countries, and later, especially in the late 80s and 90s, in the form of various types of free trade arrangements and customs unions. These are truly major departures from MFN, and the question that arises is how important these elements of discrimination have become that are embodied in preferential arrangements. Views may differ on this. But my own sense of the economic consequences of preferential trading arrangements is that these arrangements in the major countries that have used them have been welfare enhancing rather than trade diverting. They have served to re-inforce the efficiency gains that we expect and associate with liberalization of the multilateral trading system.

I turn next to a couple of points Patrick raised. First is the bargaining process that goes on and the issue of free-riding in trade negotiations. Why don't we see more uniformity in tariff schedules and NTBs? I think this is not so much a matter of free-riding but more a matter of the general point that Patrick mentioned, i.e., you have a lot of vested interests that are concerned with maintaining the status quo, or enhancing it. The absence of uniformity in tariff schedules and NTBs reflects the politics of trade policy where vested interests are still very powerful in particular circumstances.

Next is the very difficult question of "like" products. In this connection, it should be noted that economists typically try to measure degrees of closeness of substitutability or complementarity of products in terms of the cross-elasticity of demand. Such measures would help to clarify the legal implications of different aspects of "likeness." In many cases, when it is maintained that products are not alike, this may reflect protectionist influences. One example is the U.S. treatment of imports of light trucks and recreational vehicles. For some time, these vehicles have had relatively high tariff rates dating from the 1960s. These tariffs were a remnant of action taken against the European Community at that time. The maintenance of these high tariffs is an example of protectionism by the United States Another recent example is the case of certain types of lumber imports from Canada that were coming into the United States in very large volume in apparent violation of the agreement that had been negotiated between the United States and Canada to limit the quantity of lumber imports. They simply re-defined the category in this case to put it back under the non-tariff restrictions that were already existing. I would have to be convinced that there is, in many of these instances and debates, an unambiguous demonstration of some underlying social need than rather obvious elements of protectionism.

This leads me to a related point that came up in Petros Mavroidis' presentation of Bob Hudec's paper. This concerns the impact of regulation. Economists have spent many years trying to measure the economic consequences of regulation in various forms as well as the consequences of protection and liberalization. In this context, there has been a lot of work that has sought to measure the magnitudes involved. It would therefore be helpful to provide some quantitative inputs so that we could have a better assessment of what is at issue in particular cases.

Aaditya Mattoo's paper focused on mutual recognition agreements applying to personal services. I think in this context that there are a lot of other services issues that come up under the category of producer services. I am not clear as to whether the same sort of criteria of quality and the like apply in the broad range of producer services as compared to professional or personal services.

I would admit that it is extraordinarily difficult, in the services area, to come up with the kinds of economic measures to which Aaditya has referred. It is by no means simple to obtain the prices of domestic and foreign goods and measures of the barriers involved. When you have personal services, especially professional services, it is often hard to find the appropriate benchmarks that would enable you to make the economic comparisons to see whether or not and the extent to which protection is involved.

### Ernst-Ulrich Petersmann

I should like to make a comment on Bill's presentation and a question to Aaditya. Both the comment and question relate to the problem of: how much freedom should governments have in the context of national treatment, in the context of Article 3 or in the context of the GATT? What should be the significance of this aims and effects test?

I was a panel member on a small beverage panel which invented this aims and effects test. Firstly, a point that cannot be ignored, a clear aims and effects test is to be found in Article III:1 of the GATT. This says *internal taxes and internal regulations should not be used so as to afford protection to domestic producers*. This is a "should" formulation so it has only interpretative principles which is not legally binding but it has a clear aims and effects test, which cannot be ignored under recognized methods of international treaty interpretation. I find this discussion very confusing that the Appellate Body sometimes seems to put into doubt the existence of an explicit treaty language which includes the aims and effects test.

What is the impact of this interpretative principle for the interpretation of Article III:2 which is "shall" language? The text of Article III:2 in the first sentence uses two criteria: *if there are like products the imported products shall not be taxed in excess of the like domestic product*. The second sentence is poorly drafted, it refers to the principle of paragraph 1 but there is a footnote which makes it very clear that also the second sentence establishes two criteria says: *only if the products are competing or substitutable and only if there is dissimilar taxation then there shall be a violation of the second sentence*. So, in both cases of Article III:2 you have two criteria and I think the Appellate Body was wrong in saying that in ArticleIII:2, second sentence, there should be an additional third criterion, the Appellate Body says: *there shall be a separate examination of this principle in paragraph 1*. The policy question remains: What is the impact of paragraph 1 (the interpretative principle) on the interpretation of Article III:2? Here the discussion has been confusing because they have not distinguished what has happened in malt beverages and what has happened in the automobiles taxes case.

There is a very important distinction that should be made in the GATS context. The distinction is the following: The malt beverages taxes case had to deal with the situation where both parties—the complainant Canada and the defendant the United States—agreed that the product differentiation between low-alcohol beer and high-alcohol beer was legitimate, introduced for health-policy purposes, had not protectionist purposes, had no protectionist effects. In such a situation where you had a bilateral agreement I think it is legitimate to say that the purpose of Article III has been defined by paragraph 1, and the purpose is to prohibit protectionist discrimination. If both the claimant and defendant governments agree that this policy differentiation is legitimate for health policy purposes, it had not protectionist purposes or effect then it is completely in order to take this into account and to say the purpose of Article III is not to harmonize health policy regulations or to limit the freedom of governments outside the field of trade policy. The same is true in the GATS. Would you agree that if there is agreement, a mutual recognition agreement, on the conditions under which canadian doctors and american doctors are like then I think this kind of agreement should be taken into account in a dispute settlement case. It is an agreement describing under which conditions Canadian doctors might be considered equal. I think this situation has to be distinguished, which has often not been done, where the complainant argues that the product differentiation is protectionist.

That had been the situation of the US automobile taxes case. The EC argued the tax differences between various automobile categorizing the United States had protectionist purposes and protectionist effects. In this case the situation was completely different in my view. Here the panel should have applied an economic test, amount substitute ability and should have put the burden on the defendant to justify why this kind of product differentiation had not protectionist purposes or effects. To justify in the context of Article XX, why this kind of product differentiation was necessary for other foreign policy objectors. The situation has so far been not been clarified very well by the Appellate Body.

Would you tend to agree, Aaditya, there is parallel between the relevance of mutual recognition agreements in the GATS context for interpreting the national treatment requirements and the relevance of mutual agreements in the malt beverage dispute, relating to Article III of GATT? Do these two situations, mutual agreement or no mutual agreement on the product differentiation, make a big difference?

### Aaditya Mattoo

With regard to the question about producer services my example was mostly about professional services which are directly supplied to the consumer. I think the basic principles that I was speaking about would certainly apply to services producers as well. I can think of examples in financial services, for instance, if one country were to recognize the regulatory environment in country A and not in country B you could look more closely at the basis for that recognition. If it is a certain capital adequacy ratio, then you could argue that is what is relevant in determining likeness. With regard to transport services, for instance, some countries have favorable recognition arrangements with regard to aircraft maintenance and repair. They recognize these standards in some countries but not in others. In fact, there are explicit MFN exemptions to cover such selective recognition. So, I think the basic argument that if you chose to make a distinction between in what are *a priori* like then the burden of proof is on the country making the distinction and there should be a possibility to challenge that. This would apply as much to producer services as it does to consumer services.

The question: if there is a multilateral mutual recognition agreement would that influence the way you apply the GATS? That is an important point and the GATS itself says this. It creates a weaker presumption in favor of international standards, probably, than the technical barriers to trade agreement. But I think that would be a standard by which you could judge the countries that adhered to an internationally agreed standard. If on the other hand it was a purely bilateral agreement then I still think there is a problem in situations where countries differ on whether or not there is a legitimate objective. If there was agreement, as you say there was in the malt beverage case, it becomes a relatively simple case. But the problem arises when one country maintains that there is a legitimate reason for making distinctions and the other argue that it is purely for protectionist purposes. This is a serious problem. How do you distinguish between situations where protection is incidental to the legitimate pursuit of objectives and where it is, in fact, the intention of the instruments? What you said about the Cafe panel, you said there should have been an economic determination based on substitutability and then the Americans would have needed to justify it in the context of Article XX. Supposing you found that the elasticity of substitution was quite high between small cars and big luxury cars. How would the Americans justify a luxury tax under Article XX. Or would you say that they had no right to impose a higher tax on luxury cars than on ordinary cars?

### Bill Davey

On the question of defining like product. In fact panels have looked, most recently in the alcoholic beverages cases, at cross elasticity statistics. The problem with having a general practice of doing that is that often those sorts of statistics are not available. Some times you are not completely confident in the study that you have. It is further complicated by the fact that, for example, in Article III:2 you have both the notion of like product and directly competing or substitutable products. As we talked about the accordionist this morning, you can get a number that would show you what the substitutability is but how does that number relate to the different ways you are defining like product or competing products. It would be helpful, and it is looked at, but I am not sure that it would provide a complete solution to that.

On Article III on whether or not the language of the first clause, the first paragraph, *you should not use certain regulatory devices, taxation, and regulations so as to afford protection.* My problem is not that it should not be read into Article III and maybe into Article I, but more to raise the question of why would you read it into the definition of like product? Why not look in terms of the question of whether or not there is dissimilar taxation or less favorable treatment? There, I think, you could say if there is not some sort of protective effect or aim then the treatment is not less favorable in terms of what Article III is trying to get at. You can go to the Preamble of both the WTO and GATT which talks about one of the principle objectives for having the agreements, is to get rid of discrimination. So, I think there is more treaty language, in a way, to look at it in these other contexts. I am not sure I would agree there is much of a difference between the Malt Beverages and Auto Tax case as the way you should approach them. In each case I think you need to decide whether the products are like and then either go to Article XX or have some sort of other test defining less favorable treatment or a dissimilar taxation based on the "so as to afford protection" language.

### Gary Horlick

First let me congratulate the organizers on putting us in an altitude sufficient that cows grazing here will produce cheese which will meet the most classic fine-tuning of like product. 900 meters? This shows the potential of mischief of like product which is why the GATT and WTO should be properly skeptical of such abuse.

André focused a lot on terms of trade and Aaditya mentioned more efficiency and/or welfare. I think that is worth bringing out. Certainly the terms of trade article is interesting but from a US perspective it is hard to imagine the US government being able to ever negotiate that well. Historically, of course we legislated tariffs until 1930 through a process which was purely political, and our tariff structure is based on the 1930 result rather than fine-tuned strategic terms of trade. So it is hard to say the US has ever successfully followed terms of trade, or indeed has tried. The arguments that have been used in the US for unconditional MFN, certainly during the GATT period, have been efficiency or welfare gains. I do question whether that argument has much play in the US right now. When you get into arguments that are MFN arguments or free-rider you do not hear the efficiency or welfare arguments. I think economists must have done a very bad job of teaching generations of students who then go to law school. Or lawyers are too stupid.

The other argument which, historically has more of basis and not just Jacob Viner but Cordell Hull, was political, especially in the inter-war years that discrimination created political rancor. The Nazi very fine-tuned discrimination was an extreme case. Again, I find it hard to imagine in the US that that has any traction as an argument. So, the arguments for MFN that have historically been used in the US have not been very successful. Perversely, the terms of trade argument would be quite attractive in the political mode but it would not work. It is interesting in terms of the statistics that Patrick mentioned. Arguably the EU is willing to pay the efficiency costs to create an EU by discriminating against everyone else. But, I would be interested in Bob's point of view on this score. You said the efficiency gains of FTAs have outweighed the costs. It would be interested to know the magnitude of costs. What you see in terms of concentration, certainly within NAFTA, within a very short time is a great shift in terms of intra-NAFTA trade. I am surprised there is not more efficiency loss.

The US shift to unconditional MFN in 1923 was quite accidental. I think it was a legal argument. It was not a policy argument and a very protectionist administration that did it, one of the most protectionist in our history, changed unconditional MFN. It was not because of any liberal movement.

It is worth bearing in mind for WTO purposes that there are many different definitions of like products or something like it. The definition of anti-dumping is quite unique. You have to have identical unless there is no identical. Then you go up to like or directly competitive products. There are very different definitions so you cannot just talk about like products and I think that goes to the accordion analogy. In different articles safeguards would be quite different and I personally read the Appellate Body, in Japan Liquor Taxes, in some sense throwing up its hands up and saying "different horses for different courses" which is not much guidance.

Finally, I would note that implicitly a lot of GATT panels have been using an aims and effects test. The filter in the WTO and the GATT has been the plaintiffs. Only governments can bring cases unlike in the national system where anyone can go into court. What you would tend to see in the WTO, especially in an area like this, is only the most egregious cases. So the cases that get brought are cases where even if you do not have an explicit aim and effects test, you see things where that is what in fact the panel is doing. The exception would be Luxury Tax where I totally share you view.

## Kalypso Nicolaidis

Let me make a few remarks starting with services trade. First, there is an interesting historical fact that Aaditya did not mention: the importance of the modes of delivery distinction. That distinction, into four modes of delivery, was only adopted more than mid-way in the Uruguay Round. It was used, in part, because it allowed some parties to accept the MFN clause, since whether there should be an MFN clause in the first place was itself contested. Parties were reassured by this distinction in that it allows to conduct progressive liberalization. For instance, a country could chose to allow different degree of market access between a doctor's diagnosis provided through the Internet or a doctor's diagnosis provided through consumer movement and a diagnosis made as the result of the movement of the doctor himself. It is noteworthy that while the EU does not have the benefit of this modes of delivery distinction, countries have tried to use it, in order to distinguish between establishment and trans-border delivery of certain services and thus allow discrimination between countries that were prone to one mode or the other. That has been attacked by the Commission since there is not a definitional backdrop. So, I think it is worth keeping in mind the connection between MFN and modes of delivery. The concept was a two edge sward both creating momentum for liberalization and restricting its scope in many national schedules.

Second, how about MFN and Article VII on recognition? Should it be broadly encouraged while at the same time stretching the constraints as much as possible? For one, it is worth stressing the tension with Article VI of the GATS: one of the legitimatization of stretching the constraints of Article VII is to pre-empt the temptation to apply Article VI on domestic regulation and like services too far, as was done in EU. The question is whether we should rely on judicial rather than political assessment of what should be considered "like products" and in what circumstance a judicial mandate for unilateral recognition (through an extreme interpretation of future Article VI disciplines) is legitimate? Third, and in connection, he EU should not be read as a de-regulatory experience. Let us not forget as in terms of the beverage alcohol distinction, it is the European Court of Justice that first did what Petros wants the GATS to do, i.e., to extend the scope of Article 36 to all so-called "essential requirements." This was done in Cassis de Dijon, greatly expanding the scope for exceptional governmental measures while at the same time introducing judicial recognition of equivalence.

I would also add some caution there on arguing for a more "open" Article VII. For one, when Petros mentions the shift of burden of proof to say that regulatory authorities should have the burden of proof to demonstrate unacceptable differences between regulation. I view mutual recognition agreements exactly a mechanisms to shift that burden of proof. We really need to fundamentally distinguish whether there is or there is not an MRA before shifting the burden. Even once there is an MRA we do not have automatic recognition of the doctor that comes. But it is very hard to argue there should be a shift of burden of proof in the absence of an MRA. The whole point of negotiating an MRA is to create a process whereby it is not too costly to shift that burden of proof. I remember discussing this in a meeting in the OECD two years ago and Members of professional associations coming to me with the following complaint: if we have the burden of proof to decide that this University should not be accredited and therefore that the doctor coming from this University is not up to our standards, who is going to subsidize us to send people over there to check on that University? Are you establishing an obligation on us when we are private regulatory bodies? If you do that you should bear the consequences. I think we need to think concretely about what burden of proof means in this case.

Another problem with Article VII is the question of transitivity. Imagine, coming back to the US/UK vs. US/Greece example, the UK is obliged under EU law to grant access to the doctor from Greece while at the same time it has an agreement with the US for the recognition of medical diploma. Is there a transitivity obligation there? In all logic there should be. If differences between the first two are small enough and the differences between the second two are small enough then what is happening between one and three? This issue has not been addressed yet. If we think of transitivity problems and compound regulatory differences - two acceptable differences may add up to an unacceptable one-this leads to very interesting tensions between the two dimensions of our discussion in our panels today: the economic terms of trade criterion and the regulatory compatibility criterion for discrimination. Or conversely: liberalization based on regulatory compatibility vs. liberalization based on mutual market access. Despite what has been said about the irrelevance of terms of trade we still see broad reciprocity in terms of access being invoked in trade negotiations. If we confront this with the problem of regulatory compatibility sometimes the two go together and sometimes they are in complete contradiction. When is the tension greatest and what problems will this raise?

### Rob Howse

I have a question for Petros before I disagree with him. I thought I understood that he would like to have a definition of like products that would essentially, in principle, mean that any regulatory distinction would have to be justified as a kind of exception. Regardless one had pre-identified some kind of discriminatory element or trade discriminatory protectionist element in this distinction. Is this really what you are saying? No.

Maybe we have to understand a little bit more about at what point one would distinguish any regulatory distinction from one that would attract scrutiny as an exception. I would like you to explain if it is not a kind of discriminatory element that Bill Davey was suggesting, what would be the element where you could say at this point we have to subject this to some scrutiny?

The second question is about public order. Would the public order be a necessity task or would there be some lower level of scrutiny or some overlap with some of the specific has, in Article XX, if so are we getting in to different levels of scrutiny that reflect different kinds of situation?

Petros Mavroidis

Let me start from the second question. First of all I never understood what necessity means in the GATT. I come from a background where you follow, at a constitutional level, a three steps procedure. You check whether the measures are appropriate; to what extent you need to take this measure; and finally you check which measures, among the measures you need to take, are proportional. Some might be proportional some might be disproportional. This is my idea of checking regulatory intervention. If your question was *do I understand necessity when it comes to an examination of public order in the sense necessity has been interpreted in the Tuna cases?* My answer is no. Why do I say that? One of the cases that I really like in the European Court of Justice is the Reinheits-gebot case, the beer parity case. There is a very interesting obiter dictum where the Judge says any integration process is about opening and widening up our horizons. You might be producing beer in one way in German, we produce it in a different way in Belgium. If you do not check the beer from Belgium you will never know to what extent this beer is good, bad or whatever. In other words, regulatory process should not crystallize consumer habits, make them a regulation and then impose it to your partners.

On your first question it is really an issue where my thinking is still open, I do not have definite views. Let me tell you how I understand things. I began reflecting on like products more as a reaction. Why? Because when I read Gas Guzzler I was really surprised because it says *a government tells me that I have no protective aim and you have to show both aim and effect (you not me) if you want to show that the rights under Article III have been violated.* How do you show aim? Do we consult the Congressional records? If the congressional records says one says *I do it because I want to be re-elected;* the other guy says *I do it because I want to protect public order;* another guy says *I want to do it because I want to protect environment;* and another says *I do it because it makes sense.* Have you shown intent? Not to mention that you can not trace some records, they are not shown to the public being confidential. So, my thinking about like products is a reaction to this proposal.

I take Uli's point about Malt Beverages. The crucial difference between malt-beverages and gas-guzzler is what we have been discussing together. In malt-beverages we had by accident Mississippi grapes growing in Mississippi, in gas-guzzler they over-extended this paragraph and said *you do not produce small cars, you should be producing them, anyone can do it,* and you shift adjustment costs.

To me likeness means nothing. If I were to redraft the GATT Art. III, I would use one concept: directly competitive products. I would say- "check the market." Do consumers buy products a and b interchangeably? By using cross price elasticity as the sole criterion I can establish whether a and b are directly competitive products. I want to operate a regulatory intervention and I want to say "no, these two products should not be like." The WTO, the way it is now, it is not an instrument for deregulation. If this is the case, I can intervene, but I have to show that my intervention is proportional.

### Rob Howse

The initial screen being competitiveness or substitutability, I think there is a sense where we would not disagree that that should be a minimum requirement for identifying the products as like. The question is where do we go from there? It seems to me that the legitimacy of a distinction for regulatory purposes need not depend on, in any way, on whether the products are substitutable. There may be normative factors that are irrelevant to whether product A or product B are substitutable, from the point of view of the consumers, that may drive the distinction. In fact, the government may be regulating precisely because it knows that the products are substitutable but for some reason, like for example health impact, it wants consumers to prefer the one over the other. So, the question is what happens at that point? Do we then go to some kind of fairly strict screening? That would have an enormous influence on the ability to make non-discriminatory regulation by governments and then you have dispute settlement organs going over an enormous range of regulatory territory and, in some sense, re-doing the policy calculus on democratically legitimate regulators.

Of course, when they do it whether there is already an element of discrimination or apparent protection identified that seems to be legitimate because you are dealing with the core obligations of the regime. They do for any regulation because the products in question are substitutable from a consumer perspective, that seems like a potentially vast intervention.

Petros Mavroidis

I do not understand why we disagree on this. The hormones case: the EC says beef kills. Prove it to me. You want to say that. What is the danger? If I do not impose the burden of proof on the EC I create an incentive compatible structure to deviate from GATT obligations. Everybody will say hormone-treated beef kills. I do not know what kills. Anything kills. Nobody says you cannot block imports from the US. Of course you can. But when even EC scientists tell me that hormone-treated beef does not kill I think the GATT Appellate Body should have said I am sorry EC you cannot intervene. You have the right to intervene on health objectives to the extent that the objective is legitimate. My proportionality test precisely will distinguish between invocation of legitimate,—I think, maybe I am wrong—and illegitimate objectives.

Jacques Bourgeois

The title of this conference is MFN. We have not really spoken about MFN. MFN addresses the question where you have one WTO Member that makes a difference between WTO Member B and WTO Member C. We have been talking about national treatment. I have not just been making the point for the sake of argument I think that there are certain number of differences from a regulatory point of view that should be taken aboard there.

Secondly, non-conditional MFN. I listened to Bill Davey. The question which is often bothered me is when you have a given treatment, for instance in a tariff, that is conditional in a concession should that condition be extended unconditionally or should the condition that has been attached not be applied to the others?

Third point, MRAs. Of course you have the very different types of MRAs and Kalypso has pointed out that some MRAs are simply establishing a system whereby a read condition of qualifications has been made more easy. But you have also MRAs for products where there is a recognition that a product manufactured according to the rules of the exporting country will be accepted in the importing country, because it is manufactured according to the rules of the importing country. Then we have question, as far as the other

WTO Members are concerned this is quite clearly a derogation from the most-favored-nation treatment. How is it going to be justified? How is that going to fit into the exceptions of Article XX. I know that there has been a few decisions on that which seem to indicate—for instance Shrimp and Gasoline—if the West had negotiated with the third countries then those who did not negotiate, too bad for them. That sort of discrimination or derogation from the most-favored-nation treatment would be accepted. This then raises the very intriguing question: can Members of the WTO, by bilateral agreements, derogate from their obligations outside of their particular case of the customs union exception or the free trade area exceptions? These are just a few questions when I listened to the fascinating presentations.

André Sapir

I would like to come back to the question that Crawford Falconer asked: Does MFN matter? How important is it? I heard Patrick give that number which I think is a misleading number that 50 per cent of world trade in conducted on non-MFN basis, but that obviously does include intra-EU trade which one should not put there.

I did this paper recently where I looked at intra-EU trade. As you know, when you look at the partners of the EU, basically none of them is an MFN partner. But when you look in part in great detail on how much the EU trade is conducted on an MFN basis, I come with an estimate that at least 75 per cent of EU trade is conducted on an MFN basis. In part this is due to the fact that quite a bit of the trade is zero MFN duty. Therefore, we should forget that. So I think the figure of 50 per cent on a non-MFN basis is probably the other way around. It is probably that two-thirds of world trade is actually conducted on an MFN basis, obviously excluding intra-EU trade. I do not think it is small at all, I think it is the vast majority.

The second point, which comes back a little bit to what Bob was discussing, we should not forget that MFN and free trade are not the same thing: non-discrimination is not the same thing as free trade. This is a discussion we have not had here. When you look historically at discussions on MFN there has always been that element present and was even present in the great classical time in Britain. There was a discussion on whether MFN—for those who were free—is a useful device towards free trade or not. I think that is worthwhile to have today in the context of services.

The last point is the relationship between MFN, non-discrimination and preferential trading arrangements. What Bob says that on the whole about preferential trading arrangements has been welfare enhancing. That in a way comes from the discussion that yes, over the years, countries have lowered their tariffs. If you are looking from that viewpoint, yes we are going towards free trade and maybe, indeed, the preferential trading arrangements have played a role in that. On the other hand, there is something to be put in the negative column: in two words rules of origin or the custom discrimination. So, maybe tariffs are lowered, but there is a lot of discrimination around. Again, if you look in the literature on MFN, in the early literature, one of the reasons why countries wanted to have MFN was for certainty, certainty of treatment. When you look at rules of origin you are very far from certainty and that should be included here.

## Patrick Messerlin

Two questions about the Services paper done by Aaditya Mattoo. I agree with the general argument that in goods you have this issue of and you mentioned that maybe its not the same in services. I was puzzled by the fact that in services one of your core aspect was audiovisuals. But, in audiovisual it is exactly the same thing. I am talking as a Frenchman and having received my tax bill two weeks ago. The rules of origin in the movies in France are the following: the French movies are subsidized by the French Treasury. That is the official rule of origin. So, you can understand why we are subsidizing foreign producer of movies for spending more revenues, it is exactly the same. You can go on television instead of the movies and you get the same kind of revenues. I think with regard to your argument, theoretically, you have a point but empirically I am not sure

The second point you mentioned is this case of the US bank in Malaysia and the ensuing grandfathering clause. You mentioned that it is very perverse. In substance I agree but I would just like to qualify your statement a little bit. First we have done that in trade in goods. Basically some subsidies in agriculture is exactly the same kind of story. This is a grandfather clause by which we buy the old farmers silence through direct subsidies. We have the same problem in agriculture and in your Malaysian bank, the problem is that we do not put a line when the subsidies—the grandfathering—will stop. Indeed, in your case maybe the story is more advanced in the banking system because there may be re-negotiation ten years from now. So, maybe the situation is better in the US bank in Malaysia because of the possibility of re-negotiation. In Europe, agriculture subsidies are exploding because basically we gave to everybody including the new entrants in agriculture this access to all types of subsidies. Obviously this type of subsidy is going absolutely crazy.

## Aaditya Mattoo

If I can briefly respond to what you said, Kalypso, with regards to the GATS. I think the modes of delivery question is, indeed, very important. It is interesting because the scheduling practice in the GATS has created an acceptance, in the sense that services which are identical in every respect except that they are supplied through different modes, are not like services. There is no textual basis for this in either Article II dealing with MFN or Article XVII dealing with national treatment. But my impression was that this tension was much greater between the national treatment provision and the modal approach and I have discussed this at length elsewhere and I refer to this in a footnote on page 6.

Another point about Article VI which you raised, I was not quite sure what you were getting at. My impression is that part of the reason you have such difficulties in the context of Article II on MFN or Article XVII on national treatment is because your general disciplines on domestic regulations like qualification requirements, regulations, standards are not sufficiently strong in the GATS. For instance the Technical Barriers to Trade Agreement in the context of goods has supplemented the national treatment discipline in goods by also requiring that even non-discriminatory standards should not be more burdensome than necessary. Article VI of GATS begins to do this and has created a work program of mandatory negotiations which will develop such disciplines. But for the moment the real problem is that there is language there that can be read as grandfathering all existing regulations which could reasonably have been expected when commitments were made. I think it is the weakness of Article VI which causes us to worry more about discrimination in the context of Article II. Because if origin-neutral measures which escaped Article II were nevertheless disciplined under Article VI, I think there would be less cause for concern. This I discuss on page 23 of my paper.

I heard an incidental question which David addressed to Petros, which was how is it different from aims and effects? I take this personally. I think there are two important differences. First, you begin to define a category of like products on the basis of substitutability or end uses, and then if you ask for justification or distinctions. Most importantly it is different because the burden of proof is on the regulator. Secondly, you do not accept instruments uncritically, as in the Cafe panel. In this panel the Americans said *our object is to protect the environment but incidentally we decide that light trucks are not like products with automobiles*. It was allowing this sort of distinction to go unchallenged, which was a real problem of aims and effects. What we are suggesting is that you discipline the instrument, you are asked for a demonstration of necessity or economic efficiency. I think that really sets this approach apart from aims and effects.

Finally, I think what you said, Patrick, are very interesting examples. With regard to audiovisual I am not completely sure how this works. If there is an analysis of what happens with quotas in my paper and there the interesting question is who gets the rent? My argument there is that in Services, because there is less scope for intermediation, you would presume that usually the rent is appropriated by the suppliers. For instance, if you were to put down the number of American films that can be shown I think America would presumably raise the price of the films that they sell to the EU. In which case I thought what I said about domestic regulation where there is no corresponding cost in revenue lost to the importer will still hold. I think the example you gave on farming and grandfathering is very interesting.

## Thomas Cottier

Once you have three persons in the room you need it otherwise the system with initial negotiation rights would not work, the formal approach would not work and the sectoral initiatives would not work. Why do we discuss MFN now? Perhaps because moving away from tariffs we do perhaps not need it in the same way systematically. In the Services area it could be that, or perhaps it is so, national treatment is much more important: it is the main instrument of liberalization and probably, a lot of us were actually surprised when global MFN clause appeared in the text; that was not very clear during the negotiations. But, this brings me to the next point. We still are discussing on the one side the GATT, the tradition, and on the other side the new instruments, the GATS. I think the purpose of our work has to be that we work towards convergence of the two. We already see areas where it is really difficult to cut through which side it should go. Recently, we dealt with questions of liberalizing electricity. Now formally, this belongs to the GATT but if you look at it in substance, for example what has been happening within the EC, it looks more like progressive liberalization in the services area. So, we need to try to converge, and I make this point because that is, to me, very important in approaching the like-product question. Now having been involved as the Chairman of the Automobile Tax Panel at the time, I was quite happy to see how the discussions went this afternoon. I believe the way Article III is construed currently contains elements of a contrario arguments, which is not really admissible under the Vienna Convention and contemporary doctrines of interpretation. Also, we see a very intriguing divergence, for example, when you look at the interpretation of the SPS

Agreement in the Hormones case and the interpretation of like-products in terms of deference given to it. It happens to be a different agreement but the underlying issue is always the same: what level of deference should governments have in approaching their non-trade policy goals? The most striking one is environment, of course, where you have to balance it out. There are others too. But, I would argue that the overall legitimacy of the system in the long run, and that is also the constitutional challenge, really is about finding an appropriate balance between the goals of trade liberalization and the other policy goals. I think the way we construe like-products is a very, very important instrument and object and should be read in this overall goal.

Finally I would like to make a comment on conditional MFN which I read into Article VII. I think this text is very clear. It has different constellations where you have a mutual recognition agreement or you do this unilaterally. But, the third party in all cases has a right to negotiate with you. It is like, I think in the EC, where based on the Vlassopoulos jurisprudence, the person has a right to negotiate recognition. So the burden of proof, seems to me clear, the person who wants to enter the game has to demonstrate that his trainees, the Greek Doctors, are adequately trained and he has to show that. The legal problem, in my view, is where denial of justice or arbitrary responses start. What are the criteria there? May be you have an answer. Thank you.

### Piet Eeckhout

I have a comment which tries to ties in with Services from someone who first tries to read all the ECJ judgments and, if there is a bit of time left, tries to look at some WTO cases and normally there is no time left. But, one case which I did look at is the Banana's Case where both the Panel and the Appellate Body examined the issue of like services. I just glanced at a paper by Aaditya which seems to suggest that there the issue of likeness was not a very significant one and an easy to deal with. I am not sure, off the top of my head, that I would agree. The issue there, well the approach that was taken there, was to say that in wholesale supplies of bananas you should compare those supplying bananas from Latin American countries to those supplying EC bananas. Now, the issue, which I did not really discover in the reports, and I do not know to what extent it was discussed, is that you could as well say that you should only compare wholesale services suppliers of goods in general. There is nothing in the GATS Agreement which says that the like services or the like service suppliers are the wholesale service suppliers of bananas. You could have an approach which was to say all wholesale services in goods are like services and then of course it would become much more difficult to show that the impact of the banana regime was such as to differentiate between wholesale suppliers of services. Or you could say wholesale suppliers of fresh fruit. I think, in addition to your point as to the quality of service or service supplier which you illustrated with the Greek doctor and the UK doctor, there is also a question of specificity. How narrowly do you define a particular service or a service supplier? When I read it in the end it seemed to me, then again it ties in with your remark concerning the doctors, it almost seems you are creating, in relation to services, individual rights. The bottom line really is that any Greek doctor who feels that he is discriminated against as compared to a UK doctor in the United States could say, if he can bring a case of course, it is an infringement of the Services Agreement. I wondered if you had any particular comments on that? The sort of provisional conclusion which I would draw from that is that in Services I think it would be even more difficult to define like-products than it is in goods and I wonder, if I look back at the EC case law, we have a discrimination test also in relation to services and I am just thinking back to the cases, it seems like there are no cases where the products are like or not. Of course, we have moved in the direction of test-based more on restriction than on discrimination but I just wonder whether we should not also emphasize more the exact scope of national treatment and MFN, the actual discrimination clause, and perhaps the bit about like-products which I think in Services you will always be able to show that there is some degree of likeness. Whether we, in particular a number of cases that the general test of non-discrimination in the WTO is equality of competitive opportunities, which looking at it from an EC law background seems to me potentially an extremely far-reaching test. We have had to struggle with that in the EC, of course. In the Dassonville case in relation to goods we also had a very broad test. It seems to me that equality of competitive opportunities even go further than that, potentially. And many difficulties would have to be solved at that level by trying to specify and circumscribing to the discrimination test itself.

### Aaditya Mattoo

I was going to say that perhaps Bill should say something about Bananas. But, before I pass it to him, I think you are right. It is difficult to decide how many wholesalers, like what are the wholesalers who constitute the category of like services suppliers. In this case again, if you proceed on the basis of competitiveness you could argue that wholesalers of bananas, irrespective of the source of bananas who compete with each other, perhaps the price elasticity of demand between bananas and other fruit might be somewhat lower than the price elasticity of demand between bananas from Latin America. So, perhaps that was a reasonable group.

There was one thing about mutual recognition. What are the rights of the individual? I think it is a very important question because in Article VII you have in fact two provisions which counter the freedom that the first provision gives. Article VII:2 says that you have to give an opportunity to others to negotiate recognition agreements or demonstrate equivalent education and qualifications. Article VII:3 says you shall not accord recognition in a manner which discriminates. S*uppose I am the Greek doctor, VII:2 basically obliges me to approach my government or my professional agency and ask them to try to negotiate some sort of an agreement with Americans.* Article VII:3 is I think crucial. What right do I have? I do not want to negotiate a mutual recognition agreement. I just want to go to America because they are letting English doctors in and I know I am better trained and more capable. There, I think, in line with what Petros said about private rights, I do not know how you deal with it. There has to be something in this agreement which guarantees the right of a supplier from another country who might in fact be better trained than the person who is being admitted just because the mutual recognition agreement has happened to be concluded with this country.

## Bill Davey

On mutual recognition agreements in the goods area, governments have the right to negotiate mutual recognition agreements. In response to what Jacques said, MRAs would be a problem in the goods area but for the TBT and SPS provisions that allow them on conditions. With respect to bananas, my recollection is that the argument, if anything, was that the categories should be even narrower and not that it should be broad-based wholesale. There is the classification that Aaditya mentioned in his speech and it does break down wholesale into different categories of wholesale, including fruit wholesaling. There may even be sub-divisions of fruit wholesaling. If you had a very broad definition of what constituted like services you could end up with even more things being challenged because a banana wholesaler would say *well I deserve the favorable treatment that some other completely unrelated wholesaler is getting* that would lead to an even broader intrusion into regulatory distinctions.

## Paul Demaret

I would like to make one general remark and then an anecdote concerning the EC law, which relates to the mutual recognition issue. The general remark concerns the relationship between regional integration agreements, the most-favored-nation clause and the national treatment. I have made the point in other contexts but I think it is important to confirm, and I make the point after listening to André Sapir, if you have a regional integration agreement at first the regional integration agreement is an exception to the most-favored-nation clause and the regional integration agreement of the Members withhold the exception. Telling them *you do not have to extend all regimes for regional trade because you are an exception to the most-favored-nation clause*. But if the regional integration agreements become a single entity and want to be treated on the world trade stage as a single entity, like the EC wants in some respects (at least in respect of trade in goods) then it should no longer be entitled to claim the exception of Article XXIV or Article V of GATS—the exception to the most-favored-nation clause, but it should then be obliged to extent the intra-regional treatment to third countries on the grounds that it is obliged to do so under the national treatment of principles. Then, the national treatment principle applies to the region EC as such. If you accept the idea that has a lot of implications for the EC and if you try to think along that kind of lines you will realize how schizophrenic the EC is, at times. Claiming something on one ground, claiming something on another ground.

The anecdote concerning mutual recognition. There have been some cases which, at first, did not look very important, at least to me. Those were cases in the social field. But they were very important to the Germans, even Chancellor Kohl. What was at stake? German authorities, at a certain time, refused to recognize medical certificates provided by Italian doctors to Italian migrant workers, normally worked in Germany, but it so happened during the summer when they were taking their holidays in Italy they would fall ill and the family too, several years in a row. So, they were extending their holidays until German authorities said *we do not believe/trust those medical certificates which have been supplied by Italian doctors*. The Court of Justice said that under mutual recognition you are supposed to give credence to those medical certificates established by medical authorities in Italy. There was such a row in Germany that I think after that the Court of Justice in a similar case modified somewhat its case law and said *well you have really very good reasons not to believe medical certificates.* But even Chancellor Kohl intervened to say *the German social fabric is at stake here*. That is about mutual recognition in the EC.

### Tony Haniotis

Maybe I missed a lot of things. There is one aspect of the whole discussion which for policy makes perspective is important, which is PPM question—the production and processing methods which have not been as an issue here. In this context I would think that we should not forget that we have to try to find a balance between legitimate policy purposes and avoiding protection through discrimination. I believe we should make more of an effort to be more precise on the approach of the aims and effects. The consumer side definition of like product is not dealing with the PPM issues so we cannot differentiate a product on the basis of its production methods. Other characteristics which are important for policy but are not important for consumption. In this respect I would just like to bring in an element which I have not heard in this discussion.

We agree that aims and effects seem to be very arbitrary. We need some more objective criteria. How about using the criteria which exists in other places in the WTO agreements? For example the Subsidies Agreement where the test would be whether there exists a framework, a more general policy framework, within which this discrimination would be placed. So, is there a program in direction of achieving this policy goal? Within this program, this discrimination or deviation/differentiation of the product would it be placed in a more general program? This is a concept which appears in Article 8:2 of the Subsidies Agreement, maybe elsewhere in the agreements.

I would also agree with the people who said that like products should not be interpreted in the same way in every place it appears in the different agreements. There again, we should not forget that Article 1, MFN, is not to be seen as a negotiating technique, as a help to liberalization. The heart of the non-discrimination issue, in my view, would be Article 3. There we should be more careful when we look at the aims and effects texts. They should be more strict on the Article 3 interpretation or provision of like products rather than Article 1.

### Patrick Low

I would like to say two things. One is a general observation which has very little to do with MFN and non-discrimination, but I think is worth mentioning. If I read correctly Bob Howse, Thomas Cottier, Bob Hudec and perhaps a few closet greens and like-minded persons, underlying what they have to say about like products and the interpretation of that question is the feeling that by being too strict, the WTO may be behaving undemocratically.

The idea appears to be that WTO ought to be careful because there is a legitimacy problem.

If we are worried about this we should not only be looking at discrimination and non-discrimination. This idea of non-discriminatory liberalization or positive integration, which in one way or another leads to harmonized or more uniform policies, can be very intrusive. I think that the concerns we hear about this are increasingly from the developing countries, who think they have been inveigled into signing on to rules that will deny them independence of policy action. So I think we should bear in mind that it is not just discrimination and non-discrimination that may be a concern from this perspective. This is a big question for the multilateral trading system.

The other thing I wanted to mention is to apologize for being rather quick with 58 per cent as the number which I mentioned as representing preferential trade flows. The number I should have said was 42 per cent. This number is derived from a paper by Jean-Marie Grether and Marcelo Olarreaga.

### Crawford Falconer

I would just like to wrap up the session by thanking, in particular, those who have presented their papers and commented on them. Also all of you for your remarks and what was, I thought, a really wide range of discussion on a whole lot of technical issues. I thought they came across in a very clear way.

I must say in the general terms one thing that did strike me about the discussion was when MFN is concerned, the kind of issues that were discussed here have, in the last few years, changed enormously. Right up to the process and during the Uruguay Round if you had been talking about MFN the obsession would have been safeguard, gray area, and regional arrangements. Yet listening here today, and I do not think this is an atypical discussion, they have really not significantly figured in the discussion. I do not know what that means particularly but I think it has a lot to do with the fact that some of those issues were resolved and plus the fact that border measures have come down, generally speaking.

The other point that did not come up, and I am not suggesting that it should have, which is anti-dumping, an issue relevant to MFN but it is in a box of its own these days. It is not considered to be an MFN issue. It is partly in the way in which the legal regime has been restructured at the outcome of the Uruguay Round that I think when we consider MFN we think of different things than we might have done a short while ago.

The second sense that I got, I think this is also significant because it reflects something that is going out in the real world, is that the focus of the discussion has been more on national treatment than on MFN. That is very interesting. I had the impression that that is where the market is most worried. Whether this is a temporary feature, I am not sure.

The third thing, and perhaps here I am editing unduly, which did strike me is that there seems to be an enormous consensus that it is not that we have any real problem objectively with what Article III, what the like products should be about. Everybody wants to make sure that we do not mess up a good working principle because of a few exceptions but we ought to go out to do some kind of balance sheet: Not that anyone has a profound disagreement with the extent to which it is desirable to maintain competitive conditions under multilateral terms. How do you express them though in a way that resolves what appears in actual fact to be a problem? We have not really expressed that in these discussions. Can you resolve that under negotiations? I find it very difficult to see how you can get 132 Members to resolve anything let alone something so profound as this, even with the best will in the world. So, you are then faced with the question: can you resolve it juridically in a case law? Politically, even if one can come up with an approach that seems to command soft consensus—from the discussion this afternoon I do not think there is a soft consensus—would it politically stick? Or is it one of the paradoxical issues that you have to live with? The irony, it seems to me, and this is something that you said Thomas, is that MFN in tariffs seems to rest on its enforceability. Strictly speaking a tariff binding is held only by those who have initially negotiated. So though the tariff is MFN if you set aside the main supplier under the auspicious of satisfying the main supplier hence you have a supplier. In other words the legal basis which holds together MFN on tariff measure which really was not an MFN legal measure was portrayed even stronger, in the fact that you wanted to maintain reciprocity. Yet the illusion was that this was generally MFN and this was helpful. It was the glue that managed to stick together the system.

Maybe when it comes to conditions on national treatment we can face difficult marginal cases in the same way. Yet like products in whatever the interpretation takes might not be enough to see the collapse of an MFN. I very much enjoyed the discussion and now we can have dinner.

## 2. Saturday Morning

### Bob Stern

First of all, Rob Howse mentioned the least-restrictive means test. It brought to mind the way that economists think about policy making. What I mean is that there is a long tradition in the analysis of economic policy choices to focus on the source of the problem to be corrected. That is, is it a domestic problem or does it lie in external trade or investment? The way we then proceed is that, once we define what the source of the problem is, we then try to determine what the best policy is to correct that problem. By and large, most of the problems we see, with some exceptions that I will mention, are domestic in character. From that standpoint there is really very little, if any, case that can be made for applying trade measures to correct domestic problems or distortions. We try then to develop policy measures that will promote economic efficiency by targeting the policy as close as possible to the source of the problem. I think that is rather a different kind of view of policy making than would be contained in the notion of the least-restrictive means test. That seems, as I understood it, to consist of both domestic and trade measures. The types of measures that economists generally prefer are price-based measures. That is, measures that take the form of either tax or a subsidy. The reason is that if you correct the price distortion that exists in the market by the imposition of the tax or subsidy, this then gets as close as you can to the, so-called, first best solution. That is a somewhat different way of looking at these questions as compared to the approach that has been adopted in some of the cases mentioned.

Rob Howse also mentioned, in the Shrimp-Turtle and Tuna-Dolphin cases, the notion of unilateralism as sometimes being desirable as a means of achieving social objectives. The companion notion that economists use besides economic efficiency is the consideration of equity. Usually we try to solve the efficiency question first and then, if there are questions of unfairness, we consider the desirability of making income transfers. U.S. unilateralism bothers a lot of people, including myself, in the cases mentioned. First, it imposes the judgments of rich countries and individuals in those countries on the way in which firms, consumers, and others behave in poor countries. It says that U.S. environmental standards are preferred to whatever other countries may do, and the United States is going to force these other countries to adopt what the United States considers the best way of catching tuna or the best way of harvesting shrimp, etc. This is inequitable, in the sense that you are imposing your values on countries whose values and economic status may differ regarding the attainment of the social objectives. To be fair about it, you should offer these countries some kind of compensation in the form of income transfers, technical assistance, or other measures that will enable them to overcome the added costs of trying to deal with issues involved. Thus, there is no argument necessarily about there existing a problem in these cases. But it can be argued that it is inequitable for a rich and more powerful country to enforce its views on a poorer developing country. The same type of question arises in other instances like labor standards and related social issues.

When we consider public health, a similar argument can be made, except that one can think of cases where the source of a problem might be external. That is, if there was some danger of health contagion with people or unsafe goods crossing the border, it might appear that the problem is external. In this event, border restrictions might be justified. However, if there is a public health problem that is more generic domestically, then it would not be appropriate to use trade restrictions because of the distorting effects that these restrictions would impose on consumers or producers.

Ernst Ulrich Petersmann

We discussed this morning how to balance free trade rules with the need for government regulation. That is a fundamental question. In order to answer this question we looked at three levels: WTO, world-wide; regional level; and national level, United States and Switzerland. Now, I think our discussion has been one-sided and, from my point of view, disappointing. Having worked 16–17 years as a GATT diplomat I have learned to speak very diplomatically in GATT circles but here I enjoy my academic liberty and take a very critical view. Let me mention that 10 years ago I published a book on exactly the same subject, exactly the same approach. The book is called "The Foreign Trade Law and the Constitutional Law in Foreign Trade Policy in the United States" as an example of a liberal 18th Century constitution. Second example: Switzerland as an example for a liberal 19th Century Constitution and Germany after the Second World War, very modern 1949 Constitution and European Community Law—an International Treaty Constitution. The difference between my book and what we did today is the focus. We, I think all these speakers, have very one-sidedly focused on the question "what can the WTO learn from EC experience, US experience and Swiss experience?" I think we have very much neglected the other perspective. That was the title of my book: constitutional functions of international liberal rules for regional and domestic systems. That is something we have completely forgotten so far. I think that would be my invitation to all the authors to reflect on the different perspective.

Let me give you an example. I find it fascinating that both the United States jurisprudence of the Supreme Court in the jurisprudence and the European Court of Justice, have invented what you find in the GATT. That is, with regard to regulatory policies you must distinguish between non-discriminatory policies and between discriminatory policies. Both courts follow what we have in GATT with regard to non-discriminatory policies where we have a more lenient standard, Article III. With regard to discriminatory policies you have a much stricter standard. Here you have reinvented what is in GATT/WTO law. Unfortunately the European Court of Justice has taken 35 years to invent Keck. Keck is purely a reaction against the poor drafting of the EC Treaty. The drafters of the EC treaty overlooked the problem which has been dealt with in Article III of the GATT: i.e., how to reconcile non-discriminatory internal tax regulations, product regulations, production regulations with the free trade rules. That problem was overlooked in the EC Treaty. It was only answered in Article 95 with regard to Texas, which was copied from Article 3:2, but with regard to product regulations and with regard to production regulations it has been overlooked. And it took 35 years until the European Court of Justice, by re-interpreting Article 30 of the EC Treaty and inventing the Keck jurisprudence learned a little bit from the wisdom of the drafters of the GATT. That is the first point.

The second point which you have not taken into account in what you have elaborated in your papers. There is a fundamental difference between world-wide WTO rules and what you have in the US Constitution, what you have in the Swiss Constitution and what you have in the EC Treaty. This difference is of great importance. Whether you want to balance free trade rules with the need for regulation. That is to the effect, that the commerce laws is one or two sentences. The EC Treaty includes more free trade rules but only with regard to internal free trade. With regard to external free trade, vis-à-vis third countries, the EC Treaty makes the same mistake as practically all national constitutions, is very vague. But in the WTO you have 20,000 pages of rather detailed rules on free trade. The legal standard for the balancing between national regulation and international free trade it is much more detailed, much more specific in the WTO context. I find it misleading to recommend here the US Supreme Court as a model. The US Supreme Court is living in a completely different context. There you have a constitutional system based on separation of powers. Of course, in such a context, it might be wise to take a position on a political question doctrine. That the courts, here in Switzerland we have the same tradition, should respect the democratic legislation of congress or the parliament but these considerations are not valid on the world-wide WTO level. On this level we have 20,000 pages of very detailed rules accepted, ratified by national parliaments and this kind of separation of power reasoning which justifies judicial safe restraints at the national level is not applicable to the situation of panels. The panel judgments can be corrected by a new negotiations.

A third point. We find in all three levels, WTO, regional EC law, national US law/national Swiss law the least trade-restrictive standard. I have not been convinced by the paper by Rob Howse but I am not persuaded that the Thai cigarette case or the Shrimp case got it wrong. I think that the standards applied in the Thai cigarette case and the Shrimp case are exactly the same standards of least-trade restrictive measures. We also look at costs. We also look at alternatives. But I have not been persuaded that smoking Thai cigarettes is less dangerous for the Thai population than smoking American cigarettes. Advertisement regulations can be enforced both on Thai and American cigarette producers.

The same is true on the fourth point. The standard applied to non-discriminatory measures. You mentioned, for example, the US Supreme Court. I think it is interesting to see that the model of the Supreme Court is not followed, neither in Switzerland, in the EC nor in the WTO. The model of the Supreme Court is to apply a rational-basis test. Again this is influenced by the constitutional system. By traditional self restraint, vis-à-vis the other powers in EC Law, in WTO Law, in Swiss Law you go far beyond. You mentioned the SPS agreement which applies stricter standards of non-discriminatory measures. So, again I am not convinced.

A few comments to the paper of Demaret. Again, you said as a kind of model, that the interpretation of Article 30 by the EC Court is more far-reaching than the interpretation of the WTO. I think that is simply not true. The interpretation of Article 30 is not more far-reaching than the interpretation of Article XI GATT. But we have very specific detailed rules in the WTO law limiting non-discriminatory internal measures, in Article 3 in GATT, SPS Agreement and the TBT Agreement. Your example is misleading if you say that GATT law has an exception in Article 3:8 with regard to discriminatory taxes. Article 3:8 does not apply to discriminatory charges of imports. With regard to discriminatory charges of imports we do not have any exception. And with regard to the case law on Article 95, if you compare the case law of the European Court of Justice on the previous not non-discriminatory of discriminatory taxes, Article 95, with the case law of WTO on Article19, on Article 3:2, we have almost exactly the same text in both cases. I think that the case law of the GATT/WTO is much more stringent. The case law of the European Court of Justice is much more inconsistent, much more politicized which is due to the fact that the EC Treaty has no Article XX where we can correct certain problems. This exception does not exist in the EC Treaty. Article 36 does apply to Article 30 but you do not have Article XX exception for Article 95 of the EC Treaty. Here I have quite a lot of reluctance to mention the EC case law with regard to Article 95 as a model.

The EC case law is extremely introverted. You do not have legal disciplines in EC law which we have under Article III with regard to trade with third countries. The EC Court has always denied that the legal obligation under Article III which has been accepted by the WTO, by all EC Member States, has been ratified by the parliaments of all EC Member States which is legally binding in EC law and reporting to Article 208 has a legal primacy, vis-à-vis secondary EC law. The EC Court has never applied this rule. I think this is very introverted and protectionist jurisprudence.

With regard to the Keck jurisprudence. I also note that both Mr. Demaret and Mr. Eeckhout are apparently in favor of this jurisprudence. I am also in favor of jurisprudence but it is based on the GATT wisdom. Because the EC Treaty was poorly drafted and Article III of the GATT is a very important principle for balancing free trade rules and regulation. Unfortunately it took the EC Court 35 years to correct its case law but I think Keck is, as sound as Article III of the GATT and again, I think, the new development in the case law in the market access concept, you can learn from WTO law. Because you find similar tendencies in the SPS Agreement and the TBT Agreement that we go beyond Article III but here I think the balancing criteria in the EC are not more developed than what I see under the WTO rule. It is a collective learning process and my indication would be to take a more balanced perspective and ask what can we learn from the work of the WTO experience.

That leads me to the Swiss subject. Here I think Switzerland is a fascinating example of our discussion which goes much further than EC law in some respects. Take the constitutional level, Article 31, the EC constitution takes the principle of free trade which has been applied in a balanced manner. At least in doctrine it is recognized that Article 31, freedom of trade, is an individual right which applies not only to the trade between the 26 cantons but in principle applies also to the external trade, vis-à-vis third countries. I think that is an extremely important and humane citizen-frankly interpretation of this. The act on the internal market is an illustration of the constitutional functions of international rules. I think you rightly mentioned that this act on the internal market was very much influenced by EC law and WTO law and helped to liberalize internal market regulations with the help of international rules.

That brings me to the last point. I think this economic theory of optimal intervention, that we must really ask ourselves what is the true problem, is of fundamental importance. Now, I think that we lawyers do not usually apply this economic theory directly but we have individual rights perspective which tries to do exactly the same. That is to ask ourselves where is the true source of the problem. Here I think Bob you are completely right. The economic theory of optimal intervention suggests to use price-related measures, taxes, export subsidies but I think economic theory goes far beyond. There is the copyrights theory. The copyrights theory clearly says what we lawyers have said for quite a long time, that if the market participants do not have individual rights to protect their market position then the market will be distorted. Unfortunately, we lawyers are still 50 years away from discussing the true problems and I think we should focus more on this question, how to protect every market participant by strengthening his market rights? That is an approach which has been accepted in EC law but only with a protectionist focus, i.e., only for internal trade, vis-à-vis external trade, to treat the citizen as an object and that is thc position which is certainly no compatible with constitutional theory. The constitutional theory suggests that we should never treat the citizen as an object, the citizen is the source of all destination and the government should try to maximize citizen rights not only at home but also in the external relations.

But, nonetheless, I think here there is a clear trend. In WTO law we have the TRIPS Agreement. This says explicitly this is an Agreement about individual rights and from the point of the economic theory it is very interesting now to examine to what extent does this TRIPS agreement really correspond to the copyrights theory? Where should we possibly change it? What areas of WTO law or EC law should be strengthened the individual rights of market participants? Here I think EC law is extremely one-sided, i.e., with regard to trade within the EC it takes the right approach which was enormously successfully but with regard to third countries it takes a very protectionist approach. Unfortunately, also the European Court of Justice takes a rather one-sided jurisdiction.

## Thomas Cottier

I just want to make some additional remarks on the internal market in this country. I was intrigued by the papers this morning in terms of the constitutional theory. I was intrigued to see that we seem to have an inverse relationship: the more settled a system is the morc it balances trade interests with other economic interests: the more deference we observe. The more functionalist the level is, like the GATT, the more it aims at realizing free trade and the EC is somewhat in-between. What I think is really interesting is to further study the inverse relationship among these three levels and develop an overall constitutional theory to cope with this.

The Swiss case is interesting for the following reasons. Maybe it was understated. This country has a fully integrated market and this bill was enacted to overcome some specific problems and they are mainly in government procurement, that is were we you have compartmentalized markets. There are some professions that still operate with permission and there we have segmented markets. But it is the same situation as in the

United States. The big market essentially, by and large, was achieved by the end of this century and we are doing fine tuning.

The interesting thing here is why was EC law and why was GATT law influential? Because these old structures tend to move away from pushing a functionalist approach to free trade. The battle is over, you start going into balancing and all of a sudden you have a new challenge. The challenge in this country situation was Europe—the European Market. The price level in this country was too high and the export industry feared that they lost competitiveness. The same may happen to Europe in globalization and the United States. So, maybe they will get another kick someday if they lose out on markets and then Uli comes in and starts teaching us how to do it.

## Rob Howse

I basically want to give some brief responses to the useful and challenging comments on my paper. I think it would be very interesting along the lines that Gary suggested to look at the actual history rather than speculating about the influence of the anti-law revolution and for the final version I might actually try to do some work on that. As you said, at an earlier era there was much more of an integration approach and the question is what really did turn it around? Was it the anti-law revolution or was it some other form of developments? For example, the changing role of congress and the recollection of inter-State commerce.

This brings me to some of the other remarks. I think in understanding the equity issue that Bob Stern raised, it is important to distinguish situations where a country is purporting to unilaterally regulate the domestic environment of another country from the commerce problems, such as the problems that were an issue in Shrimps-Tuna-Dolphin-Turtles. Where what is involved is a shared global resource or part of the global environment. In that case there is a punitive legitimate stake that every member has in the way that others deal with the commerce. In this kind of situation you still want to look at the even-handedness of any unilateral approach. With respect to technical assistance, in the Turtles case, the United States argued that it was actually assisting dolphin countries and implementing technology that was relatively inexpensive that did not fundamentally affect the competitiveness of their industries. Indeed, there is objective empirical evidence that many dolphin countries had adopted the standard without any devastating impact on the competitiveness of their shrimp export industry. I think even in commerce cases it is appropriate to ask about equity, about the evenhandedness of any unilateral intervention. The problem in Turtles, of course, was that the panel manipulated and misused the text in the General

Agreement in order to ignore these considerations. There was an active debate between the developing country complainants and the United States about the reasonableness of the burden being imposed by this kind of regulation, given the margins of their industries. That is where some of the analysis ought to focus in properly applying the chapeau of Article 20 concerning arbitrary, unjustified discrimination.

On the Thai cigarette case: Uli Petersmann said that he was not convinced that advertising bands could not have done the job. This shows how sensitive we are to the regulatory state. Is the implication that Thailand has to try the advertising bands, get 1/2 million or a million young people addicted to cigarettes so they can go back to the panel and say *we tried these other alternatives, they do not work, now let us have an import ban.* Surely, that is unreasonable to expect that you should be prepared to take that kind of risk, especially when there was evidence from the WHO that other countries, at a comparable level of development to Thailand and with comparable sophisticated or unsophisticated regulatory states, could not bring the marketing efforts of US multinationals to their knees. Again, this relates to how much of a burden we place on legitimate regulatory efforts. That is the issue I tried to raise suggesting a thesis.

I think it is very interesting to reflect on who should learn from whom. One thing that is very striking is that there is less of a Democratic deficit in the United States and yet there is more deference. One would think, by this inference, that where you have much more of democratic deficit—like the WTO—you would want more deference rather than less deference to regulatory outcomes. But the corollary of that, to the extent that one can reduce the democratic deficit of the WTO and engage others in a more adequate way in the process of rule-making and interpretation, there may be a reason to have less deference. From this point of view, if NGOs can make submissions and participators in the process, if one extends rights of market participants to include, not just those of capital, but of labor and citizens more generally, one may find a way of reducing the democratic deficit and therefore reducing the problem to which deference of this present law—when there is some kind of institutional sensitivity to the deficit—making the appropriate solution.

## Paul Demaret

We were asked to deal with the non-discrimination principle under EC law, and that is what we did. We are not presenting EC law as a model, to the contrary, in several places in my paper I criticized the cases of the Court of Justice.

There is nothing in the EC Treaty concerning exceptions to Art. 95. That is a weakness for the internal market which I pointed out in different contexts.

Concerning Article 30. I never mentioned that Article 30 had a broader reach than GATT provisions. I simply said, and that is something which cannot be changed, that Article 30 like several other provisions of the EC Treaty has been interpreted as going beyond prohibition of discrimination.

Concerning Article III:8(b) of GATT. I think that my colleague Petersmann did not understand me correctly. The difference between EC law and GATT law is the following: under GATT law taxes which are applied in the same way formally, domestic goods and imported goods, remain consistent with Article III despite the fact that the proceeds are used to subsidize domestic products. My point was that those kind of taxes have been interpreted as falling within the scope of prohibition of charges of having an equivalent effect to customs duties. So, the result is that under EC law they are forbidden, under GATT law they are permitted.

Concerning Article 95 and its reach. I think that in some respects the reach of Article 95 is broader that Article III:2. I *do not* think that under Article III:2 of GATT you forbid instances of double taxation.

Concerning Article 36 and XX. I specifically mentioned in my paper that under Article 95, as construed by the Court of Justice, Article 36 was not applicable. There is nothing like Article XX exceptions to Article 95. That gives rise to the case law relating to the permissible differentiations. I have shown that that case law goes too far. There is a difference with Article 36 and Article XX to the extent that under that case law more public interest may be taken into account under Article 36 than under XX. That was mentioned yesterday during the discussion where several speakers mentioned there was a problem because under Article XX not enough public interest can be taken into account. So perhaps there the case law would serve as an example.

I have some difficulties to buy the idea that Keck would have been inspired by GATT. I think that under the EC Treaty you will find interpretations which perhaps could be used in the context of GATT. I think the same thing applies to GATT. There are reports which certainly will not serve as examples for the EC, for the US or for other regional groupings. Perhaps there are other reports which will serve as an example.

## Piet Eeckhout

I think Paul Demaret has responded to most of the criticism on our papers and I fully accept the point that EC law may have a lot to learn from WTO law, as indeed the opposite may be the case. It is rather a question of perspective. We looked at the title of our contribution as aimed at bringing forward the EC experience whereas yesterday we looked at WTO case law.

There is one other point that I would just like to touch upon, the question that was raised by Jacques Bourgeois, on the point of balancing. That everyone always concentrates in EC law on the scope of the provisions but not sufficiently at what the end result is and what sort of balancing is undertaken. I fully take that point. I would just like to refer to two cases and it also compares to what was said in relation to the US constitution. I think there are a couple of cases handed down by the European Court of Justice where indeed the European Court is balancing free trade to domestic regulatory interests. The best example is the Danish Bottles case which was concerned with Danish regulations on the re-use of drink bottles where the Court said: part of the system is all right because it is aimed at the environmental protection; that part of the system was ruled saying there was only a limited number of shapes of bottles which can be used to make the system even more efficient. The Court basically said *indeed we accept that this protects the environment even more than the general rule but the effects on intra-community trade are so heavy that we cannot accept it.* That is really a case where you have a balancing. It also ties in with the concept of a least-restrictive means. If you read the judgments by the European Court, the language which is used, which is the language used on proportionality, will say if there are less-restrictive means which can be used you have to use them. If you look at the cases themselves I am not sure that the Court always applies that in the same way. For example, here in Alpine Investments case, which I touched upon on Article 59 (cold-calling),the argument made by the Investment firms was that there were other means which are less-restrictive and actually exist in the UK. The system which is used to tape the telephone recordings in order to make supervision possible and it is not necessary to prohibit cold-calling as it works perfectly satisfactorily in the UK. The European Courts did not have an answer to the argument but said *the fact that in another Member States there is a less-restrictive means does not mean that the Netherlands does not have the right, in view of what happened in earlier cases, to impose this requirement and in view of the not so substantial effect on intra-community change, because there are other ways of approaching customers, we accept that this is proportional.* I think there is a lot that can be said on that. I am not sure that the case law is just looking at the tape recorder. Certainly there is more research to be done in that respect.

## David Palmeter

A couple of remarks on Rob Howse's paper. First I note that the dormant commerce clause itself is somewhat controversial and is growing increasingly controversial doctrine in the US. There is a sizable group of scholars and at least one Supreme Court Judge who thinks it is unconstitutional. Apart from that, the idea of facing GATT jurisprudence on the commerce clause is not wise. It is probably the most inconsistent, incoherent area of US constitutional law that exists. A personal anecdote: some of you from Michigan may have known Professor Francis Allen, he was the dean of Michigan Law School and he taught me constitutional law in the University of Chicago. One of my most traumatic memories was when he had me on the grill for the entire class, tied up like a pretzel trying to reconcile a series of these Supreme Court cases in the commerce clause. I went away thinking I was the most stupid person in the world and would never be a success because obviously I could not reconcile these cases and the Supreme Court said they were reconciled. The area where I was stupid was not realizing that they were not reconcilable and they are not. Almost anyone you pull out someone else can pull out an opposite one and defy you to reconcile them. The Hudec article that Rob mentioned, cites a whole series of these cases, they are called box-car citations. You decide if it is a valid exercise to the police power and if you decide that is what it is you cite all these cases. If you decide it is a non-constitutional and interferes with the inter-State commerce then you cite all these cases. How do you decide? One test that Hudec proposed elsewhere was whether the explanation of the defending party could withstand the power of collective laughter. Very often they can.

On Maine v Taylor it is a striking parallel to the Australian salmon but it has to be written somewhere, and I would recommend taking a harder look at it, it was oddly enough a criminal case. Mr. Taylor took it upon himself to import 158,000 minnows. The Maine authorities put him in the dock. But a lot of the Supreme Court opinion dealt with procedural and evidentiary issues that arose at his criminal trial. In the US it was a jury finding so you had this *junk-science in the court room* where one group of expert swearing to a lay jury that this is what the risk was and another group saying something else and the layman deciding the issue. That becomes sacrosaint. That colors a lot of it.

I can think of a Thai cigarette case but that is also a poor example. It would be interesting to apply the dormant commerce clause analogies to that case. I think, for example, that if the State of Kentucky- home of Lincoln Meyers who had a former president who used to advertise their cigarettes but fallen on harder times—if they were to say that *we can't compete with Philip Morris in Virginia and the Marlboro man, so we in Kentucky will basically impose the time restrictions on cigarettes from outside of Kentucky* I do not think that would stand a chance under any analysis of the dormant commerce clause. So I think that one way would be to take a look at some of these panels and analyze them in constitutional terms. A lot of them would not hold up.

Another anecdote is virtually all of those cases have an equivalent of an aims and effects test. The other side of that, however, is that the Supreme Court is not dealing with an Article XX. Again, the dormant commerce clause. We are dealing with a vacuum. All we have is a constitutional provision that says *Congress shall have the power to regulate inter-State commerce*. The opponents of the dormant commerce clause says that is fine. If Congress does so, this is it. But in the absence of Congress affirmatively acting then the States can do whatever they want and interfere all they chose. Congress can override that if it chooses. The dormant commerce clause applies when Congress has done nothing, has not done a thing about bait minnows, for example, or maybe cigarettes. That is the controversy there but they are not faced with the legal structure. They are not coming off at Article III, they are coming off at negative implication of the commerce clause itself and they are not dealing with an explicit Article XX.

The comparison of the analytical problems can be fascinatingly difficult. If we get back to the Hudec/Farber analysis: They have tried to reconcile the two cases in an earlier version and actually thought they were going to pose **the** solution which they could tell the Supreme Court to do in the future to get it straight and they would tell panels how to do it as well. But they came to the conclusion that it was impossible to formulate anything. I am convinced that it still is and I am convinced that sub-*rosa* there will always be an aims and effects test whether anybody says so or not.

## Rob Howse

It is useful to hear that there is a view that the commerce clause does not make sense and the judge to whom you are referring is reckless to decide consistently. That must be true. Certainly I think rancor of the censor a lot more consistent. I would simply argue that there is a way to reconcile many of these cases. But more at the level of understanding what the court might have been thinking about its appropriate role in the regulatory process, not in a more abstract or crime level. Indeed, with the environmental comments cases the way that I perceive it on the surface, at an abstract level, you cannot really reconcile these. I think the problem with the Hudec/Farber approach is that they remain at that fairly abstract level. They do not get much into the real world of regulation. Once you do get into that real world some of the distinctions the court is drawing actually tend to make more sense. We just have different views on that.

As for Main/Taylor. It was absolutely true that there was a dimensional decision that related to criminal procedure but the fundamental issue that I was interested in was they did go through and apply the least-restricted means test. I think they did it more contextually rather than with Thai cigarettes. Asking the question what the US Supreme Court would actually have done in that circumstance is not as interesting as asking what does it mean that there are differences in approaches to dealing with the demands of the real world regulation. It might well have struck down the bear. I do not know. What I do know is that US Supreme Court seems to be much more sensitive to regulatory contact than have GATT and WTO panels.

Kalypso Nicolaïdis

To relate this last exchange to Uli Petersmann's remark that the EU has come back to square one and Keck rediscovers GATT. I do hear that one of the fundamental distinctions we need to make—even if the result of implicit or explicit balancing may be the same—is between in once case a lenient Article III and less exceptions, and in the EU case this parallel evolution of a more and more expansionary interpretation of Article 30 and the increased deepening of the exception side of it. Part of what we are discussing here, is whether the WTO should go down that road, in fact a double road, a balanced road between the expansion side and the exception side. Coming back to Jacques Bourgeois' comment, if we look at the ECJ jurisprudence it is fascinating to see the real jurisprudential role of the growing exceptions—Article 36 and Article 56—especially in the area of services. Comments were made about the fact that how this applies to services is unclear. I In examining the connection between the goods and services jurisprudence in the EU, you see that most of the ECJ exercise in services is to think about how exceptions to Article 59 should lead to a different outcome than for goods. For instance, Alpine investment which was discussed in relation to Keck. Here the court defers to a very detailed political discussion that had been taking place in the liberalization of the insurance market and the distinction made between consumer—and producer—initiated transactions. This was the basis for phased in insurance services liberalization, whereby in the beginning there was no allowance for liberalizing if it was supplier initiated because consumers might not be sophisticated enough to react or protect themselves against this initiative. So, the politicians had made this call. The court gives a roadmap, but the decision has been made at the political level. So, that brings us back to Rob 's fundamental notion here. If there has been a regulatory and political debate, the European Court defers to it.

Jean Louis Juvet

This is a question to Robert Howse. Twenty years ago the direct subsidies for the origin of grants in the States were non-existing. Today, they are spanning everywhere and especially in the sub-belt area. For instance, Mercedes when it went to the States got a subsidy representing about 6 or 7 years of wages. Direct subsidy for the erection of a plant. My question.: how do you consider this from the dormant clause and how, for example, a State like Illinois reacted to the subsidies given that they are illegal from a GATT/WTO point of view? This maybe the paradox. In the States probably there was a problem to be settled between Illinois and Tennessee. How did the Federal government react and solve this problem?

Meinhard Hilf

I just want to put another question to Rob Howse. If my understanding is correct, you are refusing at the crucial state of the decision-making process a balancing test and the proportionality test in favor of a rational-basis test. But, I am still not very clear. How can you escape this balancing of these two interests: trade interests on the one hand; and public goods interest on the other side? There must be a balancing of interest in the end or not? I would just like to have further clarification on this point.

I add two other remarks on the burden of proof. There you balance with the costs involved. I found that very, very fascinating. On the issue of democratic deficit, I drop this question in deference of another afternoon. But perhaps you could given some enlightenment on the first aspect.

Gary Horlick

Briefly, on the subsidies. It is certainly actionable under the WTO of the Subsidies Agreement, there maybe even some import substitution elements involved. The interesting issue being raised along the lines of direct affect, no-one will challenge them. Is the EU going to challenge them in the WTO? I doubt it. So, the modern WTO law lapses into desertude for lack of a challenge. The interesting question whether it is legal in the US? They are legal if you read the Supreme Court cases on subsidies. This, again, puts it in historical context, when the US Constitution was written States did not give subsidies because they did not have any money. If you were writing the US Constitution in 1957, when the Treaty of Rome was signed, you would have a provision against the distortion of the market by subsidies. The US does not have one. The Illinois response to this was to offer its own subsidies.

### Rob Howse

On subsidies. The only quasi-exception is that there are some cases where if you can make a link between the subsidy and some discriminatory tax or fee as part of an overall scheme you could make a case that the overall scheme is discriminatory. But the focus is really on discrimination and the application of the tax between in -State and out-of-state actors. On the balancing, I think that is an important point. I should be more careful in using the term balancing. Obviously, in some sense what is at stake here is balancing and that there are trade-offs between conflicting values that have to be made. On the other hand what is often referred to as balancing is kind of cost-benefit analysis, where one asks under a proportionality principle, did the democratic process appropriately balance the costs in terms of the gains of trade against the regulatory benefits? There, I think the balancing in this sense of trying to redo that kind of calculus on the regulatory process goes too far with respect to the appropriate institutional role of a tribunal. So, what it simply suggests to me is that I ought to be more, in the final version of the paper, more precise about these two conceptions of balancing. Because you are surely right that in this minimalist sense, even the rational basis implies that there are competing values which have to be adjudicated.

## 3. Saturday Afternoon

### Bob Stern

I have a few comments on different aspects of each of the papers. The papers dealing with mutual recognition agreements focus on the formalization of agreements on standards and related issues. What I am interested in, though, is not only that, but rather the way in which the policy process works or doesn't work to achieve the harmonization of standards. I am sure that there have been a lot of discussions, both in the United States and elsewhere, about the need for an agreement covering labor and environmental standards, especially in the trade with developing countries, the argument often being made that unless you impose some kind of harmonization, there is going to be a race to the bottom. It is often argued in this connection that multinational corporations will tend to move to countries with less stringent environmental standards, or lower labor costs, as the case might be. Now, I think it is fair to say, historically, if you look at the evolution of the imposition of standards in a market setting, that there are a lot of reasons to believe that, as per capita incomes rise, a country tends to devote more resources to education about standards and to the enforcement of standards. From this standpoint then, you achieve a harmonization that is market driven, and not necessarily one that is tied to all these formal agreements that we talked about, between already advanced countries.

Now, is there any evidence that supports the notion that there is a race to the bottom? In the context of NAFTA, for example, in the case of environment, the tentative conclusion, at least based upon a few years of experience with NAFTA, is that it has had a favorable environmental impact in terms of the ways in which the Mexican government has approached environmental enforcement. The result is that trade has in a sense become more environmentally friendly. What I would emphasize then is that there are other important aspects of standards besides those that are embodied in these formal agreements. Related to this point is that there has been a lot of discussion recently about whether or not core labor standards should be applied to all members of the WTO. This was an issue that was discussed at some length, especially before and during the Singapore WTO Ministerial meeting in December 1996. as you know, the outcome was essentially not to involve the WTO in the imposition of core labor standards, but rather to leave these standards to the International Labor Organization.

At the same time, in the United States and in some countries in Europe, there has been a considerable movement to try to develop voluntary codes of conduct that could be applied to developing country producers of labor-intensive manufactured and related goods for export. One of the big problems that has come up, at least in the American experience with voluntary codes of conduct, is how you monitor and enforce them. In this connection, there have been disagreements between the Multinationals and the NGOs regarding these codes of conduct.

Turning to Neven's paper, I am rather confused about some aspects of the analysis as presented. First, Neven discusses the problems of measuring the impact of protection either by the rents that are created or by the price-raising aspects of the barriers. The first point I would mention is that the effects depend upon the barrier at issue. That is, tariffs would have certain effects, whereas voluntary export restraints would have quite different effects on rents and prices. So, one would have to be clear in terms of the type of protection that is being analyzed.

Next, while this may be a matter of terminology, I was bothered by the repeated reference to the way in which protection was assumed to cause an increase in the marginal costs of foreign suppliers. When I think of this kind of analysis, it is in terms of two large countries in which there are firms with market power. If country 1 imposes some kind of trade restriction that actually causes the foreign marginal costs to fall and the price to rise, the extent of change in the domestic and foreign prices will depend upon the elasticities of demand and supply.

I have further difficulty in determining the effect that a protective measure would have in this context. It seems to me that you need a great deal of information to model this kind of relationship. You need information about the market structures at home and abroad, demand relationships at home and abroad, and—even more complex in the setting where you have market power at home and abroad—you need to model the way in which firms interact. That is, I would submit that, while it is feasible, it is extraordinarily difficult in reality to undertake these measurements.

Next, Waelbroeck brought up in his remark the case of mergers, which I think lies outside of Neven's analysis. That is, if you are trying to analyze the trade implications of mergers, it is a somewhat different issue than what is involved with trade barriers.

My final point is more tongue in cheek. I am always amused to hear long, involved discussions of anti-dumping and related issues. What amuses me in particular is that nobody ever mentions how consumers benefit from lower import prices, whether they are the result of so-called dumping or improvements in foreign efficiency and lower labor costs.

## Ernst Ulrich Petersmann

I ought to start with three brief comments on the first subject by Patrick Messerlin and David Palmeter—harmonization, mutual recognition, conformity assessment procedures. I think this is an area where WTO can learn quite a lot from the regional experience. Three points:

First, I think it is fascinating to see that all these instruments—harmonization, mutual recognition, conformity assessment procedures—are already an integral part of WTO. We are confronted with exactly the same problems. An example of harmonization is the TRIPS Agreement or the SPS Agreement; mutual recognition is Article VII of GATS (here Kalypso mentioned there should be certain conditions for mutual recognition agreements but if you look at Article VII, paragraph 2 and 3 of the GATS Agreement you already find conditions for mutual recognition); and conformity assessment procedures we have very detailed rules in Articles 5–

10 of the Technical Barriers Agreement. That, I think, is the first point. We are already confronted with the same problems and we should try to avoid negative experiences from regional integration.

The second point is with regard to the substance: how should we use harmonization, mutual recognition or conformity assessment in the WTO? I think there we must follow different approaches. An example is TRIPS. TRIPS has incorporated substantive standards which were negotiated outside the WTO and incorporated these standards into the WTO. This, I think, is a good approach but leaves a lot of problems open. A year ago WIPO negotiated two additional WIPO Conventions—are these conventions also part of the WTO? Should they be incorporated into WTO law? Nobody knows. Another difference: if you take the different route of the SPS Agreement which says relevant international standards are those which have been adopted by the Codex Alimentarius Commission of the Food and Agricultural Organization. Here, I think we have a very important provision in the SPS Agreement, i.e., Article 12. This says the "SPS Committee should establish standards for controlling this kind of standard making outside of the WTO." I think, everybody knows, the FAO Codex Alimentarius Commission is dominated by industry interests. It is not controlled effectively by any parliament, it negotiates behind closed doors and, I think, this is simply not acceptable. I think here the WTO could and should use Article 12 of the SPS Agreement for negotiating disciplines and conditions under which we are prepared to apply these standards negotiated outside WTO law.

Finally, a third point in this area is a fundamental point, that is in these areas, intellectual property rights, mutual recognition conformity assessment, you must protect private rights. Here economic theories are really underdeveloped, in my view. This is a point that I tried to make this morning, that the economic theory of optimal intervention is too one-sidedly focused on using subsidy instruments and neglects the property rights theory. You have property rights theory in economics which deals with external effects—that has been accepted that individual rights are effective instruments to internalize externalities might be the optimal instrument—but I think economic theory has failed so far to develop individual rights approach with regard to other market failures and with regard to common goods. That is, for example, an economic theory whether the optimal instrument to deal with cartels is what the United States is doing, i.e., criminal sanctions and private damages. Or whether the intellectual property rights can be justified by economic theory as they have been defined in the TRIPS Agreement. Here, I think, economic theory must broaden the economic justification of individual rights and we can learn a lot from European integration, legal theory and political theory. If you look back to the political/social contract theory there

Lock rightly said that Hobbs was wrong. Hobbs said that "social contract is right where citizens give up all their rights, and we have to trust in the Monarch and the wisdom of the monarch" and we have suffered five centuries of wars and abuses of foreign policy powers. Lock rightly said "no, the social contract is a contract where the citizens retain their rights and where they have the right to resist against abuses of government powers" that is economic theory. That is an approach of using economic rights as a means to counter government failure.

Brief comment on the paper by Neven. I think Damien you should put all the blame on Petros. I think Petros gave you six panel reports and that was certainly not enough. There are additional panel reports which underline what has been said by Professor Waelbroeck, the function of Article III is not only to prevent price distortions or to prevent rend -seeking within the importing country but there are panel reports which clearly say that the function of Article III or Article XI is also to protect reasonable expectation of foreign exporters or foreign investors and to protect them against shift and of adjustment costs. Now, where to draw the line remains to be clarified, but I think Professor Waelbroeck has rightly emphasized that the function of Article III is broader. A second objection is also important, that is the exception I tried to explain yesterday, the Malt Beverages case. That is a parallel to the Cassis-de-Dijon doctrine, that is if you take into account the function of Article III as defined in Article 3, paragraph 1, then you should probably do not use Article III for situations where both governments, as in Malt Beverages, agree that the product differentiation serves a health policy purpose. I think you should put the blame on Petros and I do not blame you.

With regard to Marco's parallel, here I think I would very much underline what has been said by Bob Stern, if you analyze the dumping margin, if you analyze whether dumping has caused injury to domestic industry then I think it would make a lot of sense to use market competition approach and try to be rational. But, anti-dumping has nothing to do with rationality, with economic rationality. Anti-dumping is a selective safeguard clause in order to re-distribute rents in favor of import competing producers. Then there are good arguments against using the market concept. If you were to use the market concept, the competition concept, then this would mean you would have to impose anti-dumping duties on all competing products and that would be a nightmare for liberal trade. So, here I think we have to be careful.

The last point as a reaction to what Christoph said, I think it is an important development that also in GATT/WTO law the classic distinction between products standards and PPMs has been modified. The TBT Agreement, the SPS Agreement have drawn quite a different line due to harmonization and mutual recognition. Here I think we really have to re-think whether the classical distinction of the GATT between product standards and PPMs continues to be optimal or whether we have to draw a different line. The examples given by Christoph are good illustrations.

### Meinhard Hilf

Thank you very much for this expert-like comments on the various contributions. I give you now the list of speakers who have caught my eye: Mr. Waelbroek, Mr. Horlick, Mr. Neven, Mr. Mattoo, Mr. Falconer, Mr. Low, Mr. Bronckers, Mr. Palmeter, Mr. Haniotis then everyone can say goodbye.

### Gary Horlick

Two points. MRAs have served to illustrate a lot of what the issues are here. Take a hypothetical US/Canada situation. We are about the same size geographically, Canada has 1/10th of the population. Take a requirement that you have recycled paper in your paper and in the US this makes good sense from an environmental perspective as there is a solid waste disposal problem. If you require recycling you have less solid waste, less disposal problem. The same rule in Canada is bad for the environment. Why? Because you are spending a lot of energy trucking the recycled paper back an forth between cities and paper mills. So the exact same neutral rule has negative consequences for the environment, not even talking trade. I am just saying different circumstances create different environmental needs. Now, in a true mutual recognition situation both the US and Canada would recognize each others papers being okay and in effect it is not mutual recognition but harmonization. I have to emphasize this. Mutual recognition is really harmonization. Both standards are okay so you are harmonizing—you can do either one. The opposite, and where the trade impact comes, is if you say no we will only recognize our own standard. We, the US will only allow Canadian paper to be sold in the US if it is made in an environmentally destructive ways (in Canada not in the US). The US has a solid waste problem so it still a problem in the US. I think that illustrates the problems.

Now to go from the specific to the very general. What I take away from the two days have reminded me a lot of what has been fought out for a long time in classic public international low in terms of jurisdictional fights. This would be jurisdiction to prescribe or legislate and jurisdiction to apply or enforce. That is very traditional public international law. Add that together with more contemporary trends of assimilating to the use of force, which is the classic public international law, who can send an army to enforce where, the assimilation to that with economic force—which is what we are talking about—trade sanctions. When you put that together I would present some thoughts.

Look at first at supposedly purely international resources. Who has jurisdiction to prescribe and enforce within a territory? Take "Leg-hold" traps. In Leg-hold traps you have European consumers, through their governments, saying "we can decide what is sold here." I am not going to tell you the answer just saying the different ways of looking at it. Alternatively, you have the EU prescribing how people trap, for example in Canada. Is the EU prescribing and enforcing in the EU or in Canada? The answer to that determines the legitimacy in classical terms. Beef Hormones says the same thing. Is it prescribing what is right in the US or what is right in Europe? Within that context you have the cross-cutting issues with the SPS and TBT Agreement forcing its legitimacy. On a scientific basis, can you prescribe some answers, that is why I said this morning we have gone on beyond discrimination as there is no discrimination on the Beef-Hormone case, but there was no science. That is not treated in classic international law. In classic international law you did not have a WTO Agreement putting in a standard that goes beyond non-discrimination. We now have standards that go beyond non-discrimination. This is multiplied by ten when you go beyond internal resources to the global comments. But these are absolutely classic international law. Who has the right to prescribe for the global commons? Who has the right to enforce? The solution is multilateral agreements which is a way to avoid the fight. But if you *do not* have those I think that is where you have the fight.

If you look at the cases that have come up the WTO is not getting the hard cases yet. Look at the global common cases, the Tuna-Dolphin and Shrimp-Turtles. You do not have one on the air (CFC). You do not have a CITES case yet (although Turtles come close). So you do not have the WTO taking on something done multilaterally. They are doing the easy ones because under classic public international law a country, with the exception of agreed violation of international law, piracy etc., does not have jurisdiction over the commons. This is something where the results are unsurprising but the challenge is ahead. To conclude, most of the furor of the WTO and the environment is not about what the WTO has done. It is about what the people fear it will do because it has not happened yet. It is totally unsurprising that if you have the US passing a facially discriminatory law dealing with Dolphins the WTO panel will knock it down. That should not shock anyone. The issues comes when you deal with someone who is not a party to the Montreal Protocol and that case has not happened. I suggest that is the issue: why it has not happened and what happens when it comes?

### Tony Haniotis

As an economist I was glad to see some economic analysis here but still I feel a bit uneasy when we start to having, or looking for, economic-market definitions. Why? If we think back to the origin of the GATT in a way we *do not* trust the government because it has an obsessive desire to be protectionist, so we set up rules, the WTO rules, to limit this protectionism. Then, we continue this line and end up having courts, lawyers, and other bureaucrats examining notion such as price and cross-price elasticity as the nature of the strategic interaction between market participants, cross structures and so on. There, I see a dangerous development.

What is the conclusion? I would say that first of all we must not forget that distortionary taxation or distortionary tariffs are not normally even in the unilateral interest of a country. They are distortionary and they harm their own consumers and their own country. There is a natural limit to this sort of thing. If there is still a problem it is a political one. We should try to look at the aims and political motivation of the measures rather than doing fancy economic analysis.

### Michel Waelbroeck

I wanted to comment very briefly on what we were talking about this morning, Keck and also dormant commerce clause. We heard lots of discussion about whether the proper test should be whether the given measures restricts the access to the market. I think that is too vague. I think there is a lot of ambiguity. Really, what one is concerned about, and really the whole issue in fact, was whether it is simply market access for whom, market access for the producers of imported products or is it also market access for domestic products?

Before Keck there was a tendency on the part of the Court to want to include within the scope of Article 30 all measures which restricted market access for anybody, whether for foreigners or for domestic producers. Then the turnaround was, I think, welcome, because the court was going over board. It was assuming the right to pass judgment on legislation which did not have any discriminatory or protectionistic effect but simply regulated an industry and then it was the Court who assumed it had the right to say whether or not this was reasonable or not reasonable. This is something which is very delicate. I think it is a bit difficult for the European Court to say this is without any rational basis because then what is the government say? There have been a few cases in which the court had taken upon itself and had even condemned the German law on unfair competition on the Yves-Rocher case, for example, in which the Court said this is really nonsense. They say they want to protect consumers by preventing people from disclosing that they are reducing their prices. This does not make sense. Consumers have a valid interest in knowing that the price has been reduced.

So I think the situation after Keck is that a measure which restricts market access for imported products exactly to the same extent as the market access for domestic products escapes Article 30 even if it is completely stupid. Even the legislation has no rational basis. That is the major difference, I want to come back to what Jacques Bourgeois was saying this morning. There have been cases before in which the Court did decide that there was no rational justification. Since Keck there was Leclerc/Siplec which concerned a ban on television advertising by distributors, something that the advocate-general, Jacobs, considered had no rational basis and he recommended to the Court to strike it down and come back to Keck but the Court said no since it restricts access to television advertising both for domestic and for importers and therefore it is not discriminatory and within Keck.

## Christoph Bail

Just one reflection following what Gary Horlick and Uli Petersmann said. I think the heart of the matter is that the WTO has done one thing, namely in the context of like product definitions moved much beyond dealing with purely formal discriminations. To really look into all things which could become trade restrictive. When you do that you have to also look at the public policies in detail, the purposes and their effects and integrate that into the analysis. The WTO is only beginning to do that. It is still, a lot of people think, about trade liberalization. It is not about setting the rules of the game for competition in a globalized economy. That is fundamentally different thing. When you do that in your analysis you really have to look into these purposes and effects in the context either of your basic standard of non-discrimination or in a much more sophisticated analysis of justification for differentiation. You cannot just look in the differentiation in treatment and say everything that somehow affects the market is discrimination. You cannot say that the public policy justification is exception to the rule, and the burden of proof is on the defending government. You cannot create an *a priori* presumption that anything that looks in that sense as being discriminatory is, by definition, unjustified.

## Americo Zampetti

I just wanted to take issue with what Gary Horlick said that basically mutual recognition would be the same as harmonization. Actually, I think mutual recognition is rather different from harmonization in that the regulatory authorities that sit down establishing that a particular technical regulation of one party fulfills the public policy objectives of the other party, retain all their regulatory autonomy. What they basically establish is that public policy objectives are fulfilled in a *different* but equivalent way. And they find this acceptable.

## Gary Horlick

I say this as an observer. Take whether you have yellow or white headlight lamps and the two regulatory authorities sit down and say we do not care but we cannot muster the political effort to actually harmonize to agree on one of them because someone would be unhappy. So, we let cars drive on our streets with yellow or white headlights. I think that is harmonization. It is sloppy harmonization but it is harmonization.

Another example: let us say you have right-hand drive cars and left-hand drive cars and you let tourists drive both but its unsafe. You really would not want right-hand drive cars and left-hand drive cars circulating on the same highway. It is dangerous: I assure you—I have done it—it is dangerous. The authorities when they say we do not care if we have white or yellow headlights we are harmonizing in the sense that you can choose. You can call that mutual recognition but in fact they are accepting both. Whereas when the authorities say you have to have a right-hand drive or a left-hand drive as the case may be to drive on the highway, they are saying we *do not* want to mix the two. You can call it mutual recognition, since you work in a political body you have to, but the fact is that it is harmonization. The US/EU partnership over the last few years has done a wonderful job of mutually recognizing away unnecessary differences and I congratulate you.

## Aaditya Mattoo

I just wanted to make very brief comments on Damien's paper. First, I think it is very interesting to look at market structure in an assessment of whether a measure affords protection. Especially, in a political economy context since there seems to be much less likelihood to lobby for protection if you have a very competitive market structure in the first place. But, two very minor points. While I think it is important to emphasize rivalry it is also important to look at the supply conditions. If you, as André said, had bilaterally agreed about this, reverse the supply curves and the domestic supply curve is upward sloping and the international supply curve is competitive at constant cost, then of course you have a situation that even though you have intense competition domestically, rents are generated by an increase in foreign costs.

The second question is, really, that national treatment deals not just with measures which increase foreign marginal costs but also with measures which might confer an advantage on domestic industry. So, for instance, if I exempt domestic industry from a burdensome standard I might be acting inconsistently or discriminatorily in which case you might see protection and reduction in domestic prices. Often it might not be easy to tell the difference between what really the measure is achieving.

If I can give one final example where a situation where law and economics do not live together very easily is a situation where you introduce a standard which meets the strictest non-discriminatory requirement and that imposes an identical incremental cost on both domestic and foreign suppliers. Perhaps their initial marginal costs are different. It is not difficult to construct a model where you have protectionist effect in that domestic profits increase and foreign profits go down. In that sense I think there are real problems with applying sensible economics and interpreting it in a legal sense.

## Crawford Falconer

I do not have much to say, Gary said most of the things better than I would have been able to say them, but there were one or two things that were a bit of a puzzle to me. MRAs, to me raises some curious implications. I think what you are talking about with MRAs depends on which kind of MRA you are talking about. If you are talking about an MRA which, to put it crudely and in an ideal type, says I am satisfied that the way in which the product concerned is put into commerce and you, the exporting market, satisfies my needs without need for any other change, that is what I call a hard type of MRA. A recognition that basically if it fits conditions into your market that satisfies what my standards are into my market. That is the one that interests me most.

Take the example of, someone mentioned, Teddy bears. If I do not have an MRA and I am importing country, and I say "I am going to require everybody's Teddy bears to go through the following process to make them spontaneously combust when hugged. Then, however, I go and exempt this one country from this requirement. Perhaps somebody might say you have an Article III problem here. But if my authorities sit down with the authorities of that same country and systematically do that for everything in their tariff schedule and say that is an MRA do they not have a problem anymore because they are called an MRA? If the process they have gone through at each and every level is identical, I maybe be wrong in my presumption, is there a distinction between them other than the one that is called an MRA process because of its comprehensiveness? Is there a fundamental difference? Whatever you decide in response to that the question seems to be, does it matter? The way the practice seems to be evolving is that Members of the WTO seem to take the view that it does not matter very much. Maybe that is wrong. Maybe you are going to find third parties affected by these MRAs who demand the same treatment and not getting them and then you do have a problem, I do not know.

But, isn't this a bit analogous potentially to what happened by a different legal route? Of course, I am referring to what has happened with regional integration agreements. They are exceptional. But they have been tolerated, accepted, and one can take the view that they have contributed to multilateral liberalization. So, there has been a legal means to lead to what was a politically accepted result which was presumably not economically irrational either otherwise it would not have happened. Perhaps the same thing is happening with MRAs. Perhaps they are considered to be tolerable because politically they are trade facilitating, they are integrations. The logic is, in time, they will expand and the jury may still be out on that, but that will happen.

Now, whether there is a legal problem over all of this, in the short term, is a different question. The way in which that would seem to me to be resolved is perhaps instructive. If, as we have to think like Americo, the TBT Agreement gives you a legal basis to insulate this from a tariff. Is that the way more generally in which you deal with the kinds of problems that go outside, simply, mutual recognition area? The kind of issues that were raised by Christoph and some others about environmental arrangements and environmental measures. Yesterday, if I recall rightly, people were dubious (and rightly dubious) about whether any difficulties that exist with a like product approach and discrimination related to it, could ever be renegotiated in the context of Article III comprehensively. But, does that preclude the possibility that *de facto* you do it by grafting on, by balkanizing the issue, somewhere else? Is what TBT has effectively done for MRAs to insulate them from a problem you have with like products? In other words, will there be a decision to call off the PPM policy, for example, on certain aspects on environmental issues?

I do not know. Listening to the legal discussion it is very difficult to take any political view on any of these things at all. But, one thing that struck me from Rob Howse's remarks was this reference back to the so called democratic process and the need for the WTO system to be democratic. Well, democracy is in the eye of the beholder, but presumably the way you can be most democratic is by reaching a negotiated outcome on these matters which reflects the will of the sovereign governments which make up the contract. That is your first best solution, clearly. If it is politically impossible then that is another matter. I am not so sure that it is so easy to see that it is desirable as a matter of general interest. I just do not think there is even as much sense of acceptability coming from a judicial organ, as it were, from a national level. There is not, if you like, the political support at the national level for an activist stance on the part of multilateral dispute settlements. If anything there is more reason to say where there is a problem, where there is ambiguity, there must be most desirably a politically negotiated solution. It is a very simple view but my experience with MRAs, the way TBT has evolved, the way in which I think the International Community is going on the environmental question suggest to me that that in fact it is the most likely way to deal with some of these interpretative problems that have been discussed.

### Marco Bronckers

Well that was quite a nourishing contribution for just a few last words and perhaps I can add some technical observations to what Crawford Falconer has said, this is on the environmental aspects. I was struck by a couple of things: thinking about like products and the environmental debate. First of all, Tuna/Dolphin and Shrimp/Turtles was not decided on like products. The trouble there was that initially Tuna/Dolphin panel said that these products with PPMs were not covered by Article III. In other words, the problem was a different one, the problem about the relationship between Article III and Article XI. That is number one.

Number two, about like products: changing the like products definition taking into account some of these desirable environmental objectives: I have a problem with that. It seems to me, then again, we risk introducing into the GATT system something, that we were trying I think, to get rid of. That is to say, defining competitive relationship between products on the basis of regulatory objectives. It might sound like a good idea that we should value the environment, but what is the difference between those kind of regulatory interventions and state-planned interventions? If I could target just one problem that we see and we share, is the environment. Why not, and that I like very much what Crawford Falconer said, why not try to do the difficult thing then, that is, the more legitimate thing perhaps, to try to negotiate an agreement to resolve those problems, rather than tinkering with something that would have implications much beyond the environmental debate? That, also perhaps, is my final point. I think Christoph Bail had this interesting thought of doing to Article III what the European Court of Justice has done with respect to Article 30, that is to say add some of the public policy objectives. Perhaps that is still legitimate enough in the context of the European Union, a close knit group, etc. You can question that. But, I really have my doubts, and again that is what I have been hearing Crawford Falconer has been saying, I really have my doubts whether that is the way to go in Article III in the context of WTO.

### Natalie McNelis

I wanted to respond to something that Professor Petersmann said about the definition of "like products" in anti-dumping. My reaction when you say that we should go toward a system of including *all* competitive products is "God forbid!" Extending the "like product" category is not what we would argue for. That is why we argue that the definition should begin with the competitive relationship but we don't argue for throwing out the "similar physical characteristics" criteria that has traditionally been the way to define "like products." The reason for that is that finding physical similarity has been, in some cases, too easy. For example, in the "leather handbags case" it was relatively easy to find similar products. It was harder to make distinctions based on quality. Therefore, you had leather bags that were selling for US$2.00 being compared to leather bags that were being made for Cartier and selling for US$300.00. I think what we argue for is more of a combination of the two systems. Secondly, in response to Professor Stern's comment about "consumer interest in buying low-cost products," I can assure you that when I went to buy my new suitcase I was very glad that the EC's luggage and travel goods procedure had failed, although it might have failed in part because of too broad a "like product" definition.

### Kalypso Nicolaidis

I think the dispute between Horlick and Americo can be resolved again by distinguishing between the underlying norms and the conformity assessment or enforcement procedures. On the first dimension, there is a continuum between harmonization and mutual recognition. It depends upon what scope of the regulations parties agree should be called equivalent for the purpose of free trade. Equivalent may look exactly the same as harmonized or consist in acceptance of diversity. But on the conformity assessment side, mutual recognition is black and white. Supervision is either done at home or done in the host country. There is nothing in-between. Then mutual recognition is an alternative to host country, or to some equivalent of harmonization which would be the existence of a big multilateral accrediting body that would do something instead of the countries themselves—a supranational body. So, in this funny relationship between mutual recognition, harmonization, and home or host country (national treatment kind of approach) we must take into account this key distinction.

I am very glad to see that Crawford yesterday was talking about consensus. One of the consensus here is to examine the legitimacy of democratic process and I would add to what has been said a couple of things. Professor Stern mentioned the problem of the race to the bottom. I think the whole point of "managing" mutual recognition is to manage regulatory competition. To make sure that there will not be race to the bottom. To include clauses in trade agreements that would do that. Her again, the court again makes a black and white judgment: a measure is allowed or not allowed. Whereas negotiators can manage the race to the bottom in more fine-tuned ways. They can for instance put in place temporary or permanent safeguard clauses to apply when a country suddenly decides to deregulate beyond acceptable differences. Most importantly, they can put in place networks that can ensure that such developments are spotted in the first place.

This does not mean, however, that the courts are irrelevant. One of the lessons that we did indeed draw from the European Courts approach is that Courts might decide that "I cannot really make a judgment on this as it is a political issue, but I can give a road map to the politicians on how they should do it." For example Petros' insistence on proportionality is what we have seen the European Court doing by actually stating in many cases linked to Article 30 or 59 that proportionality is really relevant but that the Court, is not going to decide what this means concretely but point in the right direction. Jurisdictional allocation for insurance for instance should distinguish between types of consumers, for instance. The Court cannot go the next step and say "therefore there should be freedom of trade for this type of consumer and not for that type." This is an indication of what the proportionality test would do if it was then negotiated in a mutually recognition directive. We see this role played by GATT panels also, even when they do not resolve the issue in specific ways.

Finally, coming back to Marco's debate on the competitive market, it is very interesting to look at the question of whether there is a problem when a regulation is invisible to the consumer; that is why regulation started in the first place. Products seem competitive but they are not. One is more risky than the other. They are regulated differently. Christoph says that the

European Court has addressed this through labeling. Now, labeling relies on two basic assumptions. One, that the consumer is sophisticated enough to read the labels, which very often is not true (that is why we have certain regulations that did not go to labeling in the first place). And secondly, that the consumers would internalize whatever the labels say. That the public policy goal can be dealt with through labeling. But if we have externality problems then labeling is not enough. Then we really do have to come back to stricter forms of regulation.

### Peter Eeckhout

Two very short comment on what Kalypso said in relation to the European Court setting out a road map and in the end not deciding on the proportionality, for example, whether certain measures are lawful or not. I think there is a very specific procedural reason for that. That is, most of these cases come via a reference from a national court and usually the Court of Justice can only interpret European law and not, in the end, decide a case. That has to be done on national level, which is at times an advantage for the Court, at times a disadvantage. Which in some cases, gives it more leeway to set out some of the criteria. My second remark is just a short reaction to what professor Waelbroeck said, just to say that I agree entirely with the way in which he presented things. In the latter part of my paper I have tried to annualize, I think, the concept of market access in that direction. Probably in much more difficult than the very simple and clear terms he put them, but I fully agree with the analyze of the Keck and Mithouard judgment.

### Paul Demaret

Of course the ideal solution would be perhaps to do what has been achieved under the TRIPS Agreement where one finds reference to substantive provisions of the main international conventions in the field of the intellectual property rights. That would be the ideal solution to embody TRIMs the way it has been done under the TRIPS Agreement. A second remark concerning the notification requirements in the field of TBT. Here it is quite important to observe that the notification requirement first appeared in the GATT before it appeared in EC law. Recently in a the courts eventually shared the opinion of the Commission and gave a direct procedural effect to the notification requirement. What does that mean in practice? It means the following: for instance take a case where a Member state which was obliged to notify technical regulation has not done so. If you are an importer or, simply, a domestic trader and you put on the market some piece of equipment which did not comply with the domestic regulation which has not been notified, that regulation may not be opposed to you. You are free to market your products despite the fact that it is inconsistent with the domestic regulation. Simply because the domestic regulation has not been notified. That is what the court called "procedural effect." Also concerning notification requirements, one should know that in addition to the notification requirement which applies to technical barriers to trade and is enforced since 1983 and which would continuously been expanding and is now reaching information services, there is another notification requirement, more recent. It is a decision of the Council of 1985 or 86 which requires all Member States to notify remaining obstacles to trade in goods which do not fall within the notification requirements applicable to technical barriers to trade. But there, there is a debate whether there is a direct procedural effect—this is not yet clear because it fits in a somewhat different way. But I think it is quite important in terms of enforcement and practical significance of those instruments.

Now, because I have prepared something in order to give an answer to Jacques Bourgeois's question and I was asked to do so by Petros, it is a kind of quantitative analysis of the results produced by the case law of the Court of Justice with respect to Article 30 and then with respect to Article 59 because that is the question which was raised by Jacques. Here are the results. You have something like 300–350 judgments, lets say 300 if you forget the judgments concerning price regulations and judgments concerning intellectual property rights. I have divided the types of measures which might fall within the scope of Article 30 in two or three categories. Let us start with discriminatory regulations, i.e., formal discrimination, material discrimination—where there is no doubt that the measure is aimed at discriminating. The exception which can be invoked is Article 36. All the measures which have a discriminatory character have been forbidden. There are only two or three cases where exceptions were allowed under Article 36, and I think those are bad cases. The Court of Justice should not have accepted those exceptions. Example: you are to buy part of your gasoline from an Irish refinery if you wanted to distribute gasoline to Ireland. It is a typical discriminatory measure but the Court still found a way to say it was not discriminatory.

Now, measures that are distinctly applicable, not formally or materially discriminatory. But first subdivision: with a certain protective effects and I would say that now, if you look at the Cassis-de-Dijon, the core of the Cassis-de-Dijon, the protective effect is being presumed. The reason being that if you have to comply with product requirements which differ in 15 markets, there will be no common market. So there is a kind of presumption.

In the first cases the Court refers to some protective effect and then it became a presumption.

There are very many cases. Here I am referring to the typical Cassis de Dijon case. Things which directly relate to the product itself. Almost all measures of that kind which have been brought before the Court of Justice since Cassis de Dijon have ended up being forbidden. All, except two cases (And I have been helped by Michel Waelbroeck because I had forgotten the Robertson case.) It is a Danish bottle case and the Robertson case. So, only two cases out of 50–60 cases.

(Intervention from Kalypso Nicolaidis reminding the speaker of the Wood Machine case.)

Yes it could be put there too, it is a very interesting case because it could not be solved because it relates to different types of approach with respect to security and if you want to know about the case, that was the following: in Germany your approaches focuses on the training of the worker. In France, apparently, it does not focus on the training of the worker—a worker with not much technical skills is able to use that kind of machine. So, of course there is a problem if you allow machines from Germany in the French market. The Commission brought a complaint against France to the Court of Justice even though from a statistical point of view, the rate of accidents was the same in Germany and in France. The Court of Justice was afraid that someday the front page of a newspaper reads:"a french worker has been injured because of justice."

Two or three cases, not more than that, were judged indistinctly applicable with a certain particular effect. Now, if the exceptions are not only 36 but 36 plus the mandatory requirements, in fact it would be better to add unified exceptions. Measures indistinctly applicable without any protective effect: those to which Michel Waelbroeck referred to a few moments ago. Before Keck there has been something like 15 or 20 cases of that kind. In some cases it was said that they had nothing to do with Article 30. In other cases the Court said I do not know what I must do, you national judge see what should be done, and gave very bold, general guidelines without going into detail. Like the first Sunday-Trading cases. In only two cases before Keck were restrictive measures of that kind without any protective effect forbidden. They were mentioned by Michel Waelbroeck.

Now, after Keck in the field of goods in the framework of Article 30, and I speak under the control of my friend Peter Karl, I think there has been no judgments prohibiting measures of that kind. But, if you compared the situation before Keck the practical result of Keck is only that two or three cases which were the measures being forbidden, after Keck the result would have been different. For the rest, after Keck essentially I would simplify the task of the Court of Justice. It does not have to go through the reasoning process in the framework of Article 36 or mandatory requirements.

Now, very quickly services. We have something like 50 or 60 judgments under Article 59 and the free supply of services. Discriminatory measures occur on the basis of nationality or residence, nationality is not the only factor—not the even main factor. Very few measures have been allowed but there are some significant exceptions. A significant exception was in the life insurance field. An invention premium was paid to an insurance company with at least a branch on the mentioned territory and then if you are an individual you may deduct that from you tax sheet. But if you pay the premium to a German insurance company without any branches in Belgium but only branches and the main office in Germany you can not deduct the premium. So, in fact, it is impossible to supply services in the field of life insurance with that kind of tax system. That has pretty important bearing to intra-EU trade and the Court of Justice allowed that. It is a very rare instance that a discriminatory measure was this discriminatory and has been allowed.

One what basis was it allowed, one might ask. The Belgian argument was the following: In Belgium if an insurance company has at least an establishment in Belgium we are able to tax the capital at the end of the road. Whereas if the capital is being paid by the insurance company established somewhere else we are not sure that we will be able to. Advocate General Jacobs in that case had said, on the basis of Article 5 of the EC Treaty, that Belgium should enter into an agreement with the other Member States and that would be enough. We could also say okay, there is some kind of economic reciprocity in the long run.

A distinctly applicable measure: I have not made a precise calculation, probably it is 50/50 something like that. Why is it difficult to know? First, because double controls are not allowed. So, in many cases you do not know. Part of the regulation stands up, part of the regulation does not. You have to look at the content of the regulation and what amounts to a double control something which ensures that controls which have already been made in the country of establishment of the supply of services will not be repeated in the country where the service is performed. So, there you do not know.

Now, for the balance of the case it is true that a Court of Justice takes, I would say, a more deference attitude towards public policies which are behind restrictions on the free supply of services. Usually those public interests are of a more sensitive nature than, let us say, public health with regard to German beef. It is very easy when Germany bans beef for public health but Germany takes the same kind of additives in orange juice. That is quite easy. But in the field of service, it is often true that the court remains at a certain distance: for instance, in case of public lottery, public order, what attorneys are likely to do, what other persons should not do in the field of providing legal services, etc.

### Rob Howse

I just wanted to very briefly reply to Gary Horlick's discussion of the relationship between public international law and the problems posed by cases like the turtles and tuna dolphin case. I think one of the major problems in these cases is the simple failure of the panel to follow Article 31 of the Vienna Convention and to actually consider the relevant principles of public international law. The International Court of Justice in the Nicaraguan embargo case stated that there is no general principle or rule of international law against the use of economic sanctions to influence the policies of other countries. At least in the turtles case they looked at the Rio Arrangements, which said that you should try and avoid unilateral approaches to the common problems and so there is a duty to try to negotiate a solution.

Why, then, did the panel a dictum suggest that this duty had not been fulfilled by the United States? Well, they had offered negotiations but only in a diplomatic note. What do they expect? That every time the US wants to solve an environmental problem by negotiations they have to send Ms. Albright and a high level delegation to beat down the door and impress upon the countries concerned that they want negotiation?

So, even if one were to apply or use the relevant public international law, panels, like these panels, would probably still misunderstand what it means to have a duty to negotiate. So, we have really a problem in education of public international law that I think does, indeed to some extent, produce these difficulties.

### Bill Davey

I should remark, I suppose, that Article 3:2 of the DSU can be viewed only as incorporating the interpretation rules of the Vienna Convention and not any other principles of international law. It is not accepted that you would go so far. As to negotiations, the US government did not want to apply the shrimp/turtle rules to the South-East Asian countries and as a result did not go through the negotiating process with them as it went through it with other countries, which makes the issue of negotiation more complicated. It has spent years doing this with the Caribbean countries and provided them with significantly more technical assistance than the Asian countries.

## Damien Neven

I wanted to respond to the technical issues raised by my paper but I fear this is not the right time. So let me just pick up one general comment. Bob Stern is saying: well if we apply economic analysis in these trade cases we will need an awful lot of information. We will need information on the demand/cost. This is going to be terribly complicated. Haniotis, one of the few economists here, is going even further and saying we certainly do not want to have the trade cases left and being captured by some unaccountable clique of economist—better leave that to lawyers and bureaucrats.

Now, I am afraid that you do not have a choice. In the same way the anti-trust cases are more and more captured by economists, or at least in important anti-trust cases you have economists. I fear in the same way you will have economists in trade cases in the future. Economists are a very resistant species and they are here to stay.

## Meinhard Hilf

Petros has asked me, on behalf of all of the participants, to thank Petros for organizing the conference. I think we would have done that without his prompting. But we would also like to thank, as a group, Thomas the other sponsor of the conference, chairmen of the various groups and the commentators who have spoken on several occasions.

Personally, I had a lengthy concluding remark but it is not the time to do it now. However, very briefly, I want to thank you for you very intensive discussion. I like it very much that it was spontaneous. It is very rare that an atmosphere such as this is inviting for such a discussion.

If you look at the symbol or logo of the trade bar of this conference it, of course, invites to interpretation, doesn't it? I offer you four interpretations: Petros certainly taking up the micro next will explain what it really means. It could be dolphins, you see, jumping. The second interpretation could be these are ideas and problems which have already been in the past and coming back and back again with more and more weight, as you see. The arrows grow and that brings us to a remark that Mr. Horlick made, problems get more important. The third interpretation, it is MFN: if you give something here then you have to give the same somewhere else—not only in one case but in two cases. The fourth interpretation could be if you have principles, that is my remark which I make in relation to Mr. Bail, if you have principles in a national law they should be applied in international law and I do not share this view of Bill Davey that public international law general principles have nothing to do with the WTO unless they are written in the document. I think we are heading to a principle-orientated objective legal order, and that brings the question as to whether the consensus-based is still the basis of the WTO, or not. Probably we are somewhere in-between.

Anyhow, Mr. Petersmann would probably join in counter-arrow as he wants this arrow to go from WTO law back to national law. Anyhow I invite Petros to give a true meaning to the symbol.

### Petros Mavroidis

I go for Dolphins. Let me first, briefly sum up the discussion then give you my personal feeling. First of all, let me remind you of the 15 December deadline, authors and discussants to send to me the written versions of the paper.

Thomas and I would like to thank all of you because, obviously, without you this conference would not have taken place. I would like to thank the people who organized it, especially Fabienne, who went into deep, deep trouble to organize this conference. I would like to thank especially Bob Stern and Uli Petersmann for their comments, first of all for making it here and then giving us all their thought-provoking comments. Remind you that next year the topic of our conference is about intellectual property rights which is a field where Thomas knows nothing much so I would have to do it again by myself. It will take place, again, the last Friday and Saturday of August and we will focus on issues: Genetically engineering; balancing equity of TRIPS Agreement; parallel inputs; TRIPS and competition law; 2000 TRIPS agenda; relationship of TRIPS and national law—questions de facto law, and so on.

For me personally, except for everything else, and before I pass on the microphone to Jacques Bourgeois because it has become the custom that Jacques provides the concluding remarks (he did it last year with great success I am sure he will do it again), this conference was a particularly happy occasion because for the first time I had the honor and the pleasure to have my professor, Michel Waelbroek, in a conference and I hope it will happen again in the future.

### Jacques Bourgeois

I have the distinct impression that Petros wants me to pick up the pieces. We had one example here of what C. P. Snow described in one of his novels as "two worlds" the world of the economists and the world of the lawyers. We had even the pleasure of the political scientists here. I think, this is a very general remark, that the lawyers have learned quite a bit from the economists.

I am not going to say all the good I have to say about that it would be too long, I simply hope that the economists maybe learned a little bit from the lawyers, but I doubt it. My second remark is that in fact we dealt with a series of issues which, to my mind, show that the world trading system as it is established now at the WTO is facing difficult adjustments. Difficult adjustments because the world in which it applies has changed considerably. Probably to the good. There is now much more trade than it used to be. (I have not heard the word globalization today nor yesterday which is fantastic.) Secondly, because all the classical obstacles to trade have disappeared. We have now come to terms with non-classical obstacles in trade. This is indeed a difficult exercise. My third remark is that it was extremely interesting to have the comparison, have the relevant information put very succinctly, most of the time, about the US system, the EC system and about the Swiss system. To me that has been extremely illuminating. Of course, we cannot transpose the solutions, draft the solutions into the tree of the WTO—it would probably be rejected. But, nonetheless, the way in which the solutions have been thought, sought, and the balance that has been achieved has been extremely fascinating. I remember the remark made by Thomas Cottier which I found very interesting that "a system that is coherent, that has confidence in itself is much more tolerant for differences and disparities" and he was referring to the US system. Maybe the WTO system at this stage is less tolerant for differences and disparities because the danger of falling apart is much greater than in a situation like the US. My fourth remark was that my impression was that analytically everything was extremely good. We are still quite apart on a certain number of issues. But, the big advantage of this conference is that we are able to air them, that we are able to discuss them, we are able to go home and live with all that as food for thought. The last point is that I want to thank the organizers for everything. To congratulate them. Perhaps we leave with one little wish, it might be good for the next event to have the papers one month in advance because we have probably missed a few things because we are not in a position to read the papers and we have in fact to go to comment on a very short presentation by each rapporteur. That might be a good idea, if there is perhaps something on which the organization could be improved.